*My Sister
Milly*

My Sister Milly

GEMMA DOWLER

with Michelle Lovric

MICHAEL JOSEPH

an imprint of

PENGUIN BOOKS

MICHAEL JOSEPH

UK | USA | Canada | Ireland | Australia
India | New Zealand | South Africa

Michael Joseph is part of the Penguin Random House group of companies
whose addresses can be found at global.penguinrandomhouse.com

First published 2017

001

Copyright © Gemma Dowler, 2017

The moral right of the author has been asserted

For a list of permissions and credits see page 577

Set in 12.5/14.5 pt Dante MT Std
Typeset by Jouve (UK), Milton Keynes
Printed in Great Britain by Clays Ltd, St Ives plc

A CIP catalogue record for this book is available from the British Library

HARDBACK ISBN: 978–0–718–18459–9
OM PAPERBACK ISBN: 978–0–718–18460–5

MIX
Paper from
responsible sources
FSC® C018179

Penguin Random House is committed to a
sustainable future for our business, our readers
and our planet. This book is made from Forest
Stewardship Council® certified paper.

Contents

Introduction

My name is Gemma Dowler.

On 21 March 2002, a serial killer named Levi Bellfield stole my sister and sent our family to Hell. From that day onwards, Milly became an endless source of stark and shocking headlines.

My sister had a face that captured hearts. But her lovely image has been turned into a symbol of so many things gone terribly wrong. This is because what happened to Milly was not a simple murder. It was not just Bellfield who took her from us. My sister was also a victim of police incompetence, of criminality in the press and of cruelty in the so-called justice system, which puts victims on trial alongside killers.

With so many headlines over the years, Milly's name has gradually become one of those – like Marilyn's, like Diana's – that needs no surname or explanatory subtitle.

Three words came to define my sister more than any others: MISSING, MURDERED, HACKED.

Yet in her time with us, there was no such thing as 'Tragic Milly Dowler'. My sister was the most vivid girl you'd ever meet. She was the noisiest, cheekiest, danciest girl. Milly would not have wanted a minute's silence to mark her passing. She would have wanted a whole rock concert, with moshing.

So, in this book, I'm going to ask you to trade the one-dimensional Milly Dowler you *think* you know for the true girl: my funny, talented, eccentric, loving and much-loved sister.

This is also a book about putting things right. You can put something right only if you first acknowledge that it is wrong.

Bellfield is not the only one of his kind. Think of the women and children murdered since Milly was taken, some of them by Bellfield: Amélie, Marsha, Holly, Jessica, April and others. Milly didn't even get a year of being a teenager. She was doing brilliantly at it, but she'd hardly got started. Other girls didn't get to be one at all.

Think of how the families of those victims have been exposed and often judged: all the grieving fathers treated as if they'd harmed their own daughters; the mothers accused of neglect, just because their daughter, like Milly, was in the wrong place at the wrong time; the young girls labelled wilful runaways by the police, even while they were suffering and dying at the hands of violent paedophiles; the victims of press intrusion, tactless headlines, painful revelations at a time when families were in the grip of trauma and loss.

As the emblem she became, Milly has an immense power: the power to close newspapers as well as to sell them. I'm aware that, in writing this book, I'm harnessing this power.

It's not 'girl power' or commercial power.

It's moral power, the power that comes the hard way, out of tragedy survived, lessons learned.

I use it in the hope that telling our story will help stop other families suffering what happened to us.

Ever since Milly disappeared, our family's been besieged by publishers as well as reporters. We turned down every book offer – until now. It was not that we lacked material. As well as a room full of photographs, statements and documents, Mum and I have been scribbling our thoughts and feelings in mounting piles of notebooks for years.

Our family had and has plenty to say. The problem with publishing our story was one of trust. We'd been too often betrayed, mis-portrayed, made to feel like collateral damage. We shrank away from offering ourselves up for more of the same.

So why publish this book now?

I have just turned thirty-one and am acutely conscious of starting to age. Each wrinkle I have will be a privilege Milly didn't know. Each rite of passage will be one my sister cannot witness. We promised to be one another's bridesmaids. I was denied the privilege of keeping that pledge. But now there's something else I can do. I cannot bring her back, my laughing, willowy, sassy sister. Instead, it is time for me to show who she really was.

It's taken me fifteen years to find the voice to tell Milly's story, and mine. It's fair to say that over those years, some of my memories may have been blurred or distorted by the traumas that arrived one after another. Details of my recollections have sometimes differed slightly from those of Mum, Dad and other people. But I think if you ask any group of people to describe something that's happened, the individual accounts will always vary.

Now is this book's time, because previously our family could not bear to talk about what we still did not truly know. Milly would have hated for us to live so many years in such pain, wondering what had really happened to her. She would have hated Bellfield to hang on to the power of his withheld disclosures for so long. After he admitted in 2015 what he'd done to her, we could not stay silent any more. Milly would have wanted him known for what he is.

Bellfield's admissions made this project more urgent. Yet they also took many months away from it as we struggled to come to terms with the heart-breaking details and the, frankly, cruel way in which they were drip-fed to us.

It's also time for the press to demonstrate how much they have learned. We've always been grateful to the media for the way they helped us try to find Milly. And we've seen such a lovely change in the way we are treated by the newspapers. After Bellfield's trial, we felt that our ordeal had not been wasted on the press. We were right to trust them with our passionate statements in front of the Old Bailey. We were right again in 2016 when we decided to trust the media – and the public – with Bellfield's disclosures about what he did to Milly. We were rewarded with respect, compassion, insight and a well-judged amount of outrage, some very eloquent. For that reason, too, it feels safe to publish this book now.

Finally, after intensive and innovative therapy for post-traumatic stress disorder, we have at last been able to rebuild ourselves, not just as victims but as a family that was blessed with the gift of Milly. It's time for me to publish this book because, after years of being afraid of the memory of her, I have found my way back to Milly. That love is stronger than Bellfield's evil.

We hold Milly in our memories the way a child refuses to give up a fragment of its little crib blanket. She keeps us warm, dancing and laughing with us. Milly's like a hologram playing in our hearts, singing, sashaying, sassing – a little Milly, almost like one of the fairies she loved, disappearing in and out of the darkness, like the flicker of an old film.

The only book that our family can be a part of is one that will allow us to explain ourselves without sensationalizing or dumbing down, without objectifying Milly and without flinching at telling of the damage that was done to all of us. Milly would also have wanted me to take the horror out and put the music back into her short life and her memory.

Milly acquired so much personality in her thirteen years that it's survived all this time after her death, intact. She also left many lovely traces on this earth. Our family will share here for the first time photographs of Milly from our albums. There are letters from Milly herself as well as her artwork, her own essays and poetry. Milly's distinctive, evolving handwriting – and her even more distinctive spelling – are here too.

As you will read, Milly was all about music. That's why this book has playlists of the songs she loved to perform on her saxophone or sing, as well as the music that accompanied our family's progress from our former riotous happiness to shock and grief at the loss of her.

Writing is not necessarily healing. Sometimes working on this book forced me to position myself in an old familiar torture chamber and describing what it felt like. So there have been times when it has been almost too difficult to write. Sometimes I've had to drag Mum and Dad and Lovely Granny into the torture chamber too, to help me remember the things I've recorded here. There's no doubt that this book has stirred up old pain, refreshed it, made it sharp again. There have been times when it hasn't seemed fair that we should put ourselves through this, just for the sake of a book.

Then I reminded myself that some things must not be allowed to stand. So I kept writing, even when it felt like Hell.

At a certain point, I became the girl whose sister disappeared, then the girl whose sister was murdered, the girl who believed the murderer was coming after her, the girl who screamed at the trial, the girl who advised David Cameron to 'man up', the girl who told Rupert Murdoch to sort out his empire. Now I am Milly's sister again. My children will be Milly's nieces and nephews. And they won't have to read about their aunt in the press or on the internet. They'll have this instead.

Our family has pieced itself back together while working on this story. Because of that process, this book comes from a place of love.

It's time to both own and end this story. But I want to start this book with joy.

I want to start with Milly.

And, of course, the music.

Gemma Dowler, June 2017

I.

Before

1988 – March 2002

PLAYLIST

Abba	Dancing Queen
Donovan	Mellow Yellow
Louise	Stuck In The Middle With You
Elvis Presley	Fever
Britney Spears	Hit Me Baby One More Time
All Saints	Never Ever
Sarah McLachlan	Angel
Mariah Carey	Wind Beneath My Wings
Eva Cassidy	Fields Of Gold
Shania Twain	Man! I Feel Like a Woman!
Shania Twain	That Don't Impress Me Much
S Club 7	Don't Stop Movin'
Spice Girls	Spice Up Your Life
BBC TV	*999* theme
Russell Watson	Volare
Jamie O'Neal	All By Myself
Mark Knopfler	Going Home: Theme of *The Local Hero*
Michael Ball, from *Les Misérables* original cast recording	Empty Chairs At Empty Tables
Josh Groban	You'll Never Walk Alone
The Beach Boys	Surfin' USA
Henry Mancini	*Pink Panther* theme
Shirley Bassey	Goldfinger
Carly Simon	Nobody Does It Better
John Barry	James Bond theme
Petula Clark	Downtown
Jason Donovan	Any Dream Will Do
Barenaked Ladies	If I Had A Million Dollars
James Taylor	You've Got A Friend
James Taylor	Mexico
Janine Maunder	*Neighbours* theme
Cher	The Shoop Shoop Song
Susan Maughan	Bobby's Girl

Note: the playlists in this book show the particular recordings that formed our family soundtrack.

I.

Dear Milly, this is actually the bit that hurts the worst
because this is what we lost when we lost you.

xxxx Gemsie

The Christmas before Milly was murdered, Mum started using a video-camera. We got so fed up with that camera, always poking its little black snout into our lives. Now we're grateful for it. Thanks to those videos, we still have a three-dimensional portrait of our family just as we were in those last months. They show confidence, happiness, and confidence in our happiness. We were so happy together that we didn't even know how happy we were. Yes, we'd recently lost dear family members to old age. We had lost a beloved dog. We had mourned, Milly especially, as she was never afraid of feelings. So we knew what sadness was.

It's just that we never suspected anything truly evil would come our way and that it would take Milly from us.

The video-cam gradually became another member of our family. In the videos, Mum visited all our little clan and was treated to the full spectrum of our behaviours. The camera recorded our pleasures, our sulks, our eccentricities, our uproarious sense of humour. Our family was into extreme teasing. We were rarely embarrassed about ourselves. We were so tightly knit, so sure of our family-ness that we could wind one another up without mercy. We were rude the way you can be only when you know that no one will take you seriously. Or that they will always forgive you.

Those videos now exist as CDs with the Surrey Police crest on the label. They were confiscated during the house search after Milly disappeared. We did not get them back until ten years later, after the trial of her murderer. You may have seen the extracts that were screened on television newscasts again and again, first when Milly went missing, then when her body was found, again during

Bellfield's trial and the hacking scandal. Every time we had to live her murder all over again. So you will probably have seen Milly ironing her jeans, playing the sax. You will have seen that willowy frame, that delicate profile, the scrunched-up hair, those dancing eyes, that attitude.

But the video footage released by the police was silent, or muted.

What you cannot know is the happy soundtrack of those videos. There's me giggling, Mum coaxing, Milly back-chatting, Dad asserting mock authority (and real resignation) in his house of sassy women. Our home was a kind of musical comedy show with well-loved characters playing their parts. In the videos, you see us being ourselves, in our classic poses: me clearing up or sorting things out; Milly sashaying about; Dad looking mock-heroic and long-suffering. Mum had recently lost a lot of weight so everyone was entitled to joke about her 'suck-in knickers' and her sleek new silhouette.

Mum was always known as 'Mumazino'. That was her name in our mobile phones. It still is in mine. Sometimes we called her 'Mrs Tiggywinkle', after the kindly Beatrix Potter hedgehog who took in other creatures' washing. 'Lovely Mummy' was Milly's favourite, especially when she was wriggling out of trouble. 'Lovely' was a big word in our family. Our grandmother was always 'Lovely Granny'. Being Gemma, I was sometimes 'Jemima Puddleduck'. Milly was called 'Sausage' or 'Sausage Pot'. Or 'Milly Munchpot', 'Milly Molly', 'Mill Moll' or 'Herbert'. As for Dad, I'm afraid we called him a number of things that were sadly politically incorrect. He took it like a man.

Our family has always been all about music. Dad was once a part-time mobile DJ and plays the double bass. Mum has a beautiful singing voice. I'm a pretty good singer myself. Milly was both singer and instrumentalist, a thirteen-year-old with a passion for the saxophone and a talent to match. So in those family videos, there's always, always music. Uncle Pete's a proper baritone and knows how to use his voice. Milly and I warble and shimmy without even being aware of it. Mum is humming. Our little cousins sing Britney Spears songs. Even Lovely Granny's doing creditable

4

karaoke to 'Dancing Queen'. Dad's soundtracks constantly play in the background. That's the music of the sixties, seventies and eighties. Milly and I liked the current groups. We loved the 'old' music too. We have our own jukebox in the house. In the months before she disappeared, Milly's favourite songs were 'Mellow Yellow' and 'Stuck In The Middle With You'.

Milly's voice is still there for us to hear whenever we play those family videos. Even if she's off-camera, you can hear her heckling, wise-cracking, laughing. Her voice was deeper and huskier than mine. The cheeky, breathy sax music was like an extension of Milly's tongue. I'm very sensitive to sound. Milly was a bag of noise. She never stopped. Even asleep, she drove me mad by breathing through her nose. As we shared a room – through choice – my strongest memories of her are the endless chuckling and chatting until late into the night.

In one video, Mum comes into the spare room. Milly's lying full-length on the bed. She's watching a film, way too close to the screen as usual. The camera pans in on her luminous face.

It goes like this:

Milly (catching sight of Mum and the video-cam): 'You're a sad woman.'
Mum (in her coaxing bedtime-story voice): 'Have you got anything you'd like to say?'
Milly (growling): 'Go away.' (She has her deadpan face on, but her eyes are sparkling.)
Mum (cooing): 'Would you like to say something else?'
Milly: 'Yes. Go away.'
Mum (sweeter than sugar): 'Oh, you look lovely in the video.'
Milly: 'You look better with the camera in front of your face.'

And so on.

Mum filmed our pre-Christmas family party. Milly had stuck an embarrassing photo of Dad on our front door, just under the Christmas wreath. That was when the worst thing that could happen to Dad was embarrassment. He groaned when he saw it. But he's always known when he's beaten. He didn't even try to make Milly take it down.

The video-cam enters our house, all decorated for Christmas.

Milly's wearing a sleeveless white T-shirt. It's mine, yet it fits her much better. Everything does. Part of her hair is roughly bunched in a scruffy knot at the back of her head. A few tendrils escape, as they always do. This style of Milly's is officially known as 'messy bun'.

Mum films Milly saxing 'Silent Night' and 'Have Yourself A Merry Little Christmas', while I sing. Milly's face is serious: she's sight-reading these two. It's a bit more relaxed when she plays one of her favourites,' Fever', with Lovely Granny and Mum providing the sexy syncopated grunts. We're being ridiculous, as usual.

Another frame, and Milly comes dancing into the living room. Instantly she owns the camera's gaze. In seconds she's correcting Dad on his dance moves for Britney Spears's 'Hit Me Baby One More Time'. At Easter, our school was to stage a home-grown version of *Stars In Their Eyes*, a talent show in which the contestants impersonate a singer performing one of their hits. 'Hit Me' was my song, but Milly was always the better dancer. She was doing 'Never Ever' by the All Saints, with a couple of her friends. We're already deep in rehearsals.

That Christmas, the video-cam was packed in Mum's suitcase and came with us to Cuba and Mexico. So did Lovely Granny.

You see it in all the videos – Milly was a scene stealer. In the films, she barely walks. She glides, dances and sashays everywhere. While I look down, smiling shyly when the video grazes over me, Milly stares straight into the camera, raising her arms like a sunflower, giving the royal wave. Milly talks to the camera without blinking or flinching. That's her.

Sometimes Milly gives the camera a purely impudent look. Sometimes she is mastering a non-smile. About a year before she died, Milly reached a policy decision: she was now simply too cool to smile. Of course, underneath, Milly had her insecurities, her friendship issues, her hormones, some bullying from other girls. And occasionally she lost it. You don't see her cry very often; a peal of giggles is her usual lapse in cool. But Milly is disciplined. Milly knows who she wants to be. Her personal style is already sorted. So most of the time Milly is mistress of the poker-face, which, of course, has everyone else in stitches.

The camera – and the giggles, the smiles and the teasing – arrive in Mexico. We're having breakfast on a terrace looking over a glinting harbour. Then Milly, Dad and I are in a big blue inflatable, hurtling down a water slide. Looking at it now, it's hard not to see a metaphor of what would so soon happen to us. After the ride, Milly walks right up to the video-cam, her blue eye winking until her long lashes disappear into the aperture. Another metaphor.

The camera zooms in on Milly and me dawdling on some swings in proper adolescent slouches, talking about our recent swim with dolphins. Then we're suddenly little children again, tearing around the beach, throwing sand at one another in front of the turquoise waves. At that age, you can be as jaded as a thirty-five-year-old one moment (a Milly speciality) and squealing like a toddler the next. And it's all OK. It's all OK.

A little later Milly the Drama Queen is seen walking moodily along the beach dragging a dark cloud behind her by the sheer force of her personality. She's rehearsing being a sullen teenager, I guess. Being a bit of a bad girl. You can see her future as one of those teens who's always in trouble for acting out, yet always forgiven because of her ability to charm a laugh out of you even when you're furious with her. Milly struts along that Mexican beach as if she's walking towards the horizon. On her horizon, no doubt, were secret cider sessions in the park, unsuitable boyfriends, body piercings, regrettable tattoos, all-nighters on beaches. Nothing worse than that.

Mum caught that moment, of Milly on the cusp, on camera. I'm sure Milly didn't know she was being filmed.

December 2001. Christmas morning in Cancún. It's raining relentlessly. That's OK. We Dowlers make our own fun. There's Milly in yellow daisy pyjamas (mine are the same, except turquoise). She's explaining the contents of our Christmas stockings – knickers, body lotion, hairbrushes and, in Dad's stocking, aftershave.

Milly takes the camera, announcing, 'Characters include Gemma Dowler, Lovely Granny, Bob Dowler and Sally Dowler. Sound effects by Amanda Dowler.'

Milly interviews Mum about her Christmas. Mum's incoherent with giggles. The weather is awful. The food is awful. We're reduced to eating wine-gums for Christmas breakfast. Dad holds them up as the evidence of our tragic situation. We tell our stories;

our silliness is contagious. Belly laughs break out yet again. When it's my turn, I can't talk for hysterics.

'This is a real no-hoper,' growls Milly, behind the camera, including us all in her mock-disdain.

Then Mum wrests the camera back and she's filming Milly and me in our hotel bedroom, sporting cornrows fastened with bits of silver foil at the ends. Taily Ted, my childhood toy, sits on my bed. Even though I'm sixteen, he still comes everywhere with me. Everyone accepts that. No one judges. Milly has brought 'Blanky', a toy now so shredded that he is just a rather disgusting bit of fabric. He was once a pig, the first toy she ever owned. He was never pretty, but Milly loved to stroke his silky label and the insides of his ears. The more stained and ragged he got, the more she defended Blanky from Mum, Dad and the washing machine. She had another, more respectable, teddy bear, dressed in an Aran sweater, who stayed at home. Mum recorded a message and planted it in a microphone inside him. When you press his tummy, Mum's voice still says, 'Night, night, Milly. I love you.'

Disaster befalls Blanky in Cuba. A hotel maid, quite understandably, throws him away when she's cleaning our room. Milly's distraught. The whole family hunts for Blanky. Milly insists on having the hotel laundry searched. It's too late. Mum consoles Milly by reminding her that there's another scrap of Blanky still at home in Walton. That scrap will eventually be put inside Milly's coffin.

But now the video records only happiness. Milly shows off her cornrows to the camera. She gloats, 'Look, my hair is well good. Look at the back.' For Milly, everything is 'epic', 'well good', 'cool', 'well bad', 'uncool' or 'rank'.

The camera records the back of Milly's head. Watching her in the round – that vulnerable neck, the knobbles of her skull, the pale skin between the hair – that's difficult now.

Milly recounts our experiences in acquiring those cornrows. It was illegal for hotel staff to offer such services so we ended up in a backroom somewhere, with two gay guys plucking their eyebrows. Two naked women came in – 'being naked', as Milly says, deadpan – and go to the toilet. We're nice girls from Walton-on-Thames. We've never seen anything like it.

Well, actually we had. Once, on a coastal walk in Dorset, we spotted an ice-cream van in the distance. Only when it was too late did we realize it was parked in the middle of a nudist beach. Milly stopped, her mouth open in shock. We bought some ice creams. This, unfortunately, attracted a wasp that stung Uncle Pete on his lip. He's not the quietest of people. Hearing his yell, a man jumped up and dashed over with some antihistamine cream, which he kindly applied to Uncle Pete's lip. The memory of that naked man running towards us on the beach was emblazoned for ever on Milly's mind. From that moment on, she decided that nakedness was hilarious.

And nakedness kept happening to us. In Lanzarote we stayed by a surfing beach that turned out to be in the middle of a naturist reserve. We discovered this when, driving down a coastal track, we came across a middle-aged man barbecuing sausages by the side of the road. He was naked, even in what Milly usually called 'the lower *reeegions*' in her fake 'deep and meaningful' voice. The rest of us collapsed in giggles, but Milly had the wit to shout, 'Be free!' to him out of the car window.

It was something Milly used to do: take normal words and make them sound hilariously seedy. And it would all be done with her poker-face. While everyone else was dissolving in hysterics, Milly could play the straight man with amazing self-control.

In Gozo we visited the salt baths where folklore says the nuns used to bathe naked. After that, Milly would go on and on about naked nuns. She loved to say, '*Naked* nuns, naked *nuns*.' One of her favourite groups was the Barenaked Ladies, actually four guys. Obviously the name was a draw, but she also loved their rollicking song, 'If I Had A Million Dollars', about outrageous amounts of retail therapy: a house, a chesterfield or an ottoman, a car, a tree-fort with a tiny little fridge inside, pre-wrapped sausages, a fur coat ('But not a real fur coat – that's cruel'), a llama, an emu, expensive ketchup, a green dress ('But not a real green dress – that's cruel'), a Picasso, a monkey ('Haven't you always wanted a monkey?'). All four of us knew every word. We'd sing them at the top of our voices when driving in the car or cycling.

Milly could be funny about nakedness. Yet she was as shy about her own growing body as any young girl. At most, she would bare her perfect torso in her jeans or bikini.

9

Back to the hotel lobby in Cuba. Milly's in charge of the camera again. She homes in on 'the lovely old people' – our parents and Lovely Granny. Milly interviews Lovely Granny about the Latin American Spanish phrasebook she's been studying conscientiously. Listening to her new vocabulary, Milly works out that Lovely Granny is inadvertently learning how to be a heroin addict and how to pick up men.

Milly and I interview a pair of handsome Canadian boys. The flirting is shameless. The boys don't stand a chance because they don't understand that we're just joking. We do become friends with them and we're sad when we have to say goodbye. Milly tells them, 'If you want to remember me, look at the sky. We will be seeing the same stars.'

It was a mixed bag of a trip. We all suffered different injuries. But then it was funny. In the somewhat grim gardens of the Hotel Nacional, Mum decided to record a recital of our various war wounds. Milly shows a slim calf studded with mosquito bites. Mum, too, has squads of welts. I have a volleyball bruise on my wrist. Dad can offer a tiny cut on his leg. Lovely Granny wins with a jellyfish sting on her wrist *and* a burn on her finger.

Looking at these videos again, I see our family as we always were: fully engaged with one another. Milly and I are not fiddling with our mobile phones. We're three generations, yet there are no barriers between us. We're all in on the same joke. No one is on the outside. We are all each other's favourite people in the world. Later, when you're reading about us at the trial that was so cruelly choreographed by Milly's killer, please remember that. Remember that we were not dysfunctional. If anything, as a family, we were hyper-functional, hyper-joyful. Remember that Milly did not have a secret life. She lived among us as one of us. If anything, Milly was in your face, her Milly-ness demanding attention.

Lovely Granny recalls that at the trial, in his summing-up, the judge said that when Bellfield had been long forgotten, Milly's name would be remembered.

Not just her name.

2.

The newspapers would reduce Milly to a beautiful face, a mystery and a terrible crime.

But no one word can describe my sister. It takes a paragraph to get anywhere near her. Charismatic Milly of the superfast metabolism, willowy, size eight, always dancing, singing, chatting and back-chatting. Milly was a practical joker, a creative type who designed her own phone-case but never had any credit on her phone. Huggy Milly, happy Milly, naughty Milly. Your heart just went out to Milly.

Everybody's did.

As she got older, Milly just grew more watchable, more sweetly eccentric, more attractive, more her truly original self. She was growing into that rare and lovely thing: a girl who was super-cool and warm at the same time. In that spring of 2002, Milly was just coming into flower.

Now it's time to draw the tree Milly grew on.

Our father is Robert, usually known as Bob. He's tall and slim, with a comforting presence. Dad's a wonderful man to hug. It's like an encounter with a friendly bear. It's no coincidence that many photos of him and Milly show them hugging.

We sometimes call Dad 'Catalogue Man' because you can buy him anything off the page and it will fit perfectly. He eats what he likes and his body never fills out any further than the ideal dimensions for his height. Like Milly, he's just naturally elegant. Unlike Milly, he can appear quite reserved. He's also an old-fashioned gentleman, opening car doors, using your name, looking you in the eye and apologizing sincerely if he ever interrupts you.

He was born in 1951 in Hillingdon. When he was six months old the family emigrated to Adelaide under the Assisted Passage scheme. Homesickness drove them back to Britain. They lived in Hayes, west London. He enjoyed a happy childhood and was unusually close to his parents. He was a grammar-school boy, leaving at eighteen to take a job in an engineering company.

Music is Dad's guiding light. He doesn't read it – he learns by listening. He just has that knack, perhaps built from the musicality that runs deep through our whole family. He would sometimes do the discos for our birthday parties. But pretty much any day of the week, our whole house was a disco. He loved it that Milly and I were enthusiastic singers and dancers. When he turned fifty in 2001, we had a fifties and sixties fancy-dress party. Mum, Milly and I performed 'Bobby's Girl' for him, wearing matching black-and-white dresses Mum had made. We had practised the routine in secret while he was at work. Dad dressed as a Beatle with a pudding-basin wig. He thought he looked like Paul McCartney.

'Dream on, Dad,' said Milly. Her birthday card to him said, 'Now you are officially an OLD fogie.'

For some time, I think, music was the only consistent thing in Dad's life. He changed jobs every couple of years. In 1975 he was at Penguin Books, as a computer analyst and programmer.

He met Mum while he and she were working at a specialist recruitment consultancy based in Fleet Street. They married in 1984. The change to recruitment and to life with our mother clearly suited him. It seems she gave him the certainty and stability he'd been seeking. After they married, Dad settled down properly, both at home and in work. I was born two years later, Milly two and a half years after that.

Dad was devastated by the loss of his own father in 1995, followed by that of his mother in 2000. The old close family had been cut down, and it would take him a long time to recover. We were all he had, and he cherished us, bringing our mother's mum, Lovely Granny, into the fold, especially after Grandad died in 1997.

Lovely Granny is shortish, shorter than Milly and me. She has a wickedly contagious laugh. Lovely Granny was the perpetrator of most of the 'lovelys' in our conversations. Family videos show that Lovely Granny was often with us, both home and away. We particularly loved our holidays together, at first camping in the UK, progressing to Europe, then travelling further afield to Florida, Cuba and Mexico, the last big trip we made with Milly.

Dad did the discipline, but he can't have scared us much because

Milly and I didn't hesitate to play practical jokes on him. It's easy to prank the straight man, which was the role Dad played in the household comedy. He even kept spreadsheets of his colds and flu. He was very particular about the weather: he always needed to know what it was doing so he could dress appropriately. Once Mum asked him what he wanted for his birthday. His answer was 'galoshes' – the kind he could wear over his work shoes so that he could arrive at the office in pristine condition, even when it was raining.

Mum never found them, thank God. Milly and I would have been mortified if she had.

Our mother is Sally, a further education teacher, born in 1959 in Middlesex, where she spent all her young years. She did her degree in maths and statistics at Exeter, graduating in 1980. She was living in Hampton when she met Dad. They had a love of music in common.

Mum's special domain is the garden. Our parents still live in the same 1930s house in Walton Park we occupied when Milly was taken. So Mum's had more than twenty years to perfect her garden. French windows open on to it and it feels like part of the house, the most beautiful part. It is a story garden: there are gardens within gardens. The seashore's represented with planks from an old pier; there's a lyrical cottage garden; there are walks under flowered pergolas, including one Grandad built just before he died.

Grandad also built a tree-house for Milly and me. That was where we kept an old Morse code machine. Milly loved to send distress messages. Foxes and squirrels slept up there at night. The tree-house was where we used to prepare imaginary meals, especially *boeuf bourguignon*, one of our worst culinary fears. But we so loved saying the words. We even had a nickname for it – 'Beef Boginura'. Our version was made out of used teabags, mud, leaves and water. When we were pretending to taste it, we'd describe the gourmet experience with exaggerated French accents.

Mum let Milly decide which flower would climb over Grandad's pergola. She chose a yellow Banksia rose. Mum can still remember Milly tending it with her toy watering-can. The year Milly was taken, Mum acquired a new memory about that pergola. When she looked out of the kitchen window, she'd be forced to watch the police taking their cigarette breaks or nervously pacing up and down under it while waiting to be allowed to tell us that yet another body had been found.

Now, a section of the garden is devoted to Milly: a ceramic circle with a beautiful pot, both handmade by the lovely Mr Evans at the Columbia Road Flower Market. Around the rim of the pot are the words 'Forever in our hearts our darling Milly' followed by three kisses. Mum changes the flowers in Milly's pot according to the season.

Mum's petite and blonde, with big blue eyes and a quick giggle. At least, she used to be like that. She's still small and blonde, but the last fifteen years have honed her into a tighter, more watchful version of herself. Tiny as she is, Mum's the strong one, the one who has kept us all together. Mum is the proper definition of a fitness fanatic. She swims, runs, spins. Before Milly disappeared, exercise was just a pleasure for her. After Milly went, it became the way that she worked out her nervous energy.

Then there's me, Gemma. I was born on 16 January 1986 at St Peter's Hospital after an agonizing drawn-out labour. Mum still reminds me of this now, when I'm being difficult. I was christened 'Gemma Louise' – 'Gemsie' to our family. From my earliest childhood, I was a home-lover, a bubbly chatterbox, sensitive and very emotional. I've always been the one who gets up at the crack of dawn and the last to go to bed. I loved looking after everyone, making the tea, baking the birthday cakes. Like Mum, I've been changed out of sight by the trauma of the last fifteen years – into something harder yet more vulnerable. But at last I'm coming back to myself.

Milly was born on 25 June 1988. There's a photo of me with baby Milly propped up in my arms. I look like the proudest girl in the world. I was always good with babies. If anyone came over with a howling baby, Mum would tell them to give the child to me. I would stop the crying.

In one of her police statements, Mum would write, 'The girls got on very well together and there was no sibling rivalry between them.' Perhaps that was partly because Milly and I were so different. We each had our own roles to play. Like the two female leads in the musical comedy our lives so often resembled, our lights and shades were complementary. They did not cross over.

Milly was born fiercely independent, unlike me. Her stubbornness was legendary. She would consent to get into her baby sling only if she was facing outwards. The first words for which she was famous were 'Me do it!' She had to do everything her own way. You couldn't help her with anything, whether it was tying complicated shoelaces or washing her hair. If you asked, you'd get a ferocious 'Me do it!' and an old-fashioned look.

Milly talked late. She waited until she could speak in complete sentences and say exactly what she wanted to say. Her grammar and vocabulary quickly expanded. But her attitude remained just as fierce. Tiny Milly once faced off our father with her hands on her hips and the words, 'I defy you, Daddy!'

Lovely Granny remembers Milly learning to ride her bike in Bushy Park. At her first lesson, she hopped on and wobbled. Soon she was going faster and faster. Dad had to chase her. She pedalled right out of sight.

Milly definitely wasn't afraid of showing how she felt. She was fierce and brave about what she believed in. Milly was the world's best sulker. She was so stubborn that it would take her ages to finally say sorry or admit that she'd been wrong. The worst was when she and Dad had an argument – it could go on for ever because he was the same as she was. In this, Milly was very different from me. I could never stay angry for longer than an hour. I would just apologize, even if it wasn't my fault, just to clear the atmosphere.

Sulks were the exception for Milly. Most of the time she was too busy dancing, singing, teasing. She was hugely affectionate, and never held back from saying she loved you. Milly would give what she called a 'Guttural Hug', especially to anyone who was feeling down. It consisted of grabbing that person in a full-body embrace, then making a sinuous circle with your two bodies clinging together. It was important to say slowly, in a meaningful tone, 'Guttural Hug' while you hung on and pushed your whole self against them to squeeze out that last bit of love. No one ever emerged from one of Milly's Guttural Hugs without a grin on their face.

If Mum was cross with her, Milly would say, 'Mu-u-u-m, do you need a hu-u-u-g?'

If the answer was, 'No, I'm angry with you, Milly, you've been naughty,' my sister would coo, 'Mum, do you need a *Guttural* Hug? I think you do, Mum. I think that's just what you need.'

Mum would always succumb.

And then, mid-hug, Milly would purr a two-note TV jingle from a yoghurt advertisement – 'Aaah, Danone' – as her expression of ultimate satisfaction.

Her Christmas and birthday cards show the exuberantly affectionate side of Milly: 'To the best, loveliest, superest, brilliantest Mummy in the world', 'To Gemsie, love you lots like Jelly Tots!!' One exclamation mark was never enough for Milly.

Milly used to leave notes, scribbles and Post-its everywhere. We both did. We'd tuck scraps of paper into Dad's briefcase for him to find: 'Daddy, we love you.' As Milly was always in trouble, for running up phone bills or forgetting the time, she would leave 'Sorry' Post-its for our parents all over the house, and in the car. Just before she disappeared, Milly wrote me a card:

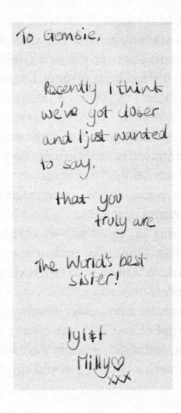

Milly always knew just who she was. Her tastes were formed early, and some of them were endearingly eccentric. She had a precocious passion for dinosaurs and was extremely knowledgeable about them. When Milly was three, Grandad and Lovely Granny came over with a gift of a dinosaur colouring book. Milly sat on Grandad's lap at the kitchen table and eagerly opened it. 'But, Grandad,' she said, 'I didn't know diplodocuses could swim!' Grandad choked on his tea.

When asked in school to write a poem about animals, featuring alliteration, Milly chose worms: 'Wiggly worm, wet worm, wonkey worm, wilted worm . . .' She followed that with an essay, 'A Day in the Life of a Worm', in which her slimy hero wakes up and finds himself in a bird's nest.

Not many girls have a favourite shark. Milly did. One of her most-consulted books was *The Concise Illustrated Book of Sharks*. Milly adored the Tasselled Wobbegong, a supremely ugly speckled specimen. It lurks on the ocean floor, ungainly as a lump of mouldy cookie dough. Milly loved the Wobbegong precisely because it was so ugly. And she thought the name was hilarious, repeating it in her 'meaningful' voice. She'd read her shark book fearlessly, even before going to sleep. However, the scary side of sharks got through to Milly in one way: she never liked murky water underneath her when she swam.

She loved hunting for fossils and special stones on the beaches where we used to walk and cycle, sometimes singing at the tops of our voices, like the family in *The Sound of Music*. Deeply, *deeply* uncool! Near Swanage, Milly found a large pebble with a distinctive heart-shaped indentation on it. Mum photographed her holding her new treasure, which Milly kept for the rest of her life.

Apart from murky water, there was only one other thing that truly scared Milly: being alone in the darkness. One of her favourite childhood books was *The Owl Who Was Afraid of the Dark* by Jill Tomlinson. Unlike Plop, the baby owl in the story, Milly never learned to like the dark. When she had sleepovers, her friends knew that a light had to be left on for her. The dark loomed large in her imagination. In one school workbook she wrote a list of things that generate suspense: 'night time in a grave-yard, on your own in a forest, dodgy street, being followed, sleepover in a haunted house . . . badly lit street . . . young girl walking home alone'.

*

Being so opinionated, Milly had a favourite everything. Her favourite had to be different from everyone else's. If it was weird, all the better. Her favourite colour was the rudest shade of shocking pink – her room was painted that colour. Sometimes Milly's tastes did not quite add up. That was something that made her more interesting. You could not second-guess what she was going to be passionate about, or what she would rubbish without mercy. Fitting in with her 'alternative' theme, Milly was left-handed, and proud of it, but she taught herself to be ambidextrous in most things.

Her favourite television programme was *999* with Michael Buerk. The show reconstructed real-life emergencies, which included a girl having her hair caught in a Jacuzzi, then being sucked under water, and a man getting his leg stuck in a crevice on a cliff edge. As *999* made Milly hyper-aware of rescue dramas, she wrote reprovingly in a school workbook:

> *Many people take part in dangerous sports such as rock climbing, mountain climbing, potholing, paragliding and parachuting etc. Therefore they choose to take part in this. It is they're choice. However some of the consequenses can be dyer and the person taking part doesn't always have to deal with them . . . what if the pothole rescue team are too late, who has to suffer then, the family. If the person dies, you then see exactly how much hurt and pain was caused by a little excitement which turned out to be a tradgic disaster . . . if they want to do it they can but then they may also make others sad/worried/go into complete utter morning.*

Given her fascination with disasters, Milly loved all things to do with the *Titanic*. The mirror in her bedroom was a simulation of a lifebelt from the doomed ship. Here's her own drawing of it:

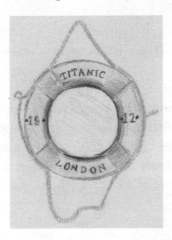

Nothing off the shelf for Milly. If it had to be bought, she would customize it, like her phone. In her Year 8 Record of Achievement, she noted that in 2001 the topic she enjoyed most was textiles: 'It showed how creative I am at art and design.' Even her bedroom bookcase was inscribed with her graffiti in felt tip and biro. Her name was in a constant state of design evolution.

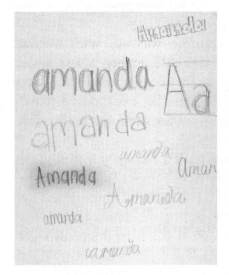

Milly loved buying rubbish and would frivolously spend her money on utterly tasteless items, even though she was perfectly aware that they were hideous. Milly could accommodate hideous, no problem. Sometimes it made me cringe. My tastes were more 'normal'. She once spent all her birthday money on a yellow hard hat with a glass on top and a curly straw so she could walk round drinking without having to use her hands.

As she claimed the right to choose *everything* in her life, Milly was also an incredibly fussy eater. She loved cheese and cucumber sandwiches. She could eat a whole cucumber, peeled, on her own. Milly also adored chips. The tomato sauce had to be on the side, for dipping. No mixing. She didn't want to eat much else, except sweets. She would absolutely not eat tomatoes, onions or carrots unless they were chopped into microscopic fragments and ground into the food. Otherwise she would pick them out. I was nearly as bad. Poor Mum. She tried to feed us healthily, but it was a real struggle. We wouldn't let a speck of Mum's 'Beef Boginura' pass our lips. Back then, Milly or I would hiss, 'Oh, no, the Le Creuset is out!' meaning that Mum was going to try some hot meaty dish on us.

Milly, in her Drama Queen incarnation, was given to writing dramatic notes to herself in her diary or on scraps of paper. She'd be tragic one second, giggling the next. Her sense of humour was far more developed than her dark side so it was best not to take the tragedy too seriously. She'd only laugh at you for it. Like any teenager, she sometimes saw things in black and white, especially if she couldn't have something she wanted.

'You've ruined my life,' she would declare, if Mum wouldn't let her have the latest model of mobile phone.

Sometimes she posed as an angry teenager, using in her diary a whole new vocabulary, one we never heard at home. It sounded terribly inauthentic when we read it later. Words like 'pull a boy' or 'snog' were not Milly. I think she was rehearsing, or going through the motions of what she thought a teenager should be. I was a hopeless role model in that respect. Too much of a goody-goody.

Any sadness in Milly seemed to come out in music. Like any teenager, she would scribble out the lyrics of wistful songs like 'Angel'. Baby pop star Milly needed to memorize the words for the singing sessions she'd record with her friends. These handwritten lyrics ended up in a Barbie-pink box at the end of Milly's bed.

Milly wasn't jealous of the things I was good at. She generally thought they were pretty uncool. I loved sport; she didn't like exercise. It made her sweat, which she hated. I was a morning person;

Milly would stay in bed until the last possible minute. I helped out in the kitchen; Milly never cooked anything more complicated than oven chips.

I was the occupant of the world's tidiest bedroom. Latterly Milly slept there with me, but she kept her possessions in her own room – a pig-sty raked over by a hurricane. Her floor consisted of her collection of sketches, beads from making bracelets, clothes she had worn for just an hour, school work and magazines. In her Record of Achievement, Milly noted, 'I have managed to consistently have the most messy room in the house all year round.'

Milly was always pushing the boundaries – the small ones, not the big ones. She wasn't a rebel. Lights-off curfews, rules on TV consumption and phone-time limits were all made to be broken, as far as Milly was concerned. Her time-keeping was not too good – maybe because Milly refused to wear a watch.

She loved prank calling, putting on silly voices. Her friend Hannah Mac remembers being in our cloakroom one afternoon when Milly started knocking on the door. Milly put on a little-old-lady voice. 'Hellooo! Hellooo!' called little-old-lady Milly. 'I'm stuck in the door. *Heeelp meee ooout!'*

Milly adored music but that wasn't enough to stop her bunking off a music lesson when she was eleven. The school wrote a letter:

Dear Mr and Mrs Dowler,

I was concerned to find that on Friday 19 January 2001, Amanda missed part of her period 3 lesson. Amanda was found in the girls' toilets with a group of friends and admitted it was their intention to miss the lesson.

I have spoken to Amanda about the incident and she has assured me that it will not occur again. She was given a 50-minute detention . . .

That was probably the worst thing Milly ever did at school. Although they put on their severe faces with her, Mum and Dad secretly struggled not to laugh. It was quite an incompetent bit of naughtiness. There were CCTV cameras in the school toilets and, not surprisingly, the absence of five girls from one lesson was rather conspicuous.

Mum pulled herself together to write a semblance of a serious letter in return:

Thank you for your letter concerning Amanda missing a lesson. We have discussed the situation with Amanda and feel she is duly remorseful.
We fully support the school's action in this case and we reinforced your actions with a one week grounding including both a telephone and internet ban.

Mum remembers saying to Milly, 'If you're going to miss lesson, why did you skip music? It's your *favourite*.'

If Mum tried to tell her off for smaller offences, Milly would coax in her 'lovely' voice: 'Come on, Mumazino, you *know* you really want to laugh.'

It was true. It would take a harder woman than Mum to stay angry with Milly for long.

Milly was christened Amanda Jane but was nearly always known to us and her friends as Milly. When we were little, my sister and I were crazy about the *Milly-Molly-Mandy* books. It was obvious to the whole family that there were very close similarities between Milly and the fictional character. Both were a mixture of fashion guru and tomboy, combining a fascination for pond-dipping and rock-pools with a love of dressing up. Both were usually at the centre of some drama generated by a bit of harmless mischief on their own part. In the middle of one of her scrapes, each girl would tough it out with her poker-face, denying any complicity at all. For a long while, Milly had the same dark page-boy bob as Milly-Molly-Mandy. Milly's flicked up at the ends too. Like her heroine, Milly loved hats. You see her wearing them again and again in the family photo albums.

Milly was a daddy's girl. And Daddy always delivered whatever Milly wheedled for. He'd laugh about it, and call it 'cupboard love', but it was real love too, and they both knew it. If Milly had been allowed to finish growing, she would probably have been tall, like Dad. Milly inherited Dad's metabolism. Industrial quantities of chocolate disappeared inside Milly without ever adding a visible centimetre to her slender frame or a pimple to her perfect skin. She was especially greedy for Maltesers. She'd consume mini chocolate croissants by the bag, not one or two at a time. I used to tease her, 'When you turn sixteen, it will all go to your tummy.'

She would reply nonchalantly, 'Oh, well, I'd better enjoy it now then,' and she'd dive into another bag of sweets.

Milly and I were both fully secure in the knowledge that our parents loved us equally. But we had these affinities and alignments of interest that distinguished our relationships with our parents. Milly and Dad would go to the Imperial War Museum; Mum would take me shopping and to a pop concert. Mum and I were swimmers. Dad was a keen angler, and so was Milly. While I look like Mum's younger sister, Milly much more resembled Dad, with the angular bone structure that photographs so well, and her daddy-long-legs frame. Her eyebrows were delicate and perfectly arched. It was almost impossible to take a bad photograph of Milly. She had all the right angles effortlessly. Her eyes, as she herself described them in a school questionnaire, were 'bluey-greeny-grey'. Her hair was 'blondy-brown'. Milly used to tease me and Mum about our closeness. It wasn't just that Mum and I are like a pair of friends, we also have a striking physical similarity. When we watched television, Mum and I always laughed or cried at the same moment.

When she was younger, rather than dressing up dolls as I did, Milly preferred spending hours digging in the mud or fishing for things in our garden pond. Each year, she and Dad would clear out the algae that choked the oxygen needed by the animals and plants underneath. Unlike me, Milly didn't mind getting her hands slimy and would happily lift fish and newts to their temporary quarters in a paddling pool during the annual clean. Our pond newts were not great beauties. They were a dark Jurassic brown with speckled yellow and orange bellies. But Milly loved them, as she loved all animals. She'd send cards from school trips addressed to 'Dear Mummy, Daddy, Gemma, Holly [our dog], Sooty [her rabbit], Snowdrop [my rabbit], frogs, fish and newts'.

Dear Mummy, Daddy, Gemma,
Holly, Sooty, Snowdrop,
frogs, fish and newts,

I am missing you all very much.
It's great here our chalet is nice. It's
cool because we have our own keys
to the chalet. To answer mum's
question no I haven't been on the
Quad bikes yet we're going on
them tomorrow (Friday)
Sorry if this card don't reach
you but I'm writing at 7:00 am
and it is sopostobe collected today!
Anyway
lots of love
and kisses your very own
Milly Molly Mandy
x x x

Newt architecture was one of Milly's hobbies. She built newt bridges out of stones. Out of a piece of slate, she made sun-bathing decks for the newts at a safe distance from any fish. She insisted on netting to keep away the newt-eating heron. As soon as she could read, Milly wanted books about newts and pond life. While she was absorbed in them, I'd be planting and harvesting flowers and watching *Gardeners' World* on television. I'd rather eat one of Mum's dreaded casseroles than pick up a newt, no matter how often Milly offered one to me.

Milly's love of animals started early. She adored Sooty, and our dog Holly, who would give us all 'lap loves' for hours. Her favourite PlayStation game was Croc, which featured foxes. Milly was always interested in everything under water. One of her earliest school pictures shows her choosing her favourite animal: 'My creature,' says Milly, 'is a fish.'

Amanda

Draw the creature from the deep

my creature IS a fish

When she was nine, Milly filled out a school questionnaire about herself. When asked, 'What do you want to do when you grow up?' Milly wrote, 'I'd like to be a vet on weekdays but a Handyman at the weekends.' She certainly had skills in that department. She had her own little toolkit. She helped Grandad build our pergola and the tree-house. Grandad also patiently oversaw Milly making a wooden bird-box for our Ginkgo biloba tree. After he died, Milly stepped into Grandad's DIY boots, helping Lovely Granny with all her carpentry needs, especially erecting flat-pack furniture. No manual was too treacherous or opaque for Milly. We bought Lovely Granny a chest of drawers to house all of her old photographs. Milly was there in a flash, screwdriver in hand, poring over the instructions.

Milly was also interested in the human body and all of its functions. She managed to persuade Lovely Granny, a former nurse, to buy her a part-work magazine called *The Human Body*. Eventually, using the separate issues, you'd be able to build a whole miniature skeleton with all its internal organs. And Milly was fascinated by lavatories. Whenever we looked at a Dorling Kindersley book with a cross-section of a castle, she couldn't rest until she'd found the toilets. On an Isle of Wight trip when she was nine, she kept a toilet diary, visiting as many public conveniences as possible. She wrote them up for style, ambience and the quality – or absence – of the toilet paper. They were rated anything between 'well good' or 'rank'. I would never go into a public toilet, even if I was bursting. I'd wait till we were somewhere decent.

Milly went through the normal childhood illnesses, including chickenpox. She had constant ear infections and suffered very badly with tonsillitis from the age of four. I was very much aware of her being in pain. Eventually Mum pleaded with our doctor for the tonsils to be taken out. When she came round, Milly's first words were 'Please can I keep my tonsils? I want to take them into school for Show and Tell.' She was gutted when the surgeon told her severely that the tonsils had gone straight into the medical wastebin. She also wanted her grommets when they were removed from her ears. That time she had her way. They lived in a little bottle on a shelf in her room so she could show friends who came round.

You needed a high tolerance of weird if you wanted to be Milly's friend.

Milly was very intelligent. Academically, she was doing much better than I was. Things came a lot easier to Milly. In spite of her eccentric spelling, she was in most of the top classes for everything except PE. She would take exams without hours of swotting, whereas I would have to spend ages studying and still not do as well.

Inside and outside school, Milly gave the impression that she was on top of everything. People who didn't know her well would have said she was very confident. It takes a hell of a lot of confidence for a thirteen-year-old girl to play snarling solos on the saxophone. And, of course, Milly was beautiful and clever. She was quick with a joke – maybe too quick sometimes. Perhaps this is partly why, for a time when she was eleven, she suffered from some bullying at school. A group of girls in her year picked on her because she was more academic than they were. They never touched her physically.

They claimed her nose was big – a lie – and said she was a 'boff'. Milly wouldn't let Mum intervene. She didn't want to make a big deal of it.

Soon enough her svelte figure and her precociously cool fashion sense would help Milly evade accusations of being nerdy.

Milly didn't make new friends as easily as I did. Large groups were not her thing at all. She would even disappear from her own birthday parties if the pressure got too much for her. She was still developing her social skills, and she sometimes mixed better with my friends than with her own.

She had a thing about always being with groups of even numbers. If there were three or five girls, Milly was afraid of being the one left out. It came to a head during a school trip to Germany. Milly was hurtfully excluded from a room shared by five friends. Instead – something we're extremely grateful for – she was allocated a room with Hannah Mac, who was also feeling left out. It was a turning point. Hannah was to become her closest school-friend and Milly was welcomed into Hannah's family as Hannah was into ours.

Hannah Mac was nice through and through, with no side to her. Both girls knew what it was to be bullied. With Hannah, Milly could relax and be herself. Hannah was a keen singer, another thing she had in common with Milly. They shared fashion and music tastes . . . head-banging, grungy stuff. Hannah's always had long brown hair. She's small with a pretty, natural face and mischievous brown eyes. At the time Milly disappeared, poor Hannah was wearing an ugly and awkward back brace that she struggled to get in and out of. Milly would help her with it when they were changing for PE, and even when she had to go to the bathroom.

My parents always welcomed our friends into the house. So Milly's chums would come round all the time. Occasionally someone would fall out of favour. Some of her friendships changed in texture and affection daily. However, when Milly met Hannah, they gelled so well that Milly had a friend for life. It turns out I had as well.

You'd expect me to say that my sister was a caring girl. But Milly's kindness went far beyond the usual cliché. It's no coincidence that so many tributes to her used the word 'caring'. The extraordinary thing about Milly's kind of caring was her empathetic attention to detail. She was kind in unusual ways, often seeming far older than she was, with quaint and formal vocabulary for important occasions.

In one of her schoolbooks, Milly wrote, 'Old people should be treated with a lot of respect whereas they aren't really now.' When Lovely Granny learned to drive at the age of sixty-five, Milly was very proud of her. In the car, she was fiercely protective. When we approached traffic lights, she'd tell everyone, 'Be quiet! Lovely Granny needs to concentrate!'

Milly was eleven when Lovely Granny made her first solo drive to our house. Instead of rushing out to talk about her new bike or her birthday party, Milly was all concern for Lovely Granny and the trauma of that journey. 'Oh, Lovely Granny,' she said, 'let me make you some coffee. Come in and sit down.'

When Lovely Granny drove, Milly always sat in the front. If I asked to have the radio on, Milly told me severely, 'In Lovely Granny's car, the radio is called the *wireless*.' Lovely Granny remembers that Milly was never embarrassed when she arrived to pick her up after school. Milly once brought her sax teacher out of the classroom to make the formal introductions. She told her teacher, 'Here is my Lovely Granny and she has just learned to drive a car.'

To this day Lovely Granny maintains, 'A kid is a baby goat. A child is a *child*.' Milly subscribed to Lovely Granny's aversion to the word 'kids' and never used it in front of her.

Lovely Granny remembers that Milly always used to curtsy after she'd had her photo taken. No wonder Hannah Mac called Milly 'Mildred'. Milly loved it: 'Mildred' was so old-fashioned that it had come out the other side and was cool. Her friend 'Eddie the Entrepreneur' called her 'Auntie'.

Milly studied *Macbeth* and *Romeo and Juliet* in the year before she died. Despite certain issues with the spelling – 'tradgerdy' and 'enimies' and 'anciet grudge' – she loved the plays' use of metaphor, noticing how Romeo describes Juliet as a 'holy shrine': 'Religious imargery is always very nice language and ausumely complimentary.'

She also adored Shakespeare's insults, writing a dialogue with her friend Cara in one of her schoolbooks:

Cara: What, shut up you cantankerous Milly.

Milly: No, why don't you, you cankerblossom, we always have to do what you want.

Cara: Oh please go wash your ears!

Milly: Oh, you're such a foolish knave!

So there was this thing about Milly: she was an old soul in a thirteen-year-old body. She wasn't so much a frilly old-fashioned girl, she was more of an old-style *gentleman* at times, so I guess it had flowed down to her from Dad. Sometimes she seemed almost out of place in this modern age; at others she seemed the perfect on-message version of a teenager in 2002.

Milly could be thirteen, and she could be a hundred and thirteen.

3.

We have a picture we love of Milly kneeling in a field of yellow flowers. It was taken during a camping trip at Selsey Bill. It brings to mind 'Fields Of Gold' by Eva Cassidy. It's a beautiful song of loss and remembrance, about a girl who takes her lover to gaze at the barley fields.

But Milly never had a lover, never made promises to a man, never took a romantic walk in a flower-strewn field. In our 'Fields Of Gold' picture, Milly is a child, on a family trip, with school-friends.

That is not to say Milly was unaware of boys, or uninterested in their potential. In a scribbled note, she declared she was engaged to one of her favourites, 'Eddie the Entrepreneur', a title he acquired at the age of eleven, when he imported Beanie Babies from America to sell at profit in the school playground. In the short engagement pact, Eddie's sophisticated entrepreneur-style signature is under Milly's. Eddie was cool and streetwise. His next business venture was always under discussion at our dining table. Milly really believed in him. The whole family loved him. But I don't think Milly ever even kissed him. The engagement note was a typical Milly joke. Closer to the truth, it was understood that Milly and Eddie were each other's back-up plan, in case they ended up single at the ancient age of thirty. Then they would marry.

Milly later had a shy interest in another boy. She never pursued it as one of her friends had a crush on him too.

Anyone who knows how to tease knows how to flirt. So Milly was fully equipped to be a heart-breaker. She just never had a chance.

There was one more member of our household: Holly. Mum, who'd grown up with dogs, introduced Dad to the concept of being a pet-lover. Milly and I were born with it. Just before my birth, Mum and Dad bought a Springer Spaniel puppy. Holly played a special part in our childhood. As she got older, one of her shoulders repeatedly and painfully dislocated. Finally the vet said the kindest thing we could do was let her go. Milly and I never got to say goodbye to her, as Dad had to make the awful decision at the vet's. Not saying goodbye properly was a big issue for Milly. She frequently talked about Grandad's death, saying that Grandad was now taking Holly for walks in Heaven.

Milly believed in some kind of higher power; that there was something out there. At least, she believed in Heaven. Hell, not so much. She couldn't believe in a God so cruel as to take Grandad away from Lovely Granny, for the two of them had shared a true love story, a lifelong romance. Lovely Granny misses Grandad terribly, but she also says that he's lucky not to have lived through what's happened to us all since 2002.

Speaking of higher powers, when Milly had a question, she would consult her beloved 'Orb of Love' – a grapefruit-sized silver plastic ball full of murky blue ink. From a hole in the top, Milly would read aloud the answers that bobbed up on a revolving bead. The Orb of Love would pronounce mysteriously, 'Very likely', 'Consult me later' or 'You can count on it'.

Milly was also keen on fairies – she usually wore a Flower Fairy necklace – and would attribute many powers to them. Insoluble problems were met with the response: 'The fairies will be sorting this out.' With Milly, you could never be sure how ironic that was. It was perhaps a way of being close to Lovely Granny, who had introduced us to the *Flower Fairy* books and used to read them to us when we were younger.

Our extended family is quite small. There's Uncle Pete – Mum's younger brother – and his wife, Auntie Jenny, and their sons, David and Daniel. There's also Uncle Bree, his wife Auntie Marilyn and their son Mark.

Uncle Bree is relatively new to our family. He's Mum's half-brother. Lovely Granny was only twelve when she lost her own mother in a car accident. When she was just seventeen, she got pregnant by a soldier, giving birth to a son. The soldier was immediately deployed elsewhere and she never heard from him again. It was socially unacceptable to be a single mum in those days. Lovely Granny was sent to an unmarried mothers' home run by the

Salvation Army in Devon. She remembers relatives writing that they wanted nothing more to do with her and that she was a wicked woman. She had no means of supporting herself or the baby. There was no help from the state. A teenager and motherless herself, she had no option but to put her child into foster care when he was six months old. Giving up her baby was unbearably painful and she had no one to talk to about it. None of us knew of Uncle Bree's existence until late 2001 when, out of the blue, he made contact with Lovely Granny.

Lovely Granny made the big announcement in November to Mum and Uncle Pete. She's always one for a dramatic build-up. She'll say, 'I have something Very Important to tell you. No, I cannot tell you over the phone. I need to see you in person.' And then she'll make us wait for it. All she would say in this case was, 'I can only tell you it's *not* financial.'

With this new Lovely Granny revelation in the offing, I told Milly, 'She's probably going to announce that she's really a princess, which means we've got royal blood too. We might be princesses!' Milly was quite sure that we would already know if we were high-born.

When she heard the story of Lovely Granny's baby boy, Milly was proud: 'Go, Lovely Granny! What a rebel!'

Mum was excited at the thought of a new brother. So were we, even if he wasn't royal. Uncle Bree was introduced to us just before Christmas. Milly and I got on with him really well, because he seemed to us just like a child trapped in an adult's body. He was charmed to have two new nieces. He took us on cool trips, including to a secret nuclear bunker. We were allowed to dress up in the old military gear in the bunker's museum. I put on a nurse's uniform; Milly chose an old WRNS outfit. The two of us dressed up our new cousin Mark as a soldier.

Uncle Bree would email and text me and Milly, just like another kid. Uncle Bree recalls how she would write little messages to him on the beer mats at his pub, such as 'You can't be cleaning this pub very well if you haven't found this yet.' He quickly formed a strong bond with her.

Milly didn't discriminate about age or sex when it came to making friends. All you had to be was interesting and open, and Milly would want to get to know you.

*

Style-guru Milly ruled our wardrobes.

It didn't start that way. As a tomboy toddler and little girl, Milly liked shorts and T-shirts: all the better for messing around in ponds. Skirts would only get in her way.

Like most sisters, we were a bit competitive about clothes. The only solution was to kit us out identically. Mum and Dad were always very fair, spending the same amount on each of us. Mum's favourite among our outfits was known as 'tomato and cucumber' – hideous green-and-red-striped shorts and T-shirts. Then there were our sailor suits. As a treat, Lovely Granny took us shopping at Debenhams to buy these outfits. The suits were navy blue with bands of white around the wide hems, which were perfect for swirling. We had white socks and navy Mary Jane shoes. The purchases complete, Old Soul Milly said, in an outraged tone, 'Lovely Granny, I can't *believe* that we're leaving the shop *without buying the matching hats.*' Milly wore the sailor dress on her fifth birthday. You can see her in the photo, curtsying in front of a cluster of pink balloons.

From sailor girl, Milly moved into a period of fake fur, the faker the better. She was careful to wear it in a way that was ironic-funny, not uncool. Even though she took fashion very seriously, she had a well-developed sense of the absurd. In one of her school workbooks, she wrote a script including stage directions: 'Man walks centre stage wearing a Tarzan costume which has a price tag dangling down, saying £12.99'. (He turns out to be Jock, who is so madly in love with Daisy that he tells her, 'The beauty of your face makes a single rose look like a moldy banana.' The lovers admire some cooing doves, which 'then poo all over them both'. After pledging their troth, Jock and Daisy run towards a horse in 'slow motion in the style of *Baywatch*' and 'galop off into the sunset'. Unfortunately Daisy falls off the back of the horse but Jock doesn't notice.)

By the time we were eleven and thirteen respectively, Milly and I were both insisting on baggy flared jeans. They hung off our bony hips and you could see the tops of our knickers. We looked more ridiculous than provocative – otherwise Mum would have stepped in. Those jeans were so long that they dragged on the ground, covering our trainers, soaking the water up to our knees. We didn't care. They were cool. Milly's were ripped and fastened with safety-pins. Instead of a belt, she would use string, a typical fashion statement.

I always feel close to Milly when I listen to music we shared. Her spirit lives more clearly in music. Whenever I hear the sax, I'm jolted. Writing this, I'm listening to a CD of Milly's group playing 'Can You Feel The Love Tonight?'.

I can feel it, and I cry.

As a musician, Milly started on the recorder. Then she found out that Mum had always wanted to play the sax but never had the chance – saxes are expensive. So Milly lived Mum's dream. She joined a group of other musos at school. They were really good. Milly's saxophone teacher found her an extraordinary girl. Craig Rickards really 'got' Milly. He later shared a memory in a letter to us:

> Amanda had passed through the music office with her sax case with her usual cheery 'hello', and after she had gone we talked about what a lovely girl she was and of how she managed to combine being typically teenagerish with being so open, warm and friendly. At the start of every lesson she would always ask how I was, how my wife and children were and about what sort of weekend I'd had. And of course she would tell me about hers. She particularly liked to chat about her holidays and family dos. It was obvious she came from a secure and loving family and she was a shining example of a young teenager who knew who she was, who lived life to the full and who had a balanced perspective on things. I think that probably the best word to describe the quality she possessed is 'Joy'. Joy in the deeper sense of the term is something like intensified meaningfulness. I think that it is of eternal substance and that it can't be destroyed.

Milly's favourite sax tune was the *Pink Panther* theme. It suited her because the film is a send-up of a detective. Milly could send up anything.

Even if the sax was not to hand, Milly would perform. She could be quite quiet until someone mentioned karaoke. Then Milly was *on*. Milly was *neon*. And you wouldn't be able to shut her up. For at least five years, every time we went away with our family friends

Auntie Linds, Uncle Ian, Laura ('Loley') and Robyn – affectionately known as 'the Dobbos' – the must-do was to find the dodgiest bar in town. Then we'd completely monopolize the karaoke. Shania Twain was our favourite. We were experts in 'Man! I Feel Like A Woman!'. We'd have two girls to a mic, aged from fourteen down to ten. We knew all the words. We designed our own dances. We flipped our hair around, played air guitar, cooed into the microphones. We knew how to get an audience going. They'd be on their feet, dancing and laughing, singing the chorus along with us. We also liked 'That Don't Impress Me Much'. It suited us. We could show some attitude. We'd shake our fingers to 'ohh-oo-oh', acting out all the little tableaux in the song, pulling pretend combs out of our pockets, miming 'But that won't keep me warm in the middle of the night'.

Then we'd do S Club 7's 'Don't Stop Movin'. We had our routine for that too, practised relentlessly at home. We'd be jumping, swivelling our hips, pointing, holding out our hands, clenching our fists, strutting, stirring the air, inscribing the S with our right hands just as the group did. We did everything but the somersaults.

In Egypt, deserted and cheap after a terrorist attack, we once stayed in the Hurghada Hilton, a notch above our usual accommodation. We met two actual Egyptian princes, Mohammed and Tem. There wasn't much to do, so Nadia, the entertainment officer, had to work with the talents we'd brought with us. She taught us the Spice Girls' routine from their hit 'Spice Up Your Life'.

Milly was practising Sporty Spice's high kicks on the marble floor in Reception when she slipped over, fracturing her shoulder. We had to pretend to Mum and Dad, who'd already told us off for these stunts, that Milly had tripped over. At the hospital they gave her a waterproof sling.

The sling did nothing to stop Milly's career as our Dancing Queen.

Just before she disappeared, Milly got too cool for this kind of thing. As she hit thirteen, her tastes changed along with her hormones. She was into Offspring and Nirvana, heavy metal and grunge, although secretly, at home, she'd still play the Carpenters and James Taylor. Outside our house, she became more self-conscious. She felt more social pressure and needed to fit in with a more sophisticated crowd. There was less karaoke and more mosh pit. Milly was a great mosher, jumping up and down on the spot, shaking her glossy hair violently in time to the music.

By March 2002, Milly had achieved epic feats of coolness – in her clothes, in her music, in her demeanour.

4.

Walton-on-Thames is such a nice place. It seems the entire community was too nice to notice that there was a serial killer, a rapist and an abuser living right in the middle of our leafy streets.

If you prefer not to look, you will not be ready for what might come out of the woodwork.

I've lived in this town ever since I was born. Walton was very quiet when my parents first moved there. The town centre boasted a Woolworths, a Safeway, a cinema, a WHSmith and Beales – an old-style department store. In fact, Walton was generally very old-fashioned. We still had family businesses: a local butcher, greengrocer, camera shop and an electrical store, the type that can fix anything. Dad still goes there. There was also a funeral parlour and Blockbuster, for videos.

Milly and I spent hours of our childhood in Walton's swimming-pool. I was in a swimming club, training three or four times a week. At Friday Fun they would put up a massive inflatable dinosaur. You had to try to run to the end of it before anyone could knock you off. Boys would be waiting on the slides at the side to grab your ankles.

Another nice thing about Walton is that it's on the Thames so we'd spend lots of time walking our dog along the river, feeding the ducks, having picnics and paddling in the water.

In Dowler-speak, Walton was 'lovely'. There were obviously places you avoided, but that's the same as any town. Very rarely did you see a policeman. I can remember once we were told off by an officer for cycling without helmets. When I was a child, I considered being a policewoman. I thought it would be a great job for me: I liked helping and looking after people. It pleased me that police uniforms were smart and never had creases. Police officers' shoes were always shiny. I thought that the police were the good guys who protected the innocent from the horrible people out there – not that there were any really horrible people, not in Walton. Not even in

Surrey. Criminals, as far as Milly and I were concerned, were on television, fictionalized in crime series.

Mum had always taught us never to get in a car with anyone, no matter what they said. So we were aware of the dangers out there.

But in your wildest nightmare you could never imagine a murder happening in Walton.

When I think back on our lives as they were in 2002, before Milly disappeared, all I remember is a kind of hilarious normality. Our lives were made up of school, home, television, sport and music, not necessarily in that order of importance.

In 2001, Mum had begun to work as a maths teacher at our school. Despite the potential humiliation, I didn't mind this as it meant she now drove Milly and me to school so we didn't have to walk to the station to catch the train.

We had two cars. Dad drove the red Volkswagen Golf estate. Mum would normally take us to school in the blue Peugeot 206, which was newer and had a CD player and radio. I had to sit in the back. Milly sat in the front so she would have control of the music: nothing uncool was to be played.

We would get home in time to watch *Newsround*, a TV current-affairs show for young people, which came on just before our favourite Australian soap opera, *Neighbours*. Milly's love for that show inspired her to write an essay, 'A Day in the Life of a Stereotipical Australian':

> *You wake up in your hammock out on your varander. You can hear the waves softly lapping on to the warm soft sand. You turn around to see it. You see a finn! Oh god! Then you hear clicking. Oh, no need to worry. It's your trusty friend flipper the dolphin.*

She also drew 'A Stereotipical Australian Person', friendly, muscled, barefoot, tattooed, wearing a crocodile-tooth necklace and carrying a surfboard.

Dad decried our soaps as rubbish, yet he knew better than to try to stop us watching them. It wasn't just Milly who liked 999, the emergency programme. We'd all mutter, '999,' when we heard the theme tune.

There was enough fun in our house – Milly didn't feel the need to go out with friends very much during the week. On Friday nights she would sometimes visit her friend Cara. They'd record themselves singing pop songs, Milly pulling faces, Cara very serious. On light summer evenings, Milly was allowed to walk the five or ten minutes to Cara's place, but my parents would always collect her if she wasn't staying over.

Sometimes Cara and Milly would walk into Walton, half an hour away at their dragging pace, and get up to stuff with other friends they met there. The 'stuff' was pretty innocent, involving hanging out with other young teenagers in the local park, and maybe drinking the occasional alcopop. We didn't have much alcohol at home, and I don't suppose fussy Milly, with her limited food groups, would have liked the taste very much. But she had social keeping-up to do, so I'm sure she would have tried one.

Other Friday nights we'd go to Blockbuster in Walton town centre to choose a video. Milly and I preferred Dad to take us, as he could be bullied into buying us at least twenty pounds' worth of ice cream and sweets. On the other side of Blockbuster was the funeral parlour. I didn't like thinking about what went on in there so I always averted my eyes.

Saturdays we spent with our friends, sometimes shopping in Kingston for hair slides, earrings or eyeliner. Sundays were our family days, when we would normally go out for a walk together, with Milly complaining all the time about how far it was. We always had Sunday lunch with Lovely Granny as that was the day she felt most lonely, missing Grandad.

In November 2001, Milly and I persuaded Mum and Dad to take us up to Regent Street to see the Christmas lights being switched on. That year the tenor Russell Watson was doing the honours. We arrived in plenty of time so Milly and I were able to jostle and burrow to near the front of the crowd of mostly middle-aged women. Milly and I stuck out like sore thumbs. We were soon singing along.

When Russell sang 'Volare', Milly and I joined in at the top of our voices. We felt as if he was giving us our own private serenade.

Putting on her deadpan expression, Milly called out, 'Russell! Russell! Have my babies!'

The faces of the middle-aged ladies were frozen in shock. Meanwhile, Russell must have heard, as he looked over. His expression was a mixture of surprise and laughter.

When I glanced at Dad, his face was a different kind of picture.

Milly moved into my bedroom just before Christmas 2001. It happened one night after we watched a scary movie together. As I've said, Milly was frightened of the dark, and the horror film had pressed all her buttons. She asked if she could come in with me. I pulled out the spare guest bed from under my own. And that became Milly's.

She never went back to sleep in her own room.

So, those last few months of Milly's life were a period of particular closeness for us. We'd go to bed at the same time and lie there chatting. Sometimes we'd text our friends on our phones. Well, I say 'our phones', but I mean mine, as Milly never had any credit on hers.

We were not angel sisters. Milly and I had our moments. We fought and teased. She had a small birthmark below her left breast. I used to refer to it as Milly's third nipple and named it 'Nubbin'. By the time she reached a body-conscious twelve, she was asking to have it removed. That didn't happen. Milly just dealt with it. She had her way of getting back at me. Because of my strong eyebrows, she called me 'Monobrow'.

Yet in those moments just before sleep, Milly and I were so very close. That's when you begin to open all your boundaries. You confide secrets. You get to hear the real story or the latest gossip. Late at night was when Milly would tell me anything she was worrying about, and I would share my insecurities with her too.

In those last months, we put in time at the family computer, looking at wedding dresses. Neither of us had ever been a bridesmaid. It was our lifelong ambition. Chatting together in our beds, we made a pact that we would be bridesmaids for each other.

We made another promise after watching an episode of a TV series called *Byker Grove*. In it, a young girl falls sick with a fatal brain tumour. In the days before her death, she choreographs her own funeral. After the service, her friends and family release multi-coloured balloons. Milly and I cried at the sight of all those balloons disappearing into the sky.

It was beautiful, and yet so sad. Milly said, 'When I die, you've got to do that for me.'

And I said, 'If I die, you have to do it for me too.'

5.

In January 2002, my birthday party – a murder-mystery that year – is held at our house.

Milly, meanwhile, is interested in the case of Sarah Payne, who had disappeared eighteen months before. Sarah, like us, was a Surrey schoolgirl, although she had gone missing in West Sussex, where her grandparents lived. Sarah's little face, pretty as a doll's, was everywhere. Sarah's body was found on 17 July 2000. Her murderer, Roy Whiting, was convicted in December 2001. He'd previously served four years for abducting and sexually assaulting an eight-year-old girl, and refused to take a sex offenders' rehabilitation course.

Milly writes about the case in her RE workbook:

<u>Religious Education</u>.   <u>Saturday 12th January '02</u>

<u>A cause for concern.</u>

I think that a deffinate cause for concern is the sad but tradgic case of 'Sarah Payne'.

Sarah was 'taken' by a man while she was on holiday in somerset with her family. Sarah was murderd and found dead naked in a 6 inch quickly dug grave.

This case surely stole the hearts of the nation.

I think it is totally wrong what happend esspicially to a girl aged 7, seven years old thats all,

In the same book, Milly writes about 'Death and Beyond':

The most important question is: 'What is the purpose of life if death is always threatening?'

I think the purpose of life is . . . to find a way to touch as many people as you can lives and 1 speacial person and touch their heart.

Milly is also taking a keen interest in history. She's studying the Second World War, the rise of the Nazis, concentration camps. She has designed a poster for a gas attack. Showing much empathy, she writes diary entries by Germans living under Hitler's regime. She copies out poems about the hardships of soldiers and the anguish of war.

Of course, our music-mad family is also up to date with what's going on in the world of pop. Westlife has topped the charts again, with 'World Of Our Own'.

On our favourite soap opera, *Neighbours*, Libby is fretting about Drew's new job as a bouncer. Rolf Harris is presenting *Animal Hospital*, which we both love. We cry at the sadness and pain of the injured animals. I'm too squeamish to watch the operations, unlike Milly.

The film *Ice Age* is about to come out, but Milly and I are above that kind of childishness. Or so we'd protest, if you asked us. Except that Milly did ask for, and get, *The Little Mermaid II* in her Christmas stocking because the first film was a joint favourite of ours. Later, I would watch *The Little Mermaid* alone, trying to be close to Milly, and find it absolutely terrifying because of the sea witch Ursula and her slimy eel minions, Flotsam and Jetsam.

Apart from our weakness for mermaids, we grown-up girls are now into rom coms, which we go to see at the little old-fashioned cinema in Walton. We're fans of *Coyote Ugly* because of the song 'I Love Rock 'N' Roll', which is automatically added to our karaoke repertoire.

I'm so obsessed with *Bridget Jones's Diary* that Milly teases me I'll end up like the heroine in the scene where she belts out 'All By Myself' in a shabby apartment. In Milly's version, my lonely spinster body is eventually found by Alsatian dogs. Milly's a champion teaser because she's so quick to take advantage of every opportunity. It's harder to get something over her. She's such a changing target, these days, engaged in a constant evolution of her 'Milly-ness'. And her expert poker-face means that you almost never get the satisfaction of seeing her upset.

Gareth Gates and Will Young are battling it out on *Pop Idol*. We love them both, but Milly and I are voting for Gareth. Milly's in ecstasy because she's going to a *Pop Idol* concert in the third week of March.

Meanwhile we're in the final frantic stage of preparations for *Stars In Their Eyes* at school. The Grand Finale's to be held just before the Easter holidays. The whole school is obsessed with the show. My group doesn't make it to the finals. Milly's does. In our living room, Milly records her friends solemnly rehearsing their moves for the All Saints song 'Never Ever'. We still have the video. Hannah Mac and the others are bouncing on their feet, stroking their hips, swinging their arms in front of their thighs. The girls wear low-slung trousers and Milly-style poker-faces.

'Never Ever' is a soul-searching song, not conventionally romantic. A betrayed girl questions her own complicity in the breakdown of a relationship. She's eating up the sadness of being alone. It's the right choice for Milly's group. This is where Milly and her friends are: they're ready to embrace the full moody tragedy of teenage broken hearts, rehearsing for it, but not quite there in person. I don't believe a single one of them has ever been in love.

In the weeks leading up to Milly's disappearance, I don't see as much of her as usual. We both have so many events on. Milly's sitting her GCSE maths module two years early, smarty-pants that she is. She's not unduly concerned about it and she doesn't need to be. All my GCSEs are coming up, with PE the most imminent.

Sunday, 10 March, is Mother's Day. We go to the Columbia Road Flower Market with Lovely Granny and meet Uncle Bree there. Mum loves primroses and daffodils so we stock up on those. Yellow is Mum's colour. It's the colour of spring, of happiness.

The following Thursday and Friday, 14 and 15 March, Milly plays her sax at a music festival organized by Heathside School. She's been practising for quite some time. One of her songs is 'Local Hero/Going Home' by Mark Knopfler. Milly, being among the youngest in the group, plays the basic tune. Ben, one of the older boys, takes on the harder part of the beautiful melody. The two saxes have a gentle conversation together. In our late-night chats, Milly's confided that she has a bit of a crush on Ben, despite the fact he's going off to university that September. She's not going to embarrass herself in front of him so at home she plays her part over and over again until she perfects it.

On the morning of Saturday, 16 March, Milly and Mum go into Kingston to buy Milly's first ever pair of tracksuit bottoms to wear the next day in a charity Fun Run organized by Uncle Bree. Milly's not exactly one to relish a run, but she's happy to let Mum invest in the accessories.

That night, Milly and I are on stage. Even while preparing for *Stars In Their Eyes*, we've been rehearsing for a fundraiser for our local amateur dramatic group, Hatton Operatic Society. Uncle Pete's a stalwart, with his opera-standard baritone voice. It would be true to say that there has never been and never will be a Dowler family gathering without someone breaking into song, and it's usually Uncle Pete. He'd have us all in tears with sentimental ballads.

For the fundraiser on 16 March, Uncle Pete sings 'Empty Chairs At Empty Tables' and 'Bring Him Home' from *Les Misérables*. After his performance, Milly gives him a big hug, asking, 'Uncle Pete, why do you always sing such sad songs?'

There's a family video of me and Milly rehearsing the Beach Boys' 'Surfin' USA' in our lounge just before the show. We're joined by our young cousins, David and Daniel, who also have the family music bug. Our routine has surfboard props. We're wearing wetsuits and goggles. Milly and I have torn up loads of paper. We tip it over the little boys to simulate waves crashing on their heads. Our choreography seems to borrow something from *The Sound of Music*, with each of us hiding behind the boards and leaping out in sequence. We're also managing to play air guitars while surfing. Milly has to nudge me to remind me to do the right hand gestures to scan the horizon for the Next Big Wave.

Milly has three spots on stage at the fundraiser. As well as 'Surfin' USA', she and Dad do a *Name That Tune* quiz. Milly plays the first line of each melody on her sax. From those few notes, the audience must guess the tune. She has a sax solo to perform too. She chooses the *Pink Panther* theme. Again, you see Milly straddling her Old Soul and Young Teenager identities. She plays like a trouper. Yet she's squashed herself right up against the music stand, almost as if she's trying to hide her slim frame behind it.

The next morning we drive to Essex with Lovely Granny, Milly's sax and her music. We dress up in our 21st Brentwood Charity Fun Run T-shirts. We all take part, even Dad. I pair with him and we get round the three-mile course in thirty minutes. Milly pairs with Uncle Bree. It takes them fifty-nine minutes, as they walk most of the way deep in chat – Milly's idea of a workout.

Afterwards we go back to Uncle Bree's pub, the Black Horse, where a live band's playing. They invite Milly to join in with her saxophone. The band members make a huge fuss of her. She's so happy that there are tears in her eyes as she plays. Milly's a perfectionist. She'll play only if she has music in front of her. The one music book she's brought along is her set of James Bond theme tracks. So she plays 'For Your Eyes Only', 'Goldfinger', 'Nobody Does It Better', 'Live And Let Die', as well as the standard James Bond theme. She's such a hit that the guys in the band just want her to keep playing. So she performs her repertoire all over again. I'd like to say thank you to that band. They made Milly feel special that afternoon.

She says in the car on the way home, 'That was one of the happiest days of my life.'

That week, the pace is relentless. Writing this now, I don't know how Milly and I had the energy for all our performing on top of busy days at school. But we did.

On 18 March, Milly stays behind at school to practise for *Stars In Their Eyes*. When she gets home from the rehearsal, she irons a pair of jeans in preparation for a *Pop Idol* concert the following evening.

Milly has never ironed anything in her life. Mum wants lasting evidence of this major historic event so she films it.

You've probably seen that video. Like the recording of Milly back-chatting to Mum from her bed, it was one of those that the police released after she disappeared. The sound was muted – and therefore so was this brief view the public had into our family life and my sister's personality.

The police edited out the beginning of the ironing video, but we still have the original full-length version. What was cut by the police? Well, I suppose it was everything that shows our family's teasing, relaxed style, the fact that we are all comfortable with our mild collective eccentricity.

I'd like to restore what was removed, leaving out only the dated slang that would sound so odd now, having acquired different meanings. The video in fact starts with me in the kitchen, chopping onions. Ever practical, I'm wearing my swimming goggles so as not to cry. I'm not thrilled to be caught on camera looking so ridiculous. Mum coos in her 'lovely' voice, 'This is Gemma doing some cooking for me.'

'You're so *not* cool, Mum,' I mumble.

'I don't think *I*'m the uncool one here,' says Mum.

In the background Petula Clark is belting out 'Downtown'. We're all moving to the music.

Mum takes the camera into the living room. There's Milly, ironing. Lovely Granny advises Mum, 'You'd better video *that*.'

Milly drawls, 'Oh, God, shock-horror. I'm ironing. It's only because Mum said she would do this for me. And she didn't.'

Mum marvels, 'This is the first time she's ever done it.'

Milly growls, 'It *isn't* the first time I've done it.'

She has her Milly-Molly-Mandy butter-wouldn't-melt face on, despite the blatant lie.

Lovely Granny says, 'I don't bother ironing jeans.'

Milly pouts. '*Exactly*, Lovely Granny. I don't even *know* how to iron jeans.'

Mum starts singing in her ironic bedtime-story voice:

> *This is the way I iron my jeans, iron my jeans, iron my jeans.*
> *This is the way I iron my jeans . . .*

Milly just can't keep up her poker-face, not when there's a catchy tune in the room. She dissolves into a smile, and she joins in.

Lovely Granny points out to the all-seeing video-cam that Milly's ambidextrous.

'Yes, I am,' Milly says, proudly. She shows off her skills, changing the iron from one hand to the other.

The soundtrack changes to 'The Shoop Shoop Song'. Mum sings along, '*Is it in his eyes?*'

Milly warbles, '*Oh no! You'll be deceived.*'

She's swinging her hips. You can see her narrow bones and her flat tummy as she's wearing her low, baggy, flared Bolt jeans. She rolls her eyes and tells Mum to go back to the kitchen.

That's where the police cut the video they released.

On the evening of Tuesday, 19 March 2002, Milly leaves school and goes straight to the home of her friend Sophie, whose father is taking them to the *Pop Idol* concert. Milly gets home at about 11.30 p.m. As it's so late, we don't really have any time for talking, but she tells me that she loved the concert. Of course I want to know every detail, blow by blow: which songs Gareth sang, how far back they were, if Gareth caught her eye. I'll have to wait.

On Wednesday, 20 March, Mum, Milly and I go to school as usual. Lovely Granny's been staying with us for a couple of days and is leaving. When she says goodbye, Milly says, 'I really love you, Lovely Granny,' and gives her a big hug.

That is the last hug Lovely Granny gets from her.

At school, Milly is given her end-of-term report. She's something of a star academically, so there usually isn't anything to worry about. Her reports have always been full of praise and high marks. But Milly has gone a bit teenager this year. The year manager notes that 'This is generally a pleasing report and it indicates that you are working well in many subject areas. There is, however, an underlying message, that you are not working to your full potential in all curriculum areas.'

There are a few comments about her behaviour. Her form tutor has written, 'Amanda can listen to others but must ensure that she's not discussing things with friends when we are working as a whole class.' Another teacher suggests that she should 'use her good oral skills to contribute towards class discussions and reading text aloud rather than communicating with her peers at inopportune moments'.

It has always been hard for the teachers to take the chat out of Milly. She knows it. In her 2001 Record of Achievement, this is her number-one target: 'I would like to try and concentrate more and not talk as much as I would like to.' Her English workbook shows where she was set to write out 'I must not talk in class' twenty times.

I must not talk in class.
I must not talk in class.
I must not talk in class.
I must not talk in class.
I must not talk in class
I must not talk in class
I must not talk in class
I must not talk in class
I must not talk in class
I must not talk in class
11 I must not talk in class
I must not talk in class
I must not talk in class
I must not talk in class
I must not talk in class
I must not talk in class
I must not talk in class
I must not talk in class
I must not talk in class
20 I must not talk in class.

That Wednesday, Mum drives me and Milly home from school as usual. We watch *Newsround* and *Neighbours*. We have the normal noisy dinner together, Milly eating a whole cucumber, refusing any meat. We catch up on *Pop Idol*. In Milly's typical Old Soul way of putting things, she tells us, 'I danced my little heart out.'

The school report must have been burning a hole in her rucksack, but Milly waits to produce it until Mum and Dad are settling down to watch television after dinner. Bravely, she offers to read it out to them. But they're tired. And no one ever seriously worries about Milly's school reports – she's so bright. So Mum says it can wait till the next day and Milly agrees, even though she probably wants to get it over with.

She knows this one's likely to lead to a family discussion about what's going on with her, especially because Mum, as a teacher, can read the code in the bland words of the report. It's hardly anti-social or serious misbehaviour, but Mum and Dad will want to extract a promise that she'll concentrate more in the future. In the meantime, Milly's not too bothered about it, and goes off to the family computer till bedtime, sending messages to her friends and playing one of her games.

After Milly and I have gone to bed, Mum and Dad have a look at the report. Mum's a bit taken aback by some of it. They groan about the references to the chattering and the not-paying-attention. That's *my* domain, the chattering. But they're not worried. There is so much praise for Milly's competence in all her subjects that the odd criticism sticks out.

Milly hasn't gone off the rails. She's just enjoying the journey a bit too much.

That is the background to the day that will change everything.

2.

The Disappearance
March – September 2002

PLAYLIST

Gareth Gates — Unchained Melody

Colm Wilkinson, from the original *Les Misérables* cast recording — Bring Him Home

BBC — Nine O'Clock News theme

ITV — Ten O'Clock News theme

Culture Club — Karma Chameleon

Jason Raize and company ensemble from *The Lion King* original Broadway cast recording — Endless Night

Faith Hill — There You'll Be

Elton John — Can You Feel The Love Tonight

6.

Dear Milly, when you went,
we stopped saying 'lovely' as every second word.
Things were not going to be lovely any more.

xxxx Gemsie

The twenty-first of March 2002 begins as an ordinary day. It's a happy one in our family, the wedding anniversary of Singing Uncle Pete and Dancing Auntie Jenny. Mum's going to babysit our little cousins, David and Daniel, so Uncle Pete and Auntie Jenny can go out.

A new anniversary will be created that day, one our family will dread for the rest of our lives.

Most readers of this book will have few exact memories of 21 March 2002. Few of us retain the trivia of our daily lives for fifteen years. And my own memories of that day would also be blurred had they not become the subject of months of relentless questioning and speculation.

Just to place us again, I turned sixteen three months ago; Milly is thirteen. She'll be fourteen in three months' time.

It's spring. Our garden always looks especially beautiful at this time of year. Mum can't resist native primroses. Once, when we were out walking our dog Holly in some woods, Mum saw a big patch of wild primroses. She squealed with delight. Then she bent down and dug up a small clump with her bare hands and carefully put them in her Barbour pocket. Milly and I were speechless. We worried that Mum might be arrested for stealing wildflowers.

All these years later, that small clump has spread and naturalized in Mum's garden. So this spring the primroses are everywhere. Daffodils, grape hyacinths, bluebells and forget-me-nots dot the carpet of primroses. It's that exciting time of year when we spot the first frogspawn. Milly and I perch on the miniature bridge, staring into the pond, counting the goldfish, looking for frogspawn and hoping to catch a glimpse of a newt.

On Thursday, 21 March, my radio-alarm goes off at 6.30 a.m., as normal for a school day. Briefly, I lounge around in bed. Milly's fast asleep, breathing through her nose as usual. The alarm clock never troubles her. Mum has woken up first and taken a shower. At seven she comes in to make sure we're awake.

I always get up before Milly. She loves her sleep. She could and would spend all day in bed if she was allowed. She groans and grumbles into consciousness.

We dress in school uniform, which consists of a short grey skirt, a white shirt, a light blue V-neck jumper, a navy blue blazer and a blue-black-and-white-striped tie. Both of us are terrors for losing our PE kit and bits of our uniform, so Mum has sewn name labels into everything from our underwear to our ties. It's only March so I wear skin-coloured tights. Milly has bare legs. She ladders her tights as soon as she looks at them. It's not worth putting them on. Anyway, she doesn't feel the cold as much as I do. She likes to fold her white socks under so as not to show over her school shoes. That wouldn't be cool. Trainer socks haven't been invented yet, so Milly has created her own version.

She's also wearing some jewellery, even though, of course, that's against the school rules. Milly has a silver ring on her right index finger. A small turquoise is set into it. She's also wearing a pink beaded friendship bracelet. She definitely isn't wearing a watch. This means that if she turns up late for lessons, she can always say, 'I didn't know I was late – my watch has broken.' With that poker-face of hers.

Milly's hair is tied up in her trademark 'messy bun', fastened with a scrappy blue elastic hairband. She sketches on some very light make-up, very natural, as we are not officially allowed to wear it at school. She would have dragged a bit of eyeliner round her lids and flicked some mascara on her long lashes. I'm wearing the same, plus a bit of blue eye shadow. Mum has given up telling us to scrub it off. She knows when she's beaten. One busy working mother against two full-time style gurus – she's never going to win.

We eat our breakfast together. It was probably cereal, one of the few kinds that fussy Milly tolerates. Sleepyhead Milly is still rather shattered from the concert two nights before. She hasn't caught up with her rest yet and she's not a morning person at the best of times, unlike me and Mum, who always wake up full of sweetness and light, jokes and teasing. If we try to talk to her, we get a few grunts out of her and some growled advice about how deeply uncool we are.

Sleepy as she is, Milly pulls herself together for the morning routine of checking Mum's outfit to make sure she's not going to embarrass us by wearing some hideously frumpy blouse or skirt. As I've mentioned, Mum's lost some weight so we want to see her out of her sad old sacks and in something that'll do her daughters credit. Today she's wearing a pre-approved outfit that consists of black trousers and a lilac shirt with a pair of black boots. She looks sleek and together. She's learning fast. Teenage sarcasm is an effective incentive.

Eventually, we pick up our school bags and get into the car. It must be 7.40 a.m. Milly's school bag is a beige and black Jansport rucksack, bought in America the previous summer. That morning, it contains her books for the day – including maths and science – and a pink Barbie pencil case. (Barbie is here deployed by my sister in a deeply ironic way.) There's also a small white purse with the ace of spades on the front so it looks just like a playing card.

We get £2.50 a day each to cover our lunch and train fares, plus £40 a month for phone credit and clothes. That goes into our bank accounts, for which we have cashpoint cards. Our parents are trying to teach us to be responsible about money. It works for me. I'm a saver. It fails miserably with Milly. Her allowance is always spent in the first few days of the month. So, by the twenty-first, that little ace of spades purse is almost as flat as a playing card.

Milly has her Nokia 3210 in her blazer pocket. Another style statement: even her mobile phone has to be different. The silver case has a blue back cover that she's customized with black pen, marking it 'Milly', surrounded by sparkles. She also has her house keys in her pocket: a Chubb and a Yale on a black-and-yellow key-ring.

Mum drives us to school in the blue Peugeot. We listen to *The Chris Tarrant Show* on Capital Radio. We're in fits of giggles as they plot to set up the Flying Eye reporter on a date. Milly and I decide to check him out later on the computer to see how fit he is.

Mum wants to talk about arrangements for getting home. Once I've finished lessons, I need to stay behind to practise trampolining for my PE GCSE. Mum's giving a maths tutorial that afternoon after school, and Milly has some art homework to complete. So it's agreed we'll meet up at Mum's office at four thirty and all go home together in the Peugeot.

Milly's plans, however, are often fluid. So that is not how our school day will end.

We arrive at school for eight.

Heathside School's a well-kept 1960s building set on a leafy side-road. It's six years since the massacre at Dunblane Primary School, where Thomas Hamilton shot dead sixteen children and a teacher. British schools have learned the hard way to take certain precautions. Mum has to report her arrival into a speaker-phone. If parents want someone else to pick up a child, documents have to be signed. I remember being terrified, at my previous school, by police coming to advise us about what to do if a Dunblane-type murderer broke into our classroom: lie still and pretend to be dead, keeping our eyes closed so as not to see the bodies of our friends.

But that morning, we have Chris Tarrant to giggle about and we're not thinking about death.

We pull into the car park and get out of the Peugeot.

The three of us say goodbye as normal.

We go to our form rooms. After that I don't see Milly at school.

In the family scenario, in our musical lives, Milly and I are very much together. We're not embarrassed by one another. However, we don't hang around together at school as we're in different years and have different sets of friends, though we all meet at our house at weekends. That's normal for sisters two and a half years apart, I guess.

But one thing is not normal that day.

When we say goodbye that morning, it will be the last time that Mum, Milly and I shall ever be together.

Mum does get to see Milly one more time. At the end of the day, after her period-six science lesson, Milly comes to Mum's office. It's just before three. She asks Mum to take her PE kit home. She finished her art homework during the lunch hour so she wants to get

56

the train with some friends rather than wait for me and Mum to finish our extracurricular activities an hour and a half later.

Milly seems absolutely fine, and no different from any other school day. Mum can remember saying, with a hint of suspicion in her voice, 'Are you *sure* you've done your homework, Milly?'

Milly responds with her mischievous playful smile, but assures Mum it's all done.

Milly leaves the school gates with a group of friends, including Cara and Danielle. They're heading for Weybridge station. The spring air is mild. Milly removes her sweater and stuffs it into her rucksack. She puts her blazer back on.

Outside the school gates, the group turns right. There's a pretty graveyard across the road on their left. Heathside School is bordered by dense woods. The students turn right again, taking the leafy path through the woods. You wouldn't want to go there on your own – I never did. But Milly's not alone. As well as her own friends, most of the school is leaving at this time. It's a beautiful place, the sunlight reaching through the foliage in misty stripes. The woods would have rung with the excited conversations of twelve- to eighteen-year-olds just liberated from a long day in their classrooms.

Coming out of the woods, Milly and her friends pass a pub and take a left into a road lined with hedges, behind which nestle some large well-kept houses. A few minutes more and they reach a short flight of stairs that takes them down to Weybridge station. That journey would take fifteen minutes at a brisk pace. Milly's a famous dawdler and chatterbox, so the walk probably took the girls about half an hour.

The last image of Milly is captured by the CCTV camera at Weybridge station. It's grainy. Her narrow body is haloed in light. You can see her hair scraped back in its 'messy bun', her long legs, the socks bunched around her ankles, her rucksack slung over one shoulder. She's still wearing her blazer.

The video shows her alone, probably because she'd had to stop to buy a ticket. As Mum usually drives us home, Milly doesn't have a season pass like the other girls.

She catches up with her friends on the platform. The teenagers board the train.

At that moment Mum's finishing her tutorial and has started

writing up some lesson plans for the following week while she waits for me to finish trampolining.

Milly is still alive, and enjoying herself with friends.

Dad's day

Dad stays at home that morning, which is unusual as he works in central London. But that Thursday he's meeting a client in Basing-stoke, then working from home so he can supervise some builders laying the foundation for a small extension to the music room.

He gets up at 6.35 a.m. as usual, shaves and showers, then goes down for breakfast with the family.

He comes out to the car to give us each a kiss goodbye. For Milly especially, a kiss goodbye from Dad is very important. On the pre-vious day, she was still asleep when he left. When he got home that evening, she told him she'd missed kissing him goodbye. No one wants to be in trouble with Milly, especially Dad, so he doesn't make that omission again today. He kisses us all properly and says he'll see us at home that afternoon.

The two workmen are digging the foundation when he leaves for Basingstoke at 9.50 a.m. When Dad gets home at 3.10 p.m., the workmen have gone, the skip outside our house has two feet of soil in it and the trench is about the size of a human body.

Dad changes out of his suit and has a cup of tea. He settles down to work in our dining and music room, which at this time doubles as Dad's home office.

Milly's afternoon

It's about a mile as the crow flies from Weybridge to Walton-on-Thames. The train journey takes about five minutes. Hersham, the next stop, is nearer to our house, but Milly, Cara and Danielle get off at Walton, along with a cluster of boys from school.

Milly's well happy. She's about to share a bag of chips with Dan-ielle at the Travellers Café on the platform at Walton station.

Milly's not a fan of walking any more than she needs to, but the chips are a powerful draw. She can still get home in time for *News-round* and *Neighbours*. If Mum does something awful, like making Beef Boginura for dinner tonight, she'll already have a nice warm full tummy.

Cara doesn't join them. She heads straight home.

Walton station is a fine blond-brick building with red-brick detailing. There's no CCTV of the friends at Walton station because the camera there wasn't working that day.

The Travellers Café has changed now. In those days, it was your usual railway caff: no patisserie, nothing healthy, no fancy coffee, just lots of bacon rolls and builders' tea. Some boys join Milly and Danielle, all pooling their money for bags of delicious greasy chips. These are boys the girls have known for years. There's no flirting: everyone's too familiar. Milly's as usual flat out of cash so Danielle has to lend her some money for her share. The others would have slathered theirs with tomato ketchup or vinegar. Fussy eater Milly has her tomato sauce on the side.

It seems that those chips will be the last food Milly ever ate. I'm glad it was chips and not one of Mum's dreaded casseroles. I'm glad Milly was happy, doing something she wanted to do, and bantering with people she liked.

Danielle's sister, seventeen-year-old Natalie, arrives. Following our family rule, Milly asks one of the boys, Chris, to lend her his mobile so she can phone Dad to tell him she'll be back a bit later.

Milly is never coming back, but none of us can know that yet.

How far do we unpick Milly's day back to the moment when her future was cancelled? To that bag of chips? What if she hadn't stopped for them?

We could go back further. What if Milly hadn't finished her art project at lunchtime? What if she had waited at school for a lift with me and Mum? What if the trains had been delayed?

The what-ifs torment us and could go on for ever.

Dad's afternoon

Dad gets the call from Milly at 3.45 p.m. 'I'll be back in half an hour,' she tells him.

She sounds happy and relaxed. It's not by any means the first time Milly has been late home from school. She always calls if she's going to be late. We're like that, as a family: we keep in touch. Dad isn't worried. Walton's such a safe place.

The walk home is only fifteen minutes. It's not even nearly dark. In fact, the sun's shining now. Dad would have driven down to the station to get Milly if he'd been anxious. But he's not. She and I have both walked that short distance hundreds of times before. It's a two-way road lined with offices and houses. And at that time of day there are still plenty of cars and people about.

Dad's conversation with Milly lasts just twenty-six seconds.

It will be the last time Dad hears Milly's voice.

He needs to catch up with work phone calls. He shuts the study door, his way of saying to the family, 'Do not disturb'. This is because his singing, dancing, exuberant daughters make more than a bit of noise when we swarm into the house after school, throwing down our school bags and PE kit and racing for the television.

Milly's afternoon

Milly's life is not going to last much longer, so each minute now is precious in our memory.

The chips have been devoured. Outside Walton station, Milly says goodbye to Danielle and Natalie. They are going left. She's the only one turning right. Milly starts to walk down Station Avenue. In front of her stands the huge 1960s Birds Eye building, like a great blue-and-white spaceship that has accidentally landed in Surrey and never managed to leave.

Music's never far from Milly so she's probably humming 'Never Ever' or 'Unchained Melody', the Gareth Gates song she sang along to at the *Pop Idol* concert. She's maybe trying *not* to think about discussing her report with Mum and Dad when she gets home.

On her right is the station car park, dozing in the afternoon sun. The commuters have not yet started coming home from London. On her left, on the other side of the road, there is a bus stop, behind which looms a thick, tall hedge that obscures an estate of flats known as Collingwood Place. The hedge is broken by various inlets allowing access into the manicured gardens. Behind the hedge, Collingwood Place is all birdsong and carefully pruned roses. It's a place of respectability and seclusion, both of which make excellent cover for a crime.

This is how it starts.

Milly is just under a mile from home.

But this is the moment when my life and Milly's fork apart.

She's about to step into Hell.

My parents and I will be in Hell for years.

7.

Gemma's afternoon

The twenty-first of March stays normal a little longer for me and for Mum. When I arrive at Mum's office, I'm not surprised that Milly's plans have changed. That's Milly for you. You just live with it. I get into the car with Mum. We leave the school at about four thirty. The route home takes us past Walton station, where, unbeknown to us, Milly has been eating chips with her friends at the Travellers Café. So at 4.40 p.m. we're passing the station, on the opposite side of the road.

Milly has already left, though. We are fifteen minutes behind her.

In our car, we're now following Milly's foot route home from the station. On our side of the road is the hedge that hides the flats of Collingwood Place. We pass the CCTV cameras on the Birds Eye building, opposite some of those flats.

We don't know that Milly isn't already home with Dad. It still haunts us to this day to know that we were so close to her, in time and place, for those short minutes, and that there was nothing either of us could do to save her.

So we keep driving. By 4.45 p.m., we're home. I hurry into the house, calling, 'Milly! Milly, where are you?'

I need to watch *Home and Away* and *Neighbours* with her. And to catch up, finally, on all her news about the *Pop Idol* concert two nights before.

Mum's first impression on arrival is that the hall is unusually tidy. Normally Milly comes home, kicks off her shoes and dumps her school bag and blazer on the floor. Mum picks them up, as mums do. I don't like creases, so I always hang my blazer up carefully.

From the tidy hall, as well as from the silence when I call out, Mum and I know for certain that Milly isn't home yet. But Mum isn't worried, because Dad is here – and she knows that Milly will have arranged something with him, perhaps to be at Hannah Mac's. She can't confirm this because Dad is in his office, busy on a conference call.

I'm not worried either. I also think Milly's probably with Hannah. I turn the television on.

Mum's babysitting for Uncle Pete and Auntie Jenny this evening. So she phones them on her mobile to check when she's wanted. It's immediately. She goes upstairs to get changed.

She doesn't want to leave without knowing for sure where Milly is. Dad's still on the phone when Mum opens the door and pops a yellow Post-it note in front of him. It tells him she's off to babysit. And it asks, 'Where's Milly?'

She tells him to ring her at Uncle Pete's when he finishes his call, so she can find out where Milly is.

At 5.15 p.m. Dad finishes his call. He walks into the lounge. Only I am there. He's annoyed that Milly has not come home during his conference call. She'd said she would be late, but not this late. He asks me where she is. I don't know.

He explains that she phoned to say she would be home at 4.15.

I look at my watch. Unlike Milly, I wear one. It is 5.15.

A shadow of a small fear falls on me, like a shiver. It's soon gone. We are not the kind of family bad things happen to. Milly's just acting out, being careless about the time. She'll be in big trouble. For a minute. And then Dad will forgive her.

I'm reassured because Dad doesn't seem really worried about Milly. He's more fed up than afraid. He's due to go out to a concert and wants to leave. But he can't, obviously, until Milly turns up.

At 5.21 p.m. he rings Milly's phone. Even though there's no credit on it, she can receive calls.

It goes straight to answerphone. Dad leaves a voicemail. He sounds unusually stern. Is worry starting to creep into his mind too? 'Where are you, Amanda?' he demands. She's not 'Milly' when she's in trouble. 'Ring me back *straight away.*'

At 5.30, a work call for Dad on the landline interrupts us. As soon as that's over, he looks in our family address book for Danielle's telephone number. Milly had told him her plan was to eat chips with her. Danielle's older sister Natalie answers. She tells Dad that Danielle's at her part-time hairdressing job. Natalie says she was also at the café with Milly and Danielle. She explains that after the chips, she and Danielle walked left to the other side of Walton station while Milly headed out to Station Avenue.

At 5.40 Dad rings Mum at Uncle Pete's house. She's just arrived. He brings Mum up to date. He assures her that he's not given Milly permission to visit anyone after school. At this point, Mum's not unduly anxious, assuming that naughty Milly is hanging out with friends and has forgotten the time.

Dad puts the phone down. He's now wondering if Milly might have stopped off at the home of her friend Cara. It's on her walking route home. He cannot find Cara's number in the address book, so he gets into the car and drives to her house. He phones Mum to tell her.

Then I phone her. I cannot keep the tremor out of my voice. 'Mum, I'm worried.'

Hearing my fear, Mum's decision is instant. She says she'll put our little cousins into her car and drive straight home. She won't leave me and Dad to deal with this on our own. She quickly fills the boys up with spaghetti bolognese, then pops them into the Peugeot.

This time I try Milly's mobile. Again, it goes straight to answerphone. I leave a message: 'Come home, Milly. Dad's *really, really* annoyed.'

At Cara's house, her mother is telling Dad that Milly hasn't been round. She invites Dad in to speak with Cara. Dad had really hoped to find Milly there, perhaps practising her singing with Cara. It hits him hard that she's not.

Dad drives home. Cara's house is just a couple of minutes away. The *Neighbours* theme tune is still playing when he walks through the door. I've had to watch it without Milly. I look up, expecting to see a contrite Milly following Dad in with her tail between her legs, having been told off for worrying us and not keeping in touch.

But Dad's alone. He looks uneasy. He's starting to look as if he's not quite sure what to think or do next.

At 5.55 Dad leaves the house again in the car. He's going out to look for Milly. This time, he wants to go to the home of her friend Rosie. But Rosie has recently moved and Dad can't find her exact address. So he starts looking for Milly in the streets nearby. He drives slowly up Rydens Grove, then Hersham Road, towards the Halfway parade of shops. He turns left at the traffic lights towards Walton station. There, he turns, then drives back down Station Avenue. No Milly.

Meanwhile, at home, I begin to message Milly's friends to see if anyone knows where she is, or if they've seen her since she left Danielle and Natalie at the station.

At 6.23, Dad phones Mum at Uncle Pete's from his car. But, of course, she's already on her way home.

It takes her half an hour. It's painful to imagine what was going on in her mind. But at least, even while confronting the worry, Mum, with her practical nature, would have been sorting out what to do next, as we always rely on her to do. She doesn't want to alarm my two little cousins. She simply tells them Milly hasn't got home from school yet and they must keep their eyes peeled for her as they drive. 'You look on the left, David. You look on the right, Daniel.'

The boys know something's wrong and both stare obediently out of the car windows.

Mum has hope, not yet despair. She expects every minute to see Milly dawdling along the road. Every minute she doesn't, Mum's thoughts are getting darker.

Milly is still alive.

At 6.45 p.m. Mum pulls into the drive. The light has faded. Dad's already back.

She finds us both in a state of agitation. By this time, Milly's whereabouts for the last two hours are completely unaccounted for.

I say to her, 'Mum, this is serious.'

Mum told me later that my voice was very strange, very deep and very frightened. It made the hairs on the back of her neck stand on end and sent a shiver through her whole body.

I explain that Dad and I have been ringing and texting all Milly's friends and no one knows where she is. This is out of character for Milly.

Mum says, 'We ought to phone the police.' She tells Dad to do it. She herself cannot simply wait. She has to do something, and I feel the same. I hop into the car with her and the boys, and we go out to look for Milly.

We drive up Walton High Street. We look in McDonald's; we check the grassy area next to Homebase where teenagers sometimes gather. We drive around all the places where we could imagine Milly hanging out with friends. Yet the truth is we don't know where these places would be. She's only thirteen and she hasn't really started hanging out yet.

Finally, we go home. We don't know what else to do, and we want to be with Dad.

At home, meanwhile, Dad has not been able to contain his fear. Instead of phoning the police, at 7.03 p.m. he phones St Peter's Hospital, where both of us were born. He asks if Milly has been admitted. She has not.

Four minutes later, he phones Addlestone police station.

He starts, 'My name is Bob Dowler. My daughter is missing.'

By the time Mum and I get back, it's 7.15. At that moment we see the police car driving down our road. It arrives at our house eight minutes after Dad made the call.

It is then that I experience a devastating feeling that I shall never see Milly again. It doesn't happen in my mind, which is not connecting with the facts. It happens in my body: a deep wave of shock.

As I've said, Milly's a practical joker. She's also very caring. She would never let a joke go as far as this. I know she'd never willingly put us through such fear and uncertainty. That just isn't Milly. So I know in my core, right then, that something has happened to her, something beyond her control.

Milly is still alive in that moment, but she is in torment.

Still trying not to alarm my little cousins, Mum quickly sets up a Disney DVD for them in another room so we can talk candidly.

I open the door to a young, clean-shaven policeman. At that moment I'm already letting go of reality. It isn't at all appropriate, and I know it, yet I feel excited, as if I'm on *The Bill*. It's the first time I have ever talked to a policeman, except that time years ago when we were told off for cycling without helmets. He introduces himself. His face is kind. He's not at all hard-bitten. He's not wearing a pre-rehearsed expression for tragedy. Instead, he has a tick-list of runaway-girl questions and a brisk sense of routine about him.

Perhaps this stops him being too nervous about stepping into the home of a family in crisis.

Later I would do some research and discover that when teenage girls go missing it's normal practice to send a personable young officer to talk to the family. It's supposed to create an atmosphere of relaxation and trust, a kind of bonding that will encourage all kinds of frankness. Frankness can be very useful to the police.

It's now three hours since Milly sat down to eat those delicious hot chips at the Travellers Café. But in police practice, young girls are not classed as runaways until they have been missing for twelve hours. So this policeman's task is to minimize the drama and find out if Milly's the kind of girl who might take off without letting her family know. She's causing trouble, by police norms. So, a hormonal and rebellious teenage girl is what the police expect Milly to be.

Even though she was last seen at Walton station, the police are not yet sending dogs there. No one is yet asking questions around the station. There's no helicopter. No one's looking for Milly, except us. Instead, there's this kind young man, trying to act normal, asking us questions that in no way fit Milly.

Milly is still alive. She's not even very far away.

Mum is worrying that all our bras and knickers are hanging on the radiators. It's not mess. It's family life. But it doesn't feel appropriate to Mum that a young male stranger should be given this view of our underwear. It seems indecent.

Mum apologizes to the policeman for the mess. This is the first time she has ever felt she may be judged as a bad mother. It will not be the last.

The policeman makes it worse, unconsciously, by asking his set questions.

'Has Milly ever run away before?'

No, we say.

'Do you have any reason to think she would run away?'

Of course not.

'Are Milly and Gemma allowed to go on internet chat-rooms?'

No, definitely not. Our computer has parental controls installed, which has never bothered us. The whole family uses that computer. It's in the hall where anyone can see it. There's no hunching over it in the privacy of our bedrooms. We have never used the computer for secrets, meeting boys or looking at inappropriate material. The only internet chatting Milly and I do is via MSN Messenger, which allows you to communicate only with people you already know personally.

'Could Milly have met someone online and gone off with him?' the policeman persists.

'No,' we say vehemently. The idea is ridiculous.

The policeman asks, 'Would Milly have got into a stranger's car, or gone somewhere with a stranger?'

'The girls know about "Stranger Danger",' Mum says.

I answer that Milly would never get into a car with a stranger unless he told her something utterly convincing, such as that one of us was in trouble. 'If someone asked for help,' I say, 'she might try to assist.'

I want him to understand how caring Milly is, yet I don't want him to think she is a stupid girl. Most of all, I want him to understand that Milly would never put us through worry if she could help it. For all her teenage cool, Milly says, 'Good night, I love you,' to me, Mum and Dad every night. Her reasoning is that if something happens during the night she will know that the last thing she said to us was 'I love you'.

'Is there anything she could be worried about?'

There's Milly's school report, of course. But Milly hasn't even discussed that with Mum and Dad yet. The mild criticism wouldn't have really bothered her. She knows she'll still be in the top sets for everything.

'Have you had an argument with her?' This question is for all three of us.

We all deny this, remembering that she was perfectly normal a few hours ago.

'Was there tension this morning?'

No. We had laughed at Chris Tarrant in the car.

The list of questions is designed to lead to the conclusion that Milly has voluntarily absented herself and is hiding somewhere. There are no questions that lead to the answer that Milly has been taken against her will.

We are distressed. We try to make the policeman understand, each of us in our own way, that Milly's no sullen runaway. She's happy, loved. We are frustrated. Why isn't he looking for Milly? Who is looking for Milly while he is wasting time with these questions? Why can't *we* be out on the streets searching for her?

The officer asks if he can look in Milly's room. That seems odd to me. I want to tell him he is wasting his time. Yet at that stage I still feel the police are there to look after me and Milly. I respect him because he's there to represent those in power, those who protect and regulate our lives. Even though he is young, I can't challenge him.

But I know Milly's not in her room. I know she hasn't been there for hours. So, a part of me has acknowledged the loss of her. The rest is in denial.

I'm two and a half years older than Milly, but fear is already sending me hurtling back to my childhood. I am regressing to a state of innocence, to a safe place where little sisters could *not* disappear. I curl up on our comfy old sofa, hugging my knees, which are bent in front of me.

Mum takes the policeman upstairs, not to my room, where Milly sleeps, but to her den where she keeps her huge volume of mess.

Like a child, I'm angry that a stranger is going through Milly's private things. I stay downstairs, acutely conscious that he might be looking at diaries or notes not meant for his eyes. I wouldn't like it if he were going through *my* things.

While he's up in her room, we all start making calls, widening the net of friends who might have seen Milly.

The policeman asks for a recent photograph of Milly. This gives us something to do at last, something to talk about, something to get our teeth into. We find one quickly, as if the urgency we feel might then translate into action by the police. We want to give the officer an instantly recognizable photo of Milly as she is now. But our latest family photos show Milly in Cuba and Mexico, wearing a bikini or shorts. We're forced, for the first time, to think of Milly through the eyes of strangers. We don't want her to look sexualized in any way. That would misrepresent her. We don't want her judged as a girl who dresses provocatively. Deeper down are other discomforts, unvoiced among us. We can't bear to think of Milly's attractiveness turning her into prey.

Knowing that we need something right up to the minute, we settle on a photo taken maybe just a week before. She and Hannah Mac had gone to a booth at Woolworths in Chertsey to take some snaps of themselves for their friendship book.

The photograph we give the policeman shows just Milly's face. She's looking straight into the camera, straight into your heart. You notice her eyes first. They are almond-shaped and slant upwards at the sides. She's wearing her favourite hoodie, with the hood tucked into her coat. Her hair is parted in the middle and tucked back around her ears in her 'messy bun', with the usual straggly strands escaping on to her cheeks. The All Saints girls, not surprisingly, often wear their hair like this. The photo does not show Milly as I personally picture her, or as I think of her now. She has a guarded, staged smile – neither the classic Milly poker-face nor her cheeky grin. This is the public Milly, not the private one. The photo does not hold any memories for us. This will prove merciful for it will become the photo of 'Missing Milly Dowler' and later 'Tragic Milly Dowler'.

We also give the policeman a picture of Milly in her school uniform. We're not keen on anyone using that one, as her skirt is short, revealing those endless legs. But it does show how she was dressed when we last saw her.

The policeman takes his leave. He's been with us half an hour. He has Milly's diary, her address book and the photographs. He tells us he's going to get in touch with her friends straight away – we have prepared a list of names and phone numbers – and that he'll report back to us as soon as possible. He returns shortly afterwards with a female officer, who quickly searches the loft in case Milly's hiding up there.

It's obvious that, in line with general police statistics, these officers believe that Milly is somewhere she wants to be. They have not been convinced by our repeated assertions that she would never run away from home.

The policeman now wants to know about Milly's bank account. Might she have enough money to run off with someone who had groomed her on the internet? No matter how much we explain that she would never have done that, this question remains in the air. It does not make any difference when we explain that Milly always spends her allowance in days. By the twenty-first of the month, her account would have been empty.

'Well empty,' Milly would say.

He tells us that if Milly doesn't turn up soon, as he's confident she will, then helicopters will use infrared sensors to look for body heat in places like sheds, allotments or derelict buildings where someone might think of hiding.

'Why would Milly be hiding?' I ask. There is no answer, as there's no reason why she would.

The policeman tells us he'll be in touch in the morning – if there's no news from our end.

In the morning? I think. *But Milly's afraid of the dark! How can the police leave Milly out there in the dark when we don't know where she is?*

I look at Mum and Dad. Their faces show they are thinking the same terrifying thing as I am.

The policeman leaves us alone with our confusion and trauma. But it's better than having him there asking questions that have nothing to do with Milly. And perhaps he's going to do something more proactive about finding her.

Before he leaves, Mum tells him he must go to Heathside School first thing in the morning – it's the last day of term: the children break up for Easter the next day. This will be the only chance to talk to them all together before they go their separate ways.

Abandoned by the policeman, we spend the rest of the evening sending MSN messages and phoning everyone we know.

Milly is still alive.

About two hours of frantic calls later, a friend tells me that Kat, a girl in my year, had been standing at the bus stop on the other side of the road just after 4 p.m. She saw Milly walking towards home, alone, on the station side of the road.

Like most of my friends, Kat's been to our house and knows Milly. I phone her. She explains to me that she and Milly made eye contact for a second. Then Kat got on the bus. After showing her pass and finding a seat, she looked out of the window, expecting to see Milly walking along. Milly was nowhere to be seen. Kat had thought it 'weird' that Milly disappeared like that. But she didn't think anything bad had happened.

Mum phones the police to tell them about Kat seeing Milly.

They don't interview Kat that evening: they say it's now too late at night. They say they'll see her at the school the next day.

In a defensive press release issued on 2 July 2002, the police will claim that within two hours of Milly's absence being reported 'inquiries were in hand to deal with fast track issues such as CCTV recovery'.

'Inquiries in hand to deal with' puts a lot of distance between the police and any actual boots on the ground, any dogs out searching the street opposite the bus stop, any helicopters overhead.

We don't see any more police after ten thirty that night.

We try to think that this is a good thing. We try to think that they are busy, that they *must* be out with dogs. They have some of Milly's possessions now so she can be tracked. Her scent must be on her diary and address book.

Eventually, we hear a helicopter overhead.

Thank God, I think. *It's looking for Milly.*

Milly is still alive.

8.

That evening Mum changes. It's hard to believe how quickly it happens. She's no longer the carefree, happy, mickey-taking Mumazino, whom Milly and I love to tease. She's turning into a statue of grief.

There's no telephone upstairs so she moves the spare-room mattress to the lounge and makes up the bed there. She doesn't use it. Mum stays up all night waiting for Milly to come home. She paces the hall for hours and hours.

Spying down the stairs, I remember thinking, *This is what a person would look like if they were going crazy.*

The floor is parquet. Back in bed, I can still hear her pacing endlessly. I imagine she's going to wear a dip in the floor. It's a nightmare sound, one foot in front of the other.

I think Mum felt that, if she ever gave up pacing, it would mean she had given up hope.

As long as she keeps pacing, Milly might come back.

That evening, Lovely Granny's with Uncle Bree and Auntie Marilyn. Uncle Bree is being awarded the Freedom of the City of London and she's attending the ceremony. They are back in Essex when we phone to say that Milly is missing. Lovely Granny is desperate to get back to us but we ask her to stay with Uncle Bree, just in case Milly finds her way there. We want Milly to have a point of reference in every possible place. It seems like the only way we can look after her.

During the early hours of the morning, unbeknown to me, Uncle Bree turns up to help search for Milly. He hasn't even told Mum he's coming. He goes straight into action. He does the one thing that is screaming out to be done. He copies Milly's last known steps from Walton station. He drives there and parks in the station car park. He notices a single police car. Two officers are sitting inside, drinking tea from a Thermos.

Uncle Bree takes a torch and a baseball bat for his own protection, given the time of night. He first searches the car park and the hedgerow that separates the train track from the large, deserted parking area, which is dimly lit. Then he walks down Station Avenue, as Milly did, towards the Birds Eye building, where CCTV cameras are visible in the moonlight.

Uncle Bree crosses the road near to the bus stop from which Kat saw Milly. He starts shining his torch into the hedges. Not many cars pass him. Methodically searching every opening, he proceeds along Copenhagen Way and then Collingwood Place.

He walks past the block that houses 23–28 Collingwood Place. A few yards ahead of him, he sees a man. Uncle Bree is large, well-built. He's been a pub landlord most of his working life. He knows how to handle himself and is not easily intimidated. He has the kind of physical presence that stops people acting out. That night he's wearing chinos and a windbreaker jacket that would have increased the sense of his bulk.

When the man starts to walk towards him, Uncle Bree is disconcerted. First, he himself is walking around with a torch and baseball bat in the middle of the night. Uncle Bree feels undermined by the confident gait of the other man, who is as large as himself. Unlike Uncle Bree, however, there seems to be something aggressive and unpleasant about this man.

The man veers away, crossing the car park diagonally towards one block, while Uncle Bree keeps on the path towards the facing building. The man does not speak to Uncle Bree, who does not attempt to say anything to him. He's in Uncle Bree's sight for a full ten seconds. It's dark but visibility is good and Uncle Bree's view is unobstructed. At the closest, the man is about fifteen feet away, at which point he looks directly at Uncle Bree, who knows immediately that he's never seen him before. The look is confrontational. The man's thick-set and also tall: at least five foot eleven. He has short dark hair. His age, Uncle Bree estimates, is between thirty and forty. His clothes are darkish in colour; nothing special is distinguishable about them in the darkness.

Uncle Bree notices that the man is accompanied by a dog that is not on a lead. It's too dark to see exactly what kind of dog it is. It's the size of a Springer Spaniel, but is more likely a dark-coloured mongrel. He sees the man pause by the corner of one of the buildings, then disappear into an entrance, which Uncle Bree assumes is to one of the flats. Uncle Bree continues in the opposite direction.

In his hours of searching, Uncle Bree does not see a single policeman other than the two by Walton station drinking tea. When he gives his statement about seeing the man at Collingwood Place, the police do not ask him to elaborate on it.

Gemma's night

While Uncle Bree is having his close encounter with the aggressive-looking stranger, and Mum is pacing the floor, I'm upstairs. I'm supposed to be asleep. Yet how can you sleep when your sister has vanished without a trace? I have a strange sensation that someone's lurking outside our house. A man. A bad man. My mind's eye even sees exactly where he stands – to the right of the driveway by a tall hedge. I keep shutting my eyes tightly, trying to close the shutters on that image. But it will not go away. Sleep will not come, and I grow increasingly terrified that this bad man has taken Milly and has now come for me. If I let myself fall unconscious, he'll seize the opportunity to grab me.

And I worry because Milly has her keys to our house with her. If that man has Milly, he's got our keys and can just let himself in. I believe in the power of this monster. After all, Mum and Dad have not been able to protect Milly from him.

I don't think that Milly is dead.

And she isn't, yet.

I believe she's been kidnapped and is being held captive. Maybe she's in the dark she hates so much. Surely she's terrified. My heart clamps on her pain.

I think that her abductor will soon be in touch, asking for money. Yet I also have a terrible sense that it's not going to work out. *I will never see Milly again.* In the meantime, I fear her kidnapper has left her tied up somewhere, so he can come and get me too.

I get snatches of sleep, then wake up seconds later, only to experience the same kick in the belly, the same realization over and over again that Milly is gone.

I want to go into Milly's room to look for clues. Yet I can't, because I know she would be cross with me for going through her stuff. But I simply cannot stay alone in my bedroom, the one that I share with Milly. Her absence is too huge. The pull-out bed that she usually sleeps in is still out, still made up with her sheets.

Mum realizes that I'm haunting the upstairs, sleepless and terrified. She tells Dad that the two of us must try to get some rest, and that I should go to their room with him so I can feel safe. Like a child, I end up in my parents' bed that night, clutching Taily Ted.

Dad's presence is comforting and familiar, but not comforting enough. I plead with him not to go to sleep. I want to fall asleep first. If he were to be unconscious, I would be alone. Mum is too far away, downstairs, lost in her pacing.

Dad's side of the bed is the one furthest from the door. On Mum's side, I'm near the door, too close to the place where I fear the kidnapper entering. My mind starts formulating a worst-case scenario: I will jump out of the window when he comes for me.

My parents' bedroom is decorated around a blue and white Spode china design. The wallpaper and sheets are striped in those exact colours. The lightweight curtains are flowered in Spode colours too. Suddenly, through those curtains, I see a searchlight raking over our garden. Then the angry roar of the helicopter surges into the quiet night. I try not to visualize Milly crouching somewhere in an allotment or a shed. Of course the image keeps coming into my mind. I've never been so close to a helicopter, or been in a situation where a helicopter had something to do with me and our family. Even though it's there to help us, its noise is brutal, like a monster. It sweeps the garden with lurid greens, transforming it into a nightmare landscape. The helicopter is like an alien creature of the night, and now we are creatures of the night too, in a dark world of danger. All the familiar places are cloaked with blackness, fear, uncertainty.

When the helicopter's roar fades away, I can still hear Mum's relentless pacing downstairs. The only time she stops is to go through the computer to check all Milly's emails and the MSN Messenger account. She also flips through Milly's schoolbooks, looking for any notes or clues that Milly might have left about some secret or planned naughtiness. There's nothing.

I try to sleep even though all my nerve-ends are thrumming and I'm struggling to breathe properly. I don't want to be awake, because that means thinking about Milly. The only relief from that agony is to be unconscious. I doze from time to time, but it's not real sleep.

The night passes slowly. We're in police time now. Police time is different from family time. It's much slower and filled with agonizing waits.

At four the next morning, we pass the 'twelve hours missing' mark. That's the point at which the police start to take a missing-girl situation seriously – unlike her family, for whom every second of those twelve hours has piled on new agony.

Mum's still pacing.

I'm getting little scraps of sleep between the waking nightmares.

Dad's struggling to rest so he'll have the strength to get us all through what's coming.

Milly is still alive.

9.

The sun has not even started to rise when I wake, gasping. The helicopter's gone. So, for one drowsy second, I'm allowed to think that this is just a normal morning. Then I notice that I'm in my parents' bed. Not in my bed, with Milly breathing through her nose in the pull-out below me.

I cannot keep back the horror. I cannot hide from myself what has happened.

I hear voices downstairs. Still in my pyjamas, I run down. I allow myself to hope that Milly will be there in the kitchen, in big trouble for giving us such a fright. Instead, I find Uncle Bree sitting at the table with the makings of a poster in front of him. It's a surprise for me because I didn't hear him arriving in the night. He's looking terrible – grey-faced with saddlebags under his eyes.

Yet his eyes are nothing like as awful as Mum's. Hers are like dark deep tunnels. She hugs me, but that feels hollow. She's wherever Milly is. She's not quite in this world with us.

Over her shoulder, I see a mountain of mugs and used teabags in the kitchen sink. The dishwasher's running, already full of cups from Mum's longest-ever night.

Uncle Bree explains how he has spent hours searching Milly's route home. He does not mention the large, confrontational man he encountered by the flats near the station. He doesn't want to frighten me.

Now that it's starting to get light again, I don't see why I can't go and search for Milly myself. I'm getting angry that I'm not allowed to. I'm sure I could recognize clues and traces of Milly that someone else would miss. I know what she's wearing and carrying.

What am I supposed to do, if not search for Milly? Drink tea? Sit around the table?

But that is all I can do. It's all any of us can do, while we wait for news from the police.

At 5.30 that Friday morning, Mum calls Glyn Willoughby, the headmaster of Heathside and a close family friend. Glyn's two daughters are students at the school, and friends of ours.

His wife Sue answers the phone with a 'Who on *earth* at *this* hour?' tone in her voice. That changes to deep concern when Mum explains what's happened.

Glyn's in the shower. Sue calls to him, 'It's Sally, Glyn. Milly hasn't come home.'

From the shower, Glyn instructs Sue to tell Mum to ring the police.

'We have,' Mum says. 'The helicopter's been out.'

Glyn comes straight to the phone. Mum lets him know that she's about to tell the police to come to the school. She's frantic, but her intelligent and analytical brain is still working at full pelt. I listen to her explaining to Glyn that she's worried because the next day is the start of the two-week Easter break so it's crucial for the police to be able to see Milly's friends and schoolmates all in one place before they go off for the holidays.

Mum being Mum, she also wants Glyn to organize counsellors for any children who are distressed by Milly's disappearance.

Glyn is saying, 'Yes, I'll hold the assembly, Sally. What do you want me to say?'

'That it's imperative that anyone who knows anything about Milly's whereabouts comes forward immediately. You need to tell them that they won't be in trouble. We just want to find her.'

I listen to Mum's voice on the telephone. It doesn't sound like her. It's so tight and precise.

She hangs up as quickly as possible. All through the previous evening she had urged us to get off the phone even when we were talking to people who might have useful information. Mum just hates the landline being occupied. What if Milly's trying to call us from somewhere?

'Where are the police?' I ask Mum.

Mum hasn't seen a policeman since last night.

It's soon agreed that I'm not going to school today. I insist on being on the spot in case there's any news. I refuse to be packed off as if everything were normal. Not a single tear is allowed out of my eyes. I'm conscious that Mum's on the edge. My visible grief would be the thing to unravel her. She, too, needs to keep in control and keep going.

Soon she's going to face her own mother, Lovely Granny. She will need to be brave for her.

I'm to go with Uncle Bree to his house to pick up Lovely Granny. I run upstairs to shower and dress. For once, I don't have Milly to give me a fashion consult, so I have to freelance. Without Milly to be my mirror, it doesn't matter what I look like. Jeans, a sweater, who cares?

I can hear the hushed voices downstairs. I'm aware that the adults want me out of the way for a little while so that they can talk frankly among themselves. They want to say things like, *In these cases, there's not much hope after the first two hours.*

Why haven't the police got dogs out everywhere?

Why haven't the police rung us? It's been hours.

Who would have taken Milly?

I'm frustrated because they're treating me like a child. Yet at the same time I still want to be a child. Being good is so much part of my nature – talking back and cheekiness are Milly's department – so I just do what they want and make myself scarce for a while. Yet, even in that, I'm still acting like an adult, taking care of *their* need to voice fearsome things without worrying about upsetting me.

I go to the computer and start checking my emails. Of course I'm really looking for a message from Milly. I hold my breath until I see that there's nothing from her. So I check to see if anyone has news of Milly. Then I ring her mobile again in desperation. Every part of my being wants her to answer. I imagine her answering. Or wanting to. It goes straight to voicemail. I can't even record a message. The inbox is full because so many people have been trying to get through to her.

Uncle Bree has a friend who is a printer. He's kindly offered to print a load of MISSING posters for us. All we need is a photo, a description and a telephone number for anyone with information to call. The printer is based near Uncle Bree's home in Essex. So we can collect Lovely Granny and get the posters printed at the same time.

Thank God, I think, *a job, a purpose for us.*

Mum, Dad and Uncle Bree talk quickly, constantly interrupting one another. No one is crying. Everyone is trying to be methodical and efficient. Mum's working out the poster text.

This is the scene that greets our new family liaison officers (FLOs), now arriving for the first time. It's 7 a.m. We crowd around them eagerly, desperately hoping that they bring news.

Jon is so tall and kind-looking that he reminds me a little of Dad. The familiarity is comforting, as is his presence, which feels genuinely caring. I quickly find out he has a little girl of his own, much younger than me and Milly. I feel he must be personally invested in the pain of a lost daughter, and that helps me trust him. Jon also lets on that he's very keen on music. I think, *Good. So he and Dad will have something to talk about.*

To my regret now, I don't instantly warm to Alice, partly because she's a smoker. I'm so fastidious about these things. She's a naturally elegant woman, who also seems briskly efficient, compared with Jon's family-man persona. But very soon I'll learn that Alice, too, is deeply kind, and is truly in our corner, even when that begins to pit her against those in power back at Surrey Police headquarters.

In the last ten years, the autobiographies of the families of murdered children have made the FLO a familiar figure. In fact, they've been around only since the late 1990s.

In 2002, Surrey Police haven't dealt with this situation before, so Alice and Jon are about to do some pioneering work in this very difficult field. They have not been in the midst of a terrified family, any more than we've been a terrified family ourselves. We're all absolute beginners. At least Alice and Jon have some training behind them. They look and act extremely professionally but know how to be compassionate without being patronizing. I think Alice in particular is already aware of what lies ahead. She's been involved in hard-hitting crime, and has worked with victims before. She knows what she'll have to do to get us through this.

From now onwards, Jon and Alice will be constantly in our house.

For Mum, they'll be a lifeline. They will be our link to the investigation. When, day after day, there's no news, they'll still have to visit. They'll bear the brunt of our frustration and distress. The more they get to know us, the more heavily this will weigh on their own feelings too. Instead of news, Jon and Alice will be forced to bring questions. They'll always have questions. The answers will be fewer. If they bring us something new, like a shoe to identify, we'll naturally be curious about any follow-up. But there will never be any answers.

I think Alice knew from that first meeting that Milly was not a runaway, not from a family like ours. She knew Milly was a victim. So she had less hope and fewer formulas, no matter how deep her training went. Her way of dealing with it would be to apologize every time she had to ask us horrible things that seemed to question our own morality and our family life. As she got to know us, she must have realized that such questions were inappropriate and irrelevant. Yet she also knew she had to ask them.

Alice would be a barrier consciously deployed by Surrey Police. Because she was doing the truly dark work with us, her seniors would never have to see our faces while she asked those dreadful questions. Or when she put to us the innocent-sounding questions that could only have terrible answers.

Alice will stay with us right up to and including the trial of Milly's murderer and beyond. I know she kept Mum alive.

Now, we think of her and Jon with great gratitude.

But at the beginning it was rough on all of us.

Alice and Jon start by asking all the same questions that the young policeman asked the night before. Alice keeps scribbling our answers in her notebook. They are the same answers we gave the young officer.

They want more detail. They want names, times of phone calls we've made when trying to locate Milly. They also want to know about any 'suspicious' calls Milly might have made from our home line.

Mum asks, 'Can't you just get our phone records?'

'That takes months,' Alice says.

Mum phones her cousin who works at British Telecom. Half an hour later a fax arrives with all the calls made from our line in the past month.

Alice raises her eyebrows but she takes the piece of paper.

I want to scream at Jon and Alice that we've answered all this stuff and none of the 'runaway' questions are relevant to the family we are and the girl Milly is. But Mum is comforted to have police officers in the house at all. It seems that someone is starting to take Milly's disappearance seriously.

They ask for Milly's toothbrush and her hairbrush. Mum takes Alice up to Milly's bedroom. Together the two of them look around the mess, trying to find any clue that has been missed.

So far it's been the police asking for things. Now it's Mum's turn. She asks the FLOs for a police telephone number to put on our MISSING posters. Uncle Bree's eager to get back to Essex. He's got the photo and description. We need our poster to be consistent with whatever the police will do – when they get round to it – so we give him the same wide-eyed photo-booth picture of Milly that we gave the young policeman the day before.

Jon and Alice explain that Surrey Police have not set up an incident room with manned phones. They're working on it, but they don't have a number yet. Of course they are not running to our urgent timeline. They're still operating on the premise that Milly has most likely run away of her own free will.

The implication is – if we're telling the truth about us being a close, happy family and about Milly being a normal, affectionate girl – that she will also come back of her own free will.

I climb into Uncle Bree's four-by-four. We don't know what to say to one another. I'm afraid to phone Mum to see if there's any news because I don't want to upset her. Yet I'm desperate to know and want to call every five minutes. We're on the M25 before I finally break, asking Uncle Bree, 'What do you think has happened to Milly?'

He says, 'I don't know what's happened. But I promise you that she'll come back.'

Uncle Bree wants to think that Milly's run away. This is his way of coping. He and Milly have a special bond because of their intense chats and bantering emails. But Uncle Bree has known her four months; I've known her all her life. How can he understand, as I do, that she would *never* run away?

After that exchange, I phone Mum, really to hear if Milly's been found but on the pretext of asking if the police telephone number is available yet for the posters. The answers are 'No' and 'Not yet'. Mum's voice is terse. I know she wants me to get off the line in case Milly calls.

Lovely Granny leaps into the car when we arrive, followed by Uncle Bree's wife, Auntie Marilyn. Lovely Granny's burning up with impatience. She doesn't even want to let me go to the bathroom – she's so desperate to get to Mum. She gives me a massive hug. She doesn't cry. So I don't cry either.

Before we can go home, we need to visit the printers. Uncle Bree's friend quickly sets up the design for the poster. It's very simple. We use her christened name, Amanda.

MISSING, it says in red capital letters. Her photo is underneath.

Amanda Dowler, age 13
Last seen Thursday afternoon 21st March
Walking from Walton Station to Walton Park
Along Station Avenue and Rydens Road at about 4 o'clock.
She was wearing her school uniform.
If you have any information, please phone . . .

Soon the poster's ready, apart from one thing: the police contact number. Lovely Granny calls Mum again to say that if we don't get the number in the next fifteen minutes it will be too late. The FLOs' response is that it takes time to organize 'that sort of thing'.

'That sort of thing' makes me furious. I think, *We're only talking about a bloody telephone number.*

So a decision is made to set the poster with our own home telephone number as the point of contact. The posters are printed very quickly on plain white paper, A4 size.

All the way back to Walton, Lovely Granny asks questions about what has been going on. I know that she knows. She knows that I know. Milly has *not* run away. Something has happened to her.

84

The Dowler family was complete with the arrival of Amanda Jane (known as 'Milly') in June 1988.

The proudest girl in the world: me with baby Milly the day Mum brought her home.

Milly's love of messing around in the water started early. By sixteen months, Milly was already in wellington boots. Her teddy bear had a matching Aran sweater, both knitted by Lovely Granny.

Even at three, Milly would win any staring competition.

Me do it!' Milly refused help to learn to ride her bike in Bushy Park.

'Night night, Gemsie. Night, night Milly.'

At six foot two (188cm), Dad provided an excellent climbing frame for his two small daughters.

For many years, Milly always curtsied when anyone took her photo. For this birthday picture, she wore the sailor suit that really needed a hat, according to Style Guru Milly.

A family of pond-dippers. Milly's fascination with newts had already begun.

Mum often dressed us in matching outfits.

Treasure: Milly found this pebble – with a heart-shaped indentation – on the beach near Swanage. When trauma stopped me from being a bridesmaid at our friend Hannah's wedding, the pebble would go in my place.

This image of us in Brecon finally came back to me, with all its happiness, in an EMDR processing session. It's possibly Dad's favourite picture of his daughters.

Milly and her rabbit Sooty: 'I promise I'll clean the cage, Mum.'

A turquoise and animal-print ensemble. Only Milly could carry this off.

Milly ready to party.

Milly starting to be too cool to smile.

For World Book Day, the other girls went as Cinderella or the Little Mermaid, but Milly insisted on being the grotesque headmistress Miss Trunchbull from Roald Dahl's *Matilda*.

Mum made these matching dresses for our 'Bobby's Girls' routine, which we practised in secret for Dad's fiftieth birthday.

Neither of us can bear to articulate it. Uncle Bree relays information to Lovely Granny in a business-like way, staring straight at the
road. I gaze out of the window, hunting for something that might
trigger a useful memory. I'm still trying to think of someone Milly
would have trusted enough to take off with, risking all this fear and
confusion at home.

There is no one. It is not possible.

Lovely Granny asks about Mum. Has she slept? Has she eaten
anything? I see something happening – Lovely Granny is becoming Mum's mum. She's looking after her own little girl. She rings
Mum to see if she needs any shopping. But Mum cannot contemplate food. She wants to ring off as soon as possible in case someone
is trying to phone with useful news.

But really, of course, it's in case Milly herself is finally trying to
make contact with us.

It's early afternoon when we get home with the posters. Alice and
Jon have gone. Uncle Pete and Auntie Jenny are there. Everyone's
trying to sit in the lounge. There isn't enough room. Uncle Pete
and Auntie Jenny are on Mum's unused mattress in front of the fire.

We're all talking at once – or we're all silent with shock.

Lovely Granny's still trying to mother Mum. But Mum's like a
teenager, shrugging off contact, absorbed in her own misery and
fear. All Lovely Granny's coaxing to eat, drink or sit down is lost on
her. She roams around the house. Her eyes are still tunnels, deeper
now. There is almost no Mum left.

Mum gets agitated if someone else tries to answer the phone.
She wants to be the first line of contact. She wants clear lines of
communication. I feel the same: it needs to be simple, just me,
Mum and Dad. In another way, it's useful to have everyone there,
as other questions come up, things Mum couldn't have thought of.
We can't afford to let a single idea get away.

The police just seem to be waiting for naughty Milly to come
home, sorry for wasting their time. This line of police thinking is,
for us, a dead end. Nothing they can say or ask will make Milly fit
inside the boxes they want to tick.

We also have the desperation of inactivity and unbearable

waiting to contend with. We hope every minute will bring us news of a police incident room and their own poster.

That afternoon, dozens of friends come round after school to collect posters. We've drawn up a map and they are assigned areas for distribution. Milly's friends take huge batches to Kingston, Woking, Staines, Guildford – places where we would go to the cinema or shopping. I'm not allowed to answer the door because we don't know who may arrive. I sit in the lounge from where I can hear the voices of Milly's and my friends. But it's too painful for me to go out to greet them. Every time the doorbell rings, I'm racked with a mad hope that it's Milly.

To all the people who are phoning to ask how they can help, we give the same answer: 'Come and get some posters, please!' They go out of the house by the boxful. Even people we don't know arrive to collect posters, once they learn they're available. Our neighbours and friends put them everywhere – on lamp-posts, fences, shop windows. People even take them on their Easter breaks so Milly's image can be spread all over the country and even beyond.

From the first, Lovely Granny decides that her job is to protect Mum and the rest of us from anyone who might hurt us, intentionally or unintentionally. Every day after that, Alice and Jon will turn up at the house. Every day, Lovely Granny will open the door to them. 'Yes?' she'll say, with arms crossed in front of her.

'It's Alice and Jon,' they'll say, smiling nervously.

'Alice and Jon *who*?' she'll demand.

For many days, Lovely Granny won't let them in until they've shown their credentials.

That afternoon we have another visitor. He's Jon and Alice's boss. We've moved into another stage of the police flow chart, promoted to contact with a high-ranking officer.

His first words on entering our house are: 'Most missing children have run away. If it's more serious, then in 95 to 97 per cent of cases, the person responsible is a member of the family or someone known to the family.'

We have to fill in the gap: they suspect that Milly has been abducted by one of our family or close circle. This makes no sense.

I think, *Is that what's stopping them looking for Milly properly?*

The officer doesn't stay long. He doesn't ask any questions. It seems his mind's already made up.

Lovely Granny goes out into the garden where Jon and Alice are now talking to Mum and Dad. Jon makes some reference to runaway children. Lovely Granny says, 'Don't be so bloody ridiculous. Of course Milly hasn't run away. She's been abducted. Clearly. Are you looking at sex offenders in the area?'

Jon's taken aback, but tells her that, yes, the police are doing that as a matter of course.

They're standing in the garden by the body-sized trench the builders were digging for the new extension the day before. Lovely Granny says to Jon, 'If you're going to dig up the garden you'd better do it before they run the concrete.'

'I'm sure that won't be necessary,' Jon says quietly.

IO.

Alice now takes me aside for a conversation that will turn out to be my most graphic piece of sex education to date. Again, I stress that Alice had been set a task by her superiors, one she surely found painful. Moreover, she and her bosses could have had no idea how innocent I was.

At sixteen, I'm painfully embarrassed about everything to do with sex. Not only am I sexually inexperienced for my age but, as I said, I'm also regressing fast back into childhood, lost in a sense of disbelief about the situation in which we find ourselves now. It's a twisted nightmare, and I don't want to be in it. I simply and impossibly long to be the girl I was, in the family I was in, before Milly disappeared. It's less than a day since all those things were taken away from me.

Alice leads me into one of our home's nicest places: the music and dining room. Here we keep Dad's jukebox, the karaoke machine, the record collection, a dresser with beautiful china. With its cosy fireplace, it's the scene of noisy, joyful Christmas dinners. It's where Milly and I watch our television shows, the ones condemned by Dad as 'absolute rubbish'. It is our family's den, a happy place.

It is about to become tainted with my shame and Milly's.

Alice must have chosen the music room because it's the only space downstairs that has a door. That is how our family lives, everything in the open. We're so close that we don't need to hide anything.

Alice shuts the door, cutting me off from our family. 'Isolate and extract': that is her mission, however little the poor woman likes it. To perform her necessary task now, she cannot afford to have my parents hovering around me protectively.

I don't like being singled out like this. It makes me feel even more vulnerable. I curl up in the tobacco-brown leather sofa, apprehensively.

Curling up is not going to save me from an experience that is a painful violation. Half an hour later I'm a wiser but even more traumatized teenager.

Recent television shows tend to have all police conversations with victims and their families recorded on video. In those days, the police officers generally had a notebook. That's all. A notebook is easily lost, pages torn out or altered. In the course of our contact with the police, notebooks, transcripts, quite a few of Milly's belongings were lost. It happens, apparently. Who knows what happened to Alice's notebook from that interview?

From my painful memory of it, the conversation with Alice goes something like this.

'Gemma, whatever you say to me is not going to get Milly into trouble. Or you. But it might help us find her. Do you understand?'

'Yes.'

'Does Milly use any chat-rooms?'

'We've told everyone already.' I can remember the childish whine in my voice, and the exhaustion. 'No chat-rooms. We just have MSN Messenger. We've *told* you.'

'Does Milly have a secret email account? Does she chat to strangers online?'

'No! We *don't do* anything secret. We all use the same computer. You've seen where the computer is – in the hall! Everyone sees what we do with it.'

Unbeknown to me, the police are right now downloading all Milly's files from our computer.

As for Milly's phone, it's just a Nokia. It's hardly a secretive device. There are no smart phones in 2002. There are no PIN numbers in Milly's phone – all you need to do is press the green phone symbol and then the star key. The Dowler family is simply not techie enough for Milly to run a secret life, even if she wanted to.

Alice starts again: 'Do you know of any secret boyfriend? Secret from your parents?'

'No.'

We all know about lovely Eddie the Entrepreneur. He's part of our family history, like Taily Ted, my plush bear. And we've made sure the police already know about Eddie, and the innocence of his friendship with 'Auntie' Milly. There *is* that boy Milly rather likes, but has kept away from, out of loyalty, because one of her friends likes him too. We all know his name. And he's also a friend.

'Do you know what happened at that party Milly went to, two weekends ago?'

'No, I didn't have time to speak to her about it. We were really busy. We've told you about the concert, the rehearsals, the Fun Run –'

'Do you think that Milly had sex at that party?'

A blush spreads over my entire body. 'No. She wouldn't.'

'How far has Milly gone with a boy?'

'Not far. I don't know.'

'Would she have let a boy touch her breasts?'

The words burn my ears. It feels as if Milly is being molested by these questions. I'm being forced to picture things that Milly would never forgive me for picturing. How can I answer? This stuff has never come up in our conversations. Milly has never talked about them even in relation to other girls and their escapades. This much I know: Milly's at a stage where anything to do with sex is pretty 'rank'.

It gets worse.

'Would she have let a boy finger her? Would she touch a boy's penis?'

I'm blushing, tearful. Words like 'vagina' and 'penis' are just not part of my vocabulary. I know what they are, of course, but I can't think of them in relation to my little sister. I don't have any relaxed or jokey sexual vocabulary to hand either, because I don't have the experience. I flinch from all those short, brutal sex words. They should be private things. They should be softened by love.

'I don't know,' I say again, hopelessly.

'You keep saying you're really close to Milly. She sleeps in your bedroom and you have those late-night chats. *Why* don't you know these things?'

My answers sound unconvincing even to me.

Alice isn't to know that it's excruciating embarrassment that's making me look so guilty. There's another thing too: I'm being made to feel I'm not a good enough sister, because I don't seem to know enough about Milly when it comes to these suddenly important things. Alice is unwittingly succeeding in making me feel that

I've never been truly close to my sister. I'm caught in the guilt trap. Guilt makes you blush and fumble. That's what I do now.

But I'm desperate to help. If this searing line of questioning is going to help find Milly, then I will cooperate, however hard it is.

In the end, I admit that Milly *may* have had a bit of mild experience with boys, though I cannot be sure. I explain the pressures on girls our age not to seem frigid. We are supposed to be relaxed with our bodies. You have to fit in, not stick out as a prude. It is a fine balance between slut and prude. Milly's socially insecure, like any girl of her age, and would have wanted to tread a safe middle ground.

My apparently evasive answers seem to spur Alice on. Perhaps she needed to shock me – maybe this is the technique she's been taught. I'm by now pretty sure she, too, is hating every second of this. I know she has already seen the tunnel eyes of my mother. She must know that Mum would be devastated by hearing this line of questioning. Alice must have found that painful too.

'Could Milly be pregnant?' Alice asks. 'Could that be why she ran away?'

'She would never – I don't know. Maybe.'

'Did she tell you that semen had actually entered her body? You do know how girls get pregnant, don't you, Gemma?'

I just stare. This is too horrible to answer, especially to a policewoman I've only just met. I couldn't have talked about this even with Mum.

The conversation plunges into the most graphic anatomical detail, with Alice trying to get me to supply words like 'masturbate' and 'intercourse'. So imperative is her need for absolute clarity that she might as well have shown me dolls, like the ones they use for the young victims of paedophiles. 'Did this go there? Did that go inside here? Did she touch it with her hand?'

I'm staring in horror, gaping like an idiot. So Alice feels obliged to explain to me what sexual intercourse is, in the basic mechanical sense. I squirm and blush. She wants to know about dry-humping, whether trousers or pants are removed, whether Milly enjoys this kind of thing.

To all this, my answers are an agonized 'I don't know'. And, secretly, *I don't want to know. Why is this awful conversation taking place? Why aren't you all out looking for Milly?*

And at the end of the conversation, the embarrassment is descending to a place of much deeper pain. I'm left feeling that the police seriously doubt my closeness to Milly. This has hurt me, when I'm already almost collapsing with the agony of Milly's disappearance.

What I've said doesn't fit in with the accusations they want to frame. They are not going to let me get away with the inconvenient truth that Milly and I are close, that we share nearly everything, that Milly loves her family and would never willingly leave us. They are not interested in the little cards Milly writes to me, or in all the singing and dancing we do. They want to see only a dark side, even though there isn't one.

I'm starting to understand that we have to carry the burden of this redefinition, because we are aching for their help. All they have to say is, 'This will help us find Milly.' Then I'll answer any question they throw at me. Mum and Dad will be the same.

At some point I'll begin to feel angry. I'll find there's nowhere to put my anger. At this stage, I still want to believe that the police are our protectors and that they are going to bring Milly home. I'll sacrifice anything to help them. My dignity has just been battered, but I would have let the police batter me physically if I thought that would help them find Milly. I also feel that the police are at the top of the authority food chain. I'm in their power now. I have to do everything they ask. Only criminals don't do what the police want.

At the end of this torture, Alice says brightly, 'Well, that's done, then. Let's go and see your mum and dad. And have a cup of tea.'

I walk back into the kitchen to face their anxious eyes. And, for Mum's and Dad's sake, I pretend that I'm completely OK, and have tried my best to be helpful to the police who are going to find Milly.

I grow up a lot in that walk to the kitchen. It's not just that I'm starting to learn to keep secrets from Mum and Dad, to protect them. I'm also learning that our family cannot stand up under the bright spotlight of relentless interrogation. I don't think anyone's family could. From now on the police are going to shape how I'm allowed to think and talk about my sister. The police will also change the girl I am. It is now inappropriate to be the Gemma I was before Milly disappeared.

I know I can't tell Mum and Dad what's just happened in the music room. I still want to protect Milly's privacy. When she comes back, I don't want to be the one who betrayed her. And of course I'm hideously embarrassed that I've had to have this sex education from a police officer.

It's quiet in the kitchen. We cannot play music. That would be too painful. For us, music is Milly. The police keep taking us, one by one, to different rooms, to answer questions. We have to tell them every single thing we've done, and with whom, and every place we've been since we last saw Milly. Not one second can be left unaccounted for. After his questioning, Dad's so silent that it frightens me. Mum's visibly carrying the burden of being the mother who has lost a daughter. Now that my sense of myself as a good sister has been undermined, I can imagine the police asking Mum why she had let Milly go to a party where there were boys. I can hear them implying, *What kind of mother loses a daughter on the way home from school?*

That night Milly's face, Milly's disappearance, is on the TV news. We sit on the sofa, watching. It's comforting to see her disappearance is being taken seriously, yet surreal to see Milly's picture filling the whole television screen. We have already spoken to all of our close friends and family but now our phone rings constantly as other friends see the news.

Twenty-four hours into Milly's disappearance, a new policeman – not Alice or Jon – comes to the house. He tells me that if my father ever sleeps in the same bed as me again, they will arrest him.

I have no idea why the police are being so cruel.

Do they want me to go to bed alone in a dark, empty room when we don't even know what's happened to Milly?

I say, 'I don't understand. Why can't Dad protect me in the night? I'll never be able to get to sleep without someone there to look after me.'

What I can't say to this hard-faced man is, *I'm not used to sleeping alone. I'm used to having Milly in the bed beside mine. How can I sleep next to Milly's empty bed, still made up with her sheets, while the man who has taken her is waiting outside to get me too?*

I plead with the policeman. I sob, 'Why are you taking Dad away from me? How can you do this?'

I'm sixteen years old, yet I'm behaving like an inconsolable toddler. Denying me my parents' care seems like denying me the right to breathe. I turn on Dad. 'Why are you letting them do this to me? Why aren't you telling them to leave us alone?'

Dad, white-faced, says nothing.

Why can't he stand up for me?

Mum looks on, also wordless, like a ghost.

The policeman's expression is impassive. He appears completely disengaged from the pain in front of him. I could have cried for ever and he would not have given in. In retrospect, I think my tears were probably considered quite useful. Perhaps I would be the weak one who would force our family to give up the dark secrets the police seemed so convinced we had.

I'm already isolated. I cannot add to my parents' troubles by telling them that I fear Milly's abductor is hiding in the hedge outside the house, waiting to take me too. I'm too innocent to read the looks on my parents' faces. Unlike me, they are fully aware of what the police are insinuating.

Mum and Dad are starting to realize that Milly's disappearance is only the beginning of their troubles.

They are starting to understand, with horror, why the police are dragging their feet. Losing Milly into an unbearable mystery is only the first blow. New blows are coming from the police themselves. It's not just that our closeness as a family has been questioned, doubted, thrown in our faces: from this very first day, Mum and Dad are being made to feel as if Milly's disappearance is something to do with us.

Something to do with Dad.

II.

With Milly still missing, Heathside School cancels *Stars In Their Eyes*.

During the night of 22–23 March, the police release the last-known CCTV footage of Milly, which was taken at Weybridge station. By this time, thirty-six hours after Milly's disappearance, our confidence in the police is dwindling and we're almost surprised to see that they have the right girl.

It's the first Saturday of the Easter break. It doesn't feel anything like a holiday to us. A police search team suddenly shows up to comb through Milly's messy room. At the end of her bed is a Barbie-pink painted blanket box that Milly uses as a general dumping ground. It's packed full of old schoolbooks, sketch pads, bits of scribbled paper, photos she's taken on school trips, jewellery, stickers, Beanie Babies, souvenirs and trinkets from various holidays, including a hideous plastic bowl with a family photo of us and Lovely Granny on a canal trip on the Costa Brava. Milly insisted Mum bought it. That bowl takes deep uncoolness to a whole new level.

The police root around, putting things into plastic evidence bags. I cannot go into Milly's room but my imagination can. Mum and I agree how upset and betrayed Milly would feel if she could see strangers going through her private things. But Mum says if it helps the police find out what's happened to her then it has to be done. They briefly search my room too and take my diary. I can understand exactly how Milly would feel: both our lives are being scrutinized with cold, critical eyes, eyes that are looking for trouble.

Every scrap of paper Milly's written on, every little note she's received, all her most personal and private stuff, is now being taken away from her bedroom.

The search team isn't there very long. They leave as suddenly as they arrived.

★

As the police haven't yet produced one, we're still focused on the distribution of our poster. Mum asks Glyn Willoughby if he can print more copies. The school takes over, churning them out on a photocopier.

I busy myself making ten-foot-long banners to hang around the local area and the school. Uncle Bree, who often organizes charity events, has brought all the necessary equipment with him. I choose bright colours to attract attention. I decorate them with stars, symbols and curly writing. I try to write as clearly as possible with no spelling mistakes. It gives me something to do.

In those dreadful hours when we feel so helpless, the poster also solves the immediate problem of what to do with Lovely Granny. It has our home number, of course, so she's given the job of answering the calls and taking the information. The music room is changed into our personal incident room. Lovely Granny takes notes by hand, being careful to ask name and number. The plan is to pass information immediately to the police. This is easier said than done. We ourselves still have no number to call. Even when we do get a number, the police often mistake Mum, Dad and Lovely Granny for cranks phoning in with bogus information.

It will take a few days for the police to set up a tape machine so we can record the calls as well as take notes. We anticipate some sort of highly sophisticated device that can trace the incoming calls and reroute the important ones directly to the police. Instead, we get an old-fashioned tape recorder. We have to push the record knob each time we take a call and change the cassette each time it fills up.

Thousands of our home-made posters are already out there by the time Alice brings us a telephone number for the police incident room. It's too late to recall our posters. So the home phone rings continually.

Who calls? Some people phone to ask if there's anything they can do. The crazy and mischievous calls start straight away, too. Alice has already warned us that our number will be a magnet to cranks and attention-seekers. She predicts that psychics will come forward with messages from Milly. She advises that such people usually have their own agendas. We must not let them mess with our heads, no matter how tempting it might be to follow any route that seems to lead to Milly.

But in that place of the terrifying unknown, you lose your normal sensible filters. Anything that offers the tiniest spark of hope becomes alluring. We are not ourselves without Milly. We are weak. It is part of Alice's work now to protect us from people who might exploit that weakness. Alice also warns us that people will phone, claiming to have Milly. They'll be lying. It seems incredible to me that anyone could be so wicked or cruel to a family in crisis.

I'm given a task: to list questions that will catch out hoax callers pretending to be or to have Milly. I suggest:

What were the names of the two Canadian boys we met in Cuba?
What did Dad do for his fiftieth birthday?
Who came first from our family in the Fun Run?
What's the name of Gemma's teddy?

I'm secretly hoping that someone will phone to ask for a ransom. Then Milly's disappearance would be solvable.

I'm never allowed to answer the phone or look at the notepad by it. It annoys me that I'm shut out. Of course I try to get a glimpse of it, and I do manage to get one look. I see that Lovely Granny has taken a call from a young man who claims he's seen a sign at St Ann's Hill, a favourite walking place of ours. It says, 'Help me. I'm trapped.' He says it was signed by Milly. He also says he heard screaming from an underground crypt.

We shall get used to this kind of call. We shall learn that it usually comes from a person who just wants to be important for a minute. For that petty glory, he or she will upset our family and waste the time of police who might have been looking for Milly.

This particular call freaks me out, partly because Milly's so afraid of the dark. St Ann's Hill is also a place I know very well. I can imagine her there. I keep asking Alice and Jon about it. They tell me that there are thousands of calls to go through, many of them less ridiculous than this one.

There is already weariness in their voices. There is no sense of urgency. They do not even entertain the possibility that this young man is anything but a prank caller. I offer to go there myself and check it out, but of course I'm told I'm not allowed to do any such thing.

*

On 23 March, the third day of Milly's disappearance, the police finally produce their own MISSING poster. *HAVE YOU SEEN AMANDA?* it says. As well as the picture of her face, they use the photo of Milly in her school uniform, full-length.

Amanda Dowler is 13 years old and attends Heathside School. She is five feet five inches tall, of slim build, with brown shoulder length hair. When last seen she was wearing her school uniform – white shirt, grey skirt and dark blue blazer – and carrying a beige and black rucksack.

Our poster has already spread all over the country by the time the police version gets its first outing. I think, *The man who's taken Milly must have driven past it so many times.* I worry, of course, that he can get our phone number from it.

Mum asks me to write down a list of anybody that Milly would get into a car with. She and Dad have already made their lists, which aren't long, and are pretty much identical. It is not until I'm halfway through my list that I realize I'm writing the names of people I myself would get into a car with. I picture the faces of all the friends and relatives I trust. I cannot conceive that any of them would do anything to Milly, or do anything to worry us. Until this moment I have lived in a web of security, of trusting relationships between adults, young people and children. I've never had to question that trust. I've never had to interrogate any of these people's characters for faults or issues.

None of them could do this to us.

It has to be a stranger who has taken Milly. Someone must have tricked her, told her that one of us was hurt or ill. He must have been so convincing that she put her fear for us ahead of her own safety.

Meanwhile the police are still coming to us with questions and evidence to support their theory of Milly the Runaway. Now they've been through what they found in Milly's room, Mum and Dad are being shown pieces of scribbled paper that – in police eyes – support police theories. These include some of Milly's rather dramatic poems or sad song lyrics or diary entries about which friends she'd fallen out and made up with. The police clearly think these scribbled expressions of normal teenage angst are evidence that Milly is a deeply unhappy person.

Then there's the note signed by Milly and Eddie the Entrepreneur to say they'll get married. When we see that scrap of paper, it's easy to envisage Milly and Eddie having a good laugh about it. It's hardly a formal document or a declaration of passion. So we cannot understand why the police think Milly was running around with boys in a serious way.

However, Alice tells us that the situation is so extreme that anything must be considered possible. Nothing makes sense and there's absolutely nothing to go on.

On 24 March, day four of Milly's disappearance, Mum and Dad go to Staines police station to do a live TV appeal.

They're not keen to do this press conference. They're afraid of what it means. They have seen appeals like this on television. They know how these things usually end. They can't face that thought.

Our FLOs and the police press officer show them in advance some of the questions they may want to address.

The first Alice mentions is: 'What was Milly like?'

Already Milly's being written about in the past tense.

Mum's brain is confused by trauma and sleeplessness. She struggles to answer basic but searching questions like that.

The press office try to micromanage the statement. They want Mum to appeal to whomever she thinks has taken Milly. Mum isn't happy about that. She's afraid that he would enjoy watching us suffer. It will give him more power over us – hand him extra pleasure. But the police insist that, if Mum fails to say those words, then it will look suspicious and strange.

Of course that works on Mum. She's terrified of doing anything wrong.

Mum's also directed to bring out the old cliché: 'Someone somewhere must know something.'

In the end, Mum tells the police that we're perfectly capable of writing our own appeal. Mum and Dad cram their grief and fear into a succinct set of words.

My task is to hand-write an appeal of my own. It will be shown on television.

Please help me find my sister.

One week ago I was looking forward to the Easter holidays. Milly was going to come shopping with me to choose my prom dress and we had planned a great big Easter party.

Since then my life has been turned upside down. Every day I wake up with the hope that Milly will return. The nights are the worst and my imagination runs wild thinking about what happened to her.

If someone has taken Milly, please return her safely to us as I am missing her very much and I couldn't wish for a lovelier sister.

I cannot understand why anyone would take or want to harm Milly, but there must be someone out there that knows what has happened to her.

Then I draw a row of hearts and stars and a big heart with *I LOVE U MILLY* in the middle. I finish with a whole row of kisses.

I style Mum for her first ever TV appearance. She wears a navy and white rugby shirt that Milly and I had given her. This goes on top of light jeans with a slight flare. I know that Milly would sign off this outfit: Mum had needed to be weaned off straight jeans, the hard way. It seems so futile and unimportant now, but Mum wants to look presentable so that, if Milly were to see her, she would approve.

Dad's wearing a blue shirt with a cream sweater and jeans. No one ever has to worry about Bob Dowler looking inappropriate.

Lovely Granny comes along to keep me company during the filming.

Early that evening, on the way to Staines police station, Mum and Dad are taken to the Birds Eye building to look at the CCTV images recorded by its camera. There's nothing to give anyone any hope or a clue in the footage that is blurred by the low winter sun that shone on the afternoon of 21 March.

Sitting on a red 1960s sofa, Mum tries Milly's phone, as she does all the time. Until now, she's always received an automated message to say it's too full to take any more voicemails.

This time she gets through to Milly's personal message, hears her recorded voice.

'Oh, my God! She's picked up her messages, Bob. She's alive!' Mum screams. The euphoria flows through her, down to her feet. She can't keep still.

Jon tells her that the police have put credit on Milly's phone. He doesn't make much of the empty cache of voicemails. He thinks that the old messages may have been automatically deleted. But Jon doesn't know the truth of the situation any more than we do.

Mum can't focus on technicalities. She phones everyone to say, 'She's picked up her messages! She's picked up her messages! She's alive!'

Staines police station is a post-modern fortress. The press are camped out on the edge of the forecourt. So Alice and Jon sneak us in round the back. We enter the station through the prisoners' entrance.

I wonder, *Why do we have to be in the same place as the criminals?*

But that will be our life from now on . . . the service stairs, the back entrance, the bin-stores. We shall be physically propelled into the places of the guilty by virtue of being the subject of relentless press attention and the family of a victim of crime.

A senior officer tells my parents that he's very nervous himself as it's his first time doing a press conference of this kind and he doesn't know what to say. He's chain-smoking. My parents are bemused that this suddenly seems to be about him and not about Milly.

While Mum and Dad are in front of the cameras, Lovely Granny and I are escorted to the new incident room. We have to peer from the doorway to snatch a look at the important people whose skills may save my sister. Surrey Police are clearly proud of this incident room. It seems as if it has been staged specially for us, like a set from *The Bill*, as if the police have made a doll's house to demonstrate how an incident room *should* work.

But there's nothing sleek or impressive about the operation. The room is about as big as our lounge. Everything is grey, institutional and worn-out. Fluorescent strips cast an ugly light. Several banks of computers hunch over old tables; not all are manned. A blackboard has pictures stuck to it, of Milly and her belongings; there's a map of Walton, with pins showing where she was last seen.

There is no sense of urgency. The room's not swarming with officers. A few calls are taken in front of us. Everything is polite and measured. I tell Lovely Granny, 'We're getting more calls at home.'

The thought keeps crashing over me: *These officers are still thinking Milly has run away.* If they thought she had been abducted, surely it would be a hive of frenetic activity in here. *Why are there any policemen in this room at all? Why aren't they all out looking for Milly?*

Nevertheless, I do my best to be conscientious, and a model sister. I examine the crime wall, trying to see if I can make any helpful links for them. I'm also suspicious. Even then I'm trying to see if there's something that the police are not telling us. I wonder if they have taken down things that they don't want us to see, and if they'll put them back up once we are gone.

I want to say, *Oh, my God, Milly, just look at all this drama you've created!*

That's partly because I don't want this to be serious. I want to think that Milly has been naughty and will be told off. I don't want to think that she's gone, and I simply cannot frame the thought that she might be dead. After all, we are constantly being reassured that she has probably just run away.

I notice how well provided the police are with tea and biscuits. That makes me feel a bit resentful. *Why are they allowed to sit around and drink tea while Milly's missing? They should be out searching and searching.*

I never thought I would be in a police station being shown an incident room about my missing sister. It's a brutal change of scene from our family home where at least I can feel close to Milly, spending time in the rooms I have always shared with her.

I don't want to be there, because I don't want to be in this situation.

Mum and Dad's appeal is televised that night. The police tell the press that they are working with sixty local volunteers to search the green areas around Hersham and the River Mole.

The camera zooms into Mum's desperate face. Dad is filmed more in the background. At the time, we could not guess that his expressions were being recorded not just for the general public but also for the police, checking for signs of guilt or lack of the right telegenic emotion.

Mum says, 'Milly, darling, if you're watching or listening to this,

Mum, Dad, Gemma and Lovely Granny want you to know we all love you and miss you very much and can't wait to have you back home with us.'

Dad explains that Milly's disappearance is out of character. He says she's 'brilliant, intelligent, witty, loving'. He adds, 'It's my wife's birthday this week. It would be the best present ever in the world if we got Milly home safely.'

Mum says, 'Someone somewhere must know where she is and we beg them to get in touch with us, let her call home or contact the police. Please, please give her back to us. We're devastated. We're just so desperately worried.'

Mum's face is scribbled over with suffering. Dad is in a clear state of shock. They are not letting their hope wear thin, but their hope is wearing them out. Mum is drained and frail. She does not have one more tear left inside her. Yet there'll be a new ocean of them by tomorrow.

If someone has taken Milly, I think, *just look at what you've done to us.*

On 25 March, Dad and I walk down our road to the paper shop. The owner knows Dad as it's where he always gets the papers on Sunday mornings, as well as his daily newspaper for the train. As a treat, Milly and I are allowed to buy sweets or magazines there too. Today the newsagent doesn't know what to say to us, especially to me.

The papers are laid out on a table. It's day five of Milly's disappearance and she's everywhere. I see the *Daily Mail*, with a picture of our family on holiday on the front. I think, *We made the front page. This must be really serious.*

Dad buys all the papers, something he'll do every day after that, no matter how much it hurts. From now on, our house will be full of piles of newspapers. Mum and Dad will hide the worst articles, if they think I can't take them.

Later a friend tells me about a different experience she had in a different newsagent that same day. Two women were looking at the headlines. One asked, 'Did you see the appeal on the television yesterday? I know it was the father because he didn't show any emotion. The mother was crying her eyes out and he just showed nothing.'

The police ask us if Milly likes camping. When we say yes, they want us to check if we still have her tent. Mum and Dad can't immediately lay their hands on it. So on 26 March, day six of Milly's disappearance, they give their consent for a search of our garage. If Milly has run away, she might have taken that tent, the police say.

They find her tent untouched in the garage.

The police tell us that they have to take away our bed sheets. This makes us feel tainted. The worst thing is that it's never anything good about Milly that interests the police, not her singing, her love of music, her affectionate nature or her sense of humour. They want to talk about a naughty Milly, who drank a bit of alcohol at a party. The police want to read something dark into everything.

When the police look at Milly's copied-out song lyrics, they see the agony of a tortured soul – Milly's. The police, not being pop-savvy, can't distinguish between Milly's original thoughts and the songs she wrote out. The lyrics of 'Angel' include the lines *'In the arms of the angel/Fly away from here'*. Words like these are now being used to support the police's theory that Milly has decided to run away from home, perhaps with an older man.

An older man? Where does that come from?

It does not suit their agenda that Milly is *also* the girl who copied out the words for 'Wind Beneath My Wings', or who wrote in her English workbook, 'In a young child, generally they find there home the most safest, nicest, familiarest place they know.'

The police come to us with a bit of Milly mischief that we'd never heard about before. Many of Milly's friends have divorced parents with shared custody. Milly had clearly worked out that there was an opportunity to exploit here. So, in her homework diary, she'd faked a note from Mum: 'I am sorry Amanda has left her homework round her father's house. Sorry again.' Milly let herself down by drawing her usual curlicue on the foot of the 'A' in 'Amanda'. It looks nothing like Mum's handwriting.

When police show her the note, Mum bursts out laughing in spite of the circumstances and says something wildly inappropriate, like,

'You little *bugger*, Milly!' The police don't think it's funny at all. They want this note to confirm their suspicion of a secret rift in our family, with Dad living elsewhere. It's hard to persuade them, as things are now, that this note just shows Milly being the acting-out version of herself, taking her first steps into what would have been, and should have been, a bit of a wild-child adolescence.

They ask us again and again who Milly might trust enough to go off with. I repeatedly tell the police that this would not happen, but they single-mindedly pursue that line of questioning, because it fits with their idea that it's not a stranger who has taken Milly. I overhear one police officer telling another about a girl who was lured into a car by a man who had deliberately broken the legs of a puppy so that its whimpers of pain were authentic. The man asked the girl to direct him to the nearest vet, and persuaded her to get into the car to show him the way. She was never seen again.

That story opens my mind to possibilities I have never considered. Milly loves animals. Milly would not be able to walk past a suffering puppy.

I don't want to talk about her as a runaway, as a naughty girl. All I want to say to the police is that I'm Milly's biggest fan. But I'm starting to doubt myself, as apparently I'm supposed to do. The police, it seems, want to make us doubt ourselves. After all, Milly has gone, and we don't have any reasonable explanations.

Growing up is partly about developing a new identity, and that necessitates some privacy. Our parents have always been understanding of that need. They look after us, and we have curfews, but they respect our boundaries and want to give us personal space. I ask you, what parent would know every tiny detail of their adolescent son or daughter's life?

As a result of the parade of 'exhibits' now thrust in front of them, Mum and Dad are being forced to find out things about Milly that they didn't know. Little things, mostly. But they hurt way out of proportion because of where we are now.

We're still in shock about the absence of Milly, and about the cold, aggressive attitude of the police towards my father. But now we're starting to realize there's a new challenge: the press.

The papers are greedy for pictures of us. Milly's disappearance has a special resonance for the British public, because of the case of little Sarah Payne, who also vanished in the blink of an eye. Milly herself had noted how the nation took the tragedy to its heart. Like Milly is, Sarah was highly photogenic. Sarah's disappearance and the trial of her murderer sold millions of newspapers.

To our horror, it isn't long before the press are linking Milly to Sarah. The perpetrator could not be the same man, as Sarah's abductor is now locked up. But the press seem to be aching to point out that what had happened to Sarah could easily have happened to Milly. The headline-writers don't seem to trouble themselves about how that might make Milly's family feel.

Daily Star, 25 March 2002; story, Gary Nicks

Just as Milly has fallen prey to an abductor, we, too, are now hunted by the press. We have something they want: raw pain and terror. Any snap of our white faces can earn them money. Any comment they can extract from us – the same. Since the second day of Milly's disappearance, the press have camped outside our house. They block the driveway and the road. They show no sign of going away. We have to fight past them if we need to go out.

Yet we need them. We rely on them to get Milly's face out there. We want them to be investigating. They may find something the police have missed.

Our lives are running to press and news cycles. The music that used to personify Milly – the *Pink Panther* theme or 'Nobody Does It Better' – has suddenly changed. Now Milly is signified by the theme music of the six or nine or ten o'clock news on television.

Journalists step out from behind hedges with questions designed to shock us into saying something quotable or misquotable. Sometimes they succeed. But mostly we cast off our former joking, open personalities and learn how to be miserable and tight-lipped. If we're seen smiling or laughing, that could be recorded and held against us, showing us to have forgotten about Milly.

With the line of questioning the police are taking, we can't afford to show a smile on any level.

12.

On 27 March – day seven – the police, with BBC *Crimewatch,* film a hurriedly arranged reconstruction of Milly's last-known movements. It's to be aired the next day, Mum's birthday. We know it's going to happen because they ask for our help, even though they don't always take our advice. We hand over various family videos, including the ones that will soon become well known: Milly dancing around with the iron, and playing the saxophone.

Desperate to do something, I offer to be Milly for the reconstruction. Of course they turn me down as I'm older and we don't really look similar. They say it would attract too much press attention and disrupt the filming, which they are trying to do discreetly. Instead of me, they get a girl from an agency and dress her up as Milly. The police try to get a replica of her rucksack for the reconstruction. Milly doesn't make it easy for them. Milly wanted a bag that no one else would have, so she chose hers in America the previous summer.

I sketch Milly's phone case so they can make a copy of it, her name written in pen with sparkles all around it. I sketch her fairy pendant too. I desperately want people to have an image of that. I have a sudden vision of someone seeing Milly's fairy pendant lying on the ground. If they saw my sketch they would never just pass by it. They would pick it up, and then we would have our first clue.

Friends make a massive banner asking people to watch *Crimewatch* on the night of the twenty-eighth. It's hung up at the traffic lights in Station Avenue, near where Milly was last seen. We want to remind each person who comes out of the station to watch the programme, to rack their brains for a relevant memory. We need everyone in Walton to have a personal stake in the show. The press duly print a photo of the banner, and we are happy because it spreads the news, makes people feel involved.

One of those people may lead us to Milly.

★

Milly's never very organized about birthdays and normally rushes out the day before to hunt down a present. But this year Milly and I had planned to go shopping together on Easter Saturday to buy Mum a necklace. Because Mum's lost so much weight, Dad's given her some money to refresh her wardrobe. My present to her is a new pink-and-white-striped rugby top.

The only present Mum wants is Milly back home safe. Instead, Alice and Jon arrive with a senior officer. Mum and Dad are ushered into the dining room.

Jon and Alice quickly say that it isn't the worst. Mum lets me and Lovely Granny know there's nothing new to worry about. Alice and Jon just want to inform us that the police would now like to search the whole house. Of course we're happy for them to do that. We'll encourage them to do anything that might help.

I notice that Dad goes to have a quiet word with an officer down at the end of the garden where he's taking a cigarette break.

Having willingly given them permission to search our house, we are then given just two minutes to find the clothing we wore on the day Milly went missing. I remind Mum she was wearing black trousers and a lilac blouse and I even remember what shirt and tie Dad was wearing.

Mum explains that we're to be sent away because the police don't want us underfoot while they search. They offer us a hotel, but we want to stay at Lovely Granny's house. We need to be with her, and together, not in anonymous rooms. We also want to be somewhere Milly knows. If she did not find us at home, Milly would certainly look for us at Lovely Granny's.

Before the search starts, I go into Milly's bedroom, accompanied by Alice, to see if I can absolutely rule out which pieces of jewellery my sister might have been wearing on the afternoon she vanished. Milly and I are accustomed to go in and out of each other's rooms, helping ourselves to clothes and accessories. Today I take a pair of silver earrings in the shape of lightning bolts. Milly was wearing them often just before she went missing. I put them on and don't want to take them off. Unfortunately, they tarnish almost instantly, and that upsets me, not just because I'm so fastidious.

We have no idea how long we'll be exiled from our home. We pack just a few things. Our priorities are crazed by trauma and strangeness. We're not allowed upstairs unsupervised to pick out our clothes. I guess that makes us nervous too. We make rushed, bad choices, of course. I take Taily Ted, my mini-disc player and the turquoise daisy pyjamas that are the same as Milly's yellow ones from the Cuba video. Mum chooses some clothes for Dad, but she's so distracted that they're left on the bed.

Our cars are to be searched too. We're not allowed to use them. So our FLOs will drive us over to Granny's.

The press are still in residence outside our drive. There are long lenses trained on us and questions shouted to us. They use our first names, as if they know us.

At Lovely Granny's, I cannot cope with the sick feeling in my stomach when I think about what the police are doing at our house. I keep gulping in. It's as if I'm taking twice as many breaths as normal.

That afternoon Mum and Dad go for a walk while I stay with Lovely Granny. It will be nine years before I find out what they discussed in that hour away from the house. While they are out, Lovely Granny and I watch the television coverage of the police searching our house. It's horrible and fascinating at the same time. Home looks so different when viewed through a camera lens pointed down at it from a helicopter.

For Mum's birthday, Lovely Granny had the local blacksmith make some wrought-iron obelisks for the garden. The obelisks, all gold balls and fancy black ironwork, had just been delivered. Now there they are on the television, standing in a line on the lawn, looking distinctly eccentric. Mum's cylindrical sweet-pea frame, which she herself designed, is waiting to be covered with plants. The wisteria has just been dug up, so there's a pile of dirt.

From the helicopter's viewpoint, Lovely Granny and I watch the police tape going up, two tents, men in white forensic suits shuffling like fat white grubs in and out of our doors. They also dip in and out of the blue Peugeot and the red VW Golf. White vans block either end of our drive.

Meanwhile, in a car park behind our house, a cherry-picker is raising a press cameraman to take a shot of our garden. Our home is turning into a crime scene in front of my eyes.

Mum and Dad come back from their walk. They join me and Lovely Granny on the sofa. They're saying nothing about what they discussed. From the looks on their faces, it has not been a comforting talk. Mum says that she doesn't mind the police searching the house. But she does not like the idea of them in her garden. We spent ages positioning her tin watering-can strategically for maximum picturesque effect. Naturally the police have already moved it, and that misplaced can seems symbolic of the unnecessary and intrusive nature of the search.

The television cameras can't go into the house, but my mind's eye sees Milly's room being ransacked once more. Mum and I agree again how upset and betrayed Milly would feel about this.

Van after van leaves our driveway, full of pieces of our lives. Many thousands of individual items will be taken by the police during this search.

The FLOs are present as much as possible, yet they're not in any position to reassure us. They are part of the police. So the pressure on my parents is crushing, even though they try to hide it from me. Mum and Dad know they are innocent of anything to do with Milly's disappearance, but the search and the attitude of the senior officers are beginning to make them afraid of wrongful accusations and even miscarriages of justice.

After all, the police have not produced any other suspects. It has not apparently entered into their calculations, as the senior officer told Mum and Dad on the first day, that anyone outside the family or our close circle might be involved. The police are thinking in percentages and statistics. Not about us as a family, as the family we are.

While we wait for the search to be over, Dad's spending a lot of his time making notes of every second of the day that Milly disappeared. He's a man for detail, so it's second nature to him to note down every work phone call he took and its duration.

Of course, the police make even his natural attention to detail look suspicious.

We're collected by car to go to the *Crimewatch* studios. Because Mum accidentally left Dad's clothes on the bed, he will have to appear on television looking less than his normal immaculate self. Mum had desperately wanted to wear the opal necklace her father gave her before he died. She thinks it might be lucky. Milly loved

Grandad so much. If she somehow sees that necklace, Mum thinks, it will give her heart. But when Mum asks them for the necklace, the police say they can't find it.

At the BBC, we're shown a preview of the reconstruction. They explain they've put the scenes together in two hours whereas normally it would have taken two weeks. To us, the actress looks nothing like Milly. Her voice, with its London accent, is quite different from Milly's. She's slim, yet not as slender as Milly. Her legs are not quite as long as Milly's. No one's ever could be, of course. The actress's socks are up around her ankles. Milly always rolls hers down, one of her trademark styles. The actress's shirt is neatly tucked in. Milly's never is. The actress doesn't hold herself like Milly does. Her gait is markedly different. Milly has a couple of ways of walking. She can do the teenage slouch. Mostly she dances, glides and sashays. As with everything she does, Milly has a repertoire. The poor actress cannot know any of it.

Our feelings are jarred by each little thing that is wrong. We want the girl to be a perfect facsimile for the sake of the reconstruction. But we are hating the fact that any girl has to pretend to be Milly. We're aware that we're asking too much of her. Yet we cannot help ourselves. Attention to detail is a big thing for me. This reconstruction is supposed to help jog memories so I know every little thing counts. Each tiny mistake is therefore a potential opportunity lost to get to someone who might have seen something useful to the investigation.

Two other agency girls take the roles of Natalie and her sister Danielle, the friend who shared Milly's last train journey. Danielle is shown with dark tights while the actress playing Milly has bare legs, which makes her skirt look very, very short. We're horribly sensitive to that, me particularly, as I know how the police have been trying to get me to portray Milly as precociously sexual. We would have liked the producers to lower the skirt length. But there's no time to protest. It's all been done in such a rush, a rush we can only support.

This is the first time we feel that the police are making a real effort, putting some urgency and elbow into it. Surrey Police are relaxing their grip on the case and letting it out into the wider world, where Milly may even be. That can only be good.

Part of the show is an interview with Mum and Dad. Now they

meet the presenter Nick Ross, who's charming and friendly. He tries to put them at their ease. He says that they'll do two practice runs and then the real thing. Dad has his arm around Mum, who breaks down at the first question.

Nick asks what Mum would say to someone who might be holding Milly,

She says, 'If someone has taken Milly and is holding her, then, please, please, give her back to us. You cannot believe the enormous grief it has caused her family and her friends . . . We are devastated . . . Please, please, give her back to us.'

Gently, Nick Ross asks what Mum would like to say if 'the worst' has happened.

Mum says bravely, 'If it's the worst that's happened, please can you give us some sort of signal so we know . . .'

Mum and Dad are immensely relieved when Nick Ross says, 'That will do as the final take.'

The police are on next. They describe all the things that Milly was wearing and carrying.

Nick Ross asks the police about links with other missing girls or women. The police say that there's nothing that links this case with any others. They're sure of that.

Nick Ross has a long chat with us afterwards. When he's run through many different scenarios, he says quietly, 'It doesn't look good.' He believes that Milly has either been abducted or fallen and suffered a bad head injury, causing her total amnesia. We quickly rule that out as someone would have seen her.

We watch the TV transmission of *Crimewatch* on Lovely Granny's sofa, as the police are still searching our house. How many times have Milly and I watched *Crimewatch* together? Milly adored Jill Dando, the former presenter, who was herself murdered. Now it's Milly up there as the victim, and my own parents are appealing for her.

There's a new feeling, an unexpected one. Our family has moved into a fresh stage. *Crimewatch* turns Milly's disappearance into a crime, whatever the police are trying to suggest to us about her being a runaway.

Suddenly *our family* is the scene of a crime. We walk around with it: we take the crime everywhere.

★

Fortunately, right from the start, the public doesn't seem to have the same attitude as the police. We feel so much more compassion coming from them. We know that many volunteers have been out searching for Milly, and we're intensely grateful.

The plight of our family clearly moves people. Mum, so tiny and fragile, seems to have become a big figure in the public's imagination. She is like an emblem for all mothers who have lost an indispensable, precious child. Mum's never self-conscious in front of the camera. She cares about only one thing: finding Milly. People respond to her sincerity and dignity. People who are not the police, that is. *Crimewatch* gives no indication of the insinuations that the police are making against my father so he is allowed to come across as he is: polite, gentle, protective. The public warms to him as well.

An hour or so after *Crimewatch*, the BBC always screens an update. By that time there have been 220 calls. A white purse has been handed in. The programme has given us hope. But hope is stressful. Hope is also unbearable. We pin so much on this broadcast. Could it make the difference?

It's a long night for us all after the screening. We sleep with everything crossed – in the brief moments when we *do* sleep. I don't feel safe at Lovely Granny's. Whoever has taken Milly might still find me there. I'm sick with sleep deprivation. The next day, my parents take me to the doctor. I need something to help me sleep. But antidepressants, anti-anxiety medication or sleeping tablets are not really on offer to a girl of my age. I'm told to try Rescue Remedy, which doesn't even touch the sides.

Meanwhile *Crimewatch*, just as the police feared, continues to bring in hundreds more calls, adding to what they clearly see as their burden.

We return to our family home on the evening of 31 March. Milly has now been missing for eleven days.

Home is not the same.

It is horrible.

The carpets have been put back but you can see from little wrinkles that they've been rolled up. Once-silent floorboards squeak.

Everything has been touched by the hands of strangers who suspect our family of something. Our papers, folders, books, bills have all been moved.

We feel as if we have been ram-raided and pillaged. Well, we have – as if we were criminals. They have been through our underwear drawers. They have checked our laundry baskets and bins. The house reeks of rubber gloves and disinfectant. Gone are the cosy smells of home. When Mum wants to go into Milly's room, just to smell the air that her daughter has breathed, she finds it sterile and cold. Milly's scent is Tommy Hilfiger's Girl. There's nothing left of it in the air. It's as if the police have erased every trace of Milly's DNA from her home. From our home.

What kind of home is it without Milly?

I can't bear to go into Milly's room to see what the police have made of her famous monumental mess. I want to remember it as it was, not as the unnaturally tidy room of a girl who could be nothing like my sister. All Milly's necklaces and earrings used to be loose and feral inside her wildly messy drawers. But the police have left her jewellery in velvet boxes in a neat heap on top of the drawers, something Milly would never do. Mum can't bear to touch them and, anyway, she's worried she will be in trouble if she does.

Our sheets, our towels, our hairbrushes (our Christmas ones, from the video) are never coming back. The police have replaced them.

The mother of one of Milly's friends brings round a CD of Gareth Gates. She thinks it will comfort Mum. Ours is a silent house now. So Mum puts on a massive pair of headphones and listens, over and over again, to 'Unchained Melody', Milly's favourite of Gareth's performances. Tears roll down her cheeks. Dad and I know she's hurting herself, but we cannot stop her.

As the empty days pass, Mum also plays and plays the video of Milly ironing her jeans.

13.

It soon became terrifyingly clear to us that Surrey Police were working on two basic templates. Template One was that Milly ran away because she was unhappy at home, with me being the daughter favoured by Mum. Runaway Milly was also supposed to be having a secret relationship with an older man. Template Two had Milly abducted by Dad, a predator who abused and killed his own daughter, under Mum's nose. Dad was the last person to talk to Milly. He was alone in the house when she vanished. Statistically, Dad did it, as far as the police were concerned. It was just a question of finding out the details. They seemed to think they'd find what they needed in our house.

The police kept Template One going even while moving on to Template Two. Template One could be twisted to serve Template Two, if that proved more convenient.

Milly, a sexually precocious and suicidal runaway? Dad, a killer? Mum, a neglectful mother? Can you imagine how their theories must have sounded in our ears and hurt in our minds? Not only was Milly lost to us, but we had these horrible insinuations to digest submissively. We were not allowed to be angry.

Our family was damaged, not deformed. To force-fit our family into their rigid scenarios, the police did the emotional equivalent of cutting off our arms and legs. We were already in pain. Their templates and their attitudes added whole new dimensions of pain and terror. If we tried to defend ourselves, we got cynical looks. Dad got threats, veiled and otherwise.

On our side, we lacked experience of evil. We had no experience of having to stand up for ourselves. We didn't understand *why* we needed to stand up for ourselves. We felt like victims. We sought and expected protection and kindness. That's what our family would have offered to anyone in our own position. We couldn't understand why anyone, let alone the police, would want to hurt us more than we were already hurting.

Our innocence betrayed us. Real criminals know their rights. They know how to cover their tracks, how to be consistent in their lies, throwing in a bit of truth when it won't hurt their case. They know how to twist questions and answers to make themselves look good.

We floundered, making ourselves look bad. We didn't even know that we were supposed to make ourselves look good. We thought our innocence was a shield. It was not. We thought the police were the good guys; that they were there to protect families like ours; that they had specialists who knew how to interview frightened young girls and terrified parents; that they knew proper, gentle interrogation techniques that would extract information without humiliating or bullying us; that they would understand that our traumatized minds and memories were not steel traps.

Most of all we believed their absolute priority would be to have hundreds of police officers out searching for Milly. We believed that everything would be secondary to finding her.

Even though we had seen the slowness of their reaction, and had experienced the wrongness of their initial brutal questioning, we didn't want to tread on police toes. We so desperately wanted to trust them. We were depending on them to find Milly, by which we meant finding her alive. We didn't even speak to Milly's friends in case we got in the way. And so those friends went unquestioned for crucial hours when Milly was still alive to be saved. We had no idea that some of her friends were not going to be spoken to for weeks.

In general, our experience was that the lower-ranking officers were extremely kind and compassionate. The more senior they were, the more arrogant they sometimes were. I often did not feel I was being taken seriously. Dad, of course, was being taken all too seriously, but for the wrong reasons. It would have been so convenient if he could have been a child-killer. Case closed. Heads shaken. You never know, do you?

Even then I understood that Milly might be seen as a route to promotion for some of the officers dealing with our case. One junior policeman posted outside had to be moved on because he fraternized too much with the reporters. Major events involving the press always saw the top brass turned out elegantly for the camera lenses. Day to day, hour to hour, we had Alice and Jon. Yet when there was a photo-call, their bosses would magically appear.

There was one particular officer who cropped up again and again in all the press coverage. It's almost like a *Where's Wally?* book. You just had to look in the newspaper picture and you'd always find him.

And we also had cause to worry and doubt when we saw how often the press appeared at moments that should have been private or forensically 'clean'. How did they know what only the police should have known?

I'd like to be more generous. I'll try. Perhaps the fact that the police deal with more bad people than good ones has in some cases distorted their ability to discern whether a victim family has some part, some accountability, in the disappearance of a child. If the minds of those in charge at Surrey Police had been more open to the idea of a happy family – not a story-book one, but a decent one – they might have rushed into action at a point when they could actually have saved Milly's life.

All these years later, we have two simultaneous timelines. One shows what happened to Milly, hour by hour. The other shows what the police were doing in those hours. If you put those time-lines side by side, a painful fact emerges. Milly was always going to be hurt and abused by the man who abducted her.

But she did not have to die.

Instead of looking for the kind of man who might abduct a young girl, the police spent the last hours of Milly's life treating my sister as a deliberate runaway.

Milly's murderer was well known to the police for his violent and predatory ways. Our family was not. For years Milly's murderer was given the benefit of the doubt. Milly's family was under suspicion the moment we reported her disappearance.

And so we lost her.

We lurch into April, scarcely breathing. Milly's been gone eleven days, twelve, thirteen . . . None of us can think about anything else but the shock, hurt, mystery and loss.

If Milly's still alive, then where is she? Why isn't she calling us? Is it because someone has her? Is he stopping her calling us? Is he hurting her? Is she thinking about us? Will she escape?

If you've lost someone the way we lost Milly, you never stop looking, even when you think you're not. You're always scanning every street, every shop, every café for a long-legged schoolgirl. You think you're concentrating on something else, but you're not. You're wondering where Milly is and what she's doing. Maybe for a minute you think your life is normal, and that you can watch *Neighbours*, but then it's the *Neighbours* theme that cuts right through your heart.

In the morning, I think, *Is Milly waking up now?*

When I go to bed, I'm wondering, *Is there a light where she is?*

Sometimes I have nightmares about what's happening to her, and the fear is so strong that I wake screaming.

On 3 April, day fourteen of Milly's disappearance, there's an appeal by Danielle, the friend who shared a bag of chips with Milly at the Travellers Café minutes before she vanished. Danielle speaks of a Milly we recognize, describing her sense of humour and her ability to comfort and understand. But in her appeal, she talks to Milly directly as if she is a runaway, asking her to make contact.

We know Danielle's genuinely trying to help, but we're too raw not to flinch when she speaks of Milly in the past tense. 'I have been remembering the times, little things that have stuck in my head, the song that we made together here at the park, with you on your saxophone and me singing. You could hardly play for laughing. I remember that you came to my house, and we did sing-along songs with Disney and you knew all the words.'

We just cannot talk of Milly in the past tense or think of her there either.

On the same day, the police brief the press that Milly's 'fairly active in the computer world, and as such, there are a number of lines of inquiry that emanate from details obtained from her computer. Surrey Police would like to stress that this is just one of many areas that we are investigating . . . There are currently no confirmed witnesses who have come forward saying they have seen a struggle. This leads us to believe that if she has been abducted, it is less likely to have been by a stranger.'

So now the media and the public have the police's preferred scenarios imprinted in their minds: Milly might have run off with someone she met on the internet. If she's been taken, it is by someone she trusts.

Posters are circulated to all the local football clubs in the area.

This is Dad's idea. One of the organizers knows Dad personally, describing him to the press as 'the most gentlemanly gentleman I know'. The man tells a television reporter, 'He lives for his family.'

The Ford Motor Company has a fleet of ten forty-foot lorries featuring giant photos of missing people on their sides. Now there's one with Milly's face travelling around the country. Her image is also being shown on screens in petrol-station forecourts.

On Thursday, 4 April, day fifteen, we're told of a body seen in a river near Motspur Park. We hardly breathe until eight in the evening, when Alice rings to say there has been a second sighting of a body in the water. Searches are taking place.

I'm having a lot of trouble sleeping. I will go to bed only with Mum. I insist she stays awake until I fall asleep. That night, I finally drop off at around 11 p.m. A little after that, the phone rings. Alice tells Mum that the search team hasn't found anything, but they're putting the nets out. It's another unbearably long night for Mum. No news comes through. We have to deduce this body has nothing to do with Milly.

Mum keeps asking the police if they have a counsellor who can help me deal with the trauma. The police say they are getting in touch with a specialist. A social worker arrives on 5 April. She has red curly hair and twenty rings on her fingers. One side of her nose is covered with a silver lizard piercing. She looks like a feral Spice Girl.

With this choice, the police show that they really haven't understood me at all. I'm a very old-fashioned teenager. Milly was the one for grunge. *I'm* not going to bond with someone like this. I'm never going to share with her dark secrets about Dad, of which there are none, or about Milly's boyfriends, pregnancies or drugs because they don't exist either. But, most of all, I'm not going to trust this woman.

The only person I want to talk to is Milly.

But I decide to make an effort with the social worker. We have, after all, been given the impression she's there to help with my anxiety. If anyone needs help, I do. My GCSEs are coming up in a month and I'm incapable of focusing or concentrating. Moreover, the police have confiscated our computer so I don't have all my course notes. Taking the computer also has the effect of isolating me from the friends I used to communicate with via MSN Messenger.

A family friend lends us a laptop. The police do not let us copy my school work from the confiscated computer to the new one. So I am really lost. I hope the social worker will help me find a path.

The first time we meet it's in the spare room upstairs. The main downstairs room is where Lovely Granny's sitting, taking all the calls triggered by our poster. We believe our own incident room is still busier than the one we have seen at the police station.

The social worker gives me an attractive zebra-skin notebook, telling me it's our private place where I can record feelings and thoughts that no one but the two of us will see. So, if there's anything I can't say out loud, well, now there will be a place for it. Then she and I can read it together and talk about it on her next visit. What she means is that I'm not to share what I write with my parents.

She makes me draw a circle of trust – family and friends I would trust enough to get into a car with them. She's trying to be cool, trying to relate to me as a teenager, trying to be my friend, trying to act my age, trying to establish that we have lots in common. Instead of answering her probing, I start asking her questions. Have they searched this place? Have they searched that one? I follow up on things that the FLOs have told us, asking for information.

I'm angry because nothing is ever answered. I'm already angry with the police in general because they never do what I think they should be doing.

The second time the social worker comes, I refuse to answer her any more. I tell her that she's not helping me.

It seems that she's in fact part of the police investigation. Her mission is to find out if I'm telling the truth when I insist that Dad would never have hurt Milly. She's been tasked with covertly observing our family relationships by talking to me on my own, all the while giving the impression she's there to help me find a way to resume my education, and to deal with the GCSEs. The 'private' zebra-skin notebook is going to be turned over to the police. We're told that a nearby house (we never do find out which one) is rigged with CCTV watching our premises. Naïvely, I find this comforting, as I think it's for our protection. Of course it's actually there to monitor our every move.

Meanwhile, on the same day, the police show the press replicas of Milly's phone, school jacket, blouse and tie, her ace of spades purse, and her shoes.

It is only on 6 April, day seventeen of her disappearance, that the hunt for Milly acquires a name. Mum notes in her diary on that day that it's now called 'Operation Ruby'. We're never told why.

The police are asking for the addresses of the two boys we met on holiday in Cuba. They seem to think it's more likely that Milly has run away to Canada than that she has been abducted by a stranger.

Meanwhile Alice takes our fingerprints, using the kitchen table. She guides each of our fingers into the ink pad, then on to a piece of paper. Unfortunately some of the ink leaks and stains the table. No matter how she scrubs, Mum will never get the ink out. In the end she'll have to buy a new table.

Sunday, 7 April – day eighteen – Mum wakes up crying. Her first thought is that, for the first time, she didn't send Milly a text message yesterday. This saddens and frightens her.

Lovely Granny is staying with us. We discuss at length every scenario we can think of to explain Milly's disappearance. We also talk about the impact that finding Uncle Bree had on family dynamics, and worry that, because he is a 'newly acquired' uncle, he may also be considered a suspect by the police.

The police come round constantly. But they have no news. Just more questions. Such as, 'Would Milly give directions to a driver?' Mum thinks she might as she's polite and considerate. Later Mum asks me the same question. Yes, I would.

Mum and Dad keep taking walks to calm themselves down. But, every time they do, Mum finds herself looking for a body.

The press coverage is doing its best to give us heart. To our minds, every time Milly's image is on the screen, someone might remember that they saw her. The police now release CCTV footage of Milly at 15.07 p.m. on 21 March, leaving her science lesson at Heathside School. She's wearing her sweater inside her blazer. In the image at Weybridge station a bit later, her jumper has gone, her tie is loosened, and her shirt's now hanging outside her skirt. But her blazer is still on. It is very sad to hear the voiceover describe the footage as 'the last time Milly was seen'. We don't want to be reminded that her classmates will be returning to school today after the Easter break – with no Milly.

At bedtime that night, Mum's with me. I can see she needs to cry but she's afraid to do it in front of me. The kind of crying we need to do now is not really something you can do quietly. In the end, Mum can't hold it back. That sets me off too. We have a bloody good cry and Dad comes in to hug us both. I think the press coverage unlocked those necessary tears. Also, we haven't cried properly for a day or two.

We have another problem, a local lady who keeps coming to the door. She has a daughter the same age as me, and she wants us to be friends. We refer to her as the 'caped crusader'. I'm frightened of her. There is something not right about her. I don't want her in our house. Even when Mum or Dad politely declines her help, she's not put off, and keeps coming.

Dad's politeness is sometimes a trap. It is now. He's not good at getting rid of people brusquely, as we've been told to do. He always engages in a little conversation. Unfortunately she feels encouraged by his courtesy.

We mention 'the caped crusader' to the police, who explain that she's known to them and that she has a history of mental illness.

We also tell them about the woman who knocks at our door and tries to give Mum her baby.

The woman is young. The baby in her arms cannot be more than a couple of weeks old. She says, 'I feel so awful for what you're having to endure. So can I give you my baby, please?' She's not crying. She's really serious.

Mum cries. A bit of Mum is thinking, *God, I'd love to have a baby.* She doesn't know which is more frightening – her own desire or this woman's offer. In the end, she says, 'I am sorry, but no, thank you. I don't want your baby.'

What Mum wants is her own baby.

We are told by the police that this girl, too, has a history of mental illness.

Jon and Alice come to take Milly's saxophone and our remote control for fingerprinting. And now the police tell us that we're to be issued with new mobiles, a special house alarm, new door locks. This is upsetting. If the locks stay the same, Milly could get in. We don't want to give up on her.

How many sets of keys do we need?

All Mum and I can think about is the real question: *Will we need a set for Milly?*

14.

I'm falling deeper and deeper into my trauma. Bedtime is a nightmare. I hardly sleep. Every time I shut my eyes I see Milly being stabbed. I also keep getting a vision of her stuck in a room with a man trying it on with her. I scream out to her and to him, but I can't do anything about it. It is as if Milly's behind a pane of thick glass.

There's talk of me doing an appeal, or writing something for a newspaper. I say straight away that the programme I would do is *Newsround*. As I'm quite sensitive, I'm often upset by *Newsround*, which deals with hard-hitting stories but usually within the context of how war or murder affects people of my age or younger. Children are given a chance to share their opinions. Young people are listened to on that programme and I know it.

I believe the *Newsround* team will take me seriously. I also have faith that they will treat me kindly. The format agreed is an interview. Milly and I are familiar with all the presenters on *Newsround*. Becky Jago, who's to be my interviewer, is approachable, pretty and friendly. Having seen her on screen so many times, I feel as if I already know her.

At last I am being given my own shot to help in the hunt for Milly and it's the biggest responsibility of my whole life. If I do badly, it may be my fault that Milly is not found.

My nerves are calmed by the fact that the interview will be pre-recorded. Also, the questions are sent to me in advance so I won't be caught out, fall silent or say something embarrassing. Surrey Police get to vet the questions before I even see them. Mum and I work out some answers. I don't rehearse, however, because I don't want to seem fake. The other young people I've seen on *Newsround* never look as if they are scripted. They look authentic, connected to real experiences. This is *Milly* I'm going to talk about. *Milly*. If I needed a script to talk about my sister, what kind of sister would I be?

My worst fear is that I might smile inappropriately. People automatically smile at a camera. We've been living with Mum's video-cam for months, and my normal reaction is to grin at it. If I do that on *Newsround*, it'll look as if I don't care about Milly's disappearance, or that I'm so caught up in being on television that I've forgotten what's really going on.

My wardrobe choice is double denim in different shades: jeans and a jeans jacket, with a hoodie underneath. My hair's pulled back but there are Milly-like straggles around my face. I refuse to wear make-up. I don't want to be stagey or artificial.

On 9 April, day twenty of Milly's disappearance, Jon drives me to the studio, along with Mum, Dad, Lovely Granny and Alice, who has to make sure that the BBC don't do anything the police might feel would interfere with the investigation. At the BBC's old White City headquarters, all the screens in the foyer are showing the Queen Mother's funeral. We're there in time for the two minutes' silence. Seeing the coffin makes me flinch. I have to look away.

We're taken to the canteen for a cup of tea and lunch with the *Newsround* team. Had I been doing *Newsround* for any other reason, it would have been a wonderful treat, something to look forward to. Milly would have loved it. All of us are conscious that we're here only because Milly's missing, and we feel a mixture of guilt and fear.

I keep trying to tell myself that this is my time to help. Perhaps the surprise of seeing me, until now hidden from public scrutiny, will make someone come forward with new information. Perhaps my grief can stir someone's conscience. Secretly, I think, *If Milly is still alive, Milly might be watching me.*

The interview is recorded in the *Blue Peter* garden. Becky and I sit together on a bench. She makes it easy for me to talk. She can't have known about the atmosphere behind our front door, about our family home now dominated by the presence of the police, their suspicions and insinuations. She could not have guessed the excruciating details of Alice's questions about Milly's sexual experience. Becky's sympathy is sincere. She isn't judging me, and she doesn't have any agenda, except to help me make a successful appeal.

Her questions offer me the relief of stating clearly how mystified the whole family is about what could have happened to Milly. My answers are not very organized, but they are truthful. The truth isn't organized at times like these. Facts and feelings get mixed up. I mostly look down, so that I can concentrate.

Becky asks how the family is coping with each day. I say, 'It's all a nightmare and I'm wondering when I'm going to wake up.'

Becky wants me to tell her the most special thing about Milly. I don't hesitate. 'The girly chats we had when we shared a room.'

I tell Becky about the lovely support from neighbours, the pain of my friends who don't know what to say to me, the impossibility of studying for my GCSEs, the helpfulness of the media in spreading the word. I get to make my personal appeal for information direct to camera.

The worst thing of all, I tell Becky, is the mystery: 'When you try to sleep you just can't get it out of your head. You keep thinking, Oh, where is she? What's happening to her? What if something's going wrong? Have I tried that place? Have I tried this place? . . . It's like twenty-four/seven. You just can't get it out of your head. What is she doing? Is she in trouble? Is she dead? Is she alive? It's just so horrible. It's the not-knowing that's worse than anything.'

15.

Walton and Surrey have lost some innocence. The unthinkable has happened. Mothers who never even met Milly start crying when they see one of the posters. It could have been their daughter gone missing. Strangers – often mothers – stop Mum in the street. Mum's not allowed any personal space, even though she's fragile as glass. Strangers hug her. Because she has this unwanted form of celebrity now, people seem to feel they know her well. They offer their opinions about what has happened, whether Mum wants to hear them or not. They tell stories of their terror when their own child disappeared for two hours. They feel better, relieved at having shared their stories, reliving their happy endings. Then they leave Mum alone, sadder and depleted. I'm sure that these people mean well, and certainly they mean Mum no harm. They just have no idea what they're doing to her.

If Mum goes to the shop, it takes ages because of all the people who want to chat to her. And it's so painful for her to pass the vegetable section without buying the usual stock of cucumbers. So, lovely friends do the weekly shop, bring casseroles and even take away our ironing.

On one occasion Mum pops into Superdrug in Walton to stock up on female monthly essentials. Dad waits in the car outside so she can run in and out. Mum fills her basket to overflowing, to put off another trip for as long as possible. Just as she's piling in the last few packets from the shelf, a man approaches her. She knows him vaguely. He flings his arms around her. They were not on hugging terms before. Now it seems that they are. Mum freezes, because the only thing separating them is a shopping basket brimming with sanitary products. The man chats to her. 'How are you? Is there any more news? What do you think actually happened?'

He doesn't seem to notice the heavy basket she's struggling to hold up. Mum's mortified. Yet when she finally escapes she's glad she had the foresight to buy us supplies to last the next six months.

I know my appearance on *Newsround* will put me 'out there' too. But I'm eager to share Mum's burden. So, when they take off my little microphone and I thank Becky Jago, I feel better for a moment. I don't feel as if I've let Milly down, which has been, and will continue to be, the way I feel after every police interview, ever since that first terrible one with Alice. Also, I haven't let myself down, or our family. I have been allowed to paint a true portrait of who we are.

After the interview, Mum, Dad and I are taken to Staines police station to identify various bits of 'evidence' handed in by the general public. The 'exhibits officer' shows us hairbands, clips, bracelets, a pair of knickers, purses, odd bits of jewellery, bits of paper. Nothing's familiar. Then we're shown a note written on a torn Joosters sweet wrapper. They hand it to us, encased in a forensic plastic sleeve. Do we recognize it?

It says simply, 'Sorry, Mum.'

Mum tells the police that Milly really likes Joosters. The two words actually look like Milly's writing. It hurts to see it again. But it's the first time we have been shown anything that might actually belong to Milly. I feel a glimmer of hope. At last, a clue.

We ask them where they found it or who handed it in. *Perhaps*, I think, *Milly left it at Walton station*. I am already responding, unwillingly, to the suggestions that the police are forcing on us. I know Milly's not a runaway, yet I can't help fantasizing that she is. Because that would mean she's still alive and may yet come back.

The exhibits officer goes slowly and laboriously through pages of notes listing all the items. It turns out that the sweet wrapper was found in the side pocket of our own blue Peugeot. I immediately return to reality. Milly's always leaving notes all over the house. And, being a 'naughty sausage', she frequently needs to say 'Sorry.'

Then I feel a little bitter, as if we have been tricked, as if they deliberately slipped her silly note from our car into a big pile of stuff handed in to the police by strangers. Why didn't they just say, 'We found this in the blue car. Can you explain it?'

Are we being tested to see if we will tell the truth? Of course we do.

The police are apparently working on the theory that this sweet wrapper is Milly's goodbye note. This is the proof they have been looking for.

Mum and I are seething with anger. Strange New Dad is just writing line after line in an exercise book. That's all he does, these days.

I want to go to the edge of a cliff and scream until my anger spreads out over the sea. But there are no cliffs close to Walton-on-Thames. So I tug the rage into the back of my mind. I try not to let it eat me up.

What's it going to take for them to realize that Milly did not run away?

Mum, Dad and I get home in time to see *Newsround* on television. We crowd on to the sofa where I usually sit with Milly – and we watch me talk about Milly. My voice sounds strange and nasal to me. I seem much younger than sixteen and my teeth look gappy. But I'm relieved to realize that I wouldn't want to change anything I said.

Friends phone and text. They tell me I was great. Lovely Granny says that I spoke 'really nicely', high praise from her. A friend suggests I look at the *Newsround* website, where they have posted the story, including a timeline of Milly's disappearance. The site is flooded with lovely comments from people my own age and younger. Many say how brave I am.

At this point, no one is saying nasty things about us or our family.

I have a sense of personal purpose at last. I've started to help. I don't regard my interviews with the police as being very helpful because they mostly seem to try to make me say things that are just not true. Now, for a few minutes, I have spoken directly to hundreds of thousands of people via *Newsround*.

The transmission is only the beginning. The television news programme shows extracts of me giving my 'loving description' of Milly. My answers will be quoted over the next week in the *Mirror*, the *Telegraph*, the *Mail*, the *Evening Standard*. My words will reach out across the nation in print as well as on the screen.

Surely, I think, *someone will read them, and call in with information.* That's what I think. That's what I hope.

Just a few hours later, I'm looking at a card that Milly wrote to me. I'm playing a sad song on my CD player and I start to cry. I fall down a well of terror and anguish. Soon I'm crying so much I cannot breathe. That is when the hallucinations start. I can see Milly. She's in terrible pain. I cannot reach her. I start screaming, not like a child but deeper, from the gut. I struggle to breathe. I can't get enough air into my lungs to feed all my feelings.

I'm losing control of my body. I start screaming, 'I can see Milly being stabbed now! Stop it, stop it!'

Mum rushes in to comfort me, but I don't feel as if I am in the same space as her. I think that Milly's kidnapper has found a way to drug me secretly so he can take me tonight. I fight against his drugs, exhausting myself.

Mum and Dad are petrified. No matter how they try to reach me, I am lost in the terror and Milly's still being stabbed in front of me. This continues for over an hour. Then Dad tries to be a bit firmer. He tells me to pull myself together. That's when I really lose it. Mum phones the emergency doctor. A locum arrives. I've never seen him before. I don't trust him and scream at him too. I cannot communicate because I'm still totally engrossed in fighting off the drugs that the kidnapper has got into my system. I have to win that battle, or he will take me just as he took Milly.

The doctor looks scared. 'I'm a religious man, Gemma,' he says. He falls to his knees and starts to pray, as if he's performing an exorcism.

That just makes me scream louder.

Mum tells the doctor, 'Get out of my house.' She gives me a diazepam. Soon I'm almost euphoric because the hallucination has lifted and I'm in a blanket of not-feeling. I ease into sleep.

The next morning, Mum rings the social worker, who explains I've had a panic attack. She tells Mum how to manage panic attacks by making me breathe deeply into a paper bag. Jon, too, diagnoses a panic attack. We wish we'd been advised that this could happen. The police have warned us about all kinds of things, mostly the potentially bad results of non-cooperation on our part.

They have not told us that we might become traumatized and what the symptoms would be.

16.

The police have seen the same happy family videos from Cuba that I've shared with you in words here. They've examined our computer, our drawers, our letters. They are practically living in our house. We cannot go in or out without their knowledge. And who knows what type of listening devices have been installed in our home?

So, the police can see who we are. They see our closeness, our grief, our shock. But they are still choosing to hunt for evidence that Milly is depressed or somehow alienated from the rest of her family and has run away. Or that Dad has done something to her. The real reason the CCTV camera's outside, I suspect, is to monitor if Dad is going out at night or behaving in any way that might seem culpable, such as disposing of something incriminating.

The police continue to turn Milly's private life inside out. They are going through her schoolbooks. Those little books will finally come back to us full of stickers that mark out words, phrases, song lyrics that the police thought pointed to evidence of Milly as a runaway, or as the victim of paternal abuse and maternal neglect.

The media spotlight is on the police and they are making sure that the press have plenty of action to record. The day after *Newsround,* they drop leaflets on cars at Hersham and Walton station car parks. That afternoon they interview commuters leaving the stations.

We feel desperate about reports of a girl seen crying or upset between the station and our home on the afternoon Milly disappeared. The witnesses claim that the girl matches Milly's description. There's another report of a girl seen talking to a man in a blue Saab in Station Avenue at around the time Milly disappeared. Why are we learning about this only two weeks later?

Surrey Police issue a press release. A hundred police officers are working on Milly's case. There are helicopters. There are divers in the River Mole. And now there are dogs. *At last* there are dogs.

Mum has repeatedly asked for them. Hannah Mac's dad has a friend in the dog team at the Metropolitan Police. Their services were offered very early on but we were fobbed off with, 'Well, the dogs tire very easily and are a very expensive resource.'

If the dogs had been deployed straight away they definitely wouldn't have got tired. It's well known where Milly was last seen – just yards from the station. The trail is stale now. By the time the dogs are used, they follow the now well-beaten path to our house that all the press and police have been traipsing up and down for days.

Suddenly, now that it may be too late, Surrey Police have set up what will become one of Britain's biggest and longest missing-person investigations.

But they still have their sights set firmly on us.

The twelfth of April, day twenty-three of Milly's disappearance, it's my turn to be cross-examined by the police.

Alice collects me from home. A non-relative adult must accompany me as I'm only sixteen. I choose Auntie Linds, as she has daughters of the same ages as me and Milly. She won't judge me and she knows Milly through and through. And loves her.

We're driven to a police 'safe house' in Weybridge. It turns out to be on the route that Mum takes to school. The building is one of a set of four two-storey brick council houses with front gardens, well kept and looking like normal homes. They are for families or children at risk or in witness protection programmes, an environment away from the police station.

The domesticity of the house is immediately confusing to me. This is to be a day of formal interrogation. I'm not expecting homely sofas. Alice is told to leave. Auntie Linds and I are left with a male and a female officer, both much older than Alice. The female officer is a bit too friendly for my liking. The male officer scares me. I don't understand why there needs to be a man present.

They put the kettle on, making a point of letting me see the posh chocolate chip cookies that await me, presumably as a reward if I am a good girl today.

The questioning is to take place in the living room. It will be filmed. The cameras are visible but only when the officers point them out. I'm told that the male officer will monitor the interview from a control station in one of the bedrooms upstairs. I'm shown that room too. In fact, the comfort of the house and the fake kindness of the woman just seem all wrong. It is like a horrible doll's house. I am afraid they're going to move me around and play nasty games with me.

The policewoman starts with the well-worn questions, the ones that Alice has already asked, all focused on Milly's sexual experience. There's so little to tell: a little bit of cider drunk in a park, a party Milly hadn't told our parents about. Innocent things compared with the crime of whoever has taken Milly. The atmosphere changes as the policewoman starts to talk about Dad.

She asks, 'Are you scared of your father?'

That's a new one. Of course I'm not. Dad? *Scary?*

Naturally Dad is slightly more scary than Mum, which isn't saying much. Dad is the ultimate resort of discipline. Mum invokes his coming home from work as the time of reckoning if Milly and I have been bad. Like any father, like any mother.

'What does he do when he gets angry?'

Dad's tone changes, I tell her. He raises his voice, rarely, but that's what makes it very effective. He never has to do more than that for me. Milly pushes a bit more.

'What happens when you do something he doesn't like?'

'We get sent to our rooms, or they ration our time on the computer, phone or PlayStation. Sometimes we're grounded.' But I hesitate. I'm not clear. I'm fearful. I don't like the feeling that my tears and confusion are being watched. It feels like a trap. I have only to make one mistake and I could get Dad arrested.

The policewoman is not satisfied with my account of an ordinary father with no-more-than-normally-naughty teenage daughters. She wants me to express some kind of fear about my father. Does she not realize how cruel that is? I'm a girl who has lost my sister. I'm already very frightened. I'm terrified that whoever's taken Milly has hurt her. And that he might come and hurt me too.

It's the same questions, again and again. She mixes up the order to try to catch me out. She has whole sequences and seams of questions that seem designed to destroy my confidence in all my relationships – not just with Dad, but with Milly herself, Mum, and even Lovely Granny, all the people I love and need the most.

What? You don't remember what Milly did at that party, Gemma? What kind of sister are you, Gemma? What – your mum let Milly go to a party like that, Gemma? What? You don't care that Milly drank some cider, Gemma? What – your parents let Milly go out dressed like that, Gemma?

Any 'yes' will lead me deeper into betraying the people who are my world. The police are melting down my memories of happiness, ripping up our family photo album, or at least pouring darkness on it. It seems that we are, in their eyes, a truly bad family just pretending to be good.

Every time I make a little mistake I'm losing confidence.

'Don't worry, Gemma, we know you're trying your best,' the female officer says.

The police are putting themselves in the position of my protectors, the ones who really understand me. They are portraying me as a poor, insecure, confused girl. 'You're safe with us, Gemma,' the policewoman says.

The implication is: *You are not safe at home. Milly wasn't safe at home. You see now?*

I feel as if the police are breaking me down. That isn't so hard in the state I'm in. I can't focus. I can't hold the woman's words in my head. I get lost between the beginnings and the ends of her tortuous questions. I'm also worn out. I've hardly slept since Milly vanished.

I'm still not offering up the answers she wants. So she launches into something new. It's about something that happened about nine months ago. I guess Mum or Dad must have told them about it. Like me, they are not just willing but *eager* to tell the truth. We would all do or say anything that would help the police find Milly.

The officer wants to talk about the time Mum sent Milly upstairs to fetch a clean handkerchief from a chest of drawers in my parents' bedroom. Milly accidentally pulled the lowest drawer so far out that it slipped off its rollers. Underneath she found an adult magazine. Milly didn't like the way the girls were posing in it. Milly and I are very straightforward with our parents. Dad was out, so Milly brought the magazine down to Mum. She wanted reassurance, and Mum gave it. 'It doesn't mean Daddy doesn't love me,' Mum told her.

I was babysitting. Milly phoned to tell me, but she was fine by the time I came home. She didn't raise it with me again. She talked it over with a couple of friends. There was no major upheaval in our house about the magazine. Afterwards, Milly and Dad were the same towards one another as ever.

I can remember very little about it because it blew over so quickly. Now the policewoman will not leave the subject alone. She wants me to frame it as a major drama in our household, as something so terrible that it would make Milly run away almost a year later. I've been trying to cooperate. But when the magazine is dragged in, I suddenly lose faith in the police. By treating it as important, the police are barking up the wrong tree, just trying to make us look bad, wasting precious time, not trying to find Milly.

I clam up. I look at the floor. I groan under my breath mutinously. I want to run away. But they are the police. They are the ones in charge. What can I do? I'm trapped in this room, with the curtains drawn, allegedly for my own safety and privacy.

The policewoman's response is to express disappointment in me. She implies that my behaviour will make it harder for them to find Milly.

I ask to call my mother. I think, *Mum will persuade them to let me go.*

She will not let me speak to Mum. Or Lovely Granny. Or anyone. Poor Auntie Linds is not allowed to intervene.

The questioning goes on all day.

It almost feels as if the policewoman is bored when I tell her the truth about how normal things were in our family before Milly disappeared. She tunes out. She tunes in again only when she thinks I might be offering something that interests her. We go round in circles. I have to fight so hard to keep stating the truth. It is exhausting.

I want to ask some questions of my own. Like *Why don't you believe me?* Like *Why do you keep asking me the same thing? Over and over again? Are you trying to brainwash me?* I want to scream at them, *You have no idea what a happy family we were! Stop questioning me and find the kidnapper!*

But they are the police. They are in charge. Even Auntie Linds cannot stop them. I can see how she is suffering, forced to listen in silence to all this.

Painful cracks are forming in my sense of myself.

And, worse, they have battered my belief in Dad so hard that I feel tiny cracks forming there too.

It isn't until the end of the first day of questioning that I really understand that they're trying to make me say that Dad is the one who's done something to Milly.

I defend Dad. I defend the truth.

My punishment is to be a second day of interrogation.

At home, I plead with Mum, 'Don't let them take me back. I don't want to go there again. I don't know what they want me to say. Can you tell me? Have I forgotten something important?'

Mum's making me a cup of tea. I can't meet her eyes, not after what I've been forced to say to the police about the magazine, not with the thoughts that the police have put into my mind. Mum knows me inside and out. She knows that I'm harbouring some kind of terrible secret.

'How did it go, Gemsie?'

Silence.

Mum repeats, 'What happened there?'

I break. 'Mum, I don't know how to get it right for them. They make me feel as if I'm wasting their time. They want me to . . .'

'Say something?' asks Mum. 'About Dad?'

She knows. Even though I forbade Auntie Linds to talk to her about the first day of questioning, Mum just knows.

I blurt it out, 'Mum, don't tell anyone I said this. Don't tell Dad . . . but do you think there's any chance he did it? Or is involved? Or something?' Even as the words come out of my mouth, I feel sick with shame. I know they are wrong. I hate my lack of self-control, my weakness, the fact that I have allowed the police to manipulate me.

I'm shaking. Too ashamed to meet her eyes, I stare at the terracotta tiles on the floor – the ones Grandad laid for us. It's so wrong that those tiles now have to bear the tramping feet of police officers who think my dad is a murderer. It's so wrong that Milly's not dancing and slouching around on those tiles, practising her 'Never Ever' routine for *Stars In Their Eyes*. Then I fix my eyes on the cooker, a green Rayburn, where Mum filmed me wearing swimming goggles while I chopped onions for supper . . . just before she panned in to Milly ironing for the very first time.

Only three weeks ago – now a whole lifetime ago.

I feel a huge desire to clean that Rayburn, clean everything, get rid of all the terror and sordidness of the police questioning.

My question still hangs in the air. Not my question, the police's. *Could Dad have done it?*

I can rely on Mum. She knows this isn't me, that these words have been put into my mouth. She understands I feel that I'm betraying my father.

Mum had exactly the same treatment the day before, so she can guess what I've been through. She must have been devastated to discover that the police have reached so far into my mind as to plant this obscene idea. Of course she doesn't want to traumatize me further by interrogating me. She doesn't want to make me feel guilty for anything that the police might have dragged out of me. She must have been terrified at the police's power to distort the trust and love in our family. But she manages not to show any of this.

She says firmly, 'No. Of course not. You know Dad. You know he isn't capable of anything like that. You know how close he and Milly are.'

It's true. He's my dad. Milly's dad. Dad with spreadsheets for his colds. Dad who always strokes my forehead when I have a nightmare.

I tell Mum, 'I can't do another day of this. Do you think if I tell them I think Dad did it . . . will they leave me alone?'

I hate what I've said. I want to take the words back straight away.

Mum says, 'Gemma! This isn't you talking. This is the police. This is what they're doing to you. They are trying to make you . . . You just cannot say those words. They are *not true*. But even though they are not true, the moment you say them, Dad will be arrested. And that would be wrong. It would be a lie. They can't make you lie. And if they arrest Dad, and stop looking for whoever has really taken her, *then we will never find Milly. And you will lose your dad.*'

*

On the second day, 'Lizard Nose', the much-pierced social worker, replaces Auntie Linds as my 'safe' person in the 'safe' house.

All my safety nets are being cut apart. They have taken Dad. They have taken our home. Now they have taken Auntie Linds away from me.

The policewoman who drives me to the house tries to set me at ease with pop music on the car radio. 'Do you like this music?' she asks, pretending to groove along. It's completely unconvincing.

Do you think I'm stupid?

Back inside the house, I'm on my own with the police and the social worker whom I already know to be a direct line to the police.

The curtains are drawn. The camera begins to run. I see its red light winking.

My first line of defence is to keep asking the police what they are doing to find Milly.

'It's not your place and this is not the time for you to ask questions, Gemma,' I'm told. 'You are here to answer them.'

Then it's back to the same questions about the magazine.

I lose my composure. I'm angry; I cry. Sometimes I'm sarcastic with the policewoman. Sometimes I'm rude.

She doesn't care, because she doesn't care about me. That is hard to face. I've grown up in a family where love is freely given and no one would dream of emotionally abusing a child. The policewoman reproaches me for not helping them. She piles on the pressure.

Don't you know your sister, Gemma?

Anything I do admit is twisted to her purpose. She softens me up in order to harvest whatever 'useful' fragment I can give her.

There's a sinister light being cast on all the things that are perfectly normal to our family. It's like being in a snow globe. That would have been a helpful image at the time. I wish I'd had it. Our family is at the core and the police are turning us upside down and shaking us, with white flakes of interrogation paper flying around, hitting our faces, making us unclear, sore and distorted.

All those pieces of paper that Milly has written on – they are turned into paper arrows to throw at us, to hurt us. Nothing is innocent. In police eyes, if Milly wrote a note to apologize for using my phone credit, it's because she was arranging a secret rendezvous. If she copied out a sad song lyric, she was expressing a desire to run away and put an end to herself. And in these interviews, the reason behind all of this is supposed to be Milly's burning desire to get out of our unbearable family. Even death is supposed to be better than living at home with us.

I picture myself as a statue, strong, unyielding. I'm like one of the creatures in Narnia turned to stone by the witch. No matter how much the policewoman distorts the facts and tries to make me voice the words she wants, I just can't. There is something about me that she can't understand, which is working against her: I could never lie to the police. That is part of being a good girl.

But I'm falling apart, incoherent, sobbing and shouting. Eventually I start to make so much noise that it's no longer productive for the policewoman to pursue her line of questioning. It's not the right kind of noise. The one sound she wants to hear is of a girl betraying her father in a flood of tears. I'm no use to the police. They let me go. They don't try to make me feel better – no one has told me I have done well. The implication is that I have done nothing to help Milly.

Alice comes to drive me home – what's left of me.

Lovely Granny opens the door and takes one look at me. The colour drains from her face. She makes me tea, wraps me in a blanket. I phone Auntie Linds's daughter Loley.

A little later I hear the front door slam and see Lovely Granny marching across the drive to talk to a senior officer who has just pulled up. Of course I listen from inside the door to what happens next.

Granny says to him, 'I'm glad you're here because I've got something you're going to need to listen to. I've just heard Gemma say to her best friend, "Be prepared for the police to ask you if you've ever slept in the same bed as your father." '

The officer makes an attempt to placate her. He says, 'Shall I take you somewhere for a coffee and we'll talk it over?'

'No, the road will do very well,' Lovely Granny says loudly and forcefully. 'Why the hell do we have to go inside? I don't care if the press hear what I have to say. It's the truth. Gemma is very damaged already, having lost her sister, and you are just making it worse. You are making me *very, very* cross. I don't like what you are implying. We are not stupid and in my day we called it "incest".

'How *dare* you say what you've been saying about her father? How can you take someone's father from her when she needs him? How can you be so cruel? Gemsie needs her dad. What kind of police force are you? Don't think you can behave like this, and that no one's going to pull you up on it. Because I will. Because I am.

'And why aren't you out searching for Milly, instead of beating up Gemma, Sally and Bob with these ridiculous questions? It's a charade. Stop it.'

After that, the officers of Surrey Police go in fear of Lovely Granny. They are more respectful when she's around. Having Lovely Granny in the house is like being tooled up with a mighty forcefield.

Lovely Granny doesn't care what the police think of her. She lost her mother in a car crash at twelve. She was forced to give away her baby. She has recently lost her beloved husband. She has lived her life the hard way. Her adored granddaughter is missing. She can see that her other granddaughter is falling apart under pressure from the police. Lovely Granny isn't having it. She's going to protect me and our family, in the way that Dad and Mum can't because they're going through the same torture. Lovely Granny's going to stand up for our happy family, or at least the memory of it.

After that day, Lovely Granny demands identification from every police officer who tries to enter the house. Even Mum's friends are interrogated as to their reason for bothering Lovely Granny's family.

Lovely Granny prides herself on being well organized and efficient. She doesn't suffer fools gladly and generally is happy to voice her opinion. When she's told to report to Walton police station for her own initial questioning, the officers struggle to make the recording machine work. After too many exasperating minutes, they get it going. Then there's a further delay as they can't find an empty tape to put in it. Lovely Granny's a committee member of the Sunbury Women's Institute, where she helps run the PA sound system. She thinks that Surrey Police should at least be able to rise to the WI's level of technical competence. I would have liked to be a fly on the wall during that session. Apparently Lovely Granny uses the word 'ineptitude'.

Lovely Granny's second police interview takes place some

months later at her house. Two officers arrive to question her about Milly's Flower Fairy necklace. They ask Lovely Granny where and when she bought it. It was a long time ago. She can't remember. As the officers are leaving, having taken her statement, one remarks that Lovely Granny has photos of Milly on her wall.

Lovely Granny says, 'Well, she's my granddaughter. What do you expect?'

To which the reply is, 'Oh, we didn't realize you were related.'

This doesn't go down well with Lovely Granny. Again the word 'ineptitude' floats in the air.

Later, I discover that the police have given Lovely Granny a nickname: 'The Rottweiler.'

She's proud as hell of that.

17.

I don't see Dad after my first day of questioning. He's gone back to work. His work has fed and clothed us and kept us in CDs, petrol and lovely holidays. I guess he's seeking the only kind of normality available by returning to the office where he has worked for fifteen years. At least it isn't patrolled by police officers. It is all he knows how to do, to try to keep himself together. He cannot shed the habit of responsibility, of providing for his family, no matter what the police are trying to imply about him.

He struggles to focus, of course. His presence in the office is seen as distracting to others. By July of that year his company will sign him off on paid sick leave. They are being kind. But the collateral damage is to Dad's self-esteem. And his career prospects are wiped out. He's too old to try for a position anywhere else. And his face is all over the newspapers. When he does eventually go back to work in January 2004, it will be in a reduced position, but the company continues to be generous to us all in one crucial thing: much-needed health cover is extended to all three of us.

Mum does not go back to work. She will never be a teacher again, a huge loss to Heathside. She has been a popular and accomplished member of staff. Letters pour in from her students, saying they miss her, some even apologizing for bad behaviour in her classes. One of Milly's friends writes a particularly affecting letter, describing Mum's talent in the classroom.

The next night I have to greet Dad in the knowledge that I've been bullied into doubting him. This betrayal is also a betrayal of myself. The old Gemsie would never have stood for anyone criticizing her family, especially if it was a lie. And the lie has now forced itself between me and Dad. The shadow of that lie will hang over our relationship for years.

I decide not to discuss my questioning with anybody – not even Mum. I'm too ashamed of the place to which the police have led me. People who are ashamed of themselves tend to act out. They have lost their self-respect and they behave badly even towards those they love, because secretly they don't believe they themselves deserve love. They want to test the love of their family. So from that time on, I give in to tantrums, to shouting at our family, particularly at Dad – purely because in my heart and in my conscience I know that I have done him an injustice.

There's a song from *The Lion King* called 'Endless Night':

> *Father, I feel so alone*
> *You promised you'd be there*
> *Whenever I needed you.*

It's sung by the lion cub Simba, mourning his lost father. It describes how I feel then. I love my father, but he is missing, like Milly. It's too much to lose all at once. Home doesn't feel like home any more. Someone has turned out the lights, and I have no safe place to go.

Dad has started to self-edit. He will not allow himself to show me the old open affection in case it's misconstrued by the police. Because of my own questioning, I'm half aware of the problem, yet I can't totally see Dad's point of view because that would mean facing up to the enormity of the accusation against him. As I can't understand it, I'm simply devastated by his withdrawal. I turn more and more to Mum, who is not restricted in her cuddles or words of love. In turning to Mum, I'm turning my back on Dad.

And I force Mum to turn her back on Dad too. I insist on sleeping in the bed with her. Dad has to sleep elsewhere. He's so tall that he has to use my bed, the next biggest in the house. Even then, his feet hang out through the ironwork at the end. He must feel as if he's in prison.

Half our family has gone missing, even though Dad still lives with us.

*

Missing Milly 'hoax' outrage

SICK WOMAN HAS POSED AS YOUNGSTER

BY SARAH ARNOLD

THE hunt for missing Milly Dowler took a shocking twist last night when it emerged a deranged woman has been posing as the missing youngster.

Police believe the sick hoaxer called into a recruitment agency pretending to be Milly.

Staff at the Midlands bureau failed to recognise the name as that of the missing girl and took the woman on their books.

It is thought the hoaxer even gave the agency Milly's real mobile phone number. Police believe she may have got it by gaining the trust of people who knew the schoolgirl.

The agency used the number to contact Milly, real name Amanda, when a job vacancy arose and left a message on her voicemail AFTER the 13-year-old vanished at 4pm on March 21.

Twisted

It was on March 27–six days after Milly went missing in Walton-on-Thames, Surrey–that the employment agency appears to have phoned her mobile.

The 'twisted' creature also contacted TV's Crimewatch programme, claiming to be Milly.

Police say the hoaxer has hampered the investigation and previous high-profile inquiries. Officers have now been briefed on how to spot her.

A senior officer involved in the hunt said last night: "Our inquiries and those of other forces have been plagued by a professional hoaxer who has much experience of the practices of the police and investigation methods.

"The chances are extremely high that the individual concerned is a rather disturbed lady who needs care.

"This individual has been to a number of force areas and has been quite devious in the attention-seeking methods employed."

●ANYONE with information about Milly should call Surrey police on 01372 471212 or the National Missing Persons Helpline on 0500 700 700 or Crimestoppers on 0800 555 111.

NEW PICTURE
THIS party snap of Milly was released by a pal yesterday to jog memories. It is an image of a sparkling girl with no hint of the torment to come

HUNT: Police officers search for clues

PLEASE JUST CALL US

MILLY'S distraught godmother yesterday appealed for help in finding the missing teenager—and begged her to get in touch if she has run away.

Maths teacher Sarah Ford, 42, of Farnham, Hants, said: "If she's run away, whatever has happened can be resolved.

She added: "If somebody is holding Milly against her will they must release her and let someone know what has happened.

"Someone must know something – she can't have disappeared without trace.

"Her parents are being torn apart by not knowing. They are coping but they're devastated."

APPEAL: Sarah

News of the World, 14 April 2002; story, Sarah Arnold

On 14 April, day twenty-five, the *News of the World* prints a story by Sarah Arnold headlined 'Missing Milly "hoax" outrage'. It says that police believe 'a deranged woman' called a recruitment agency, pretending to be Milly. She arranged to be put on the agency's books as a job-seeker, giving Milly's mobile number as her contact. The agency, the story says, failed to recognize the name, despite the nationwide publicity. It left a message on Milly's phone on 27 March,

144

inviting her to a job interview. The *News of the World* says 'it is thought' that the 'twisted' hoaxer got hold of Milly's number 'by gaining the trust of people who knew the schoolgirl'.

The story, while horrible, is not a big thing to us at the time. Our whole lives are focused around the painful gap that is Milly's disappearance. We miss her so deeply. We crave the sight of her sashaying across the room, the sound of her gruff little voice singing.

Everything we hear runs through one single filter: *Does this mean that Milly might still be alive?* If it doesn't have any relevance to that, then it's just irritating background music and possibly worse than that because it might be wasting the time of police who should be working without cease to find her. This *News of the World* story falls into that category. We know that Milly would never run away to seek employment. So the *News of the World*'s 'hoax'-outrage piece is just another distraction from the real task of finding Milly.

A little later, the *News of the World* journalist who wrote the piece gets in touch with us personally. At that time, many newspapers are having couriers deliver letters that we're forced to go to the door to sign for. They're from reporters asking us to give an interview. Sarah Arnold has already done an appeal, including an interview with Hannah Mac. Her letter – very like those of all the other reporters – starts, 'Few words can describe how you must be feeling as a family at the moment and my heart goes out to you . . .'

Dad spends 16 April – day twenty-seven – at the so-called 'safe' house being interviewed by the police. He comes back grey and drawn, but he won't talk about it. Mum's also interviewed again. She, too, is silent. Later I'll discover that both of them have been blamed for Milly's disappearance.

Dad is still the only suspect. It seems Surrey Police are just waiting for him to admit it.

As for Mum, her interrogations at the hands of the police can be summed up with one question, which is put to her repeatedly: *What kind of mother do you call yourself?*

18.

On 19 April, day thirty of Milly's disappearance, a call comes through on our fax number. The fax machine has a receiver and different number from the one we put out on the posters. Unfortunately the fax number is not ex-directory, and is listed in our name. So a few determined callers have got through already – generally cranks or journalists.

So, when that phone rings, we're pretty sure it's not going to be good news. Mum says, 'Oh, God, what now?'

I'm secretly thinking, *Could this be Milly? She's got that number.*

It's early evening, and we're all at home. Alice and Jon are there too. I go with them and Dad to the fax phone.

Dad picks up the receiver. Only he can hear the person on the other end of the line.

A girl says, 'I've got your daughter Milly with me.'

The line is crackly. Dad says, 'Oh, so you've got Milly with you, have you?'

He's letting us know what's going on.

I'm dying to grab the phone. Mum and Dad have by now answered so many pointless and cruel calls that they have little confidence in this one. Their faces are hard. But I think, *Milly must be somewhere. Why not with this woman?*

Dad stays completely cool. He asks, 'May I speak to Milly, please?'

'Milly doesn't want to speak to you. She's afraid to.'

Dad repeats this, to keep us in the picture.

'Milly's run away. She's frightened,' says the girl.

Dad asks again to speak to Milly. The girl says, 'She can't. She's in the bathroom. She's crying.'

'Let me just speak to her,' pleads Dad.

The girl starts whimpering. Now she's trying to make Dad believe that *she* is Milly, incoherent with distress.

Bullshit, I think. *How sickening is this?*

If it were me, I'd drop the phone. But Dad keeps her on the line,

146

doing his job, prolonging the call so the police can track this person down.

Alice asks if Mum will speak to her. Dad hands over the receiver. Mum hears only the whining and sobbing. She knows straight away that this is not Milly. She looks sick to her stomach. She gives the receiver silently to Dad.

It's hard not to shout out what I feel about this cruel hoax. I force myself to stay silent. Alice and Jon are giving me warning looks. I know they would rather I wasn't in the room.

The girl switches back to being Milly's keeper. The whimpering stops. She repeats, 'Milly just can't talk right now.'

Dad says, 'If she won't speak to us, can you just ask Milly a question, please?' Amazingly, he's still keeping his tone calm and polite. 'What's the name of Gemma's teddy bear?' he asks, using one of my secret questions to which only Milly would know the answer.

The girl just cries some more.

Alice and Jon, in turn, take the phone and listen. This is so that they can write up the call as an incident.

Dad finally hangs up on the false Milly. He shuts himself into the music room. He and Mum won't subject me to a display of their own distress. I don't want to worry them by telling them how much it has disturbed me. We have these invisible walls between us, built out of trying to protect one another from hurt.

This is not the only hoaxer. We also receive letters and many, many calls. Some are kind. Some are frightening. Here's a brief sample of our phone log:

25/3/02 A woman. Her son knows Milly. Search the gravel pits. She has a strong feeling about them.

2/4/02 A lady from Molesey rings to say she will do anything for us, washing, shopping, etc.

11/4/02 A man says he has seen a small tent in a tiny park in Stompond Lane less than half a mile from where Milly was last seen: someone was camping in the bushes.

Mum phones that one through to the police immediately. We don't get any feedback, so later that day she and Dad drive down to the park to check it out themselves. They find the police there.

Mum and Dad get a severe reprimand for potentially contaminating a crime scene.

14/4/02 Mrs RP says she had a very vivid dream ten days ago that Amanda's body was near a lake in Chertsey next to St Peter's Hospital. She has visited the site today. She's never been there before yet has found it exactly as she had pictured it. She saw nothing in the immediate shrubbery near the lake but did not search thoroughly. Sorry for appearing to be a crank.

20/4/02 A lady says that a man on a train on 19 April p.m. was pretending to be a reporter, and said they had found Amanda's body in a ditch.

24/4/02 A psychic (Miss S) says she did a drawing the day after Amanda's disappearance was announced. Drawing shows rough ground, a lane with a tight bend, pot holes, farm buildings within two miles of where she went missing.

26/4/02 A man says he wants to speak to the police. Says the investigation is a waste of money.

26/4/02 A local man says he has seen a white Transit van. He has told the police 3 times and they have not got back to him.

1/5/02 A police officer phones to say they have just been advised by two Dutch tourists that they had seen Amanda on a tour bus in London.

23/6/02 A caller says, 'Don't give up.'

5/8/02 A private detective offers his services.

Our FLOs tell us that all this is 'normal'. It's just part of our job experience as the family of a victim.

The police are pressing us for another appeal. We're all used up at the moment, and perhaps a new face will jog new memories. We want to make sure it's someone nice, well-spoken and reliable. So that same Sunday, Milly's godmother, Sarah, makes an appeal for her return.

Our school tries to do its bit to help find Milly. Alison Price, a teacher at Heathside School, speaks to the press. Hannah Mac, with our permission, does an interview with the *News of the World*, published on Sunday, 21 April.

When the police first searched the house, they had left our mattresses. Now they want to take them away. They provide new ones the same day. Mum airs them thoroughly and puts our familiar sheets back on them. She doesn't want me upset by alien smells. I'm also spared the sight of the switch taking place. But I am still outraged. Milly's and my mattresses are new. It was lying on those mattresses that Milly and I had our best late-night chats. Don't they have Milly's DNA from her hairbrush and her toothbrush? I'm still not getting it: in spite of Alice's questions, I'm still too innocent to understand why the mattresses might be so useful to the police. No one wants to explain.

I sit on my new mattress and it doesn't feel like mine, any more than my whole life feels like mine. It's not as good as my old mattress. They have taken away my sleep and the place where I used to be able to sleep.

I go to my box of special things. Inside, there's a blue birthday card 'to the world's best sister'. The police haven't taken that away. I feel a stabbing pain in my chest. I start crying, a deep crying that feels almost nice, almost like relief. Then it escalates. I start to howl, a noise like an animal dying. Something is squeezing my chest, sucking the life out of me. I try to calm down, but fear is eating me up.

Mum starts to have visions during her long sleepless nights. One of them is that she inadvertently passed Milly when she was driving along Station Avenue on 21 March. She's remembering – or is it fantasizing? – that she saw a group of schoolchildren on that street. Is it possible that Milly was among them? She knows Kat saw Milly walking alone, there one minute, gone the next. Could Kat have been wrong? Could there be lost minutes? Mum's mathematical brain is calculating not just in minutes but in seconds.

After a night of torment, she phones Alice before dawn to ask if the timings can be double-checked. Is there any more CCTV? Are there any other witnesses? Alice promises to come to see Mum and go through it all again.

Mum's desperation clearly disturbs Alice, who calls our doctor and asks him to do an emergency home visit. Lovely Granny infuriates the doctor, making him wait until the police allow him in.

Mum confesses to Alice that she's beginning to wonder if she should see a hypnotist to recover any shreds of memory she has lost. Alice warns against it. Often those people have their own agendas, she explains earnestly. Her eyes are wide with worry.

Mum persists, 'Is there any chance I could have seen Milly? *Was* there a group of schoolchildren at the Halfway crossroads?'

Alice admits that a group was seen there. She explains that those students are being interviewed. This drives Mum to a new pitch of desperation: it seems like confirmation that Milly has been there. She's fusing possibilities and hopes into something concrete. Her mind is starting to play tricks on her. She's beginning to visualize Milly in that group. It is only hurting her, not helping.

Alice reinforces the visualization by letting Mum know that a boy in Milly's year has claimed he saw Milly in the group. Mum asks the name of the boy. When Alice gives it, Mum sighs. He's well known for attention-seeking and fabricating the truth. He's already claimed that Milly was meeting someone at the Halfway shops to collect some drugs.

Mum's hopes come crashing down again, even more painfully than before.

Alice and Jon come every day, with new questions, but no answers.

Mum has endless lists of questions for herself.

Who would Milly get in a car with?

1. *Family friend?*
2. *Teacher?*
3. *Someone in uniform? Policeman?*
4. *Unknown male? No, not without a struggle.*
5. *A school-friend's father or vague acquaintance?*
6. *Taxi driver saying he had been sent to collect her? (But we have never done that.)*

7. *Older brother of a school-friend?*
8. *If a school-friend was already in the car?*
9. *Was the abductor parked in the station car park?*
10. *Car or van? Maybe a well-known logo like BT. A workman says,
    'Could you pass me something?'*
11. *Could she have got on a bus? Very unlikely.*
    How could someone get her in a car without a struggle?
    Invented a story about a sick mother?
    Maybe she met someone on the train and stayed with them?
    They drugged or threatened her with a knife or gun?

Meanwhile our lives seem to be one long sequence of identifying things in plastic bags. Alice and Jon arrive daily with photos, usually blurry, from the public or CCTV. We never have any doubts: none of these girls is Milly.

They also bring us objects to identify as Milly's. We're shown shoes. We're shown images of a pink make-up case. We have to provide samples of the kinds of keys that Milly carries. They keep asking us about the jewellery Milly's wearing.

Milly owns numerous pieces of costume jewellery. At one point Mum thinks Milly's wearing her Flower Fairy necklace, which she rarely takes off. But later she finds it in Milly's room. Subtly infected by what the police continually imply, she wonders why Milly took it off – perhaps to have a bath. Then Mum feels terrible because she simply cannot remember if Milly had a bath the night before she vanished. What kind of mother does not remember that?

Mistakes like this make us look bad, at a time when looking bad is both delicate and dangerous. Every time our credibility is undermined, we are made to look guilty, as if we are the kind of family who might harbour a dark secret.

19.

When Milly was nine and I was twelve, we went on a theme park ride known as the Tower of Terror. It's in Florida's Disneyland, inside a simulation of a grand ruined building called the Hollywood Tower Hotel in the Twilight Zone. You enter as if you're a guest and then you ride thirteen storeys up in haunted lifts. You have stepped into a nightmare, a dimension of shadows and uncertain substance. You have a bad feeling. The hairs at the back of your neck are standing on end. At a certain point, the lights flicker and cut out. You suddenly drop. The terror is not just the fall – it's that you never know when you are going to drop, or when you are going to hit bottom.

That's what losing Milly is like.

When Milly first went missing, friends would look at me differently, not knowing what to say to me.

I go back to school for a few half-days. I'm struggling, so my teacher says I can go into the old music room with some friends: we can do our work there. I'm thinking this is cool as I don't have to be in class: I can just doss with my friends and chat about normal things.

It isn't like that. We don't chat about clothes or parties or the prom or anything nice. My friends sit very silent, afraid of hurting me. Now even known bullies are nice to me. It's as if I've become suddenly popular or famous.

My unwanted fame earns me privileges. I don't take my GCSEs. I'm given a special dispensation, awarded a merit based on my mock exams the year before. Part of me is relieved as I'm in no state to concentrate on school work; the other part regrets that I never earned the merit properly. I've skipped over a rite of passage. I'm cut off from the normal life of a schoolgirl progressing through the syllabus and all the extra-curricular life lessons too. I have been kicked off the path of my life.

I'm isolated from everyone I know, yet over-exposed to them too. The intimate details of our family life are out there for

152

everyone to read. No one else at my school has parents in the news. No one else's name is splashed all over the newspapers, with their family photos – holidays, celebrations – turned into some kind of spectacle of horror.

No one else has a missing sister. No one else goes home at night to a bedroom with an empty bed, or to a house afflicted by terror and grief. My situation makes me an object of whispering and speculation. So I'm lonely, when I most need friends.

The normal preoccupations of a teenager are replaced by ugly thoughts and terrible images. I still believe a man is lurking in the bushes outside the house. He's the man who has taken Milly, and now he is coming back for me.

Hannah Mac is suffering too. People dare to be mean to her because it isn't *her* sister who is stolen. Her friendship with Milly is belittled by those who want the glamour of being the best mate of the girl in the headlines. I know what's happening to Hannah Mac, and she knows what's happening to me. But we can't reach out to one another. We're frozen in our separate shattered states.

Fiona Bruce interviews Hannah for the news. First, the presenter walks the places where Milly was last seen, marvelling at how safe and normal Walton seems. It is, she says, impossible to imagine any-thing bad happening here. Yet, she notes, the posters for Milly are everywhere. 'You cannot miss them. You cannot miss that this town has lost someone from its heart. Not since Sarah Payne has the agony of a missing child been brought so acutely into focus.'

In her interview, Hannah Mac says she finds it really hard to think for herself. If she had a problem she would go to Milly and Milly would do the same with her. Hannah Mac says, 'It's really not like Milly. She's never done this before . . . It's really out of character.'

When she heard Milly was missing, she knew something was wrong straight away. Terrible things were going through her head. 'It's like a nightmare. I cannot tell the difference between the night-mare and the reality,' says Hannah.

Fiona Bruce asks her what she would say to anyone who, God forbid, might have taken Milly.

'Just find it in your heart somewhere to let her go,' says Hannah Mac, 'and give her back to her family. The pain, the emotion running through the family, the friends, is unbearable.' She adds, 'I think of all the good times Milly and I have had, and I think we'll have them again.'

And she smiles hopefully, that sweet Hannah Mac smile.

It's my cousin Daniel's seventh birthday on 22 April, and Milly has been missing for thirty-three days. He writes a card to say that all he wants for his birthday is for Milly to come home. He hangs it in our hedge. Before Milly disappeared, we would have thought that charming. Now we have to make him take it down because it's attracting other cards, turning our hedge into a shrine. Then it's impossible to walk past them, as if you're ignoring Milly, which you could never do in real life. So my parents and the police remove the cards as soon as they appear.

Writing our birthday card to Daniel reminds us freshly of our loss. We've always signed birthday cards with 'Bob, Sally, Gemma and Amanda'. It's too impersonal to write 'The Dowlers' but Mum will eventually learn to do that.

On Tuesday, 23 April, day thirty-four, Dad's at work in London. Mum and I are at home – with our usual press contingent parked outside. Alice and Jon turn up at the door – which they do once or twice a day with questions or things for us to identify. This time they say they are going to wait in the garden until Dad gets back from London. We watch them from the window, Alice looking anxious and smoking furiously under the pergola that Grandad built, now covered with hundreds of little yellow roses.

We have no idea what's going on. But we guess and fear that it's important.

When Dad arrives back from London at about 6.45 p.m., Alice phones her boss, who comes round immediately. This, we shall learn, is a characteristic procedure of the police: senior officers would insist that they have the 'glory' of giving us news, rather than the family liaison officers whom we know and trust, having formed a relationship with them over many hours and days.

All of us are in the lounge. A terrible atmosphere hangs in the air. The silence is broken only by Mum, Dad and me letting out straggly breaths that we've held in too long. The senior officer asks to speak to Mum and Dad in the dining room – without me. I'm furious to be excluded, as ever. I have to stay with Alice. I hate being an adult when it suits the police – capable of answering the darkest questions – and a child when it suits them too.

I'm terrified they're going to arrest Dad. I batter my phone, texting friends. I start shouting when I receive a text from Uncle Bree: *What's this about the body in the Thames?*

Unbeknown to me, Uncle Bree's texting from a police station where he's been called in for questioning. Meanwhile officers are lifting the floorboards of his pub. He's heard about the body in the Thames not from the police but from his petrified wife, Auntie Marilyn, who's seen it on television.

I turn on the TV. A camera crew at Walton Bridge, fifteen minutes' drive from us, is filming a police boat. The subtitle is 'Breaking News – body found. Could it be Milly Dowler?'

I scream, 'Alice, what's going on?' I cannot believe that I'm sitting here with a police officer and I still have to hear the news from my uncle and the TV.

The senior officer is, with great difficulty, telling Mum and Dad about the body found at Sunbury Lock. All Mum and Dad want is the truth, without ornament or hesitation. You don't really hear all the frills in that situation anyway. You hear only words like 'body' or 'Thames' or 'dead'. He tells Mum and Dad that there's a team on site, and that the media have got hold of it.

All Mum asks is, 'Is the body naked?'

He doesn't answer except to say that he still doesn't know if it's male or female.

On the 9 p.m. news, they screen the body being hauled out of the Thames. Mum and Dad don't want me to watch it. I beg them not to exclude me. I'm trying to work out if the body in the bag is the right size for Milly. I'm guessing which stretch of the river is being shown. How could Milly have got there? Dad says conclusively that the bag is too big for Milly. But we are still petrified. I lose all restraint, asking questions that my parents can't or don't want to answer.

I sleep with Mum. I still won't let her go to sleep before me. I force her to stay awake till I'm fully unconscious. At midnight I'm woken by the telephone. The police are calling to ask if Milly has any capped teeth, so we know they're doing a post-mortem on that body.

When Mum says 'No', they confirm that the body is not Milly's. It's believed to be that of a very old woman who's been missing for months.

The agony does not abate for more than a second. I don't want it to be Milly, but if it had been, at least she would be in a place where no one could hurt her any more.

I ask Mum to phone Lovely Granny and the family. I ask her to text the mother of Hannah Mac as I know she, too, must be in torture.

It is really late, so we don't phone and text everybody. We think that no one will be upset because the press will print the correct information that the body is not Milly's.

Nevertheless the next day, 24 April, the *Daily Mail*'s front page headline is 'MILLY: BODY FOUND IN THE THAMES', with a half-page picture of her.

Daily Mail, 24 April 2002; story, Ben Taylor and Stephen Wright

The *Mirror*'s front page also says, 'MILLY ... BODY FOUND IN THAMES'. Inside it prints a large photo of the body being dragged out of the river, with the headline 'IS THIS MILLY?'.

Even though it's not Milly, that photo forces me to confront the idea of Milly being a body rather than being alive. It's awful to have this new scenario in my head.

After that day, we ask the FLOs to tell us of any other bodies themselves. We want to hear the worst news from them, not from the top brass.

Dad does not ask the police if he can have legal representation because he does not think he needs it. He is innocent. However, after several more interviews, he's very shaken. Finally, he tells us he's been 'cautioned'.

Lovely Granny persuades him to go and see a lawyer.

Where on earth do you find a lawyer who specializes in criminal law in this area? We have no idea. After phoning around, Dad goes to see one in Chertsey.

Three days later, the police are at the door with questions that have only bad answers.

Why did you go behind our backs for legal help, Bob?

Do you know how we found out, Bob? Well, your lawyer had a word with one of the officers who had questioned you to find out what else was going on in the investigation.

Why didn't you ask us, Bob?

What have you got to hide from us, Bob?

Dad's reply is, 'I know I am innocent. But you don't seem to be listening. I need to protect myself.'

Why do you need to protect yourself, Bob?

'I'm painfully aware that you are not looking for anyone else,' Dad says. 'I have to protect myself so I can be there for our family. I can't do that if I've been arrested.'

If you carry on this way, we will leak it to the press. How will that make you look, Bob?

Mum has to rush out of the room to vomit.

★

We're back to nothing again. No leads. No sightings. No information.

Into that vacancy come the cranks, the mystics, the profiteers. A man even registers Milly's name as a website. We are grateful the FLOs have prepared us, explaining that people would exploit our vulnerability with crank calls and strange letters. Because of the delay with the police incident room, our phone number is public knowledge. Just our family name and 'Walton-on-Thames' will get a letter to our door.

Mum is very level-headed and, under normal circumstances, wouldn't be interested in psychics. But, in the midst of this unbearable mystery, she is tempted. By this time, her relationship with Alice is growing stronger. Alice advises her gently that psychics are not likely to be of help. They're more likely to prove emotionally abusive, whether they mean to be or not.

The phone rings constantly. The police suggest we change our number.

But I keep hoping that Milly will call it. I can't bear for her to find it cut off.

On 25 April, day thirty-six of Milly's disappearance, Mum, Dad and I are taken to the Missing Persons Bureau in East Sheen. It keeps a database of lost and missing people. They explain what would happen if Milly rang them. They show us the process of answering calls from runaways, reassuring them that they are not in trouble.

These are good people, kind people, but I'm angry that the police are stubbornly refusing to contemplate any other scenario than the ones that suit their preconceptions yet in no way fit our family.

Next we're summoned to Surrey Police headquarters at Mount Browne. We're shown CCTV footage – three still shots – of a girl walking past the Birds Eye building in Station Avenue at the time Milly was last seen. We gaze at her in the blurry shots. Then each of us has to say whether, in our opinion, she is Milly.

If it's Milly, she got further towards home than was previously thought, based on what Kat saw. If Milly passed those cameras, she could have been abducted from within a wider area. If she did not, it will be clearer that she vanished seconds after Kat saw her. And if that is the case, the point of her disappearance can be isolated within a fifty-yard stretch of Station Avenue and all searching can be concentrated in that spot.

We know what's at stake here. So we fix our eyes on the footage. I'm desperate for this girl to be Milly. That would be something. Just a glimpse of her.

But our statements show that Dad and I agreed this girl was 75 per cent unlikely to be Milly. Mum gave it 60 per cent.

That leaves us with the conclusion, and ought to have left the police with the conclusion, that Milly vanished within a tiny, well-populated area, which should have been the focus of the investigation from the moment when we called the police. We can't understand why that spot is not *already* the focus of intense and sustained scrutiny.

On 30 April, day forty-one, Surrey Police tell the press that pop-up messages have been put on several internet chat-rooms popular with teenagers. They claim they're still keeping an open mind as to the reason for Milly's disappearance. They say, 'It is likely that there are still things we don't know about Milly.'

And I think, *The only thing you don't know about Milly is who took her and what they did with her.*

The weather echoes our mood. Rain is falling on the thousands of posters around Walton.

Milly's face is being washed away.

20.

On 3 May, day forty-four of Milly's disappearance, there are two different headlines. The *Evening Standard* says that the police have ruled out abduction in Milly's case. Our local weekly paper, the *Walton Informer*, says fears are growing that Milly has been kidnapped. What are we supposed to think? That same day we're told that the *Sun* newspaper is prepared to offer a massive £100,000 reward – if we'll just give them an interview. They'll also print six million posters about Milly to distribute all over Britain.

Mum and Dad are worried that offering a reward could attract even more cranks and actually hamper progress. They'd been warned as much when Uncle Bree's and Dad's companies offered to put up rewards.

For me, however, the reward is a massive thing. Somehow it rekindles hope that has been seeping away over the last six weeks. I want to think that someone is still holding on to the truth about Milly – and that this money will tempt them out into the open. Even evil people might betray other evil people when such a lot of money is involved.

But new hope is cruel. The thought that Milly might come back gives me sudden access to feelings I have prohibited in order to keep myself under control. Her absence is suddenly terribly immediate again. The moment I feel a tiny spark of hope, I feel guilty about the times when I have given up.

We're also unhappy about the way the police announce the news. It seems to cast more suspicion on Milly herself: *There may be secrets about Milly or her life – we need to know what these secrets are.*

We are not in contact with the *Sun*. The contact number given in the paper is for the police. We pester the police every day for any news. But the reward, it seems, brings in no leads that they think worth pursuing.

On 7 May, day forty-eight, we release a new picture of Milly: the 'Fields Of Gold' picture. We also issue one of me and Milly with our arms around each other.

Mum and Dad release a statement. 'Someone out there must know something. It is like a living hell. We need to know where Milly is and what has happened.'

Two days later it's my prom at Heathside. It's been months since I went to normal classes, but I'm determined to go through this important rite of passage.

Milly, Mum and I were supposed to find my prom dress during the Easter break. It was going to be a proper girls' day out. Now Mum can't face the people who will inevitably stop her to talk. Uncle Bree and Auntie Marilyn want me to have my 'princess' day of shopping and spoiling, including a lovely lunch. Uncle Bree says he'll treat me to whatever dress I want. Everyone is being super-careful with me. So no one tells me when I choose the wrong dress, settling on a purple taffeta number that Milly would never have allowed.

Mum's video-cam comes out for the first time since Milly went missing. It records Auntie Jenny doing my hair and make-up. Mum's voice is sweet and coaxing as usual on the voiceover. We're all trying too hard, smiling too much, and no one is mentioning Milly's name. But she's there with us, by her absence, and all the pretending is almost too painful to bear. In the background you see the fridge, covered with photos of Milly.

Making a strenuous effort at normality, I pose for Mum's camera, my hair dragged up into huge heated rollers. My friend Lizzie's there too, as well as Lizzie's mum, Auntie Marilyn and Uncle Bree, who has brought our corsages. He's going to drive us to Hampton Court jetty, where our prom boat awaits. He's in full white tie and has borrowed a Bentley. There's champagne cooling in an ice-bucket inside. Nothing is too good for Uncle Bree's girls going to a prom.

In the middle of the preparations Mum disappears for a moment. Only later will I discover that she's taking a call from Alice, who wants to know about any identifying marks on Milly's body. A torso has been found in Scotland. Mum suggests checking the dental records, and then the penny drops about what a torso means. Mum mentions that we still have the X-ray of Milly's broken shoulder in Egypt. She also tells Alice about the small birthmark below Milly's left breast – the one I nicknamed Nubbin. Mum puts down the phone and comes back to the prom preparations with a smile fixed on her face. She refuses to spoil my night.

Fully dressed and made-up, Lizzie and I parade for Mum's camera before the Bentley backs out of our drive.

Mum and Dad are the only parents not joining their sons and daughters at the Hampton jetty. I've forbidden them to come as I know they'll be mobbed by well-wishers with an endless stream of questions.

Yet, when it comes to it, I really wish they were there with me. I'm surrounded by friends, but I feel alone. I'm an alien in the midst of these excited, happy families.

Friday, 10 May, day fifty-one of Milly's disappearance, Dad gets a call from Mum on his way back from work. She wants to meet him at Walton station and walk back together the way Milly would have gone. Mum lets Alice know that she's going to do this. She cannot bear the thought of being out of contact for even a second.

Mum and Dad walk slowly along Station Avenue. Every single lamp-post and tree bears a poster for Milly. Just after the traffic lights, Mum stops and touches a poster on a tree.

Two days later, there's a picture of that very private moment in the *News of the World*, with the headline 'The Longest Walk Home'. Mum's livid about the invasion of privacy and immediately phones Jon. She knows the photo has been taken covertly with a long lens and she wants to know exactly how the paper knew where she and Dad were going to be.

Yet my parents don't make an issue of it. They are purely focused on finding Milly. The press are constantly violating our privacy, turning up in our garden, following us around. But we can't afford to be uncooperative or unfriendly. One of these journalists, or one of their articles, might be the catalyst that helps unlock the mystery. We need the press on our side. They are already helping us. The *News of the World* is a sister paper to the *Sun*, which has offered the reward. We let it go.

That month it's decided that I won't go back to school. There's a leaving do for my class, on the London Eye. It's the first time I've gone so far from home without Mum and Dad, an FLO or Lovely Granny.

Setting off home after the Eye, we're at Waterloo station when I see Milly's name all over the *Evening Standard*. I read the words 'MAN ARRESTED'. I'm shot through with hope that Milly's been found. Then I feel guilty that I've been in the Eye, far away from our family, enjoying myself, while important events were taking place. My teacher won't let me read the newspaper. She tells me she's had a phone call from my parents and that there's nothing for me to worry about. Sadly, there is no real news about Milly.

Nevertheless, by the time I'm back in Walton, the press are out in full force, pressing themselves against the car windows. I feel I'm being judged for having an evening out while my sister is still missing. I fear they might have pictured me with my friends at Waterloo.

This is the story: eight weeks after Milly went missing, a thirty-six-year-old man has been arrested – the first arrest directly related to Milly's case. His house is being searched, including the building site in the garden. He is being interviewed at Staines police station. All the usual footage rolls out, Milly ironing, the CCTV images of her at Weybridge and Heathside, the reconstruction showing 'Milly' in a short skirt, a busy and efficient-looking incident room, students walking through the school gates at Heathside.

The man is soon released without charge. This is a pattern we shall get used to.

On 31 May, day seventy-two of Milly's disappearance, the *Walton Informer* says the police are denying that the hunt for Milly is being scaled down. But in the press there's much criticism of Surrey Police, saying they are not equipped to deal with such a massive inquiry. There are reports that the police have called in the army.

During the days in between, you can imagine how it is for our family – to read in our trusted local paper that the police have effectively given up on Milly as the case is too hard. My feelings towards the police are coming to the boil. I have seen how wrong their thinking is. Now I'm wondering about their competence too.

Mum and Dad are always polite. I, however, give Alice and Jon a hard time. I say what I think about their little black notebooks full of questions we've already answered, but which they keep on asking, as if we are liars to be caught out.

I'm still Gemma the good girl, but I no longer believe there's any point in being good with the police.

21.

Milly, there's a secret RAF spy plane looking for you!

xxxx Gemsie

The army does indeed come to look for Milly. The *Sun* prints an article stating that 'a secret RAF spy plane' is using heat-seeking technology to search for her.

On Sunday, 23 June, day ninety-five of Milly's disappearance, the *Mail on Sunday*, the *Sunday People*, the *Sunday Times* and the *News of the World* all report that Surrey Police have virtually given up hope of finding Milly alive. The journalists flock to Walton again, and also to Staines, home of the police incident room. Beautiful young women with perfect make-up and lacquered hair talk in grave tones about my sister on the television news. It's all so bland in the context of our turbulent fears and grief.

By now we're very familiar with the members of the press who are regularly working Milly's case. We even have our favourites. Mum likes Clarence Mitchell from the BBC. Milly would have known his kind face as he was very involved with reporting the death of Jill Dando. Clarence was the reporter who collected the ironing video of Milly. A very kind BBC engineer helped prepare the recording for TV.

At Walton police station, Clarence Mitchell once asked Mum if she would be filmed walking along outside the police station with him, to validate his report. 'I don't like being an actress,' she told him.

Mum doesn't want to be famous. All Mum wants is a Guttural Hug from her younger daughter. But of course she'll do anything if it might help find Milly.

Milly's fourteenth birthday's coming up on 25 June. People are asking us if they should send cards. We don't know what to say.

We're asked to supply yet another photo of Milly. It's so hard to choose. We don't want precious happy images destroyed by seeing them used to illustrate articles claiming that she is dead. We select one from a family holiday in Cyprus the year before. Milly's at the helm of a speedboat we hired. We crop the picture to her head and shoulders as we don't want to expose her body in a bikini. Her hair is scraped back, as it was on the day she went missing. The two little straggles of hair are hanging down in front, as usual. She's smiling.

We also release video footage of Milly swimming with dolphins during our Christmas holiday. Milly's beautiful smile is plastered all over the news: she splashes through the water, confident and happy, surrounded by the friendly dolphins. But the voiceover to this image reports, 'Her family have been informed that there's now little hope she's still alive.'

We feel betrayed. We did not give out our private video for that.

We've been racking our brains about what to do with Milly's birthday. We usually celebrate her birthday with a barbecue party round our above-ground pool. Milly might have wanted karaoke this year. Her birthday presents would have been music albums. Maybe she would have received a video-cam or a digital camera of her own because she's always snatching Mum's. She loves doing the voiceovers and narrations. She likes to stage the scenes, work out the lighting, record her new style statements: 'Effects by Amanda Dowler'.

In some ways, Milly's birthday will be no different from any other day since she vanished. Our lives are just one long scream. Milly's birthday without Milly just adds another layer of pain and sadness. Yet the date also offers a chance to make a new appeal because we'll have the full attention of the press. Surrey Police have a media plan for Milly's birthday. So Mum and Dad release a picture of Milly, in her sailor suit at five, and a new statement: *It would have been inconceivable if, when Milly first went missing, someone had said we still wouldn't know what's happened to her by her birthday.* Mum and Dad thank everyone: the people who display posters, the press, the postmen, the well-wishers who've sent letters and even the police.

Everyone is so kind. We've not been able to get back to all those people but we want to say thank you. Your support is appreciated. Milly's birthday is a very reflective time for us. Hearing that there are so many people thinking of us, every day, does help.

Dad says:

Last week I got a taxi and the company wouldn't take any money from me. The driver said they felt they couldn't do anything to help, and this was one thing they could do for us. It was genuine and heartfelt.

They're frank about how hard it is to cope:

We're struggling to fill the days – we try to set ourselves a project yet it's hard to remain motivated: we end up going through the motions. But we have to try to hold it together for Gemma.

It's frightening when we realize how many people are feeling this too. Lots of other people are hurting for us, and not necessarily people we know. We find that very touching.

Mum says:

I still send her text messages every day just in case, and then just wait for the 'failed Milly Mob' message to come back. I find it really difficult every time I buy something for Gemma. It's a horrible feeling, because I should be getting something for Milly.

Mum and Dad describe the gap left by Milly's vanished music:

There are so many things we miss, especially her playing her saxophone. The lack of noise is very noticeable – the house is so very, very quiet now. When Gemma has a friend round we remember what it's like having two in the house, and how it should be.

Because of the posters, Mum and Dad still see Milly's image everywhere they go:

We know it's good to have so many posters all around, but it's also very hard. We just can't believe that it's our daughter. We drive past and wonder, 'Will they still be here in six months?'

The media arrive in force for Milly's birthday. The television cameras roam around Walton, looking for sound-bites to record. A mother says, 'You just don't know, do you? There could be someone lurking around the corner.'

Girls of Milly's age are interviewed and speak of their fears.

The news coverage notes that parents in Walton are picking their children up from the station, afraid that there's a child-killer on the loose. 'This is a town on its guard.'

Our family is not in Walton for Milly's birthday. We cannot bear to stay at home. Instead, we take a walk along the cliffs at Poole Harbour, not far from the nudist beach. My cousins David and Daniel come with us. While walking, we gather a large bunch of wildflowers. Eventually, we approach the beautiful view of Old Harry's Rock. We stop and gaze out to sea. Then we throw the flowers over the cliff and into the foaming water.

None of us can actually speak. Each of us wants someone else to say something and for it to be the right thing. But what is the right thing to say? None of us knows. Instead, we stand there with tears streaming down our faces, saying nothing and thinking, *These flowers are for you, Milly, wherever you are.*

The next day, the newspapers give Milly a lot of space. 'Where are you, Milly?' asks the *Evening Standard*. The *Daily Mail* asks, 'Do we send a birthday card?' The *Walton Informer* shows a rare lapse of taste, headlining 'Milly Parents' Birthday Blues'.

The drawing pins are getting rusty on the MISSING posters. But they're still there: on lamp-posts, shop windows, even inside the back doors of vans.

And now – as we approach the hundredth day of Milly's disappearance – the press are also starting to write Milly off. Making a breath-taking jump from 'missing' to 'murdered', one news station invites in a clinical psychologist to profile her killer. He points out that 'millions of males' could be suspects now. He appeals to girls who suffer or have suffered attempted abduction to report it to the police.

He points out that the killer is likely to have done this before.

Which means that he'll do it again.

22.

For the next few weeks, the local newspapers turn their attention to Surrey Police. Scorn is poured on the first four months of the search for Milly. The *Evening Standard* and the *Metro* join in. An article in the *Sunday Mirror* on 30 June is so scathing about Surrey Police that the force feels obliged to issue a formal rebuttal.

At this point, I'm with the newspapers. Alice and Jon have Mum and Dad's confidence. Beyond them, I have no faith at all. When I see the huge headline 'Chaotic and Rudderless', I feel it's pretty accurate. The *Sunday Mirror* lists various major 'blunders' in Surrey Police's handling of Milly's case. The two that stand out for us are these: 'failing to treat her disappearance from the outset as a potential murder inquiry' and 'issuing conflicting statements about whether Milly was abducted, had run off with an older man or had been murdered'.

The article explains that the police have told us that Milly is probably dead, but in the absence of a body they are treating the case as one of a missing person rather than a murder inquiry. Yet since 1954, police forces have been allowed to mount murder hunts without a body, and many have done so. In Milly's case, 'It is feared that vital evidence could have been lost by the delay.'

Mum and I are getting into the car when a photographer jumps out from behind the hedge. He says, 'What do you think about there being a new head of the investigation?'

It is, of course, the first we've heard of it.

Mum tries not to look amazed and replies with the usual 'No comment'. Once we have pulled away from the kerb, Mum says to me, 'God, I hope that reporter was right, Gemsie. That can only be good news. Perhaps the new head might believe we didn't do it.'

Gone: the man who has overseen an investigation that heaped extra pressure on us, an investigation apparently fixated on the idea that the only really worthwhile line of inquiry was Dad. We had to wonder if this man believed it was just a matter of time before Dad would be shown to be the killer.

Enter: new 'head of investigation'. Hallelujah, we think. Fresh eyes might also see something that has been missed.

Indeed, the new man is more engaging and humane. Although I don't exactly warm to him, at least he assures us that he is going to concentrate on the area where Milly was last seen: the old garage that does tyres and MOTs next to the station, the taxi rank outside the station, the buildings in the immediate vicinity, like Collingwood Place.

At last someone is using their common sense and about to do some real police work, we think.

Mum asks him outright if Dad is still a suspect.

' "Suspect" is a very strong word, Sally,' he waffles.

He's adamant the investigation should stay as a missing person rather than a murder inquiry. He talks about the constant need to try to stay one step ahead of the press. His parting comment is that he'll be reviewing the database as it's often the case that the person responsible for a serious crime is already on the system.

Well, we think, *not brilliant, but a damned sight better than twenty-four hours ago.*

Then, on 12 July, day 114, Surrey Police issue a set of hypotheses for Milly's disappearance. The top of the list: self-harm and running away. They've added in suicide and injury. The very last theory on the list is abduction.

The police rule out running away on the grounds that Milly has never done it before, and that she's made no cash withdrawals from her account. No clothes are missing. And Milly's on Mum's passport still.

Suicide is judged unlikely in a thirteen-year-old. Apparently, someone of that age is more likely to make attempts that are really a cry for help, or to kill themselves in such a way that their bodies will be found. The police say that Milly's unlikely to have drowned herself – because she doesn't like murky water.

The abduction theory is at last given proper consideration. It is, they say, 'a real possibility'. But they still insist that the abductor could be someone she knows. They say that they are interviewing local sex offenders as well as people who know Milly.

The FBI has joined the team. American officers have been drafted in to examine CCTV footage from the Birds Eye building opposite the place where Milly vanished. These are the same images we looked at months before. They're interested in a man walking with a guitar case and a woman with long blonde hair.

On the same day, Surrey Police make a new appeal for information from the public. Among their questions is this one: 'Has anyone suddenly moved out of Walton and surrounding areas or been keen to quickly get rid of a car?'

The *Sunday Express* reports that the police have been approached by 450 psychics offering their help. The newspaper has called in one to explain what has happened to Milly. His name is Craig Warwick. The headline is: 'FBI tracker claims vanished teenager's spirit led him to a gravel pit grave. Milly had a crush on her killer, psychic tells police.'

The psychic claims that Milly got into the man's car. They argued about their relationship. The man, whom Mr Warwick believes to be in his thirties, 'then became violent – strangling Milly and dumping her body near a gravel pit'.

A self-styled psychic stops Mum in the supermarket. She says she's had messages from Milly. Mum freezes. She politely excuses herself, saying that our family is not pursuing that line of investigation.

That's the last time Mum goes to the supermarket for a very long time.

At the end of the month, a forty-seven-year-old local man is briefly arrested in connection with Milly's disappearance. This is the third such arrest. A fifty-two-year-old prisoner was also questioned in June, and a thirty-six-year-old man was arrested in May, but released the next day. We usually hear about these things the day before reading them in the press. And we hear very little more than we read on those pages.

Heathside School closes for the summer holidays. It feels like one more door shutting on the investigation: we hate the fact that now all the students who might be asked about Milly will disperse for many weeks.

My friends are going to Newquay for their first grown-up holiday after their exams. I was a part of the plans but I'm not part of the trip. I have shut myself away. I'm still terrified that whoever took Milly will come back for me. I barely leave the house on my own. Mum and Dad have to drive me everywhere.

Finally I get a summer job at Thorpe Park, an amusement park in nearby Chertsey. The job suits me – I'm the one who looks after lost children, who meets and greets, who cleans up the vomit at the X No Way Out ride. I'm out in the world again. I make friends. I even get interested in a boy for the first time. He takes me to the cinema. He's at my side at the weekly socials at Thorpe Park. For hours at a time, I'm busy and can almost forget what has happened to my life.

On one of the busiest days, I'm chatting to one of my fellow workers, a man in his fifties. He says, 'Look at the state of these girls!' He points to a young teenager in shorts and a strappy top. She's not dolled up – no high heels or make-up. She's just a pretty girl, ready for a summer day in an amusement park.

She's Milly's age.

My shoulders tense. I ask him what he means. He says, 'Look at those shorts. It's no wonder these girls go missing. Like that girl Amanda Dowler. I've seen the photos. Her school skirt was way too short.'

He has no idea who I am. I'm shaken: *Is this how people are thinking about Milly, but are too polite to say to us?*

'She's my sister,' I hiss at him, shaking. 'How dare you say anything about that situation? You have no idea of what's gone on.'

I storm down to the manager's office. By the time I arrive, I'm bawling uncontrollably. Yet I manage to tell him what happened. Mum comes to collect me. Alice and Jon talk to the man.

After that I go back to work, but they keep me away from him.

I've lost something, though. Until that day, I enjoyed my job. Thorpe Park was a safe and happy place for me. I thought I might be allowed to snatch a bit of normality.

The incident has proved that I'm not allowed to.

23.

On 4 August, Holly Wells and Jessica Chapman, both aged ten, disappear from the village of Soham in Cambridgeshire. Of course we read everything we can about the case. We're fully aware of what the families must be suffering: the agony of not knowing, the shock, the simple, painful missing of a beloved child.

Milly has now been gone 137 days.

Mum and Dad send a message of support.

Our hearts go out to both sets of parents. It is hard to imagine that anyone else would have to suffer the pain and anguish and desolation we have experienced since Milly went missing on 21 March . . . We deeply hope that both girls are found alive and well. We also hope that it is not too long before they find out what has happened to Holly and Jessica because the 'not-knowing' is so very difficult.

Naturally the press are drawing comparisons between Holly and Jessica and the other most missing girl in the country – ours.

There's one enormous difference. To us, everything going on in Soham seems to mock the relentless emptiness of the Surrey Police search for Milly. The television shows the police swarming all over the village. The helicopters go up immediately. The sniffer dogs are out within a few hours. It looks urgent. We guess that the poor fathers are getting their share of suspicious attention, but it's obvious that the search net is much wider than the family. And there's no accusing the girls themselves of being runaways.

The burned bodies of little Jessica and Holly are found in a forest less than two weeks later. The school caretaker, Ian Huntley, is arrested for their murder three days after that. It's sickening, but at least it's swift, even though we know the families will never get over it.

I have a private worry that the whole world will forget about Milly because of the media frenzy generated by the Soham murders. We watch the television obsessively. A woman speaks to the cameras, saying she has seen the girls. After all our exposure to hoaxers and cranks, we've acquired some skills. We're like lie-detector machines now. I know instantly that she's a fake. I point at the screen and say, 'Liar!'

I'm right.

A Surrey Police website update on 21 August reiterates the mounting statistics for Operation Ruby: 5,000 calls from the public, 1,700 statements taken, 50 kilometres of waterway searched; 320 sites combed.

We silently add, *Results: zero.* It's now been 154 days since Milly disappeared.

A former high-ranking officer of Surrey Police admits in an interview that the Milly Dowler case is difficult: there's no evidence, no witnesses and no body. We understand that he's defending Surrey Police against comparisons with the Cambridge force's quick response to the Soham murders. The officer insists that Surrey Police is big enough to handle priority cases. He says the force also has access to the National Crime and Operations Faculty and a national 'Murder Manual' as well.

We've never heard of these things. A murder manual? Is it like the *Dummies' Guide to Excel Spreadsheets*? Or the *Dummies' Guide to Trigonometry*? We look at him in despair. Lovely Granny always says she has never recovered from that particular officer kissing her by way of a greeting. In Lovely Granny's world, people call her Mrs Wood, *not* Ann. They certainly don't kiss you on first meeting – and without permission.

Before Milly went missing, we'd booked an August trip with the Dobbos to the Algarve. The police say we should still go. They think it's worth checking to see if a runaway Milly, more interested in a holiday than her family, will turn up at the airport. We treat that suggestion with the scorn it deserves.

Leaving the house seems inconceivable. Milly has a key. How can we leave the phone unattended? The idea of a 'holiday' is totally impossible. How can we enjoy ourselves in the midst of this agonizing mystery?

But Auntie Linds and Uncle Ian persuade us that we need to get away. They keep working on us, promising that they'll look after us. Uncle Ian even undertakes the awful task of phoning the airline to explain the situation. Mum cannot bear to cancel Milly's ticket. The airline is compassionate, agreeing to keep the ticket open.

At the airport, Mum automatically counts her little flock and our bags. As a mother, and as a teacher, you are always counting your charges to make sure that no one is missing. It doesn't add up. It will take years for her to stop counting Milly.

We stay in a blindingly white villa with a pool. There's an inflatable in the shape of a killer whale. I burst into tears when I see it because it reminds me of our trip to Florida, when Milly was there. Mum and Dad do everything they can to make it nice for me. But the struggle is visible on their faces. Mum's missing Alice. Trust has built up between them. Alice is also Mum's main source of information. Not enough information, ever – but that isn't Alice's fault.

I love the Dobbo daughters, Loley and Robyn. They've always been part of my life. Loley's the same age as Milly. Loley and Robyn still have each other, but I don't have Milly. It's just too hard to deal with. I can't even share a room with them, as in the old days. I have to sleep with Mum, so Dad is exiled to another bedroom.

We three girls try to avoid the subject of Milly. Yet she's there, everywhere we are. It is probably a stupid idea to go to a karaoke bar. We sing and dance a bit, but our hearts aren't in it. Mum hasn't brought the video-cam. We don't want to record a trip without Milly.

The time passes too slowly, despite all the immense kindness we are shown. We're aware of how hard this is on the Dobbos, and we feel guilty too.

Hannah Mac and her family are also in Portugal. We arrange to meet them at the beach where they're staying. Mum and Hannah's mother, Sara, go for a five-mile walk. Mum opens up to Sara. She tells her she's terrified that Milly will never be found.

We slip back into England, unnoticed for once by the press.

24.

No one in the family or the press misses the fact that the six-month anniversary of Milly's disappearance is approaching. The police still come to Mum and Dad with questions, questions, questions. And no answers. Much of the time, Mum and Dad are still made to feel that they are under suspicion. Meanwhile Mum's mind is forced to consider every possible option, some of which are unthinkable.

She has barely slept or eaten since 21 March. The adrenalin constantly pumps through her body. She's exhausted. She's living her life as if in a trance, while remaining constantly in a state of high alert in case the phone rings. She operates on a minute-by-minute basis. She cannot make any plans for the next day, let alone the future. Something might happen. She's doing her best to hide it from me, but she's really hovering on the brink of a breakdown. The 'not-knowing' is excruciating. Mum feels as if she's in a constant battle to stop herself being sucked into a deep dark hole with slippery sides. She knows that if she lets go it will be the end. So for my sake, for Dad's, she keeps trying not to go under.

Mum's a highly qualified maths teacher. Now all her abilities seem to melt away. By September, her mental arithmetic is non-existent. Her sense of direction has gone. She's frightened to be left anywhere in case she gets lost. People she's met in the past need to remind her who they are. Mum's once excellent memory seems to have been obliterated. Things that had previously come automatically to her are difficult now. These include basic functions, like driving, cooking and even communicating.

She feels as if the damage may be irreparable.

Then she's called to Heathside to receive the results of the maths GCSE that Milly took two years early.

She passed.

★

FBI experts have enhanced the images from the Birds Eye building, removing the sunlight's glare. Surrey Police say they are very pleased with the result: a stick figure standing next to a dark-coloured saloon car near where Milly was last seen. If it's Milly, then it's from seven minutes later than the last known sighting of her – by Kat at 4.08 p.m. And the stick figure talks to the person in the car for forty-two seconds. In the next image, the car and the figure have gone.

The media have put out that the police now see Milly as the victim of a chance abductor. We don't know if they're aware of what the police are saying to us about Dad.

Mum and Dad record an interview for *Tonight with Trevor McDonald*. They tell the interviewer that 'unlikely as it is,' they can't help hoping that Milly is still alive. Mum says that she has a permanent sense of churning in her stomach and of her heart racing. Dad talks of the roller-coaster of emotion. They explain how they worry about leaving the house in case Milly comes home. This piece for *Tonight* will not be broadcast immediately.

Meanwhile, Surrey Police want us to do a major interview with Rebecca Hardy for the *Mail*. As ever, they want to orchestrate the whole thing, including the questions. We're actually grateful. We've simply run out of energy. There's not much fight left in us now. As the interview takes place at home, Rebecca Hardy will get to describe the private places of our grief, which have so far been hidden from the press by curtains and blinds. She makes notes about our lounge, our books, our framed photos, Milly's teddy bear that says 'Night, night, Milly' in Mum's voice, when you press its tummy. The journalist is friendly, but nothing is going to make this a comfortable experience.

It's 9 September, day 173 of Milly's disappearance. Mum confesses to still listening to Gareth Gates and watching the ironing video continually. She says to Rebecca Hardy,

> *Right now if you asked me what happened, I'd say Milly's been murdered. But I haven't really gone beyond thinking, She's been abducted and she's dead.*
>
> *What's happened in between is a gap. I can't bring myself to think about that bit. Until we find out for sure what's happened, it's too awful to contemplate. Sometimes your mind starts churning and you think: What if she's been abducted and the person who's got her realizes how nice she is and he looks after her? – but you know that's just a fantasy. You know that logically she has to be dead, but there's still an element of doubt.*

Mum and Dad tell Rebecca Hardy that since Milly vanished they've always left two lights burning all night, one upstairs and one downstairs, in case Milly ever comes home.

Dad talks of the struggle to keep going and the guilt this entails.

Anything we can do to introduce something like normality into such an abnormal situation can only help us – otherwise we'd just go mad.

Is it wrong to laugh and enjoy yourself? You show me the rule book, tell me what I should do now. We have to focus on Gemma. I can't do anything about Milly disappearing, but I can try to make sure that as a family we're as together and as strong as we can be for Gemma's sake.

I do my own interview with Rebecca Hardy. I tell the journalist about the music that was always in the house and how hard music is for us now. Music makes Mum weep. 'The sad songs are sad and the happy songs are sad too, because Milly isn't here.' I say that I sometimes wonder if I should learn the sax, in order to heal the saxophone silence in the house. Then I fear it would hurt my parents more than help them. I tell her, 'Sometimes I dream Milly's still in our life . . .'

The journalist draws me out, and I speak frankly of my fears and the dreadful images that stop me sleeping. 'Every time I shut my eyes I could see Milly being stabbed . . . I also kept getting visions of her stuck in a room with this man trying it on with her and I couldn't do anything about it.'

By now, I should have known better. I should have known that the papers would take those words and turn them into headlines.

I make an appeal of my own. 'Whoever's done this to Milly must have a family as well. Let's switch the situation. Would you like me to take your family from you? If I stole one of your family members would you be able to feel how hurt we are? Anyone who suspects a member of their family should come forward.'

The first job I ever wanted was as an air hostess. The idea came to me when I was ten, taking my first plane trip, in 1997, to Florida. The job seemed to combine my two favourite things of looking after people and travelling. I wanted to work for British Airways: my grandfather and my mother had done in the past.

In September 2002, when so much else has changed, I'm still clinging to my old idea of being an air hostess. I enrol in a travel and tourism course at Brooklands, a further education college next door to Heathside School. Mum has also worked there. It seems like a safe place to be. None of my school-friends is on the course. It seems that the Brooklands students have been briefed to be tactful around me. They are almost too much so. I crave some independence and freedom.

Milly's the one who struggles to break into new friendship circles. I've never had this problem before. I want to talk to her about how to deal with it. I feel like an onlooker when it comes to college life. My fellow students are enjoying getting their driving licences, trying cigarettes and alcohol. No one else has to check their phone constantly to see if the police have called. No one else must keep their phone on twenty-four/seven in case their mother rings. By now Mum has five mobile phones, each one on a different network. Three were provided by the police for emergency contact. Mum cannot bear the thought of Milly – or anyone important – not getting through to her. No other student at Brooklands has journalists waiting at the bottom of their drive. No one else has parents coming to pick them up at the end of the day. I cannot replicate Milly's last known journey – the walk to Weybridge and the train to Walton: the press still hang around the station whenever there's a new lead in the story.

I do, however, have a boyfriend. The relationship is only a few weeks old, and it's lovely. He's quiet and gentle. He bears with my mood swings without complaint. He's shy with my parents, but he's not afraid to meet them. I feel safe with him. We go to Brighton and Selsey, to breathe sea air and look at high skies. It is amazingly helpful to have a safe pass out of Walton.

At home, I am learning how to be an only child. It is more like being a widow who has lost a life partner than being a teenager who has grown up without a sibling.

As well as sending loving texts to Milly's phone, Mum keeps putting pocket money in Milly's account every month. That's her way of showing that a small part of her has not given up hope.

Now, that money is my wedding dress fund because, in September 2002, Mum has to stop putting money into Milly's account.

3.

Discovery
September 2002 – March 2003

PLAYLIST

Craig Rickards (Milly's saxophone teacher)	For Milly
Judy Collins	Amazing Grace
Eva Cassidy	I Know You By Heart
The Beatles	In My Life
Queen	No One But You (Only The Good Die Young)
Chicago	Wishing You Were Here
Colin Blunstone	Don't Feel No Pain No More
The Isley Brothers	The Highways Of My Life
Justin Hayward	Forever Autumn
Elton John	Come Down In Time
Kevin Colson from the original cast recording of *Children of Eden*	The Hardest Part Of Love
Miss Lea Salonga and Simon Bowman from the original cast recording of *Miss Saigon*	The Last Night Of The World
The Beach Boys	'Til I Die
Bread	If
Leonard Cohen	Sisters Of Mercy

25.

'Minley' and 'Milly'. They sound so similar.
Is that why he took you to Minley Woods?

xxxx *Gemsie*

Thursday, 19 September: Milly has been missing for 183 days. Mum's doing voluntary work at Wisley Gardens, furiously digging flower borders. Dad's out sailing with Uncle Ian in the Solent near Chichester. I'm at college, planning to see my boyfriend in the evening.

That afternoon, knee deep in mud, Mum receives a call from Alice. 'Remains' have been found, this time in Hampshire, about twenty miles from Walton. Alice says, 'There's nothing to link it to Milly.'

By now, we've had five bodies, one at Hersham station, one in the Thames, one at Morden, the torso in Scotland and another body on the Isle of Wight. Five false alarms.

Mum's still shaken by the call. She leaves Wisley immediately. On the way home, she phones Lovely Granny. She can't get hold of Dad. The boat is out of telephone range. She calls Auntie Linds, hoping to get a message to Dad as soon as he comes ashore.

Mum drives back to an empty house. She takes a shower, then sits on her bed, having a quiet cry on her own.

The phone rings. It's Rebecca Hardy from the *Daily Mail*. The journalist wants Mum to check her article before it goes out. 'You sound upset,' she tells Mum, with a question-mark in her voice.

'Just one of those days.' Mum manages not to give anything away.

Two minutes later the doorbell rings. Mum opens the door to Alice and Jon. They're clearly ill at ease. When they find out that Dad's not there, they say they'll wait for him. Mum knows that when the police come round without prior warning, it's because something serious needs to be communicated to us. The fact that they want Dad to be there adds weight and tension to the situation. If it were good news, they would not need to wait for Dad.

When Mum phones me to say that I need to come home, she doesn't say why. But the tone of her voice tells me something bad has happened.

I think, *Is this the moment things are going to change?*

I need to get home as soon as I can. Yet I don't want to go. The waiting and not-knowing have been unbearable. *But knowing*, I suddenly realize, *is probably going to be worse.*

In the meantime Auntie Linds has arrived at our house. She's spoken to Uncle Ian. He and Dad have altered their course to come back directly. Unfortunately they've missed the tide and managed to run aground. They won't be home for hours.

As my boyfriend and I turn into our road, Alice and Jon's unmarked police car is parked outside. I'm relieved to see no cameras or press. We pull into the drive. I don't want to get out of the car and face what's coming next. Whatever is going on inside the house, I can't bear to be a part of it. What happens next will change for ever the home where Milly and I lived together as loving, uproarious, musical sisters, where we played, fought, dressed up and dressed down, where we shared a bedroom and so many late-night chats.

In the end, I peel myself off the car seat. Auntie Linds opens the door – she's already at the window, scanning for the inevitable arrival of the press. She wants to make sure I get into the house safely.

A few minutes later Lovely Granny appears.

There's a new atmosphere in the house. We have arrived, I understand, at the next stage of this vile journey. Alice, Jon and Mum look strained. I can see that they're worried about me. Of course, it is better to worry about me than about Milly. About me, they can do something helpful. Me, they can hug. To me, they can hand steaming mugs of tea. They can't do those things for Milly.

I don't think my boyfriend needs to go through what's coming next, so I tell him to leave. I think he's lucky to be able to get away and go back to a normal home.

Mum explains about Dad being trapped on the boat. She says again, in that dark voice, 'There's a body.'

I cannot think about Milly as a body. I can only think of her as Milly, alive and sashaying about, being cheeky.

Now they know Dad has run aground, Alice and Jon are forced to tell us more about the new body. Alice starts by saying 'it' was found the day before, in some woods in Hampshire. For the first time I hear the name 'Minley Woods'. To me, this sounds like 'Milly Woods'. Which gives it a terrible credibility as a place where she may have ended up.

Jon adds quickly, again, that there's still nothing to indicate at this stage that this is Milly's body. They know that the discovery will lead to the usual Milly feeding frenzy in the press – that's why they needed to let us know.

'But you're here,' I point out. We all know that there's a reason for that. There must be something they're not telling us.

I want to ask if 'the body' is clothed, and if it still has skin. I'm ashamed of my morbid curiosity, and I don't want to make it worse for Mum. I don't know what awful images are in her head. I must not add to them. So I keep quiet.

Alice and Jon leave, saying, 'Please phone the moment Bob gets home.'

Mum has taken to pacing again, which is what she always does when it gets tough. It was what she did the whole night when Milly first went missing. It's the only way she knows how to bear her pain.

I want to turn on the television to see if there's anything about the body. We're accustomed to getting more answers, more quickly, from the TV than from the police. But it's 4 p.m. and we're in a lull in the daily news cycle: there won't be anything till six.

For the next four hours, we phone the people in our inner circle – Hannah Mac, Uncle Pete, Auntie Jenny and Uncle Bree. We can't give them any answers; they understand from our voices that they can't ask us any questions.

We can't check the internet. Our family computer never came home after the police search. A friend of Mum's has lent us a laptop but we have only dial-up, and we can't get through to any news sites. So it's the six o'clock news that finally feeds us the first pictures of Minley Woods and Yateley Heath, with maps showing how close they are to Walton.

I hear one TV journalist say, 'I don't think there is a person in the country today who would change places with Milly Dowler's parents.'

Dad eventually arrives home at about 8 p.m. He phones Alice immediately as instructed. That call ends very quickly. The next is from a senior officer. They greet one another on first-name terms. Despite the excruciating situation, Dad's as polite as ever, asking the other man how he is.

I hover by Dad. The call seems to go on for ages. Dad is making notes on the edge of our diary. I'm trying to read his expressions but it's impossible.

This is the phone call, I think, *that will change everything. It will tell us whether they have found Milly or not.*

I can't bear the waiting to hear. I interrupt Dad. 'Get off the phone and tell us what's going on.'

'Thank you very much for phoning,' Dad tells the officer at the other end of the line.

I shout, 'Don't fucking thank him for phoning with *that* information.'

Dad is silent.

'Is it her?' I demand. 'Is it Milly?'

Finally Dad tells us exactly what the officer's told him. He speaks slowly and methodically, as if he's not talking about his own beloved daughter. His job at this moment is to tell us the facts.

At a first look, the broken shoulder and dental records of the body in Minley Woods seem like a match. Work will continue overnight at North Hampshire Hospital in Basingstoke.

Mum's sitting on the sofa and desperately asks the obvious question in a low rasping voice, 'Is it female?'

The answer haunts the room. 'Yes, it's a female.'

Mum screams. I see her hope dwindle into thin air. Lovely Granny has her arms around her. I'm curled up almost foetally on the opposite sofa. It feels as if I'm looking at this scene from the outside. Gemsie has well and truly left the room. For the foreseeable future.

I have split into at least two Gemmas. One despairs. The other refuses to give up hope. The police never seem to give a definitive answer to any question. We're always left in the dark and uncertain of how to feel or digest information. So my thoughts and feelings seesaw.

They haven't positively identified this body. Lots of people have broken shoulders.

Another Gemma, a sadder and wiser one, is looking down a long tunnel of loss.

The television stays on. We watch the reporters massing in Minley Woods. The press see the arrival of one senior Surrey Police officer at Minley as signifying that 'the remains' might be Milly's.

I finally voice my thoughts from earlier. 'Minley Woods,' I say senselessly. 'Perhaps he knows she's called Milly and that's why he took her there.'

So now he's in the room with us: the 'he' who took Milly. I'm shocked that these words have come out of my mouth. I have brought Milly's death into the room. I have brought the killer into our house.

Mum speaks quietly from the depths of Lovely Granny's arms, 'Gemsie, you need to understand that . . . he . . . wouldn't have spent long enough with her to know her name.'

So there is no relationship between the woods, Milly and the person who put her there.

Except there is.

I go to bed – in Mum and Dad's room. Eventually Mum comes to lie down next to me. She doesn't stroke my hair. She doesn't hug me. There's nothing left of her.

I am stressing about people we need to tell. I don't want to leave out anyone important, who could be hurt and shocked by what they see in the paper.

Mum says, 'It's all right, my darling sweetheart. We've told everyone who needs to know.'

26.

We haven't got Dad a card. Should I even wish him Happy Birthday?
It won't be Happy without you.

xxxx Gemsie

When I wake up in the morning, I'm alone. I look out of the landing window. There's a police car in the street again, as there is every time something new happens. A policeman is standing in the drive to stop the press ringing our doorbell. But the press haven't arrived. They are at Minley Woods instead.

It's Friday, 20 September. Dad's birthday. He's fifty-one. I can't give him the card I've written. Milly and I should have written one together, as usual.

Dad has already been out to get the newspapers. By the time I come downstairs he's edited out the worst coverage and hidden it from me. It's still bad enough.

By coincidence – or maybe not – it's the same day that the Rebecca Hardy article goes out. Her interview is featured on the front of the *Mail*. Half of the page is taken up with a photo of Milly hugging Mum. The piece mentions that a sixth body has just been discovered in woodland twenty miles from our home. On another page of the same newspaper, there's an article headlined 'Milly hunt: Body found in woods'.

The *Mail* seems to have shared some of Rebecca Hardy's interview with Mum and Dad. The *Daily Express*, the *Telegraph* and *The Times* all print parts of it. *The Times*'s headline is: 'Milly's parents accept that their daughter is dead.'

I put the television news on. No one stops me. At this point it's all still speculation, journalists with solemn faces mouthing 'might' and 'could be' in front of a cluster of trees.

It isn't until the afternoon that the home phone rings. Dad's the only one allowed to answer it. It's the same officer. Again they greet one another on first-name terms. Despite the even more excruciating situation, Dad's still as polite as ever, once more asking the officer how he is.

I hover by Dad. He carries on the conversation, making more notes. But this time he has his hand over his forehead. This is a pose he adopts when he hits rock bottom, when all hope has gone.

'*Get off the phone, Dad*,' I scream.

When he does, he says, 'This time the dental records are a fit, Gemma.'

Why was it that officer who called, not Alice or Jon? How can this be allowed to happen when we've asked so often that anything crucial should come from them, our family liaison officers, whom we know and trust? The role of the FLO is supposed to be as a safety net for the victim's family. Moreover, this kind of information is not supposed to be transmitted via a phone call. It should be handled face to face, with physical and emotional support on hand.

Mum runs into the garden in an attempt to escape the horror of what she has to hear. Lovely Granny follows her.

The doorbell rings. It's Jon and Alice, looking more shocked, more upset than I've ever seen them. They were not aware that the senior officer would take it on himself to go against our wishes and make these revelations himself, and by phone. The truth is that they've been sitting in Walton police station since they left us that morning. They've been preparing themselves to be the ones to deliver the blow, as gently, sensitively and humanely as possible. I see the distress on their faces. They're on the front line; they've put six months of their lives into our family, taken calls from Mum and Dad at all hours of the night, dealt with our unruly grief, including all my acting out. Now they've been betrayed. And they will have to deal with the nightmare that has just been unleashed.

I run to Mum in the garden, followed by Jon and Alice.

'It's Milly,' I say.

Alice and Mum are friends, of course, but not today. Mum screams at Alice for the first time ever. 'You promised you'd be there. You promised you'd be the ones to tell us.'

That is the last thing that flies out of Mum's mouth before the torture of the last six months hits her. She falls to the ground.

I feel as if I'm falling too. Everything is dropping away. The terror seems bottomless. I need to be with Mum. Yet my feet won't let me move. Dad is frozen.

Alice and Lovely Granny prop Mum up and half carry her back into the house. Mum has started to scream and sob. We need to get her inside and shut the doors. The press may be somehow filming this scene in the garden, using cherry-pickers hidden in the trees.

I'm desperate to get to Mum's arms, but everyone's around her, trying to take care of her. I feel alone, excluded. Mum needs my help. My job in life has always been to look after people, most of all our family. There's nothing I can do to make this any better for Mum. I can't stop her making those noises of grief that I've never heard before.

What am I if I can't comfort my mum? What kind of daughter am I? And I'm all she's got now. Milly's not coming home.

Dad's also excluded by the tight circle around Mum. He's not able to move, anyway.

I don't know the right way to react. I can't do anything right. *Should I be relieved that Milly has been found? Should I start to grieve?*

Lovely Granny, as always, has a practical answer. She says that Mum needs tea with something strong in it. I go to make it.

I'm alone in the kitchen. I'm alone in the family – is how it feels. *Milly won't be with me to be my bridesmaid. She won't be with me to nurse our parents when they get old. She won't be with me ever again.*

My hands are shaking. But I busy them with the tea because I cannot bear the images coming into my mind. There are things to do with teeth, and dental records. There are images of bones. There's Milly's face laughing at me.

If they are looking at teeth, does that mean Milly doesn't have a face any more? Is her face a skull?

Alice offers to help me make the tea.

'No, Alice,' I say. 'It's fine.'

It's not fine. It will never be fine again. I don't want Alice to look after me. I want Mum. But Mum needs her own mother at this moment. Lovely Granny is with her, and that's how it has to be for now. I know Mum will be there for me as soon as she can.

Alice and Jon are frantically making calls. They go to sit in the car outside so what's left of our family can have a little privacy.

We know that the press will go large on 'the remains' found in

Minley Woods. We make another round of calls to the important people, to brace them for what they will read the next day and hear on the news later this evening. Hannah's mother, Sara, says to Mum, 'At least no one can hurt her now, Sally.'

This thought comes mother to mother. It's how Hannah's mother would have felt if it were her own daughter found. Mum is grateful for that thought. She takes it into her heart. I will hear her repeating it over the dark days ahead.

Eventually Alice and Jon come back into the house. They give us more details, starting from the beginning, as if it is a story. They say that the people who found Milly were picking mushrooms at the time. They say that only 95 per cent of 'the remains' have been found. No one explains why, so I am left wondering what has happened to the rest. In my head, there are still two things: Milly's beautiful little body and 'the remains'. I cannot reconcile the two because 'remains' are gruesome, muddy, inhuman things with blood and bits of flesh. I want to go on the computer and google images of skeletons found after six months.

'That's not a good idea, Gemsie,' I'm told.

Alice and Jon tell us that no clothes have been found with 'the remains'. It's not that the clothes have decomposed. It is because she was dumped there naked.

That's the hardest detail to deal with. The ultimate indignity – to leave Milly alone without even a decent covering, or one of her familiar possessions.

No, nothing. No decency at all.

The image of Milly's naked body is too much to bear. If it is Milly – and one part of me's still not accepting that – then I want her little body covered with a blanket at least. Mum grabs my hand, and holds on to me. That's her new abbreviated form of hugging. That's all she can do.

Dad's taking notes, as he always does. His hand isn't even shaking. He's going to be strong for all of us.

I'm thinking, *This isn't my house. This isn't my life. I don't want to be living this. This isn't how you're supposed to live when you are sixteen years old. These walls aren't made for hearing these things. These walls are made for dancing, and singing, opening Christmas stockings, being together.*

I want to believe in time travel, to go back to a time when this was a proper family home and not a scene from some horrifying murder documentary.

'There is some hair,' Alice tells us. I think of Milly's lovely glossy light brown hair scrunched up in its 'messy bun'. If it *is* Milly, I know that the hair will not be glossy now. *That* hair belongs to something else, to 'the remains'.

The body has been disturbed by animals, Jon explains. More bones may yet be discovered. I cannot visualize this at all. Skeletons in science classrooms are all in one piece. I like everything tidy. I need to think of everything that way, more than ever now. *What animals have been there? Was it foxes? Did a fox eat some of Milly's skin? Did foxes fight over her and pull her apart? Is that why some of her is missing?*

Each piece of news is a blow. It's like a bulldozer running over us, coming back and doing it again. My family is crying, and shuddering. Every face is contorted with pain. There is so much emotion in the room. It's too small a room for all of this. There are too many people in the house. I can't take it all in because of the confusion of voices, tears and exclamations.

Mum and Dad, strangely, are experiencing relief. I see it on their faces and I don't understand. They try to explain. For them, the not-knowing is starting to be over. That is all they can think about. Unlike me, they understand that this stage must be over in order for grieving and healing to begin.

I feel alone because I cannot get anywhere near that kind of acceptance. I don't even really believe that the 'remains' are Milly. Alice and Jon look at me, clearly worried. Of everything they are saying, the only bit I cling to is this: they have not said, 'a definite match' – which means that I can't yet let go of crazy little flashes of hope. I'm so distrustful of the police now that I find it hard to believe anything they say.

At 5 p.m., we turn on *Channel 5 News*. On the left-hand side of the screen there is a picture of Milly – it's the one from the MISSING poster. The presenter crosses live to a press conference at Minley Woods. The screen goes to two plainclothes policemen, one from Surrey, the other a detective superintendent from Hampshire Police. They are standing in front of a tree-lined meadow, facing a battery of clicking cameras.

The Hampshire officer announces the results of the dental comparisons. 'We can now confirm that the remains are almost certainly those of the missing schoolgirl Amanda Dowler. DNA tests will be carried out as soon as possible to confirm this.' He says that Hampshire is now handing over the investigation to Surrey Police. The officer says, 'Our worst fears have been confirmed. The search for Milly has changed from a missing-person inquiry into a murder investigation.' He adds that they are now much closer to finding out what happened to Milly and who did it. He continues with the usual clichés – no stone will be left unturned in the hunt for Milly's killer, condolences for the family, and so on.

My first thought is, *Now you can't bloody say any more that she's a runaway.*

The camera's eye moves to a journalist in the wood. We want to see all we can of the scenery behind him yet we want to cover our eyes too. It's a beautiful place, grass rippling in the sunshine, a field surrounded by a rim of leafy trees. It's like a place where we would take our dog for a walk. It does not look like a place where you would dispose of a murdered little girl.

Then the camera pans in on a group of people clad in white and wearing masks in the middle distance. There's a glimpse of an area closed off with blue and white police tape. Then the usual images are shown: Milly dancing around the ironing board, her hair shining; Milly in Dad's arms; Milly and Mum together.

We watch this in silence. We have trained ourselves never to speak over the news because we might miss something that the police haven't told us. One word resonates repeatedly over and above the others: *naked, naked, naked.*

We are sitting in exactly the same place as Milly did that ironing. The walls are still the same colour. In the video, the paintings behind Milly's head are still the same. The same Brambly Hedge china's on the shelf, including the special cup and saucer that was always used by the birthday girl or boy in our family. It's Dad's birthday today. For once I haven't served his coffee in it. It's the same room but we are millions of miles away from it.

I go into forensic mode. It is more bearable than being the sister of a girl whose 'remains' have just been discovered. I try to see if the people in white suits are moving anything. I just can't comprehend or accept that Milly's just a skeleton now. I still imagine her as the Milly I know. The coverage of the living Milly is too fresh – it doesn't make sense that she's not as she was when I last saw her.

I'm desperate to understand if we as a family have ever been to this place. Dad gets out the *AA Road Atlas*. He assures me we've never been there.

The house is frenetic. We're prisoners inside because the press are suddenly camped outside again. They've shown the world the woods. Now they want to show the public our shocked and grieving faces. Alice and Jon are in and out, coaxing Mum and Dad into drafting a new press release.

Alice brings us supper – including the vital supplies of Ben and Jerry's Caramel Chew Chew ice cream. We live in dread of the local supermarkets running out of that. It does happen, but it just can't happen today.

The television is on the whole time. We can't afford to miss a single broadcast.

At last I dare to ask Dad, 'I can't understand how they can identify her from dental records. Can you explain?'

He tries to give me the Disney version, all prettied up, which leaves me mystified.

I end up in Mum and Dad's bed, as usual, that night. Dad has to sleep in the spare room.

The television has finally been turned off, and the house is silent. All day I've wanted everyone to leave. Now that they have, I can't bear the quiet. This quiet is made up of absence. Milly's voice isn't there. And it's not going to be, ever again.

I just want them to find all the bones and put her back together again.

27.

On Saturday, 21 September, the newspapers have Milly on all the front pages. The *News of the World* prints a picture of Milly flexing her muscles just before the Fun Run. It doesn't represent the real Milly, who hates exercise. For the camera, she's just pretending to be sporty and at the same time poking fun at the concept of sportiness. That's Milly. The headline is 'Milly's Poignant Last Goodbye'.

I think, *Stop it! That was never meant to be a goodbye.*

Do the sub-editors ever give a thought to how her family might feel when they publish headlines like 'I KNOW MILLY'S KILLER' and 'MPs say hang the killer'? Some papers talk of a 'shallow grave'. Yet we've been told that Milly wasn't buried. The press have resorted to the usual clichés. The *Sun* does what it does: 'WE'LL NAIL MILLY'S KILLER. Cop: Bones are her.' They quote a policeman: 'Leaving Milly in such a lonely place was the final insult.' Another officer is quoted as saying that Milly's body could have lain undiscovered for years had it not been found accidentally. The *Sun* prints an aerial photograph of the crime scene, showing the white vans. They give more detail than we can bear to read – about two ribs being found next to the skull. The *Sun* also feels the need to say how much our family house is worth.

Mum and Dad protect and distract me from this kind of thing as much as possible. Mum takes me to the local jeweller. I pick out a gold ring shaped like a wave. I ask him to engrave on the inside 'sisters forever'.

Meanwhile the television shows Walton station, where Milly started her last walk towards home, now lined with flowers. Teddy bears and bouquets have been left in Walton Park, and at Heathside School. People come to the house too, but have to hand the flowers to the policemen guarding our drive.

We have to look at more gruesome images of the forensic team in their white space suits picking over the glade in Minley Woods.

These images are superimposed on the pictures in our mind created by what Jon and Alice have told us.

Mum and Dad release their statement. *At last the long agonizing wait is over. Now we can bring her home and say goodbye.*

Of course, we can never bring her home now. Yet the words of the song from *Les Misérables* have come to the top of our minds. Mum and Dad finish by describing how things are now that the not-knowing is over: *A feeling of relief but so very, very sad. No one can hurt her now, darling Milly.*

If only they had been right about that.

Prayers are said for Milly in all the local churches on Sunday, 22 September. Milly's maths teacher is a part-time priest at St Mary's Church, where a candle has been lit for her every Sunday since she went missing. We agree that Milly's teacher should conduct a service for her there and that Mum and Dad will attend.

A senior officer accompanies Mum, Dad and Lovely Granny, standing so close that he is in the press photographs. He even sits himself down in the front row next to Lovely Granny, something he will be made to regret.

I can't make myself go to the service. I've become uneasy about churches since Milly disappeared. My faith has never been strong. I'll attend weddings and funerals, and I believe in Heaven and Hell. I'm not certain of where I stand on deeper questions of theology. I'm sure of only one thing: I'm angry at any God who could allow this to happen to Milly.

Also, I don't want to put my personal grief on display in front of a crowd. I know that the people of Walton are sincerely sad and shocked about Milly – and so many of them helped search for her. But I need to shelter my pain from view. No one puts pressure on me to go. They are, perhaps, afraid that I'll do something unsuitable, like shout at a policeman or scream during prayers. They have every reason to be afraid. I don't even want to hear about the service when they get home. But I'll see the accounts in the papers the next day.

That's how I'll learn that Mum collapsed when the priest said, 'We thank You that she is in Your gentle and loving hands, far from the cruelty and violence and harm of our world.'

The service reduces everyone to tears, of course. At the height of the weeping, Lovely Granny the Rottweiler turns to the high-ranking policeman who is sharing the front row, uninvited. She says, 'You shouldn't be here. Get your finger out and go and look for whoever did this.'

Also in the papers that day is my own interview with Rebecca Hardy for the *Mail*. It has been 'pooled' by the Press Association. The other papers mostly lead on the fact that Milly said 'I love you' to everyone in our family before she went to sleep – in case something happened in the night.

This is the interview in which I talked of seeing her stabbed, or stuck in a room 'with a man trying it on'. Those words are repeated in all the Sundays, sometimes as a headline, their impact multiplied by the fact that now Milly is 'remains'. My face is everywhere – a photo of me looking unlike my former self. My eyes and mouth are harder. For once I look my age, or older. I gaze intensely into the camera. I want answers.

Surrey Police do not apologize to Dad for the months they wasted with him as their suspect. Perhaps they still think he could have killed Milly. At this point, besieged by journalists, the police say again that they are interviewing known paedophiles. They also make a new appeal for information and show replicas of Milly's uniform, purse and phone. They think that these things might have been dumped somewhere between Walton and where 'the remains' – I still cannot think of them as Milly – have been found.

These objects are all harder to see now that we know Milly is never going to need them back.

The press are once again a fact of our lives. Every time we step out of the house, there they are, cameras flashing.

Something has always mystified us. We were first told about the body the day after it was found – Thursday, 19 September. By Friday, the twentieth, Dad's birthday, the identity was confirmed to us. By Saturday, the twenty-first, it was already in the press. *How did they know about it so soon?* They must have known when we did, to publish so quickly.

One front page upsets me more than the rest. Fortunately, I

believe that this would never happen now. But in 2002 the *Daily Mirror* shows a woman police officer in a white decontamination suit, her eyes apparently wide with horror. The article implies that this is the moment Milly's body is discovered. This is the headline:

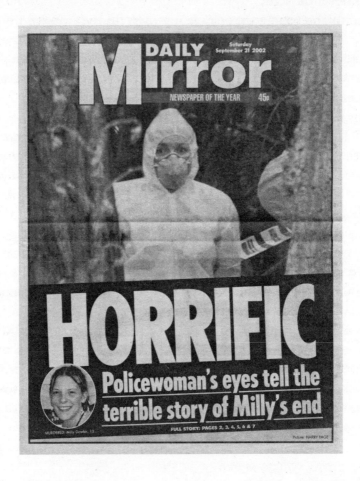

The paper represents my beautiful sister as an object of horror. That's the worst thing, but there's more. What were the press doing there to record that moment? Before Milly's family is even aware of the discovery? Or have they grabbed this photo and distorted the timing to make a better story? Is the caption simply a fudge?

Whatever happened, it shouldn't have.

Suddenly my sister has a new name. She is 'Tragic Milly Dowler'. The *Sunday Express* has Milly on pages 1, 3, 4, 5, 6 and 7. It quotes an interview with an expert on child sex criminals, who has given the police a list of suspects. Ray Wyre warns that Milly's murderer will kill again, if he hasn't already. Mr Wyre says that the killer is also 'forensically aware' – making sure that none of his DNA is at the scene. He's right – the police have told us that. He profiles Milly's killer as someone who feels powerful in taking a life, and enjoys the fear and pain he creates. The *Sunday Express* publishes the theory of how a murderer may get sadistic pleasure from living out a brutal sex fantasy that leads to a child's death. This is printed right next to a half-page picture of Milly and Mum.

Are we supposed to have no feelings?

The *People* leads on a theory that Milly knew her killer. This story upsets us too. If Milly knew that person, then we know them too. We don't believe anyone in our tight, loving circle would do this. Of course this theory reawakens residual worries that the police might still be trying to blame Dad for the crime.

The *Sunday Mirror* leads on 'KILLER IS A LOCAL', saying that only someone with intimate knowledge of our part of Surrey could have bamboozled Surrey Police for so long.

For a while, we are allocated two police officers to stand at the front of our house to keep the press away and to ward off unwelcome visitors. Alice turns up one day and parks out the front. As usual, she's laden with bags and paperwork. When she leaves, an hour or so later, she finds her car has a parking ticket. The two officers hadn't realized it was hers.

The same day our neighbour Fiona sends a text, saying, *I'm in Tesco. Is there anything you need?*

Yes – doughnuts, I reply tersely.

Arriving back in our street, Fiona approaches the officer guarding our driveway. Not wanting to disturb us, she asks him if he could give us the bag of doughnuts.

'I'm afraid I'm not permitted to do that,' he replies. 'But you may knock on the door.'

When Fiona rings the bell, I open the door only the tiniest slit – just enough for her to squeeze the bag of doughnuts through.

Of course, this is exciting for the press. A scoop. The next day there's a photo of Fiona on our doorstep delivering the family sugar fix.

Even at a time of such sadness and despair, this still raises a smile.

By this time I have different feelings about our front door. It is a beautiful door and until now I had always insisted that it stayed the same in case Milly ever came back. It's wooden, with panelling and a cord for the bell, which rings with a lovely musical sound.

The doorbell is starting to be tainted. Apart from the arrival of those doughnuts, it never opens to anything good. It just announces the police coming to torture us with more insinuations or unspeakable news.

Monday, 23 September, sees a new press release from Surrey Police: they have a hundred officers working on the case. They've received around four hundred calls from the public since the discovery of Milly's body. But it will take time to process all the statements made.

They're still combing Minley Woods, now with the assistance of six victim recovery dogs from the Metropolitan Police, the forensic orthodontist who identified Milly from dental records, a forensic archaeologist, and a soil and vegetation expert. They are also continuing to work with profilers and psychologists.

Dogs now, I think. *Dogs, the day she disappeared, might have found her alive.*

Alice phones. They've still found no clothing or personal property belonging to Milly or anyone else. A metal detector has come up with nothing. Dad makes notes of the bones they have found. How can Milly be described as 'a vertebra, tibia, left collarbone, left shoulder blade, sacrum, skull and sixteen ribs'?

How many people have to take this sort of telephone call? I wonder. *Very few, I hope.*

Alice says the reason there are no clothes might be because the animals ate them. She reassures us that house-to-house questioning is in progress and that the police have visited a nearby Traveller community. Meanwhile CCTV footage from the Minley Woods area is about to be harvested.

On 24 September, the *Newsround* website reports on the discovery of Milly's body.

Kids of around Milly's age leave comments. Charlotte, fourteen, from Workington, writes, 'Just think six months ago she was just a normal school girl going home from school. She was special, special to her friends and family, and now she's been taken away to be special in Heaven.'

On Thursday, 26 September, Alice calls to say the bridleway at Minley Woods will reopen tomorrow to the public: 'If you want to visit before everyone else does, then we have to do it now.'

I want to go there. I want to see if I can find any clues that the police have missed. Yet I flinch from seeing the place where Milly's skull was found, even though I know that the police have now taken the bones away.

Mum and Dad are fuming that yet again we have no time to prepare. Dad rushes home from London and I scramble back from college. We're aware we'll be photographed. We're learning to dress the part. We're actors now in a new stage of a drama that seems to have captured the heart of the nation. The press will be greedy for images of us visiting the place where Milly's body was left; they need pictures of us in an appropriate tableau of grief.

We don't want to wear black. We cannot mourn the fact that we now know where Milly is: Minley Woods has offered an end to that part of our ordeal. And we are not ready to mourn Milly. In spite of the long-awaited evidence, I don't think any of us can quite, quite accept that she is dead. Mourning is what comes after disbelief, then acceptance. We're such a long way from there.

The old instincts kick in: I want to wear something that Milly would recognize, and consider cool enough. But in the end there's no time. I have to wear what I put on for college that day. Mum wears pale blue trousers and a zip-neck top that Milly and I chose for her. At the last minute, she's grabbed a long-stemmed white rosebud from one of the bouquets that have been delivered to us. She hasn't even had time to make a loving choice of a flower from her own garden, one as pretty as Milly. The anonymous rosebud is wrapped in a piece of wet kitchen roll and cling film.

Dad wears a zip-neck top too, in a brighter colour. His trousers are dark.

Alice and Jon drive us. The five of us won't fit in the usual car: both Dad and Jon are giants. A twenty-mile drive is too long for them to cram their legs into a tiny space. So the police have to hire a people-carrier. Sitting in the back, I put my earphones in. I don't want to sit there making small-talk on this trip. Dad offers advice about the best route to drive: as ever, he's getting comfort from being efficient, or at least he's distracting himself. Mum doesn't even try to pretend that this drive isn't the worst of her life. She gazes out of the window with empty eyes.

It takes almost an hour to get to Minley Woods. Tension builds. It's as if we are about to do an exam that none of us has studied for, an exam no one should ever have to take.

Six months' waiting for Milly to come home is no preparation for visiting the place where her murderer dumped her.

28.

Just before the woods, there's a mini roundabout. As we turn into the road, we see that the public has got there before us. The police have cleared everyone away from the road for our visit, but we find the way lined with teddy bears, flowers, handwritten notes and angel dolls. There must be thousands of tributes, three feet deep, going on for a hundred yards. They continue right up to the place where police tape blocks off the road, the place that's just for us.

A gentle rain falls on everything.

I think of how it must have been here before we arrived. There must have been *crowds*, to leave so many tributes. I know that the gifts come from the hearts of people genuinely touched and shocked by what has happened to my sister. This is their way of offering us support, showing us how important Milly has become to so many in this country, that she won't be forgotten. But I cannot connect with this public grief.

More desperately, I cannot connect to Milly.

I stay in the car as a high-ranking police officer takes Mum and Dad to do their duty by the press, which must have its photo opportunity. There's an unspoken bargain to be fulfilled. They will leave us alone for a few minutes at the site where Milly was found but, first, we have to give them something in return.

Mum and Dad hold hands as they walk along the row of flowers and tributes left for Milly. They're shadowed by photographers. I'm hoping they barely notice it. I'm hoping they take comfort from this handmade display of support, even if I can't. Mum and Dad spend half an hour looking at the tributes. I'm wondering how much they're doing this for themselves and how much is a public thank-you to all the people who have been so kind. Every second of not breaking down must be agony for Mum. I'm glad not to be under that scrutiny – but I also feel guilty because I'm safely out of the limelight.

The press must have their one unforgettable image for the next day's papers. So Mum places the single white rose on a grassy verge about eighty yards from the real place where Milly lay all those months. There's no note. Just the long-stemmed rosebud. It's hours since we left home, and the rose is wilting slightly, which just makes it look sadder.

The press want Mum and Dad to react to the tributes, so they kneel down to read some of them. Tears are wetting Mum's face, but she doesn't break down. Dad puts his arm around her. Next they visit a Portakabin in which the police have placed a book of condolence signed by thousands of members of the public.

Mum and Dad return to the car, their hair and clothes damp. We drive straight to the place in the road where a bridleway forks off to the right. As we climb out of the car, a small group of policemen bow their heads in respect.

I still cannot feel the appropriate matching sadness. Instead I have a sensation as if my chest is being crushed. My heart seems to be beating higher up than it should be and twice as fast as normal. I feel sure I'm going to fail at this new test.

We're greeted by another senior Surrey Police officer, one of the more humane men. I believe he's been at this crime scene since the first, and that he really knows the terrain. He's drawn the short straw today – who would want to accompany a family to the place where their murdered daughter and sister was found?

It's very quiet. Even the police are quiet. The mood is solemn. The soft quiet rain matches our work today. I walk underneath an umbrella, as if it can shield me from what we're about to do. The senior police officer explains that he is going to take us to the spot. It's just him and us. Uniformed officers patrol to make sure that the press are keeping away from the immediate vicinity. We walk down the bridleway in silence. The murky sky's obscured by tree branches meeting overhead.

The officer turns off the path. He guides us between trees and shrubs. There's no path, but it's clear that police activity has thinned out the foliage here. We're literally walking in the footprints of the forensic team: I can see them in the disturbed earth. The damp ground is littered with brown leaves. The tree trunks are grey.

To keep myself calm, to bring myself back to reality, I concentrate on finding a clue that the police have missed. I don't even trust them to have gathered all of Milly. I worry that I'm going to walk on something – on a part of Milly they haven't found yet.

I don't even know how I'm going to deal with what comes next. I still cannot make this alien scenario fit with the person I think I am, with the life I thought I had.

What sixteen-year-old has to walk through a forest to see the place where her murdered sister was dumped?

I ask if they have searched the woods all around for the missing bones. The officer tells me they have gone into a 'fingertip' search. He says, 'Our conclusion is that the missing bones were eaten by animals.'

Bile rises in my throat. Milly *eaten?*

I'm afraid that I'm going to vomit on this place where we need to be so solemn. I fight to keep the bitter liquid down.

Mum will tell me later that all she wanted to do was sit down and scream, sob, howl. But I'm there, and she has to protect me from the sight of her breaking down. So she and Dad walk right up to the place where Milly was.

I can't make myself take another step forward. To me, this place is like all the forests of our childhood, where we used to play hide and seek, where our singing would echo through the trees. I'm in shock that Milly has lain here for so long undiscovered. We're so close to the bridleway. The foliage isn't dense. It's so open that I feel embarrassed again for Milly's dignity, her naked body exposed to the sky while it . . . No, I can't bear that thought at all.

Wasn't it enough for him to kill her? Why did he have to do this to her too? Is he this sick? Or is he this evil?

He is both, I realize.

The hairs at the back of my neck suddenly rise. I feel as if the murderer is there in the trees, watching, enjoying what he has done to our family. *That's just what he'd do, gloat, isn't it?* Now would be a good moment for him to take me too. Mum and Dad are lost in their own world of grief. This one police officer is never going to save me. I spin around, checking every shadow. I can't see him, but I feel his presence.

Twenty yards on, I see a dried water course. It's about eighteen inches wide and meanders through the forest out of sight. To the right is a field, bathed in light. Half in the field, and half in the water course, there's a bald patch where the leaves and soil have been cleared. It's very subtle. Apparently the police have had to be wary of press helicopters or even tall cherry-pickers homing in on the spot.

There is no grave, shallow or otherwise. There never was.

Instead, there's a yellow rose wrapped in cellophane on the damp leaf-strewn soil to show where Milly was left. It's tied with a yellow ribbon.

There's another yellow ribbon a few yards away, tied in a simple bow like the ones you get for Cancer Research.

The officer explains that, when Milly was dumped, there would have been up to two feet of water in this place. But a hot August has just passed and now it's dry. The running water, however, carried one of her arms a few yards away. The presence of water, he adds, would have made the decomposition happen faster.

I'm confused. They told us before that animals took away some of Milly's bones – not water. *Why can't they be consistent? Don't they understand what terrible abysses open in our minds? That we can barely support one thought, one image, one idea?*

I look, but my mind veers away from what I'm seeing. I don't want to see the place. I don't want to look at the ribbon. From the open skies above us, I can see that the murderer has had no care for Milly's humanity. But I do. I know she wouldn't want me here, picturing her here.

I had such hopes that I would feel Milly's presence in this place, hopes so secret that I had not named them even to myself. Yet I feel nothing. My hopes crash and I feel worse for losing them.

This should be a special place. There's nothing beautiful here. There should be music to express our emotions – both the essence of Milly as she was, and the darkness of what has happened. There should be something to mark how terrible this is. Instead it is just a normal grey drizzling English day, and an ordinary field, and trees that you'd see anywhere.

Mum bends down at the first spot. She's weeping inconsolably. Dad puts his arm around her. He catches my eye and mouths, 'I love you.'

I have come empty-handed. I had no time to grab something for Milly. I should be crying like Mum, but I can't.

Maybe the policeman will think I didn't love Milly because I can't make myself react the way I should.

My confusion is covered with a thick coating of shame. I'm ashamed of myself because I want to ask about the position of Milly's body when she was found. *Was she face up or face down? On her side?* Milly used to sleep on her left side as that was normally the one facing the door. So, if anyone came in, she would see them immediately.

How long does a body take to decompose to bones? Would there be anything left apart from bones by now? Does that mean Milly died six months ago, or was she kept captive for a while? Can we at least be certain that her terror was quickly over?

A child would ask these bold questions – not an adult. Children are not afraid and not ashamed of being curious. I can't ask such things aloud. The grown-up part of me knows they're not the appropriate questions to ask in this moment, which is supposed to be sad and dignified. The newly experienced part of me, which has endured the last six months, knows that the police won't give straight answers anyway. The protective part of me – the old Gemma – doesn't want Mum and Dad to have to hear such questions and such answers. What they know is already too much for Mum.

I won't ask anything more here. I'll look it up on the computer, alone, at home, when no one's looking.

The police officer bravely turns to me. I don't say anything, but I guess he's seeing me as I'm seeing myself in that moment, as a frightened child. I'm not sixteen. I'm ten, and getting more child-like and more frightened every minute. Without being able to utter a word, I'm obviously transmitting all my distress and confusion. Perhaps that is why he says, 'Maybe think of it like this, Gemma. Remember the movie *Snow White*? When she's asleep after eating the poisoned apple? All the animals come to care for her.'

Fairy tales, at this moment? You take a sixteen-year-old to see the place where her murdered sister's body was found, and you want to talk about Snow White?

I turn an incredulous face to him. Poor man. He's only trying to be kind. He wants to make it seem cosy, but you can't cover this scene with Disney fairy dust. Animals – I don't want to hear about them now. He's just told me that animals ate parts of Milly.

Does he want me to think that Milly's going to wake up and there will be a happy ending?

Hearing about *Snow White* in this context doesn't make me feel safer. It just makes me hate *Snow White*.

The officer withdraws to the path to give us a moment alone. He probably needs a moment to himself too. Having a ringside seat at an exhibition of what trauma looks like: that's a trauma in itself.

I'd like to think he was also examining Surrey Police's part in this picture.

Without speaking, Mum, Dad and I go to stand together in the space between the yellow ribbon and the rose. Mum's in the middle. Dad and I have our arms around her. We remember how she fell to the ground when she heard about Milly being found in this place. We know we need to hold her up. Sheltering in one another's arms, it's a moment for us to cling to the memory of the happy family we were before Milly was taken. We know that when we leave this place, we'll be different people. There's a finality here. The mystery is laid to rest. We're the family of not a lost but a murdered child. That's what we shall always be from now on.

Mum makes a low kind of wailing noise. This makes me cry. 'Stop,' I beg her. 'You're frightening me!'

Mum repeats under her breath, 'You're safe now, Milly. No one will hurt you any more.'

I stumble away from Mum and Dad, needing my space.

Mum takes three pictures of the place where Milly was found. Then we walk back to the car, and I climb inside. I'm done now. I don't want any more human interaction for a while. Jon's there, but I just put my headphones back on. I'm playing Eva Cassidy's 'Fields Of Gold' at top volume, and Faith Hill's 'There You'll Be'.

Before we leave Minley Woods, Alice presents each of us with a little purple box. I can see she's really invested time in finding these boxes. Milly's room is decorated in purple and pink. Inside each box is a lock of Milly's hair tied with a pink ribbon. This is not part of police procedures. Alice must have negotiated this gift from the forensic team. She must have cleaned the hair, combed it, and tied those tiny bows herself. I'm sure she also paid for the boxes and the ribbons.

It was so kind of her, but I don't want the hair. I want Milly.

I don't want Milly to have her hair taken away. Her pretty hair. I still cannot deal with this separation of the Milly I know from 'the remains'. For me, Milly is still my beautiful, dancing, luminous sister, not a corpse that has decomposed, abandoned, in a forest. Milly needs *all* her hair for her famous 'messy bun' style.

Mum is moved that Alice has done this for us. She hugs her.

We get back into the car, holding our little boxes of Milly's hair.

That is all we can take home from Minley Woods.

29.

For the next few days, we see our visit to Minley Woods described in compassionate headlines. We see photos of what it was like at Minley Woods before we got there: a carnival of people with flowers and balloons. People have gone to lay flowers and candles because of the pain in their hearts for Milly. And then there are the people going to see all the flowers and candles and teddy bears.

The police let the press know that twenty officers have searched the site for clues as to whether it was a murder, suicide or natural death.

Suicide? Natural death? How can those theories still have a place on a Surrey Police press release? How would Milly get to a forest miles from home? How would she physically kill herself?

They also take away forty sacks of leaf matter from the area where Milly's body was found. Six months later they will still be examining it for evidence.

When we go home after Minley Woods, it is to a house to which Milly will never return, a bed she will never sleep in again, clothes she will never wear.

Mum wants to address that.

Her room has been rifled by the police and left in a state of clinical tidiness that means it just isn't Milly's any more. I simply never go in there. Mum has a different attitude. She doesn't want it to be a shrine, and wants me to help her sort it out. But I just can't force myself to touch Milly's things. Dad can't do it either. The only person who is strong enough to help Mum is lovely Auntie Linds.

Milly's mirror, in the shape of a *Titanic* lifebelt, is among many things Auntie Linds takes away, at Mum's request, to go to the charity shop. Loley and Robyn return from school to see Milly's mirror in their hallway. This throws them into hysterics that are a mixture of shock and tears.

Now, looking back, I am sad that I couldn't join Mum. I should have been there for her. I also should have made the most of the chance to touch Milly's things for the last time. Mum keeps all the important things, of course, like the hundreds of loving cards Milly wrote and received within the family, her schoolbooks, her reports, her music, her sax and one or two pieces of clothing, the pebble with the heart-shaped indentation Milly found on the beach near Swanage.

Now Mum buys a running treadmill and puts it in the garage. The relentless turning of the belt seems much like the way her mind churns.

After that, all night we hear the pounding of Mum's feet on that treadmill. She runs through the pain, as if it is her just punishment for losing her daughter. It doesn't matter if she's tired or sore. She runs. But she can never outrun the pain. She's running on the spot, making no progress, just hurting herself. She keeps going until she seriously injures her knee. Years later, that knee will require extensive surgery to fix the damage she starts inflicting on herself now. She also puts in fifty lengths at the pool and gives the machines at the gym a hard time. Dad, in contrast, tries to lose himself in mindless television.

Just lifting our post is heavy physical work. The condolence cards have started to arrive, thousands of them from all over the country and from all over the world. Mixed among them are a few nasty crank letters. Mostly we are overwhelmed by kindness. People want to express their sadness and horror about what happened to Milly. She has touched the hearts of so many people.

There's something approachable about our family. People write to us as if they know us. Perhaps this is because they have seen us on the screen; they, too, have lived our mystery and agony for all these months. I believe it is also because they see clearly what the police were unable to recognize for so long because of their tunnel-vision templates of runaway girl and guilty father. The public has seen our faces and read our words in the newspapers, and they have drawn their sad and frightening conclusions: that Milly came from a loving, decent family, who had nothing to do with her death.

The unspoken implication is: if this could happen to a family like ours, it could happen to anyone. Deep empathy, not just sympathy, runs through their letters.

Mum, of course, wants to thank Jon and Alice for all their special kindness to us. She writes to Jon's beloved Charlton Athletic to ask for a T-shirt signed by all the players. It arrives with a Letter of Authenticity that says, 'To Jon, from all your friends at Charlton Athletic'. Jon has the T-shirt framed. For Alice, Mum chooses some really stylish keep-fit clothes, as Alice is taking part in various sporting activities.

It's only now that ITV screens the interview Mum and Dad did for Trevor McDonald's show before Milly's body was found. It's become a half-hour special appealing for new information or witnesses.

'It's the little things that can be so hard,' Mum tells the interviewer. 'The other day, I was chatting to someone I hadn't met before. She didn't know who I was and asked how many children I had. I couldn't answer. I just cried.'

30.

From the day Milly's body was found, flowers began to appear on the green next to Station Avenue, outside the school. It's lovely for us that so many people have thought to do this. Flowers are a good way to remember Milly. The sight of these fields of flowers makes us feel cared for and even loved.

But we can't bear the thought of those beautiful flowers starting to die and turn brown. So, before that can happen, Mum and Dad go out and scoop up all the flowers to bring them home. They buy five enormous compost bins, and make a space at the end of the garden for them. Eventually that compost goes to nourish more flowers in Mum's garden.

The sacks of mail don't stop arriving. People are writing to us to ask how they can send a donation. We appreciate their thoughts but we don't want money for ourselves. Meanwhile, Mum's desperate for something to do, something into which to throw the nervous energy that has devoured her since Milly disappeared. Until Milly was found, Mum could concentrate on the search. Now that part of our ordeal is over.

She decides to set up a charity. With her organizational and mathematical skills, the whole thing takes her just days. Mum's idea is that there's lots of material about 'Stranger Danger' for very young children. There's less for teenagers, who are possibly more at risk. The charity is to be called 'Milly's Fund'. Its aim is to promote personal safety for young people by the provision of training and education to teachers, youth workers and children themselves.

Milly's Fund is working with Diana and Paul Lamplugh, mother and father of the missing estate agent Suzy Lamplugh, who vanished without a trace in the year I was born, 1986. Her mother later founded the Suzy Lamplugh Trust, which campaigns for personal safety. Mum and Dad already know the Lamplughs. They were incredibly helpful in the early days when Milly went missing. Diana even taught Mum how to identify a body, should it ever become necessary. Diana learned the hard way, even though her daughter has never been found. The best coping strategy, Diana told Mum, is to look once very quickly, then look away. And then take another look. You need to slowly accustom yourself to what you are seeing. This is supposed to traumatize you less than one long look at a corpse.

I've gone back to Brooklands, and try to focus on my college studies. That, however, is not the only reason why I don't get very involved with Milly's Fund. I'm proud of Mum, but I'm also missing her full-time attention. I know that Milly's Fund is a wonderful cause, and something has to be done with the money that's flooding in. Yet the part of my character that has regressed to childhood wants Mum spending every minute with me. She's a brilliant multi-tasker, but it's just not enough for me.

The police still have the 'remains' so we cannot give Milly a funeral yet.

However, on Tuesday, 8 October, there's to be a service for Milly at Guildford Cathedral. It's intended as a celebration of her short life. There's a frantic rush to prepare everything: the order of service, the choice of music and who's to play or sing it, the eulogy. All these endless, dragging months of waiting for news and now we have to prepare Milly's service at high speed.

Mum asks Ben, who had played 'Local Hero' with Milly, if he'd be kind enough to perform at the service. He tells her he feels privileged to be asked and travels all the way back from Newcastle for the service. He will not accept any money for his train fare.

I want to write something, a tribute to my sister. But words fail me. My old confidence is gone: for so long, I've been made by the police to feel an inadequate sister to Milly. Relentless cross-examinations have torn my words to pieces, along with my belief in what I thought I knew. I have learned to lock my sacred private memories of Milly away from the police.

Now when I desperately want to share those memories, I don't have access to them. I sit helplessly, looking at a blank computer screen. I can't even find something written by someone else that

Karaoke Queen: Milly singing 'Man! I Feel Like a Woman!' by Shania Twain, along with Loley.

n charge in Cyprus.

Minutes before we strayed unawares on to a nudist beach: Milly and I with our Singing Uncle Pete, Dancing Auntie Jenny and their boys, David and Daniel.

Milly playing Christmas carols on the sax, December 2001.

Three ladies in Cuba, Christmas 2001, the last holiday we'll have with Milly.

Well good' cornrows in Cuba. Milly wore her Flower Fairy necklace, as usual.

Milly with Lovely Granny, whom the police would come to call 'The Rottweiler', because of her ferocity in protecting our family.

The 'Fields of Gold' photo of Milly, taken on a camping trip to Selsey Bill.

tyle Guru: hat and matching
gloves, of course.

The young Style Guru has
achieved total black.

Yes, I have done my homework,
Mum. My bedroom's really tidy.
Now can I go out?'

Retro flower-power flower-child with her fashion drawings behind her.

Milly wearing the famously ironed jeans: 'Go away, Mum!'

Double denim.

Another dance move.

Milly gives Mum a
'Guttural Hug'.

Cupboard Love:
guaranteed supply of
Maltesers.

would be appropriate. There doesn't seem to be a word, a prayer or poem to represent the complexity of my feelings. I'm bad at spelling, bad at grammar, bad at writing. Nothing I can write will be enough to show the world how much I miss her and how little I can bear the thought of not having Milly at my side to share whatever life is going to bring.

I'm telling myself that I'm not good enough.

Maybe, I think, *if I had been a better sister, we wouldn't be holding a memorial service for Milly now.*

There are only dark thoughts running through my head as I dress for the service. This time, Dad, Mum and I choose black, a colour I've never worn before. Milly was the one for fashionable black. The rest of our family has always loved a pastel palette. But today we know the eyes of the world will be on us via the lenses of the press. We want to be judged sober and dignified. Anyway, there's certainly no colour in our lives now.

I wear a high-necked ruched top, of which Milly would have approved, on top of a mid-length pencil skirt. My hair's pulled back in elaborate coils I've styled myself. It's the opposite of Milly's famous 'messy bun'.

We've ordered bouquets for me and Mum from Dandini Flowers. Mum craves sweet peas but it's not the season. The florist has assured Mum she will somehow track some down. She has done so – by flying them in from South Africa. And she refuses to charge us for them. I will carry white ones; Mum has pale purple.

An hour before the service, two people-carriers arrive at our house. Lovely Granny's already there. Uncle Bree, Auntie Marilyn and Mark, Uncle Pete and Auntie Jenny join us, along with their sons. We set off promptly. We're a punctual family – except for Milly – and there's no way we're going to be late for this occasion.

It's a beautiful day, bathed in light. Guildford Cathedral is perched on a hill overlooking the peaceful Surrey countryside. I feel honoured that we're allowed to celebrate Milly's life in this magnificent building. But, when I see how big it is, I also worry that there might be embarrassing empty seats. There's no need to worry. There will not be enough room for everyone who wants to come.

As we draw up, we hear the bells, already tolling for Milly. We see a huge crowd waiting on the grass in front of the cathedral. We're taken around to a car park to the left. When we park, it's among dozens of television vans. As usual, we don't go in through the front door. We're let in at a side entrance.

I'm overwhelmed by the never-ending height of the cathedral's roof. The blond stone seems to enfold us like a forest, though forests are hard to think about now. The cathedral is rigged up with sound and video equipment as if for a royal wedding. There are pens of press positioned at different vantage points in the church. One glass-fronted pen is just a few feet from the pew where we will sit. I'm afraid they'll film me crying, and spoil my time with Milly. Alice reassures us that they are not allowed to focus on our faces. Their cameras are trained on the altar. No clicking or flashes will be permitted.

The people outside are now allowed to enter.

The first thing they see is a pair of large photographs of Milly mounted on easels. One shows her driving the boat in Cyprus; the other is Milly in a classic dance move in our garden. She's wearing her hip 1970s psychedelic top and her horrible jeans.

The vast cathedral seems to fill instantly. I want to say, 'Look, Milly! Look how many hearts you've touched!'

Twelve hundred people have come to pay their respects to Milly. Heathside School has closed for the day so the pupils can attend. In the back rows are Milly's friends, dressed in the height of teen fashion in tribute to the style guru she was. Many wear black. Others have decided to celebrate Milly's vivacious personality in full colour.

A coachload of police files in, along with representatives of the fire service, who assisted in the search. Officers of both forces are in full dress uniform. They look so smart.

Milly, I think, would have loved this array of red, dark blue and gold braid.

I'm grateful to the police for that. For once, the place seems safer for their presence. I think, *If a fire breaks out, if something happens, we'll all be protected.*

I'm grateful, yet I can't help thinking, *Milly's being protected right now, more than she was when she really needed it.*

I don't know if they're here, but Mum and Dad have also invited the mushroom-pickers who found Milly's body. My parents are grateful to them because they have put us out of the misery of not knowing.

On their seats, the people find the order of service we've designed. Its title is *Remembering Milly*. For the picture on the front, we've chosen the one of her driving the boat.

We follow the bishop and the dean down the central aisle to take our places. The dean welcomes everyone and offers thanks to all the many people who have helped us over the last six months. Then Dad, Hannah Mac and Auntie Linds go up the steps into the chancel. Hannah and Auntie Linds walk hand in hand. Dad's towering over them.

Hannah reads a poem she has written. She's slender and sweet-faced in a dark trouser suit with a crisp white shirt. Milly would have loved the expert eyeliner. Hannah reads her poem perfectly and bravely, with the light and shade of sincerity. In her dreams, she says, she's still with Milly, happy and full of laughter. She smiles at the memory. Then her face grows sad. 'If only that were real.' Hannah's composure is almost perfect, with only one visible gulp when emotion threatens to overwhelm her.

Auntie Linds also wears elegant black and white. She tells the congregation, 'I first met Amanda Jane Dowler on the day after she was born. As a toddler she soon showed the traits that would form part of her personality as a young girl. Endless hours of dancing and running around the lounge, singing at the top of her voice to *Joseph and His Technicolour Dreamcoat*. The ever-present intellect and the imposing questions she wanted answering. Instead of the normal child's cry of "Why, why, why?" we were bombarded with "What are bricks made of?" or "How does blood stay in the body?" '

Auntie Linds recalls holidays, karaoke and Milly's famous baggy jeans. 'I thought they were disgusting. My daughter Laura thought them to be "cool".' Auntie Linds says she's discussed with her daughters what to say today, because of the importance of the friendship between the four girls – me, Milly, Laura and her younger sister Robyn. 'Loley could share her deepest secrets with Milly with the knowledge that that trust would never be broken.'

Auntie Linds makes a subtle reference to all the rubbish that has been written about Milly, including the insinuations made by the police. She knows all about that – she was there at the first unspeakable day of my cross-examination at the so-called safe house in April. So I understand Auntie Linds's defiance when she describes Milly dancing at the ironing board: 'The smile on her face that comes from her eyes' – here Auntie Linds breaks down a little – 'her constant need to be dancing or moving as she sways with the ironing, her inherent coolness. Actually, it *is* the girl I knew – and the girl we all miss dreadfully.'

She reiterates, 'For those of you in here that never knew Milly in life, but have now got to know her since she was taken from us, I promise you that the girl you have seen is the girl she was – no doubt.'

She remembers an evening when she, her husband and my parents discussed the future careers of their girls. 'When it came to Milly we thought maybe a vet, a presenter or even an entrepreneur. This evil deed has taken away my opportunity to watch Milly grow, but I have seen enough to know we were shooting too low. Milly would have made a real mark on this world, a real difference. I am thankful that we finally have her back to allow us to say a proper goodbye.'

Auntie Linds struggles to get the last words out. Dad puts his arm out to steady her.

Last, Dad reads his tribute to Milly. Being Dad, he's rehearsed it until he's word perfect. But the size of the congregation unnerves him. His hands are shaking as he holds his notes, and his voice falters more than once. He bites his lip to keep himself under control. I'm so proud of him, and so grateful that he has the strength to represent our family here. Mum and I could not have done it.

I think of Milly listening to Dad's familiar voice, speaking about her. Despite the time and the place, this is somehow reassuring. Dad shares the joy of having Milly in our lives. 'What will we miss? We will miss Milly's fantastic sense of humour. Sally will particularly miss Milly referring to her as "Lovely Mummy". Milly always offered constant words of encouragement and advice if you were feeling a bit sad. I will miss asking her where my missing CDs are as she often borrowed my 1960s music CDs. Sally will miss her untidy bedroom, definitely an award winner.

'What are the special memories we will have of Milly? Her laughter, joking and mimic skills. So many people have said how much Milly used to make them laugh. Often her jokes were at our expense – particularly mine. Trying to instil some table manners often reduced Sally, Gemma and Milly to helpless laughter . . .

'What we are proud of: her talent for music – Milly loved to sing and dance and play her saxophone. We were especially proud of her saxophone playing. We also feel proud of the things other people have said about her and particularly the things that Milly had said about us that we may never have known. The way she supported and helped her friends, the lovely memories that other people have of Milly. One card we received was a lovely note written to Milly and at the end her friend wrote "PS Milly, I bet you are loving all this attention." In the nicest possible way we can just imagine it!

'We are so grateful that Milly was able to pack so much into thirteen happy, healthy years and bring us so much happiness, and that she was able to realize at least some of her potential. Milly – we know that your memory will live on.'

What most of the people sitting in the cathedral don't know is that Dad has spent the last six months under suspicion of her murder.

Our friend Glyn Willoughby, Heathside's headmaster, reads from 1 Corinthians.

Of course there's plenty of music. Uncle Pete opens the tributes with 'You'll Never Walk Alone' from *Carousel*. The acoustics of the cathedral amplify his superb baritone voice, lifting the words to the roof. It's as if he was born to sing in such a beautiful place. He makes us feel every single word. He does Milly proud.

I remember the last words Milly said to him: 'Uncle Pete, why do you always sing such sad songs?'

We sing Milly's favourite hymns, including 'Amazing Grace'. Eight students from Milly's school saxophone group play 'Can You Feel The Love Tonight?' which Milly first performed at Lovely Granny's ruby wedding celebration, and 'Nobody Does It Better', the last piece Milly ever played in public.

It's the first time I have heard the saxophone since Milly went missing. It stirs me to my core. I look at the players. Some are older than Milly, and are friends of mine. I can't help being jealous they still have all their sisters and brothers, and their innocence, and their everyday lives. Yet I love them for giving their all to Milly. Like Uncle Pete, they put on a show-stopping performance. They don't hold back. They don't play sadly. They play sassy. They play like Milly.

It's strange to attend a service for Milly, something very like a funeral, but without a coffin. 'The remains' are still with forensics and we have no idea when we'll be able to bury her. I'm glad that almost nobody in the cathedral knows that Milly's body is to be subject to its official post-mortem in two days' time. The inquest will open on 17 October. I don't want people picturing 'the remains'. I want them thinking about Milly as she truly was.

The Right Reverend Ian Brackley, Bishop of Dorking, speaks movingly of Milly being taken when just on the threshold of adulthood. He asks the parents in the congregation not to let the forces of darkness close in, not to become overprotective or suspicious.

When the service is over, Mum, Dad and I walk down the aisle to the main door. Now I see up close the faces of all the people who've come. There are people we haven't seen since years before Milly went; others we haven't seen since our lives changed from fairy tale to nightmare. Everyone is strong. No one is weeping. They meet our eyes.

I keep myself together enough for the two tasks I have agreed to perform. The first is the photo opportunity requested by the media. I lay my sweet peas in front of one the photographs of Milly in the nave.

Then we move outside on to the grass. Close friends and members of the family follow us. Hundreds of journalists and photographers are already stationed outside. Some are on stepladders and others are weighed down with telescopic lenses. The cameras start clicking immediately.

This is my chance to honour the promise I made to Milly more than a year before, when we watched that sad episode of *Byker Grove* in which a young girl dies of a brain tumour but plans her own funeral first. So now, just as I told Milly I would, I snip the ribbons to release twenty-five blue, pink and yellow balloons to sail up into the air and away. In that moment, I am the closest to Milly that I've been since she disappeared.

Mum hugs me. And Dad enfolds us both in his arms.

The press are told, and duly report, that this is our way of launching Milly's Fund.

The promise I made Milly – we keep that to ourselves.

31.

Heathside School has made a Book of Remembrance for Milly. It's a huge, beautiful volume bound in paper rippled with leaves, tied with an apricot-coloured ribbon. The pages are crowded with messages in all kinds of handwriting: borderline sophisticated to childish, some in biro, some in glitter ink. There are many hearts and stars, much underlining, little drawings of Milly's smiling face. Also glued in are the cards, some handmade, that accompanied flowers and teddy bears that the children and teachers brought to the memorial service at Guildford Cathedral.

Some messages are to me, Mum and Dad:

Bob, Sally and Gemma, Milly's absence is an infinite loss. My prayer is not that you forget that loss, but that you find peace with it and abiding joy with her presence in your hearts.

Mrs Dowler, you are the best teacher ever and I hope you come back soon.

To the Dowler family, I cannot even think how you feel. All of Heathside know the sun won't shine without her.

Amanda had so much hope + life ahead of her & it grieves us all that it was taken so pointlessly.

Others are to Milly herself, with people remembering her smiling and joking, her supportiveness and her fear of the dark. One of her teachers writes of her last memory of Milly dancing around the room, excited – presumably about *Pop Idol*. Even children who did not know Milly personally show how they've been touched by the last six months of mystery and suspense, and their sad conclusion.

But those who did know Milly – you see a portrait of her in their eyes. This is the portrait that we as a family can recognize, far from the one the police have tried to create. It is also a portrait of the generation of schoolchildren who've had to grow up knowing that a child's life can be ended for no reason that makes sense. You see them trying to frame their own concepts of mortality and the after-life. There is childlike hatred for the 'sick' monster who took Milly away.

I've kept the spelling and grammar authentic here, no matter how eccentric it is.

Hannah Mac wrote:

Milly, You are my bestest friend in the whole entire world. Make sure the angels keep that light on at night! You did <u>NOT</u> deserve this. I love you so much! Watch over me, watch my children grow, watch me progress. We will meet again. Deepest love and hugs + kisses.

Cara wrote:

Milly . . . you were a true angel. You took me under your wing when I was weak. You made me laugh 24/7.

Eddie the Entrepreneur wrote:

Dear Auntie Milly, words can't describe how I feel at this time. All I wanted you to know is I will never forget your smile, laugh and your gift on the sax. Rest in peace milly I'll always love you.

Other messages were:

You were the smile of the year.

You always sang like and angel + now you are singing with them.

I don't understand why you're not still doing your ape impression or being on the phone constantly to Hannah. I guess we never will, but oi, we'll never forget the good times, yeh?

Even the hours we spent in your bedroom pretending to be teachers with the white board – I'll never forget. You were always little Milly-Molly-Mandy & I still cannot comprehend that you're not coming back.

You made me laugh so much, I'll never ever forget you. Those prank calls at hannahs house, that was so funi.

Dear Milly, I remember the good times we had when we were young. Eating cheese and chips in your tree-house, watching TV in the dark, in the middle of the day, and doing the three legged race at sports day.

I have so many memories of you but there are a few which will always stay in my heart: - the thoughts of you, me, Gem & Hannah dancing to silly songs in your living room (with hairbrushes as microphones).

Milly I remember the time when you came and sat next to me when I didn't look to good and started talking to me saying if I was ok and I was thanks to you.

Amanda, you were loving, caring, kind and the most gracious person in the world. You are so brave.

To Milly, It is relly upsetting that someone somewere has been so craul to take you away from us.

I don't know who could be so mental to do such a thing. You will be in the nations hearts forever and floods will be cried for you.

Ace saxophone players never get forgotten.

> *If I knew it would be the last time*
> *We'd practice our All Saints song*
> *I would bring the performance forward a week*
> *Knowing 'Never Ever' could feel this long.*

I hope and pray they catch the sick individual who snatched such a talented, beautiful, genuinely kind and innocent 13 year old girl away from where she felt safest.

One student finished her message, 'P.S. WHY?'

32.

On 15 October, the *Evening Standard* runs a story about a witness who claims to have seen a girl resembling Milly walking in Minley Woods with two men. The girl was dressed in school uniform, including a grey skirt and blazer. The group of three were sighted at around 5 p.m. on the afternoon of the day Milly disappeared seven months ago. Given the known timeline, it would have been possible to drive to Minley from Walton by that hour.

But this story implies that Milly knew the men and had agreed to go there with them. Without calling us? That's so unlikely that we discount it immediately. It's just another theory based on someone Milly absolutely was not.

The inquest opens. The coroner reports that the police do not know how Milly died. The post-mortem has failed to produce any evidence that would point to the manner of her killing. Mum and Dad are called to Woking police station and are given the coroner's Interim Certificate of Fact of Death.

It hurts like hell to see the bald words 'Name and Surname of the Deceased'. Then Mum and Dad are distracted by the fact that the 'Date and Place of Death' are listed as 'Nineteenth September 2002, Yateley Heath Wood, Minley Road, Fleet'. Anyone looking at Milly's death certificate would assume she had been alive on 18 September 2002. Yes, we'd have loved that to be the case – and us all happily living together in blissful ignorance of the danger and the evil on our doorstep. But it's not true.

Mum is angry. Milly almost certainly did not die there, and she did not die on that date. The state of her remains shows that she had been dead for months. Mum and Dad cannot understand how such an official document can contain a blatant inaccuracy.

The coroner tells Mum that it's simply procedure and cannot be changed. But the police questioning has taken its toll. Mum's conditioned to feel guilty most of the time. She's distraught that she can't even ensure that the date is correct on her daughter's death certificate. Helpless, she feels she has failed in her last duty as a mother.

I don't want to see the false death certificate, or have anything to do with it. It just seems more rubbish, more lies, more insults to Milly's memory; one more piece of chaos, inaccuracy, carelessness.

Chaos, inaccuracy and carelessness: without those things clouding the search for Milly, she might not have ended up in Minley Woods.

Even with this travesty of a death certificate, we still can't have Milly's body for burial. The police are continuing to comb Minley Woods and will not release her until that search is finalized.

There's a second post-mortem, as inconclusive as the first.

The search in Minley Woods closes. The police are still going through forty sacks of leaves and soil from the site. The only news is that DNA now absolutely confirms that the body is Milly's.

I have written to Prince Harry, asking him to be a patron of Milly's Fund. He's involved in various charities, and he's my age. I know he understands bereavement, having lost his mother when he was just twelve.

I receive a handwritten letter from Eton College. He writes, 'I believe that we share something similar, even though I can never imagine how dreadful it was for you and your family.'

He's sorry but he can't become a patron as he's under orders to concentrate on his school work and not undertake public engagements. However, he says he hopes to meet me when his exams are over. And he asks me to write and tell him how Milly's Fund is getting on. I do feel that he is sincerely sorry.

Christmas looms. Christmas without Milly seems unthinkable. Home is so empty without her. It's not an option to spend Christmas there. We don't want to go to a hotel, because we couldn't bear people pointing and staring at us. Mum asks Diana and Paul Lamplugh how they coped with their first Christmas without Suzy. We also ask Alice and Jon for advice.

In the end, Mum, Dad and I fly to Oman on 11 December. We stay with the parents of dear family friends. Sue and Bernard take us under their wings. They look after us so well, filling our days with activities, trying to keep us busy. Sue takes us to a jeweller, who makes Mum a necklace with the word 'Milly' shaped in gold. Mum has asked our former neighbour Anne to design it so that the name is not immediately distinguishable at first glance. That way Mum can wear it without attracting unwanted attention. The jeweller also adds a tiny diamond as the dot over the 'I' in 'Milly'. It is perfect.

I've brought with me Milly's lightning bolt earrings. They're too tarnished to wear but I like to keep them close. Mum suggests that the same jeweller should make a facsimile pair in gold. He notices my 'sisters forever' wave ring from Walton. He offers to clean it for me. I don't want to take it off my finger, as it would seem like a letting-go I am not ready for. He persuades me, though, and makes it sparkle.

In Oman, I cannot sleep. The image of Milly being stabbed wakes me up constantly. I feel less and less safe. The alien landscape frightens me. I feel as if I am sinking.

I wonder if I should offer to go fishing with Dad, as that's what he used to do with Milly. Would it cheer him up to have another daughter beside him? But I don't feel I can ask. It might be too much for him.

On 22 December, the *Sunday Mirror* reports an exclusive. Just how do they learn that we have gone to 'a country where Christmas isn't celebrated'? The headline is 'Milly's Family Flee to Escape Xmas Agony. They've nothing to celebrate'.

The paper quotes a 'close family friend'. We guess it's more likely to have been a tip-off from the police.

And it's wrong. We're already back in the UK.

33.

My first birthday without you.
Wish you were here to hold my hand through it.

xxxx Gemsie

January 2003 brings us the trial of the female hoaxer who pretended to be Milly on the telephone. Leanne Newman is only twenty-one, which is why she was able to impersonate a weeping schoolgirl. Just four days after Milly was taken, she started telephoning – four calls to the police, and later Heathside School. On 19 April, she started on us. She pleads guilty and is remanded for psychiatric reports. Her barrister tells the court that Newman has been diagnosed as an 'attention-seeker'. She will eventually be jailed for five months.

Mum and Dad have had birthdays without Milly. Now it's my turn. For my sixteenth birthday party, last year, I'd had a murder-mystery party. We'd laughed and played at the whole idea of murder. Birthdays are always a big thing in our house but this one is very subdued. Milly's not going to be allowed to grow older. I don't want to grow older without her. Driving lessons are my birthday present. Before this year, I'd imagined being the cool older sister picking Milly up from parties. I remember how proud Milly was of Lovely Granny when she passed her test after Grandad died.

My mind is so scattered by trauma that the driving lessons go badly. My eyes won't rest on the pages of theory long enough to memorize any facts. I fail the theory test three times. But I pass the practical first time.

On 4 February Alice rings Mum to say a girl has been murdered in Hampton, six miles from us. She reassures Mum that there are absolutely no similarities between this case and Milly's. The *modus operandi* of the murderer is quite different and there's nothing to suggest any connection. 'I'm just telling you because it's local, and you'll be hearing about it in the press.'

The press duly fill in the gaps about the attack on Marsha McDonnell, just a hundred yards from her home. As with Milly, there's a *Crimewatch* reconstruction of Marsha's last known moments. Marsha stepped off a bus around midnight. Within a few seconds, she was bludgeoned from behind and died shortly afterwards in hospital.

Inevitably the press are quick to point out that this murder happened just five miles from the place where Milly was taken ten months earlier. Marsha's father tells the press, 'Anyone who could be so cruel as to do this to a girl like Marsha has to be stopped. No one should have to go through what we are experiencing.'

Mum and Dad protect me from seeing most of the reports. Personally, I don't link Marsha with Milly. At nineteen, Marsha seems grown-up to me. She was taken at night, and left for dead in the street, whereas Milly was abducted in broad daylight and left twenty miles away. Marsha has two sisters and a brother. The oldest is the same age as me. We know how her family must feel. We know there's no consolation. Naturally our thoughts go out to them.

Then Marsha's father Phil makes contact via our FLOs. He has refused to speak to any counsellor or therapist, saying, 'The only person I want to talk to is Bob Dowler.'

We remember how helpful Diana and Paul Lamplugh were to us when Milly first went missing. Dad agrees to see Phil. Their first meeting is very emotional for both of them. It turns out the two fathers have music in common. Phil has been a tour manager for Fleetwood Mac, and now runs a freight company that serves the music industry. Dad learns that Marsha, like Milly, had loved music. Where Milly played the sax, Marsha was a talented violinist.

Ute McDonnell has the consolation of a strong faith, but her husband is struggling. Dad reaches out to him, as much as he can. Although Phil had asked to meet because he hopes Dad can help him, I think that the meeting helps Dad too. A special and lasting bond is now created between these two fathers. Sometimes they don't even need to speak to one another, just to share a space.

When Mum meets the McDonnells later, I remember her saying over and over, 'They are just an ordinary lovely family and this is so unfair.'

I reply, 'Mum, we are just an ordinary lovely family too.'

She looks startled. 'Yes, sweetheart, you're right. I hadn't thought of it like that.'

Somehow it helps to meet other people hurt by tragedy. The decent, lovely McDonnells are the right people to whom the wrong thing has happened, just like us. Dad says it's like being members of a really exclusive club, one that no one wants to join.

At the time, these two grieving families have no idea exactly how much they have in common.

34.

Mum is fixated on the idea that Milly's funeral must be held on 21 March 2003, exactly one year after she went missing. It was always going to be an unspeakable day, so it seems right to focus our grief on it. Initially the police suggest that this isn't a good idea. They're not sure they'll be able to release Milly's remains by then. This makes Mum even more determined. She insists that they do.

Milly's funeral is to be private, unlike the service at Guildford Cathedral. This time, it's not a rush. We can prepare properly. We choose the Woking crematorium where Grandad's service was held. Mum designs the order of service. It's simple in black and white. Milly's saxophone teacher Craig Rickards has composed a song for her. It's called, simply, 'For Milly'. The hymn will be 'Amazing Grace' again. Both Mum and Dad are going to speak. I won't be able to do that.

If I were to speak, it would mean I had given up all hope that I would ever see Milly again. I can't stand there and say things about her. My brain is trying to preserve, in this way, every pure and lovely memory we shared. I want to keep Milly safe in my head, even if I didn't in real life. But there's an even darker truth – I just can't find those memories and this makes me feel like a worthless sister.

Of course we go back to Dandini's for the flowers. At first I don't want Milly's name picked out in flowers beside the coffin, which, we're told, is what usually happens when a child dies. I argue with Mum and Dad that this must be a properly private occasion and we don't want to draw attention to the hearse as it rolls through Walton. I warn, 'The press will turn it into a circus. It's supposed to be *our* day.'

But why should Milly's name be suppressed just because of the press? I don't want that either.

In the end, we do ask Dandini's to spell out Milly's name in small white roses. Uncle Pete's floral tribute is a large musical note formed of the same flowers with a red rose at either end. Mum, Dad and I have bouquets of pink roses to take to the service. Uncle Bree commissions an arrangement in the shape of a saxophone. He tucks a huge box of Milly's favourite Maltesers behind it.

There will be neither a gravestone nor a grave.

We've decided not to bury her. We need to truly lay Milly to rest. We can't bear the thought of Surrey Police demanding to exhume her bones for some reason, months or years from now. And a grave is a public place. The cranks and the press would be drawn there as if by a magnet. We don't want any kind of impromptu shrine being shown on the news to remind us of our loss.

We want Milly safe and away from everyone. Mum, Dad and I decide to scatter her ashes in a place that will always remain secret.

Woking crematorium is not large. Neither, therefore, is the invitation list. It's just family and really close friends. We know some people will be offended not to be asked, and we're sorry.

We choose songs. Sadly, we pass over Eva Cassidy's 'Fields Of Gold' because we cannot have its back-story of a girl writing to her lover. Also Mum's aware of the frequency with which it's played on the radio. She doesn't want the song to cause us – or anyone who attends Milly's funeral – an extra jab of pain when least expected. So we select another Eva Cassidy, 'I Know You By Heart'.

We decide to wear the same black outfits as for Guildford Cathedral. We know we'll never be able to wear them again, so it's better not to have two sets of clothes that bring back unspeakable memories. It's colder now than it was in September. So Mum and I simply add smart jackets to those tops and skirts. I think, *How practical we've learned to be. How experienced we are in the mechanics of grief these days.*

We decide that the funeral will commence with our following the route of Milly's last walk, the one she never completed.

We want to see her safely home one more time before we cremate her.

The day before the funeral, Dad, Mum and I write our cards to Milly. They will be tied on the bouquets that we'll carry to her funeral.

I don't want to write in black ink. It's what you use to fill out forms: plain and boring. Milly wasn't either of these things. I use blue, and my best writing to say, *To Milly, I wish I could just have you back for five minutes to tell you how much I need you and miss you. But now you have been taken away I will live life for the both of us! I will always love you! Love you loads, Gemma. Xxx.'*

Mum writes, '*Goodbye my beautiful Darling Milly. I will always love you. With fondest love, Mummy. xxxx'* She draws a heart above the last x.

Dad's card reads, '*Dearest Milly, a part of me will always be missing now that you are no longer here, but the lovely happy memories I have of you will always help me through the rest of my life. All my love. God bless, darling. Dad. Xxx.'*

Lovely Granny writes a poem for Milly, and also a card: '*Darling Milly, If only I could have taken the bullet for you. I will never forget how you helped me, and lit up my life. Your light will always shine in my heart. From Lovely Granny.*

Dad makes sure that our shoes are shining clean. Mum checks that everything is beautifully ironed. I lay out an unladdered pair of tights, with five back-up pairs just in case. Grief has made me clumsy. I'm constantly dropping and bumping into things. No pair of tights is safe since Milly went.

The night before the funeral, Milly's remains wait at the chapel of rest. The funeral parlour is in Walton town centre, opposite the Surrey Police station and next door to Blockbuster where Milly and I used to choose videos and bully Dad into buying sweets on a Friday night.

The funeral directors, Frederick W. Chitty, are discreet and protective, fully aware of the inevitable press interest. Being local, they know every detail of the last year. They, too, have woken up every day to newspapers talking about Walton, about Milly, about the police.

Mum gives them some things to put in the coffin. There's a card. There are some scraps of 'Blanky', Milly's fragment of a toy pig. She would have liked more of Milly's special things, but they are still in police custody. Mum asks me if I want to put something in the coffin. I don't. I just cannot cope with the idea of the coffin or the idea of Milly being in it.

Mum and Dad are asked if they wish to sit with the coffin the night before the funeral. Alice thinks it might help. When Alice asks if I would like to go, I snarl, 'Why would I like to go and sit with bones? That is *not* Milly.'

Dad goes late at night, to avoid the press. I'm happy that Milly, for at least part of the night, will not be alone. Mum stays at home to look after me. She knows I'm terrified of what goes on behind the thick white curtains of the funeral parlour. I don't share the thoughts going through my head.

What do they do behind those curtains?

How is Milly being treated?

Is she being left in the dark, which she hated?

Did they clean the bones?

Did they arrange them back in the shape of Milly when they put them in the coffin?

Are there any other bodies sharing the room with Milly?

Who are they?

Will they be kind to her?

Years on, I will regret that I did not go with Dad. So will Mum.

Every time I drive past there, even to this day, it still haunts me that I left Milly alone that last night she was on earth.

35.

I didn't realize how small you were. Now I have seen your coffin.

xxxx Gemsie

The morning dawns grey. I don't want to get out of bed. Today is going to be another step into the dark tunnel. We have Milly's body, yet the person who killed her is still at large. Surrey Police have given us no reason to hope they are going to solve this crime. So the funeral will not draw any kind of line under Milly's death.

Why are we even bothering? I think. But I can't share that darkness with anyone.

Lovely Granny has stayed the night. I did not want her to be on her own the night before Milly's funeral. When I go down, she's busy in the kitchen with Mum and Dad. I'm in my pyjamas still. I know I can't face the day with nothing in my system to sustain me. I also know that everyone will worry if I don't eat. Even if I can't focus on Milly, I want them not to be having to deal with me. So I swallow bran flakes and drink a cup of tea.

About twenty people will be taking the walk from Walton station with us, so other family members are arriving, clinking cups and saucers, talking in low voices. But it's too loud for me to bear. I retreat to my room.

As I dress in my ruched top and skirt, I think, *This is the worst day of my life so far. It's Doomsday. It's the pivotal day that concretes the fact that Milly is dead and never coming back.*

I put on the gold lightning bolt earrings that are replicas of Milly's old silver ones. I wear a plain silver heart pendant.

Looking in the mirror, straightening my skirt, I see very little of the Gemma whom Milly would remember. This Gemma is dark. She's not interested in being the good girl any more. She's still angry about the way she's been treated by the police. There is no more of that smiling Gemma who was always looking after

233

children. Once I could calm down any child and find the reason for its distress very quickly. Now I can't even settle the childlike part of myself, the part that shared a childhood with Milly.

I am becoming a shell. There's nothing good going on inside the coat of armour I've acquired. It's built from fury, determination, pain, betrayal, hurt. I'm not sure if I even want to be able to please people the way the old Gemma did. I have lost the ability. I can barely be civil. I can't even be bothered with the normal small courtesies.

I go into Milly's room. It's tidy, of course, without Milly to mess it up. The bed is still made with Milly's old quilt cover on it. Only Mum has ever dared to sleep in it.

I am saying goodbye to these four walls as 'Milly's room'. A person who is cremated cannot have a bedroom any more.

Mum joins me. She's wearing a locket given to her by her dad.

She tells me that we have to leave now.

'I don't want to go,' I'm sobbing like a small child. 'Please, Mum, I want to stay here. I can't do this. I don't want to go to a funeral. I can't say goodbye to Milly.'

Mum says quietly, 'You have to come, Gemma. You don't have a choice.'

Out of the window, I see the hearse pulling up with Milly's name spelled out in flowers in front of a coffin. A moment that I shall never forget.

It's the smallest coffin I have ever seen.

Mum literally drags me down the stairs. Tears are still rolling down my cheeks. The voices downstairs hush when people see me. There's pity on their faces. I hate it. I want to shout, 'I'm the sister who survived! Don't be sorry for *me*. Think of *Milly*!' But I say nothing. I pull myself together and wipe my face. I get into the car with Mum, Dad and Lovely Granny. It's the first car behind the hearse. I cannot look at the coffin.

While I was writing this chapter, Mum looked out the invoice from the funeral directors. It lists four limousines, the crematorium fee. They refused to charge us for a 'child's funeral service'.

The hearse leads the way to Walton station, where we all get out of the limousines. There's an arrangement of lilies waiting for us there – as well as a battalion of press. We have released details of the walk only hours before it starts. We do not want the public waiting and watching, even to wish us well. They would be kind, but we cannot bear kindness from strangers at this moment. We have released no details at all about the private service that will follow.

The press have scrambled quickly. Our walk will be streamed live to news channels and websites. The journalists are respectful, though. For once, they don't call out our names to attract our attention. The spectacle of our grief is enough. They can find their own words.

The families make up the agreed formations, as choreographed in advance by Mum.

The hearse is first, preceded by a man from the funeral director's wearing full mourning and a black top hat. On top of the hearse is an enormous canopy of white lilies, roses, freesias and phlox. Milly's name is spelled out in soft ivory roses.

Mum, Dad and I are in the front row. Dad walks on the side closest to the press, to shield me and Mum a little. I'm in the middle, and Mum's on the side of the bus stop where Kat stood when she saw Milly.

Then come Lovely Granny, Uncle Pete, Auntie Jenny, David, Daniel and Uncle Bree, Auntie Marilyn and their son Mark. Lovely Granny refuses to use her stick. She's going to do this walk for Milly without any help.

The next row is Auntie Linds, Uncle Ian, Laura and Robyn. There follows a very small group of our most trusted friends, including Hannah Mac and her parents. And behind them all walk the police, though the press will mention only one of them. There are twenty-three mourners in all.

I ignore the press. I draw my thoughts in. I focus everything on this walk.

Our pace is regulated by the speed of the hearse we are following. I still cannot look into it. I keep my eyes averted.

Mum, Dad and I walk with our heads held high. Dad and Mum cross their hands in front of them. I march like a soldier, with my arms at my sides. I repeat to myself, *This walk will not break me. This walk will not see me fall. This walk will not make me expose the emotion I need to keep safely inside.*

Back at the house, Uncle Bree gave me some advice. I think about it now. He said, 'Best thing to do is focus on the spot where you think she went and put every ounce of your thinking there. And maybe the Higher Beings will make the perpetrator feel some guilt.'

Uncle Bree, of course, knows the walk very well because he searched every inch of it the night Milly went missing.

We pass the bus stop, the sign to Collingwood Place, then the hedge that shields the flats from the view of the road. Someone has put a bunch of white flowers at head height in a tree by the place where Kat last saw Milly.

I vow, *I will not break in front of the world's press and probably Milly's murderer too. He's probably watching it on television or even here, getting off on this.*

I have to keep my composure intact for just a little longer. I know that the press will leave us at the traffic lights and we won't see them again today. Alice and Jon have reassured us that the press have no information about the next stage of proceedings.

Four hundred yards ahead, I can see our limousines waiting for us. The public ordeal will soon be over. I haven't been able to think about Milly properly because it's been such a struggle to stay dignified. Now I start to see the careful work that Mum, Dad, the funeral directors and the police have put into this day. The police have organized six motorcycle outriders, so it's like a royal wedding or a presidential visit. Station Avenue is closed to all traffic except ours.

'Milly would have loved this bit!' I tell Mum, as we get into the car.

I have tried not to think about what comes next, but at least I know it will be private. I hope that my thoughts will at last have some peaceful time alone with Milly.

It's half an hour's drive to Woking. The police escort, lights flashing, clears the road in front of us.

I remember the crematorium from Grandad's funeral. It's a quaint little painted chapel, all terracotta and Gothic windows, set in a small park. The approach is so leafy that you don't see the chimney amid the tall gables and pines. But I don't like the place. I don't like the word 'crematorium'. I don't like fire. I am petrified of it. To this day whenever I stay in a new place, I check on the fire escape route and make my own plan. As the limousine purrs into the crematorium's drive, I feel each yard brings me closer to something dreadful. The hearse takes a side-road, taking Milly with it, away from us.

I'm briefly distracted by a group of our family and friends who were not part of the walk but have been invited to meet us here. Vicky catches my eye. She automatically smiles lovingly at me and waves. I can't cope with her friendliness now. Vicky is a part of my childhood, and a friend of the Gemma who went missing when Milly was lost to us. I give her an empty smile.

When Mum, Dad, Lovely Granny and I walk inside, everyone else is seated. Compared to the magnificence of Guildford Cathedral, the crematorium is like a cottage, or even a mouse-hole inside a cottage. A painted, vaulted mouse-hole. It's completely full. In the intimacy of the confined space, I can hear the voices of all our friends and family.

I had hoped to find a space here to grieve quietly and privately for Milly. But I'm still not connecting with Milly or myself. It's just my clothes, my hair, my skin and my organs present in this chapel.

I don't see the coffin until we are halfway down the aisle. Dad, Mum, Lovely Granny and I are directed to the front row, and the white coffin is there, just a yard away, placed on a marble plinth. Lovely Granny is closest to the archway which, although I don't realize it then, leads to the furnace and the chimney.

The coffin terrifies me. I feel inadequate, a poor sister, because after all these months, I still have not been able to reconcile 'the remains' with Milly. 'The remains' are something to do with horror. Milly is to do with dancing, singing, cheese and cucumber sandwiches, laughter, late-night chats. It's inconceivable that all her joy and cheekiness is now still and silent inside a coffin.

Yet the coffin is in front of me, and I have to give at least the appearance of addressing it with dignity. I remember the advice Diana Lamplugh gave Mum about identifying the corpse of a loved one. I give the coffin quick glances, then look away. Suddenly the image of 'the remains' inside the coffin tries to enter my head. I shut it down immediately.

I'm barely aware of my parents. I can hear their voices but I'm miles away from them. I don't know what they're thinking, and it's better they don't know what is going on inside my head.

The celebrant is a kind lady, the Reverend Margaret Callow, the minister from Walton Methodist Church where Milly and I were both christened and Mum and Dad were married. The service commences with her welcome and a reading from the Scriptures. Then we sing 'Amazing Grace'. We say a prayer.

Mum speaks first. 'No one ever expects their child to die before them, least of all in such horrific circumstances. The hurt and despair are unimaginable but preferable to the not-knowing. She is safe now and no one can hurt her.' Then Mum focuses on the pleasure that Milly brought us, and especially the fun that always surrounded her. 'My beautiful lovely daughter Milly will always be remembered for her kindness, her patience, her musical ability, her wonderful personality and her fantastic sense of humour. She had a knack of being able to cheer you up if you were feeling a bit sorry for yourself.

'Sometimes, we would cry with laughter over the dinner table as Bob was trying to instil some table manners into the girls. She would spend ages trying to teach me a dance routine, which, without fail, I always managed to get wrong. Milly enjoyed baking cakes but had rather a limited repertoire of foods she liked eating. Her favourite tea being a hunk of cheese, a whole peeled cucumber and chips.

'The house feels very different without her. It is so quiet. I cannot tell you how much I miss her. She was truly full of character and she certainly made a mark during her very short lifetime. She has left an amazing legacy.'

At the end of her tribute, Mum talks about me: 'Gemsie has been very brave and we are extremely proud of her and Milly would be too. We cannot let the monster who committed this appalling act ruin Gemma's life too, so we must continue to find the strength to carry on and try to remember all the lovely times we had together because there's nothing we can do to change what has happened.'

Mum's kindness is infinite. She knows I feel guilty about being mute at this service. So she includes my contribution in her speech, reading out what I wrote on the card for Milly's bouquet. She explains first, 'One of the hardest jobs to do in the lead-up to this funeral was to write the cards for the flowers, as I'm sure you all know. When Gemma wrote her card she reduced me to tears on the spot.'

Mum manages to get through the whole thing without breaking down.

It's Dad's turn now. 'A few months before she disappeared, Milly asked me which was my favourite song. I replied that it was "In My Life" by the Beatles.' He reads the words of the song, 'which help me express my love for Milly'. He, too, is calm and does not break.

Then it's Eva Cassidy's 'I Know You By Heart'. This is when the doors in the archway open and the coffin starts to move slowly to the right. I had no idea this would happen. I don't even know why it is happening. Terror flushes through my entire body. I'm shaking. Then everyone stands, so I stand too.

How do they know what to do? Why am I the only one who doesn't understand?

The still, silent coffin was frightening enough. Seeing it move, creeping inch by inch towards the door, is unbelievably awful.

I want it out of my sight – it has scared me so much. At the same time I realize that when it leaves, Milly will be truly gone too. For one unbearable second, Milly and 'the remains' are fused in my mind. It's too late for a proper goodbye. I don't know what's beyond the doors. Instead of the healing sadness, instead of any sense of a proper farewell, my brain is jostling with inappropriate un-askable questions.

Is the fire right there beside us? Is it dark out there? Will they burn her while we're sitting here? Or will she have to be alone again after we leave?

In the end, it is not me who breaks. It's Mum.

At my side, she suddenly makes a noise that doesn't even seem human. It's loud, low and long. This awful poignant moan continues the whole time the coffin is moving relentlessly towards the door. Lovely Granny pushes me gently out of the way, rushing to take Mum in her arms. Dad's on the other side of Mum, trying to calm her. Mum's struggling against them both. It seems for a moment that she is going to throw herself on the coffin, as if she wants to be burned alongside Milly's bones.

People would say to me afterwards that they had never heard a noise like the one Mum made then, and they hoped never to hear it again.

Mum, Dad and Lovely Granny form a tight cluster. I'm left alone – like a little hedgehog caught in headlights on a deserted road. Inches away from me, the last of the coffin disappears.

A new sound comes into the chapel. It's the wordless saxophone solo that Milly's teacher has composed and recorded. It's beautiful. But it seems to me too beautiful for this ugly moment. I block it. I block our family. 'For Milly', the song is called. And Craig Rickards has written a fine work. It truly evokes her teasing, sweet spirit. Yet there's no bringing Milly back. There is no bringing our family back now.

We cannot bear it but we have to let Milly go.

We have to let her go. It is 365 days since she last woke up in the bed next to mine, 365 days since Dad last kissed her goodbye; 365 days since Mum last asked Milly if she had *really* finished her homework; 365 days since Milly wiped the chip grease and salt off her lips, shrugged her rucksack on to her left shoulder and set off for home, *Neighbours*, family dinner, homework and a midnight chat with me. It is 365 days since she encountered pure evil, a man who really isn't human, who stopped all our lives in their tracks.

A few days later, during a very emotional conversation, Auntie Linds tells Mum that at that moment she saw Milly's spirit rise from the coffin in the chapel and that she was smiling.

I so want to believe her, but it's too painful.

If only I too could have had that comforting vision.

36.

Outside the chapel, the funeral directors have set out all the flowers. We go to look at them and read the cards. Among them is a letter from Loley. She writes to Milly just as if she's talking to her.

Hello baby! I hope those angels are treating you well.

You were always there to help, after all what are best friends for? But right now I need you more than ever. So I'm trying to follow my heart and do what I think you would have told me to. If only I could see you once more, but you know what, I will. I'll see you in my dreams and in my heart where we can be together again.

We're all holding onto you, and we'll never leave you. Don't think of this as a good-bye forever, just a good-bye to this past dreadful year. I will see you again to dance, sing and laugh.

You'd better still be playing your sax. I wanna hear you play it to me again, and with me, like how we did at your Grannies. That was such an amazing week-end, just the two of us, we had such a laugh! You better remember, matey!

We had some great laughs, like all our holidays, scary theme park rides, karaoke, fast boats, the sightseeing and most important the fun we all had together.

I'm going to cling tight to all our memories and promise never to forget a single one! I could write to you for ages so instead of doing that I'll talk to you in my prayers. So listen to them!

Rest easy, beautiful, we'll be reunited again in heaven.

Love you,
Loley xxxxxxxx

There are flowers with cards from so many kind people, including heart-breaking notes from our young cousins. In their shaky childish handwriting, Daniel says, *Milly I love you and wish you were still here with us.* David writes simply, *I will always love you Milly.*

After the funeral, Mum writes to Surrey Police to thank them for all their help, especially with the police outriders, whom Milly would have loved. She asks the chief constable to thank everyone involved on the day with security, the traffic and the press. She also takes the opportunity to thank our FLOs, Alice and Jon, for their tremendous support: 'If there is any type of award I could nominate them for,' she asks, 'please let me know.'

She adds, very generously in my opinion, 'The motivation and determination of Surrey Police during this investigation has been unquestionable.'

On the same day as the funeral, Surrey Police offer a £50,000 reward for information that will help them find the person or persons responsible for Milly's murder. At this time they are homing in on Milly's clothes and possessions, which have never been found.

They list again all the items that have been mentioned so often: Milly's school uniform, her 'Pod' shoes, her customized Nokia phone, her Jansport rucksack, her keys and her purse.

Back at the end of January there had been a new flurry of police activity. The police had removed another haul of clothes from her bedroom. Then they announced that they had matched DNA found on Milly's clothing with a sample found three hundred miles away at St Paul's Church, Ryhope, on the outskirts of Sunderland, where a thief had snatched the collection tray. The DNA was found on a cup used by an accomplice who distracted the cleaner by asking for a drink of water.

Milly was found naked. So the item of clothing with the DNA match had been taken from our house.

Surrey Police released a statement, 'It's a very odd coincidence that we need to find an explanation for.'

Forty-six male members of the congregation are asked for DNA samples.

Inquiries are made as to whether anyone in Ryhope has connections with Walton.

We're deeply unhappy about the way the information is released and the slant that some sections of the press are quick to take. The *Daily Mail* writes, 'The DNA match may renew the theory that the youngster had a "dark secret" and was seeing someone none of her friends or relatives knew.' The paper also feels the need to remind readers that DNA can be harvested from hair, saliva, blood and semen.

We are so tired of these insinuations about Milly. She's dead and can't defend herself.

Now there's also much dwelling on a black top Milly bought at New Look for a Halloween party. In fact, she never wore it, but it's the item on which the police have found the DNA linked to the coffee cup in Sunderland.

The police release a picture of the black top, which makes us groan because we know how the press will fall on this garment. They won't care that it was fancy dress. They'll want to reinvent Milly as a girl who habitually wore provocative clothing. They'll prefer the theory that Milly knew the man whose DNA has been found on it.

Sure enough, the *News of the World* slants the story as best they can: 'Police find man's sweat on bodice in her bedroom.' The implication seems to be that the man was actually *in* Milly's bedroom. We ask Surrey Police to stop feeding the press words and ideas that can only make things worse for us. We feel certain that Sunderland is just a side-show and we want to know what's going on in the real investigation.

After all the publicity that rages around that top, the police eventually come to tell us that there was a mistake in the laboratory. This non-story, of course, never makes it to the newspapers, so those false impressions of Milly, generated by incompetence and spread like the wind, go uncorrected.

The police have finally dismissed as unreliable the supposed sightings of two men leading a schoolgirl across a field at Minley Woods. They explain that a team of thirty to forty officers is still working on the case, and that the incident room is still live. By this time nine thousand people have offered information, 2,700 vehicles have been checked, over five hundred items have been brought in for forensic testing and 3,300 statements have been taken. They are still working on the forty sacks of leaf matter taken from Minley Woods.

And just yards from Walton station, on the anniversary of her abduction, pupils from Heathside School hand out leaflets asking for help in tracing Milly's killer.

4.

The Waiting
March 2003 – 2010

PLAYLIST

Pink Floyd	Brain Damage
Abba	Slipping Through My Fingers
Peabo Bryson and Regina Belle	A Whole New World (*Aladdin* theme tune)
Samuel E. Wright	Under the Sea (from *The Little Mermaid*)

37.

There commences a period of waiting. Waiting for information. Waiting to resume our lives and find some kind of resolution. Waiting for justice.

What we can't know in March 2003 is that it will take another eight years before that process can even start.

Six months after the funeral and a year after Milly's body was found, the police say they are working on new leads. Yet there's nothing specific. Can it be that the media are tiring of Surrey Police's press releases? There's not much coverage.

On 28 September, the *News of the World* gives two pages to a possible link between Milly and the so-called 'Costa Killer' and rapist Tony Bromwich, also known as 'the Holloway Strangler'. Surrey Police tell the press that they are keeping our family updated about the 'Costa Killer' link. In real life, this means police inform us on a need-to-know basis, or they tell us when the press have got hold of some information.

It will be the same with the 'M25 rapist', who is also, briefly, connected to Milly's case. As is Ian Huntley, the Soham murderer, and 'the Beast', a Polish serial killer, 'the Wolfman' and 'the New Year's Day Murderer'. Their faces are printed huge in the papers, next to Milly's. For a while, the press keep the connection alive. Eventually, slowly, Surrey Police eliminate each of these men from their inquiries.

I don't want to know about these monsters. I don't want to have anything else awful to think about in 2003. For me, this is the year of Milly's funeral and nothing else. It draws to a close with no clues, no leads, no idea what happened to Milly.

Mum invites the whole family to us for a Christmas lunch. She's hoping that if we're all together it might somehow feel a little easier. But Mum, when socializing, has a cut-off point when suddenly she's had enough and urgently needs to be alone. We come up with a plan. Mum makes a life-size replica of a 'Stop/Go' traffic sign, using cardboard and a bamboo cane. I paint it red one side and green the other, then carefully add the lettering.

Everyone arrives laden with gifts and food for Christmas lunch. Mum explains the 'Stop/Go' sign rules to our guests. We eat, drink and try to be merry. It's just too hard. Mum silently holds up the 'Go' sign.

Our guests think it's a joke. They start laughing. Uncle Bree says, 'We've only been here an hour and a half, Sally.'

'Yes,' replies Mum. 'And now it's time to go.'

More tittering. I come to the rescue, warning our guests, 'If you don't go in the next few minutes Mum might well use the bamboo cane for other purposes.'

Everyone evacuates, fast.

Left alone, Mum, Dad and I cry for Milly.

We live in a vacuum. There's no news that amounts to anything.

Into the vacuum comes mischief. The *News of the World* can always be relied on to give us grim news. On 11 January 2004 it publishes a double-page spread with a life-size pencil sketch of a man with short cropped hair and a large chin. 'IS THIS MILLY'S KILLER?' the headline asks. 'The cold, staring face above could be the last thing that murdered schoolgirl Milly Dowler ever saw,' continues the story.

The portrait in the *News of the World* has been drawn by a court artist based on a psychic's description of his vision of Milly's killer. This time the psychic is Dennis McKenzie, 'the grandson of a true Romany gipsy'. He's already been 'active' in the Soham murder case.

McKenzie tells the reporter, 'Milly isn't the first child this man has killed. He's done this four times before – and he'll do it again within the next five months.' The psychic gets his information from spirit guides. They've told him that Milly's killer is white, between twenty-eight and thirty-five, with cropped brown hair and piercing, staring eyes. He has a round full face and is stockily built. He's not a loner, and does not live alone.

You can imagine how I feel when I read that Mr McKenzie's murderer lives within a fifty-mile radius of our house and that he always kills close to home.

As this is a *News of the World* story, it soon gets sexual. The psychic has intuited that Milly's killer likes his women to play dead during intercourse. His method of murder is strangulation.

We try not to read this story but get sucked into doing so.

Mr McKenzie has also been 'in contact with' Marsha McDonnell. He sees her killer too as a local man. So, not for the first or last time, Milly's face appears with Marsha's on the same page of a newspaper.

Meanwhile, the second anniversary of Milly's disappearance arrives. Surrey Police appeal to anyone who has noticed a change in behaviour by a family member. From experience, they say, someone who commits a crime like this will tell someone, unless they are a total loner. So someone knows something. 'That person has lived with that knowledge for almost two years now. The time has come for them to come forward.'

Lovely Surrey is not feeling safe, and neither am I. In broad daylight, a man tries to abduct a girl near Brooklands College, where I am studying. In April, a girl named Edel Harbison is attacked near Twickenham Green. Early in May, close to our house, a man in a car tries to block the path of a fifteen-year-old girl. He gets out of his car and follows her. She breaks into a run to escape.

Surrey Police tell us that some of the reported incidents may be attention-seeking. Milly's case is so huge: young girls may be wanting some kind of fuss.

That seems disgusting and bizarre to me.

Who would willingly court the kind of attention we've had to put up with? Don't these people know that a real girl died?

38.

On 28 May an attack leaves another girl almost dead. Kate Sheedy, who has just turned eighteen, looks remarkably like Milly. Like Milly and Marsha, Kate's an accomplished musician. Her instrument is the flute. She's been head girl at her convent school.

Like Marsha, Kate alighted from a bus near her home late at night. Her assailant appears to have stalked her in his white van. Despite its blacked-out windows, she noticed a man sitting in a white Toyota Previa with the engine running. Something about that car seemed wrong to Kate, so she crossed the road to get away. The driver suddenly revved up, performed a U-turn and ran her down, stopping the car on top of her body. Then he reversed over her, leaving her for dead. By a miracle, Kate managed to call the emergency services and her mother.

Her injuries are horrific and life-threatening, but somehow she has survived.

I'm trying to get on with being an adult. I pass my travel exams. On 1 July, I join First Choice, training to be a holiday rep specializing in looking after children. Even more than air-hostessing, this seems the ideal job for me. When I'm with children, I can lose myself in their games and their needs. I know how to make them happy. And I have no trust issues with children.

Soon I'm off to Ibiza on my first posting. I work from 10 a.m. till 10.30 p.m. I run the karaoke evening, the chocolate quiz, the mini disco and the 'Crash Out Club', a crèche. It suits me to be so busy. I even sleep, through sheer exhaustion. It's just as well I'm busy, as the resort is even less lively than Walton. I write to Mum and Dad that the food is 'well minging'.

Mum and Dad visit me there at the end of August, the same month the 'M25 rapist' is ruled out of the inquiry into Milly's murder. But now we have a mentally ill man harassing us with letters and emails that Milly is alive and working as a stripper in Eastern Europe. He mentions teen porn websites, attaching a picture of a blonde girl in transparent underwear: one of Milly's new friends.

My parents and Heathside School decide that there should be a place of reflection and celebration of Milly's life. 'Milly's Garden' opens next to Heathside's playground. Created by landscape construction students from Guildford College, it's a heart-shaped clearing with two green benches facing one another in a sociable way.

It suits Milly, the great chatterbox.

On the night of 19 August, Amélie Delagrange, a pretty French student, steps off a bus in Twickenham, not far from Walton. She's blonde, twenty-two, yet very petite and looks much younger. She's been in London just three months, improving her English. To her family and close friends, she's known as 'Lili'. When I read about that, I shall, of course, think that it sounds like 'Milly'.

Amélie misses her stop, perhaps having fallen asleep. She gets off the bus and starts walking back. CCTV captures Amélie's image at 10.01 p.m. Minutes later her bludgeoned body is found on an unlit piece of ground on Twickenham Green. She's unconscious but still breathing. Amélie is pronounced dead in hospital.

Her parents, Jean-François and Dominique, arrive from France. Their pictured grief strikes home to us. Like Station Avenue and Minley Woods, in Milly's time, Twickenham Green fills with flowers.

Five days later, police searching for clues pick up a signal transmitted by Amélie's phone. It leads them to a stretch of river near us at Walton, a mile and a half from where Milly disappeared. Under Walton Bridge police divers find Amélie's purse, keys and Walkman.

Mum and our neighbour Fiona go out for a run that morning. They run right into the police cordon. They see the divers under Walton Bridge. They don't ask. They just keep running. It's not until they get home and put the television on that they realize this search is to do with Amélie.

The press are already linking Amélie to Marsha McDonnell,

killed in February 2003, also in Twickenham, also with blows to the back of the head.

Detective Chief Inspector Colin Sutton leads the Metropolitan Police's investigation into Amélie's murder. It's known as Operation Yeaddis. Recently I heard Colin Sutton talking about the case. He said that many nights, even after a long day at work, he would drive to the scene of Amélie's murder, just hoping to find a clue in the passing cars and pedestrians, as if staring at the scene would bring some kind of revelation. And when he did so, he would spot some of his men, in their own clothes and in their own time, doing exactly the same thing. It would never be mentioned the next day at work.

At this stage we do not know exactly how important Colin Sutton will be to our lives. But we like the way he talks. We listen attentively to the statement he makes, explaining he believes that the killer must be on film, and that it's just a matter of finding out which man it is, which car he is driving.

By the third week in September, the Met is working on connections between the murders of and attacks on various girls and women in the south-west of London. Ute McDonnell confirms that she thinks the attacks on Marsha and Amélie are linked.

Colin Sutton identifies the make of white van almost certainly driven by Amélie's killer. In sifting through twenty-four thousand such vehicles, he's had two pieces of help. A woman has come forward to say that her former partner is violent and capable of killing girls. He drives just such a van. And a phone record shows that a man who drives such a van made a call to police denouncing some neighbours he did not like – as terrorists. It is the same man, and the same van.

In the early hours of 22 November 2004, the police drive up to a number of separate addresses, looking for a man who is known at all of them. One group arrives at a semi-detached council house in a cul-de-sac called Little Benty in West Drayton. The police bang on the door of number 11, shouting the man's name. When there's no answer, they use a metal battering ram to break the door down.

The man has leapt naked out of bed, run to the landing, pulled out a chest of drawers and climbed on top, opening the hatch to the attic. He hauls himself up into the roof space. As the *News of the World* will later report, the 'naked monster HID in his LOFT when cops stormed his home'. He's eventually found wrapped in a roll of insulation material.

There are pictures of the moment of capture taken by a press photographer. They will be published with the boast, 'The *News of the World* was the only paper present during the early morning raid.'

It is early o'clock – what is a newspaper photographer doing in that cul-de-sac at that time?

The pictures won't be published until much later. They will reveal a bloated man with several chins, an incongruous tuft of dark hair, a blue T-shirt and a pair of handcuffs. He's taken in for questioning. He refuses to answer. He's angry to be detained, and complaining that the loft insulation is making him itch.

There is not yet enough evidence to charge him with the murder of Amélie Delagrange. But several of the man's previous partners now come forward. There is sufficient evidence to charge him on 25 November with three rapes, which is enough to keep him detained. On 9 December he's charged with assaults on a woman in Twickenham between 1995 and 1997.

Meanwhile, the police are investigating the many cars this man has acquired and disposed of and his many mobile phone numbers, one of which is known to have been in use in Twickenham on the night that Amélie Delagrange died.

While looking through the files on the man who is his chief suspect in Amélie's murder, Colin Sutton notices something.

He makes a call to a colleague at Surrey Police.

39.

Jon rings Mum to say that the police are searching a property in Station Avenue. 'We've been made aware of an address,' he says. This is the usual phraseology – a bit pompous, a bit vague. It's what he has to say.

Jon knows that we drive past that area all the time and he doesn't want us to have any unpleasant surprises. He doesn't make a big thing of it. Neither does Mum. It's been months since we've had news that amounted to anything.

Mum's doing a school assembly for Milly's Fund that day. On her way back she passes through Station Avenue. Despite Jon's warning, shock courses through her body when she sees exactly where the police cordon is: right by the bus stop where Kat saw Milly. The red and white tape curves out in and around the hedge, into the estate called Collingwood Place, then loops out around the bus stop. There are quite a few police cars and officers.

Mum has to swerve into the wrong side of the road to avoid the obstruction. She can barely control the steering wheel. She veers to the kerb and stops the car. She takes some deep breaths. This is the most real thing that has happened in the investigation since Milly's body was found.

She phones Dad, who plays it down. He and Mum have trained themselves not to get excited about new leads. Nothing ever comes of anything – that's their experience. Mum calms herself down enough to drive home. But when she's there, she phones everyone: Lovely Granny, Uncle Pete, Uncle Bree, the Dobbos.

There's no doubt in Mum's mind that whoever lived in that flat in Collingwood Place is the man who took Milly. There's no doubt in my mind either. Only Dad stays cautious, afraid of investing too much in what might turn out to be yet another false lead.

Mum goes back to look at the photographs of Milly's funeral, when the cortège passed that hedge at Collingwood Place. Lovely Granny had ordered copies of the press photographs, which show me, Mum and Dad walking behind Milly's coffin at the exact place where the cordon now hides the police search.

Mum wants to know everything about what is going on at Collingwood Place. Wanting answers and getting them are not the same thing. With Surrey Police, our role has always been to give answers, often disbelieved.

But now we have questions that will not wait.

Alice and Jon come to see us. No, they can't tell us the name of the person who lives in the house being searched. They say there are new people in the property since Milly was taken.

Mum asks, 'So who *was* living there in March 2002? Do you know?'

Yes, they know. No, they can't tell us the name.

'You'll only look it up,' they say. What they mean is, *You'll go too far and get into trouble.*

We get one small piece of information to work over. Number 24 Collingwood Place is a rental property. The same sofa is still there from the time when Milly was taken. Fibres are being removed from it as part of a full forensic sweep. We wait in an agony of impatience, all the while knowing how painfully slow everything to do with an investigation is likely to be.

Alice phones Mum, who is driving.

'Suggest you pull in,' says Alice.

Alice tells Mum that the former partner of the tenant of Collingwood Place has come forward. There's a lot of work to be done, Alice tells her, but there's now reason to suspect that this is the man who abducted and murdered Milly.

Alice gets to us with the information just hours before the press break it.

It is still a huge shock.

The *Daily Mail*'s headline on 27 November is 'Suspect's link to Milly. Man quizzed over murder lived yards from where schoolgirl vanished'. It's confirmed that Surrey Police are liaising with officers from Operation Yeaddis, the investigation into Amélie's murder. We're told about various places being searched, including a lock-up somewhere. We're brought a couple of hairbands from the lock-up.

We don't think they are Milly's. What we don't know is that police have now moved diggers into the garden of the man's house at Little Benty, and they are digging up every inch of it. They cannot be looking for Milly's body but perhaps they are worried about other missing girls, looking for items belonging to murder victims.

Of course we wonder why it has taken two and a half years to make the connection between the man at Collingwood Place and Milly. Was this man not questioned by Surrey Police in their door-to-door inquiries immediately after she disappeared? He still lived there then.

We ask ourselves the same questions, over and over again.

Where did he go?

How could he have slipped through the net?

But Surrey Police are still following an official line, saying that the murders of Milly, Amélie and Marsha are not formally linked. They say Collingwood Place is only one of several sites they are searching in relation to Milly.

Given how it makes them look – the connection between Milly and Collingwood Place – I'm sure they want to play it down.

40.

We're still getting sacks of post from well-wishers. Even if the address says simply 'Dowlers – Walton', it still arrives. Yet not everyone wishes us well. Being well known attracts obsessives and troubled people. It also attracts malice.

Walton's close community tries to take care of us. This includes both the local sorting office and our lovely postman. Before he delivers, Chris checks our mail for anything that looks suspicious. He makes sure to hand anything like that not to me but to Dad or Mum. He gives some items straight to the police to check.

But on 29 November, all our safety nets fail.

It happens when I am in a reasonably good state. I've recently returned from six months in Ibiza. It's been healing to work with happy children, to be in the sun, to be away from tragedy and among holidaymakers who have no idea whose sister I am. I'm tanned. I've been swimming in the sea. I am starting, at last, to feel comfortable in my skin. There are glimpses of the Gemma that Milly would remember.

When I come home, it's not just Mum and Dad waiting for me. Milly would adore the latest member of our family – a cream-coloured Cocker Spaniel. Holly, our old Springer Spaniel, brought so much joy to our household and Mum hopes that a new pet will do the same. Dad has taken some convincing. Mum and I listed pros and cons for the acquisition. On the pro side are 'lap-loves' and 'wagability' to make us happy.

Dad gives in, of course.

Mum doesn't write this down, but the dog is also intended to open up our world a bit. A dog needs walks. That will get us out of the house.

We call her 'Maisy' – the only name Dad will accept from the list Mum and I prepare. He absolutely refuses to call 'Pebble', 'Splash' or 'Sprinkles' in public. The puppy's name, of course, sounds a lot like Milly's, which wasn't intentional yet is actually rather nice. In fact, Lovely Granny sometimes gets their names confused, and calls for Milly when she means Maisy.

Maisy turns out to be nothing like Holly. She won't sit on anyone's lap, sulks ferociously and takes seven months to house-train. She gets herself banned from the grooming parlour for bad behaviour. Every single night, Maisy wets her bed. Our vet tells us that he thinks she needs psychiatric help.

Mum says, *'Even the dog?* Is there no one sane in this house?'

Of course we love her all the same.

On 29 November, I'm at home puppy-sitting Maisy. Dad's at work. Mum's doing a Milly's Fund presentation at Scotland Yard. I'm watching television when the post arrives at about 11 a.m. I pick up the bundle of letters and take it back to the lounge.

I hear my phone ringing in the kitchen and get up to answer it. First my attention's drawn to a white envelope addressed to 'Mrs and Miss Dowler'. There's something strange about the envelope. The writing is messy and hard to read. The shape seems to indicate a card. Yet it's nobody's birthday in our family.

I carry it into the kitchen where I answer the phone. It's Mum. She's just about to give her speech. While chatting to her, I start opening the letter. It's handwritten on prison letterhead. The logo is HM Prison, Liverpool. I ask, 'Mum, why would a prisoner be writing to us?'

Mum says quickly, 'Don't read it, Gemma!'

It's too late. My eyes are already scanning the page.

The writer says he wants to tell Mum that he has nothing to do with Milly's murder. But he hopes one day that their daughter Gemma will also disappear and stay missing so long that, if she's ever found, it will be impossible to identify her body.

'Mum,' I say, 'he hopes I'll go missing like Milly.'

Mum tries to persuade me that I must be reading it wrong, and that he hopes I *won't* go missing. Yet worry's tensing her voice. She's at least an hour and a half away, with a speech to deliver at Scotland Yard. She knows Dad's in Stevenage, two hours' drive from home. She says she's going to phone Alice. She tells me I should call Lovely Granny.

I keep scanning the letter. He's demanding a large sum of money, or he will kill me. I shout at Mum, 'You must pay him. You've got to pay him. Mum, he's going to kill me.'

Then I arrive at a sentence that will haunt me for the rest of my life.

The writer says that he's really looking forward to skinning me alive and cutting off my nipples. He wants to cut me up in tiny pieces and leave them all over the country, so no one will ever be able to put me together again.

I can't say the words aloud. So Mum has no idea how terrible the letter is. I'm still shouting, 'Mum, he's coming to get me!'

Mum doesn't understand what I'm crying about. Keeping her on the line, I try Granny's home line with the other phone. There's no answer.

'Try her mobile,' says Mum.

I say goodbye to Mum and promise to dial Lovely Granny on my mobile.

There's no answer there either.

I call Maisy into the house. I lock and bolt all the doors. If this man is coming to kill me, I'm not going to get taken unawares, like Milly was. This letter has triggered all the fears I've tried to put away through years of hard-working therapy. I might as well not have done them. My attempt to establish self-control is useless. I'm going into shock. I'm hyperventilating. I start to scream.

Still screaming, I dial Mum again on my mobile. Gasping out the words, I tell Mum that the letter is threatening my life, but I don't give her any details. I still can't say those things aloud.

Mum's struggling to understand what I'm saying. Now the land-line is ringing. It's Lovely Granny. I shriek, 'Lovely Granny, you must come round! Now!'

My words come out garbled with tears. Lovely Granny can't make out what I'm saying. She just understands that I'm in distress. She's too upset to drive and too afraid to hang up on me. So she uses her mobile to call Uncle Pete to bring her over. Uncle Pete rings me on his mobile, and I try to tell him what's in the letter. It comes out in incoherent whimpers and cries. He keeps saying, 'Gemma, calm down. I can't understand what you're saying.'

'Get here, for God's sake!' I scream. 'Someone's trying to kill me!'

The doorbell rings.

Trembling, I rush to look through the letterbox. It's Alice and

Jon outside. Jon's so tall I can see only his tie and shirt. He leans down to talk to me through the letterbox.

'It's us, Gemma,' he says, in his reassuring Dad-like voice. 'We're here to look after you. Let us in.'

But I'm in a delusional state. I don't trust even Jon and Alice. I think that the killer has got to them and they've come to help him finish me off. The letter's on official prison letterhead. I believe this man has the authorities under his control. And I'm here alone.

It takes Alice a long time to persuade me to open the door. Then I won't let them near me.

Jon asks, 'Gemma, where's the letter?'

I point to it mutely. I cannot touch it any more. It's as if it has potency of its own and can transmit images of my fear to the killer, telling him what I'm doing.

Jon pulls on gloves and puts the letter in a forensic bag. The words are still visible through the plastic. They can still hurt me.

Lovely Granny and Uncle Pete arrive. I've neglected my puppy-sitting duties so they have to carefully step over the puddles on the kitchen floor. I'm too exhausted to talk, so Alice and Jon brief them. Lovely Granny asks Alice to go to the doctor's surgery for diazepam. I'm desperate for some relief from the panic, so when Alice gets back with it, I swallow it obediently.

By this time, Lovely Granny's set me up on the sofa in the music room, wrapped in a blanket with Taily Ted tucked in beside me. The diazepam shuts me down. I don't have the energy to protest any more. I am wearily relieved to be out of the grip of my panic attack.

So I don't see Lovely Granny reading the letter inside the transparent evidence bag. She will never tell me what she thinks about the content. To this day, that is an off-limits subject.

For eighteen months, without even knowing it, our family has been subjected to a campaign of hate letters from this prisoner. This is the only letter that gets through. The rest are intercepted before they leave the prison or are caught by our lovely postman and given to Surrey Police. *They* haven't felt the need to tell Mum and Dad because they think, as usual, that they have the situation under control.

The source of the letters is a paedophile named Paul Hughes, who's serving a fifty-six-month sentence for a violent assault on a twelve-year-old girl. He'd previously been convicted of indecently assaulting a very young girl over several years, for which he received only a probation order. In April 1999 he was convicted of making threats to kill, obscene phone calls and sending letters to his young female victim. He told her she would get 'knifed'.

In 2002 Paul Hughes received not the maximum sentence of ten years but only five.

While in prison, he became obsessed with Milly's case. He could not have killed Milly because at the time of her disappearance he was two hundred miles away at a probation office in Warrington. However, he wrote at least ten letters saying that he did and insisting that he was going to do the same to me.

Given that the others were intercepted, you'd think that a special supervision would be kept on Hughes's outgoing correspondence. But it appears that he was able to get this letter through the prison's screening process by a simple ruse. He put it in an ordinary envelope rather than using the usual prison-issue one, then seems to have passed it on to a prisoner to put in another wing's post box. It's not rocket science, is it? But it was cleverer than the prison service.

Mum's police statement says:

I found the contents to be absolutely sickening and extremely distressing. The fact he wrote about wanting to kill Gemma was bad enough but the graphic description of what he would like to do to her dead body was both shocking and utterly vile . . .

As a result of this letter, Gemma has suffered what I consider to be an immeasurable setback. Her symptoms include severe anxiety, fear of being left alone, inability to sleep at night and the onset of terrifying graphic mental images brought on by the description given in the p.s. of the letter. Since Gemma's sister Milly was abducted and murdered in March 2002 Gemma has feared the perpetrator will get her too. This sick and depraved letter has heightened her level of fear and her life can only be compared to a living nightmare.

Mum and Dad also write directly to the governor of HMP Liverpool:

The questions we need answered are as follows:

1. *How is it possible for us to receive a letter of this nature from a prisoner?*
2. *Why wasn't it checked, especially as we understand that the prisoner in question has done this type of thing before?*
3. *How can someone who openly writes about his desire to skin a young girl and cut off her nipples etc ever be released back into society?*

By this time, our family has learned more about the darker side of human nature. We know better than to expect that this psychopath will be sorry for what he has done. So Mum and Dad conclude the letter:

We hope that Paul Hughes can be kept unaware of the distress that this letter has caused because we feel quite sure that someone as sick, depraved and perverted as he is will find the thought of our pain and anguish immensely satisfying.

Lovely Granny writes her own letter to the prison governor about the effect of the letter on me.

Medically, I think it could take at least six months to anywhere near repair the damage . . . I cannot put into words how angry I am. After all this family has been through, that letter, something that could have been avoided, has so carelessly happened. Please do not mention this man's human rights to me, as to have human rights, surely you have to be human first.

41.

When you read the chapter about the day Milly went missing, I'm sure you knew there was something important about Uncle Bree's close encounter with a bulky confrontational man in Collingwood Place the night Milly disappeared.

With the help of Colin Sutton, Surrey Police have finally joined the dots. So on 19 December 2004, the police take Uncle Bree back to Collingwood Place. They make him retrace his steps so he can provide a new statement about what he saw. They press him for details about the appearance of the man and his dog, the location of the door where the aggressive-looking man paused and the numbers of the flats concerned.

Thirty-two months after that night, Uncle Bree, whose observations at the time were not considered important, is suddenly under pressure to exhibit a photographic and faultless memory. He does his best, but it isn't easy.

We're desperate to know what the man from Collingwood Place looks like. It's even possible that we know him by sight. Mum could have taught him or his children, for all we know. Maybe we would recognize him from an event we'd been to. Maybe he has even been involved in something to do with the charity – all terrifying thoughts.

We ask Surrey Police if we can see a photo. The answer, inevitably, is no. Both the name and the face of the man who lived at Collingwood Place are still being withheld from the press. We have no more status than the press, and fewer resources.

Mum tries again with Alice, who makes it clear that she is really, really, really not allowed to tell us anything more at this stage. Poor Alice. This must be torture for her. All we can be told is that the man who lived at Collingwood Place in March 2002 is in the custody of the Metropolitan Police and is being investigated for crimes under their jurisdiction. This means that Surrey Police are not yet allowed to question him about Milly.

As the third anniversary of her disappearance approaches, Surrey Police release their usual tally of statistics on the Milly Dowler case. They don't seem to see the irony in these huge numbers. Not one of the 4,288 statements they have taken so far has made any difference. The only lead that has any relevance whatsoever is the one that came from Colin Sutton at the Met about the man who lived at Collingwood Place.

Alice and Jon reassure us that the Met are 'building their case'. Our sympathies go out to the Delagrange family, who must be waiting in an agony of impatience that we know only too well.

One new piece of information emerges. There's now a car, as well as a man and an address, in the picture. Three years on, FBI-enhanced CCTV images from the Birds Eye building have revealed a red N-registration Daewoo Nexia. It's recorded parked near the station half an hour before Milly vanished, then again later driving away, with just one person inside. The car, too, has vanished and the police think it might have been disposed of – for example, by crushing.

On 13 March, the *Sunday Mirror* has a headline on page 7, 'Milly Murder: DID KILLER USE AN N-REG DAEWOO TO GET RID OF BODY?'

Mum and Dad look at the images of the Daewoo car, wondering if Milly's body lies unseen in the boot. Despite only one person aboard, the car sits low on its springs, as if heavily laden. They have the necessary awful conversation and conclude that Milly could not have weighed down the boot – she was far too slight.

The Times makes the link on 15 March. Their crime correspondent writes, 'A serial killer may be responsible for the murder of schoolgirl Amanda "Milly" Dowler and the killings of Marsha McDonnell and Amélie Delagrange.' The same man, the paper writes, may also be responsible for attacks on four young women in south-west London in the past three years.

The next day the *Evening Standard* links the same serial killer to the hit-and-run attack on Kate Sheedy on 28 May 2004. Kate Sheedy is the girl who looks so much like Milly that it made us jump. She's made an amazing recovery from injuries sustained when a man in a white people-carrier ran her over, then reversed back on her body.

We release a statement through the police to mark the third year since Milly went missing. Mum and Dad don't want to appear ungrateful now that it looks as if something might really be happening at last:

> The anniversary of Milly's disappearance is always an extremely poignant time. This year her friends have embarked upon their A Levels and watching them grow up and start to think about their futures is a constant reminder of what Milly might have been doing now.
>
> Three years on, we would urge anyone to come forward with any information that may help Surrey Police with their investigation. We need to know the name and see the face of the person who murdered our beautiful daughter. It feels like a very painful waiting game but one day we feel confident that the diligence and hard work of the police will pay off.

By the end of April, the police report that more than four hundred people contacted them about the red car. They're optimistic about finding Milly's killer.

All these people are coming forward now, three years later, so the number does not give us any kind of hope. We are dubious and sceptical.

On 21 May, the lead suspect in Amélie's killing is granted bail for the murder but remains in custody on suspicion of rape. He's listed as 'of no fixed abode'.

This is the first time we see his name.

It is Levi Bellfield.

42.

Knowing Bellfield's name does not help. We can do nothing. We're not allowed to ask Surrey Police about him. We're not supposed to talk about him to anyone else.

He is not the only paedophile in our world, unfortunately.

The case comes to court of Paul Hughes, author of the death-threat letter to me. There's no way that I am going to give evidence. I cannot be in the same room as that man. I can't afford to have him seem so real. So, on the same day, I leave for my summer posting in Gran Canaria, to spend time helping families with children to enjoy themselves and keep safe. Mum and Dad don't attend the trial either. Even the police think it's not necessary to put them through that. My identity is to be kept out of the press.

The defendant is found guilty and sentenced to five years.

The Home Office has launched a high-level investigation into how Hughes was able to send the letter from prison. For all its 'high-level' status, the investigation comes up with an explanation that does not sit well with us: 'human error'. Hughes claims he thought the letters would never get through. He admits that the letters were 'disgusting' but excuses himself on the grounds that he was going through 'a bad patch'.

Bad patch? *Bad patch?* Our whole lives have been a bad patch since March 2002. In Hughes's statement you see the thing that distinguishes a psychopath from a human being: an utter lack of empathy. Other people are not real to psychopaths. Other people's pain may even be something to enjoy.

I'm not doing well in Gran Canaria. I manage my job, but every time I leave the pleasant chaos of the Kids' Club, I fall apart. I don't feel secure. A holiday rep has been drugged and raped. I'm afraid to go out. I drink alone in my room, trying to blot out my feelings about events at Guildford Crown Court. I phone Mum all the time, in tears.

My apartment's in a dodgy area a good twenty minutes from the hotel. Finishing late in the evening after the mini disco, I'm terrified by my walk home alone. My flatmates are rarely there. I'm determined to make a go of it, however, and I do – until something happens that means it is no longer bearable to stay.

On 15 May, a picture of me and Milly appears on the front of the *Sunday Express* with the headline, 'HATE MAIL ORDEAL OF MILLY'S FAMILY'. The paper has applied to overturn a judge's order forbidding my naming as the girl targeted by Paul Hughes. In an editorial, the paper claims to respect my privacy and our family's suffering, and that 'Our heart, like that of everyone in the nation, goes out to them.' Then the paper justifies itself:

> *But it is our duty to tell in full how a prisoner was allowed the freedom to terrorize a citizen. Gemma was let down badly by the prison service. The publicity generated by revealing the story may stop such a terrible occurrence happening again and causing more suffering.*

The other papers profit from the 'duty' performed by the *Express*. My name and photo are on the television news too. Mum and Dad warn me not to read the papers that arrive in Gran Canaria, or to look on the internet. There's every chance that a picture of Paul Hughes might be in the paper, next to mine.

Of course I look.

Mum and Dad have to get on the next plane to Gran Canaria and bring me home.

In June, I have an interview with British Airways for a position as a customer services agent. I get the job. It seems such a triumph at the time, something like a turning point.

In July, at the Hampton Court Palace Flower Show, Mum and Dad exhibit a garden in aid of Milly's Fund. It wins the Tudor Rose award for Best Show Garden and the Royal Horticultural Society Gold Medal.

Mum has always loved sweet peas. She has grown them since she was a little girl. And they were Milly's favourite flowers, which is why we carried bouquets of them to her memorial service back in October 2002. In the Milly's Fund garden there are sweet peas galore, of course.

Feeling buoyed up by the success of the garden, Mum approaches

Matthewman Sweet Peas of Leeds with the idea of naming a flower after Milly. It turns out that Matthewman have been inundated with inquiries about the varieties we've used in the Milly's Fund garden. Moreover, David and Pauline Matthewman have a new variety that is as yet unnamed. They agree then and there to call this new sweet pea 'Milly'.

Thousands of people visit the Milly's Fund garden. One of them is Kate Sheedy, who comes with her grandparents. She asks if they may speak to Mum.

It's a deeply emotional moment between the two families. Then Kate's grandfather says, 'Don't you think Milly and Kate look similar?'

Mum stares at Kate. There she is, a beautiful, extremely well-spoken young lady, who has suffered and survived unbelievable damage.

Well, yes, Mum thinks, *I certainly do think they look similar.*

But Mum's barely able to speak to Kate – she's so scared of Surrey Police saying that she shouldn't be talking to a witness. At least she can give the tall, slim girl a hug.

In September Milly's Fund is amalgamated with the Suzy Lamplugh Trust. Mum's raised over £800,000 and has done what she set out to do, producing a safety video called *Watch Over Me* for mass circulation in secondary schools. There's also been a campaign called Teach UR Mum 2 TXT, encouraging parents and their teenagers to keep in touch by mobile.

Meanwhile the kindness and generosity of so many members of the public who donated or raised money is beginning to restore Mum's faith in human nature.

43.

It is not until 2 March 2006 – fourteen months after that dawn arrest – that Levi Bellfield is charged with Amélie Delagrange's killing on 20 August 2004 and the attempted murder of two other women, Kate Sheedy on 28 May 2004 and Irma Dragoshi on 16 December 2003, as well as the attempted abduction and false imprisonment of a fourth woman, Anna-Maria Rennie, on 15 October 2001. The police have managed to keep him in prison all this time because of various rape charges. Keeping him in prison has meant that his partners have felt safe to talk about him.

Bellfield speaks only to confirm his name and date of birth. When remanded in custody, he applauds.

For the fourth anniversary of Milly's disappearance, Lovely Granny gives an interview to the *Surrey Informer*. The journalist there has cultivated a friendship with Lovely Granny via a mutual appreciation of her dog, Scrumpy. She tells him how she sometimes drives her car to the place where Milly was last seen. She parks and watches children walking home down Station Avenue, as Milly did.

> *I sit there and hope that something will come to me, but it doesn't. I look at the schoolchildren and see what they do, but it doesn't give me inspiration . . . I want to know, if someone took her, how they did it. But it doesn't get me anywhere . . . March is a bad month but you know it's coming. You just have to get through it, don't you?*

Another journalist who calls on Lovely Granny does not get his story. He gets a sore ear instead. His mistake is to approach her with the words, 'Are you Milly's nanny?'

He's informed, 'Milly never had a nanny. A nanny is a *goat*.'

The reporter is dismissed. Lovely Granny's not going to waste her time with someone too inept to know the difference between a goat and a grandmother.

*

On 25 May, Bellfield is charged with the murder of Marsha McDonnell.

So now five attacks on girls are linked to him. We have known – since the search of Collingwood Place – that he's also linked to Milly's disappearance. We are sure that Milly should be on Bellfield's charge sheet too.

Surrey Police, however, are behind the Metropolitan Police in the queue for Bellfield. The Met got there first with their arrest and their charges, even though most of those crimes post-date Milly's murder. Via Surrey Police, we hear that the Crown Prosecution Service considers Milly the 'weak link' in the chain that leads to Bellfield. Unlike the other girls, Milly wasn't found until six months after her death so her body yielded no forensic evidence. This means that the case against Bellfield for her murder can be proved only by five-year-old circumstantial evidence. The CPS doesn't want to compromise Bellfield's trial for the other murders, for which Colin Sutton at the Met has accumulated good evidence. Moreover, the attacks on Marsha, Amélie and Kate were quite different from whatever happened to Milly.

So justice for Milly – and justice for us – will have to wait until Bellfield has been tried for the later murders. It is so hard to accept this, but we have no choice.

The case against Bellfield for the attempted abduction of Anna-Maria Rennie in 2001 is important to us, however, because, if proved, it will show he has a history of trying to snatch a girl before Milly vanished.

We have still not seen Bellfield's face. We're trying to keep our memory of Milly safe from images like that. I'm trying to preserve my old image of a dark figure with no face. A face would make it worse.

Instead, at the end of May, we celebrate the launch of the beautiful magenta sweet pea named in her honour. Now the flower – simply called 'Milly' – lights up the Chelsea Flower Show with a magnificent display. It will be in full bloom for Milly's birthday on 25 June. And twenty pence from every packet of ten seeds will go to the Suzy Lamplugh Trust.

Mum tells the press, 'It is such a lively, vibrant flower – it has lots of Milly's characteristics.'

Here, at last, is a photo-call that we can enjoy. There's a genuine smile on my face as I pose in front of Milly's sweet pea, and real pleasure in Mum's as she takes a deep breath of the fragrance.

One visitor is Alan Titchmarsh, the television gardener. He's already come to see Mum's garden at home, and is such a gentleman that he's managed to forgive me for accidentally serving him stone-cold tea that day. He gives the 'Milly' sweet pea a lovely mention on *Gardeners' World*.

Mum plans to twine our own Milly sweet peas up one of the black iron obelisks that were a birthday present from Lovely Granny the year Milly was taken from us.

In September, another cruel hoaxer revisits our life. This is Gary Farr, who sent obscene emails to my parents, claiming that Milly's disappearance was a cover-up – and that she was alive and well, and working for the Polish Mafia in Gdansk as a stripper. For this, the English teacher had appeared in court in August 2003 and was bound over to keep the peace for two years. But in August 2004, he started again, also targeting a couple who had the same surname as one of Milly's friends, as well the chief executive at the Suzy Lamplugh Trust.

His lawyer tells the court that he became obsessed with Milly's case. It appears, however, that Farr was also hoping for a share of the generous reward money out there for information about Milly. This month he admits harassment. The court is told that he has a history of paranoid schizophrenia. He's sectioned indefinitely under the Mental Health Act.

We don't go to court. We have no wish to see this man or to hear more of his emails. It appears that the magistrates have the same idea. After hearing some extracts from his correspondence, they ask the prosecution to stop reading them out.

Meanwhile, something is changing at last for the better at Surrey Police, as far as we are concerned. There's a new officer in charge of the investigation into Milly's murder. Her name is Maria Woodall. A game-changer, this woman is not egotistical like some of the male officers we've encountered. In fact, she's been on the case since the beginning, but not in a senior capacity. So we have not met her until now.

She comes to our house to introduce herself. We see a slim blonde woman, extremely attractive, with a pleasant voice. We find that we are able to chat with her. Maria Woodall is a dog-lover, with a new dog of her own. That doesn't stop Maisy barking at her, but they soon become friends. This is a good sign.

The thing about Maria Woodall is that she answers our questions as fully and frankly as she can. That's new for us. The usual response to one of our questions has been 'I'll take that away and get back to you'. Maria gives us answers, even if they are horrible or hurtful. But the real differences between her and the other senior officers we've dealt with seem to be that she is hell-bent on bringing Milly's murderer to justice – and she knows categorically that it isn't Dad.

Those two things raise her a gigantic level above her predecessors in our estimation. There won't be any more time-wasting. There will be progress. We just know that.

And, apart from anything else, Maisy likes her.

We all do.

44.

On the fifth anniversary of Milly's disappearance, I write her a letter.

Dear Milly,

I am writing to you five years down the line and it still feels like yesterday that I lost you . . .

I loved you so so much and I will never stop loving you. Everything is different without a sister. I'm not sure I can cope without you anymore. I can't cope without a best friend, maid of honour, an auntie, and most of all a sister. I miss the way you used to make up funny songs and poems which would always make me laugh. I miss our midnight chats . . .

I wish my memories would come back as I can't remember what happened on the day you went missing. What kind of sister does that make me? None of this is your fault. You were just in the wrong place at the wrong time. I know that but that doesn't make it OK. I am sorry you were left all on your own in that horrible wood. It was really scary when I went to see it. Like the trees were whispering to me. Like they all had eyes and had seen it all happen . . .

Life no longer seems to have any relevance; there is never anything to look forward to. The sunshine has gone and now every day seems to be a rainy day. I have dreams about you nearly every night but I end up dreaming that you have come back. Then it's like someone ripping your heart out when you're still alive. There is always an empty chair at the dinner table . . .

I've begun to work again, as a business travel consultant at Ian Allan in Shepperton. I had spent the two previous years at British Airways, as a customer service agent at Heathrow. I've always wanted to work for BA, but I can't follow my dream of being an air hostess. I need to be close to home, and to Mum. In the end, I find I can't deal with shift-work either because it means driving in the dark to the airport. I cannot face going outside the house, alone, in the middle of the night.

The new job in Shepperton is ordinary office hours, and only ten minutes from home.

At BA, I made a friend for the first time in ages. Lauren and I stay close, even when I change jobs. She's a little younger than me, with a Milly-like sense of the ridiculous. Lauren's traffic-stoppingly beautiful, yet completely unaware of it. She's also truly stylish. We get on really well.

The only problem is that Lauren lives very close to Minley Woods, where Milly's body was found. I try not to think about that when I go to stay with her.

Two weeks after I start my new job, on 13 May 2007, the *Sunday Times* prints an article about 'the main suspect' in Milly's murder. Illustrated with a photo of Milly, the story does not name or show the man, but it explains he has a track record of violent sex offences. It also states that he was living not far from Walton station at the time she went missing.

The internet is my best friend and my worst enemy. It's easy to work out that this suspect is the same man who is about to stand trial for the murders of Marsha McDonnell and Amélie Delagrange. So I know why they can't name him in the article: it could prejudice the trial. For the same reason, his picture is still not out there.

Meanwhile, there's another lost girl in the news. On 3 May, little Madeleine McCann disappears from her bed at a holiday resort in Portugal. Her parents are on the news, begging for information about her. I look at the anguished faces of Kate and Gerry McCann. I hope they won't have to wait as long as we still are to find out exactly what has happened to their daughter. Like us, this family has to expose its vulnerability to the media because they need the media's help. I can see what it's costing them, these decent, intelligent people, who love their beautiful daughter and cannot bring themselves to believe that she may be lost to them.

Lauren and I attend the Concert for Diana, and are invited to a lunch there with Prince Harry. Afterwards I write a thank-you letter: 'I think you and your brother were very brave organizing such a huge event and I think your Mum would be immensely proud of you both.'

The next day, Lauren, her sister and I fly off for a girly break in Crete. I feel as if I am doing well. I feel as if I am doing a really good impression of someone who is normal, someone who is coping with the fact that Bellfield's trial is soon to start.

Then a reminder of the truth comes out of nowhere.

45.

It's 27 July 2007, a Friday night. I'm out with Lauren and a few friends in Fleet, a small town a stone's throw from Minley Woods. I'm enjoying myself. I'm not minding how many drinks I have while we tell everyone about our holiday in Crete. The evening starts in a bar. Later we progress to a club. It's hot inside. I want some air. I try to tell Lauren where I'm going, but the music's too loud.

Outside on the street, I realize she hasn't followed me. I'm alone in the dark, past midnight, on a narrow lane. Something washes through me. It's a sudden shattering sense of loss, as if the happiness switch has suddenly been flicked off. My sense of safety jumps over a cliff. I start to sweat. My heart judders around like a battery toy.

How could I be so stupid as to lose Lauren in the crowd?

That makes me angry.

What if Lauren is really lost to me?

That makes me desolate. Just thinking that makes the loss real. *My friend, who is so much like Milly. My friend, the only person I've been that close to since Milly. She's gone. I shall never have a friend like Milly. Perhaps I'll never have a real friend again.*

Instead of doing the sensible thing, and going back in to find Lauren, I drop to the pavement with my back to the wall. The panic rises. I can't do anything to help myself.

I can no longer suppress my thoughts about Minley Woods, only a few miles away. The emotions of Minley Woods mix with the pain of lost Lauren. I lose control of my breathing.

By the time Lauren comes to find me, only five minutes later, I'm crying so much that I can't even see her properly. I recognize her by her voice. Lauren asks, 'Gemma, where have you been? What's happened?'

It's too late to bring myself down now. I can't talk. I can't even breathe.

Lauren takes my hands and pulls me to my feet. With her arm around me, she guides me to the taxi rank a few yards away. But it's empty. We sit on the bench together.

This panic attack is different from all the old ones. It's accompanied by new hallucinations. I'm at the scene of Milly's murder. I'm with her, but the killer cannot see me. This scene is much more real to me than the road in Fleet and my friend beside me. I see a man grabbing Milly in Station Avenue. It's the same shadowy man who was always hiding in the hedge outside our house. I scream at him to stop it, to let my sister go. He just drags her away. He can't hear my screams or he doesn't care about them.

Lauren, however, can hear my screams, and so can other people in Fleet high street. People are staring. They probably think I'm drunk. I gasp, 'Lauren, I need a paper bag to breathe into.'

Army barracks are just outside this town, and there's a lot of Friday-night drinking here. As a precaution, an ambulance makes regular late-night patrols of the streets. By chance, one arrives now. Lauren runs to flag it down.

At first I'm calmed by the sight of the ambulance and the uniformed staff, a woman and a man, who seem to be the same age as my parents. But I'm still voicing my hallucination, pleading and crying, 'Don't take Milly!'

Following some kind of protocol, the man shuts Lauren in the front passenger seat to question her about what drugs I'm on. The woman turns to me. She also assumes I'm on a drug trip. She doesn't have any sympathy to spend on me. 'What have you taken?' she shouts. 'How much?'

I cannot answer this aggression. Now I'm worried that the man in the front is going to take Lauren away. I run to the door and pull at it, screaming, 'Let her out!'

The back doors of the ambulance open. The woman orders me to get in. I yell, 'Has Bellfield sent this ambulance? Is this his way? Is this how he's going to get me? Are you helping him?'

She pushes me in. From inside, I can hear Lauren explaining to the man about what happened to Milly. The woman, who has now shut the doors, also hears. I put my hand on her arm. 'Can you please help Milly? Can you stop him hurting her?'

'But is she on drugs?' the man persists.

'No,' says Lauren. 'Don't you understand? This is her life.'

As the ambulance revs up to drive, I'm seeing myself in the murderer's car. He's finished Milly off. Her body is slumped beside mine. There's no blood but she's absolutely gone. And now the murderer is driving us both to Minley Woods, so close to where we are.

Even though I know Milly's dead, I keep trying to wake her up. 'Milly, come on! I'm here!'

The murderer cannot see me, so I still think I can save her.

The woman tries to clamp an oxygen mask on my face to help with my breathing. She doesn't understand that I believe she's working for Milly's murderer and that she wants to smother me.

'This is a situation that everyone needs to know about! It's got to be stopped!' I keep screaming, wanting to attract attention, and help.

The woman tries to bring me back to earth by asking routine questions about my address and age. Lauren has to answer as I'm miles and years from Fleet, from the ambulance, from 2007. I'm back in 2002, somewhere near Station Avenue in Walton-on-Thames, and my sister is being murdered.

The ambulance staff are so alarmed that the man phones Mum and asks her what he should do to calm me down.

Ten minutes later, we're at Frimley Hospital. They open the ambulance doors. The man, the woman and Lauren take my arms to help me out. From the door aperture I see a massive tree by the entrance to the hospital. Bellfield's standing behind it. He jeers at me, 'I knew I could get you here. Do you really think you're safe? You're so stupid, if you think these people are going to protect you. The minute you step out of that ambulance, I'm going to get you.'

As he tells me these things, I repeat them aloud. But my voice is blurred by weeping, and my breathing is still out of control. No one can make out what I'm saying.

A doctor comes to meet the ambulance. He takes Lauren into the entrance of the hospital. She goes out of my sight.

'He's out there!' I scream. 'Where's Lauren? Has he got her?'

'She's with the doctor,' the woman tells me.

I cling to the seat in the ambulance. Eventually they prise me loose and put me in a wheelchair. My head is in my hands, and I'm weeping, 'He *will* get us, you know. This is just what he wants.'

The ambulance crew still believe that this panic attack has been exacerbated by my taking illicit drugs, so the hospital won't give me medication to tranquillize me. They wheel me into a small room with a large air-conditioning duct in the ceiling.

My hallucination expands to a new chapter. Bellfield is in the duct, crawling on his hands and knees towards me. He's watching from above. He's got me just where he wants me. A doctor enters the room. I shriek at him, 'Get the hell away from me! You're part of Bellfield's team, aren't you? He's got you all working for him. I know. Well, you're not going to get me! I'm not Milly. I'm not going to disappear without a trace. I will scream until the fucking end!'

The doctor looks petrified. Part of me can see the effect of my terrible words, even while another part is living the uncontrollable terror.

He flees.

Mum, Dad and Lauren now come into the room. Lauren is ashen-faced. Bravely, she's not crying. Mum's by my side in a moment. 'Gemsie, I'm here. Dad's here. You're safe. You're in a hospital.'

I know that they're there. I know they want to protect me. But in that moment I believe more strongly in the evil that took Milly. I believe in Bellfield above me in the air-conditioning duct. I believe in his power to get me. Marsha's family loved her; Amélie's family loved her. Bellfield still took them. So many people loved Milly too, and tried to find her – yet Bellfield got her and did what he wanted. She was not safe. I'm not safe either.

A young female doctor arrives next. I am more in the room, more in the present now. I still carry the fear of the hallucination, but I'm able to talk to her. She persuades me to stay still enough for her to set up a cannula and drip. This is to flush my system of any drugs. Even if I haven't knowingly taken any, she explains, someone might have slipped something into one of my drinks. Mum demands that they test me for those kinds of drugs. She notices the young female doctor has tears rolling down her cheeks.

Mum promises me, 'The sooner you calm down, the sooner we can get you home to your own bed, Gemsie.'

It takes what Mum later describes as a horse tranquillizer, administered intravenously, to finally loosen the grip of this attack.

*

We cannot let this pass. The hallucinations were far too vivid. I can't forget them. I cannot dismiss the attack as an unfortunate one-off. What if it happens again?

I go back to work. I try to put it behind me. But I'm laid low by the aftershocks of this panic attack for months afterwards. They're usually triggered by apparently harmless and even happy events, like an office birthday party. I can't protect myself because I don't know where the next trigger will come from.

I'm still attending sessions with a therapist who uses cognitive behavioural therapy as a way of grounding me in comforting reality as opposed to the terror of my hallucinations. Of course it works – when I'm not actually in a panic attack. But when the attacks come, I'm too distressed for methodical thinking.

I tell the therapist I cannot cope with my job. My activities there – in a jolly office – are so alien to what's going on in my head and at home. The trial of Bellfield, for Marsha, Amélie and Kate, is looming ever closer. I'm drinking far too much to blot out my fear. I say, 'I can't keep myself safe any more.'

Mum's with me that day, because things are clearly coming to a head. She needs to bear witness about my behaviour in the last month, and to make sure that what I say is being taken seriously. After sitting in at the start of the session, she goes to wait in the car. Coincidentally, at that moment, Alice rings to tell her that the prison-letter man, who wanted to skin me alive, is about to be released from jail.

Mum wasn't able to protect Milly and now she feels unable to protect me.

Meanwhile I'm trying to explain to the therapist that I'm not threatening to hurt myself. It's that I cannot anticipate when my irrational fears will next overwhelm me. I'm not in control of my emotions, and I'm afraid of them. I don't have a lid to put on the sensations boiling up inside me. I'm walking on broken glass all the time. I'm aggressive with everyone. I scream at the least thing, like a knock at the door. If a friend doesn't text me back in an instant, I hate them. I swear and rage about the house. I am heartless about the way Mum and Dad are suffering, even though I'm aware of it. It's all or nothing: I'm either laughing like a crazy woman or shouting like a crazy woman.

I'm wild and foul-mouthed one minute, weeping like a child the next. I gravitate towards mostly unsuitable boys, as if I don't deserve someone decent in my life. If they hurt me, then I take it out on Mum. It's messed up, and sometimes I know it. I don't like it. I don't know how to get off the roller-coaster that is my emotional life.

Here's a list of the things I cannot do: walk in the dark, sleep in a house on my own, take Maisy for a walk in the evening, go somewhere alone even in the daytime, be around a man I don't really know, wait in a queue in a shop, drive.

My friends and family look afraid of me, as well they might be. Everyone who cares about me is under strain. I know it hurts them to see me in this state. I don't want to put another friend through the ordeal Lauren suffered.

46.

There was no psychiatric support available to me immediately after Milly was taken. I had the much-pierced social worker who nominally filled the role of counsellor but it was hard to trust her as she was part of the police machinery.

Mum used her considerable resources to try to track down help for me, especially after the panic attacks started. Our local doctor warned us off antidepressants because of the side-effects. Mum was allowed them only after Dad literally carried her into the surgery, screaming and sobbing. For me, they were still ruled out on the grounds that insufficient research had been done on their use by young people. I was offered some mild over-the-counter sleeping meds.

As I've written, two weeks after Milly disappeared, a locum doctor offered to pray for me, as if performing an exorcism. Mum was on diazepam. Despite misgivings, she gave me a tiny dose, which helped. After that, Jon suggested I breathe into a paper bag to control my panic attacks. From that point on, I rarely went anywhere without one.

But a paper bag was never going to sort a trauma like the one I was going through.

After Milly's body was discovered, Mum found a mental health charity online: SAMM – Support After Murder and Manslaughter. The lovely people at SAMM recommended the Traumatic Stress Clinic, where we found David Trickey, a tall, approachable man who made me feel at ease. Going to the clinic was at first daunting because it meant taking a train from Walton station, one of many toxic places for me. Mum had to accompany me, and I gave her a horrible time. She herself would end up in tears. Tears attracted attention from strangers because Mum's face was too well known.

But David Trickey was worth the journeys. He gradually earned my trust with his obvious understanding of what I was going through. He helped me with my recurring living nightmare of a man lurking in the hedge. In May 2004 he wrote a very perceptive analysis of my mental state.

Gemma has been coming to the Traumatic Clinic since 21 November 2002 in order to receive treatment to assist her following the traumatic killing of her sister.

We know from research and also from our clinic work that traumatic incidents such as this affect people in a number of ways. The strong emotion that they elicit has a long lasting physiological effect, sometimes described as chronic hyperarousal. The effects of this are that the person has difficulty paying attention during the day, and problems sleeping which can lead to tiredness during the day. Furthermore, people who have experienced a trauma are often preoccupied with thoughts about the event, which exacerbates their concentration problems . . .

But when I turned eighteen, I was technically classed as an adult in the British mental-health system. This meant I was no longer allowed access to David Trickey.

Mum did not find herself a therapist until October 2004. And this therapist wanted to trace the origins of Mum's problems to events that occurred in Mum's own childhood. What was wrong with Mum had happened on 21 March 2002. Too polite and too needy to stand up for herself, Mum obediently attended this therapy for years. She thought she had to, because Dad and I needed her so much. So Mum and I were fumbling on without the right help and only getting worse.

Six months after my sessions with David Trickey finished, I started with a new female therapist. It is two years later, while I'm seeing her as an outpatient, that I suffer the catastrophic panic attack on the street in Fleet. My therapist happens to work at the Woking Priory Hospital. She tells me that I can choose to become an inpatient there. She takes me and Mum on a short tour of the parts of the complex I've never seen as an outpatient. I like the Victorian section of the building and the security arrangements but I'm unhappy that the facility is surrounded by woods.

At the end of the tour, Mum and I are left alone to think about things.

Slowly, I say to Mum, 'I think this is where I need to be.'

Mum and Dad agree. Dad's company is still kindly allowing its private health plan to cover our medical treatment. Their insurance agrees to meet the costs of my stay.

A week later, on 8 October, I move in. My bags are searched for drugs, sharp or pointed objects, and my phone is confiscated. I fill in a sequence of admission questionnaires.

Mum and Dad have kissed me goodbye many times before, when I've been travelling for pleasure and for my work. This goodbye is much worse. When they leave me in my comfortable little room, my heart plummets. Has it really come to this? That I have to live in a mental hospital? That I'm no longer fit to live in society, or to work, or even to live with my parents?

That evening Mum and Dad are due to go and see Auntie Linds and Uncle Ian. When they turn up, Auntie Linds is so shocked at how they look that she wraps Mum in a blanket and just holds her tight for a long time.

The dining room is busy when I go down for my first dinner at the Priory. I'm the only new girl and the youngest by a long way. I don't know what my fellow patients are in for. I look at each one in turn, wondering, *Is it depression? Is it drink? Are you here for drug dependence?* I know there won't be anyone with my type of problem.

Everyone is quiet. So quiet. When I get my own meds that night, I start to understand why. I guess that many of us are heavily sedated.

Starting the next morning, I sleepwalk through a full schedule of CBT, art therapy, building self-esteem, managing anger, learning about self-awareness, drama therapy, healthy lifestyle, sleep management, and learning about anxiety and relapse prevention. I respond poorly to group therapy. I'm impatient, have no tolerance of others.

I'm given a 'Grief Wheel' to help me understand the nature of my particular negative spiral – the way the tiniest moment of feeling abandoned reminds me that I'm alone, that I'll probably never be good enough for anyone, that I'll never have a friend like my sister, that no one will ever know me like Milly did. That leads to thinking that I shall always be alone, feeling angry, sad, worthless and unsafe.

I doodle all over the worksheets they give me. I draw little-girl images of fairies with wands, kittens, hearts. In art therapy, I draw a shining sun. But its body is a garishly coloured snake.

I make a diagram of what Paul Hughes said he would do to me. I've become obsessed with the detail of the man skinning me alive slowly with a potato peeler and a cheese grater. For cutting my nipples, I picture a knife with a serrated edge.

The drugs initially stop the panic attacks. They also suppress inhibitions and rational thought. My swearing goes into overdrive.

One of the fellow inpatients tells everyone he's ex-army and a trained assassin. He and I get on quite well.

After a couple of days, I'm allowed to phone Mum. 'Don't worry, Mum,' I tell her. 'I've got some good news for you. I've met a trained assassin.'

There is silence at the end of the line.

I'm wondering, *Why doesn't she see it? We can get him to take out Milly's murderer.*

It will be years before Mum and I can talk about the Priory. This is what she has recently told me about her experience of leaving me there.

'Not only had I failed to protect and look after Milly, now I couldn't even look after you either. Clearly I was not fit to be a mother, just as the police told me. I felt completely helpless and surrounded by doom from all directions.

'Mental health was not really talked about in the mainstream at that time. It was something often brushed under the carpet and there was a real stigma attached to it. I had visions from the film *One Flew Over the Cuckoo's Nest* and of very old mental institutions with strait-jackets and men in white coats. Of course, the Priory was nothing like that.

'But we had no history of mental illness in the family and so no previous experience of depression or trauma or how to deal with it. It was utterly terrifying.

'All that kept me going was thinking, Well, these guys are the experts so at least they will know what to do for you, Gemma. But I was so shocked to see your belongings being searched and your phone being confiscated.

'When we visited you a day or two later, we were horrified. You were in bed and so heavily sedated that you could barely string a sentence together. I remember the fraud department from your bank had phoned, urgently needing to speak to you. Of course they could not give me any details.

'So there we were: you drugged up to the eyeballs and me asking for your phone-bank password. If it hadn't been so sad it would have been funny. It turned out someone had fraudulently put a £1,100 payment through on your card.

'Why are they pumping you so full of drugs? I thought. I could do that at home. At least that way you wouldn't have to join the queue for meds with the little white paper cups and then be checked to see if you had swallowed them.

'You were twenty-one, so technically an adult and therefore, because of patient confidentiality, I was not allowed to be told anything by the medical staff – including how long you'd be there.

'I felt as if I might have lost you too.'

My lovely friend Vicky bravely comes to visit me in my room. I fall off the bed but don't even realize that I am on the floor. After she leaves me, Vicky sits in her car and cries for an hour.

On 5 November, one of the other inpatients manages to walk out of the facility and into the forest. The place goes into instant lockdown. An alarm goes off. I'm in Reception, about to go to yet another group-therapy session, when four police cars arrive, their lights flashing. I run out of the building towards the cars, full of fury. Then I hear the police helicopter overhead. That only makes me angrier. Since the night of 21 March 2002, neither Mum nor I can bear the sound of a helicopter.

I think, *This woman has been missing for two fucking minutes, and the police are here, there's a police helicopter here. It's probably got heat sensor cameras! Why didn't they bring out the cavalry for Milly in two minutes? Milly was missing for hours before they took it seriously. If the police had reacted like this, Milly might not have died.*

By chance Mum's in the car park, bringing me some clean laundry. She runs to grab me before I get to the police cars. She hauls me aside, still screaming.

This panic attack clarifies my situation for me. After four weeks, I still can't relate to the issues of any of the other patients. The Priory's a good place but there's no good place for someone in my condition. The drugs are turning me into a sleepwalker, while failing to manage my anxiety. My stomach hurts. I'm resentful, angry all the time. I can't stop swearing. It's time to leave.

Somehow, I don't think they're sorry to see me go.

As a family, we lose confidence in therapy for a while. But we keep going, trying different people. No one gets through the trauma to the real issues that are still destroying us. I keep an anger diary. I note how short my fuse is. In November 2007, I write down the symptoms of an anger attack, which are the same as those for a panic attack: tension, sickness, heaving, heart palpitations, flicking the switch on, fight and flight reactions, sweating, a huge knot in my stomach.

I've gained some insights, but few coping strategies. I'm aware that I behaved badly at the Priory. I know they tried to help me. I know that I need to channel my anger into something productive instead of just lashing out and shouting. So I list the things that make me angry. The first thirteen are about Surrey Police. So are many of the others. I even hate the police colours of yellow and blue stripes. I hate the leaking of information to the press. I also hate that they seem, to me, to be forgetting about Milly.

Of course the thing that underlies all this trauma, the thing that is tearing me apart, is the trial of Levi Bellfield, which started on 12 October.

We're asked not to attend in case jurors and press recognize us. We know we would not be able to cope with it, even if we wanted to go.

Bellfield pleads not guilty to all charges.

The papers cover the trial day by day. Dad buys them and spreads them on the kitchen table.

We read the accounts of witnesses to the murders of Marsha and Amélie. On 26 November Kate Sheedy weeps as she relives the ordeal of being run over twice and left for dead. Despite her injuries, she managed, of course, to call both an ambulance and her mother. Her mother's statement reveals how Kate told her that, if the ambulance did not arrive soon, she would die. Mother and daughter both said, 'I love you.' Kate's father, summoned from nearby, arrived in time to hear Kate say that she loved him too.

It emerges that police officers reviewing CCTV tapes from a nearby pub neglected to look at the crucial one, which had only recently been found. It revealed a white vehicle following the bus from which Kate emerged, only to be run down.

But the evidence that seems to be game-changing is that of Emma Mills, Bellfield's girlfriend, who asks for a curtain to be placed between her and the father of her three children. That's how afraid she is of him.

There is a break in the trial for Christmas. Bellfield goes back to the cell paid for by the taxpayer and probably eats a hearty Christmas dinner, unlike anyone in the Dowler family.

I think, *How can a multiple murder trial just stop for Christmas?*

At the end of 2007, Mum writes a letter to Milly.

My darling little sausage Milly,

Perhaps not so little now as you would be eighteen and very beautiful I am sure.

It's hard to know where to start but perhaps I should start by telling you I miss you so much and that not a day goes by when I don't think about you. You are often in my thoughts and I'm thankful that during your short life we had some very happy memories.

Mum lists the memories. There are so many and they are so lovely – all about Milly's musicality, her sense of humour, her affection. Some of them are in the first chapter of this book. But after two pages, Mum's thoughts darken.

Of course my mind dwells on the horrific circumstances in which you found yourself on that dreadful day and I can only hope that it was all over very quickly . . . With hindsight it's so easy to say why didn't you come home with me that day or why didn't Dad pick you up but sadly that didn't happen and the consequences were absolutely unthinkable. This weighs heavily on my mind and my heart as I deeply feel I was unable to protect and look after you as I should have done. I honestly would have given my life for you if only I could have taken your suffering away, my poor darling Milly.

The desperation we all felt during the months before you were found was too difficult to describe but I can say I was relieved when your body was found as I feared we would never find you. The thought of you being left dead and naked in Minley Woods is truly harrowing . . .

I have missed not only your wonderful sense of humour but your warm and kind nature and that wicked glint in your eyes when you were teasing me. I have even missed your little paddies and tantrums and would give anything to have them back. Remember the performance at mealtimes, what hard work! All was OK if cheese and cucumber was on the menu but heaven help us if it was a cooked meal!

My heart aches for you my darling. I worry about Gemma so much too as she doesn't deserve this any more than you did . . .

I can't understand why this had to happen to you.

47.

Bellfield's trial continues, so our lives must continue too. We're desperate for it to be over, so that Surrey Police can get on with investigating him for Milly's murder.

I have tried not to follow the trial obsessively. I'm still struggling after my breakdown the previous year. The courtroom drama is not good for me. It's not good for Mum and Dad to read about the discovery of the bludgeoned bodies of Amélie and Marsha. The more we hear about this man's way of dealing out violence and death to young women, the more he frightens us.

I'm appalled to hear about Bellfield's behaviour in the courtroom. He laughs and jeers, has winked at Kate Sheedy's boyfriend, and told the parents of Amélie Delagrange, 'Fuck off, you fucking leeches!' He gives threatening stares to people in the public gallery. He makes obscene gestures. He blows kisses to Marsha's sisters. But he's cunning enough to do these things only when the judge and jury are out of the room.

I note that he has not been stopped.

I imagine how it must feel to be Kate Sheedy, standing in the courtroom, in front of the monster who tried to kill her. Bellfield did not run me over, as he did Kate, but he might as well have done. That is how it feels, as if he ran our whole family down when he took Milly. By hiding her body and leaving us suffering for so long, he ran us down again. How brave Kate is to face it without breaking down. I know Bellfield's in a Perspex cage, surrounded by security, yet I'm sure his evil must leak out.

When it comes to my turn to face Bellfield, I hope I can show as much dignity as Kate does.

On 25 February Bellfield is convicted for the murders of Marsha McDonnell and of Amélie Delagrange, and of attempting to murder Kate Sheedy. Unfortunately the jury have *not* been able to reach verdicts on whether he attempted to murder the hairdresser Irma Dragoshi or to abduct and falsely imprison Anna-Maria Rennie.

The latter is devastating for us, because Anna-Maria correctly identified her attacker as Bellfield. A guilty verdict would have confirmed an attempted abduction in broad daylight just months before Milly was snatched, demonstrating a propensity that would make a conviction for Milly's killing more possible.

We've been horrified to read that Anna-Maria has been subjected to a terrible ordeal in court. She's had to suffer the humiliation and terror of not being believed, has been accused of taking drugs and being unreliable. In court, a policeman admitted that he did not originally take her claims seriously.

Now the trial is over, we see, via the press, the face of Levi Bellfield. The courtroom artist sketches had not seemed real. Now there are actual photos all over newspapers we find almost impossible to look at. Indeed it is only in researching this book that I have really forced myself to fully read the coverage which dominated the press for days after the verdict. Mum and Dad protected me from a lot of it at the time.

People have asked us to remember how we felt when we realized that this was the face of the monster who took and hurt Milly. But the fact is, individually and collectively, our family has nothing to say about the moment we first saw Bellfield's face. In retrospect, I think trauma made us disassociate then, and we have stayed disassociated. It is the safest place to be. That image is best buried. We simply do not want to relate that thing to Milly.

As Dad says, if we started to do that, we would be crossing the Rubicon. If we did that, we would be granting Bellfield some humanity, some right to live in the same world as us.

He has no such right.

★

It must be hard on the parents of Marsha, Kate and Amélie to see how the press leap straight from their tragedies to an obsessive focus on Milly. We're embarrassed and hurt for them.

'WILL HE GET AWAY WITH MILLY'S MURDER?' screams the *Daily Mail* headline on 26 February. Yet in doing so the paper actually makes that very thing more likely. The police have warned us that such reporting could be seen as prejudicial to a fair trial for Milly's murder. We're even frightened to look at these papers ourselves in case we are somehow compromised as witnesses. With every headline, we worry that the press will rob us of our chance to see justice done.

The journalists must know what they are doing, I think, and how risky it is for any further conviction. So why do they do it?

The *Sun* splashes on the Milly connection, giving it a whole inside spread.

Sun, 26 February 2008, pages 4–5; story, Mike Sullivan

The *Sun*, like many papers, is not slow to pick up on the sad contrast between Milly's lovely delicate features and Bellfield's bloated, ugly ones, between Milly's dancing eyes and his reptile-cold ones.

We shall always feel pain every time we see Bellfield's face close to a picture of Milly. In the case of the image above, the faces are cut and pasted as if the two of them are actually standing together. We've wished so many times that the newspapers would think about the messages this sends. The overlapping or juxtaposition of those two faces seems to imply that Milly actually knew her killer, had something to do with him. That's a cruel, dishonest implication.

But, most of all, couldn't the press have thought about how we, her family and friends, have felt every time we saw that brutal face next to hers? Could they not have spared a thought for Kate Sheedy and for the families and friends of Amélie and Marsha every time they put Bellfield's mug-shot next to the faces of those pretty girls, whose only connection with Bellfield was of being stalked and violently assaulted by him?

Because of the risks to a future trial, we have mixed feelings when many of the papers echo the *Sun*'s detailed conclusions that Surrey Police failed to spot so many clues linking Bellfield to Milly, leaving him free to keep murdering girls for years.

They print aerial photographs showing the proximity of 24 Collingwood Place to Milly's route home. They mention the attempted abduction of another girl just one day before Milly's disappearance – by a fat-faced man in a red car. That report was 'lost in the system'. They write of the 'fat white man' who exposed himself and tried to grab a girl in Station Avenue a month before Milly's abduction, another case the police failed to link to Milly; that Bellfield knew Minley Woods well; that he suddenly moved out of Collingwood Place immediately after Milly was taken.

The police have never prepared us for Bellfield's appalling back-story. And it was not admissible in court. So it is via the press that all the families of his victims get to know a thousand details about their girls' killer, details that hurt like knives.

Out they come, all the stories about Bellfield drugging girls with ketamine or buying them with cocaine. About his liking for girls way below the age of consent. About his aggressive pestering of women and girls in the street, of luring them into vans where he kept a mattress and a baseball bat. According to the *Evening Standard*, 'In the two years before Milly's abduction, Bellfield was reported to the police a total of 93 times for alleged indecent assault, obscene phone calls and physical assaults.'

Ninety-three reports. That means Bellfield was hurting and terrorizing people, mostly women from the sound of it, almost every week, and hurting them so badly that they sought the help of the police. Not just a punch or a kick, but a beating or a rape.

And how much more pain was he allowed to inflict in the two and a half years *after* he took Milly? All this time, that man has been driving our streets, treating Walton as a buffet for whatever he fancied.

I think, *He must have believed he was untouchable.*

Now that Bellfield is safely put away, his terrorized girlfriend Emma Mills can talk without fear. In the *News of the World*, she gives an interview in which she tells how he beat, strangled and raped her. Even during their relationship, he was having an affair with a fifteen-year-old schoolgirl. She tells of a pattern of disappearing cars, and sudden holidays.

For the first time, we see some words that will chill us, and will one day chill another courtroom. Emma recalls how, on the day Milly vanished, Bellfield was missing for hours, with his phone turned off. He turned up late at night in different clothes from those he had been wearing when she saw him in the morning. She tells of his disposing of the sheets from the apartment in Collingwood Place, claiming the dog had had an accident. The next day, when she questioned him on his movements, he joked, 'What – you think I done Milly?'

How, we think despairingly, *are we going to find a jury that doesn't know about this?*

She explains that Bellfield had her car that day. 'I feel sick to think my car might have been used.'

So do we.

A week later, Bellfield told her that the car had been stolen from outside a pub where he was drinking.

Johanna Collings, another Bellfield ex, talks too. She gives an exclusive interview to the *Sun* on 27 February in which she speaks of how, when they were together, he boasted of regularly raping girls. As for herself, Jo Collings tells the reporter that Bellfield repeatedly raped and battered her, strangling her with a belt, burning her with cigarettes and attacking her with a claw hammer.

Another ex, Becky Wilkinson, talks to the *Daily Mail* of eighteen years of rape at knifepoint and beatings by Bellfield, with whom she has four children. 'They are ashamed they are related to him,' she says.

The newspapers put the spotlight on other possible victims, including Patsy Morris, a fourteen-year-old found strangled in 1980 when Bellfield was only twelve. He's said to have been her boyfriend. There's Edel Harbison, horribly injured in a hammer attack near Twickenham Green in April 2004. There is Sonia Salvatierra, attacked in Twickenham in November 2002. There's seventeen-year-old Jesse Wilson, beaten with a blunt instrument in Strawberry Hill in January 2003.

On 26 February Bellfield is sentenced.

The judge pronounces that Bellfield will not be considered for parole and will spend his whole life in prison. The court rings with applause.

The murderer himself refuses to appear to hear his sentencing. He's in his cell, having a tantrum about all the bad publicity in yesterday's papers. As the *Daily Express* puts it, 'Hammer maniac Bellfield cowered in his prison cell yesterday as an Old Bailey judge condemned him to death behind bars.'

Editorials rail against the fact that the British justice system allows convicted murderers to do this. The *Sun* thunders,

Bellfield's final act of cowardice insulted the relatives of his victims and sickened the rest of us.

Why was this monster allowed to exploit the law by refusing to attend court to hear his sentence?

He should have been dragged, kicking and screaming to the dock. In a
straitjacket if need be.

Within minutes of Bellfield's convictions, Surrey Police offer the reward of £50,000 for information leading to a murder charge for Milly's death. They hope 'people who were previously too afraid to speak' may come forward. Unwritten are the words 'now that Bellfield will be locked up for the rest of his life'.

Mum and Dad add their plea, with a statement issued on the anniversary of Milly's disappearance:

Six years ago our beautiful daughter Milly was callously murdered and still no one has been brought to justice. How can we find peace? How can we ever understand who could commit such an evil act and why? Imagine not knowing how your daughter died, or where or when and by whose hand, and imagine how we as a family live . . .

In 2006 Milly would have been eighteen. All her birthdays are anguish for us but this was particularly hard to bear and made us think what could have been. As all her friends go off to university and carry on with their lives we wonder about what she might have studied, the boyfriends she might have had, the places she might have lived; the day-to-day trivia we would have shared and above all how her many dreams and aspirations may have unfolded . . .

We are pleading for anyone who knows anything to have the courage to speak up. Nothing will ever bring Milly back, but even six years on you can still help start easing our pain by letting us know, finally, what happened on our daughter's final days.

A few days later I meet Kate Sheedy for the first time. She comes to our house for tea. She's such a beautiful, intelligent girl – it's impossible not to wonder how Milly would have been at her age.

Bellfield's van tore open Kate's lower back, breaking ribs and her collarbone. Her liver was crushed and fractured; one lung was punctured and the other collapsed. Doctors managed to save her life, but there followed months of physical rehabilitation. She also lost her life as a carefree teenager, reduced to physical pain and weakness while her friends were getting on with their lives. And the psychological scars went, if anything, even deeper, with the panic attacks, nightmares and flashbacks that are the key symptoms of post-traumatic stress disorder. It took until late 2004 for Kate to be diagnosed and treated.

Kate and I have this in common: our lives were torn apart by Bellfield. So I want to see if she has found some ways to claim back control, to achieve some kind of peace. I want to know if seeing Bellfield convicted has helped her in any way.

Four years have passed since the attack, and Kate is twenty-one now. Her physical injuries still trouble her, yet you'd never know it to look at her lovely face. She's studying politics and history at the University of York.

Kate says that she, too, struggles with being alone on the street or even at home. Like me, she does not want even to utter Bellfield's name. To her, he is just an inhuman thing. Kate knows her attacker is a suspect for Milly. She believes him capable of anything.

How brave she is to relive her trauma by coming to talk to me about it. She's gentle and kind with me, but she's also inspiring in her courage and determination.

I feel better after meeting Kate. She's helped make it real that Bellfield will never ever leave prison.

48.

Dear Milly, Thank you for arranging the dolphin for Mum's birthday.

xxxx Gemsie

Mum and I have discovered a new form of therapy.

The water has always been a special place for us, even before Milly was taken. Afterwards, we found a kind of salvation there. Milly, of course, loved marine biology and it might have been her career, had she been allowed to grow up. Milly always championed the underdogs of the underwater world, with her newts, her sea-slugs and her Tasselled Wobbegong shark. But she also loved dolphins, and that was something Mum and I could share with her.

Since she went, dolphins and Milly have fitted together in our minds. Knowing that, Alice and Jon thoughtfully adopted one in Milly's name up in Scotland.

Mum and I do a diving course. There seems to be no peace for us in this world, but together we find it under water. There's something about its quietness – only the sound of breathing and bubbles, and the parrot fish crunching up the sand. Diving forces your mind to take a break from hideous thoughts. And the concentration required wears you out so you sleep the whole night through. That's a blessing for us.

I'm a little pleased with myself because I've been able to retain new knowledge, a huge challenge when your brain is fragmented. And I'm better at diving than Mum. For once, I have a chance to help her with something. I also use much less oxygen under water, so if Mum ever got into trouble, I could look after her.

Having done all the theory back in the UK, we head for Sharm el-Sheikh, to meet our instructor Duncan, Glyn Willoughby's nephew, and to do the real thing.

Our first proper dive's at a famous reef called Ras Mohammed. We both jump in, brimming with excitement and adrenalin. At that moment, something changes. There's a whole new world down there, incredibly beautiful and peaceful. The fish are amazing: electric blue, bright yellow, stripy, spotty silver, pretty, ugly, and some really funny-looking ones that Milly would have loved.

Duncan leads us through the water to a place where a lemon shark rests on the ocean floor with a remora gently cleaning its skin. There's something sacred about these great fish in their own environment. They're not disturbed by us, so we watch them for a long time. Eventually the lemon shark rises. Inside our masks, Mum and I are in tears at the elegance and grace with which it sashays away.

It is just so Milly.

As usual, we cannot bear to be at home for the anniversary. Mum and I fly back to Egypt in search of some more underwater escapism.

On 28 March – Mum's birthday – we're bimbling around in the sea when we see a dolphin swimming towards us. He's between five and six feet long. He swims right up to us, until he's only about two feet away. He plays with us, circles us. The dolphin accepts us as one of his own. We don't touch him; we just share his space. It is magical.

It's Milly, I think. *She's arranged this.*

I want to put my arms around him and hug him. He's sleek and cheeky, just like Milly. But this time, unlike the shark, he doesn't seem to *be* her. He's more like a message from her.

The underwater paradise continues to help me and Mum through tough times, giving us something to plan, to look forward to, to learn. Part of the diving qualification is a fish identification test. After each dive, we memorize the fish we've seen. Our fish ID book is soon well thumbed.

It's not enough, though. I always seem to leave the wonderful feelings behind when our plane hits the tarmac at Heathrow. I'm so depressed that I'm put on anti-psychotic medication.

The only thing that comforts me is the fish ID book. When I can't sleep, Mum comes to sit with me and we go through it together, repeating the names, like a strange and beautiful prayer: 'Parrot Fish', 'Crocodile Fish', 'Lemon Shark', 'Masked Butterfly Fish', 'Angel Fish'.

Mum puts on her special comforting bedtime-story voice as we remember the fish we've met and the different dives when we saw them. Sometimes it takes minutes; sometimes it takes an hour. Sometimes it takes all night.

The fish safety blanket is the only one that works for me.

49.

Our long wait moves into its eighth year. We hear more from the press in 2009 than we do from the police, who continue to inform us on a need-to-know basis only. We are aware that Surrey Police are building a case against Bellfield but very little more than that.

On 18 January, the *Sunday Times* says that the case is in advanced preparation, and that now Bellfield's been convicted of the other murders, prosecutors will be able to present details of those cases to a jury. The only delay is being caused by Bellfield, who's attempting to mount an appeal against his convictions.

On 4 February, the *Sun* says that Bellfield has vowed to beat up Roy Whiting, the man who killed little Sarah Payne in 2000. Now that he's close to being charged with the murder of a thirteen-year-old himself, it seems that Bellfield has a sudden hatred for paedophiles. Incredibly, the story says that Bellfield has told fellow prisoners he has met with Sarah Payne's family and wants to hurt Whiting as a matter of 'honour'. Even more incredibly, someone has believed the murderer, and a newspaper has printed the story.

The *Daily Mirror* reveals that 'MUMMY'S EVIL BOY' calls his mother up to four times a day.

The *News of the World* reports that Bellfield has been attacked by a 'fellow lag' in jail. He was punched in the face and knocked to the floor. He's had stitches for a split lip and been transferred to a special protection wing, the paper says, because of his alleged connection with Milly's murder.

Mum's furious when the *Sun* prints a story with a headline that at first glance is terribly upsetting: 'Milly killer "my dad".' Of course we fear the old lies about Dad are being aired once more. The story is in fact about Bellfield's daughter, Bobbie Louise Wilkinson, who says, 'I believe he killed Milly Dowler.'

And again, we fear and worry: will all this prejudice a trial? Will we be allowed justice?

*

Maria Woodall comes to see us. She confirms what we've been reading in the press – that the case against Bellfield is almost ready. She gives us more news too: the trial will not just be about Milly. Surrey Police are now, finally, linking Bellfield to two earlier incidents: the 'fat white man' who, a month before Milly vanished, exposed himself to a girl in Station Avenue, and a man 'with a fat face' who attempted to entice an eleven-year-old schoolgirl named Rachel Cowles into his red car *the day before* Milly was taken and just three miles away.

Maria explains that these two cases are important, because they would establish propensity – if, that is, they can prove that the fat white man in both cases was Bellfield.

At this time, we are under the impression that we may have some choice about whether or not Bellfield will be tried for Milly's murder. We're told that our opinion on the matter will be taken into consideration. So Mum, Dad and I allow ourselves the luxury of opinions, something we are not used to when dealing with the police. We are increasingly torn about it. We want justice for Milly, but Bellfield will never leave prison. Mum and Dad wonder what would be served by another life sentence?

What if the papers have prejudiced the case so much that we'd go through the ordeal of a trial for nothing?

How can we even face Bellfield, be in the same room as him? The idea is terrifying.

We cannot talk of 'peace of mind'. We shall never have 'peace of mind'.

Milly is gone.

50.

When Surrey Police finally question Bellfield about Milly, he answers, 'No comment,' in a high womanish voice. He smirks. His attitude to the murder of a little girl is simply contemptuous.

The police try to find a way in, even challenging Bellfield to defend himself. Their voices rise. They hector him with the obvious – where was he the day Milly was taken?

'No comment,' he says, to every question. It seems to be a game for him, and he's winning by withholding.

By now a couple of years have passed since Uncle Bree was summoned to Woking police station to identify the man he saw at Collingwood Place the night Milly disappeared. There Uncle Bree was met not just by the police but also by the solicitor for the accused, who was female. The 'identity parade' consisted of Uncle Bree looking at computer images. First, the solicitor checked out the picture selection, removing several. The pictures Uncle Bree was allowed to see showed only the suspect's head and neck, not the whole shoulder width. As one of Uncle Bree's main observations had been about the man's thick-set body and aggressive stance – the most noticeable things about him – it's hardly surprising he was unable to identify the right man that day.

Now that there seems to be a chance of Bellfield being charged, Uncle Bree feels terrible, as if he has let Milly down. We try to reassure him. He's not the only link in the chain that leads to Bellfield.

The CPS has called a press conference. Minutes before it starts, Maria Woodall calls us. She *thinks* it will be announced that Bellfield will be charged with murdering Milly.

We've been waiting so long for this that we almost don't believe it will happen now.

We watch it on television: the press conference taking place at

Staines police station. Maria stands next to the man from the CPS. Proudly, he makes the announcement that Bellfield will, indeed, be charged with Milly's abduction and murder.

Mum gets up from the sofa and sees the first press van arriving, before even Alice can get to us. The reporters and photographers wait until they're made to understand that no statement is going to be generated from our front door, and that we are not going to give them our shocked, grieving or angry faces to photograph and comment on. We know the drill.

Dad says, 'Oh, X and Y reporters will be off to Walton station now.'

He's right. The swarm settles on the usual places – Walton station, Heathside School. They'll interview anyone who will talk to them about it. And the old footage of Milly ironing, the pictures we released to the press, parade across the screen again.

We have never, of course, been involved in criminal proceedings before. We think that we are the victims and the accused is the criminal; that the trial should expose the crime, and we should have the comfort of seeing things put right, or as right as possible. I'm still thinking that way, in my innocence. But Mum and Dad have kept an eye on press coverage of Bellfield's prosecution for Marsha, Amélie and Kate. Dad has met with Phil McDonnell, Marsha's dad. He knows how Bellfield lied and lied in the dock and how those lies were faithfully printed in the press the next day, almost making them seem true.

I think Alice and Maria were even then aware that it would be not just our mental health at stake in this trial but our privacy, our lives, our reputations and even Milly's reputation. We ourselves could not know that. Our fear was that the police's initial suspicions about Dad might come out in court. That was painful enough to live through once. And at that time it was private – between us and Surrey Police. It would be different in a trial. We don't want to relive it through headlines in the press.

Mum and Dad are wondering how much more we can bear. But it's not complicated for me. I simply want Bellfield up there, being tried as a child-killer. I know that this will be a game-changer. 'Nonces' are given very different treatment by other prisoners from killers and rapists.

Two weeks later we have our own meeting with an official from the CPS. It's the first time I've been to Staines police station since the early days of the inquiry. I hate the place. Again, to avoid the press, we have to use the prisoner entrance, as if we are the guilty ones. We're ushered into a meeting room and are introduced to the man we saw on television.

At the outset he's friendly and sympathetic. This meeting is theoretically to consult us about the trial. So Dad's first question is, 'Why are you consulting us about the trial if you have already decided to go ahead?'

This isn't really answered.

My question is, 'Will Bellfield's defence try to frame Dad for doing it?'

'No, Gemma,' the man says smoothly. 'Your dad was unaccountable for only twenty minutes the day Milly went missing. He wouldn't have had time to kill her and dispose of her body.'

It sounds very logical, but there's something rotten here. Not having the time is not the only reason why Dad didn't kill Milly. *Why is that not being acknowledged?*

'Can Bellfield plead insanity and get off that way?' I ask. I'm worried that he may end up in a comfortable psychiatric prison, where his behaviour will be attributed to traumas in his childhood. Traumas in childhood are what Bellfield inflicts, not what he suffers.

We're told, 'No. He can't plead insanity because he didn't do that when he was tried for Marsha, Amélie and Kate.'

'But could he get off? Could the jury say he didn't do it?' I ask.

Well, the answer is, this trial *does* present a risk, because all the evidence is circumstantial and not forensic. This is code for words that people don't like saying to us, partly because they're so gruesome, partly because it makes us angry to remember that Milly's body was so decomposed and the trail had long gone cold by the time Surrey Police found out where Bellfield lived on the day Milly was taken.

After the meeting, Dad asks to have a word on his own with the CPS official. I imagine that it's about the twenty unaccountable minutes. I go off, unwillingly, to the horrible police canteen for some undrinkable tea with Alice.

Dad appears to get some reassurance. Yet I can tell that he's not quite right when he comes to find me.

But that's just Dad, I think, *perfectionist and worrier.*

We're being kept in touch with details about the case against Bellfield. Complicated legal manoeuvres are going on to do with plea and case management. We're told that there is, at this stage, the possibility that he will plead guilty and save us the trauma of a trial.

From what we know of Bellfield, that possibility seems non-existent.

We learn that the case of Rachel Cowles is shaky because, like Uncle Bree, she failed to identify Bellfield several years on from the day when a fat man in a red car tried to entice her into it.

In October, Maria Woodall flies to Spain to speak to Anna-Maria Rennie.

Bellfield had already been charged with her attempted abduction and false imprisonment in 2001. She was able to identify him correctly in a video parade four years after that. After she was undermined as a witness in court, the jury failed to reach a verdict. Now the police want to re-try her case. But Maria Woodall can't persuade her. Her mauling at the previous trial traumatized the girl so much that her psychiatrist insists she must be excused.

Nevertheless, on 6 October 2010 – just before the eighth anniversary of the service at Guildford Cathedral – Bellfield appears at the Old Bailey and is told that he will go to trial for Milly's murder.

5.

Trial and Punishment
January – June 2011

PLAYLIST

The Who	Behind Blue Eyes
Eric Clapton	Wonderful Tonight
The Band Perry	If I Die Young
Simon and Garfunkel	Bridge Over Troubled Water

51.

Mum, Dad and I meet Surrey Police on 18 January to discuss trial logistics. We suddenly realize the smallness of our place in the grand workings of the police and justice system. At this point, we're told it's highly unlikely that Mum and I shall have to give evidence. Do we even want to attend? We get the impression it would be easier for them if we did not. After all, we're just the family of the murder victim. The lead role, it seems, belongs to the defendant. We're also told that if we insist on going then we must take public transport to the trial in London, which may go on for twelve weeks, including the pre-trial arguments. There is no funding available for our transport.

I think, *But we have to see Bellfield in a courtroom. Maybe he'll taunt us the way he did the families at the first trial. We might still have to give evidence! We'll be upset! And then we just have to get on the train with people who'll have read all about us in the press, who will recognize us. The press will follow us on to the train. We'll be taking the train from Walton station, where Milly was last seen.*

So we have to take the train while the taxpayer pays for private transport for Bellfield, who wakes up in a bed paid for by the taxpayer, eats a breakfast paid for by the taxpayer and dresses in clothes provided by the taxpayer? How is this right?

I let the police know exactly how I feel. I won't let it go. In the end, the police agree to give us a car. It seems a big victory at the time.

On 11 February, we have a police briefing about how we are to behave in the courtroom. We're told that it's vitally important to show no emotion, no matter what we hear, because it could be seen to prejudice the jury.

I feel as if this is for my benefit because I am the one who's always shouting at the police. I'm the one who no longer cares what she says to them.

'A courtroom is not like real life, Gemma,' the police tell me.

'You cannot scream at the barristers or the witnesses if they start talking about Milly in a way you don't like.'

We're also told that we are not allowed to look directly at the jurors. If the defence sees us doing that, we might be accused of emotional blackmail. We are not allowed to tut. If we need to cry, we have to tell Alice, and proceedings will need to be suspended while we excuse ourselves. This would be bad for the case.

I ask where Bellfield is going to be. 'How close to us? Will we be facing him? Will he be in a cage or a box? Will we, for protection? Where will the press be?'

Mum wants to know if Bellfield will be in chains. The police laugh. It's not funny for us.

At the beginning of March, Mum and Dad have their first meeting with Brian Altman QC, the prosecuting barrister. He successfully prosecuted Bellfield for the murders of Amélie and Marsha and the attempted murder of Kate. So he's the natural choice for this case too.

Mum's first question: 'Is there any chance of Bellfield *not* being convicted?'

'Nothing can be guaranteed,' says Altman.

Then Mum asks, 'Are you going to take the jury to where it happened?'

Of course she's anxious that the jury will see with their own eyes the tiny number of yards between the hedge on Station Avenue and Bellfield's flat at Collingwood Place.

The answer is yes. But Alice tells us, 'Unfortunately that means they have to take Bellfield too.'

Mum makes notes about what they're told: that the trial itself will last five or six weeks; that before there will be legal arguments for up to two months; that Mum, Dad and I are to be called as prosecution witnesses after all.

I'm glad when Mum tells me that I can have my say. I can tell the world how wonderful Milly was and how lovely our family was before this happened.

When Mum receives the call from Alice, we are at Uncle Pete's, having a barbecue. It's a rare day out for Mum, who has pretty much confined herself to the house, haunted by a sense of foreboding about the trial. A call from Alice usually means something gruesome. And, of course, the call starts with the usual, 'This is really sensitive information, Sally.'

Mum's irritated at being disturbed when, for once, we're trying to get on with a normal family occasion. But, as Alice explains, the news comes from something she calls 'Operation Weeting'. Mum's never heard of it.

I hear Mum repeating, 'Can you say that again? . . . No, we were never told that at the time . . . No, we never heard that before . . . *Why* weren't we told?'

Alice is silent. Unusually, she cannot offer any reminders.

Mum puts down the phone and comes to me and Dad with an astonished face. 'The *News of the World* hacked Milly's phone when she was still missing.'

At first, the seriousness of the situation does not sink in at all. We don't even know exactly what hacking means. And none of us is particularly astonished to learn people had been listening in on our phone calls in 2002. We suspected that all along. The police, we assumed, were bugging us because they wanted evidence on Dad. But we are stunned to hear that Milly's own little phone had been *hacked by a newspaper* in the early days of her disappearance.

A meeting is fixed for a few days later at Walton police station. Operation Weeting investigators are coming from London to talk to us about the phone hacking.

Meanwhile Mum's head churns with agonizing thoughts: *How could someone get access to Milly's phone? They would know things before me and that's not fair! Could they know things before the police?*

The violation of our privacy, of Milly's privacy, is horrifying.

Mum's also remembering what was supposed to be a private walk that she and Dad took seven weeks after Milly vanished. It was a last-minute idea. Dad was travelling back from London. Mum rang him to suggest that they meet at Walton station so they could walk home together following the same route Milly started towards home. Mum, always needing to be contactable, also let the police know they were going to do the walk. On that day, there were for once no reporters hanging around at the station. Mum and Dad managed to do the walk unnoticed – or so they thought.

Then, the following Sunday, a large picture was printed in the *News of the World* of Mum 'tenderly stroking a poster of Milly'. In fact, Mum was checking to see which telephone number was on the poster. It had curled up in the rain so she was unfolding it.

In those days, we were constantly being asked for press interviews and photos. We were as accommodating as possible because any publicity might lead to some new information about Milly. But, in this case, the picture was taken without Mum and Dad knowing, from quite a distance, at a time when the press mêlée had somewhat quietened down and the police station was no longer knee deep in reporters. Now Mum remembers thinking that our phones must have been listened to for anyone else to know what was happening, especially as it was such a hastily arranged walk.

'I wasn't going mad after all,' Mum says to me and Dad.

The other thing that immediately comes to Mum's mind is how, in the first few days, she was continually ringing Milly's mobile and receiving an automatic message that there wasn't room to leave a voicemail. Yet at the Birds Eye building, a few days after Milly was taken, Mum suddenly got through to Milly's personally recorded message. She believed Milly must have listened to her messages. That, Mum thought, was the reason why there was space for new ones.

Mum had cried out to Dad, to me, to everyone then, 'She's listened to her messages! She's alive!'

It was a moment of false hope.

But it was the only hope that Mum had, and she had clung to it.

Now, nine years later, Mum and Dad are ushered to a small room at Walton police station where they are joined by Maria, Alice and two Metropolitan Police officers.

The two Met officers look exceedingly uncomfortable. They don't want to be the ones telling us about this situation – for two reasons. First, the Met has had this information for at least four years. Second, Surrey Police have known about it since April 2002.

Mum remembers watching a bead of sweat roll down one officer's nose as he begins to tell them how a hacker working for the

News of the World had accessed Milly's voicemails, listened to them and written them down.

Sheets of photocopied handwriting are fanned out in front of Mum and Dad: pages and pages of scribbled messages, along with the names, telephone numbers, addresses and dates of birth of many of our friends and family members. It looks like the Dowler family address book.

'These pages are from the notebooks of Glenn Mulcaire,' the police tell Mum and Dad. They remember his name: Glenn Mulcaire is the *News of the World* operator jailed back in January 2007 for hacking the phones of royal family staff.

The officers from Operation Weeting explain that the Metropolitan Police seized these notes during Mulcaire's arrest in August 2006. They had not deemed them worth further investigation. However, the new operation is taking a rather different view.

'You're telling us that the hackers were in Milly's phone?' Mum asks. 'They were in all our phones?'

She has to keep asking because she needs to make sure.

Even though they are completely focused on the trial, Mum and Dad know that this is important. They try to concentrate as they are given just a glimpse of Glenn Mulcaire's pages. Their requests for copies are firmly refused.

Mum and Dad are now reminded by the officers that, three weeks after Milly disappeared, the *News of the World* had printed a story about an employment agency in the north of England that had called her number and left a message on her voicemail about a job interview. The paper claimed that this happened because a female hoaxer had given the agency Milly's number, having tricked it out of people who knew her.

Mum and Dad now hear how that story really came about. Having hacked the job-offer message on Milly's phone, reporters from the *News of the World* had staked out the agency, doubtless hoping to find a runaway Milly and bring her home in triumph. But the agency had denied all knowledge of contact with Milly. The *News of the World* then tried the story on Surrey Police, who advised that a female hoaxer may have been involved.

We had seen the published story back in April 2002, of course. It did not occur to us then to wonder how the *News of the World* had obtained its information about what was on Milly's voicemail. Back then, we were absorbed in our shock and grief. Even now, the significance of the story is very slow to dawn on Mum and Dad.

It was not about a hoaxer at all. This was about the *News of the World* hacking into Milly's phone.

Mum's first thought is, *Why the hell didn't the* News of the World *tell us when they thought they had found Milly? Why didn't the police tell us? It was a lead! When there were no leads! Every second of every hour without news was agony to us. A scoop on Milly was just money to the* News of the World, *but for us – we were barely breathing, we needed information so badly!*

Mum now shares her memory of the photo that the paper had shot of herself and Dad taking that supposedly private walk home from Walton station a few weeks after the hoaxer story appeared. She also tells the officers about the moment, at the Birds Eye building, when she suddenly got through to Milly's voicemail after continually being unable to leave a message.

Now Mum and Dad are given to understand that the reason why there was space on the voicemail just then was that the older messages had been deleted. Mum asks, 'Does that mean that the hacker deleted them? To make room for more messages to hack?'

The answer comes, 'That's the sort of thing they do.'

The Weeting officers are operating under the assumption that we were briefed by Surrey Police about the hacking when it happened back in 2002. Of course this Operation Weeting meeting is attended by none of the Surrey officers involved at a high level back when Milly went missing. Those officers have moved on now, so there's no one to ask about why we weren't informed.

Mum and Dad are hardly surprised to be told in no uncertain terms that the hacking information is 'highly sensitive'. We're not to say a word. *Not a word.* Otherwise it might compromise the trial of Bellfield, only weeks away. The police know that this will work on us.

As they walk out of the police station, Mum says to Dad, 'Did they really just say that a hacker deleted Milly's voicemails?'

He nods. He can't speak.

The enormity of what they've just been told begins to sink in. However, Mum and Dad know that they must obey police orders and keep it to themselves. They have to focus on the trial.

But the hacking continues to gnaw away at Mum. She can't sleep. She can't rest. She researches the hacking scandal so far. It makes disgusting reading. Celebrities, sports stars, actors – all hacked. Now we are a part of that story. Mum feels tainted. She gets progressively angrier. She thinks, *What type of person hacks into a missing young girl's voicemails looking for a story?*

I'm not at the Operation Weeting meeting. I just can't take any more time off work. I'm saving up all my time for the trial. When Mum and Dad tell me what they've seen and heard, I struggle to take it in. I feel a sense of sickness and wrongness, but I'm preoccupied with facing the living murderer in a courtroom in the not-distant future. Some sordid newspaper hacking Milly's phone – what can be done about that now?

Milly cannot be saved.

52.

Bellfield's trial for Milly's murder will take place in Court 8, one of the three largest rooms at the Old Bailey. We're reminded that we may not show any emotion or reaction in court. The force with which this message is delivered makes it seem that compliant behaviour on our parts is much more important to the prosecution than anything we may be feeling.

Even though Bellfield is already a convicted murderer, it becomes increasingly clear that the police are anxious about this trial. The murderer made sure to leave no traces at the scene. Bellfield is not just forensically aware. He's legally aware now too. He sits in prison calling for any kind of law book he wants. Law books that cost hundreds of pounds are his – he just has to demand them. He doesn't have to work. He's fed and housed without lifting a finger. So he has all day every day to prepare. Specifically, Bellfield is aware of court procedure. He's already been the subject of one trial. We fear his deviousness. Whatever else one might say about Bellfield, he's not stupid. He's cunning. It took cunning to get away with his crimes for so long. For years, he was cleverer than Surrey Police.

We're told that he has access to the material from Surrey Police's investigation. We obviously have no idea what 'full disclosure' might really mean for us. Of course, there's much I myself do not know about what was found in the house searches. My preoccupation is that Bellfield might be allowed to touch Milly's things. That seems obscene to me. But I'm learning that Bellfield has rights I could never dream of.

Mum and Dad are briefed now about the barrister who will be defending Bellfield. Just as I've chosen not to identify specific officers of Surrey Police, I have decided not to name this man in my book. He will be known simply as 'the defence barrister'.

By a strange coincidence, the defence barrister has made his name clearing the man initially convicted of killing Jill Dando. Milly had composed an essay about Jill Dando in her English workbook, another item confiscated by the police and therefore available to Bellfield when preparing his defence. This is what Milly wrote, on 12 October 1999, a time when her spelling was still evolving:

I think Jill Dando should be a modern legend because she was very kind. She was also a television presenter. She stard in The Holiday Show, *the* News, Crimewatch UK *and* House Inspectors *she filmed just before she died. There was quite a big discussion if they should show the series but in the end they did. I think that it was a good idea because people don't have to morn her. They can just watch and think about her good points and be positive and not sad. It was also good because people who weren't all that interested in her can see her qualiteys.*

She would also make a good modern legend because she wasn't just a television presenter she was more. She was kind giving and pleasant. Many of the people who loved her, her family, friends and even people who she had never met were devestated by her death. Many people including me were also very sorry for her feonsay.

If Jill Dando could of had any heroic qualities I think that hers would have been to be able to fight against crime. She kind of had this qualitie already but it would have been great if she could have stopped all the crime.

Jill Dando actually died because she was shot in the head walking out of her front door. Nobody actually knows who shot her but I think that it was somebody off Crimewatch *for she uncovered many storys and put many people into jail. It was a great loss of a great person.*

We know we have to give evidence. This means that we shall not be allowed in the courtroom until after we've delivered it. Mum now resolves to attend this trial from that point through to the end. She will see Milly's killer convicted, whatever it costs her, whatever she has to hear, even the evidence of the pathologist, even the words of the murderer, if he chooses to speak.

Unlike us, he has a choice.

Dad's not so sure. He's struggling with the idea of actually being in a room with the man who murdered Milly. You'll remember that we have cut ourselves off from the image of Bellfield's face. We don't even want to breathe the same air as he does. Dad wants to be there for me and Mum, but he's afraid.

As for me, I'm determined to be there every minute I can.

I want to see justice done for Milly. I still believe the trial will do that.

We're now offered a chance to see the courtroom at the end of one day, so we won't have to deal with the public. This visit is supposed to prepare us for what will happen there. I'm relieved.

Our scheduled visit on 27 April is cancelled at the last minute because Court 8 is still being reconfigured to accommodate the large numbers of press who want to attend. I don't realize it at the time, but precautions are also being taken to keep Bellfield out of the sightline of the place where our family will sit. There is, moreover, one key witness who will need 'special measures' to shield her from Bellfield's sight. We wonder who she is.

Another scheduled trip to the Old Bailey is cancelled at short notice. Finally, on 1 May, we're taken into the building, via the bin-store. We have to wait by the bins for quite a long time, until a person from Victim Support comes to escort us inside. A filthy service lift takes us up to their office. We stand away from the walls to keep our court clothes clean. We soon discover that the impressive exterior of the Old Bailey is nothing like the inside – which seems to be like a mouse house, with separate burrows, hundreds of tiny doors and narrow corridors. I'm suddenly afraid that, after the trial begins, we could bump into Bellfield at close quarters. There seems to be nothing to protect us from that.

This is my own first meeting with the prosecution barrister, Brian Altman QC. He's intimidatingly intelligent. I feel quite subdued in his presence. Even though he is not *our* barrister – he acts for the Crown – I feel as if he must be there to defend us and Milly, simply because he's there to prosecute Bellfield.

Altman is tall, but not as tall as Dad, which is somehow satisfying.

The police warnings about our courtroom behaviour are still ringing in my head. I think I have to be the same here, in the chambers: no emotion, no raised voices. I'm twenty-five years old now, yet I am there, like a child, to be seen and not heard.

The barrister tells us that the courtroom will be cool, at his request. Without any apparent irony, he says that it must be so for his brain to function at the highest level. If the temperature rises or falls below his specified level, he may well ask for proceedings to stop.

Holy shit, I think. *His brain must be some kind of precision instru-ment. Note to self: bring warm clothing to the Old Bailey.*

But a precision instrument's just what I want in the prosecution barrister. This imposing man seems our only hope of seeing justice done for Milly. We've heard too many times that the physical evidence against Bellfield is not comprehensive enough for a certain guilty verdict. This barrister will have to shape the shreds of evidence into a convincing narrative.

Altman talks to us about the fight ahead. It becomes clear that he sees it somewhat differently from the way we do. *We* see it as justice for Milly and closure for ourselves. *He* sees it as a battle between two outstanding legal minds – his and the defence barrister's.

It's becoming clear that the trial's emotional impact on us is not on this barrister's agenda or even on his radar. We are not his problem, unless we misbehave and somehow make his great work more difficult.

We are going to disappoint this man so much.

Our Victim Support helper now escorts us to the witness suite, two floors above the courts. Witness Services, a part of Victim Support, are provided by a team of kind-hearted volunteers. They look after vulnerable people in a cluster of rooms where witnesses for both the defence and the prosecution wait before they are called to give their evidence.

We're told we won't have our own room. I'm shocked. How will we be able to cope with the emotions the trial will generate with no privacy? At this point, we still have no idea of what line Bellfield's defence will take. We don't know what witnesses they will call. Will we be sharing this space with members of Bellfield's gang? His fellow nightclub bouncers? Car-clampers? Some of his paedophile friends are in prison now. Yet there are surely others. There'll be other trials going on at the Old Bailey too. Witnesses supporting criminals of all kinds might be there.

In the end, they agree to *try* to reserve a small room for us. They cannot guarantee it. That room, with its grey walls and beaten-up furniture, reminds me of a police questioning cell. There's a tiny sofa and a desk, a few shabby toys on a bookshelf. With Alice, Jon, Mum, Dad and me inside, there'll be no room to move. Unfortunately, the room looks over the car park where the vans arrive carrying the accused from their prisons. I immediately start worrying that Bellfield will look up at me when he gets out of his van.

In the corridor there's a place to make tea and coffee. The trial will cost millions; the investigation has cost millions. Now our family will excavate our own small hole in the public purse with our frankly greedy consumption of strong cups of tea over the coming weeks.

We're next taken to the canteen on the same floor, but told that we won't be permitted to use it as jurors, clerks, press and lawyers have access to it. We are not allowed to mix with them. Everything seems to be designed to show us how few rights we have and how low our status is in the legal pecking order.

On my first look into Court 8, I'm surprised at how small the room is. It's painted white, with wooden panelling. Beyond a low entrance space, the ceiling is high and vaulted. Turning around, you see that the public gallery is above the entrance, with its own separate access.

I make a map in my notebook. The judge is at the front, of course. Immediately in front of him or her, but sitting lower down, are the clerk recorder and the witness box. The jurors will be sitting to our left, and will have sight of us, Bellfield, other witnesses and the press. The jury must see everything.

Suddenly I realize just how close I shall be to Bellfield. His Perspex-and-wood box is just two yards away from where we shall sit, to our left.

There's a TV screen for showing images such as maps. I don't need to be told that it will also stop Bellfield being able to see the row of chairs where our family will sit. He won't be able to blow kisses or wink at me, as he did to the families and friends in his first trial. But will the screen stop him whispering obscenities to us?

I stay quiet, intimidated by the serious building and our serious guide, who is now showing us where the press will sit. The woman tells us they're expecting a lot of press interest. They'll be issuing tickets.

I think, *This is going to be a murder trial. It's not a bloody show.*
I'm wrong.

In the build-up to the trial, I'm drinking too much, burning myself out. As David Trickey diagnosed back in 2004, I'm in a state of 'chronic hyperarousal', unable to concentrate, unable to sleep. My mind constantly ticks over images that shouldn't be there. I'm furious all the time. Everything that the police tell us about the trial makes me angrier. I'm even more hypersensitive to noise, which is a nightmare for everyone, as the least disruption – such as someone crunching a crisp – sends me storming off, or starts me screaming, 'Shut up, shut up!'

Our domestic preparations for the trial are in sharp contrast to what we are about to face.

Crying is inevitable. I google for the world's most waterproof mascara for me and Mum. Milly would never forgive us for black tracks down our cheeks. Mum and I buy clothes in various shades of black, cream and navy blue, far from our normal pastel palettes. I'm glad Milly isn't here to see how uncool these clothes are. My arms are covered; my necklines are high; my heels are low. I can't articulate it to Mum and Dad, but I feel these clothes need to send a message to Bellfield, when he watches me on the witness stand.

I may be young, but I'm not a sex object. Especially not for you.

We'll need to bring packed lunches with us because we won't be allowed to leave the court once we arrive there. Lovely Granny and I will prepare ham rolls and salads each morning. Our neighbour Fiona makes a huge box of shortbread, to be replenished every day. A family friend, Julie, is delegated to deliver M&S Rocky Roads and Percy Pigs.

While we're at the Old Bailey, Lovely Granny will look after Maisy and prepare supper for us. She's a world-class expert in comfort food. Her picnics have always been banquets. During the trial, she will feed us quiches and wonderful tomato salads. There will be days when only a grease-fest will do, so she keeps the freezer stocked up with scampi and chips. Dad needs piles of boiled potatoes and other vegetables to fill his tall frame.

Mum will bring knitting with her to the Old Bailey. She always needs a project, the bigger the better. This time, she's making a real fish safety blanket for my bed. Each square will have a different creature knitted into it. There will be a newt, a Tasselled Wobbegong shark and a sea-slug, another unlovely creature Milly used to care about. There will be a dolphin like the ones we swam with, and a starfish.

I'll be bringing a huge cross-stitch pattern, a gift from Alice. She knows I love shopping, so it shows some girls having coffee after a spree, surrounded by bags. Typical Alice thoughtfulness, and certainly a personal, not an official, gift.

A member of our family, Carole, has kindly offered to help us in a particular way. It's a huge offer and we agree gratefully. Apart from the judge, Carole will be the only person who attends every single day of the trial. Sitting up in the public gallery, her role will be to keep Lovely Granny briefed on everything, truthfully, not distorted by any sensationalizing on the part of the press. This will also mean that Mum, Dad and I will not have to break our legal silence by discussing the case with Lovely Granny before we have given our own evidence.

It goes deeper than that. Carole knows that Mum needs all her energy to keep herself in one piece and to help hold my fragile pieces together. She's offering a quiet and constant support. Carole too has a knitting project to help her through. It is a hedgehog postman for Uncle Pete's new grandson. Mum's favourite land animal is a hedgehog. She has a collection of ceramic ones. Carole is hoping that the hedgehog postman will be good for Mum's morale: she'll be able to watch him take shape as the trial progresses.

Dad's preparations are characteristically minimal. He has headphones and his iPod. The headphones are huge, and powerful enough to cancel out every noise around him. He's made a playlist just for the trial. The song he'll play over and over is by The Who: 'Behind Blue Eyes'. The words of that one will soon acquire a special, painful resonance for him. Others are sweeter and gentler. He's going to need every note and every word of comfort on those tracks. He's going to need to remember Milly as she really was.

Mum's playlist includes Eric Clapton's 'Wonderful Tonight', which reminds her of Milly. She also listens to Simon and Garfunkel's 'Bridge Over Troubled Water', an old favourite. When Milly and I were children, she often sang it. We used to think it was a bit uncool. But then, on one episode of *Pop Idol*, the contestants were asked to sing it. Suddenly it wasn't uncool any more. And Milly and I were well pleased because we already knew all the words.

The song I listen to over and over again is the Band Perry singing 'If I Die Young'. The singer, Kimberley Perry, asks for many beautiful things. Milly, who died young, never received any of them.

> *If I die young, bury me in satin*
> *Lay me down on a bed of roses*
> *Sink me in the river at dawn*
> *Send me away with the words of a love song*
> *Uh oh uh oh*
> *Lord make me a rainbow, I'll shine down on my mother*
> *She'll know I'm safe with you when*
> *She stands under my colours, oh and*
> *Life ain't always what you think it ought to be, no*
> *Ain't even grey, but she buries her baby . . .*
> *The sharp knife of a short life,*
> *Well, I've had enough time . . .*

For the next six weeks, we shall ram our earphones in every day as we're driven to and from the trial. We'll all be listening to different songs.

We should have made a playlist for Milly. We would have done, if we'd known in advance that her character was also going to be under attack in this trial. It would have had 'Never Ever' to show her sadness at the undeserved cruelty that befell her; it would have had all the James Bond themes to show her indomitable spirit and Martini-dry wit; it would have had 'Bobby's Girl' to remind her how much she loved Dad; it would have had 'Unchained Melody' by Gareth Gates.

Mum and I make arrangements with our personal trainer Sam at the local gym. During the trial, Sam will act as a kind of counsellor, looking out for us both. Mum will also go to spinning classes, burning out her energy so that she can sleep.

Sam tells me that I can call him at any time, and he'll come into the gym to work with me. He provides the best form of therapy so far – an unbiased ear and full-on support. I will be all cramped up with misery. But he will help me let my toxic fury out. What I'll do is pull on leather gloves and fly at the pads he holds up in front of me with all my strength. Night after night during the trial I will go to the gym and let fly, screaming, until I collapse, exhausted. I can trust Sam to witness this. He won't go to the press and sell the story of my anger. Of course he will be approached by a journalist wanting a story. As with all of our true friends, his comment will be 'No comment'.

On 6 May, the inquest into Milly's death is formally adjourned by the coroner at Woking while Bellfield stands trial for her murder. We don't attend. Alice texts us to ask how much Milly weighed. That simple question, no doubt required by the barrister to build his case against the large, fat Bellfield, sends us into a rage. How are we supposed to remember that, nine years on? We also feel guilty because we can't immediately remember Milly's weight. And, of course, the question brings unwelcome pictures into our minds.

By the time of the trial, my appearance has changed yet again. I have darkened my hair, cut and straightened it into a helmet. My eye make-up is harsh. I'm a warrior, even though I cannot know at the start of the trial that our family is about to be plunged into a new war on our sanity and our reputation.

We are petrified about the evidence we have to give. What if we misremember something and it's made to look as if we didn't really know Milly? We're used to our answers being treated with disbelief or cynical expressions on police faces. We know how undermining that is. It makes you flounder. That makes you look guilty or unreliable. We don't want to falter in front of the jury. What if we make a mistake that gives Bellfield an advantage?

Our cross-examinations will be based on our police statements from nine years ago, statements we haven't seen since we signed them off. They will be returned to us briefly to refresh our memories.

Alice will bring those statements to us. Along with them will come cautions. We must not try to memorize them or even study them too closely. If it looks as if we are reciting material, our words will not seem credible.

This confuses and worries us. We're not professional criminals with a slick answer for everything. From the accounts of the first trial, we know Bellfield has a talent for smokescreens and fluent lying. Unlike Bellfield, we have never been interrogated by a barrister in court.

We're not really aware that Bellfield's been entitled to sight of much of the material taken from our house during all the police searches. He's had nine years of knowing what really happened, and access to thousands upon thousands of documents to set up his defence.

We shall have ten minutes and a few pieces of nine-year-old paper to prepare ourselves for what is to come.

53.

When Milly's schoolbooks finally came back to us – nine months after this trial – they were dotted with green stickers. From these, we understood fully for the first time what the police were thinking back in 2002. They were crafting the image of a desperately unhappy Milly to serve either of their two templates – that Dad had killed her or that she had run away.

The poems of First World War writers she'd copied out were considered by the police to offer useful evidence of Milly's state of mind, even a poem about soldiers sitting in a trench with rats. Milly's red-ink fingerprints in her science workbook were apparently somehow seen as suspicious or indicative of a forensic state of mind, as were her velocity equations and answers to questions on electromagnets or her comments on the planets in the solar system. The police stickered anything that might – in their minds – make it seem that she was troubled.

This material would be used by Bellfield and his lawyer to try to incriminate my parents in her death. Bellfield didn't even have to read all the material harvested from our house. The police had conveniently pointed out the relevant passages with their little green stickers. Thus their old template, of Milly as runaway or even incest-murder victim, became Bellfield's. So, like the police, Bellfield's defence produced a confusing twin-headed attack on our family.

Remember Marsha's and Amélie's parents were spared the ordeal of appearing as witnesses at the trial of their daughters' murderer. Was that because the fathers were never suspects? Perhaps full disclosure of the Met's files did not produce anything like as much exploitable material as Surrey Police's did.

I hate it that Milly's murderer had access to her personal papers, her secret notes and private thoughts. To my mind, letting Bellfield read that material was another way of murdering my sister. In what way is it right that a paedophile should be allowed to know so much about the girl he had killed? To see her handwriting? How can it be called justice for a sadistic murderer to know Milly's adolescent doubts and sufferings?

What do we have here? A thug with a thing about schoolgirls. Let's give him a box full of notes in schoolgirl handwriting, complete with schoolgirl spelling, to remind him how young she was when he took her. Give him copies of her little exercise books, the handwritten lyrics of the songs she danced to. Who knows what enjoyment Bellfield might have derived from this new and deeply personal access to his victim years after he killed her? Through the police, Bellfield got to know so much more about my sister, and I fear that they gave him an opportunity to relive repeatedly the pleasure he had taken in abusing her.

I have another question. Why did the CPS assure my parents that initial suspicions about Dad would not be aired in court? Why did they *not* warn us that Milly's sad private notes would also be exposed while none of her lovely affectionate letters and joyful writings could be shown to balance the picture? Did no one think to tell us that Mum could stand accused – as she had been by the police – of being a bad mother who preferred me to Milly?

At the Old Bailey, we had no counsellor on hand and not enough information. All we had was diazepam to get through this trial. And music. And the support of our friends and family. And the steadfast presence of Alice and Jon.

But even they will be shocked by what happens.

Bellfield's trial for Milly's murder has been reported extensively. Several books have been written about him since then, the authors including the words spoken by the prosecution and defence. Our own statements have been printed in full or in part in these books and in the press. Our posture and clothes have been described. The expressions on our faces have been summarized by journalists, often with compassion, occasionally with the compassion of hungry vultures.

This over-supply of words has left me with a decision to make about how to cover the trial that so many will remember well because of its sensational aspects. I have concluded that my work here is to show what no other writer could – how it felt to be on the inside and behind the scenes of one of the most searing criminal trials of the century so far.

I'm including some short extracts of the 'public' material, to keep things in context, but also because it will look different now: you will be reading it afresh, this time through my eyes.

Just before the trial begins, my friend Vicky sends me a box. Inside is a mass of little parcels, each one prettily gift-wrapped. There's a present for me to open every day of the trial. There's a candle to light when I feel dark. There are DVDs of happy or rollicking movies to distract me from sadness, forensics and death. There are tissues for crying into. There's a bottle of bubble bath to wash away the stains of a dirty day in court. Each gift comes with a loving note.

On 4 May we go to the Old Bailey for the trial preliminaries. We don't even get to the courtroom. Maria Woodall comes to tell us that she's really sorry but it has been decided that the opening speeches may give us information that could change the evidence we are to present. So we stay penned up in the witness suite.

This is the fourth change of mind. But there's no one to complain to. We don't even know who we can talk to about what's going on. We're afraid of making trouble. We still want to be compliant. After all, we are the good guys.

Aren't we?

So we are *quietly* furious that we've come all this way to stare at four small walls. We can't slip away because the press are outside, lying in wait for us. We have to wait for our official police transport. We're told that the day's proceedings will be short and that we can soon go home. But we end up waiting six hours, mostly because Bellfield's defence turns out to have such a lot to say.

It will, in fact, be another twelve days before any of us goes into court. Because first the jury must hear the opening arguments on both sides and then the case against Bellfield for attempting to snatch eleven-year-old Rachel Cowles the day before Milly was abducted. Now twenty-one, Rachel's going to be a witness. The defence is particularly keen to dismantle her evidence because it can be seen as a demonstration of Bellfield's desire, back in March 2002, to snatch a schoolgirl.

Nevertheless, we travel to the Old Bailey every day, only to sit in our grim little room.

In court, there's much discussion of Bellfield's quarters at Belmarsh Prison. Until now the nature of the charge in this case was not officially known to other inmates because of press restrictions. The trial will lift the restrictions and Bellfield will be known as a suspected child-killer. This means that he has 'justifiable' fears for his safety and demands segregated accommodation. His lawyer also wants to make sure that all Bellfield's papers will be transferred to his new cell.

Carole is the only person in the public gallery that day. This is the first time she sees Bellfield in the flesh. He's even uglier than he looked in the photographs she has seen. He's shaved his head. His face is flabby and strangely flat. He has lost weight since he posed for the photographs that the press love to use of him. Perhaps in prison he's not had access to the steroids that – according to the media – bulked him up to twenty stone.

Carole feels that his eyes bore into her. She feels his need to know – *Who are you?* She recalls, 'At that moment I took the decision: "Stare at me and I will stare back, as long as you want. After all, I'm free to get up and walk away whenever I desire. *You* are the prisoner in the dock, already a convicted murderer."'

At times during the trial Carole will get the impression that her continued presence in the gallery either bothers or offends Bellfield. *Good*, she thinks. Yet she worries, too, in case Bellfield tries to get her removed. Carole has signed on to 'serve' Lovely Granny for the whole case, however long it takes. So she must be as compliant as necessary to ensure she can stay.

Carole had planned to take notes. But she's immediately ticked off by court security. Again, she's afraid of Bellfield whistling up his defence to get her excluded. So she stops writing and has to rely on her excellent memory instead.

This is also the first time that Carole sees both the defence and prosecution barristers. Her impression of Altman is that he is calm, measured and authoritative. He has a certain dignity. To Carole, the defence barrister seems no match for Altman in his use of language and his manner. But he has an air of success about him.

The sixth of May is largely devoted to jury selection, which will need to be done twice. One of the jurors suffers a bereavement over the weekend and is excused. On 9 May the jury is reselected with a new member.

The judge gives the usual strict instructions to the jury on keeping themselves away from media reports and social media. Facebook is cited as a particular no-no. He warns that failure to observe this rule may result in a charge of contempt of court. At this stage, the jury do not know what crime is to be tried.

Altman's opening speech on 10 and 11 May crafts the whole story of Milly's abduction and murder in a logical and measured way, dovetailing Bellfield's movements and Milly's. The jury are allowed to hear about Bellfield's previous convictions for Marsha, Amélie and Kate, and about the alleged attempted abduction and false imprisonment of Anna-Maria Rennie, who identified Bellfield in a line-up. Altman speaks of patterns: Bellfield's choice of small young females as his victims; unplanned family holidays and cars suddenly lost or sold after girls are murdered; phones turned off at the times of the killings; the suddenness and speed of the attacks.

However, it has previously been decided, away from the public court, that none of the other allegations against Bellfield, about alleged rapes, the drugging of young girls and antisocial behaviour – all those already written up so graphically in the press – will be mentioned in this trial, despite the ninety-three times he was brought to the attention of the police in the two years before Milly was taken.

The defence goes for a more scattered approach. There's no single angle or point of view. This will prove an accurate representation of what is to come. I don't think anyone ever seriously doubts Bellfield's guilt. So the purpose of the defence seems simply to muddy the situation.

On 10 May Dad is referred to in court as 'nearly a suspect' and matters to do with the house search are also aired. Carole is, of course, in the public gallery that day. She knows the whole story, including certain things that as yet I don't. In her daily call to Lovely Granny,

330

she sends a message: 'If there's anything that Gemma doesn't know about Bob, tell her now.'

Dad calls me into the lounge. Mum's sitting in an armchair. I go to sit on the sofa, so we are in a triangle.

It should have been a circle, with Milly there too.

Dad sits with a notebook open in front of him. He meets my eyes. He doesn't hold back. He's clear and concise, totally to the point. He starts by saying that he'd hoped this conversation would never happen. He tells me that, once the police identified Bellfield as the real suspect, they assured him and Mum that what he's about to tell me would never be used against him. Those promises continued all through the trial preparations. It was not just the police, he says. The CPS have also always told him and Mum that there would be no reference in the trial to what he's about to tell me now.

'Tell me *what*, Dad?'

Dad won't be rushed. 'The promise the police made may be about to be broken, Gemma,' he tells me. 'I want you to hear it from me, now, not in the courtroom.'

This is what Dad tells me: when the police came to search our house they found a box in the loft. It contained fetish videos and magazines. They also found some bondage gear.

'No!'

'Yes. Yes, it was there, Gemma.'

I'm simply not taking this in. I cannot see Dad, my old-fashioned gentle, gentlemanly father, like that. But I don't have time to think. There's more.

It's not just what was in the loft. There were a few minutes missing from Dad's scrupulous account of his day on 21 March 2002, when Milly disappeared. Dad, of course, had openly told the police he had stopped at some motorway services. They then seized CCTV footage of the services and found him looking at soft-porn magazines.

Dad hangs his head. I don't need to look at him to understand how much pain it is causing him to speak these words to me. He's pale and tired. The thought of this conversation with me must have haunted him for years.

I stare at him. 'For God's sake, Dad! Why didn't you just get rid of that stuff when you knew the police were coming to search? You had plenty of time.'

A week passed between Milly's disappearance and the detailed house search.

'Dad! You made it so much worse for yourself.'

Now I remember how the police questioned me over and over again about the magazine Milly had found about nine months before she was taken. As I told the police, the incident had not cast much of a cloud and was soon forgotten. It would have stayed that way, had Milly not disappeared.

Suddenly I'm angry with Dad.

But I'm older now. I've been around a bit. I know how men can be. I say out loud, 'I think if you looked in the attic of half the men in England you might find stuff like that.'

Dad says humbly, 'That doesn't make it OK, Gemma.'

'When did Mum find out?' I ask. I don't like it that they've been keeping secrets from me for years. At the same time, I'm reluctant to engage with the details.

'I told her while they were doing the house search. When we moved in at Lovely Granny's. Mum and I went out for a walk. Do you remember?'

I do. I hate thinking about what it must have done to Mum to find out about this – and at the same time that Milly was first lost.

'What did Mum say?'

'She was absolutely devastated, but her main priority was to protect you. She knew if we split up it would have been the end for you.'

'Bloody hell.'

Yes, I'm furious with Dad. But I'm in warrior mode and very focused. The upcoming trial has targeted my hatred on the real villain. And that's not my dad. That's the person who murdered Milly.

There's been enough anger in our lives. We don't need to direct it at one another.

Now I'm achingly sorry for Dad. At last I understand why the police were able to treat him so badly for all these years. They had something over him. And they used it. Surrey Police must have thought they'd struck gold.

So must Bellfield now, I realize. If he wants to use it in his defence.

So this was why Dad never stood up for himself against the police's insinuations that he might be Milly's killer. Mum had retreated behind her tunnel eyes, unable to connect with the world. Dad reduced himself to a mouse-like character, a non-Dad, nothing like the tall, strong man who had been a climbing frame for his young daughters. When we were on his shoulders, Milly and I felt that we were on top of the world. That man had crumbled away, leaving me nothing to hold on to all these years.

'Why didn't you tell me, Dad? I didn't understand why you didn't stand up to the police.'

Dad says very quietly, 'I didn't want to lose another daughter.'

He has been afraid of my judgement on top of the police's contempt for him.

But I don't judge my father. If Mum has forgiven him, then I can too. He needs our support.

If anything, it's the CPS's betrayal that makes me angriest. They assured us this would not be used in court. They, too, have let him down.

'How can this happen?' I rage.

Dad has no answer to that.

So, even though Dad is not a suspect any more, he can still be put on trial within the trial of his daughter's murderer.

Everything Bellfield needs to do has been prepared for him by Surrey Police.

On 12 May, there's an away-day for the whole court, including Bellfield. They go to Station Avenue, where Milly was last seen, and Collingwood Place, where Bellfield lived. It makes us feel sick and shivery to know that Bellfield's allowed on our streets for a few hours. Even handcuffed and escorted by police officers, he seems dangerous to us.

The whole area is brought to a standstill when twelve jurors, the lawyers and the judge arrive in Walton. A rolling police cordon accompanies them around Walton station, the Travellers Café, Station Avenue, the bus stop where Kat stood, the Birds Eye building. The jurors are also taken to see 24 Collingwood Place, though they do not enter the ground-floor flat.

Before that, they inspect the street, three miles away, where a fat man in a red car accosted Rachel Cowles.

A local reporter describes Bellfield that day: 'And there, in the middle of the scene, casually dressed and in good spirits, was the imposing handcuffed figure of the murderer Bellfield.' The same reporter notes that, when the jurors stood at the place where Milly was last seen, Bellfield was 'smiling and swapping comments with his security detail'.

Only now do I understand why Bellfield was in high spirits that day.

Bellfield knew what was about to happen to Dad and Mum in court.

On 13 May, the jury hear evidence in the Rachel Cowles case. Rachel describes how a man driving a red car had pulled in beside her as she walked home from school. He told Rachel that he'd just moved in next door to her. He was large, balding or shaven and with a 'chubby head'. The car had two child seats in the back and was messy with magazines and sweet wrappers, like the red Daewoo Nexia that Bellfield was using. The man asked Rachel if she wanted a lift. Sensibly, Rachel refused. A police car passed at that moment, and the man in the red car also drove off. Rachel was extremely distressed by the encounter.

Her mother dialled 999 to report the incident. According to later reports, Diana Cowles was worried for other children in the area. But the information was not passed on to the Milly incident room and was not connected with Milly's disappearance the next day. Three years later, with Bellfield and the red car in the news, Diana Cowles again tried to contact the police about what had happened to her daughter. But it took two calls and a letter before there was any police follow-up. By then it was years too late for Milly, Marsha, Amélie and Kate.

Even though I'm not allowed in court until I've given evidence, I still want to go in each day. We crowd into our poky quarters in the witness suite. It's a bit like sitting in a relative's room in a hospital when they're dying. You know there's nothing you can do but you cannot leave.

Because I insist on going, Mum or Dad or both need to be there as well. I'm in such a feverish state that I can't be at the Old Bailey without them. I buy a pretty childlike notebook with a tree and birds on the cover. In it, I start writing things, reacting to what I'm being told about what's going on. Later I will record my reactions while sitting helplessly in Court 8 listening to proceedings.

One entry shows Milly's name inside a heart. Radiating off it are all the lovely things about her . . . *pretty, slim, understanding, bubbly, lovely, vivacious, intelligent, sparkle in her eye, funny.* I write of happy memories, dancing and singing 'Bobby's Girl' for Dad's birthday, sharing a room, the Fun Run, Cuba, swimming with dolphins.

Soon my notes grow increasingly dark. I will write things like 'Does jewellery burn? . . . Does a mobile phone burn?'

There's another notebook, with jolly coloured dots on it, which I share with Mum. We will use it for drafting our end-of-trial statements and, when we are finally allowed in the courtroom, for passing notes to one another, such as 'The lady on the X row at the X end of the jury looks about to fall asleep!'

Up in the public gallery, Carole spends a lot of time watching the press. They seem to walk in and out of the courtroom as they please. They use their mobile phones, albeit silently. The judge has given them explicit instructions about social media. They are allowed to tweet fact but not opinion. Yet who is checking?

The case against Bellfield for the attempted abduction of Rachel Cowles continues. Carole watches sadly as the defence barrister makes much of small discrepancies in the evidence of Rachel and her mother, who crumbles under his mocking, ferocious cross-examination.

Carole notes that the defence barrister loves to ask, 'I am right, am I not?' when he's most painfully undermining a witness.

Dad is due to go into the box on Monday, 16 May.

54.

At the beginning of that day, before the jury are summoned, Altman makes a final attempt to stop Bellfield's defence deploying the items found in our attic.

Two hours later, Maria Woodall comes to find us in the witness suite. Jon and Alice are making tea in the corridor. We're told that the attempt has failed. Mum screams at the top of her voice, 'Operation Destroy the Dowlers' Lives Even More!'

Jon and Alice come rushing in to help.

Dad has to go off to the witness stand at 2 p.m. As he leaves, Mum presses a little gold ring into his hand. It's Milly's ring, which we bought for her in Hurghada. Mum had it enlarged so she can wear it. Now she wants Dad to have it in court. She says, 'If you feel like you're stumbling, hold on to it. Milly will look after you.'

By now Carole has been joined in the public gallery by various people. Some will turn out to be relatives of Bellfield. They are not on his side. There are also people who just enjoy a good murder trial and are regular attenders at the Old Bailey. There are others whose presence she cannot explain. People see Carole sitting in the row reserved for family and close friends of the participants. They surround her and start asking questions about Mum. A man follows her all the way home to East Croydon one evening. In the end, she's given some protection by the court.

Carole, surrounded by strangers, watches Dad arrive at the stand. As always, he carries himself with dignity. To her, he seems calm, yet it's clear that he knows what's coming. Carole glances at Bellfield. He knows what's coming too.

First Altman asks Dad about what happened the afternoon Milly disappeared. It's all straightforward. It doesn't last long.

Now Mum goes downstairs to sit outside the courtroom. Alice is with her. Mum's next up, so she needs to be close at hand for when she's summoned. We've no idea how long Dad's questioning by the defence will take. I long to go with Mum, but I have to stay upstairs in the witness suite with Jon and my cross-stitch.

The defence barrister starts, not by talking about the events of 21 March 2002, as the prosecution did, but about Milly herself. He doesn't even mention Dad's transgression. He will come to that in good time. First he needs to set the scene so that Dad's transgression can be used to maximum effect.

He makes his position clear with his question to Dad, 'Milly had her demons, did she not?'

Is 'demons' the appropriate word to use about a girl who has been murdered?

Dad replies, 'I think she had natural childhood fears.'

To be misrepresented is something Milly would have hated and feared. She had defined her personality so clearly – in the family, at school, among her friends. Milly was Milly, the coolest, warmest girl in Surrey, the dancer, the singer, the fashion icon, the family girl, the occasional Drama Queen, the Guttural Hugger. Now Milly's about to be reinvented as a suicidal, miserable character who is nothing to do with Dad's daughter, a girl with a secret double life.

Milly didn't need a secret double life. She was perfectly happy with the one she had, with us.

The defence barrister reads out two notes scribbled by Milly in a couple of her Drama Queen moments. I've never seen these notes. It's the first time for Dad too. Mum's seen only one of them, or a part of it.

They were found in the police search of Milly's room back in spring 2002. The police must have believed they illustrated their pet theory that Milly had run away. They were not interested in Mum's observation that the handwriting on the note she saw was different from the kind Milly was using at the time she went missing. Milly had customized her writing over the years, changing it just as she changed the way she dressed. It had gone from laborious to cute and curly, to no-nonsense serious Young Adult. Mum reckoned that the note she saw was 'curated' in Milly's eleven- or twelve-year-old writing, with curls on the footers. It was also lettered very carefully, almost as if it were a creative-writing homework exercise. It did not *look* like the passionate outpourings of a tortured soul.

Milly herself did not date these pieces of writing so there's no way to explain how we, or the police, or the defence, can know if they were up-to-the-minute productions. By Bellfield's defence, however, they will be treated as if they were written at the exact time of her disappearance.

We would later be accused by the press of being naïve about the character assassinations that were about to take place in Court 8. Apparently we should have known that the defence would take this tack. But how were we to know, when even the huge-brained prosecution barrister did not appear to be prepared or armed with evidence against this line of questioning?

The defence barrister has a habitually hectoring tone. To read the first note from Milly, he adds a reproving one. It's as if he's asking Dad to face up to what he drove his daughter to write.

> *Dear Daddy and my beautiful Mummy, by the time you find this letter I will be gone, up there or down below you.*
>
> *I have always been that way, below other people.*
>
> *I am sorry, you deserve a better daughter, so I should have left. If anything, you should be happy now, you can concentrate on lovely Gemsie, without me getting in the way.*
>
> *You should have had an abortion or at least had me adopted, then at least I would not have made your life hell as well. I think it would be best if you try and forget me.*
>
> *It's nothing you have done. I just feel I had to go. Please don't let any harm get to any of you, Mum and Dad, please look after Gemma. I am sorry and goodby.*
>
> *Lots of love, as always, your little disappointment, Amanda*

Bellfield's barrister next reads a poem Milly apparently wrote:

> *I don't know what it is I do,*
> *They all just seem to hate me*
> *All they do is slag me off*
> *And force everyone against me.*
> *I know I am pathetic and helpless*
> *And I know I'm not pretty or fit.*
> *But what do they have that I haven't?*
> *Let's face it, I am just totally shit.*

I know what people think, I know how they feel.
What the fuck, I don't know
What do I do to make them hate me.
Maybe I should just go.
Sometimes I think how life would be without me
For Mum and Dad to have a beautiful little girl who is
*   something like Gemma.*
She would be everything I am not, everything I dream to be,
*   pretty, smart, intelligent, wanted loved.*
Then I hit myself and wake up to reality and how bad
*   school's going to be in the morning.*
I hate it but not nearly as much as I hate myself.

Mum and Dad did not expect those notes to be used against them in court by Bellfield. That's how innocent they both were. So to see them is an enormous shock for Dad. He's unnerved, partly by the notes themselves but also because Milly's murderer has been allowed to read them, and to use them and, for all Dad knew, may even have been permitted to have his hands on the originals.

The defence barrister is now going to make use of the disorienting effect of that shock. I think he expects a protest. He expects a quick opportunity to demolish Dad's credibility and to cow him. But he doesn't know Dad, any more than he knows Milly. Dad doesn't rise. He waits politely for the next question. I'm sure this was not lost on the jury: Dad's persistent dignity.

It is also, of course, the first time that Carole has heard these notes. She's a mother. She knows that this is the kind of thing young girls write. They're the kind of notes that she herself wrote as a teenager, the kind of note a teenager writes when she's not allowed to go to a gig. To a teenager, every little denial is like the end of the world. Carole also knows that Milly loved music. Song lyrics are so often melodramatic, often dark. Milly knew the words to a thousand sad songs. She borrowed feelings from them when she was upset or frustrated. That's probably why her poem sounds like the draft of a lyric.

Carole knows that these notes totally misrepresent Milly and that they are being used to misrepresent our family. It angers her. But she can say nothing. Like the witnesses and the jurors, Carole has been sternly briefed to make no comment and to show no emotion. She cannot do anything that will prejudice the case. She has Bellfield's eyes on her. She cannot afford for him to pick her out as a disruption and have her ejected or banned.

The jury have no way of knowing the contents of the first chapters of this book. The jury cannot know who Milly really was, and how inaccurate, how inadequate and misleading a portrait of her is drawn in two short pieces of writing she produced at unknown dates for unknown reasons. Bellfield's lawyer is not going to present to the court any of Milly's hundreds of loving, exuberant notes – because the police were not interested in those when they did the searches – and neither would such happy truths be of interest to Bellfield's defence team. They are allowed to use these notes against Dad.

That's how the justice system works.

The prosecution does not seem to have been prepared to have Milly and her family prosecuted right back. The prosecution has prepared to present none of Milly's 'Love you lots like Jelly Tots' cards or her affectionate happy letters to the family addressed also 'to the frogs and newts'.

Meanwhile, Dad's had no time to ready himself, emotionally or mentally, for this encounter with two heart-rending pieces of writing. Even if he'd had time to think about these letters, to question the timing of them, to mention the handwriting, we know that the defence barrister would close off any such comments.

In front of me and Mum, Dad did not cry when Milly went missing, or when her body was found. He managed to speak at the funeral service without breaking down. This was not because he is a cold man. He is the opposite. He is a man full of fiery love for his family. He puts us first. He knows that Mum and I need to vent our feelings. He's needed to be the calm one, the shoulder to cry on, the strong arms around us. He's always looked after us, keeping his own feelings under the strictest control. So now, listening to these unbearable pieces of writing, brought up in this literally judgemental context, he finally breaks.

Before the defence barrister finishes reading the two notes, Dad is weeping silently. He brings a crisp linen handkerchief out of his pocket. After wiping his eyes, he straightens up and gets ready for the next blow. He's behaving like the gentleman he is.

Dad is crying for Milly, not for himself. She is long gone, yet he still cannot bear her pain, any more than he could when she was alive and scraped her knee, impaled her arm on a stick, or suffered bullying at school. Dad has one agenda: justice for his daughter. The defence barrister has another: demolishing my father.

For Dad, it is not a game: it's about Milly. He doesn't need to win or score points, just tell the truth. Unfortunately he has to listen to Milly's words while directly in the line of Bellfield's sight and at the same time as the jury and the world press. Bellfield is clearly fascinated. This is power, to see the father of his victim suffering like this. This is the man who has already put Dad through six months of loss and not-knowing, the dreadful hours in Minley Wood, two years of mystery and nine years of grief. This is his reward: to watch Dad suffer.

Equally unfortunately, Dad has to look at the defence barrister while he listens to the words. This means that Bellfield's in his sightline too. Dad does not deign to give him a glance. It is just that there's a monster-shaped blob in the left-hand corner of his vision.

Only now that the courtroom is full of teenage misery, and a father hanging his head in sorrow is on display in front of the jury – *now*, the defence barrister brings up the fetish magazine Milly found, by accident, under a drawer.

So, silently, Carole watches Dad being pulled into a trap. It is horrifying, she thinks, the lengths to which the defence will go. She recalls, 'It seemed to me that it was nothing more than a weak diversionary tactic, steer the jury and, because of press coverage, the public away from the horror of Bellfield's crimes.'

There is absolutely nothing in the content of the two notes to connect them to Milly's finding the magazine. But Bellfield's lawyer can be creative about that. All he has to do is mention them together: the magazine and the Drama Queen notes.

Dad knows exactly what's coming next. It's the thing he has feared, but for which he has prepared himself. What he didn't realize is that it could be, and would be, put into a sinister light by juxtaposing it with some of Milly's private thoughts written at a completely different time.

Dad acknowledges that Milly would have thought the magazine 'horrible and disgusting'. He is forced to admit keeping the magazine was irresponsible of him and 'a complete betrayal of her as a father'. Yet that's not actually what Bellfield's lawyer is making Dad admit. This is not really about the magazine. The lawyer is using the magazine to get Dad to make a much more holistic statement about his relationship with Milly: that he was, across the board, across time, 'a complete betrayal of her as a father'.

And Bellfield's defence barrister knows that now he has got these words out of Dad's mouth the press will helpfully spread them all over the newspapers.

Dad doesn't have the opportunity or the spirit left to point out the obvious – that the magazine had nothing to do with Milly's death, and that he himself is not supposed to be on trial for Milly's murder. The actual person on trial for that crime is sitting in his cage. And no one's blaming *him* for his sexual history, spectacularly coercive and violent as it is. That's not allowed to be mentioned in this court.

The defence's next objective is to make Dad name himself as the first suspect in Milly's murder. Just getting those words out there will take attention away from the man already convicted of killing two young girls and trying to kill a third. So the defence barrister then goes on to supply to the court the full inventory of what the police found in our attic. His slant is that Milly *might* have found these items too and her distress at the discovery could have made her run away.

There is no evidence for such a thing. He plants the image anyway.

The defence barrister and his client are not going to spare Dad anything. So now the QC brings up the video footage of Dad looking at soft-porn magazines at a motorway service station on his way home the day Milly disappeared.

I simply don't know how the defence barrister did what he did next. I don't understand the mentality that agrees to destroy a man whose beloved daughter has been killed. I know it is not the defence barrister but Levi Bellfield who is directing these proceedings. Still, the barrister allows himself to be the murderer's filthy mouthpiece. He then suggests that Dad went home aroused by the magazines and masturbated in the bedroom before he got on with his work.

I could have left these words out of my book. I thought about it. God knows I don't want to put Dad through any more. But both Dad and I think it is important that we tell the truth here. Because it is only by putting these words on the page that we can start to convey what it was like in that courtroom. I also want to give you a chance to judge whether you think that this is an appropriate way for a defence barrister to cross-examine the father of a murder victim – in front of the paedophile who killed his daughter. And, unlike Dad, that man can decide whether or not he wants to take the witness stand.

You can read this in a situation of safety and privacy. No one is watching or judging you. Dad is facing these questions in the highly charged atmosphere of a courtroom, with his daughter's murderer listening to every word. And the world's press are busy scribbling down the whole thing. They are not thinking about a murdered girl any more. They have been given an angle of a salaciousness they could previously only dream of.

Meanwhile, Bellfield's sexual history has been put away and wrapped in cotton wool to protect him from prejudicial treatment. Ruled not admissible: the ninety-three reports to the police about his aggressive, predatory behaviour in the two years before he took Milly. Ruled not admissible: previous girlfriends' statements about being beaten, kicked, burned with cigarettes, strangled and raped. Ruled not admissible: allegations of gang rapes of under-age girls.

If the defence wanted to put Dad in the frame, should it not have acknowledged that there were no victims to what Dad did beyond the hurt it gave Mum and me? Bellfield's victims are many. They'll probably be traumatized for the rest of their lives. Some are physically scarred. Some are dead.

But that is not how the law is working in Court 8 today. The judge does not ask the defence barrister to desist from this line of questioning. With so much stacked against him, Dad is beyond defending himself.

Carole recalls that the defence barrister 'had a belligerent stance and later during the trial he almost became bullying when cross-examining the witnesses. I emphasize "almost". He never quite crossed the line to being bullying. He was never admonished by the judge and, however we felt about his tactics, it's worth remembering that his line of questioning was not closed down. It is my firm belief that, with this judge, if he had overstepped the acceptable legal bounds for cross-examination he would have been stopped.'

It has been offered as theory that the judge let the defence barrister go so far because he wanted to fend off any line of eventual appeal by Bellfield. In other words, the court had to push Dad to the limit because it was necessary to demonstrate that Bellfield had been given every possible means of defending himself. If so, well, it's a commendable *idea*. Perhaps, in legal terms, it's like the principle of chemo- and radiotherapy – you need to kill the cancer by throwing every poison at it. Yet the effects of the treatment are so appalling that you shut down the disease only at the expense of nearly destroying the patient.

The defence barrister still has not finished with Dad, who now has to admit that he was once a police suspect in Milly's disappearance, and why. At least he gets to point out, 'I was very concerned because I knew, if they only focused on me, they absolutely needed to be focused on someone else.'

The 'someone else' sits in the dock. It is nine years, and at least two murders later, partly because Surrey Police's focus was fixed on Dad when it should have been on the twice-convicted killer in his Perspex cage.

Nevertheless, reactivating the police's old, wrongful template, the defence barrister now reads out part of Dad's police interrogations back in March 2002.

'Are you in any way responsible for Milly's disappearance?' Dad was asked then. His reply was, 'The only way I can be responsible is if she had seen some of this material and decided to run away. God forbid she decided to take her own life or run away. I have no involvement in any other way.'

But Dad isn't going to falter again. He has prepared himself for this part, even though the police and CPS assured him so many times that it would never happen.

Nothing that the defence can throw at him now is going to crack Dad's grief. This is not the worst day of Dad's life. The worst day of Dad's life was, and always will be, the one when he lost Milly.

We can only hope that the jury understand this.

Carole recalls, 'I don't think that the defence barrister had factored in how dignified Bob would be throughout his cross-examination. Yes, there were tears, yet at no time did he lose his composure and he just took on the chin the accusations about his private matters. It was dreadful to watch but I remember saying to Sally later, "You should be so proud of how he conducted himself, a true gentleman." I meant it. Would I have been so composed under such duress? Would anyone? Very, very doubtful.'

The defence barrister sits down, satisfied. He has indeed done a marvellous job for his client – if his brief was to make cruel caricatures of Dad and Milly, and divert attention from the scattered bones of a naked, murdered thirteen-year-old girl found in lonely Minley Woods, and how she got there.

If he could have, I think the defence barrister would have patted himself on the back just then. He has indeed done splendid work for his client.

But has the defence barrister done a splendid job for justice?

Now it is the turn of Brian Altman, the prosecution barrister.

'At every step of the trial,' Carole remembers, 'Altman was quietly measured and never raised his voice or lost his composure. The defence barrister, on the other hand, often became animated during a particular point and had an unfortunate unctuous inflection when addressing the judge. He would say "my lllawd" as though there were several ls at the beginning of the word and "aw" instead of "or". I have often been told that a good barrister knows the answer to every question he puts to a witness before he asks it. Was this part of the difference between the two barristers? Nothing appeared to surprise Brian Altman.'

Altman tries to limit the damage as best he can, giving Dad a chance to explain that Milly's behaviour was not changed by her discovery of the magazine nine months before she went missing, and that she was never afraid of him or unwilling to be alone with him in the house.

When I hear about this, I scribble in my notebook, *Milly didn't want to be in the house with Dad only? What a ridiculous statement. It makes me sick. Is that really where the defence wants to go?* I think, *Milly LOVED being in the house with Dad. He's the soft touch. With Dad, she could get away with not eating all her dinner and still being allowed pudding.*

Milly herself had written in her English book, 'In a young child, generally they find there home the most safest, nicest, familiarest place they know.'

That's because that was how it was to us.

If I had been there, and if it had been my little brain under the white wig, and not Altman's enormous one, I would at this point have asked a different series of questions. I would have asked Dad to recall all the things that happened in our family between the finding of the magazine and Milly's disappearance. It would have taken a long, long time, and all the many stories would have added up to a detailed picture of a happy family, on holiday in Cuba, swimming with dolphins, singing and dancing together at home and for Hatton Operatic Society, all the family walks, the sitting together watching videos, the birthday parties, the Sunday lunches, the Fun Run. It would have taken so long to recount *all* the happy family occasions that an almost *physical* distance could have been established in the jury's mind between Milly finding the magazine and Milly being killed.

Those questions would have also redrawn the portrait of Milly created by the defence. It would have shown my sister for who she truly was.

Unfortunately the information that would accurately portray our family is irrelevant in the game of brains being played out by the defence and the prosecution. The prosecution's job is not to defend our family. It is purely focused on getting a watertight conviction for the murderer. So Dad has been claimed as a pawn by Bellfield's defence. He's been knocked off the board with a flourish. The prosecution cannot worry about that now. Onwards and upwards. Dad has been a necessary sacrifice. Dad has even accepted his fate, conveniently. The bigger picture is winning the game, with other pieces.

As the defence knows, the press have their story now, and nothing is going to make them hold back on their headlines, not even the sight of Dad bravely admitting to everything and making not one single excuse for himself. They have the words, but they are going to need a picture to illustrate it.

They will work it out.

And Dad? Leaving the witness box, discarded by both the major players, Dad feels relief. He will tell me later that he finally felt free. After that day in court, the police and press will no longer have anything to hold over him. All of us have been virtually black-mailed by the police for so long: 'If you do that, we cannot stop the press getting hold of the info . . . If you do that, your career will be over.'

Dad has been brow-beaten for nine years because the police had the trump card of what was found in the attic. It's been played now, finally.

The trouble is, it's been played by the defending team of Milly's murderer.

Is that really what the police wanted?

Dad does not look at Bellfield when he leaves Court 8. He will not show Milly's murderer the pain in his eyes.

Carole remembers Dad's upright dignity as he left that devastating scene. He had told the truth, and he had done it for Milly and our family. All Dad wanted to do was behave like the father Milly knew, even in a situation that would have mortified, humiliated and horrified Milly herself. And that is just what he has done.

Mum and I have no idea yet, but the full cunning of Bellfield is now dawning on Dad. As he walks out, he can hear the whispers and shuffles of the press, their clicking iPhones and Blackberrys. Dad's aware Bellfield knows that today's revelations will take the moral spotlight off him. Dad understands that the press will be more interested in sex than in murder.

Dad keeps walking towards the door. He knows that Mum is waiting behind it. He has nothing to lose now for himself. From the moment he leaves the stand, he's thinking about just one thing: how to protect what's left of his family. Having just been emotionally dismembered, he is terrified about what Bellfield and his clever minions will do to Mum. Even though he was ambushed by unexpected and terrible material, Dad has been able to take it. But will Mum? He knows how fragile she is.

Even without being in the room, Mum's been able to guess at

some – though not all – of what's been happening to Dad. Now Dad's face, as he exits the court and walks towards her, tells her that it's been worse than she could have imagined.

He needs to give Mum Milly's ring for her turn in court. But he is not allowed to talk to Mum or touch her. So he hands the ring to Alice, who silently gives it to Mum. Fitting the ring back on her finger, Mum's already in tears as she is led into the courtroom.

Dad comes up to the witness suite, accompanied by Jon. He is very quiet. He gives me a hug. I know from his face that he won't speak to me about what has just happened to him. He's not allowed to; he also doesn't want to. It does not need to be said.

Jon quietly leaves us to it. Dad and I cram our headphones on. I pull the cross-stitch out and stab wildly at the fabric. Dad looks down at his knees. He sits there motionless for the rest of the afternoon.

Remember the song on Dad's iPod? Pete Townshend's 'Behind Blue Eyes'. If you don't know it, it goes like this:

> *No one knows what it's like*
> *To be the bad man*
> *To be the sad man*
> *Behind blue eyes.*
> *No one knows what it's like*
> *To be hated*
> *To be fated*
> *To telling only lies.*
> *But my dreams*
> *They aren't as empty*
> *As my conscience seems to be.*
> *I have hours, only lonely*
> *My love is vengeance*
> *That's never free . . .*

Dad has only the music and his love for family. There's no satisfactory vengeance to be had for Milly, not in this system.

Back down in Court 8, Carole is watching as Altman encourages Mum to talk about what a happy girl Milly was, letting Mum's sincerity and loving nature become clear to the court. No one can be in a room with Mum without understanding those things about her.

Then he asks her about the day Milly disappeared. Mum answers fluently but there's a tremor in her voice. Finally he asks her about the magazine. Mum tells the truth, that Milly was taken aback at finding it all those months before she went missing. Milly didn't hide her feelings and they were able to discuss them frankly. Mum says, 'I told her, "It doesn't mean that Daddy doesn't love me."'

Then come the familiar questions about whether Milly would get into a car with a stranger.

The very stranger himself sits there watching Mum suffer. Unlike Mum, he knows full well that there's more acute suffering to come at the hands of his barrister, at his own direction. That's power, for Bellfield, knowing horrible things that other people can't even guess at, leaving them to the torture of speculation.

But the murderer's treat is delayed. It's been a long day and Mum's cross-examination by Bellfield's barrister is postponed until the next afternoon.

Mum, Dad and I meet up in the witness room. So many terrible feelings crowd into that small space. Mum is mid-evidence so she cannot talk about what she has been through. Dad is catatonic. I know better than to ask questions.

Alice and Jon hurry us down to the bin-store where our car is waiting. It pulls out of the Old Bailey drive. Jon's at the wheel. Dad's in the front seat, the only place that can accommodate his long legs. Mum and I are in the back with Alice. I'm behind Dad and Mum's in the middle. Even though I've been told nothing, I'm sitting there thinking, *This is the worst day since Milly went missing.*

Jon tries to turn left as usual. 'What the –?' he shouts. Mum and I turn to Alice, who looks worried. When *Alice* looks worried, *we* have learned to be terrified.

The press have found a way to get the picture they need to illustrate today's sensational story.

The road is blocked by a lorry that has halted crossways just in front of us. The press are waiting for us. Swarming around all four sides of the car, they get all the photos they need of Dad looking devastated. He covers his eyes with his hand. Unlike Bellfield, Dad's not a professional criminal. He doesn't know that this gesture can be described as the body language of shame, not pain. On the television coverage after the case, you can see me flinching away and crying out in terror from the cameras that are rammed against the glass. I look like a cornered animal.

Mum had brought some scarves for herself and me, knowing how both of us feel the cold, and thinking that we would need the comfort and warmth at the end of the day. Mum and I grab those scarves and hold them up to our faces. It's too late for Mum: the press have already caught her stunned, sorrowful face behind Dad's. The press want above all an image of them together at this point.

Dad doesn't want a scarf. He has accepted what happened to him in court. He has accepted what is going to happen to him at the hands of the press.

Jon does his best to manoeuvre the car out of the press scrum. He drives as aggressively as he can without running anyone down, no matter how provocatively they position themselves for their money shots. We reverse back towards the bin-store. The door is still shutting, with its usual tortuous slowness, so we can't get back inside. All this time, we are at the press's mercy.

At last the lorry moves and Jon accelerates out of the road. He says sincerely to Dad, 'I'm so sorry I couldn't stop that happening. That's the last thing you needed.'

Dad says, 'It's not your fault, Jon.'

I don't know yet exactly what has happened to Dad. I cannot believe what the press have done in order to get a photo of him.

Why, I wonder, *are they not surrounding Bellfield's prison van like this?*

Then I realize: *Of course, Bellfield is protected from press scrums like this. By the police. By the law.*

We drive home in silence. It is the legal silence of fully bound witnesses, and the silence of people who are speechless with shock.

Later we are told that some journalists paid the lorry driver to block the road and trap us. That shows just how good a job the defence barrister had done on behalf of his client. He'd created a feeding frenzy in the press. This was a story that *needed* a photograph of Dad looking despairing and Mum looking wretched. The press do not always resort to stunts like this. But that day the press, like children pumped up on too much sugar, took to acting out.

Lovely Granny is waiting. By the time we get home, she has received her briefing call from Carole, so she knows what Mum and Dad have been through and we don't need to contaminate our witness silence by explaining things.

Normally we eat. Tonight Lovely Granny has to coax food into us.

The trial is all over the television news. Passing through the hall to get some tea, Mum's unlucky enough to glimpse the 'goodbye note' from Milly on the screen. It should not have been shown and I'll never know how it got there. She starts screaming. Even her knitting cannot soothe her. I don't watch the news: it's against the law. I still have my evidence to give.

Mum and Dad carefully don't tell me about the two sad notes from Milly. They don't need to rile me up any more. Alice and Jon have enough to do at this moment, just keeping me from making any kind of outburst. I am a powder-keg and everyone is rightfully afraid of me. The real target of my fury is protected by the court, and his representative doesn't care how I feel. So I lash out at everyone else.

After supper, I do what I usually do. I watch mindless television – carefully avoiding the news – until midnight, trying to trick my mind into a vanilla state.

The papers the next morning have a feast of Dad. Of course they're kept from me, for both legal and emotional reasons. I've read them for the first time while researching this book. Mum writes in her trial notes, 'All the sleaze and salacious details they want.'

As directed by Bellfield's legal team, the press have obediently linked Milly's disappearance with Dad's magazine, even though the defence did not – because it could not – make any timeline link. No one in the press cares. This is a *story*. No one seems to care that the very trial of Bellfield demonstrates clearly that Dad's magazines are nothing to do with Milly's death.

The *Daily Mail*'s subhead on 17 May is 'Daughter found sleazy magazine and left tormented notes, jury told.' The *Daily Star* headlines, 'MILLY FATHER HAD A STASH OF PORN & BONDAGE GEAR.'

Only the *News of the World, The Times* and the *Sun*, the Murdoch papers, are a little bit careful, a little bit delicate. And only our family knows why, but we are not allowed to mention it to anyone yet.

There's even a bit of sympathy in the *Sun*: 'DOWLER DAD WEEPS IN COURT. MILLY'S AGONY.'

The next morning Court 8 is out of action for administrative reasons. So Mum will not be on the stand until the afternoon of Tuesday, 17 May.

Before being collected in the cramped car, Mum goes for a run along the river with Maisy. They go from Walton Bridge down to Weybridge and back. But the stress hasn't dissipated. She phones Lorna, a friend from her knitting club. Lorna picks up the phone and hears Mum weeping inconsolably about Milly's notes. Lorna's heart is breaking. She tells Mum the notes are 'typical teenage angst. Everyone does it'. I'm not sure why Mum needs reassurance, because she knows this is the truth, but Lorna's words give her the strength to carry on.

At the Old Bailey, we sit in silence in the witness suite, waiting for Mum to be called. With us are Carole, Julie, Auntie Linds and Loley. They all want to support Mum today. Julie has brought extra Percy Pigs; Loley has brought a make-up kit to make sure Mum's got the most extreme waterproof mascara; Carole's on the final stretch with her knitted postman hedgehog. They'll all be up in the gallery, fixing their love on Mum when she answers to the defence barrister who pilloried Dad.

This time, when Mum goes in, I shall be the one waiting outside the courtroom. And Dad, who has now been cross-examined, will be able to go into Court 8 to watch proceedings. He will sit next to Bellfield, with only a couple of yards and a screen between them, so he can watch, helplessly, what the murderer's defence barrister is going to do to Mum.

55.

Even without reading a word, Mum knows that our family has been held up for humiliation and that millions of newspaper readers have digested Dad's shame over their breakfast. She can guess what the world has been told to think of her husband and her marriage. This is our fear: after Bellfield's cunning move, propagated by the press, how many people will still have wholehearted sympathy for us?

And how many people on the jury will have been influenced by what they saw in court yesterday? Will they understand the attempt at manipulation? Will they see that there's no link between Dad's magazine and Milly's murder?

Mum's going over her dates and times in her head, not wanting to be caught out deviating from her police statements, hoping to be a calm and competent witness, eager to help the process of justice, still wanting to believe in the process of justice. She's hoping that being sure of herself will help her control her feelings. She turns Milly's little ring around on her finger.

When Mum is called, I actually feel relieved. The waiting is over.

By the time Mum walks into Court 8, everyone else is there. Bellfield is in his dock, the best seat in the house for watching the continued annihilation of the Dowler family. The judge is there; the gallery is full. The jurors and counsel are ready, too. The press are re-energized by their exciting day yesterday. Their pen is full to bursting.

At first, Mum stands steadfast in front of the defence barrister. She refuses to look at his client. Afterwards she will tell me that she felt him staring at her so intently that it seemed as if his flat eyes were piercing her skin. He is the ultimate predator, able to project fear on to anyone. He has already taken Mum's child: now he has power over Mum herself. This is wrong: he seems too powerful. Bellfield has only two reptile-like eyes, but it feels to Mum as if he has a thousand, all trained on her.

Bellfield's line today will be that Mum was a bad mother who preferred me to Milly and who failed to protect her daughter from a bad father. Milly was therefore so miserable that she ran away and came to harm, or even fatally self-harmed. And thus, in Bellfield's logic, Mum and Dad were effectively Milly's killers, causing her death through their failures in parenting.

The defence barrister asks Mum with theatrical sympathy, 'Would you like to take a seat?'

'No,' says Mum. 'I'm fine standing.'

In truth, Mum's channelling Lovely Granny. She's thinking, *I'll stand even if it kills me, you bastard.*

The defence barrister starts straight in on the magazine and how much it must have upset Milly. Mum says that Milly's mood might have changed a little after discovering the magazine but it had certainly returned to normal and was normal at the time she vanished.

The defence barrister takes the opportunity to insinuate that Mum may have shut her eyes to the material and its effect on Milly. Neither is Mum allowed to distance the magazine from Milly's disappearance. It worked the day before – the press took the bait – so it's not surprising that the defence barrister then pounces on the Drama Queen notes, especially the one that says Mum and Dad should 'concentrate on lovely Gemsie without me getting in the way'.

The defence barrister asks her, 'Have you seen this letter before? Would you like me to refresh your memory?'

Mum says, 'I saw it on the television last night.'

I'm sure the members of the jury flinch at that. But perhaps they understand how Mum felt, seeing Milly's handwriting and words in that context.

Mum says truthfully, 'A lot of girls write that kind of stuff. It's not unusual. I'm a teacher. I see them scribbling this type of stuff all the time.'

She has fallen into a trap. 'But did it produce a picture of your daughter which you did not recognize as her mother?'

In other words, the defence barrister implies, Mum never really knew Milly. In other words, poor Milly suffered a sense of exile within our family. In other words, poor Milly was allowed to grow up miserable, without Mum even knowing. That's because Mum was busy enjoying herself with her perfect other daughter, me.

The questions that follow are leading, insinuating, horrible: 'Were you aware that Milly may have felt that you favoured your elder daughter over her?'

It's a classic 'trap' question to which every direct answer is incriminating.

If Mum were to answer 'Yes,' she would be damned.

If she were to answer 'No,' she would be damned.

What kind of question is this to put to a woman grieving for her murdered daughter?

Mum simply screams. Then she cries. 'But it wasn't true. It was not true at all.'

Up in the gallery, Carole, Julie, Auntie Linds and Loley are in agony, and in tears. They came to support Mum, yet they are helpless at this spectacle. They are outraged, almost unable to believe what they are seeing and hearing. Carole recalls, 'The defence was like a predator *playing* with its prey.'

The defence barrister hasn't finished. His client has directed and he has agreed to do some more 'work' on the case against Milly herself. This one's a bit of a stretch. It is going to be hard for anyone to prove, as much as they'd apparently like to, that Milly got herself to a remote field twenty miles from home, stripped off, disposed of her clothes far from the site, returned naked and lay down to die on purpose.

Instead, they are going to paint her as the kind of girl who was 'asking for it'.

Asking for trouble. Asking for a man to snatch her off the street and murder her. Asking to die, beautiful, smart, thirteen, with *Stars In Their Eyes* just days away.

The morality of this? Again, I cannot tell you because I shall never understand what made an intelligent lawyer agree to torture my mother like this, and to slander my dead sister. Of all the bad surprises our family has suffered over the years, this is one of the worst.

Carole is worried about Mum. The suggestions are outrageous. No matter what Mum says, the defence barrister has mapped out his path of destruction and he's not going to deviate.

He's also deploying his special trick for undermining those he cross-examines. As Carole has noticed, his 'I am right, am I not?' makes witnesses doubt themselves. It makes them flounder. It makes them make fools of themselves. It makes them sound less than credible.

Carole is finding it hard to breathe. How much more can Mum take?

She's going to have to take a lot more, because it's going to get worse.

Bellfield's defence now introduces the idea that Milly had a 'double life'. He brings up the name of her email account (in fact a jokey play on a line in an old Tom Jones song). He suggests that Milly was a regular in internet chat-rooms, and that she counteracted her feelings of being rejected, ugly and bullied by finding her fun outside our family.

Mum explains that Milly used just MSN and spoke only to people she knew.

The barrister brings up Mum's request to be hypnotized back in May 2002 when she wanted to see if she might recall anything useful, especially a sense of perhaps having seen Milly in a group of schoolchildren the afternoon she disappeared. Mum withdrew that request after two weeks: this too is now made to look suspicious.

Mum's forced to admit, 'I was on the brink of insanity, my mind was going over and over. I had a nervous breakdown, for God's sake.' Then she says, 'Hang on a minute. Is this about the time when I phoned Alice at about four in the morning completely desperate and so distressed at not being able to answer all the police questions?'

The question Mum's really asking is, how does Bellfield's barrister know about that?

But Mum has fallen into another trap. That word 'insanity' will make a good headline. A good headline about Mum will divert attention from Bellfield.

Another tick in the box for 'Operation Destroy the Dowlers'.

The insinuations of the defence sound very familiar. This is because we've heard them before. Most disappeared girls of Milly's age come home, shamefaced yet safe. Milly's murdered body had

MISSING

Amanda Dowler, Age 13,

Last seen Thursday Afternoon 21st March walking from Walton Station to Walton Park along Station Avenue and Rydens Road at about 4 o'clock. She was wearing her school uniform.

Milly and Hannah Mac went to a photo booth at Woolworths in Chertsey to get pictures for their Friendship Book. We gave this one to the police the night Milly went missing as it was the most recent picture we had of her. We also put it on our own MISSING posters. We used our home phone number because of delays in getting an incident room number from the police.

The first appeal after Milly's disappearance, Monday 25 March, 2002.

Still missing. Months of desperation were etched on Mum's and Dad's faces in this photo taken for an interview with *Good Housekeeping*. On the left are the photos of Milly that were still all over our fridge.

The police left these flowers to show us where Milly's remains had lain. You can see me among the trees, desperate not to be here.

Dad and Mum held me after Milly's memorial service at Guildford Cathedral on 8 October 2003.

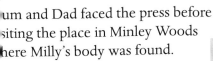

um and Dad faced the press before siting the place in Minley Woods here Milly's body was found.

After the service, I kept a secret promise to Milly by releasing twenty-five coloured balloons.

Milly's funeral on 21 March 2003, the first anniversary of her disappearance. Lovely Granny walked just behind me and Dad. At the time, none of us knew what had happened to Milly. But we were pictured here passing the place where Bellfield snatched her.

Outside the crematorium. For the coffin, Milly's name was spelled out in white roses. Uncle Pete designed a musical-note tribute and Uncle Brian had a saxophone made out of flowers, tucking a bumper box of Maltesers behind it. Hannah Mac went for bright colours to show Milly's vibrant personality.

alking our dog Maisy just before the death-threat letter arrived. After that,
ould not walk the dog or go anywhere alone for a long time. At one point
ery member of the family was in therapy, including the dog.

helsea Flower Show, where the 'Milly' sweet pea won a gold medal in 2006.
ou can see 'Milly' between Alan Titchmarsh and Mum.

Mum changes the flowers in
Milly's pot each season.

With my friend Lauren. This
lovely girls' night out in 2007
ended in a horrific panic attack
and hospitalization.

Mum and I found peace and happiness in encounters with dolphins and fish on our diving expeditions. Our diving teacher montaged this picture and sent it to help us through the trial.

Before and after the trial, Mum tried to expend her restless energy on endless spinning at Hampton Pool. As for me – I pulled on boxing gloves.

Craft-therapy during the trial. Mum was knitting her famous fish blanket; Lovel Granny's 'court correspondent' Carole (left) was making a hedgehog postman. At a particularly dreadful point in the trial, the hedgehog postman would get it in the eye with a knitting needle.

The blanket Mum knitted at the Old Bailey. Characters she sewed on to the squares included Milly's favourite shark, the Tasselled Wobbegong, a dolphin like the ones we swam with in Cuba and our dog Maisy, as well as a sea-slug an a jellyfish.

been found, yet still the prosecution is being allowed to insinuate that our family had driven her out of her home to meet her fate at the hands of anyone but Bellfield. The point the defence barrister seems to want to make is: if we had not been such a bad family, then Milly would still be alive.

As with Dad, the defence is using the police's own templates against us.

But the police had set them first. That should never be forgotten.

The defence barrister stands down.

Carole has silent tears running down her face.

She remembers thinking, 'How was that allowed to happen? What the hell am I going to say to Lovely Granny?'

Carole still finds it very difficult to revisit that episode. 'My precious Sally had dealt with so much sorrow and these vile people had destroyed her all over again.'

Altman is now allowed to put some questions to Mum. He tries to help her re-establish the truth about Milly, a girl who never spoke of running away, a girl who was absolutely not dark or depressed.

'She was happy. We were a happy family,' says Mum.

You, the reader of this book, can judge the truth of that.

Released from the witness box, Mum gulps, as if she's trying not to vomit. She screams, a low-pitched growling noise from the pit of her being. The last time she made a noise like that was at Milly's funeral when the coffin began to edge towards the furnace.

As Mum leaves the witness box, her legs buckle. She can't walk a step further. Instead, she begins to fall. Dad rises out of his seat, but he knows he's not allowed to go to the witness stand. Alice is. She puts both arms around Mum and guides her towards the door, quietly saying, 'You did really well, Sally, really well.'

Mum's determined to keep herself together until she's out of the court, but, just before they make it to the main doors, she collapses on the floor, weeping and flailing her arms and legs. Now Dad rushes to her. So does the court matron. Mum's so out of it that she doesn't really know who they are. She tries to fight them all off, screaming and making incoherent noises of rage and distress.

Mum on the floor at the Old Bailey.

Mum's in danger of being trampled by the press, who have another spectacular front-page story to file. The matron and Alice pull Mum to her feet.

Dad is not an angry man. At this moment he experiences the greatest rage he's ever felt. He feels as if he has just watched his wife being physically assaulted in public, and that nobody helped. Nobody has expressed the outrage that should have been expressed. Everyone, apart from our friends in the gallery, sat silent and impassive, obeying the court rules. This has all taken place in front of Bellfield, who has already almost destroyed our family – and in front of the press.

I'm waiting for my turn outside when I hear Mum's scream.

It sounds primitive, and I have a primitive response. *'Mum!'* I cry out, like a child. I try to rush into the courtroom. I'm thinking, *Just let me in there – I'll tell that jury what they need to know.*

I'm restrained by court officials. I have not yet given my evidence so I'm not allowed in. Outside the courtroom door, I have a full-blown panic attack. I, too, end up on the floor, screaming in front of the media.

One reporter shows compassion, handing me a bottle of water.

From inside the courtroom, Dad's throwing me agonized looks, but his hands are full with Mum. How can he choose between us? The law decides. He's not allowed to talk to me. Auntie Linds and Loley run down from the public gallery. Auntie Linds takes me in her arms and hustles me away from the press.

By now Mum's upstairs in the witness suite, heavily dosed with diazepam and being looked after by Alice. She's so exhausted that she falls unconscious – I wouldn't call it sleep. That would be too kind, too restful, for her state. At least she's allowed out of the nightmare for a time.

Back in the courtroom, the defence and the prosecution are in a huddle. Mum's meltdown is being discussed. The defence barrister wants it on the record that he did not bully my mother into a collapse. He insists that catching a glimpse of me through the swinging doors of the courtroom was the reason why Mum broke down. It was not his questioning that made her lose control: it was the sight of me.

A little later, Carole spots the defence barrister in the street outside the court.

He is smoking a cigarette and his hands are shaking.

Milly and I were not allowed to swear as children. If we said 'bloody' we'd be in real trouble. 'Sugar!' was the prescribed exclamation.

When Milly disappeared, everything changed. Mum and I descended into foul language. It was as if we had lost our connections to the old decencies. We were breaking down, and so were our words. We didn't have enough of them to describe how we felt. The hard, brute consonants of swear words were our crude blows to defend ourselves.

Dad held on to correct language until the trial of Milly's killer. But on the day that the defence barrister paints Mum a bad mother, Dad changes.

Mum's in our Witness Services cell, her head on the table, barely conscious. In another suite of the Witness Services space, Dad and I are waiting to see the prosecution team.

I'm fuming. Dad is livid. We are joined by Altman, his aide, and Maria Woodall, who looks devastated by what she's just seen.

Altman addresses me, 'Gemma, I know how you feel.'

I say, 'Shut the fuck up. You do not know what I feel. How can you say that you know what I feel? You don't have a clue what you have just let happen.'

Dad holds up a hand. 'Gemma, stop it.'

I look at him. There's something different about him. His authority is returning. He's growing back into the man he used to be, the man Milly would recognize. I know I can rely on him to protect us now.

Then Dad raises his voice – something so rare in him. He raises it in his special way. It's the tone he would use to tell me and Milly off for something really shameful. Quiet as he is, I'm sure everyone in the whole witness suite hears what he says next. Perhaps he even feels relief at finally coming to the boil. Until now we have tried to trust those in authority. We have taken their bait and behaved in the way they wanted us to. And this is where it has led us. There is no way back now.

My father says to the prosecuting team, 'You let them tear my wife apart. Whatever happened to me, I was willing to take it. But how could you let *that* happen to Sally? Watching my wife go through that – no, that is not acceptable. If you bring my wife and daughter into this – *no*.'

Altman takes a step back. Dad stands very close to him. 'You will listen to me and you will listen well. My wife collapsed. My daughter is on a knife-edge. Both of them are distraught, mentally and physically. Who can I go to? How can I make this better for them? I was willing to accept whatever line you took with me. That was my fault. I will take that. But what you allowed to happen to my wife in that courtroom is *unforgivable*.'

Altman says quietly that these have been the two worst days he has ever seen in court.

Then he says that I cannot after all be a witness in this case. He tells me I'm in no emotional state to do it. It's hard to argue with this. Yet hearing it just makes me angrier. I'm being deprived of my one chance to say what I think of Milly's murderer. And now there's this unexpected new and urgent need to defend our family against the slanders of Bellfield and his lawyer. I also have to defend Milly's character from the attack that has just taken place, something we never expected.

I *need* to stand up and let people know we were just an ordinary happy family before Bellfield turned us into a spectacle of grief and betrayal. Mum and Dad have been annihilated. They can't defend us any more. But I was there! I know the truth. Now we know the line that Bellfield is taking, I'm the only one left who can tell the world that Milly grew up in love and safety. Who if not me is going to remind the jury that Milly's killing is the real point of this trial – not nasty slurs against Mum and Dad? And Milly herself.

Altman tells me, 'Your police statement from 2002 will be read in court.'

'That's not acceptable. *You* don't get to decide that,' I tell him. 'Why are you the person who plays Almighty God in that courtroom?'

He says, 'It has been agreed with the defence that you will not appear. If you give evidence now, the case can be thrown out. Bellfield's defence team can say that you have been in this meeting with your father, and with myself. You can be seen as a "coached" witness.'

Ah, so this whole meeting has been a trap, I think.

That's Dad, Mum and me safely locked up. There won't be any more trouble from the Dowlers. Is that it?

The next day there are pictures of my stricken face, and headlines like 'TORTURE'. And Mum gets her own headlines: the *Sun* goes for 'MILLY'S MUM IN COURT COLLAPSE'. The *Daily Mail* chooses 'Milly mother: I was on the brink of insanity'. The *Mail* also goes for a panel entitled 'A SECRET LIFE ON THE INTERNET'. The first line is 'Milly had a "double life" away from the eyes of her parents, it emerged yesterday'. The *Daily Mail* has swallowed Bellfield's defence, or at least chooses to give it credibility for a good headline now.

Later, when it makes a better headline, the papers will compete to show compassion for our family and our torture by cross-examination. Yet, at this moment, Bellfield's defence has the better tune and all the good songs. They're so catchy that the press are practically humming them under their breath.

My notebook says, 'My mental health has severely deteriorated and all of my hard work over the past year with my counsellor has been undone and I'm right back to where I started from.'

As for Mum, an extraordinary thing happens to her that day. She loses her sense of smell. For ever after her cross-examination, Mum will not be able to smell the flowers in her garden, my perfume, Lovely Granny's scones. It is as if the accusations, false as they were, stripped her of one of her senses. Perhaps the accusations were, as Milly would have said, so 'rank' that Mum never wanted to be able to sniff anything so disgusting ever again. No amount of therapy has been able to undo the impact of that day.

Thanks to the man whose defence has turned into our torture, Mum has lost a daughter, nearly two daughters, and half the pleasure of her one consolation, the beautiful garden at our traumatized home.

56.

I'm allowed into court for the first time on Wednesday, 18 May, to hear my police statement read out by Altman's junior, a man.

I sit in a row with Dad, Alice and Jon. Mum's still shattered by what happened to her yesterday. We've left her at home with Lovely Granny to mother her.

I notice that the court is cold, and think, *No doubt to protect the workings of Altman's mighty brain.* For the rest of the trial, we shall often wear our coats in court.

This is the first time I'm in the same room as Bellfield. Mine is the nearest seat to his. I'm less than two metres from him. I want to look at him, but the screen is angled to block any line of vision between us.

I hold Dad's hand while my words are read out. At the moment, I'm trying not to think about Bellfield. I'm just thinking about my sixteen-year-old self, the words I spoke then being uttered now with no emotion. Bellfield is allowed into my head, not my heart. Milly must be kept safe there. That's where I keep my beautiful memories of our shared childhood. So, while my statement is read out, I'm not thinking about Milly either. I'm trying to keep her out of my mind. I don't want her in the same room as Bellfield ever again.

I notice that the defence barrister is assisted by an attractive young solicitor and that she's sitting very close to Bellfield's cage. That's what *he* gets to look at. I'm particularly sensitive to the fact that her skirt is surprisingly short. I wonder how she can work in the defence of that man. He seems to get everything he wants. It feels as if he is in charge.

This is the first time I see the jury, which is composed of seven men and four women. One has had to leave the trial through illness. They look like pleasant, educated people, with steady jobs and stable families. They are well dressed. Like me, the women appear to have taken care not to dress provocatively. They appear to be the kind of people who might live in Walton-on-Thames. They don't look like the kind of people that Bellfield used to hang out with – car-clampers, nightclub bouncers and paedophiles.

I've been warned not to meet the eyes of anyone in the jury. So I carefully give them only the briefest of glances. Looking straight ahead, I see the judge, who is older than I had expected. To my left and right are the pens where the press sit. Everyone else in the room is still and respectful. Only the journalists are rustling like teenagers in a maths lesson. They get up and wander in and out of the court. Hypersensitive to sound as I am now, I find their noises distressing. They fiddle with their mobile phones. I'm disturbed by their fidgeting. It seems to me that some of them are forgetting that we are all in this room because an innocent girl died and was dumped naked in a forest.

I can't believe that they're allowed to send tweets with no one to check on the truth or suitability of what they say. I'm acutely aware that if they say something wrong, this whole case could be declared prejudiced and that Bellfield could get away with murdering Milly and escape the label 'paedophile'. I'm thinking of Lovely Granny, who keeps televisions on in two rooms, each tuned to a different channel so she doesn't miss anything. What if a journalist tweets something to their network and Lovely Granny hears something awful from the courtroom without us being able to talk to her because we're trapped inside?

We, of course, are not allowed to bring in our phones or send messages.

The judge and the counsel speak. Every time they say something that would cause obvious distress to me and Dad, the press swivel their heads to us, looking for a reaction to note down. The heads all move at the same time in the same direction, like people watching the tennis at Wimbledon.

At the end of my statement, they play the video of Milly ironing. I still don't know how or why this has been allowed to happen. It seems like a gift for those of us who loved her.

The screen is positioned next to Bellfield. So everyone in the jury, the press and the public gallery gets to see Bellfield's face next to Milly's. I'm glad that the jury can see this. The video tells the jury what we have not been allowed to say because, so far, Milly has been one of those pawns sacrificed by the prosecution to the defence, who have been allowed to show her as a miserable suicidal girl.

Moreover, the image of beautiful, happy, dancing Milly is screened next to a troll of a man already convicted of two murders.

Even more surprising, there's sound in the video. You can hear us all singing and chatting. This video brings back the music that has been missing so long. The family banter's there too – me chopping onions in the kitchen wearing a pair of swimming goggles to stop myself crying, Milly ironing and Mum singing some silly made-up song. The video paints the real picture of us.

Milly's face and body speak for themselves. You see no darkness there. You see a lovely young girl dancing around an ironing board. Her humour is irrepressible. No one could see that girl as 'ugly' or 'depressed', no matter how hard her murderer's barrister has tried to portray her as those things. That teasing, smiling, confident girl is the real Milly, not the one whose character the defence has presented as beset by 'demons'.

I sit proudly next to the video of Milly. That's my sister. No one can take the truth about her away from me.

Bellfield is not happy about the screening. He passes notes through his little hatch to the pretty young woman on his defence team.

It's clear this video is undoing several good days' work for him in court.

My statement has not taken long. Also on the eighteenth, Danielle gives her testimony about saying goodbye to Milly in Station Avenue after sharing a bag of chips. Of course, she too is questioned about Dad's magazine. She insists that Milly always found a way to laugh things off. The defence barrister keeps digging. The more time he spends spouting this rubbish about Milly, the more he is serving his client. There is only one explanation that will make sense of what happened to Milly and it won't be heard from the defence at this trial.

On 19 May, Hannah Mac is in the witness box wearing her own suit of armour. She's elegant and immaculately groomed. Milly would have gasped at this spectacle of propriety. All the chokers, the thick eyeliner, the baggy flares – none of that is going on today. I'm glad. Nothing that we shared as teenagers should be here in the courtroom. Everything here will be tainted.

Hannah holds her own. She's so well educated and so articulate. She stands up for Milly so well. Her answers are incisive. She's not rattled by the little tricks of the defence barrister. She refuses to be undermined. She knows where the truth is, where it was, where it always will be.

Of course the defence wants Hannah to talk about the miserable notes Milly wrote. But Hannah will in no way support the theory that Milly was a suicide risk. She says briskly that all teenagers have melodramatic moments. Hannah admits that Milly had once told her about trying to slit her wrists with a dinner knife after being bullied at school. I've never heard about this before, and it sounds shocking in the court situation. It's designed to do so. Again, it seems that it's Milly who is in the dock, not Bellfield. Yet I'm not devastated by this information. Not for one second do I think that Milly would have been serious. I can just picture her playing around with a dinner knife in one of her Drama Queen moments. If she had actually hurt herself, I would have known about it. We all would.

It sounds like what it no doubt was: an experiment on the dark side. Milly couldn't go through with it because the darkness was not truly inside her. Also, this incident must have happened at least two years before Milly disappeared because that was when the bullying happened – something we had known about, and something that Milly had dealt with in her own way, chiefly by moving away from the set who bullied her, and beginning the deep friendship with Hannah.

We're not allowed to show emotion. All I can do is squeeze Dad's hand tightly. Our hands cannot be seen by the jury or the press, so this is safe. *Dad*, I'm saying with that little squeeze. *This is Milly, for God's sake. Mum probably wouldn't give her extra telephone time or something. Doesn't anyone round here know what young girls are like?*

I scribble in my notebook, 'Milly is not here to defend herself . . . Milly, I'm so sorry about the way you have been portrayed. I wish you could help. I really wish you could.'

I suddenly have an inkling of what the police, back in 2002, must have done to Dad and Mum in their questioning. Did they ask them about this? Did they make something silly seem like something serious?

But we can count on Hannah Mac. She's one of us. Hannah knows the truth and she knows how to tell it. She dismisses the knife as a typical Milly dramatization, noting that it took a year for Milly even to mention it to her. And she tells the court that Milly had admitted she didn't even break the skin. Hannah deftly smashes the suicide theory, making it seem as shoddy as it is.

No matter how Bellfield's barrister pushes her, Hannah Mac has an answer, a good answer, a true answer. She says, 'She was a joker. She would always make you smile. She had funny voices that she used.' Again and again, Hannah scores against the defence barrister.

I keep thinking, *Good answer, Hannah!*

Hannah says that Milly was looking forward to a music gig the next weekend and to seeing a boy she liked. Nothing Hannah says makes Milly seem like a potential runaway. Hannah is completely clear that Milly was 'just a normal thirteen-year-old'. She throws cold water on any idea that Mum and Dad preferred me to Milly.

Hannah's not providing what Bellfield wants. The defence barrister soon gives up on her.

Carole remembers, 'Milly's friends were fabulous. Nine years after the event, they were young women. They conducted themselves impeccably. They all appeared well prepared and did not fall into the traps the defence tried to lay for them during cross-examination. The defence underestimated them. Hannah almost rounded on the defence, telling him she could not possibly know the answer to one of his leading questions as she was not a mind-reader – brilliant!'

I'm proud of Hannah Mac, yet I'm furious as she leaves the stand. This is the first time I have seen the defence barrister in action. Like a child, I want to cry out, *That's not fair!*

Now I can see how he lines up things that have nothing to do with one another, making it look as if they do. Separate things happened in Milly's crowded little life. He picks out a few that suit him, and cobbles them up together as if they make a coherent story. This way he can create a whole alternative universe far from the truth. I can't understand why this is allowed.

What is the point of this trial? I'm thinking. *This is not the truth.*

My mind is working fast. I know all this is rubbish, but do the jury? Will they be able to understand the timelines? Will they understand that the bullies and the knife incident, like the magazine, took place many months and even years before Milly was taken?

I'm also starting to worry how much the press will love this story.

Indeed they do. Even the *Daily Telegraph* headlines with 'Milly tried to cut her wrists, friend tells murder trial'. By the third paragraph, the report admits 'it was not a serious attempt' and by the fourth, it comes out that the incident occurred two years before Milly went missing. The vast disparity between the headline and the content shows what some sections of the press wanted from this trial, and how neatly Bellfield and his defence team have supplied it.

Other friends of Milly testify to her being normal and happy, with nothing strange about her behaviour or mood in the days leading up to her disappearance.

The defence barrister keeps digging. We shall leave it to his conscience as to why he decided to proceed in this way. I suppose you could say that he was just doing his job. But in my notebook, I write:

> *The past month has been a complete and utter nightmare and a living hell. I can honestly say that my strength and trust in the legal system has been tested to the absolute limit, and if this is how the legal system treats victims and their families then I'm completely shocked.*

The twenty-third sees my friend Kat and Uncle Bree in the box.

Kat describes how, when waiting for a bus, she saw Milly walking on the other side of Station Avenue. She explains how, the moment she boarded her bus, Milly suddenly disappeared from sight. 'It was quite weird I hadn't seen her. I could see quite clearly down the road but I still couldn't see her.'

Uncle Bree falls prey to the defence barrister. Lovely Granny and I are in court to see his evidence. It's the only day Lovely Granny comes to court. Before the judge enters, she briefly leaves her seat, walks in front of the screen, and looks Bellfield in the eye. When she gets back to her seat, neither Alice nor Jon dares to reprimand her.

Like Dad before him, Uncle Bree now seems compliant and submissive in the hands of the defence barrister. I'm not used to seeing this confident authoritative man so nervous. He stumbles even on the oath. Then he makes a small mistake about the timing that night. The defence barrister uses that opening to undermine everything else Uncle Bree says.

Carole remembers, 'Poor Bree seemed to fall into every trap that the defence laid for him. If only he had understood that by admitting he had got his timings wrong he would not alter the facts he was giving . . . Bree had wanted to do his best for the family and for Milly but the reality of giving evidence was very different from his expectation.'

Under the barrister's unrelenting questioning and undisguised mocking of his answers, Uncle Bree is made to look unreliable, which he's not. He's been left vulnerable because he failed to identify Bellfield – and now everything he says is open to doubt.

The jury do not know that Uncle Bree was made to look at a close-cropped screen image of Bellfield's face, not the bulky body and swaggering gait that were the most easily identifiable things about him that night. The jury do not know that Uncle Bree was not asked to pick out Bellfield until five years after he saw him in the dead of night at Collingwood Place.

With horror, I watch the defence barrister ritually dismember Uncle Bree. Can anything be worth this kind of cruelty? Can defending a convicted double murderer be worth it?

I don't even recognize my uncle when he leaves the stand. His head hangs low and his shoulders slump. Poor Uncle Bree has been made to feel that he has failed us. So he feels as if he has failed Milly.

Actually, it's the police who have failed both Uncle Bree and us. If they had taken him seriously when he first called in his encounter at Collingwood Place, he would have been able to identify Bellfield *at the time*, when Milly was still alive. After all, Bellfield was well known to the police as a sex pest to young girls. And Uncle

Bree's detailed description should have linked him to the man who had tried to abduct Rachel Cowles just the day before.

After his testimony, Uncle Bree disappears. I want to give him a hug, but he's gone. He goes to sit silently in front of a soft drink in a pub for four hours, trying to rebuild himself. Later, Uncle Bree will describe his experience with the defence barrister: 'I'm over sixty years of age and it was the most harrowing time in my life. I can't even put into words how sick I felt. He came at me like a rugby player.'

The defence has taken another pawn. That's too many now. Mum, Dad, Uncle Bree.

The inconceivable seems to be happening: Bellfield may get away with it.

Maisy's been off her food and she's struggling to walk. On 19 May, she won't even eat her favourite, a piece of carrot. What's left of Mum knows this is serious. The vet sees Maisy immediately. Mum suddenly cannot remember why she is there. She breaks down and starts to weep. The vet says, 'Sit down, Sally. Let's do this by a process of elimination.'

Gently prompted, Mum gradually remembers Maisy's symptoms. She tells the vet, 'I have to go to the Old Bailey today.'

The vet reassures her that he will look after Maisy. He asks, 'Is there anything I can do for *you*, Sally?'

Everyone's always asking that. There is never anything that anyone can do to help us. But in that moment, there's something that this man can do.

'Yes,' says Mum. 'I need to know the name of a drug that instantly kills someone without leaving any trace.'

Mum's speaking with the seriousness of a child. She doesn't want to use that drug. She just wants to know that it exists. That would be a kind of comfort in a dark place. Of course, she's expecting a politically correct and reproving reply.

The vet knows what's going on. He doesn't judge her. He silently scribbles 'Polonium' on a piece of paper, folds it in half and hands it to her. He understands Mum's sense of impotence and desperation. We shall always love him for that.

It is just what Mum needs – a straight answer, for once. Even if it's a humorous one. And what's more, the vet gets Maisy well enough again to resume her diva ways.

At this point we are so traumatized that we have all reverted to childhood. Mum and Dad amuse themselves by marking up with highlighter pens each time the papers get their ages wrong. It feels like the only power they have.

Then Mum remembers something else.

Operation Weeting's been making some high-profile arrests at the *News of the World*, which has set up a compensation fund for hacking victims, with apologies on both its website and its newspaper pages.

After her traumatic questioning at the trial, Mum starts to look online at information about legal representation. She can't yet force herself back into that courtroom so she thinks about tackling the hacking. After the pain and helplessness of the trial, she knows we need someone who is on our side, someone with no vested interest in anything except finding out the truth about what happened and having it put right.

One name comes up a few times: Mark Lewis. Mum looks at a photo of the lawyer. He seems like a decent sort of chap. There's even a direct telephone line to reach him.

Mum stares at the screen. This is a pivotal moment for my parents. They are both thoroughly exhausted, totally disillusioned and barely have enough strength to communicate with each other, let alone a complete stranger, a very clever one. Mum knows, too, that a solicitor at this level does not come cheap. We don't have that kind of money. Mum hasn't been able to go back to work, and a crippling amount is being spent on my mental health.

Mum takes a deep breath. She calls up to Dad, who's now set up his office in a spare bedroom. 'I've found a lawyer who's done lots of phone hacking stuff. I'm going to call him.'

Dad's voice floats down to her, quiet and resigned. He's the only breadwinner and he can guess what this will do to our family funds. 'OK, darling. You do what you need to do.'

Even with Dad's blessing, Mum hesitates. To pick up the phone takes every ounce of energy that she can muster. If, in that moment, the doorbell had rung or Maisy had barked to go out, Mum might have lost her nerve. She also has the usual sense of fear and guilt – she will be disobeying police orders by talking to anyone about the hacking. Through all these nine years, our family's had only one conversation with a solicitor. That was when the police made it clear they were not looking for anyone except Dad in connection with Milly's disappearance. When the police found out that Dad had spoken to a lawyer, they told him it implied guilt – or could be seen to do so if the press found out about it. (And how would the press find out?)

But the doorbell doesn't ring and Maisy sulks silently on her beanbag, as usual. So Mum picks up the receiver and dials Mark Lewis's number. It clicks to voicemail. She leaves a message. 'I'm the mother of the murdered schoolgirl Milly Dowler and I'd like to talk to you about phone hacking.' When she hangs up, her hands are shaking.

She definitely needs to stock up on Caramel Chew Chew ice cream. In the fifteen minutes it takes for her to get to Tesco and back, Mark Lewis has phoned and suggested a meeting.

Mark Lewis's offices aren't far from Waterloo, where Mum and Dad worked together years ago, so the geography is familiar.

Mark comes down to meet us. He's as nice and decent as he looked online. We all squeeze into a tiny lift to go up one floor. It feels odd and frightening. He ushers us into a room with high ceilings and a big conference table in the middle. Once we're settled down with tea and coffee, Mark explains that everything we say is in the strictest confidence. Nervously, Mum starts talking. She tells Mark about the Operation Weeting meeting and the evidence she and Dad were shown from Glenn Mulcaire's notebooks. Mark's assistant is taking rapid notes, while Mark gives us his full attention.

At the end of Mum's account, Mark expresses his sympathy for everything we're going through. 'It's deplorable,' he says sincerely. He says that, if we would like to work with him on the hackings, he will represent us on a 'no win, no fee' basis.

He tells us we're entitled to compensation for the invasion of our privacy at a terrible time. He explains that the *News of the World* is paying large sums to victims of hacking as a way of nailing down a lid on the scandal. Mark Lewis says that in our case, if he were Rupert Murdoch, he would hand us a chequebook and let us write out whatever sum we wanted. Ours is not like the cases of celebrities and politicians who've been hacked. The revelation that *Milly Dowler* was a victim would change everything.

'So what are you looking for?' he asks.

This is an unfamiliar question. No one ever asks us what we want. We've been made to understand, forcefully, that the trial is not about us. Also, the talk of the chequebook is disturbing. Would this be blood money? That feels unbearable.

It's easier for Mum to say what we *don't* want. 'The last thing we're looking for as a family is more publicity. We don't want Milly to become a figurehead for another press rampage or campaign.'

Then there's the question of going to court. We can't take on *two* trials. Mum says, 'No way we're doing that. We desperately need a quick out-of-court settlement with a minimum of fuss.'

Mum leaves Mark Lewis's office knowing it was the right decision to call him.

Now she can go back to court.

57.

Emma Mills takes the stand on Wednesday, 25 May. She was Bell-field's official girlfriend at the time of Milly's disappearance and some of the other crimes. She took up with him at seventeen, after meeting him at a nightclub. When Milly was murdered, Emma Mills was the mother of two of his children; another was born after Milly died.

Emma Mills spent ten years with Bellfield, on and off, including time in a women's refuge. After his first trial, she spoke to the press about his domestic regime of rape and abuse. Even though he's been locked up for ever, she's still so terrified of him that she will not take the stand unless she's allowed 'special measures', which consist of setting up black curtains so she can give her answers without seeing or being seen by him.

Carole remembers, 'When discussions took place about Bell-field's former partner, Emma Mills, giving evidence, his body language changed again . . . The judge made a suggestion that Bellfield would have to sit in a different seat in the dock. So unhappy was he with this suggestion that he declined the judge's invitation to move seats and ended his diatribe with "Fuck off".'

Unfortunately the curtains will not provide sound protection. Bellfield is aware of that. As Carole recalls, 'Miss Mills gave her evidence from behind a screen but it was very noticeable that Bellfield developed an annoying cough during this time. It cleared up pretty quickly, in fact as soon as Miss Mills left the court.'

My parents don't want me to hear Emma Mills's evidence. Mum insists on being there. Without the testimony of Emma Mills, there might not be a case against Bellfield.

In the end Mum agrees that I can come.

We don't see Emma Mills in the witness suite that morning as she's being kept in a separate room, away from everyone. The first time we see her is when she enters the courtroom and goes behind the curtain. Emma is thirty-three, and tiny, compared with her former partner. Her demeanour is that of a terrified mouse. With straight brown hair and a face bare of make-up, she could be a child herself.

Even at a brief glimpse, her terror is visible. Her knees shake. All these years later, with Bellfield in a cage surrounded by guards, she's still petrified, as if she knows he'll find a way to hurt her. Even before starting her evidence, she's on the edge of breaking down. I know that if, somehow, Bellfield gets to her in this courtroom, it's game over. She won't be able to go on.

Until this moment I have wondered how Emma Mills could keep Bellfield's secrets for so long. Suddenly I understand a little more. If, while living with him, she had done anything against his interests, she must have feared he would kill her. Maybe she was afraid that he would harm her family, or even her children. Instead of feeling badly about her, I realize that hers is another life brutally ruined.

I hope that the jury see what I see: this terror. I want them to know what it's like for a woman who really knows Bellfield. She's a living embodiment of the fear he inspires.

Once Emma's in place in the witness box behind the curtain, Bellfield is led in.

First, she gives all the logistical background – that she and Bellfield had lived together at Little Benty, West Drayton. She explains that 24 Collingwood Place was rented in her name with her mother's help after she had ended up in a women's refuge. Her mother also bought her a red Daewoo Nexia. But the relationship with Bellfield resumed. He moved into Collingwood Place, along with his dog, a Staffordshire Bull Terrier. He started using her car.

In the week Milly disappeared, however, Emma and the children were not at Collingwood Place. They were staying at a friend's house in West Drayton, near the Little Benty property, which was being redecorated as they planned to move back in. Emma explains that, on the day Milly went missing, she struggled to reach Bellfield on the phone. She was trapped at home as he had the Daewoo Nexia. He eventually returned to the house where they were staying at about 10.30 p.m., and in different clothes from the ones he had worn that morning. Those clothes must have come from Collingwood Place so she knew he had been there. He stayed with her just a couple of hours, getting up between 3 and 4 a.m. He said he wanted to go back to Collingwood Place 'for a lie-in'.

At 8.30 the next morning, in a 'happy and jokey' mood, he told her in a phone call that they were not going to wait for the lease on Collingwood Place to expire or for the work at Little Benty to finish. They were going to move straight away and she was to go and pack up.

At Collingwood Place, she discovered the master bedroom's bed was missing its sheets, pillow cases and duvet cover. When she phoned Bellfield to ask about it, he told her that the dog had had an accident on the bed and he'd thrown the bed-linen away. Emma knew that this was a lie. She suspected he had been with another woman.

I scribble in my innocuous-looking notebook – questions which the court seems to need answered. 'Were those the black bags that he disposed of Milly's clothes in? . . . What clothes did Emma see Bellfield in on that day? . . . Were there any stains on the mattress?'

Emma explains that the whole family immediately moved back to Little Benty.

It is at this moment that Bellfield coughs. It's a deliberate, loud clearing of his throat, not an involuntary cough.

Emma falls silent. The whole court falls silent.

I can't see Emma. Only the jury and the judge can. But it's obvious to everyone what is going on. There is no screen thick enough to block out the effect of Bellfield's cough on this tiny, terrified woman. Emma's terror is such that she simply cannot speak any longer. The court, as Bellfield wants, is dismissed for a pause.

Poor Emma has to stand, quaking, in the witness box, until the jurors and Bellfield have left the room.

I'm seething. Bellfield has just got away with intimidating a witness. Did no one notice that cough? Or is it more convenient not to notice it?

We troop back to the witness suite. Emma Mills is somewhere we can't see. We're all in shock at Bellfield's cough, and how far his power still extends in the courtroom. We are traumatized by hearing what was happening, unknown to us, during all those hours when we were desperately searching for Milly. Everything hits us hard: the fact that Bellfield had 24 Collingwood Place to himself that day, that he had use of the red car, that he destroyed the bedding, that he changed his clothes.

I'm not picturing Milly in those contexts. I'm working on a timeline in my head. I'm repeating the words, trying to make them stick. Only later will I process them into what they mean to me and my sister. In my heart, Milly and Bellfield cannot occupy the same space. If I let the two of them meet, I will not be able to go back into the court. So I keep my compartments rigidly separated.

We're very aware that Emma Mills's mental state is fragile. She has told half of the story. We're terrified that she will not be fit to tell the rest. That cough may have finished her off.

But Emma Mills is determined. She wants to get this over with. Half an hour later she's back in the stand. She explains how she became aware of the police search for Milly. Without making any connection, she questioned Bellfield about what he had done during the missing hours that Thursday night. She was still suspicious that he'd been with another woman.

'Why do you keep going on?' was the response. 'What – you think I done Milly?'

A chill falls on the court. There has been silence in the room before, but not like this. Even the press, for once, are quiet and motionless.

I feel goose-pimples forming on my arms. I think, *Even if she can't do any more, even if she has to flee now, she's done it. Emma's done what we needed.*

I'm aware of the imperative to show nothing of what I feel. If Mum or I were to react, this priceless opportunity might be lost. If I were to take Mum's hand, she might cry. Then I might cry.

Emma Mills is asked how she reacted to 'What – you think I done Milly?'

This gives Altman a chance to repeat the words.

Emma explains that she did not question Bellfield any further on this subject. She had learned that it was better not to do that. She thought it was a horrible joke. 'I was used to him making horrible remarks.'

Her last piece of evidence is about the Daewoo Nexia. A few days after their abrupt move, Bellfield told her it had been stolen.

I scribble a note to Mum: 'Would you mind if we requested to see Emma Mills after this, to say thank you? Or would that be weird?'

There's no answer from Mum in the book. We are not supposed to be passing notes.

We do get to meet Emma Mills. At the end of the day, we're taken to a little witness room that has been set aside for her. She has given her permission and she is expecting us. The witness officer knocks and leads us in. He introduces us to Emma. Of course, hidden behind the black curtain, she was unable to see us in court. We've had just glimpses of her being led to the stand.

She's trying to compose herself for our sakes, but she's distraught. She's white, shaking convulsively.

I say, 'Emma, we just wanted to thank you so much for what you just put yourself through.'

She clearly wasn't expecting our thanks. She protests. She tries to apologize for how long it took for the truth to come out.

I stop her. 'No. Just thank you for what you did.'

Mum says, 'We are just so grateful that you were brave enough to come forward.'

We leave the poor woman in as much peace as she can ever have. I hope it gives her some kind of relief that she has done the right thing, for having the courage. I hope she feels safe because Bellfield cannot hurt her any more.

For once, the headlines go against Bellfield. Few copywriters can resist his comment to Emma Mills: 'What – you think I done Milly?'

The defence barrister spends many hours trying to undermine Emma. She does not succumb. A statement by Emma's mother, Gillian Mills, is read out to the court. She did not like Bellfield, saw him as a bad influence on her daughter. She has written, 'I would describe Levi as a big, fat lump with a high voice. He had no neck.'

I'm not in court that day. Maria Woodall has organized for me to be pre-recorded for a documentary that will be aired when the trial is over – if a guilty verdict is reached. My interview for *Taken* is filmed at a hotel. I'm interviewed about my memories of Milly and our family. It is strange to do this in the middle of the trial of Milly's murderer. Yet I'm relieved. I'm able to voice all the things that I was prevented from saying when it was decided that I would not give evidence at the trial. Hannah Mac is also interviewed, as is Maria Woodall herself.

I'm in court on 6 June for the testimony of another former girlfriend of Bellfield. Johanna Collings doesn't ask for special measures. She's not afraid of Bellfield any more.

Johanna Collings says she used to go to horse trials at Yateley Heath with Bellfield in the 1990s. Yateley Heath includes Minley Woods. He would take the dogs rabbit-hunting there. She also explains that Bellfield used to get through a lot of vehicles and attended car auctions near Yateley.

Once the jury is dismissed, and in the moments before Johanna Collings leaves the room, Bellfield swears at her. He is not reproved.

The trial grinds on.

There are other testimonies – for example, about Bellfield's telephone on the afternoon Milly disappeared. His phone was 'unavailable' between 3.28 p.m. and 4.48 p.m. He called his mother at that time, from a place close to her home in Hanworth. His phone was also switched off between 1 a.m. and 8 a.m. on Friday, 22 March.

We don't go back to court ourselves until Monday, 13 June. We come to hear the testimony of the pathologist, Hugh White, who conducted the post-mortem examination of Milly's body.

The pathologist says that the state of Milly's remains indicated that she had been dead for months rather than weeks. He explains that he could extract no evidence of the cause of her death as only bones remained. She might have been strangled or suffocated, but there's no way of knowing. The only thing he can say for certain is that she was murdered.

I'm relieved that his evidence rules out suicide. The defence barrister looks unhappy.

Despite a three-week search of Minley Woods, not a shred of clothing was found there, the pathologist points out. 'This is a girl of thirteen years found in an environment where she could not have got to by herself – and she was without any clothes.'

The court next hears details of the murders of Marsha and Amélie, and the attempted murder of Kate. But Bellfield has a 'migraine' and has to leave court that day. He manages to get across to the jury that the prison service has denied him the proper medication for his headaches: it's *their* negligence that necessitates his departure. He finds ways to take control, a man who should have no rights left at all. He feels entitled to compassion, this man who has shown none to his victims.

A headache? I think. *Or does he not want the eyes of the jury on his face while they hear what he has done to other young girls? Why aren't they tying him to the chair and making him listen to this?*

Then Surrey Police give their evidence. They are forced to admit that, out of all the occupants of the fifty-two flats in Collingwood Place, only the people who lived at number 24 were not interviewed. Officers knocked eleven times. The eleventh time, a new occupant answered the door. Yet no inquiries were made with estate agents to trace the previous tenants of number 24.

Eleven times. And no follow-up, I think. *Of course, they were busy harassing Dad.*

And so Bellfield was left free to kill Marsha and Amélie, and to try to kill Kate, to beat and rape Emma and to attack or sexually pester other young women.

In the next session, Rachel Cowles sits next to me. My chest constricts. I can't look at her. I write a note to Mum and pass her the notebook. 'Why can't I cope with sitting next to Rachel?'

Mum writes, 'Because she lived.'

58.

Throughout his trial for my sister's murder, Bellfield yawns, flicks paper fasteners, shuffles his notes and jeers at the public gallery. No one stops him. He kicks a chair when he's told that Emma Mills will not have to see his face while she testifies. He swears audibly, though under his breath. As the case progresses, his behaviour degenerates. He's even heard shouting at his own counsel.

He acts as if his security detail is his personal squad of bodyguards. He chats and laughs with them. His guards stand behind him in his glass box throughout proceedings. One of them is a woman. When I see her giggling at something he has said, I wonder how she can do that.

Bellfield behaves like this, of course, only when the jury are absent from the court. When he's in their view, he keeps quiet. He sits making notes, as if he is engaged in the respectable work of defending his innocence.

Carole remembers, 'He was in the dock, on trial for the abduction and murder of a child. Also, not forgetting Rachel, the attempted abduction of another child. His demeanour at the beginning of the trial was one of self-importance and utter contempt for those other people involved. He gave the appearance of believing he was on an intellectual level with his legal team, often impatiently writing notes and banging them on the wooden part of the dock in order for them to be collected by the pretty young lady and handed to the defence barrister. On other occasions Bellfield would sit tilting his chair back with his finger rammed firmly up his nose.'

During the latter part of the trial, many days are spent by the expert witnesses giving evidence of painstaking analysis of all the records provided by the phone companies and phone masts. Lists of calls made and received on Bellfield's phones are cross-referenced and fitted to a timeline. Sitting in the cold courtroom, we find it hard to concentrate on this detail. We can have no idea that this information will become important, long after this trial has finished.

Up until Thursday, 16 June – six weeks into the trial – we always thought that Bellfield would give evidence and submit to cross-examination. He did so at his last trial. But now the defence barrister announces that Bellfield will not testify.

At that moment, Carole is knitting her hedgehog postman up in the witness suite. When she hears that Bellfield's not going to testify, the postman gets it in the eye with a knitting needle.

She remembers, 'I was outraged that this was allowed to happen. Sally and Bob were compelled to give evidence: they would have faced arrest had they failed to turn up. They could be humiliated in court and, as Sally said, have every aspect of their lives inspected. Yet the defendant could not be forced to utter one single word.'

Of the three of us, Dad is the angriest. He spends hours ranting about how bitterly unfair the system is.

Nothing astonishes Mum or me any more.

That morning Brian Altman begins his closing speech. The first thing he does is point out to the jury that Bellfield's refusal to speak has deprived them of the opportunity to hear him explain all the evidence that put him at the scene of Milly's disappearance and the unusual behaviour documented during the night and day that followed.

Bellfield has not grasped the opportunity to explain his innocence, Altman continues. 'The reason you may think he has not done so is that he does not have an innocent account to give.'

Altman shows repugnance towards the way Mum and Dad were tortured in the witness box, on Bellfield's instructions. He then lays bare the ridiculous threads of the defence case. 'As we understand it, it's going to be suggested that Milly was a runaway who did not want to be alone in her father's company that day, so she hung around in or about Station Avenue only to slip away without being noticed into the hands of another killer, at another time, and at another place, so that Levi Bellfield cannot have been her abductor and killer.'

He goes on to demolish the 'evidence' that Milly was unhappy, unprotected by Mum and still upset by a magazine that she'd found nine months before she was taken. He gives a portrait of Milly we recognize: 'an intelligent girl, top set at school, interested in all the topics a thirteen-year-old girl would and should be'. He describes her as very close to her family, adored by Mum, and looking forward to the rest of her day, the rest of her week, the rest of her life.

He notes that the defence has not been able to excavate any evidence of a threat to run away from Milly. 'At thirteen to run off like that with not a penny or a purpose or a plan? Utter nonsense.'

He describes what might have happened by the hedge at Collingwood Place. 'It was then a short step and a simple thing for a big man to get or drag a slight thirteen-year-old into 24 Collingwood Place . . . it would take seconds for a big man to have manhandled a small girl inside without screaming.'

Altman is doing wonderful work, but the weekend is looming and I'm worried that all this brilliance could be forgotten by Monday.

The defence barrister has continually shocked us with his audacious tricks. *What if he has something else up his sleeve? Can Altman defeat him?*

We finish for the day. The next morning, Friday, 17 June, Altman starts with the red Daewoo car. He points out how its disappearance mimics that of a Ford Courier van that Bellfield 'lost' in 2004.

Regarding the geography of the crime, he says, 'So Milly disappeared from an area where the defendant lived and at a time when he was actually present, and her remains were found in an area with which he was familiar. What are the chances of that being a matter of pure coincidence?'

Altman speaks fluently for two days.

On Friday afternoon the court goes into recess. Once the jury have left, Bellfield shows his fury that his own barrister is not going to be able to start defending him until Monday. He complains that he will have a terrible weekend.

To distract ourselves, we spend the weekend working on a post-trial getaway. We need to be out of the country the minute we can, somewhere the press cannot follow us, somewhere we won't be recognized. There are no holidays offered in underground secret bunkers, unfortunately.

On Monday morning, the jury file back in and the defence

barrister begins an informal, almost rambling sort of defence, far less structured than the rather old-fashioned address given by Altman. He runs through the now-familiar slanders of Dad, Mum and Milly. He accuses the prosecution of cobbling together a case from tailored evidence and parading Bellfield in front of the court as 'the local serial killer'.

Is there something wrong with that? I think. *He is local, and he is a serial killer.*

Compared to Altman's two days, the defence barrister's speech is just three hours long.

I'm not surprised. *He doesn't really have much to go on, does he? He's impressive when it comes to undermining cowed witnesses, but he can't take Emma's words out of the jurors' memories.*

He spends quite a bit of his speech talking to the jury about their responsibility not to be bamboozled by a laborious prosecution case. He constantly reminds them that the burden of proof must lie with the prosecution and that their case is flimsy and circumstantial. I feel that he's trying to make the jury feel bad about themselves for believing what they've been told and shown.

The judge begins his summing-up the same afternoon. He will spend the next day, Tuesday, and part of Wednesday, 22 June, reminding the jury of all the evidence they've heard. His voice is without emotion. He lets the facts speak for themselves.

Carole is sitting on the edge of her seat. She remembers, 'I felt more relaxed after the judge's summing-up. One thing sticks in my mind. He said, "You may rely on the fact Milly intended to return home that day," or words to that effect. *Good,* I thought. *The evidence of the school-friends has done its job.*'

Just after midday on Wednesday, 22 June, the judge sends the jurors to consider their verdict.

While the jury are out, we're told that we need to prepare statements to read outside the Old Bailey once the verdict has been given. We have to produce statements for both a 'guilty' verdict and a 'not guilty' one.

Mum tells Altman, 'If Bellfield is found "not guilty", then the only option is a joint suicide pact.'

Silence falls on the room.

I am only twenty-five. I have hardly started my life. I don't want it to end.

Not surprisingly, the police are keen to 'help' us with our speeches.

Not surprisingly, we won't let them near what we write.

I don't want to write a 'not guilty' version, as I can't fathom that possibility.

I spill my outrage into my pretty notebook. There's nowhere else for it to go.

There are no ways to describe how I'm feeling at the moment. Probably I'm still in shock. Closure – what does that word mean? I cannot tell you how many people have said, 'You will now have closure.' Really? This will not give us closure. I believe the only way I could get that would be to know exactly what happened to Milly. The court process is mental torture and has no regard for the families involved. I feel like I have been in a soap opera or an ITV drama. However I'm sure they wouldn't have written it as bad as it has been.

Now I'm realizing that Bellfield will never be brought to account for what he did to our family in the arena of that court. The law did not protect us. Our innocence and naïvety did not protect us. These things only facilitated his malice. And the law facilitated it too. Then I think, *This whole spectacle was unnecessary. What did Bellfield have to lose by pleading guilty? He's never leaving prison. He doesn't have a reputation to lose. The newspapers splashed his violent sexual depravities across their pages after the first convictions. He's already a known monster. Adding Milly to his tally isn't going to change that.*

If he wanted his day in court, and a fight, Bellfield could have drawn on the lack of forensic evidence. But Bellfield and his defence chose to use our family as his shield – let us be exposed, mocked, censured, accused – instead of him.

This is not just the lack of empathy you'd expect from a man who beats, rapes and murders. This is sadism, which probably didn't surprise anyone who knows what he did to the women who lived with him.

The shock, I think, lies in the fact that Bellfield has been allowed the pleasure of watching his victim's family tortured in front of him.

Bellfield's barrister served him with as much talent and energy as if he had been defending an innocent man. He put all his considerable intelligence, aggression and theatrical skills into the work of effectively destroying our family. Even if the defence barrister believed implicitly in his client's innocence – was putting Mum and Dad on trial the right way to demonstrate it?

Why did he choose to take the path that Bellfield was innocent because our family was guilty?

59.

The jury spend just one afternoon and the following morning – eight hours altogether – deliberating on what they've heard and seen in Court 8.

Meanwhile, the jurors have been asking questions. Each time the jury raise a question, everyone must return to court. Their requests are detailed and intelligent, which gives us hope. The defence barrister minced up Rachel Cowles and her mother on the stand, trying to undermine their part of the case against his client. So the jury quite naturally want some things clarified regarding that charge.

Of course we can't know how long the jury will need. So each hour is a lifetime for us. After what we've seen of justice in these weeks, there's no guarantee in our minds that Milly's murderer will receive the verdict that we know he deserves.

And will Bellfield even turn up to hear it? Will he want to know what the jury, the judge or anyone else thinks of him? He's brave when it comes to hurting small women and girls. He's a hero when he's got a car and his rape kit, a claw hammer in his hand, and it's late at night, with no one watching. When it comes to standing up like a man, and hearing the truth about himself, Bellfield is a proven coward.

I suppose Bellfield has to balance that in his mind against the pleasure it will give him to see the suffering of our family when they have to hear it confirmed by a jury that their lovely daughter died at the hands of a thing like him. He's had a good long look at us already. Court 8 has been a sadist's cinema. He's been able to watch an expensive barrister hurt, humiliate and diminish Dad and Uncle Bree. He's heard his young victim's character dragged through the mud. He's seen her mother collapse in agony. He must also have enjoyed watching Milly's beautiful friends on the stand.

The day the jury retired, Bellfield had indulged in some coughing to show how unwell he was. This was different from the menacing throat-clearing that so terrified Emma Mills. This was 'poor me, I'm so unwell' coughing – too unwell to hear a verdict, perhaps?

But on Thursday, 23 June, he does attend the court. It seems that Bellfield believes the jury have yet another question to put to the judge.

Mum, Dad and I have come in that day, knowing only that the jury are still engaged in their deliberations. Alice has told us that this could go on for weeks. For all we know, we're making the first of many days' futile pilgrimages to the witness suite, to sit there – with our headphones and our painful soundtracks – and relive the horrors of this trial.

There is nothing more for us to do. We have drafted our statements for 'guilty' and also, with heavy hearts, the unthinkable 'not guilty' verdicts. We've agreed that if the verdict is 'not guilty', we shall not make a public appearance. Our statements will be read by Alice and Jon.

It's the waiting game again, a game we know so well. Waiting and not knowing go hand in hand. Waiting for Milly to come home. Not knowing what happened to her; not knowing if we would ever find out. Waiting to find out who murdered her. Waiting for Bellfield to be tried for Marsha, Amélie and Kate, sitting on our hands, unable to speak. Waiting for him to be charged. Waiting for this trial. Waiting to give evidence.

This wait is different. My greatest fear is that the way this wait ends will be the difference between Mum wanting to live or die. This fight has taken so much from us all, but Mum has suffered the most. It is quite evident in the way she carries herself. Thin as she is now, she's also weighted down. She's been fighting for nine years and now every step seems to be taking her closer and closer to suicide. She won't talk about it in front of me. Yet I know it is in her heart. She cannot survive another blow.

I wish that the jury could somehow know that they hold Mum's life in their hands.

We are full of fear that Bellfield might get away with it. We have been cowed and terrified by the process, which has shown us how unimportant we are compared to the defendant and his legal rights. Most of the details of Bellfield's street-prowling, girl-drugging, raping lifestyle have been pronounced inadmissible so he's been protected from the revulsion of the jury. The press, while fully aware of what Bellfield is, are not allowed to mention it in their day-to-day reporting. They would be prosecuted and fined if they did.

Meanwhile *our* rights to a private life have proved non-existent. Dad's the one who's been portrayed as a virtual sex criminal. Mum's been depicted as a bad mother. Even Milly's true character has been mere collateral damage. She's been slandered while Bellfield's dark and violent history with women and young girls is kept under wraps.

Everything that was supposed to protect us has let us down and worse.

We know in our hearts that Bellfield is guilty but by now we don't have much faith in the justice system. We have to rely on the individual jurors to see the truth.

The trouble is that, in too many ways, they will need to read between the lines to find it.

So, on 23 June, we're in the witness suite, preparing ourselves for another long day. Carole, Julie, Loley and Auntie Linds are there with us. We now have a well-organized system. As ever, I'm trying to keep a neat and tidy space – it seems the one thing I can actually control. Our biscuits are in one corner on the windowsill, where we can reach them easily to have with our tea. The lunch boxes are placed in the fridge by the tea-making facilities.

Mum takes a photo of us there. It is for our own records, to show where we are, physically and emotionally, at the moment when it seems our lives are hanging in the balance. We're looking as scarred as we feel: pale, tense and exhausted. I don't look like a girl who has much of a life in front of her. How will I ever work again after this? Dad looks like a ruined man.

We still have a grab-bag for court, like a hospital case for a heavily pregnant woman. Along with Mum's knitting, our food supplies and our headphones, our bags are now stuffed with scarves to protect us from the press cameras, make-up and deodorant (we now operate under the slogan 'Don't deny, reapply'). We have spare pairs of tights, tissues, sweets. A glasses case holds the vital diazepam. There's also a white paper bag to breathe into in case of panic attacks.

Mum's still working on the fish blanket, but she's not making anything pretty now. Instead of the fish and animals she's brilliantly created, she just knits plain squares in dark colours. Struggling to concentrate, I've abandoned the cross-stitch. To numb my mind, I've got a colouring book. It's not the sort of colouring Milly and I would do as children. I'm lashing on the colours with venom, pressing hard. There's no careful shading going on, as in the fashion pictures you'd see on Milly's wall. What I do is just a mess, worse than a five-year-old's work. I can't stay within the lines and I don't want to.

Shortly after lunch Alice hurries in to say that the judge wants all parties in court. That includes Bellfield. She says it's probably that the jury have more questions, but there's something in her voice.

Carole remembers, 'I think we had all thought that this was going to extend into another week . . . I suddenly felt very ill at ease. What was going on? This was very quick. Surely it could not be a verdict.'

Down in Court 8, the press seem to know something's up. Their pen is full to bursting. You can barely move in the room. Reporters are even spilling out and blocking the entrance. Lovely Kate Sheedy is there. I recognize Amélie's parents in the front row of the press pen. I think, *If this trial had taken place back in 2002, the Delagranges would not be grieving and hurting now.*

Then I wonder, *But why are they here for a jury question to the judge?*

Mum, Dad and I walk into the courtroom with our arms around one another. We sit down in the front row. Rachel Cowles and her parents take their places silently beside us.

When the judge enters the room I can barely make it to my feet. I'm shaking, grasping on to Mum's hand with everything left inside me. Mum's in the middle, leaning forward, her face taut. I'm closest to Bellfield, knowing his bloated profile is above my head. Mum and I are both dressed in black. I've turned away from the murderer, and I'm sobbing into a handkerchief. Dad sits back, grim-faced, his eyes fixed ahead. His foot is tapping nervously.

The judge asks Bellfield to stand. As an experienced convict, this must be the moment when Bellfield realizes he has been lured into court for the verdict.

I'm not an experienced murderer so I don't know what it means.

All I know is that he's never been asked to stand up before. Now, above the screen, I can see one side of his bald head.

I break all the rules and whisper to Mum, 'Is this it?'

She says, 'Yes,' and takes my hand. Hers is trembling.

So Bellfield has not got his own way – he has not managed to avoid hearing the verdict. He has been outwitted. For once, things have stacked up in favour of what is right.

He should hear what he is, I think. *He should hear the words out loud.*

I realize that I'm counting on a 'guilty' verdict.

But that's not a safe thing to think, I remind myself.

The clerk to the court asks the jury if they have reached a verdict on count one, the attempted abduction of Rachel Cowles.

The foreman of the jury says, no, they have not come to a verdict.

A cold flush runs through my body. Mum has no colour in her face.

This is bad. This is really bad.

It's like Anna-Maria Rennie all over again. This means that the jury has not agreed with the prosecution that Bellfield was on the hunt for a schoolgirl back in March 2002. It has not been shown that he had 'propensity'.

Mum's hand must be fossilizing – I'm holding it so tight.

Now the clerk asks whether the jury has come to a verdict on counts two and three of the indictment.

Counts two and three are the abduction and murder of Amanda Dowler.

The foreman says quietly, 'We find the defendant guilty on both counts.'

We have been silenced for so long. All through the court case, everyone in the gallery has been under the strictest orders to be quiet. Even our expressions have been edited. We have not been allowed to show disgust, fear, hatred or even grief in case we prejudiced the jury.

But now all restraints are gone. And not just from our family.

When the verdict comes through, everyone can at last make as much noise as they want. There are people gasping and shouting, including us. Mum and I both cry out, 'Guilty! Guilty!'

Dad is very quiet and remains the upstanding gentleman that he is. He has filled his pockets with packets of tissues. He has the medication he knows we'll need. He has prepared for this and he would never fail Mum and me. He will not give in to the way the police, the justice system, the press and Bellfield betrayed Milly. He will keep his standards.

I look over at the press. It's like a children's party in the pen. They are excited, delighted. They're chattering, packing their bags. They will have by-lines on the front pages tomorrow. They will be on the news tonight.

The next day the *Daily Mirror* will note, 'Even experienced detectives had tears in their eyes after the verdicts were read out.'

They must be describing Maria, Alice and Jon, who are not, of course, allowed to hug us.

I ask Mum if I can climb over the bench and tell the defence barrister what I think of him. She physically holds me back. I'm convinced that this will be the last time I'll ever see Bellfield. I take my chance. I scream, 'You fucking child-killer. Burn in Hell!'

I want Bellfield to hear those words from the sister of the girl he killed.

I know that Bellfield hears me. He's only yards from me, in the same place where he has listened to all the witnesses. They were speaking in quiet or normal voices, and he took in every word, scribbling notes for his counsel. I, in contrast, am screaming at the top of my voice. It's got to get through.

Carole tells me later that the whole of the Old Bailey, not just Court 8, could hear what I shouted.

Good.

Mum wants to do the same but she's too distressed to utter coherent syllables. She screams and falls to the floor. After I've said what I needed to, my energy suddenly evaporates. My knees give way and I fall to the floor too. Dad rushes to help me and Mum. We simply cannot get up. We cling to one another, sobbing.

Our tears are of relief. My mind's eye sees Bellfield being escorted back to a prison where everyone will now know that he's a child-killer. I see him in a dark room, afraid. I see him angry and frightened. This is one fight he didn't win, no matter how dirtily he fought. His curiosity and desire for more juicy details have drawn him into court – and have let him down. Instead of more wordplay, he has heard judgement.

Mum and I have lost it again, and once more it's with the world's press standing ten feet away. There's also at least one writer in the room at work on a book about Bellfield. We know that too. At that point we never dreamt that we might have a chance to give our version of events.

From where I lie on the floor, all I can see is the feet and legs of the press stampeding out. Reporters are scrambling out to record their accounts of the breaking news. Articles that have clearly already been written are being uploaded to all the news websites. The press simply ignore the sight of our collapsed exhausted bodies. No one helps us. They push past us. Our vulnerability has already given them the show they want.

Eventually Alice, Jon and the matron of the court fight their way through to me and Mum. Alice is clinging to Mum and Jon is clearing the path. Their one object is to get us out of this mêlée and back up to the witness suite as quickly as possible.

Later, I'll read that the only person *not* in a state at that moment was Bellfield himself. He was made to stand up for the verdict. Now his only reaction is to ask if he can sit down.

As Bellfield is led away, he lets out a protracted yawn.

Carole remembers, 'The bastard Bellfield yawned. He yawned. How dare he? He sauntered out of the dock as though nothing had happened.'

Alice, Jon and Dad deliver us back to the witness suite. I'm in a dizzying vortex of anger, relief, despair and sadness. As usual, it's the anger that takes a grip. Then I feel a sudden pang of guilt.

Lovely Granny! She's on her own. We haven't made any preparations for her because we were not expecting this to happen today. And Carole has just dropped her phone in the tea-making sink because her hands are shaking so much.

Lovely Granny has the TV news on in two rooms. *Was anyone there to hold her hand when she heard? Was she crying? Was anyone there to look after her, like I had promised Grandad I would? Did she have anyone?*

I want to go home and tell her. But I can't. She's two hours away.

We were given the news about Milly's body in a phone call. Now Lovely Granny has to find out about Bellfield's conviction that way.

Mum texts her: *Guilty.*

Lovely Granny saves that message on her phone. She still has it. Unlike me and Mum, she never doubted that the jury would get it right.

Lovely Granny doesn't cry. Bellfield is not worth her tears.

The first words spoken in the witness suite are between Dad and Jon. Dad says, 'I can't believe this has happened. I mean, that he was in court to hear it.'

Jon says, 'They knew Bellfield would never turn up for a verdict. But his need to hear all the jury questions would get him there.'

Dad says, 'It worked eventually – one for the Dowler family.'

I text to everyone in my address book: *GUILTY.* It is the easiest way and there isn't any more to be said.

Julie, Loley and Auntie Linds join us in the room. Auntie Linds folds me in a big hug. I relax into her arms. It's a new feeling after all these weeks. Auntie Linds says quietly, 'Justice, my darling Milly.'

I reply, not to her, but to Milly, 'We have got him and now you're safe and he will always be known as a child-killer.'

Shortly after that, we're driven home.

We're a lot more prepared this time and have the scarves ready. We have learned to wind up the electric windows, stuffing the edges of the scarves in at the last moment so they are fixed to the insides of the car like pretty curtains. But this time the road is clear. The press already have what they need.

When we get home, everything is different. The sense of doom seems to have lifted. Some of the tension is gone from Mum's face. Yet I'm not sure what's going on behind her eyes. I'm still not certain that she has abandoned her suicide fantasy. Will she still be there for me and Dad? Will we ever heal? Milly's killer is behind bars, but Milly's still not coming back.

On television that night, the main story is Milly, on every channel. All the TV stations point out the very few yards between Bellfield's home and the place where Milly vanished off the face of the earth.

They all explain how he stripped the flat and moved out immediately after Milly vanished. They all say that the police tried his door eleven times, yet did not follow up on who lived there on the date of the abduction. They all tell how, after letting Bellfield slip through their fingers, the police focused on Dad as the suspect, that we have had to wait nine years for justice and how, in the interval, Milly's killer was able to murder two more girls. They all describe how Dad and Mum were 'wrung out', pilloried and humiliated in court, as Bellfield's defence tried to make it seem that our family was responsible for Milly running away. They recount how, at the verdict, Bellfield merely yawned. They also say that he's now being investigated for up to twenty other attacks and murders of women.

Of course, we are not the only family bereaved by Bellfield.

The parents of Amélie, dignified and serious, speak through an interpreter. Dominique Delagrange tells ITV, 'It's true there is the question that if the same thorough investigation had been carried out in the case of Milly, then Marsha and Amélie would still be alive. That question remains.'

Of Bellfield, she says, 'Well, to me he is not human. He has no humanity. He is without remorse.' She says she does not dare think about it: to do so stirs too many unbearable thoughts, because 'it cannot be put right'.

'Nine years of bewilderment and grief,' says ITV. They describe me and Mum screaming and crying in court, and show the court artist's picture of the moment that the verdict was given.

Bellfield's troll face looms out of the screen, torturing us. He's shown smirking as he repeatedly says 'No comment' to the police interviewer, and arrogantly turning his back on the police camera in the interview room.

Uncle Bree is interviewed on *Channel 4 News*. He recalls his meeting with a large, intimidatingly confident Bellfield, while he himself was frantically searching for Milly at Collingwood Place in the middle of the night after she disappeared.

'What do you think he'd been doing?' asks the interviewer.

'He wasn't just taking his dog for a walk,' says Uncle Bree. Then he pauses, and horror fills the pause.

Uncle Bree remembers Milly's singing, her dancing, the loving, funny little notes she'd write on the beer mats in his pub, and the 'happiest day of her life' when she played her sax there on the Sunday before she was taken. 'She grew two inches!' He agrees with the interviewer, who suggests that the letters read out in court were just the stuff of normal teenage melodrama. 'The way Milly was portrayed in no way represented her life, her love for her sister, her mum. Her mum was like an elder sister *and* a good mum. And Dad – Milly thought he was great fun.'

He says, 'If you'd known Sally and Bob before this started, you're looking at two different people now. They're struggling to live through this and I just know that the court case and the way it's been portrayed has damaged them yet again. And it's going to be years before they can try and even smile at each other after what the defence counsel tried to portray.'

ITV interviews Colin Sutton, the Metropolitan Police officer who made the vital link between Bellfield's address and the date and place Milly disappeared. We shall always be grateful to him for this good old-fashioned bit of proper police work. The disgust on Colin Sutton's face is clear when he talks of the man he and his team finally hunted down. 'Levi would commit anything. He effectively did exactly what he liked . . . He has no regard at all for the law, or even for morality.'

Everyone points out that Milly's family still does not know exactly how she was killed.

Only Bellfield knows that.

The interviewer asks Uncle Bree, 'If she were still alive, what would Milly be doing now?'

'She would have gone to university, she would probably have some stunning colour hair to shock us all. And I'm sure she would have been in some music band. I'm positive of that.'

As the interviewer points out, Milly wasn't allowed to grow up.

We watch the television for hours, mesmerized by the fact that the press do actually understand what went on. They understand that Surrey Police's lapses left Bellfield free to kill again. They understand that we have waited nine years for resolution. They even seem to understand our courtroom agony.

That night I go to sleep with a little comfort.

He has been found guilty, so Mum will want to live? Won't she? That was the pact?

60.

The next morning's papers focus intensely on the verdict. Describing every word and gesture of our collapse at the Old Bailey, the *Sun* comments, 'The suffering released by Sally and Gemma Dowler produced one of the most heart-rending scenes ever witnessed at the historic court building.'

Other press coverage is more reflective. There's much sympathy for us, with commentators pointing out that the jury – unlike Surrey Police – had no trouble in swiftly dismissing the preposterous idea that Dad was somehow responsible for Milly's death. 'Justice at last for Milly Dowler as "monster" is found guilty of murder,' writes the *Daily Express*.

But has it really been justice for Milly, what happened in that courtroom?

The *Daily Star* goes for a long headline: 'AS MILLY MUM SOBS HER HEART OUT EVIL KILLER JUST YAWNS.' Unfortunately they put big photos of Milly and Bellfield side by side underneath. The *Daily Telegraph* does the same thing.

Quite a few of the newspapers are keen to dwell on the failings of Surrey Police and Operation Ruby. For all its budget of £6 million, its hundred officers taking 5,600 statements and its long-running incident room, the press note the one very basic mistake that allowed Bellfield to continue murdering after taking Milly. It was, as the *Daily Mirror* notes, the failure to follow the trail of who lived at 24 Collingwood Place that permitted Bellfield to get away with his crimes for so long. Marsha and Amélie might also have lived if the police had harvested and linked up information about the attempted abduction of Rachel Cowles, the day before Milly, three miles away, at the same time of day, by a round-faced man in a red car. Rachel Cowles belonged in the same incident room as Milly. But, as the papers note now, her report never made it there.

The *Sun*'s editorial rages,

What is it with our police? . . . Mistakes in the Milly tragedy were elementary and demonstrate failures of training, management and leadership – to say nothing of a lack of brain power . . . Policing must be made more professional. Lazy and dim officers must be rooted out.

But it's not over yet. We must now return to the Old Bailey to hear Bellfield's sentencing.

Carole recalls, 'Overnight the media had gone mad. The reports in the press about the guilty verdict had expanded to Bellfield's violent behaviour towards others. It had all been put in the public eye.

'To my utter shame, I did not consider how this would affect Rachel Cowles, so wrapped up was I in our family's feelings. Inevitably, when we got into court, the defence barrister had a pile of newspapers and immediately made an application to the judge that the jury be discharged in the case of the alleged abduction of Rachel. He said it would be impossible for them to reach a verdict in which they had not been influenced by what the media had put out there. The judge agreed. That was that. No verdict for Rachel.

'During all of this there was one noticeable absentee: Bellfield. He had declined to leave his cell at HMP Belmarsh. What a coward! However, this was hardly a surprise.

'The judge then began his sentencing remarks. He was very complimentary about Milly, saying she was intelligent and sparky, among other nice comments.

'During all of the judge's sentencing remarks, he addressed the empty dock. This is the usual way when a defendant is too cowardly to return and face his fate.'

Altman seems to take everything in his stride. He's been here before with this defendant. The defence barrister, Carole notes, 'looked as though he had swallowed a wasp during the judge's complimentary remarks about Milly and the family. His defence tactic had failed spectacularly and "my lllawd", like the jury, had been unconvinced and – it would appear – unimpressed by the defence fabrication that this was a dysfunctional family.'

This is what the judge says about Bellfield:

He is marked out as a cruel and pitiless killer . . . he has not had the courage to come into court to face his victims and receive his sentence. He subjected Milly Dowler, a thirteen-year-old schoolgirl, to what must have been a terrifying ordeal for no other reason than she was in the wrong place at the wrong time . . . He robbed her of her promising life, he robbed her family and friends of the joy of seeing her grow up. He treated her in death with total disrespect, depositing her naked body without even the semblance of a burial, in a wood, far away from home, vulnerable to all the forces of nature, thereby, as he clearly intended, causing her family the appalling anguish for many months of not knowing what had become of her . . .

He abhors the fact that Bellfield told his lawyers to expose to the world all Milly's most private adolescent thoughts, secrets and worries,

thereby worsening the anguish of her family, particularly her mother, Sally Dowler, in ways which were made dramatically clear to all in court.

But he has failed in what he intended. Milly's memory will survive and be cherished long after he is forgotten.

Bellfield's sentence is, once more, life imprisonment without parole. He's already serving the same sentence for his crimes against Amélie, Marsha and Kate. This makes him the first criminal in history to have whole-life terms from two different trials.

This is what we wanted, yet we are left feeling empty. It's not just that we have been drained by the insults of the defence barrister, and stunned by the press. It is that we cannot really take in the result. Yes, it's right that he has been found guilty. Now no one can doubt he is a child-killer. It sounds good, a life sentence. But we have a life sentence too. We're sentenced to life without our beautiful Milly.

We need to compose ourselves quickly as we now have our one chance to say something about what happened. On the steps of the Old Bailey, we shall read out speeches we have prepared.

Alice comes to say that she doesn't yet know when we'll face the media. Mum telephones Lovely Granny to update her.

'But we're not sure when we're going on television,' Mum says.

'Yes, Sally,' Lovely Granny says. 'I know. You'll be on the steps of the Old Bailey in seven minutes.'

Mum laughs – it's par for the course. Lovely Granny knows before us because Sky News knows before us.

You may have seen us on television, outside the Old Bailey. I am proud of how we were that day – Dad, Mum and me. Given that one chance to speak at last, we did it with dignity, yet without hiding our grief.

Rachel Cowles goes out first, with her dad. She reads a brief statement about her feelings – angry and hurt – that her case has been dropped, precisely because of the press jumping the gun and printing all their back-stories about Bellfield. She says she has been robbed of justice. She talks of reliving her trauma in court. She expresses her pleasure that Milly's family has at last had justice.

Maria Woodall speaks now, in her quiet voice. She reiterates some of the words of the judge: 'Milly was a funny, sparky and enthusiastic teenager. Milly's memory will survive and be cherished long after Bellfield is forgotten.' She adds that he has never shown a shred of remorse. She talks of the near-decade of hell he has put our family through, not to mention a long and difficult trial.

About the performance of the police, she says that lessons have been learned and changes have been made to procedures. She explains that, even if it had been a perfect investigation, it's unlikely that her predecessors would have been able to find Bellfield straight away. She says that they had to follow every lead, as any lead could have been the right one.

Maria Woodall has done her best for us. And her best has been so much better than what went before. Mum has made sure to mention that in her speech.

Now it's our turn.

We file out into the street: Mum, then me, then Dad. A ring of press surrounds us, some but not all of them held back by metal barriers. A bank of microphones is positioned where we are to stand. I have never seen so many cameras. For once the press are silent, not shouting our names or questions. They don't want to compromise the sound quality of their recordings. They need to make sure they get our every word.

The final drafts of our statements are quieter than our earlier ones. Even without the police to edit them, we have decided to be as dignified as we can manage. The fact that they contrived to get

Bellfield into court to hear the verdict – that has endeared the police to us more than almost anything they have done in the last nine years. Our statements, I think, reflect that. We might have used this platform to criticize the investigation that allowed Bellfield to continue his killing spree for so long. We don't need to. The television news and the papers are already on that case.

We have agreed that Mum will speak first, then me and then Dad, in order of the most fragile. Jon and Alice stand by us, as they have throughout, looking as kind and compassionate as they are. I'll be glad to see their faces on the news that night and in the papers the next day. They deserve much more recognition. They know they have our gratitude and affection – but we have no idea if their empathy's appreciated inside Surrey Police. The job of the FLO is harrowing – the closer they come to the family, the more painful it gets for them.

Mum has pushed her glasses to the top of her head. She wants to look the press straight in the eyes. Her face sets in a hard expression. She doesn't seem like her gentle self at all, as she says,

We are relieved to have this verdict returned and would like to thank the jury for their decision. At last the man responsible for the cruel murder of our darling daughter so many years ago has been found guilty.

However for us, the trial has been a truly awful experience. We have felt that our family, who have already suffered so much, has been on trial as much as Bellfield. We have had to hear Milly's name defamed in court. She has been portrayed as an unhappy, depressed young girl. Ordinary details any mother would recognize have been magnified into major problems. The Milly we knew was a happy, vivacious, fun-loving girl. Our family life has been scrutinized and laid open for everyone to inspect and comment upon. We've had to lose our right to privacy and sit through day after harrowing day of the trial in order to get a man convicted of this brutal murder.

To actually see that man in court, a man capable of such a vile and inhuman crime, has been grotesque and distressing for us.

I put my hand on Mum's shoulder at this point. I want to show how much she is loved and supported while she talks of this experience. I feel a tremor but she continues bravely, fuelled by the need to get her feelings out there. Those feelings have been trampled by

Bellfield's defence. Yet Mum is not defenceless, and she's going to show that to the world:

The length the system goes to to protect his human rights seems so unfair compared to what we as a family have had to endure.

I hope, whilst he is in prison, he is treated with the same brutality he dealt out to his victims and that his life is a living hell.

For a mother to bury her child in any circumstances is truly agonizing but to bury your child when you know she died in such an appallingly awful way is terrible.

The pain and grief, the damage he has done to our family and friends, will never go away. We have just had to learn to live alongside it. A day does not pass when we do not think of her and the life that she might have led.

We would like to make a special mention of our FLOs, Alice and Jon, who have been with us from day one. Their incredible support for our family has gone well beyond the bounds of normal duty. Also, after DCI Maria Woodall took charge of the investigation, we at last felt that progress was being made and Maria made every attempt to correct some of the mistakes of her predecessors. For this, we are very grateful.

Mum's voice stays strong. Lucy Bannerman will report in *The Times* the next day, 'The message loaded between the lines of her statement was clear. It was "How dare you?"'

Mum steps back. It's my turn now. I am not nervous at all.

Lucy Bannerman recalls how I lay howling on the floor when the verdict came through – and how different I am today: 'By the time she faced the release of camera shutters, the smartly dressed, striking young woman was completely composed.'

I'm glad to my core to have this opportunity at last. For so long we've been muzzled by the police. We've had to be good and silent. We've rarely been told enough, and usually too late. Now we've been punished in court. I don't believe I'll have another chance to say what needs saying in front of reporters who will carry my words to the world. This is it.

The past few months have been some of the toughest times for the whole family. I can honestly say that the day my mother and father were questioned by the defence QC was the worst day of my life. It is hard to believe, but it was worse than when I heard the news that the remains were that of my sister Milly.

The way my parents were questioned can only be described as mental torture. Have they not suffered enough? I will remember that day for the rest of my life: seeing my mum collapse in court and having to be carried out by my father and our family liaison officer. I was waiting to give evidence, so couldn't even comfort my own mother.

The way they can portray my lovely sister as a depressed teenager has shocked me terribly, the worst part being that she isn't here to defend herself. To have to listen to that was emotionally scarring.

My voice starts to tremble here. Mum reaches out an arm to steady me.

The scales seem to be tipped so much towards the defendant rather than us, the family who have suffered an almighty loss. It feels like we are the criminals and our family has been on trial.

I take a deep breath, brush my hair out of my eyes and continue.

She was the best sister anyone could ask for: she was a shoulder for me to cry on, a fashion guru, a person who could make you laugh even when you felt sad, and she would light up a room as soon as she entered. She really was a star, and on dark nights I look out at the sky and there almost seems to be a star shining brighter than the rest. I am sure this is Milly watching over me.

When this all happened nine years ago I was sixteen. I had no other choice but to grow up. I feel I have missed out on some wonderful teenage years. I waved goodbye to the happy family we were and I realized life would never be the same again. The past nine years have tested our relationship as a family; there have been extremely bad days but we still manage some good days. Sadly it's those good days when we realize that there is somebody missing and then I will spend the next day feeling guilty for enjoying myself . . .

I, too, thank Maria Woodall, saying that we would not have got to trial without her. Then I say:

I often asked why, why us, why our family, and most of all why Milly? I now know the answer and that is simply Milly was in the wrong place at the wrong time and there's nothing I can do to change that.

With regard to the question of justice, in my eyes justice is 'an eye for an eye'.

403

You brutally murder someone then you pay the ultimate price . . . 'a life for a life'.

So in my eyes no real justice has been done. He took away my beautiful sister and he will now spend the rest of his time living off taxpayers' money.

It's Dad's turn now.

We are pleased that a guilty verdict has been delivered by the jury and that Levi Bellfield has been convicted of the murder of our daughter.

However, we do not see this as true justice for Milly, merely a criminal conviction. Our family has had to pay too high a price for this conviction.

The pain and agony that we have endured as a family since 21 March 2002 has been compounded by the devastating effects of this trial.

Prior to this trial, my family and I had only an ordinary person's understanding of the legal process. However, during the past seven weeks, our eyes have been well and truly opened. The trial has been a truly mentally scarring experience on an unimaginable scale – you would have to have been there to truly understand. Things that you wouldn't believe could ever happen did in fact happen.

During the past nine years there have been many occasions when the police investigation has left us in despair. The trial has been a truly horrifying ordeal for my family. We have had to relive all the emotions and thoughts of nine years ago when Milly first went missing and was then found murdered.

During our questioning, my wife and I both felt as if we were on trial. *The questioning of my wife was particularly cruel and inhuman, resulting in her collapse after leaving the stand. We despair of a justice system that is so loaded in favour of the perpetrator of the crime.*

It has often appeared almost incidental that this is a trial concerning the murder of our daughter.

We would like to pay tribute to all the witnesses who so courageously gave evidence for the prosecution.

This is in stark contrast to the cowardly behaviour of Bellfield, who was allowed to decline to give evidence and chose instead to hide behind his defence QC, to challenge the testimony of every witness. Where is the fairness in a system which allows such behaviour? *The defence inferences about myself and my wife were hugely distressing.*

And yet again Bellfield has been spineless and gutless by not attending his sentencing in court.

Thank goodness that we have so many close and wider family members and friends who have supported us through the past nine years.

Tomorrow, Saturday, 25 June, would have been Milly's twenty-third birthday, and, as always, we will remember the happy, fun-loving and talented girl that she was . . .

At this point I come to Dad and put my arm around him. He continues,

. . . but who was never allowed to fulfil her potential. This is a gap in our lives that can never be filled.

We would ask now to be left alone to try and put the pieces of our life back together and try and look to the future.

Thank you.

That night it rains, drenching Wimbledon. The deluge is refreshing for us all.

Bellfield announces, through his lawyers, that he is going to appeal.

No one takes much notice.

Instead, our Old Bailey statements are reviewed on the night's and the next morning's television news. Everyone agrees that it is 'powerful stuff'.

'Nine years of anguish flowed from Milly Dowler's family,' says Sky News.

The *Independent* shows me, Mum and Dad on the steps of the Old Bailey. The headline is 'Failed by the law, the police and the media'.

61.

At least the press are on our side now, which makes us feel so much less alone. There's a swelling outcry about the way we have been treated.

Good, I think. *Maybe no other families will have to suffer as we did.*

Meanwhile, however, darker and more upsetting matters are also being aired, things that we can't bear to read about. Now that he's safely condemned, Emma Mills and Johanna Collings feel free to talk about Bellfield to the media, as they did after his first murder trial.

In the *News of the World*, Johanna Collings says that he may have assaulted as many as a hundred girls during the time they lived together – sometimes one or two a night. He boasted about it, making her scrub the car clean of forensic evidence.

The *Sun* writes that eight women have come to them with stories of being raped by Bellfield. Some have reported his attraction to very young girls, and his liking sexual partners to dress up as schoolgirls. He's said to have described schoolgirls as 'slags' and 'asking for it'. Blondes were 'sluts' who 'deserved to be messed around with'.

The *Daily Express* writes, 'Monstrous serial killer Bellfield was suspected of being involved in at least five drug-assisted gang rapes of girls aged between 14 and 16.' It explains that charges were never pressed because none of the girls, often vulnerable and with drink or drug problems, would make reliable witnesses in court. It adds, 'In one sickening attack in 2004, Bellfield, now 43, was believed to be one of a gang who filmed each other as they took it in turns to rape a 14-year-old girl they had drugged. She told police she was stripped naked and dressed in the school uniform belonging to the daughter of one of her rapists.'

Writing in the *Daily Telegraph*, Gordon Rayner says, 'Bellfield was a man for whom the phrase sexual predator could have been invented. Despite his 20-stone frame, incongruously girlish voice and Neanderthal habits, he believed women should fall at his feet, and relentlessly pestered women and schoolgirls for sex. To him, women were a commodity to be used for his own gratification and discarded . . .'

The *Daily Mail* points out, 'Although the Dowlers suffered brutal cross-examination about their family secrets, Bellfield himself enjoyed the protection of the court. His lawyers persuaded the judge to rule as inadmissible damning evidence.' It notes how unfair it was that Milly's private correspondence was laid bare while 'the jury was never told how Bellfield, who cruised the streets leering at young women waiting at bus-stops, was known to force his girlfriends to dress like schoolgirls. Evidence that he beat and raped them was also ruled inadmissible'.

I'm sure that there is no thought of hurting us in the minds of Emma Mills or Johanna Collings, or any of the women who now speak to the papers or the male and female reporters who cover what Bellfield's said to do to girls.

The trial has harrowed us. Our feelings are so very raw that we cannot bear any more. We can't bear to hear what Bellfield did to these poor women. We want them to stop talking about how he burned them with cigarettes, how he beat them and how he raped them, how he knocked them down the stairs, how he strangled them.

But they won't. Not for years.

Louise Casey, the commissioner for victims and witnesses, comes out in support of us, and all the families like ours. She tells BBC News, 'I'm trying to make it a watershed moment.' She says that, like everyone, she has been 'profoundly moved' by what happened to Mum and Dad, but that it was not an isolated case. 'Inhuman treatment of witnesses is somebody's problem in a courtroom . . . Nobody seems to stand up for them. We have codes. We have charters. We have guidance. But what we don't have at the moment is a line that says, "You have gone too far."' She says that if a woman collapses in court under a battery of questions – then that is going too far.

We are stunned by the media coverage. Mum's pleased that the wrongness has been recognized.

In television interviews, lawyers point out that barristers act under the instruction of the client. It is explained that protection is not guaranteed to the family of the victims. Justice has to prevail over the sensitivities of families. The evidence has to be tested, forcefully and fairly, in the interests of justice.

Later, in the press, Louise Casey will assert that if everyone behaved according to the rules in that courtroom, then it is the rules that need to change. Speaking of Mum and Dad, she says, 'No one in this country can think what happened to them in that courtroom was right.' She also says, 'It is time the system takes a look at itself. If the message from today is "Do not go into a courtroom because you will be ravaged, your entire life will be torn apart, that people go too far, all in order to ensure due process for the defendant" – then I think a wake-up call needs to happen.'

The then director of public prosecutions, Keir Starmer QC, also speaks out: 'This trial has raised some fundamental questions about the treatment of victims and witnesses in the court process. Those questions require answers.'

The *Daily Mail* points out that the defence of Bellfield in his various trials has come with a total price tag of £4 million to the taxpayer. We're sure the prosecutions have cost much less.

A few journalists now show sympathy to us, particularly to Dad. It is noted that Dad took his punishment like a man when it came to having details of his private life revealed to the world, but what made him break down was hearing Milly's miserable words in the letters. The one thing he could not bear was the thought of his daughter being unhappy.

No one at all is sympathetic to the flawed police investigation.

The *Daily Telegraph* notes that 'No one has been disciplined, and the force says it has no plans to refer the case to the Independent Police Complaints Commission for an independent review of the inquiry'.

Surrey Police announce that they have apologized to the Dowler family. I have struggled to remember the words, yet I can't. Obviously they did not come from Maria, who has nothing to apologize for, but from the top brass. And it was, as usual, a waffling, confusing non-apology.

★

Lovely Granny writes to the Ministry of Justice too. She's particularly outraged that Bellfield was allowed to avoid hearing the judge sentence him:

> To achieve justice, he should have been dragged into court to hear his sentence, and let the victims cheer, after the way he behaved. If he is allowed to refuse to go to court legally, then the law should be changed.

Bellfield does not slip out of the news. The *Daily Mirror* reports one more fact about him. He's not Bellfield any more. The paedophile murderer has converted to Islam and changed his name. According to the *Mirror*, he's been given the necessary reading matter by the 'fearsome Muslim Boy Gang, who protect anyone they convert'. The headline is 'Milly Dowler killer Bellfield trying to save skin in prison by turning to Islam'.

On 3 August, the *Daily Mirror* is back with 'MILLY KILLER COMPO OUTRAGE' on the front cover. Milly's murderer is suing the prison service for £30,000 for failing in its duty to protect him when he was jumped outside a bathroom, suffering minor cuts. According to Bellfield, he should have been kept away from other prisoners who might want to hurt him.

The attack happened at Wakefield Prison the previous September, while he was on remand awaiting his trial for Milly's killing. Bellfield is within his rights to make these claims. He apparently brags to fellow prisoners that he is going to buy a holiday caravan with his pay-out. He thinks he will successfully appeal against his convictions and wants the caravan there to enjoy when he gets out.

The paper points out that Bellfield enjoys a private cell now, a TV and a kitchenette. He makes up to ten calls a day to relatives and friends. As the family of one of his victims, we are apparently entitled to sue him for damages due to loss of life and loss of enjoyment of life. But, no, we don't want Bellfield's money. In fact, we don't want to dirty our hands or our minds with him ever again.

We want to attend to our mental health and try to recover our happy memories of Milly.

We want to do that far from the scrutiny of the press.

If only we had been allowed to stick to that position.

6.

Scandal

July 2011 – 2012

PLAYLIST

Vangelis   *Chariots of Fire* theme

62.

Milly became the face of the hacking scandal that brought tumbling down the old cosy relationship between this country's politicians and its newspapers. For us, however, the hacking was among the least of the traumas that followed her abduction.

Compared to the searing pain and terror of Milly's disappearance, the bleak sadness of finding her body, the intense darkness of the trial, our feelings about the hacking were more in the region of astonishment and disgust. The whirlwind of the hacking scandal took our breath away, yet its emotional impact was insignificant, compared to what we were put through by Bellfield's barrister at the Old Bailey. In the context of what we'd suffered for so many years at the hands of Surrey Police, the whole shabby hacking story was just par for the course.

Compared to losing Milly, the scandal was only background noise. In that summer of 2011, our heads and hearts were still full of pain for what our girl had suffered. Our trauma was unresolved. The wound of Milly's loss was continually ripped open every time we thought we might at last start healing. Quite simply, we missed Milly like hell. The hacking was just one more thing to deal with.

The hacking scandal has long roots and many twists, some of which still remain hidden from sight. Our family was drawn into it at a time when the trial had reduced us to such a pitiful state that it was hard to focus on the incredible developments that now unrolled day by day, sometimes hour by hour.

So this chapter has been especially difficult for me to write, and I've needed Mum's and Dad's help perhaps more than in any other place. It was Dad who bought and read the newspapers and who recorded the television coverage for us to watch later, when we might be able to take it in properly. He was the one who attended the Leveson Inquiry, even on days when he and Mum were not giving evidence.

This new strength in him can, I think, be put down to the fact that the trial had in a sense liberated Dad, as well as subjecting him to so much hurt. In spite of all the vileness thrown at him, he had stayed dignified. He had been strong for me and Mum when we needed him. He was coming back to the man I knew before Milly was taken. The police no longer had anything they could use over him. Milly's murderer had been convicted and the world knew that no one else was responsible in any way for what had befallen her.

Meanwhile Mum, of course, kept meticulous notes of meetings, copies of press releases, letters and photographs for our family archive, which has been such a wonderful resource when writing this book. So, special thanks to Mum and Dad for helping me to shape these pages about the hacking scandal and our place in it during those bewildering months just after Bellfield's trial.

Until 2011, we had a complicated relationship with the press. They were there for us when we desperately needed their help to publicize Milly's disappearance. At that time, we wanted everyone on the planet to know what she looked like so they could keep an eye out for her. The press soon made sure that Milly's face was completely recognizable. We'll always be endlessly grateful for that.

Sometimes, indeed, the press were far more proactive than the police in keeping us informed of developments. In fact, often it seemed that the police informed us of developments *only* because they knew that the press were about to reveal them. They would even admit as much: 'We're telling you this because it'll be in the papers tomorrow.'

We are an ordinary family, not attention-seekers or natural celebrities. The intrusions of some journalists upset us. So did tactless headlines. But after nine years the press were a fact of our lives. We even had certain favourite reporters who were always scrambled to deal with Milly news. They had a job to do, and they were more experienced than our family at dealing with the abduction of a little girl. Precisely because we'd had so much empathetic coverage, we'd been disappointed to see how some papers feasted on the interrogations of Mum and Dad in the witness box. Then we'd been buoyed up by their compassion after the trial. That was truly empowering, when we'd felt so helpless for so long.

Of course we had wondered for years how some papers seemed to get exclusive photographs and scoops so regularly.

After 2011, we did not have to wonder any more.

When Milly and I were little, the *News of the World* was not the sort of newspaper that my parents would buy, or that we children would be allowed to read, any more than we would be permitted to go to an X-rated film. That newspaper was all about things that were alien to us. Young girls posed half naked. Other people's sorrow and shame were often entertainment on its pages. It seemed to be all about sleaze, preferably celebrity sleaze. That much we knew. What we never understood – until 2011 – was that its circulation of 3.5 million made it the best-selling newspaper in the country and possibly the world. This gave the *News of the World* not just influence but a certain hold over institutions and people that we thought were beyond any kind of corruption or bad behaviour.

Ironically, we started to buy the *News of the World* after Milly went missing – precisely because it seemed to be able to tell us things that the police couldn't or wouldn't share with us. It seemed to get to news first. It seemed to know stuff.

Then, just weeks before the trial, we found out that they had hacked Milly's phone in the early days of her disappearance. It was at first impossible to process this new information, or to swallow it. We didn't want to accept that Milly had been treated with such cynicism at the same time as she had also suffered the worst abuse and violence.

After the police finally told us about the hacking, Mum took to pacing the floor again, as she had on the night Milly first went missing. We felt sick and tainted. We were suddenly having to confront the fact that our whole family had become part of something so dirty during the most vulnerable and terrifying moments of our lives. We also had to deal with knowing that the police had been aware all along about this violation and had been keeping it secret from us for years.

When Milly first went missing, we were made to feel afraid of the police because they seemed determined to find us guilty of something: bad father, bad mother, bad sister – that was us, in their eyes. Yet now it seemed that the police themselves were afraid of the *News of the World*. They were certainly more afraid of the newspaper than they were of us. While the police were using bullying, intimidation and blackmail on Dad, was it that someone was doing the same to them?

Milly would, as I've written, become the poster girl of the hacking scandal. But Milly was no longer here. So it was for Mum, Dad and me to deal with this drama. To us, our part seemed very small in what came out: a picture of press, police and politician co-dependency in which it seemed that the press were actually the most powerful of all. We were just a normal family, yet we would receive more attention than the TV and film stars who were hacked. Our ordinary sorrowing faces would be the living proof of the damage done by reporters and editors who valued a scoop over human pain.

And, of course, the timing could not have been crueller. We thought we had done with publicity after the sensational trial. We thought we'd be left alone to get on with our grieving, which had so often been interrupted. This was exactly the wrong time for us to have to step up to the cameras and the shouting reporters again.

I would like to say a couple of things here on behalf of other victims of hacking. There are thousands of us, and very few will be privileged to have the platform of a book to express what it feels like. Of course, it's different for everyone. But we non-celebrity hacking victims do have a few things in common – which is that we became persons of interest to the hackers precisely because we were *already* in agony.

The families of the victims of terrorists, the wives of soldiers – many innocent, suffering people – became the targets of News International's hacking machine. What should have been private became the public property of the *News of the World* reporters. After illegally and secretly eavesdropping on our sorrows and shame, News International then peddled them for profit.

It never seemed to be about helping the police. All the technical talents of the hackers – why could they not have turned them to solving something? If the *News of the World* had hacked in a spirit of helping our family, well, we might have been able to deal with their casual invasion of our intimate lives. Yet the fact that they did not even tell us when they really thought they had found Milly – it shows where their priorities were.

We have never known when or if the hacking of our phones stopped.

Once you have been hacked – just as once you've lost a family member to murder – you never quite feel secure again. Even while working on this book, I have thought it possible that someone was watching my emails and listening in on my telephone. One of my reasons for writing is that I want to say these things in my own voice, without my words being stolen, or twisted or cut to fit someone else's version of our lives. So it seemed very important to try to keep my words safe until I was ready to publish them. We had not been able to keep Milly safe. And our desperate messages to her, when we thought she might hear them, were not safe either.

So, I took a lot of precautions while writing what you are now reading. The words have been typed into a computer disabled from ever connecting with the internet. Mum nicknamed it the 'Bat Computer' and that has stuck. Chapters of the manuscript were never sent to my editor electronically. We used hard copies and memory sticks exchanged hand to trusted hand. We had code names for people involved in the book. Dad burned all our early drafts. We set up new email aliases. On Mum's suggestion, the making of this book was called 'Operation Wobbegong' after Milly's favourite shark.

It all sounds rather cloak-and-dagger, yet if we had not been so careful, you might not be reading our real story for the first time on these pages.

Of course, when we were finally told about the *News of the World* hacking Milly's phone, we tried to remember what we'd said to her voicemail when she first disappeared, when we hoped and wanted to believe she was still alive.

I flinched to think of that self-righteous little message I left for Milly when she'd been missing just an hour, 'Come home, Milly. Dad's *really, really* annoyed.' What if the hackers listened to that? What if they thought I was a bossy bitch who didn't get on with Milly? What if they thought it showed Dad was a scary man and that Milly was afraid of him? What if those words had been passed on to the police? In the early days, the police were always trying to get me to say that Milly and I were frightened of Dad.

All those voice and text messages Mum, Dad and I sent to Milly – a cynical hacker got to hear them when she didn't. She had already been murdered by the time the *News of the World* got into her telephone.

Milly's phone was like a sacred object to us, in memory. She was mildly addicted to it, like most teenagers. Even at school, it was always tucked inside her blazer pocket, where she could feel it vibrating with a message during class. It was our way of being in touch with her. It had 'MILLY' emblazoned on it by her own hand. To this day, it has never been found. We hated the idea that someone else, even by remote, had been handling it for dirty motives of profit and sensation.

And, of course, that phone had given Mum false hope when she discovered that there was space for a new voicemail three days after Milly had vanished. For a brief moment Mum had believed that Milly was still alive and had heard our messages. That there was suddenly space was, in the end, possibly nothing to do with the *News of the World*, but the fact remains that the paper had hacked its way in to hear messages intended only for Milly.

These are the kinds of messages that we sent in those early days of mystery and terror. Did anyone in the newsroom at *News of the World* feel even an atom of guilt at reading transcripts of these pleas, these outpourings of love and desperation?

Until the voicemail filled up, Mum texted Milly day and night: *Night, night Milly. I love you,* Mum wrote. Or she spoke to the machine: 'Come home, Sausage. We love you.'

Dad's messages said, 'We're not cross with you, darling. Just come home. Love you, darling.'

When I couldn't sleep, I would send Milly new messages. I would think, *Maybe she's at last free to answer it.* Even if she wasn't at the end of the line, it was like a way to talk to her. I could imagine that Milly might be listening, even without being able to answer. I could feel close to her as long as my voice was talking to her. I would say things like, 'I really, really miss you, Milly. Please come home.'

Other members of our family, and our friends, were also leaving messages. And the *News of the World* was harvesting their numbers too, hacking them, gathering more information.

Of course these were just normal messages of love from normal people in an abnormal situation, and not of interest to the *News of the World*. The message that caught their attention was from a stranger at a recruitment agency. They thought it might be a story. And so they went after it.

Here's something I've thought about a lot. What would *Milly* think and feel about being hacked?

Well, in a sense, she had already been hacked by the police in a worse way. They had rifled through her pink blanket box on a mission to find a reason for her running away. Her private notes had now been read out in court, and published in newspapers – notes she never meant to send or to be seen.

Milly would have hated what the police and the newspaper did to her. She would have thought that everyone is allowed a certain amount of privacy and dignity. What the police took from her blanket box was used in court to hurt her own family. She would have been distressed by that. What the *News of the World* hacked from her phone was just to make money out of her ordeal and death – and that was something Milly specifically disapproved of: *using* a person.

Milly was very keen on people looking out for one another. She disliked people who exploited others. Just before her last Christmas, she was asked to compose a definition of 'My Ideal Person'. This is what she wrote:

> My ideal person is someone who is loyal, a good friend, trustworthy, loving, caring, friendly, generous, doesn't use people, doesn't have to be popular or gorgeous or even good-looking, as long as you know they will be there for you and stand by you.

So much love and fear poured into her little phone in the days after Milly went missing. So much soppy unselfconscious family sentiment. Neither were her friends in any state to filter their feelings. I think Milly would have been shocked by the exposure of everyone's pain and confusion. As she was always looking after people, I think she would have worried for our embarrassment. She would certainly have hurt to see how devastated we were when we discovered what had happened to her phone while she lay dead in a forest.

Just as Milly thought that the killing of Sarah Payne was 'a deffinate cause for concern', she would probably have written a dark essay in her RE book about the hacking of a dead girl's phone. She would have analysed the whole thing with her excellent logic and her terrible spelling.

Like us, I think Milly would have thought of the hacking of her phone as one more violation of something that should have been innocent and safe.

63.

For our family, the first part of 2011 is, of course, dominated by the upcoming trial of Bellfield. After the first briefing by Operation Weeting officers, we notice when new hacking victims are named, including the actress Sienna Miller, the RMT union leader Bob Crow and the MP George Galloway, Sarah, Duchess of York, Princesses Eugenie and Beatrice, Steve Coogan and others.

We still have no idea that we ourselves shall be swept into the very heart of the hacking scandal.

During the trial, our anger levels soar. It feels to us as if no one in authority is on our side. No one, apart from Alice and Jon, is looking out for our emotional welfare. We never wanted to be fighting anyone or anything. Yet now we seem to be up against so many parts of the establishment – especially the police and the justice system.

Even at the Old Bailey, Mum finds her thoughts interrupted by memories of the meeting with Operation Weeting officers. We know we'll be invited to read our comments on proceedings at the end of the trial. In spite of all the cautions about secrecy, Mum wonders if her speech might be a good place to let the press know what happened with the *News of the World* and Surrey Police in the days after Milly went missing.

In the end, we decide to keep the hacking revelations out of our post-trial speeches. We don't want to dilute what we have to say about Bellfield by bringing in another sensational angle. We want the press to concentrate on the murderer and his crime.

Mum meets with our lawyer Mark Lewis one more time during the trial. He offers to check our statements to make sure we don't say anything that might bring down more trouble upon us. He reads them quickly and reassures us that there are no problems. So we speak from our hearts and don't hold anything back.

Once the trial of Bellfield is over, we long to fade into the background and get some badly needed rest. We plan to leave Mark Lewis to get on quietly and discreetly with our privacy complaint.

We have lived in the spotlight long enough to know we won't be left in peace after the trial. Our speeches gave the press something to chew on but we fear they'll soon be looking for fresh material. We cannot cope with the thought that our home will be under siege again.

Mum's idea of rest is running, swimming and sunbathing without being recognized – all the more important after the over-exposure of the trial. Dad's concept of peace is a shady spot where he can be close to Mum while reading a musician's autobiography with the songs playing on his iPod. For me, the water is always healing. And I have a huge need to simply sit in the sunlight.

So we allow ourselves a short break in Turkey. But the sun and water fail to perform their usual healing magic on us. In the evenings, we take a ferry across to another town for dinner. Often, as we cross the bay, the sun is setting. Mum takes photographs. Yet none of us is truly in the right mind to see and feel that beauty ourselves.

In Turkey, Mum and Dad get new wedding rings made. The trial has not destroyed their marriage. Bellfield has not destroyed their marriage. Bellfield's barrister has not destroyed their marriage. They are damaged, yet they, our family – what is left of it – are determined to survive. If we crumble now, Bellfield will have won. The most binding thought of all is this: Milly would be appalled to think of her family falling apart as a result of her murder.

Of course we cannot escape entirely. Other holidaymakers are buying English newspapers with pictures of us on the front pages.

On the day after we get back from Turkey, Mark Lewis tells Mum that the hacking of Milly's phone is about to be outed by the *Guardian*. We're terrified. It seems too much, too soon after the trial. A few days of sunshine cannot heal all the damage done in Court 8.

The investigative journalist who breaks the hacking story is Nick Davies. He's spent years working on unfinished business after Glenn Mulcaire, the *News of the World* hacker, and Clive Goodman, its royal editor, went to prison in 2007. The case was considered closed, a matter of a 'single rogue reporter' behaving badly. This was confirmed by the paper, the police and the Press Complaints Commission, all of whom claimed to have investigated the hacking.

Nick Davies never really bought the 'single rogue reporter' angle. In 2009, he broke a story about the *News of the World* making huge pay-outs to gag other hacking victims. A secret contact made him aware there were many more *News of the World* journalists involved in criminal interception of voicemails, many more hackers, many more methods of 'blagging' – gathering illegal information from British Telecom, mobile-phone companies, banks, the DVLA and even the police. And Nick Davies has learned there were *thousands* more victims – not just a few royal ones.

Operation Weeting is proving itself the first really effective police investigation into the hacking. From February to June, it dismantles the walls of secrecy and obstruction that previous investigations ignored.

By now our relationship with the police – apart from with Alice, Jon, and Maria Woodall – is in a very bad place. We don't feel we were sufficiently briefed about what would happen to us in court. It seems to us that Mum and Dad were expendable pawns in the CPS's edgy game with Bellfield. We're not interested in working with Surrey Police on a press release about the hacking,

Somehow, the trial verdict and the post-trial press sympathy have given us courage that we did not have before.

With Mark Lewis to help us, we are going to tackle the hacking. We draft our own statement and Mark gives it to the *Guardian*.

At 4.29 p.m., on 4 July, the *Guardian* breaks the story of Milly's hacking on its website. The next morning's paper edition goes out with the headline '*News of the World* hacked Milly Dowler's phone during police hunt. Exclusive: Paper deleted missing schoolgirl's voicemails, giving family false hope'.

From the *Guardian*, we learn much more than we have previously been told. The story explains that the *News of the World* first hired a private investigator to obtain home addresses and numbers – including ex-directory ones – of families with the name 'Dowler'. The ex-directory ones were 'blagged' illegally from British Telecom. One was Milly's. Others belonged to members of our family.

Glenn Mulcaire, a full-time 'investigator' for the paper, then hacked into Milly's phone. He listened to and recorded the messages flowing in, allowing the reporters access to the desperate words of Milly's friends and family. Among all those loving messages was one left by that recruitment agency, in Telford, Shropshire, on 27 March, six days after Milly went missing: 'We're ringing because we've got some interviews starting. Can you call me back? Thanks, bye.'

The News of the World thought its hacking had tracked down Milly, a runaway looking for work. However – and this is the part of the story that upsets us more than anything – instead of alerting her family or the police to this evidence that Milly might be alive, the newspaper despatched a team of six or seven reporters and photographers to Telford to stake out the small family agency.

It seems that the News of the World believed this would bag them a sensational scoop – of *their* hunting down Milly working illegally, being under-age, in the north of England and *their* bringing her back in triumph, with plenty of 'exclusive' photographs and headlines. This potential scoop was more important to the newspaper than our desperation.

Under menacing siege from the News of the World posse, the employment agency checked out their records. No Milly Dowler.

Nevertheless, the News of the World persisted. A reporter approached one of the agency's top clients on a golf course, telling him that the agency was employing under-age girls. The company feared it would go under in this sea of lies, but it stoutly maintained the truth: that they'd had nothing to do with the missing girl, Milly Dowler.

Finally the News of the World must have realized they had a non-story on their hands. So they decided to try it out on Surrey Police. Their reaction might provide an angle.

There followed various phone calls and meetings between the News of the World and Surrey Police. I'm not sure why the police told them of the existence of a female hoaxer instead of demanding to know how the paper had obtained access to the message from the employment agency.

The piece the *News of the World* published on 14 April was just 300 words tucked away in the back pages. They framed it as the hoaxer herself extracting Milly's number from one of her friends, then using it to register at the employment agency.

Well, indeed *someone* was using Milly's number illegally, but it was not a hoaxer. There was absolutely no legal way that the *News of the World* could have obtained that agency message, so it took great complacency and confidence for the reporters both to tell Surrey Police and to publish their story, even hidden behind the smokescreen of the hoaxer angle. But that was how it was then. Things were so cosy between the press and the police. Probably the paper could also count on Surrey Police being worried about what potentially embarrassing information had been uncovered in the suspected hacking of the police's *own* phones.

'Sources' at Surrey Police admitted off the record to the *Guardian* that the force knew that the *News of the World* had got into Milly's phone, but there was just so much going on with the investigation that there wasn't time to deal with it. They didn't see the hacking, apparently, as important.

Meanwhile, as we know, the police are now claiming that they kept us informed about the hacking at the time.

The *Guardian* article includes Mum's moment of false hope at the Birds Eye building, when she suddenly found space to record a new voicemail. The story also alleges that the *News of the World* was so greedy for fresh material about Milly that it deleted the cache in order to let more messages in.

Reading this, we remember what the police officers told Mum and Dad in April: 'That's the kind of thing they do.'

The article points out that Rebekah Brooks was the editor of the *News of the World* when the hacking took place, although she will maintain ever after that she was on holiday in Dubai that week. She is now, July 2011, chief executive of the paper's parent organization, at this point called News International. Andy Coulson, former head of communications for David Cameron at Number 10, was the deputy editor of the *News of the World* at the time of the hacking of Milly's phone.

Nick Davies quotes our statement: 'It is distress heaped on tragedy to learn that the *News of the World* had no humanity at such a terrible time. The fact that they were prepared to act in such a heinous way that could have jeopardized the police investigation and give them false hope is despicable.'

On the inside pages, the *Guardian* reveals that Operation Weeting is now alerting all the victims listed in Glenn Mulcaire's eleven thousand pages of notes. The number is likely to be more than three thousand. The 'single rogue reporter' cover is blown apart.

Only one part of Nick Davies's story will remain subject to doubt. It will turn out that the *News of the World* may not actually have deliberately deleted the messages to Milly. Its operative certainly listened to and recorded them, but the messages may have been deleted automatically by the telephone company after they had been played either by the police or by Glenn Mulcaire. Or the telephone company may have deleted them via some automated system – even though its employees were aware of the investigation into Milly's disappearance.

None of those explanations are good enough in the context of a hugely high-profile police hunt that would turn into a murder investigation.

Otherwise, everything that Nick Davies wrote about the hacking of Milly's phone was absolutely true.

The *Guardian*'s story drops like a bomb.

Labour MP Tom Watson tells the Commons that targeting Milly's phone was 'a despicable and evil act that will shock parents up and down the land to the core'. Labour MP Chris Bryant also hurls abuse at those responsible: 'This is the most horrific, depraved story yet in this catalogue of extensive criminality. Not only did the *News of the World* clearly think that they were above the law, they were prepared to play God with the emotions of the Dowler family.'

The hacking of Milly's phone dominates the front pages and is the lead item on the TV news. Nick Davies's allegations are explored from every angle, unfortunately focusing on the one thing that cannot be proved – who, if anyone, deleted the messages, and why.

Milly's ironing on our television screens once more, and playing the saxophone, sitting in the field of gold flowers, sporting her cornrows. Mum, Dad and I are shown again, reading out our 'memorable' statements, just ten days before, in front of the Old Bailey. Our request not to be contacted is respected by the press, for which we are grateful. Fortunately no one prints images of Bellfield's face. Instead, on every network, Milly's face is shown next to that of Glenn Mulcaire, the way she used to be shown next to Bellfield.

We're just too fragile to face another press onslaught. Sensitive to this, Mark Lewis offers to be our spokesperson. We accept, gratefully. Soon he is plastered all over the television and the newspapers.

Behind all the news commentators and talking heads Milly's beautiful face is blown up to billboard size. Now she's joined in some broadcasts by the faces of Hugh Grant and Gwyneth Paltrow and other celebrity hacking victims. This is the starry company Milly runs in, these days.

Mark Lewis is so passionate, so genuinely outraged by the hacking of Milly's phone, that we have to rein him in a bit. We agree with how he feels but we desperately crave a little peace. Mark quickly understands that we don't want to comment on every development. 'That's why I'm your lawyer, Sally,' he tells Mum. 'I take instructions from you.'

This is another new experience for us – someone who is there to do what we want them to do. We're grateful beyond words to have a human shield. For a little while, we are able to maintain our stance of not appearing in public.

For a little while – and then everything escalates again.

64.

Milly was not, of course, the only non-celebrity victim of the hacking. Other papers join in with their own investigations. It turns out that the parents of the Soham girls were also hacked, as were some of the families who lost loved ones in the London terrorist bombings of 7 July 2005. And now it's not just hacking. Scotland Yard announces an investigation into claims that police officers were paid by the *News of the World* for inside information.

We think, *Yes, that would explain some more of those Sunday scoops.*

On 6 July, there's an emergency Commons debate. David Cameron says, 'Lessons must be learned from this disgraceful episode. We are no longer talking here about politicians and celebrities, we are talking about murder victims, potentially terrorist victims, having their phones hacked. It is absolutely disgusting what has taken place and I think everyone in this House and indeed this country will be revolted.'

Meanwhile Ed Miliband, then leader of the Labour opposition, wants to halt the full takeover of BSkyB by Rupert Murdoch. Photographs of Rebekah Brooks are everywhere. She's still CEO of Murdoch's UK company, News International, which owns the *News of the World* and the *Sun*. There are many calls on her to resign. However, she's a friend of the prime minister and she's sticking to her story that it was 'inconceivable that I knew or, worse, sanctioned these appalling allegations'.

Waves of revulsion flow through press and social media at the hacking of Milly's phone. A Twitter campaign bombards the *News of the World*'s advertisers with demands that they stop spending money with the newspaper. WHSmith is the subject of thousands of re-tweets of the message, *Do you consider it ethical to stock a newspaper prepared to hack a murdered girl's phone?*

On Thursday, 7 July, comes the announcement that the *News of the World* will be closed down. The following Sunday will be its last edition, with no advertising and all revenue on sales going to charity.

We are sad for all those who in an instant lose their jobs at the paper just because a few people behaved in a criminal manner. It seems such a ruthless move. How hard will it be for the innocent employees to find new jobs? It is not their fault that the *News of the World* has become a toxic brand. They have been collateral damage in a massive public-relations exercise.

We know what it feels like to be collateral damage.

The decision to close is not, it seems, entirely voluntary. Dozens of its core advertisers have decided to boycott the paper. The *News of the World* is 168 years old. Nevertheless, it cannot survive the national disgust generated by its hacking of Milly's telephone. Who would want to be seen reading a paper like that now?

The *Daily Mail*'s headline is 'PAPER THAT DIED OF SHAME'. It asks, 'But is it a cynical ploy to save Sky deal and executive skins?'

The great survivor is Rebekah Brooks, staying on in her position while she tells 250 employees that they have lost their jobs. James Murdoch, son of Rupert, is also keeping his place.

Meanwhile, the scandal gathers pace and acquires some teeth. On 8 July comes the arrest of Andy Coulson and, again, of Clive Goodman, the former royal editor.

We buy a copy of the last edition.

The *News of the World* is not going quietly. It bestows on itself a heroic sad finale. Its own obituary is 'The world's greatest newspaper 1843–2011'.

'THANK YOU & GOODBYE' is splashed in massive letters over the images of some of its sensational covers.

When Dad puts the paper on the kitchen table, we gather around it and say, 'Go, Milly!' We toast her with cups of tea.

Inside, the paper celebrates its crime investigations, its vice stories, its celebrity exposés, its paedophile hunts, its royal coverage, its cads, its hookers, its adulterers, its drug busts and its page-three girls. As for its wrongdoings, the editorial says, 'Quite simply, we lost our way.'

But the story is not shut down with the closure of the paper. It continues to reverberate loudly. Rupert Murdoch flies in to take control of the situation.

On 10 July, Mum gets a call from Mark Lewis on his mobile. As usual, the reception's bad and she struggles to hear him. He says, 'Would you be interested in going to a meeting with Nick Clegg?'

'Who?'

'Nick Clegg, the deputy prime minister, Sally.'

Mum's hesitant. We don't want any more meetings. We're looking for a chance to get off the roller-coaster now. Mark reassures her, 'I'll be there. And a few other people who are hacking victims like yourselves. And Hugh Grant will be there.'

Suddenly Mum can hear every word. 'Did you say *Hugh Grant* will be there, Mark?'

'Yes, Sally.'

'I'll check with Bob and Gemma,' Mum says. But it's a done deal.

Mum hangs up, then turns to me and Dad. She says casually, 'Mark asks if we'd like to go to meet the deputy prime minister tomorrow.' As if as an afterthought, she adds, 'Oh, and Hugh Grant will be there.'

I squeal. Dad frowns. Mum and I tease Dad. We haven't had much of a chance to giggle about anything for such a long time.

'What shall I wear? Do you think Hugh likes blue?' coos Mum.

'Well, I think this calls for new outfits, Mum.'

Dad remains stony-faced.

'Gemsie and I are going, Bob,' says Mum. 'You can come if you like. Or stay at home.'

In the end, Dad agrees 'to meet with the deputy prime minister'.

That day Mum, Dad and I meet with opposition leader Ed Miliband as well as Nick Clegg. We tell them both that we have been made to wash our dirty linen in public, and that politicians must now do the same: find out the truth and sort out what has gone so wrong that the police and the law stood by and let the *News of the World* get on with hacking thousands of innocent people. Both men are genuinely outraged; both give undertakings to get to the bottom of the scandal.

It feels good to be taken so seriously. The only disappointment: there's no Hugh Grant at either meeting.

Mark now takes us to a hotel. We're ushered into another big room with another big table. The only person there is Hugh Grant, who looks just like he does in the movies. Mum goes into full swoon instantly.

In front of Hugh Grant is a delicious-smelling bacon sandwich, and he's about to tuck into it. It's not your normal greasy-spoon bacon sandwich. This is a posh West End version, tiny and crust-less, with a lot of garnish. It still looks very inviting.

Hugh jumps up to greet us. He kisses me and Mum, and shakes hands with Dad. He seems nervous. It's amazing that this Hollywood actor could be intimidated by us.

Mum and I are blushing and grinning, but Dad can't take his eyes off the bacon sandwich. It's been a long day and we haven't eaten for hours. Hugh notices immediately. He offers us the plate with the small exquisite sandwich. Mum and I don't want to eat in front of him. Dad, however, can't go on any longer without sustenance. That sandwich, plus learning that Hugh was a rugby player, puts Dad in quite a different place with the actor.

The campaigners from Hacked Off join us in the room. It all gets very technical, about strategies to deal with the emerging picture. Hugh is articulate and gets his points across very well. We don't need to say anything.

Just before we leave, I pluck up courage to ask Hugh, 'If we're invited to meet with David Cameron, will you come with us?'

But Hugh is aware of the impact of his role as a British prime minister in *Love Actually*, in which he famously dances down the stairs at Number 10. He says, 'I'm afraid that it wouldn't be appropriate. The press won't be able to resist doing something about me, and I'm not the point.'

Another small matter is widely reported. It is a statement by Scotland Yard's deputy assistant commissioner. He says that our family should have been told by Surrey Police that our phones might have been targeted. Mark Lewis adds, 'Why they didn't tell the family at all is a matter for Surrey Police to answer. What it does show is that this relationship between the police and the press is not restricted to the Metropolitan Police.'

Meanwhile Hugh Grant says that people feel 'viscerally sickened' by what happened to Milly's phone.

Channel 4 News talks of politicians lining up to bite the hand that once fed them so well – that of Rupert Murdoch, the unofficial twenty-fifth member of the cabinet. David Cameron has reinvented himself as the scourge, not the friend, of News International.

Rupert Murdoch's biographer, Michael Wolff, tweets, '*This is chicken-with-head-cut-off time. I think Rupert Murdoch has no idea what he should do.*'

By 13 July, Rupert Murdoch has withdrawn his bid for BSkyB.

Yet that's nowhere near the end of the story.

The hacking scandal, so close on the heels of the trial, means that, as Milly's family, we have a new label to add to the package of fame that we never wanted.

Exhausted and frail as we are, our instinct is to try to use this unwanted currency for the good. If the ripping away of Milly's and our own privacy can be deployed to improve the situation for others, we're up for it.

The trial has torn us apart, yet it has also strengthened us. Now we feel that we may be able to wrest back some control and some sense of self-worth. We want to believe that what has happened to us in the courts and in the press might be prevented for others. From the sacks of mail we still receive, from the money that poured into Milly's Fund, we've known for years that we have the compassion of the public as well as their intense curiosity. Everything to do with Milly is charged with electric interest. So we shouldn't be astonished that now the party leaders seem to want to meet and talk with our family – and other victims of crime – more than they want to meet with the starrier people in Hacked Off.

On 13 July, Mark tells us, David Cameron will announce a judge-led inquiry into press ethics and behaviour. It seems that he would like our blessing to set a seal on this new direction. Dazed and broken as we are, we decide to support this move.

We are going to Downing Street to meet the prime minister.

65.

I choose a grey dress, with a grey-and-white-striped jacket. Mum wears blue-and-white stripes with a blue white-edged jacket. Dad's in blue stripes too – his shirt. It may look like it, but I don't *think* we're consciously adopting a prison uniform.

First we go to the public gallery in the House of Commons to hear David Cameron announce at Prime Minister's Questions what will soon be called 'The Leveson Inquiry'. It is named after its leader, Lord Justice Leveson. Its task will be to investigate illegal activity at News International and other media groups. It will also look into the culture, practices and ethics of the British press, including over-cosy or financial links between politicians, police and journalists.

We march over to Downing Street, accompanied by Mark Lewis and various members of Hacked Off. Mum gets to lift the Number 10 door-knocker and rap it smartly. Of course, it's just ceremonial. There's someone already waiting right behind the door to let us in.

I have to suppress a giggle as we walk up the stairs of Number 10. Hugh was right: it's impossible not to remember him dancing down them in *Love Actually*. We're shown into a room lined with cream bookshelves. David Cameron stands up to greet us – shaking hands with everybody. At his touch, the usual painful thought runs through my mind: the honour of speaking with the prime minister has come at the expense of Milly's life.

He immediately says that he's absolutely outraged about what has happened to us. Then he moves swiftly into a discussion about the logistics of a public inquiry. Again, it's very technical, and I drift into my own thoughts.

David Cameron comes across as a very well-to-do man, and extremely well educated. Looking at him, listening to his confident voice, it seems impossible that such a successful politician, at the top of his powers, has apparently been unable to do more to prevent or stop hacking. I've also read the stories about how much he socializes with his country neighbours Rebekah Brooks and Elizabeth Murdoch, Rupert's daughter. I know that when he employed Andy Coulson as his press secretary, a former *News of the World* executive ended up in one of the most influential jobs in the country. *That* does not seem to me to be a piece of excellent statesmanship or judgement now that Coulson is under arrest.

Why, I've wondered, is everyone so afraid of Rupert Murdoch, that they cut their own throats to keep him happy?

After giving his speech to the campaigners, David Cameron asks, 'May I see the Dowler family in private now?'

Everyone files out except Mark, his assistant and ourselves. A couple of prime ministerial advisers stand at the side of the room. We're given tea. Biscuits are served on bone china. They are not chocolate biscuits like the ones served to Hugh Grant in *Love Actually*.

David Cameron says he is very sorry for our loss. He adds, with dignity, 'I know what it's like to lose a child.' His own son Ivan, a severely disabled little boy, died in February 2009. He was just six years old. We express our empathy.

I know we are principally there to allow our prime minister to show compassion and respect for us. I know there will be an official photograph to immortalize this moment. Suddenly I'm tired of being passive and pitied. I'm tired of listening. We've seen heads shaken sorrowfully before, most notably since our ordeal at the trial. The vestiges of Good Gemma are pretty tattered, these days. There is something I need to say. While my parents sip their tea, I feel sentences building in my head.

Out they come.

'You know, we can all sit around for ever discussing the pros and cons of a public inquiry. But that's not really the point,' I tell David Cameron. 'You've got to face up to the Rupert Murdochs of the world. This behaviour is completely unacceptable.'

The room falls silent, apart from my insistent voice. Mum and Dad's faces are frozen. But this is 2012. I can't be sent to the Tower for what I say. Knowing that, I say plenty. I look the prime minister in his blue eyes. '*You* could be the one to make the changes! *You!* If you just aired all this dirty laundry, and did something about it, people would respect you more. You need to man up!'

I glance at my father. 'My dad didn't have any choice as to whether his dirty laundry would be aired in front of the whole world. Especially since Bellfield was allowed to see that evidence, even though it was irrelevant. And he was allowed to have it used in the trial.'

I tell David Cameron about the police's harassment of my father, when their only theory was that Dad killed Milly. I tell him about the senior officer who said that Surrey Police were not looking for anyone else in connection with Milly's disappearance. I tell him about the police saying, just after Milly went missing, that if Dad ever slept in the same bed as me they would arrest him – this at a moment when I was hysterically afraid of being alone.

At that David Cameron flinches. I'm suddenly sure that he knows what it is to comfort a distressed child at night, that he's stayed by a distressed child until he or she finally falls asleep. He asks me, 'Do you want to take this further?'

I say, 'I don't want to put my parents through that.'

I have wandered off topic. I return to the matter of press hacking. 'Why can't *you*,' I urge David Cameron, 'be the leader who sets a new precedent for press ethics?'

David Cameron promises, 'It's already in motion.'

'Good,' I say.

The meeting is over. My parents thank the prime minister for his time.

As we're leaving, one of David Cameron's advisers puts a hand on my arm reassuringly. 'That was an amazing speech, Gemma. I truly felt the *Chariots of Fire* music should have been playing when you finished!' He adds, 'You could have a good career in public speaking.'

This is when I dare to think for the first time that maybe, just maybe, what I have said could actually make a difference. You can see it in the photo. I'm looking at David Cameron. Mum and Dad look serious, but I have a different expression on my face. I look like a girl who has just woken up to discover that she's not quite as helpless as she thought. My eyes are super-alert. What you see in that photo is a girl who has just realized she can speak truth to power. She's not afraid to do it. In fact, she insists.

Outside Number 10, my bravery collapses in tears. I *can* put on that truth-to-power face and voice. For a few moments. There's a cost. Afterwards, I feel hollowed out, exhausted. The press are waiting for us in the street, of course, so now there's another picture, showing my naked vulnerability. Mum strokes my wet cheek. Dad bends over us both, his face soft with concern.

In the meantime, we fulfil our end of the unspoken bargain. Mark releases the statement we've prepared:

> The Dowlers are delighted the Prime Minister has announced a full, judge-led inquiry, and that politicians for all three parties have reacted so quickly . . . in response to the outrage of the public in respect not only of Milly but all the victims of such unlawful practices, and failures in the pursuit by the police and failures by the politicians.
>
> This shows the power of the public, however big an organization is, to stand up and say 'something isn't right'.
>
> Like most scandals, this wasn't about malign conduct. It was about the attempts to cover it up. When people cover up things, they are not fit and proper to run something.

The words 'fit and proper' are the ones that News International least wants to see at the moment because if it is judged not 'fit and proper' then it can never claim the prize of BSkyB.

We go home and watch ourselves on television yet again.

What has Milly done? Rupert Murdoch has held politicians in his grip for decades. ITV's political editor, Tom Bradby, says, 'In terms of British public and political life, this is the end of the world as we know it, and the beginning of something new.'

Over a video of Rupert Murdoch dodging the press and of Milly playing the sax, the economics editor, Daisy McAndrew, says, 'When the corporate history books are written, *this* man's biggest humiliation will be inextricably linked to *this* murdered thirteen-year-old, because the moment word spread that *her* phone seemed to have been hacked by *his* employees was the moment his seemingly unstoppable rise to world media domination was halted.'

Mum phones me. 'Would you like to meet Rupert Murdoch? We've been invited.'

We've been given two hours' notice. It could have been less: his PR people have suggested to Mark Lewis that Murdoch could come to our home to meet us. Mum doesn't want that circus on our doorstep. 'We'll come to London,' she tells Mark Lewis.

Would I like to meet Rupert Murdoch?

There's no question in my mind that this is something I want to do. Rupert Murdoch himself is the person who ultimately has to take responsibility for the hacking of Milly's phone.

Prime ministers, like David Cameron, come and go, but press moguls like Rupert Murdoch seem to last for ever. For years, Murdoch's been adding tabloids, broadsheets and television stations to his empire, to the point where his media companies can sway the minds of nations. If his papers throw their weight behind a political party, it can make all the difference to the result of an election. Then the leaders of that party owe the media something. De-regulation of the press, for example.

But now Rupert Murdoch's empire seems to be coming apart at some of its seams – and we see that today in two more resignations, that of Rebekah Brooks, and that of Murdoch's aide for over fifty years, Les Hinton. It's a terrible day for Rupert Murdoch. And on that same day he has to meet the family of Milly Dowler.

But this meeting is not about money, or power, or politics.

It's about saying sorry.

Mark Lewis has been negotiating damages for the violation of our privacy by the *News of the World*. It remains very hard to think about. It feels like blood money, and at the beginning I don't want any part of it.

However, the stress and grief of the trial have by now eroded my mental state, which has never recovered from the abomination of what happened to Milly and the way the police dealt with us. Because of them, it's going to take years to repair things with Dad, quietly, step by step. I feel as if I'll have to live at home for ever, trapped in my childhood, because Milly's murder has put insurmountable damage in the way of my growing up. I know that I still need some serious therapy. Intensive psychiatric help has a hefty price tag. My bills are already at five figures. We don't have that kind of money. Moreover, while I have the therapy I need, I won't be able to work full time or maybe even at all.

Meanwhile, Mum and Dad are still ghosts of themselves.

Our once happy, anonymous personal lives have been publicly dismantled by all the crimes against Milly – her abduction, her murder, our virtual trial for her murder, the hacking of her phone. Our privacy has been wrenched away. It is an ordeal to walk down the street. People point at us, as if we can't see them. They talk to us as if they know us. We have the taint of victims. Will we ever be recognized again just for our own talents or hard work? Who will give me a mortgage so that I can have a home of my own?

On the other hand, the *press* have profited financially from our loss. Milly's murder has sold tens of millions of newspapers.

That is the state of mind we are in as the minutes melt away before our meeting with Rupert Murdoch.

After Mum's call, I rush home and plaster on the war paint, trying to cover up all signs of my true vulnerability. I'm going to be Gemma the young woman who has recently told David Cameron to 'man up' – and who got respect for it.

I wore grey to David Cameron. For Murdoch I choose a black dress as a mark of respect to Milly and the damage done to her reputation in the trial. I decide to wear a gold necklace that Lovely Granny bought for me – the pendant is the initial M. Normally I keep it inside my dress, close to my heart. On this day, it's fully visible. I want to show the world that Milly is constantly with me. Mum's in white with a yellow jacket. Dad, as always, looks immaculate in a suit with a blue-striped tie and shirt.

We board the train, taking our seats among passengers still reading the day's papers. Most of the front pages are saturated with the story of phone hacking. Milly's on every front page, all over the carriage. As we travel in silence towards London I put my earphones in. I'm desperate to distract myself from everything that is going on in my mind. Every so often I catch the eye of someone whispering to the person next to them.

'Look, there's the Dowlers!'

Of course, they have no idea we're on our way to see Rupert Murdoch.

We're due to meet Mark Lewis at a coffee shop. The site of the Murdoch meeting is to be kept secret until the last minute. Mark Lewis is very clear on how we are to behave. This is one occasion, he tells us, when we don't have to hold back our emotions. Dad immediately looks uncomfortable.

Our lawyer tells us that Murdoch is very close to his family, particularly his mother. I'm not sure why, but this seems like useful information to store away. I'm still trying to think of the meeting as a way to make a difference.

I don't think about the financial settlement that is under discussion. I'm aware that an amount will be given to us to help secure our futures. If I actually think about the real reason we're getting the money I would never be able to accept it. Or I would feel constrained to go into the meeting feeling humble and grateful.

That's not how I want to be today.

We are here to receive a public apology, which is due not just to us but to a whole nation.

Mark receives a text setting the meeting's location: One Aldwych, in the Strand.

As we walk to the hotel, the coast is clear, a relief. Then I think, *Of course unwanted press will not be here. Rupert Murdoch will make sure of that.*

I'm feeling jittery. I still don't know exactly what I'll feel when I see him, or what I shall say.

When I examine my feelings, I realize I'm angry that he has allowed journalists to behave in the way they did. Yet in the context of the trial we've just been through, Murdoch is small fry. Compared with the trauma of sitting in a room with Bellfield, this doesn't even come close.

Come to think of it, I wonder, *why don't Murdoch's papers hack criminals? Why did they not hack Bellfield? Perhaps they did. Yet they didn't use the information in any way that I've noticed.*

The hotel is minimalist. The walls are white and hold the light, giving the impression that the reception area is huge. We're escorted to a meeting room on the first floor. By contrast, it's so dark in there that at first we cannot see the man we've come to meet. This room is painted black and has mirrors on one side. The only illumination comes from dimmed spotlights. I'm wondering if

Murdoch himself has chosen the lighting. Is it because it will be flattering? Or is it that he doesn't really want to see the expressions on my parents' faces, and mine?

Of course he doesn't understand all that we have been through, and that to us the hacking is just one more thing piled on a great bonfire of our feelings that started burning nine years ago. Hacking's making lots of flame and smoke now but, as far as we're concerned, it's just having its moment in the limelight.

This meeting is different from the ones we've had with politicians. There are no microphones or cameras set up. It is just the six of us: four on our side and two on his.

Murdoch's assistant is a good-looking City type, in a slim-fit suit and a skinny tie. He's a very pleasant chap and makes us a cup of tea. He seems somewhat out of his depth.

Our eyes readjust so we can focus on Rupert Murdoch himself. He's wearing a navy pinstripe suit and thick black-rimmed glasses.

He looks so old, I think, *that if he ever went out on a windy day he would simply blow over.*

The man is clearly very uncomfortable. He keeps putting his head in his hands and sighing. He repeats several times that he is sorry for what happened. Every time he apologizes, he strikes the table with the side of his hand. He keeps glancing at us, as if expecting a response.

I wonder, *Is he waiting for us to thank him for apologizing? If he is, then let him wait.*

Instead of acknowledging his words, Mum is radiating anger. She gives him one of her long disapproving looks.

I think she's making him nervous, because he suddenly says, 'My wife sends her apologies for not being here. She wanted to meet you too . . . but she couldn't make it.'

That doesn't go down well. Mum still glowers at him in silence.

He seems far too frail to be dealing with any of this. For a moment, I feel sorry for him. As I look at him, and his adviser dancing around him with the tea, I think, *You are just a weak old man. You are nothing for me to fear and I don't have any respect for you or the business you own. You may have lots of money and own a lot of the media yet to me you look like any other old man.*

Rupert Murdoch looks down at the floor, avoiding our gaze.

There are some things you can accept an apology for – someone spills your drink, or misses an appointment, or bangs your car: an accident happens. You can apologize for a misunderstanding, hurtful things said in the heat of the moment. An apology for intercepting your missing sister's voicemails doesn't really come into any of these categories.

'This is the worst day of my life,' he says in a feeble voice.

He does not sound like a press baron. He sounds like someone who is very sorry for himself.

If it's the worst day of your life then you're bloody *lucky*, I think. *If only the worst day of my life was a meeting – and not the one when my mother was taken apart in court. Or was it my sister's funeral? Or was it the day she was taken?*

I feel as if we are just one more thing on Murdoch's job list for the day. *Go and meet the Dowlers and say sorry. Tick!*

There is silence in the room. Eventually, our lawyer speaks for us. He wants to make it clear that the reason we are here personally is to make sure such a thing will never happen again.

To our faces, Rupert Murdoch says, 'I had no knowledge of these practices going on in my company. I wasn't informed. If I was informed, it wouldn't have happened.' He adds, 'I am appalled that this happened. This is not the standard set by my father, not the standard set by my mother. I'm sorry. This should not have happened.'

His father, our lawyer has briefed us, was an acclaimed war correspondent and newspaper proprietor, Sir Keith Murdoch.

I remember the press parked day after day in Station Avenue and outside our house. Some of them worked for this man. I can't hold myself back. I say, 'Let's be honest. If the *News of the World* had been in charge of the investigation into Milly's disappearance, things would have been very different. It's a shame you hacked Milly's phone and not Bellfield's. Then the police would have found him before he killed Milly and other girls. That would have saved lives.'

No one on our side tries to quieten me down.

Now is the moment to make use of what Mark Lewis told us – that Murdoch is close to his mother. I take it upon myself to raise a new point. 'How would *you* feel, Mr Murdoch, if your last conversation ever with your mother was hacked by some seedy reporter?'

He cannot meet my eyes. I can't really blame him. If I were him, I wouldn't want to look straight into the eyes of the sister of the murdered schoolgirl whose phone his company had hacked.

Tears appear on Murdoch's wrinkled cheeks. I think, *So now you're going to cry? Really? You are far too old for this. You must be fed up with all of the reporters chasing you around. You should be enjoying your retirement. You need to stop.*

He says very quietly, 'I am appalled that this has happened. What can I do?'

Mum speaks at last: 'All this press attention is *not* what we want. We just want things sorted as quickly and quietly as possible so that we can get on with our lives. We don't want to be dragged through the court system again.'

The young assistant says, 'We'll liaise with Mark, of course,' which I take to mean that the settlement will be out of court.

Murdoch adds, 'We will get things settled as soon as possible.'

No mention is made of money. That will be for Mark Lewis to deal with.

Dad is staying quiet. Words are not needed – not from us.

I remember the impression that I made with my speech to David Cameron just two days before. Now I'm sitting in a room with someone who is actually in a position to implement the necessary changes to stop this dirty cycle of invasion of privacy and profiting from information gained in that way.

Rupert Murdoch doesn't even need to make a law, I think. *He can just send a memo.*

He agrees that he can make changes. He sounds half-hearted.

I do feel he's ashamed. But it's not exactly for what he has done to us. He's ashamed because he has let his parents down so badly and because he has been made to look bad in the eyes of the world.

The next step is to prepare a statement for our lawyer to read outside the hotel. Murdoch's adviser suggests that we all stand together on the steps. This is not an option that appeals to us. We don't wish to appear as a united front. We decide that we'll go first.

We walk back into the hotel reception area. There it becomes apparent that Murdoch has not after all been able to control the secrecy of our meeting. The lobby is swarming with journalists, photographers and cameramen.

It is now Murdoch's turn to face a press feeding frenzy.

This time it's Murdoch himself who is their prey.

As he appears, the press lurch forward in a mob, almost smothering him. There must be a hundred reporters and photographers. It seems as if they're going to knock Murdoch to the ground. I see the strain on his face as he struggles to stay upright. He makes a brief statement. But no one lets him get a word out. They are screaming at him.

From the back of the press scrum, a man yells, '*Shame* on you!'

The next day, 16 July, Murdoch takes full-page advertisements in various papers, including the *Guardian*:

> The News of the World *was in the business of holding others to account.*
>
>> *It failed when it came to itself.*
>>
>> *We are sorry for the serious wrongdoing that occurred.*
>>
>> *We are deeply sorry for the hurt suffered by the individuals affected.*
>>
>> *We regret not acting faster to sort things out.*
>>
>> *I realize that simply apologizing is not enough.*
>>
>> *Our business was founded on the idea that a free and open press should be a positive force in society. We need to live up to this.*
>>
>> *In the coming days, as we take further concrete steps to resolve these issues and make amends for the damage they have caused, you will hear more from us.*
>>
>> *Sincerely*
>>
>> *Rupert Murdoch*

The non-Murdoch press have a field day with his apology to us, especially on the length of time it has taken him to face us since 4.29 p.m. on 4 July when the hacking of Milly's phone was exposed.

The *Independent* describes 15 July as Murdoch's 'Day of Atonement'.

66.

Lots of people are atoning now. Rebekah Brooks is arrested on 17 July and released on bail. Sir Paul Stephenson, Metropolitan Police commissioner, resigns. So does John Yates, assistant commissioner, the man who hadn't thought there was anything much worth investigating when it came to the hacking scandal, although he had been specifically asked to review the standard of the Met's original investigation.

This seems a fitting place to finish talking about the big beasts in the hacking scandal for a while, even though their names will fill the newspapers for years yet.

It's time to get back down to our level, the humble level of victim.

There's an article in the *Daily Mirror* on 22 July by Paul Routledge. It's entitled 'The manipulation of Milly Dowler's memory must stop'. It's the most empathetic piece of writing we've seen.

> *It must be dreadful for the Dowler family, reminded every day of their lost daughter by endless screening of her picture on television.*
>
> *Milly ironing her jeans, Milly among flowers, Milly laughing and larking about. Terribly poignant images of an innocent teenage girl, murdered by a sub-human brute.*
>
> *Sometimes I have to turn away. What must their anguish be like?*
>
> *And the worst thing is, these emotive shots are simply used to illustrate the hideous, but quite distinct story of phone hacking by unscrupulous hacks working for Rupert Murdoch . . .*
>
> *Milly's life, Milly's fate, has nothing to do with these low-lifes. I wish the TV people would stop exploiting her image this way . . .*
>
> *Unfortunately, and quite by chance, Milly achieved more after her death than a thousand investigative journalists . . .*

Sadly, our family is not yet done with phone hacking. On 21 July 2011, Mum and Dad have a meeting at Mount Browne police station with Maria Woodall and a senior officer from Surrey Police.

This officer wants to talk about Operation Weeting. He says that they have now had a chance to look through their old notes. Previously they had not wanted to get those notes out of order because of the trial. This sounds odd, but we're used to things sounding odd at Surrey Police. Now they have discovered some recordings of where they had tried to pick up Milly's voicemail and there were lots of clicks on the line. They themselves, they discover, still have recordings of the messages from family and friends.

The difference is that the police are now saying there's no evidence to suggest the *News of the World* had deleted messages. They tell us that it is impossible to prove either way. Mum and Dad are now informed that they were *not* told in April that messages had been deleted.

Another U-turn.

A handwritten note is produced with an ambiguous statement on it. Mum and Dad are told that this is proof that Dad was told about the hacking back in 2002. The piece of paper does not jog any memory of such a thing happening. We know we'd remember if we'd been told of it. Our memories would not need jogging.

Mum and Dad have brought some questions of their own. They insist on raising the question of leaks to the press by Surrey Police back in 2002. They are informed that one 'loose-lipped' officer told his friend about the case. He was immediately dealt with. They insist that there's no other information to suggest that anyone was in collusion with the press. If we find out otherwise, they promise to investigate.

There is talk of previous officers with leading roles in the investigation. One, we are told, was removed simply because he was not experienced enough to deal with this type of case. It had nothing to do with Mum complaining about his attitude and failure to keep us informed in a timely way. There is discussion of certain other officers who have been removed from the case, but there's no conclusion.

Mum and Dad are left confused about what this meeting was really about. One thing is sure as hell: it was not an apology.

It is one more blow on top of so many others. Mum breaks down when they get home. The whole thing is so toxic, and so huge. It's five days before she stops shaking. Meanwhile, we hear that Bellfield is indeed appealing his conviction.

Of course we want the hacking stopped. What we know now cannot be allowed to stand. We want justice meted out to anyone who is guilty in regard to Milly. That includes police officers who weave webs around truths that we know, and make us feel as if we're walking in quicksand.

No more, we decide. Mum tells the police that we shall no longer deal with them directly and they must work through our solicitor, Mark Lewis.

Mark has negotiated a settlement for us. The papers are full of speculation about the sum, quoting numbers far bigger than reality. Let's get it straight here. Our family receives £2 million with an additional £1 million going to charities we nominate. There's a condition that the charity money will be paid directly by Rupert Murdoch.

It crosses my mind that Rupert Murdoch needs to be seen to give us this money possibly more than we need to receive it.

But we need it too. And so do others. We put a lot of thought into the six charities that will benefit.

The £1 million that morally belongs, in our eyes, to Milly is to be given to charities that feel right for her. We start with Shooting Star CHASE, a children's hospice near our home that cares for local families who have a child or teenager with a life-limiting condition (£500,000), and Child Victims of Crime (£100,000), who provide material and therapeutic support for children up to the age of sixteen who have been victims of, or traumatized by, any criminal offence within the UK and nominated to them by serving police officers. Both of these choices reflect that Milly was a child when she was murdered.

For Cancer Research, there's £100,000 for pancreatic cancer in honour of my dear grandad, David Wood, Lovely Granny's husband. Braintumouruk.org receives £100,000 in honour of Ray Ford, Milly's godfather, who died young of a brain tumour. We give £100,000 to Hampton Pool Trust. Milly and I used to swim there and it's still a place of solace for me and Mum. Finally there's £100,000 to the Suzy Lamplugh Trust, which provides practical help and guidance to reduce people's fear of crime and to develop skills and strategies for keeping themselves safe. The Suzy Lamplugh Trust's founder, Diana Lamplugh, did so much to help Mum and Dad when Milly first disappeared, and this was, of course, the trust that had absorbed Milly's Fund.

From our own share of the money, we need to pay our legal fees, amounting to £360,000, though Mark Lewis has earned every penny.

The residue is to be divided between Mum, Dad and me. It's going to need to last a long, long time, and stretch a long way, with the therapy bills still mounting and both me and Mum still unable to work.

I want to buy a pair of Jimmy Choo shoes, because that's what Milly would have wanted. Mum talks me out of it. This is not money for joyful extravagance. Anyway, in my current state, I barely leave the house, so where would I wear those shoes?

I remember how, as a family, we used to sing 'If I Had A Million Dollars' by the Barenaked Ladies, at the tops of our voices. Milly loved that song.

Now we have a million dollars but we don't have Milly.

67.

On 1 October, the mood changes, briefly. I do a photo-shoot for *Cosmopolitan* magazine's December issue. I've been nominated as 'Ultimate Family Girl' because of my bravery at the trial and throughout the hacking scandal.

Mum comes with me to the photo-shoot, which is the coolest thing. She gets styled and made up too. After the year we've had, we are allowed into the happy, bubbly world of glamour for a brief moment. Milly would have loved picking through the rail of dresses. The photo-shoot is full of laughs. I'm in a flaming red, drapey off-the-shoulder red number. It's way over the top, but in a good way. It has been a way over-the-top year, after all. I have chandelier earrings, a chunky bracelet and of course I wear the M necklace.

On 3 November, Mum and I attend the official *Cosmo* Ultimate Woman Award dinner at the Banqueting House in London. I dress edgy for this occasion: a black plunging number with lace. We meet other nominees, including Lisa and Louise Hawker, who campaigned for justice for their sister Lindsay, murdered in Japan in 2007. Lindsay was raped and strangled. Her Japanese murderer then tried to dispose of her body in a particularly gruesome way. This summer, the family has had to sit through a harrowing trial in Japanese. One of the sisters had by that time taught herself the language so that she could translate proceedings for the rest of the family.

Lucy and Louise have won the Editor's Choice Award. We spend time chatting with the sisters and their mother, Julia – Jules. We pose for pictures together.

Accepting the Ultimate Family Girl Award, I read a short speech about how I plan to draw a line under the terrible years that have passed. As I listen to the applause, I think, *If only it could be that easy.*

We leave with Lisa and Lindsay Hawker and their mother. They're staying at the same hotel as Mum and me. The banquet supper was very light for a group of healthy young women . . . too light, so we stop the taxi on the way back to the hotel. We emerge from it in our posh dresses and invade a McDonald's. We fasten our Ultimate teeth around Big Macs and strawberry milkshakes. Holding up our Ultimate Woman statuettes, we blag a free bag of chips. The award is already proving its worth.

Back at the hotel, the Hawkers come to our bedroom for more talk. We sit on the beds, trading our intense and terrible experiences, asking questions. Mum's dress is tight, so she sheds it, and continues chatting in her slip. The conversation would, to an outsider, seem bizarre. Yet who else can you ask but another victim family when you want to know something like 'How long does it take to strangle someone?'

The answer is three and a half minutes. Louise tells us that in the trial of Lindsay's murderer, the court was made to sit in silence for exactly that time. It felt like ages. She explains that this was done to demonstrate that a strangler has plenty of time to change his mind, to decide not to kill.

Lucy, Louise and Jules are serious and knowledgeable. We are all candid with one another. I'm so grateful to those brave women.

The next day Mum and I are invited to breakfast with Samantha Cameron. I pose on the steps of Number 10, wearing a red dress with a gold belt and a smile that the press have not seen all year.

The Leveson Inquiry begins on 14 November. Dad attends the first days. He hears the barrister David Sherborne talk of how our family was betrayed in a 'terrible intrusion'. The barrister adds, 'Probably there are no words which can adequately describe how despicable this was.'

Preliminary panels have heard that it was likely Surrey Police's own phones were hacked by the *News of the World*. Knowing the fear that the paper inspired, it's becoming understandable to us why it had so many scoops. There were clearly two routes to those scoops: letting officers know that potentially incriminating private matters could be exposed, and finding out where and when to be in order to get the best photographs.

It emerges that our lawyer, Mark Lewis, was also placed under surveillance back in 2010 by the *News of the World*.

Mum and Dad attend the Leveson Inquiry on Monday, 21 November. They are the very first witnesses, and their evidence will be the most incendiary.

It's packed with press in Court 73 at the Royal Courts of Justice, reminding them of Court 8 at the Old Bailey. To add to the tension, this is the first time Mum and Dad have given evidence since Bellfield's trial, only six months before. The wounds of their mauling at the hands of the defence barrister are still quite visible on their pale faces.

Mum ends up sitting next to Hugh Grant, much to her delight. They both admit to being very anxious. He teaches her the seven/eleven breathing exercise to help her nerves: 'Breathe in for seven seconds, breathe out for eleven.'

Lord Leveson greets Mum and Dad courteously and thanks them for agreeing to appear.

Mum tells the inquiry about the electrifying moment when she believed that Milly must still be alive because her voicemail cache was emptied. She doesn't say what everyone in Court 73 must be thinking: that at that moment her daughter's body was lying naked and dead in the forest where her murderer had dumped her.

Mum also recounts the effect on her when she was finally told about the hacking of Milly's phone so many years later: 'I didn't sleep for about three nights because you replay everything in your mind and just think, Oh, that makes sense now, that makes sense.'

One of the things that made sense was how the *News of the World* acquired photographs of Mum and Dad retracing Milly's last steps. They had arranged that walk with private texts and calls between them, seven weeks after she vanished. Mum says, 'That Sunday, that photo appeared in the *News of the World*. I remember seeing it and I was really cross . . . How on earth did they know we were doing that walk on that day? It felt like such an intrusion into a really, really private grief moment.'

Dad tells the inquiry, 'Fundamentally, everybody's entitled to a degree of privacy in their private life, and it's a deep concern that our private life became public.'

Mum is also honest about the fact that we had needed so often to rely on the press in the early days of the search for Milly. 'We were really, really desperate for some information about Milly, and the press were in a position to be able to help us and they did get the message out that she was missing and lots of information came in to the police headquarters.'

She explains how we learned to see the press as a double-edged sword: 'But on the other hand, the persistent being asked questions and being door-stepped and everything else that's associated with it, and all the letters that you get requesting books, films, interviews . . .' She recalls how hard it was to leave the house without being accosted by reporters. 'They would come up to you when you're least expecting it, so as you're sort of lifting stuff in and out of the car or something, and then they'll fire a question at you without introducing themselves, and so you have to train yourself not to answer.'

Lord Leveson thanks Mum and Dad. 'I can only sympathize with both of you for the appalling losses that you have suffered and for the traumas that you have undergone.' He asks Mum and Dad if they have any ideas about how the press could be better regulated.

Mum has another Lovely Granny moment. She says quietly and politely that this is Lord Leveson's work, not ours.

As they make their way home that evening, Mum's phone buzzes with dozens of messages of support from friends who have watched the live broadcast, knowing what it must have cost her. Replying to Fiona, Mum mentions that she picked a piece of lint from Hugh Grant's trousers.

Well, I hope you kept it, Fiona texts.

Moments of silliness like this are what keep you going when things seem impossibly tough.

The next day, the press give Mum and Dad the front and inside pages again. There is praise for their steadfastness. The *Daily Telegraph* writes, 'They remained assured and dignified throughout their half-hour appearance before a packed Court 73.' Simon Carr, writing in the *Independent*, describes how his notes were 'swimming' because he was so moved by their testimony. He describes my parents well: 'Mr Dowler, by the way, is a large, quiet man with a resonant voice. I hope Mrs Dowler won't mind my saying her manner shows something of the last decade. They refer and defer to each other with quick glances.'

Meanwhile, the hacker himself, Glenn Mulcaire, insists that he did not delete Milly's messages. Quite reasonably, he asks why he would do so.

By 12 December there's a new row brewing over exactly who deleted Milly's voicemails. Suspicion in the press briefly points to Surrey Police, who certainly listened to and transcribed the messages just as the *News of the World* did, though not, of course, illegally. The police claim that neither the hacker Glenn Mulcaire nor the *News of the World* journalists are likely to have deleted the voicemails deliberately. And, of course the police themselves did no such thing. But it's also possible that listening to messages set an automatic deletion deadline of seventy-two hours – whoever listened. This evolving information disturbs the proceedings of Leveson. New investigations are requested.

Yet was it really the *deletion* of Milly's messages that closed the *News of the World*? Was it not the *hacking* of Milly's phone that caused the outrage and revulsion? It is certainly what caused ours.

Fortunately Lord Leveson quickly and sensibly makes it clear that the deletions and 'false hope' moment were not and are not the only reason for establishing this inquiry into press standards.

Just before Christmas, Mum makes some notes about where she is now. Those two pages of blue biro make such sad reading. Just in this year alone, Mum writes, we've had to face the trial, the hacking, the new confrontation with Surrey Police, the encounters with the Metropolitan Police and the Leveson Inquiry. She goes on,

I'm starting to doubt anything I say. I'm too scared to say anything. I feel completely helpless against two police forces, the justice system and News International . . . exasperated at the costs and complicatedness of it all . . . Will the News of the World *ask for the money back? Gemma at crisis point again . . .*

7.

Breakdown and Recovery
December 2012 – May 2015

PLAYLIST

Amy Grant	Carry You
The Beach Boys and	
Lorrie Morgan	Don't Worry Baby
Billy Joel	Lullabye (Goodnight, My Angel)
The Moody Blues	Om
2Cellos	Benedictus
Santana	Europa (Earth's Cry Heaven's Smile)
Alison Krauss and Union Station	A Living Prayer
The Judds	Love Can Build A Bridge
Rascal Flatts	When The Sand Runs Out
Tim McGraw	Live Like You Were Dying
Judy Collins	Miracle River
Eagles	Seven Bridges Road
Rascal Flatts	Bless The Broken Road
Vince Gill	Go Rest High On That Mountain
Josh Turner	Long Black Train
Barenaked Ladies	If I Had A Million Dollars

68.

On 30 January, Surrey Police finally return all of Milly's possessions that they took away almost ten years earlier. Among them are Milly's daisy pyjamas, the ones she wore in the Cuba video. When Mum had asked for them back, ages ago, the police said they had been incinerated. They even produced a note they said bore Mum's signature, authorizing the destruction of the pyjamas. There's no point reminding them of that. Officers come and go at Surrey Police, meaning that gaps of memory will never be filled.

The pyjamas are a rare *good* mistake. Mum washes them immediately to remove the fingerprints of the police exhibits officer. She wears them that night.

Milly's things come home in lots of cardboard boxes. They're not neat inside but that's OK – nothing in Milly's room was ever neat. At least that's consistent. This is when Mum discovers all the little green stickers on Milly's schoolbooks. We see how the police inadvertently helped Bellfield's defence by marking up anything that looked even a little bit sad as potentially suspicious.

We keep the schoolbooks, poems, sketchbooks. Only Mum dares to look inside. It is lovely for her to see Milly's writing again after all these years, and to rediscover her cheeky sense of humour, her amazingly eccentric spelling and her clever designs. It's sad to think we have been denied these for so long. Having Milly's things back inspires us to take the old family video tapes to be digitized so we can watch them again, and see her laughing, singing and chatting.

Meanwhile, the hacking scandal is not over. On 13 March, Rebekah Brooks and her husband are arrested on suspicion of conspiracy to pervert the course of justice.

By April 2012, I'm seriously worried about Mum. Her mood is not good. She's not sleeping. She feels as if her mind is playing tricks on her. She suffers from headaches. She does not want to talk to anyone. She closes down conversations, withdraws from social situations and has difficulty communicating even with me and Dad. If she has to be sociable, she soon falls asleep from the mental effort it has taken.

Mum also spends too much time worrying about the *News of the World* money. It sits in our bank accounts as if it's radioactive. The only thing I've bought with it is a blue Mini, and that was because my old car was falling apart. Mum buys a new collar and lead for Maisy: red with white spots on it. Other than that, it's hard to touch the money.

It certainly doesn't feel like happy money or buy-yourself-a-nice-dress money. After all these months, it still feels more like if-you-touch-me-I'll-make-your-life-miserable money. Or remember-why-you-got-me money.

Mum's buffeted this way and that by advice about what to do with it. The money represents material security at a time when she's too fragile to take any more disruption. Because of it, she and Dad will not be forced to downsize. They can pay off their mortgage. And I will one day be able to have a home of my own and, in that way at least, can start to catch up with people of my generation after all the years lost to trauma.

Mum tries to distract herself by watching television. She finds she's just not absorbing anything. If a show has more than three or four characters, she cannot follow it. That's on top of avoiding any dramas including police, court appearances, murder or violence. Given these strict criteria, it's hard to find anything safe to watch.

Instead of getting better, Mum seems to be declining further. Decisions are impossible. She can't even choose pond plants. People keep asking her if she's seen her counsellor lately. I hate it when that happens as I know how much she recoils from that question. They have no idea that they are lucky Mum doesn't punch them.

Mum knows something is wrong, but even her mathematical brain cannot work out what triggers these painful responses. I go with her to see our psychiatrist. Afterwards she breaks down in tears because she now realizes that so much of her misery can be attributed to anger about what the police have done. She's constantly ruminating about them. She dwells on the ineptitude and dishonesty about Milly's pyjamas, which seems so insulting and is such an echo of the original investigation. Mum finds herself obsessing over what happened to her and Dad at the Old Bailey. Then there's the murderer himself. Now that she has been in a room with him, Mum finds that horrific thoughts about him suddenly explode inside her mind. In her drowsy muted state, she's powerless to shut these images down.

We go to Egypt to seek solace under water.

We find it there, and in the hotel, which is so beautiful and by now familiar. Arriving there is like coming home to a place where we are safe. Diving with the multi-coloured fish, we feel the weight lifting from our shoulders. We don't care that it's temporary. In those moments, it feels so good.

One day Mum and I swim to a private beach. We write an enormous 'Milly' in the sand and arrange some pretty shells all around it in the shape of a heart. Apart from diving, we spend most of our week sleeping. We don't understand it yet, but this is a normal symptom of post-traumatic stress disorder.

Sharm el-Sheikh airport almost undoes all the good of the trip, taking its usual chaos to a whole new level. In order to cope, Mum does press-ups in the departure lounge. We don't care about people staring. We're used to it. We do what we have to do in order to survive.

We return to see Milly's ironing video on the news again. There are pictures of all three of us. And our inboxes are full of inquiries from the press to do with the Leveson Inquiry. Meanwhile the hacking scandal continues, with more layers unpeeling.

On 14 June David Cameron himself gives evidence to Leveson about what kind of regulatory system the press needs, in the wake of the hacking and police corruption scandals. He says,

> I will never forget meeting with the Dowler family in Downing Street to run through the terms of this Inquiry with them and to hear what they had been through and how it redoubled, trebled the pain and agony they'd been through over losing Milly. I'll never forget that, and that's the test of all this. It's not: do the politicians or the press feel happy with what we get? It's: are we really protecting people who have been caught up and absolutely thrown to the wolves by this process?

Andy Coulson is charged on 24 July with conspiring to intercept communications. On 28 October, the trial of Rebekah and Charlie Brooks begins. One of the first things to emerge is her affair with Andy Coulson, her deputy and then successor at the *News of the World*. It all seems so sordid. We don't really want to know more about the private lives of these people who had been so interested in ours when newspaper sales were at stake.

I have decided that looking after children will be the best job for me now. Being with children was the best part of my previous work as a holiday rep. I have been able to lose myself in their games, their needs. I'm still mistrustful of grown men. In October, I complete a child-minding programme and in November I start working as a nanny for a German family.

Part One of Lord Leveson's report is finally published on 29 November. Millions of words, many of them about Milly. As 'core participants', Mum and Dad are invited up to London to look at it before it's released to the public. The brief is to give their comments, if any.

There's a vast amount of material to read and check in two hours. It feels like an impossible exam. Other victims are sitting in the same room, with the same brief, the same pressure. Mum's next to Kate McCann. Also in the room is John Prescott. Mum finds herself being kissed by him.

There's nothing for Mum and Dad to add to these hundreds of pages. It is hard even to concentrate on them. After about an hour, Mum's had enough. She finds the room oppressive and she doesn't want anyone else to kiss her, unless it's Hugh Grant, and he's not there today. Dad keeps reading, while one of the Hacked Off organizers kindly accompanies Mum downstairs to the foyer. There's a massive crowd of reporters and photographers waiting outside. Mum needs to get away but she's terrified of running the press gauntlet. The lady from Hacked Off tells Mum that she can get her out unnoticed – via the laundry chute. It makes a change from all the prisoners' entrances, bin-stores and toilets.

The conclusions of Lord Leveson are that there was an 'arguably over-cosy relationship between the press and the police . . . There have been leaks and briefings that were paid for either in favours or cash. Reporters and photographers have claimed prized scoops because of insider information from the police.' Lord Leveson wants a new and properly independent regulatory body set up to supervise the press and to investigate ethical and criminal breaches. He wants something with legal powers and teeth. There's a howl of pain from the media. They claim this will interfere with a free press.

I think, *Look what the press did when it was free.*

But the newspapers will pre-empt any statutory moves by setting up IPSO, the Independent Press Standards Organization, in 2014. It is tasked to protect the innocent from the worst behaviour of the press.

And when we need it – which we shall, sadly, some years from now – we shall find that IPSO can help us.

Just before Christmas we go to a wedding in North Yorkshire. It's a huge distance to travel at a time of year when the roads are difficult. The prospect of being stared at by wedding guests is also challenging. But we love Rebecca, Mum's goddaughter, and we want to be there for her. Rebecca's mother, Sarah, was one of Milly's godmothers and made a television appeal for us in the early days of Milly's disappearance.

The wedding is being held in Yorkshire because Rebecca, a GP, has been posted there. Milly was so good at science and not squeamish about anything. She would have made a great doctor if she wasn't a vet or a marine biologist. Rebecca was born in the same year as Milly. As Mum and I plan our outfits, we are acutely conscious of that, and of the empty space there'll be at the table, in the car, in our hearts.

I have quarrelled with my current boyfriend, which adds extra heartache to this wedding. Not for the first time, I'm going to a wedding with my parents instead of a date of my own. And this in turn reminds me that Mum and Dad aren't always going to be here for me. There is hardly anything left of our family after the events of the past years. We're all trying to keep it together and be strong for each other. Since the publication of Leveson, the press have calmed down a little and Milly's picture has been given a break from the front pages.

The journey takes hours. I'm boiling with silent frustration at Dad's cautious slow-lane driving. I think if he were ever pulled over, it would be for going too slowly. Eventually we arrive in a quaint Yorkshire village. Mum has booked us into a little B-and-B rather than the hotel where nearly everyone else is staying so we can have some space for ourselves.

It seems she's decided not to take up her suicide pact, but she's not really living. She's just going through the motions of life. She has lost even more weight and looks very tired. I wish I could wave a magic wand and let her have one night's sleep in which she isn't haunted by her cross-examination at Milly's murder trial, the face of Milly's killer and her constant worry about my own well-being.

As it's nearly Christmas, the B-and-B is festooned with decorations, as our home should be – but isn't. We haven't had the heart to do it this year. The owners are friendly and very kind. They recognize Mum, letting her know in an empathetic way so it doesn't hurt.

I have chosen a soft pink dress and a fur coat (fake, of course) to wear today. I begin getting ready before Mum and Dad as I take much longer than they do. And, of course, I have to get ready alone. I hate this! I always get ready on my own now, without Milly to style me. But I don't think I shall ever get used to it.

The service is at the church, followed by a reception at the hotel next door where the other guests are staying. Some of them haven't seen us since the trial and they want to offer some consoling words. Dad and I are on high alert, making sure no one lingers near Mum for longer than need be.

We take our places for the service. The two most difficult parts of a wedding for me are always the church readings and the speeches at the reception. The church readings are hard to hear because I still can't connect with a God who let so much harm come to a child like Milly. Wedding speeches always reminisce about past times. I cannot do that about my childhood. I don't know where the memories are. Yet the duty of a good wedding guest is to look happy for the bride and groom and their families.

I brave a wave at our friend Vicky, the bride's sister. Reading the order of service, I see that Vicky's playing the flute. That makes me well up. Milly should have played the sax at my wedding. When

Vicky walks down the aisle behind Rebecca, Mum and I daren't look at one another. If a tear creeps out of my eye, Mum will be sobbing in a second, and vice versa. Poor Dad knows the drill now. His suit is filled with multi-packs of tissues. He's perfected a multi-arm high-speed tissue-delivery service for me and Mum.

We manage the service without crying until the minister mentions Vicky and Rebecca's late father Ray, Milly's godfather. Then Vicky stands up and puts the flute to her lips. The music fills the beautiful church. My friend is glowing with pride for her sister and her new brother-in-law. That's when I lose it. The tears streaming down my face are not of grief or joy. They are tears of helpless frustration because something so lovely can be going on yet I still can't enjoy it. Vicky finishes and catches my eye. She mouths, 'Sorry.'

Through my suppressed sobs, I mouth back, 'No, you nailed it! I'm so proud.' I hate that she is feeling bad for me at her sister's wedding. It is not Vicky's fault.

We make our way out of the church towards the hotel. I'm at a table with Mum, Dad and Rebecca's two brothers. I sit there stiff with dread. Ben, who is in charge of the music for speeches, has warned me that we may be in for a tough listen.

The speeches start off fine. I smile and clap along with everyone. But then an uncle starts to talk about Milly, Rebecca and their fire-fighting skills, recalling a time they set fire to our tent on a family camping holiday in Brittany. I don't usually mind people talking about Milly; in fact, I enjoy listening to stories about her as my memories seem to have failed. Today it's just too hard. I want to look at Mum and Dad yet can't for fear that if our eyes meet then mine will fill with uncontrollable tears. Then the uncle mentions Ray, Vicky and Rebecca's dad.

Oh, no, I think. *This is definitely going to send me over the edge.*

The uncle says he would like to dedicate a song to Rebecca from her father. It's Billy Joel's 'Lullabye'. The music starts up and the first words play out into the room.

> *Goodnight my angel, time to close your eyes*
> *And save these questions for another day.*

This is the tipping point. I look at Mum and whisper, 'We need to get out of here.'

We're right in the middle of the room. There's no way to escape discreetly. The situation is getting worse with every repetition of 'Goodnight my angel, time to close your eyes'.

Abruptly, Mum rises from her seat, heading for the door. Dad politely stays for the rest of the song. I go to comfort Mum and be comforted by her. She's already sobbing. I help a very exhausted, depleted Mum on to a large armchair in the hotel's reception area. I need to get diazepam into her. Over Mum's increasingly loud weeping, I ask the receptionist, 'Please can we have some water?'

The receptionist quickly returns with a glass. I say to Mum, 'Take these and then we'll go back to the B-and-B.'

It's only then that I realize Mum has no shoes. She has left her wedding heels under the table. I ask the hotel if they have a pair of slippers we could borrow. Cold cobbles on Mum's stockinged feet would not be a good idea. Mum seems to have lost her sense of where she is. Her normally fairly restrained crying has taken on a whole new dimension. The tear vaults have opened. Dad rushes over to us. He says the speeches are over now.

'We need to get Mum back to the B-and-B ASAP,' I tell Dad, who immediately goes into Superman mode. A friend helps him pick Mum up and, between them, they carry her over to the B-and-B. Her cries are very loud now. She has lost every vestige of control. The diazepam has not yet kicked in. When I open the door of the B-and-B, the couple who run it look aghast. Dad rushes Mum through into their room.

I need to get tea and biscuits organized. That is my job: it gives me my focus. As I go into the kitchen, the lady is waiting to hear what she can do. When I ask for tea, she points to a bottle of whisky, asking, 'Are you sure you don't need something stronger?'

'No, thank you.' I haven't got the words to explain the healing power of tea for our family.

She starts making it, asking, 'What on earth happened?'

'I'll explain later,' I promise.

I deliver the tray of tea and biscuits. Dad helps lift the cup to Mum's lips. Her teeth are chattering. She can't speak. I just put my arm around her and cuddle her. After a while, I say, 'I should probably go back to the wedding, collect Mum's shoes and see Rebecca and Ashley.'

Dad says, 'Are you sure you can manage that, darling?'

'Yes. I think I should go and tell them that Mum is all right.'

'I can't leave her.' Dad takes my place with his arm around Mum.

When she comes back from wherever she's been, Mum tells us that she's mortified. She feels so guilty and desperately hopes she hasn't upset Rebecca and Ashley. The last thing in the world she would want to do is to make a scene on such a special day for them.

Mum needn't have worried. By the time I get back to the hotel, everyone is dancing. I catch sight of myself in a mirror. My make-up is smudged with tears. I'm past caring. My urgent need is to be brave for Rebecca and try to make her feel better about what happened. The bride and groom are both lovely and very understanding. They make nothing of the fact that one of their wedding guests has had to be carried from their reception sobbing.

Driving home, I think, *Why did they have to play that song 'Lullabye'?*

But the real question is, why – after all these years – can't our family cope with that song?

69.

Milly has been gone for ten years. But her absence is bigger and more painful than ever, and so is the damage. What I witnessed in Yorkshire is a cry for help from Mum, and I don't know how to answer it. Moreover, when Mum broke down, it felt as if she was doing it for both of us.

Christmas is a blur. All I can see is my grey mum looking as if she has aged twenty years overnight. Mum hardly sees any point in her existence. If it wasn't for me, there would be none.

Yet I'm in crisis myself.

Mum and I are locked in the old symbiosis. My being down drags her further into depression. Her anxiety about my long-term future is acute. She also worries about me from hour to hour, with my moods and dramas. I have broken up with my latest boyfriend. I react with anger, pull on the boxing gloves. I also react with panic attacks. The diazepam comes out again.

I know I sounded brave and fierce as I challenged Rupert Murdoch and David Cameron. But I did those things as an automaton. Whenever I talked about Milly I felt guilty because, in my state of suspended animation, I was talking about a stranger to strangers. I felt guilty because I was so distant from Milly, yet my whole life had been defined by her for the last ten years. Every time I thought of Milly, I thought of her murderer.

There seems no way to cleanse her memory of that brutal face.

Mum's the same.

We have tried everything. We have medicated ourselves with sun and water on foreign beaches. We have tried not to be the Dowler family, the ones whom everyone recognizes in the street. All the reasons for recognizing us are sad ones. We're the victims of a child-killer, of a cruel trial, of phone hacking. It is so disempowering always to be the victims, our fate always decided by someone else.

Over the years, we have tried quite an assortment of therapies.

Mum put effort into 'psychodynamic therapy', which related all her trauma to childhood experiences. But she had enjoyed a very happy 'normal' childhood and she couldn't relate any previous feelings to the utter despair, desperation, confusion and anxiety she felt after Milly's disappearance and death. Not being a quitter, she stuck with the therapy for years even though it didn't seem right for her. When you are vulnerable and unwell, it's really hard to realize you need something different and to pluck up the courage to ask for a change.

In August 2009 Mum started working with a practitioner specializing in cognitive behavioural therapy and mindfulness. She much preferred this type of treatment. Her new therapist provided her with some valuable coping strategies. For a couple of years, this worked reasonably well. It gave Mum something to focus on and got her through some tough times. But, really, it was only putting sticking plasters on to a large and festering wound. The breakdown at the wedding had merely demonstrated what we all really knew.

Now, combining therapy with ever-increasing doses of numbing drugs, Mum's at her wits' end. Since the wedding, she's struggling not to cry all the time. She's not sleeping. She doesn't want to talk to anyone – not even her best friends. She cancels all social arrangements. She only wants to be around me and Dad.

Like me, Mum has no tolerance for noises. The least annoyance makes her feel hysterical. Sometimes she just lies on the sofa with a blanket over her head. She feels guilty at being a burden to me, Dad and Lovely Granny. Her headaches are terrible, allied to a strong sense of foreboding. Just breathing seems to use up her entire capacity for living. There is no room for anything else, except frenetic physical exercise, which is so exaggerated that it's starting to tear her body apart.

We know there's something very wrong with us, yet none of the psychiatrists, none of the drugs, none of the therapies have even touched the dark heart of the problem.

There is no hiding that Mum and I are broken. We've never been fixed, just tinkered with.

The final resort for Mum is lithium. I don't want that to happen. At the Priory, I saw what that stuff did to people. That is not what I want for Mum. I want a way out of her pain.

Straight after our disastrous Christmas, Dad makes an appointment for Mum with our lovely new GP. Dr Ratcliffe is very concerned when he sees her. He contacts the Priory to say Mum needs an emergency appointment. Mum gets a call to say her usual psychiatrist is away on holiday but she can see his stand-in.

It's not ideal, but Mum's beyond caring. Her appointment is booked for New Year's Day.

Happy New Year, I think.

The emergency psychiatrist, Dr Joe Muguisha, asks Mum what he can do for her. She's barely able to string a sentence together so she has made a long list of her symptoms. She starts reading to him from her notebook.

The doctor interrupts, 'But you have post-traumatic stress disorder,' he says. 'You need EMDR.'

He tells her that eye movement desensitizing and reprocessing is a strong therapy and she'll need her existing psychiatric team to declare her fit enough to take it.

That's scary, Mum thinks.

Yet she feels a sudden warmth of hope. This doctor seems to be taking her seriously. He's not offering some new miracle drug to numb her pain. He's not trying to tell her that the reason she's depressed is because of something that happened in her childhood. This doctor has actually listened to Mum. It feels as if it's the first time that a doctor has really heard what she's saying.

'I think I know the right person for you to see,' Dr Muguisha says to Mum.

We cannot know it at the time, but this is going to be the beginning of something good.

70.

That weekend, at Sunday lunch, Mum tells me about EMDR. The letters send a shiver down my spine, because I think it must be electric-shock therapy. I saw one woman go through that in the Priory and she told me she had forgotten her children's names.

Mum, please don't forget my name.

I want to google the therapy. But Mum's been advised by the doctor not to do that. He told her, 'You must go in with an open mind.'

As Mum's willing to try, I know I have to support her, no matter how cynical feel.

By 8 January, Mum has been pronounced fit for treatment. Our neighbour Fiona drives her to the clinic in Woking. Fiona has packed biscuits and sweets for the trip.

At Woking, Mum meets Michelle Calvert, who has helped victims of serious crime, as well as those who have been emotionally abused to the point of self-harm. Michelle is a delicate and beautiful woman. Her voice is soft and sweet. Yet she will have the power to pick up the entire Dowler family from the dark and dangerous place where we've ended up. She will have the power to make us focus long enough to see the light. She also has the power to make us feel we are entitled to that light.

And so it begins, the process of getting there.

In their first session, Michelle talks calmly and understandingly to Mum. She explains that trauma is like a grenade going off in your brain. Everything gets fragmented and scattered about. Also, certain events or situations can trigger extremely painful thoughts. Her first task is to find out what Mum's trigger points are.

Mum finds Michelle easy to talk to. She doesn't feel self-conscious and this means that she can be completely honest, even when honesty takes her to appalling places.

By the end of the session, Michelle has extracted a long list of Mum's triggers. They include:

1. Milly's body in the woods, maggots and animals
2. Rape
3. Mum's police interview
4. Being regarded as a suspect by the police
5. Her cross-examination at the trial
6. Seeing Bellfield in court
7. Being recognized by the public
8. The initial period of 'not knowing'
9. The house search by the police
10. The *News of the World* hacking Milly's phone when she went missing
11. Worry about my future

That's only a start. Twenty-one trigger points are identified in that first meeting.

Fiona picks Mum up after her session. From Spud-U-Like, she brings Mum a cup of tea that is cold enough to moan about. But the best thing is that Mum feels empowered to moan at all. The car journey home starts well enough. Then Mum develops a severe headache and nausea. She asks Fiona to pull over as she needs to be sick. In the end, she merely retches a little. Mum tries to blame it on the tea. Both Mum and Fiona know that has nothing to do with it. Her nausea is the result of dragging up those bitter and painful thoughts.

Mum's beginning to understand why Dr Muguisha said she would need to be fit to undertake the new therapy. By the time Fiona gets her home, Mum has a full-blown migraine. Her head is in complete turmoil. Fiona force-feeds her a diazepam and tucks her up in bed. The next morning Mum does not get up at dawn to go spinning at the gym. This is unheard of.

After Mum's first appointment, I know that something has changed. She's not radiating optimism, but there's definitely a sense of weight lifted. There is someone listening to Mum at last.

A week later Mum has her first actual EMDR session with Michelle. This treatment entails reliving a traumatic experience while watching either lights or the fingers of the therapist moving backwards and forwards. You live and relive and re-relive the experience in this way, noticing the reactions in your body, until its impact on you diminishes to a point where you can remember without melting down in fear or pain. EMDR does not cancel out terrible events – to pretend that could be done would be a lie, so it wouldn't help. It enables you to learn how to accept them and live with them.

In that session, Mum and Michelle visit Minley Woods together. Gently, Michelle takes Mum back to the day when we went to see the place where Milly's body was dumped.

These are Mum's first memories:

I want to be there on my own, not surrounded by police and press.
I want to lie down on the ground.
I want to wail.
I am a terrible mum.

Michelle constantly takes her back to the painful memory and asks Mum what she's feeling and where in her body she feels it. Then, at key moments, Michelle moves her fingers backwards and forwards in front of Mum's face. Mum's eyes have to follow her fingers. It requires intense concentration to focus on those fingers. As I've said, Mum's not a quitter and she gives it everything she's got. Soon she's crying, shaking, shouting, swearing and making very angry growling noises. She's utterly exhausted by being asked to go back to the initial memory over and over again.

Every time Mum says, 'I can't do this any more,' Michelle says, 'You're doing well, Sally. Keep going.'

Mum's learning how to relive the experience with her body, to allow all that has been repressed to come to the surface and ease its way out. It's messy. The horror, the fear, the naked need of a mother for her daughter: none of these things simply flow out of Mum. They come out painfully, with weeping and screaming. But out they come.

At the end of the session, Michelle briefly massages key acupuncture points on Mum's hands. It is soothing.

When it's over, Mum feels dazed. Yet she's determined to persist. She understands now that the darkness inside will only get worse unless she peels away everything.

Meanwhile I'm still on my downward spiral. One night I have a nightmare that Mum commits suicide. In the morning, when I wake, it feels as if she really has. I'm hysterical. I force her to promise that she would never do that – unless we do it together.

Mum asks again if I would like to see Michelle. But I cannot muster any enthusiasm. I've had so much therapy, some as an inpatient at a mental-health facility, and nothing has really helped me. I still crash without warning. I still fear that Milly's killer will get me. My life is circumvented by all kinds of things I cannot do, especially be alone for any period of time. I don't believe that therapy is the answer for me. What I'm really expressing is despair. I'm happy for Mum, yet I don't believe that anyone will ever fix what is broken in me.

Mum starts an intense therapy recovery timetable. All she does in the next three months is process, sleep, eat or spin. Mum reckons that an EMDR processing session uses up more calories than a spinning class as it's so mentally exhausting.

At her EMDR session on Wednesday, 13 February, something unexpected happens. Mum's surprised and a bit annoyed to find that she has to return to Minley Woods. Yet this time it's completely different.

Michelle taps her hands while Mum goes back to her feelings. A vision comes into Mum's mind in which she lies down in the place where Milly was found. But now she's cuddling Milly, who's alive and smiles at her. It is beautiful.

Mum's crying deeply, yet her memories are lovely. Her mind travels over Milly's love of cheese, cucumber and chips. It hovers over Milly's wonderful kind nature and her cheeky sense of humour. In that spirit, Mum finds that she can say goodbye properly to her beautiful daughter in the knowledge that Milly really loved her, and that Mum herself was a lovely, not a terrible, mother to her younger daughter.

In eleven years, Mum has not experienced a happy dream or daydream about Milly. This is the first time. She's euphoric when she leaves Michelle. She realizes that something has altered in her breathing. It doesn't hurt. She hadn't even realized that it hurt her to breathe – she has become so used to it.

She writes in her diary,

Please let me remember these feelings forever:
I am a good Mum

I cuddled her
We said goodbye
I told Milly how much I loved her.

On Valentine's Day, Mum feels brave enough to listen to one of Milly's favourite songs: 'If I Had A Million Dollars' by Barenaked Ladies. It's been years since she dared to play it. Instead of raw pain, it sends a wave of comforting sadness over her. She remembers the whole family driving along in the car, singing it at the tops of our voices, racking up the purchases – a tree-house, a llama, a monkey. Most of all – love. Until that moment, the Murdoch settlement has felt like 'blood money', but now – suddenly and vividly – there's a connection to Milly, one that makes Mum laugh with joy.

On Saturday, 16 February, Michelle tells Mum that they are going to process Milly's murder.

All sorts of vile images flood into Mum's mind. Some are familiar old nightmares. Others are new ones, seeming to come out of the blue. Michelle insists on processing Mum through every single one. Sometimes there are false endings. Mum thinks and hopes it's over. Yet Michelle says they need to return time and time again until everything is cleared out. Mum goes deep, so very, very deep. She growls hate for Bellfield. She screams her ferocious anger at what he did.

Mum feels bad about exposing Michelle to all this horror. Michelle just encourages her, gently repeating, 'Don't hold anything back, Sally.'

Mum and Michelle go over the final moments of Milly's life many times. Eventually the fear begins to dissipate and turns into something surprising: relief.

It's over now, Mum finally knows. *She's dead. He can do no more harm to my beautiful girl.*

Mum's limp and completely numb.

Michelle asks how she's feeling. Mum says, 'It's as if I'm in transition during labour.'

More fond memories start to stir: Milly fishing with Grandad; Milly helping Lovely Granny learn to drive; Milly and me checking Mum's outfit before school; Milly pretending to frown and saying, 'Oh, my God, Mum, you're not wearing *that!*'

Mum's aware that, now she's found them again, she must hold on to those beautiful memories. They are what she has left of Milly.

Mum goes home feeling good. But after dinner she suddenly crashes. Her brain seems to fracture into the old vile images. Her head aches. She takes a diazepam, watches a mindless film.

She realizes it cannot be that easy. There is still more work to do.

On 2 March, Mum starts another batch of intensive EMDR. March is always emotionally testing for us as it includes the anniversary of the day Milly was taken, Mother's Day and Mum's birthday, all close together on the calendar.

And now it looks as if the Leveson Inquiry will come to nothing. On 16 March, Mum and Dad issue a statement: 'Given the considerable investment of time and money in the Leveson Inquiry, we are very disappointed to learn that Lord Justice Leveson's proposals may not now be taken forward if the politicians choose to ignore the recommendations . . . that were aimed at preventing the sort of abuses that we and so many others suffered.'

Mum's spending time sorting through Milly's possessions that the police returned. In one of the evidence bags, she finds a note Milly wrote, listing the good qualities of everyone in the family – honesty, generosity, kindness and so on. Mum discovers Milly has given her ticks for everything, apart from 'stand up for what I believe in'.

She talks to Michelle about this and takes the thought with her to another meeting with the police, this time about the Independent Police Complaints Commission, who are examining the work of a certain officer who was high up in the original investigation into Milly's disappearance.

Something in Mum has turned. She's not going to stand for the usual bullshit. Mum wants Milly to be proud of her, even now. She wants to stand up for what she believes in. So she says just what she thinks and feels about the senior officers who worked on the original investigation, about the way in which the media was used as a constant threat when they wanted our compliance, about the way in which she and Dad were treated as if they were guilty, and the horrible portrait that the police tried to build up of Milly as a 'bad girl'.

Mum's in top form at last. She speaks eloquently and emotionally.

The words 'smarmy tosspot' are deployed. After the meeting, she feels as if the investigating officers have had their eyes opened.

We know nothing will come of this. The police, in our experience, do not own up to mistakes. They simply move the goalposts and the person who has done wrong is quietly transferred elsewhere.

Nevertheless, Mum writes in her notes, 'Milly would be proud. Gemma would be proud too.'

On 23 March, two days after the anniversary of Milly's disappearance, Mum writes a letter to Milly.

My dear beautiful little sausage Milly,

It was eleven years on Thursday since the day you went missing.

I'm not really sure what to say apart from you have left a huge hole in our lives and I miss you so very much.

On a general basis, we 'get by' but life is so very different and difficult since you have gone.

I have been having some new therapy called EMDR and for the first time in eleven years I have had a few happy memories break through. (It was so wonderful to see you smiling and laughing.)

Gemsie is a constant worry to me. She struggles but is managing. I think she feels isolated and alone as well as an overwhelming sense of guilt for not being there.

It is hard when I see your friends/peer group and see what they are doing. Hannah and Loley have been to uni and now both have steady boyfriends. I love them both but of course it is tinged with sadness. Why can't it be my daughter doing those things?

It's just not fair. We were just an ordinary family getting on with our lives and then one day this unimaginably awful tragedy happens to us.

My heart aches for how you suffered, my Darling, and I always wish it had been me instead. One of the first things that changed was our house went from being a happy vibrant home full of lots of friends to a quiet, desolate bereft building, no laughing, no music, no arguing, no nagging to do homework, no moaning about what was for tea!! No singing, no taking the piss out of Mum, no saxophone playing 'Local Hero', no extremely messy bedrooms, just an enormous sense of loss and the huge weight of 'not knowing'. Desperation for six months. I used to text you every day and each time the message would fail. When your body was finally found, it was such a relief. A relief to know that no one could hurt you any more.

As for the police – well there's such anger and such resentment there that it's hard to bear.

Basically everything stems from losing my beautiful, sunny, smiling kind-hearted daughter. Your presence is still felt and missed and I so wish you were here (to help Gemsie) because life without you is shit.

My little curly haired baby/toddler shouting 'Me do it!!' With that little determined face. We now have a little cocker spaniel called Maisy who has a very similar look and I'm sure I know what she is thinking.

Today I'm about to start phase II of my EMDR treatment so a tough week ahead but I know I will feel better afterwards.

We are 3 weeks into an extension being built – this has involved knocking down half the house (literally). Your bedroom has been rebuilt – you are having a new bigger one instead!

I'm off to do the Bushy Park run this morning. (It will be my 40th one today.) Then it will be back home for a bath and some hot toast.

I'm hoping I might see you later – just a glimpse of your beautiful face and your expressive eyes.

With fondest love
Mummy xxxx

A week later, Mum has a session with Michelle that's hard but turns out to be magical and moving. They're working on the trial, in particular the cruel cross-examination of Mum by Bellfield's aggressive barrister with reference to Milly's 'Drama Queen' notes. Mum brings copies with her.

When she's looking at them with Michelle, new things emerge. For example, in the letter, Milly calls Mum 'beautiful Mummy'. The word 'beautiful' is very powerful. Mum believes that Milly meant that she was a beautiful human being rather than being physically beautiful. Mum knows that this is what she must take away from the note. She allows herself to start believing what she has always really known – teenage girls are hormonal and it's part of their development to push boundaries and say things like 'I hate you' or 'You are ruining my life' over even trivial things, like being told off for overuse of the phone. Such words are just snapshots of a moment of anger that usually passes quickly.

Having looked at the notes in this new light, Mum then processes the trial scene. The notes seem different now. They are not there to shame Mum. They exist because Milly was a normal teenager. Both Mum and Milly were put under an unfair, selective focus to serve the legal team of a murderer. That is horrible. Yet it does not mean that Mum is a bad mother. It means that something is wrong with the legal system.

Towards the end of the session, Mum feels bathed in a bright and warm light. It's like the sun that she and I love so much. The warmth suffuses her body and she suddenly sees Milly smiling her mischievous little smile with her dancing eyes. Milly holds out her hand, and says, 'Come on, Mum!' They run through a meadow with Maisy bounding alongside, her blonde ears flapping. When Milly leaves, Maisy sits on Mum's lap for what we call 'a love' in our family.

It is not that Maisy replaces Milly. It is that Milly's love is still there.

Mum writes in her diary afterwards, 'The bright light, the warmth, the love, the happiness and the joy of seeing her again and holding her beautiful hand. That's what I must cherish.'

71.

An independent investigation has concluded that Surrey Police 'at all levels' knew about the hacking of Milly's phone by the *News of the World*. But nothing was done for nine years. It was only when the Metropolitan Police launched Operation Weeting that we were made fully aware of it. Of course, by now, the Surrey officers involved have moved on to other posts.

The Independent Press Complaints Commission says that the hacking of the phone was a crime and should have been acted upon by Surrey Police. Deborah Glass, of the commission, says,

> *Former senior officers, in particular, appear to have been afflicted by a form of collective amnesia in relation to the events of 2002.*
>
> *This is perhaps not surprising, given the events of 2011 and the public outcry that the hacking of Milly Dowler's phone produced. However, it is scarcely credible that no one connected to the Milly Dowler investigation recognized the relevance and importance of the information Surrey Police held in 2002.*

The IPCC notes that the force's focus was on finding Milly. But it also mentions claims of an 'unhealthy relationship' with the media. We ourselves had seen how this worked. Why were the press apparently present and taking photos, for example, when Milly's body was found at Minley Woods? How did a photographer come to be present at Bellfield's arrest?

All that happens is that one senior officer receives 'words of advice', the lowest possible sanction. His successor in the job receives the same, even though she was not at all involved in the events or the 'amnesia'. We are furious for Maria Woodall. In our opinion, she deserves praise, not 'words of advice'.

Not long afterwards, Mark Lewis lets us know that it has been established that a Surrey Police officer or officers took money from the press early in the inquiry.

We finally receive a background briefing about the events in the hacking scandal. The story that brought down the *News of the World* started with a wrong number. The employment agency in Telford had a woman called 'Nana' on its books. Nana phoned on 26 March 2002 to give the agency her new mobile-phone number, but a mistake of one digit was made either by Nana or the person who took it down. That one digit changed Nana's number to Milly's. That was why the agency left a job interview message on Milly's number on 27 March.

And that was the message that Glenn Mulcaire hacked.

Michelle gives Mum a week off to rest. Mum, Vicky, Fiona and I fly to Marrakesh. Before leaving, Mum writes a letter to Michelle.

When I see the letter, I discover that my lovely Mumazino is still alive in there, inside that shell of a woman. Michelle has found her. I realize that Michelle is also going to bring Mum back out into this world.

Dear Michelle,

The help you have given me over the past couple of months has been immeasurable and the results so far have been profoundly moving. For the first time in eleven years I have felt a morsel of hope and have had the absolute joy of some memories breaking through. Things that I had forgotten that were previously totally blocked by the trauma. I have also been able to feel a bit of a connection with how Milly used to be.

Before I came to see you I would describe my existence as barely functioning with regard to communicating with people. Recently people have commented on how much 'lighter' I seem and my Mum thought I must be taking some new stimulants!!

My previous thoughts of suicide being the best thing that could happen to me have changed considerably and a little bit of hope for the future seems to be manifesting itself. (An emotion I have been starved of for so long that I'd forgotten what it was like.)

The two sessions I would describe as truly inspiring were when we finished the scene where Milly's body was found in the woods and when we finished the cross examination in court. I would never have believed it would be possible to accept such things with such a sense of calm and just a deep sadness for my daughter rather than all the self-loathing, guilt, pain, blame that had become part of my everyday life without me realizing.

It has been so long since I have slept peacefully that to get two consecutive nights after Saturday's session was wonderful.

You do an incredible job, Michelle. You must never underestimate what you are able to do for people.

Things I can do now that I couldn't do before

1. Listen to music and feel sad but sort of in a nice comforting 'closer to Milly' type way
2. Think of Milly and smile about some of the happy times we shared together (which is an enormous breakthrough)
3. Breathe more easily and without pain
4. I have started to feel a bit of excitement about our new house extension and that is another new emotion for me. (In fact I woke up with a strange feeling and I didn't know what it was and it was actually excitement)
5. I think it has also helped me recognize when our family are displaying some of the symptoms I did

I feel rather like I suspect a 'stroke patient' might feel. It feels like I'm learning about positive emotions for the very first time and it's very, very tiring.

I feel like my brain has been damaged and you are very gradually helping me repair it.

My mind seemed to be being tidied up and that has made it possible to find some old memories previously completely blocked.

I have yet to see if this sense of relief and connection with Milly will last but I really hope it does.

I await our next phase with a bit of trepidation but also a growing optimism that EMDR will continue to work.

I'm sure you get many letters of thanks for the work you do but this letter comes from the bottom of my heart.

When I first started with you, I told Gemma and Bob that I thought you could help me. After our first phase of treatment, I told them I loved you more than I love the newly opened Tesco Express just down the road! (The reasons I loved the Tesco Express were because you could always get a parking space, it's nearly always empty inside and no one comes up to me and talks to me . . . three major positives.)

This should give you a measure of my gratitude!

With my heartfelt thanks and very best wishes
Sally x

I watch with joy and fascination as Mum begins to regain colour in her face. More and more often, there are glimmers of the Mum I remember, *the Mum Milly would remember.*

Mum starts playing a song by Amy Grant. It's called 'Carry You'. Until recently this song would have been too emotionally danger-ous for her. This is partly because Milly might have grown up to look and sound like this beautiful singer with the tendrils of dark hair that straggle around her cheekbones, her black turtlenecks and her slender frame. In this song, Amy Grant sings again and again,

> *Lay down your burden, I will carry you.*
> *I will carry you my child, my child.*

The singer says that she's weary of watching her child struggle on her own. She's watched the sleepless nights, the tears. But this mother has special powers. She's seen the darker side of Hell and she's returned.

Mum sees Michelle as the person who is carrying her to safety now. She has at last started to grieve. This is very, very sad. Yet the tears she sheds now are comforting to Mum, whereas before they were just a way of emptying her head.

The processing has allowed her to put the past in some sort of order, thereby making a little bit of room for ordinary things. This is so wonderful for her. For example, now when she is running by the river, she is able to appreciate the beautiful surroundings as well as the exercise.

Mum has also developed her own 'processing playlist'. That's an invaluable tool and helps to calm her down if she gets agitated. Mum has wisely planned her playlist so it starts off fairly sombre and reflective but finishes with feel-good songs.

One Sunday lunch Mum broaches the subject of my seeing Michelle Calvert. I am one of Mum's triggers. The Gemma prob-lem needs to be resolved too. Mum explains that she has already asked Michelle if she could possibly help me. That's a big ask, given how much time and energy she's devoting to Mum. It must be exhausting for her. Can you imagine the burden of treating both me and my mother for the trauma caused by all that has happened to us: the abduction, the body, the funeral, the police, Bellfield, the trial, the hacking?

Michelle, however, understands that Mum and I are entwined in a symbiotic relationship and that she cannot, in fact, help one of us without the other. She agrees to take me on too.

When she heard that, Mum tells me, she felt more hope than she had for the past eleven years. She describes it as the sort of hope that she'd felt when I was first born, when she was thinking about all of the exciting things that lay ahead for her gorgeous little daughter and all I could achieve.

I stare at Mum. This is painful to hear. Because we both know that, at this point in my life, and in my mind, I haven't actually achieved anything.

'Gemma, this therapy is a chance for you to have a life, to have a future that's not haunted by Milly's murder. It will be a chance for you to be you.'

A little piece of me is angry that Mum can even think like this. *Does she want me to forget about Milly?* The rest of me is resolutely cynical. *Another therapist*, I think. *They're all the same. I can't keep explaining to all of them why I am the way I am. I don't want to go and 'talk about my feelings'. I just want to hide away. I want the world to stop moving on when I'm stuck in quicksand, in a whirlwind of emotions but gradually sinking lower and lower.*

I still don't know much about EMDR therapy other than it's working for Mum. She's reconnecting more and more with 'normal life'. Her eyes don't look so bleak. She's slowly emerging from the darkness. I'm happy that Mum is finding a path, and slightly jealous as well. The main thing is that I'm so full of self-loathing that I don't believe what works for her will work for me. I'm a write-off, in my eyes.

I'm not able to do paid work. I have started some volunteering at a couple of local playgroups in Walton. I've lost weight, which makes me happier with my appearance. Yet that doesn't make me feel any better. I spend most of my time angry at everything and everyone. My hearing has become even more acute: everything seems too loud now. So I keep my headphones on as much as possible, listening only to the music I choose. I don't want to hear the noises of a world carrying on without Milly.

'Behind Blue Eyes' – Dad's soundtrack for the trial in which the defence case put him and Mum in the dock as bad parents.

A press photographer captured Dad devastated after his humiliation at the hands of Bellfield's barrister. To get this photograph, the press arranged for a lorry to block our escape route.

3 June 2003. Mum and collapsed when the reman of the jury ronounced Bellfield uilty' of Milly's bduction and murder. lelping Dad with us, on he left, is lovely Alice arr, one of our Family iaison Officers.

Rehearsing the speech I woul
deliver outside the Old Bailey

Dad, Mum and I read our statements in front of the Old Bailey after Bellfield's conviction for Milly's murder.

ver tea in fine bone china I told Prime Minister David Cameron that it was me to stop talking and start acting on hacking. Look at my expression: this is e face of a girl who has just realized that she can speak truth to power.

he cost of bravery: as soon as we were out of 10 Downing Street, the tears oured down my face.

With Hugh Grant, who became a friend through the hacking scandal, of which he was also a victim. This picture was taken in July 2011, on the day Hugh literally saved Dad's bacon.

My second visit to Downing Street in four months: breakfast with Samantha Cameron to mark my Cosmo Ultimate Family Girl award.

um and Dad giving evidence about phone hacking to the Leveson Inquiry, ovember 2011.

One of Mum's relentless personal keep-fit challenges, this time a five mile run with Fiona in the Olympic stadium in 2013.

Mum and I with Michelle Calvert at the International EMDR conference where Mum was a keynote speaker. It was Milly's birthday that day.

In 2016, on the anniversary of Milly's disappearance, I went back for the first time to the secret place where we scattered her ashes, taking this card and primroses from Mum's garden.

This last year has brought Milly's saxophone back into our lives – you can see it behind me in this photo taken in January 2017.

Milly would be astonished to see how well Dad plays the double bass now.

Mum, Lovely Granny, Dad, Maisy and me on the Chesterfield,
one of the items on the wish-list inspired by the Barenaked
Ladies' song 'If I had a Million Dollars'.

I'm like a child who holds her breath because she cannot have what she wants. I have not learned to want anything new, so the only thing I want is to have Milly back. No one can give that to me. I'm also like a child who holds her breath for a dangerously long time. I'm in self-destruct mode. I don't want help. I can manage on my own. Everyone has let me and our family down, so why should this therapy be any different? I'm accustomed to specialists promising me a future, yet ending up writing another prescription for antidepressants.

It's only for Mum's sake that I agree to try Michelle. I cannot say no to Mum.

She drives me to my first appointment. She's probably afraid that I won't turn up unless she escorts me. I'm reluctant even to enter the building. The first thing I notice is that Michelle is much younger than I thought she'd be. The next thing that strikes me is her mane of beautiful dark curls.

Mum sits in with me for the start of the appointment. I'm already crying. I tell Mum one of my fears: 'If you get any better then you won't need me any more.'

Of course Mum rushes to hug and reassure me. But then she has to leave. This is my appointment, and I've told Mum I'll do this.

Now it's just me and Michelle. I sit in my chair doing everything possible to avoid eye contact. Ten per cent of me wants to listen to her, after all she has done for Mum. Ninety per cent is just angry at having to be there.

This is an assessment rather than a processing session. I cannot be forced into EMDR. Not everyone responds to it. Just because it's working for Mum doesn't mean that it will unravel my knots too.

I don't make it easy for Michelle. I'm sulky and hostile. I answer her reluctantly. When she tries some relaxation exercises on me, I tell her to 'fuck off.' I guess I'm testing her. She does not falter.

I rudely make clear that I'm not buying into the idea of a saviour. But Michelle doesn't want to be my saviour. The truth is that she knows post-traumatic stress disorder when she sees it. Quietly and slowly, she makes me understand that this is something I'm doing for myself and for Mum and Dad.

Michelle is patient with my aggression. Like a lion-tamer, she waits until I'm ready to make my move. I'm a bad-tempered lion, shaking my blonde mane, snarling. I don't want to let her tend my wounds. I prefer to go on holding them tight to my chest. Perhaps there's a part of me that is afraid of letting go of my trauma because it is all that I have.

Michelle's voice is clear and sweet. I start to be aware of a maternal feeling coming from her. She's seen through my smart clothes and make-up. Without talking down to me, Michelle connects with the scared girl I've tried to hide. It is as if she's talking to sixteen-year-old Gemma, the one whose life was ripped apart in 2002. She talks to the frightened Gemma, who's still so stunned and sick with the loss of her sister that she's not even able to grieve. Michelle talks to this Gemma kindly, and she doesn't expect too much from her.

Yet.

Then Michelle says something that terrifies and elates me at the same time. She says that by doing this therapy I will be able to get closer to Milly again. It won't be easy. But if I work hard, I'll be able to remember the childhood we had together without the contamination of the pain and fear of losing her.

I'm dazed. In just a few minutes, this woman has identified my greatest need. I see that Michelle has the gift of seeing who I really was before the grenade exploded my life. Michelle can actually see *the Gemma Milly knew*. She thinks she can reconnect me to her.

I cannot say no to that.

I don't ask Michelle whether she has children. She volunteers that she has a little girl who's now a similar age to Milly when she was taken. This reassures me. No previous therapist has ever openly talked to me about their own life. It's as if she has offered an olive branch of transparency that no other doctor or therapist ever thought worth giving to me.

As Michelle had done with Mum, she now works with me on a plan of action. She quickly identifies that my most overwhelming feeling is of being unsafe. This will be a recurring theme throughout many sessions. She's so patient with me, and constantly reassures me. Some of my fears are completely ludicrous and many people would have told me to stop being so ridiculous. Michelle just listens.

One of the hardest parts of the therapy is letting go of the anger and allowing the grief in. That's something I have never done. I used to imagine that if I let in the grief all my tears would fill the room and I would drown in despair. I learn from Michelle that anger is a secondary emotion. Normally it's masking a deeper, truer feeling.

I have to acknowledge that for years I've been doing everything I can to make sure I stay angry. I'm always angry. It's an easier emotion to exhibit. Sadness is too unpredictable, and shows weakness and vulnerability. Anger, on the other hand, reliably makes it seem as if I'm scary and unbreakable.

Michelle and I work our way through so many painful scenes, starting with the night Milly disappeared. During processing, you go into a kind of freefall, talking to yourself without any self-consciousness. Like this:

Why am I always searching?
I'm trying to find her.
Where is she?
She isn't at the woods.
She isn't at home.
Where can she be?
I MUST KEEP LOOKING.
I MUST NOT GIVE UP.
I don't want her to be alone.
I don't want the darkness to descend and for her to be left there.
Don't give in to the tiredness.
It's all right. The helicopters will find her.
This can't be happening.
Stop this now please.
Let me wake up from this nightmare.
This is not a nightmare.
I'm the only one left looking.
Everyone has given up.
I can't be here without her.
I try to concentrate really hard on trying to see if she is giving me a
  message.
She is not there.
I check her room – she is not there.

Where is she?
I ring her mobile – no answer, straight to answerphone.
Where is she?
I hate this pain.

I know it sounds like a cliché when people talk about having a breakthrough moment in therapy. But logical Mum, maths-degree Mum, sensible Mum had described to me a moment that sounded like something out of a fairy tale, when Milly came back to her, loving and laughing.

My moment comes too, and it's not at all what I expect.

It happens when Michelle and I are revisiting the day we went to Minley Woods. I have done sixteen hours of processing on this particular event, as it's one of my sharpest triggers. But this time the fear disappears. I feel only acute sadness. I give in to a deep surge of grief.

Michelle holds my hand and talks me through it. I'm so grateful for her gentle company in those dark woods. Her quiet voice can explain things more clearly and less scarily. All of a sudden, the image changes. I'm no longer seeing the bleak forest and the cellophane-wrapped yellow rose the police left there. Instead, I see Milly alive! There she is, laughing, in memories of Cuba, memories of family Christmases together. They all flood back. I'm not afraid to experience them, because they are not tinted with any darkness. There's just light. The love our family had and still has suddenly shines in a clear path through all of the evil that has suffocated me for years.

After months of hard work I have finally begun to feel a difference. It's a disorienting, euphoric feeling. At first I thought that this was just another new and scary emotion to deal with as part of my processing. I'm wrong. What I feel is simple happiness.

Of course, I also experience sadness. But now I understand that this is normal and it won't kill me.

I have my own processing playlist too. It includes the Beach Boys singing, 'Don't Worry Baby'. In the version I play, Lorrie Morgan accompanies them. I try and try to believe the words, that everything's going to be all right.

I'm in the process of buying my own home, using some of the

settlement money from the *News of the World*. I cannot live there, however, for another six months until Michelle has removed all the unsafe feelings.

I'm working as a nanny, looking after three adorable small children. Now I can bear to be reminded of my own wonderful childhood, the childhood I had subsequently lost. I look after those children as if they were my own. It is partly thanks to this kind of work that I feel able to mature into an adult naturally – the kind of adult I was once destined to be: caring, thorough, sensitive. I will not be misshapen by the evil that has happened to me and my family.

Looking after children is also good for my self-esteem. I'm aware that a parent has entrusted me with their most valuable possession. I must be worth something if they let me look after their children.

On one occasion, I prepare an Easter egg hunt for the children. The oldest child reads the rhyming clues to find each egg. The last one is hidden in their book bags. They find all the eggs within fifteen minutes. One asks, 'How did Gemma manage to hide the eggs in our book bags, when we had them with us?'

The little boy, four at the time, answers, 'Because she's magic.'

I have created a safe and loving environment, just like Mum did for me and Milly when we were young.

Mum is a great thanker of people. Our personal files are full of copies of thank-you letters she has written to every conceivable person who helped us on our long, dark way. Mum wrote to thank the police for arranging the motorcade for Milly's funeral. She has, of course, written to Alice and Jon. To people who helped with Milly's Fund. To so many people.

Her letters are special. She always identifies the exact way in which the person has helped. She has a real talent for that. She has already written to Michelle but now, after seeing my progress, she wants to find a new way to thank her. She wants Michelle recognized for all her hard work. In June, Mum contacts the EMDR Association to tell them what Michelle has done for her and me.

I believe Michelle Calvert to be a truly inspirational woman and I
wondered if it's possible to put her forward for some sort of award/

recognition as she has helped our family so much and has worked above and beyond the call of duty. I believe she has actually saved my life. She is one of the most caring and compassionate people I have ever met with an abundance of infectious positive energy and spirit.

I understand there is a conference in June next year and if you are interested I would be prepared to speak at your conference about my EMDR treatment. I feel it may help other trauma sufferers to find the right treatment quickly and give them some hope for the future when they are in complete despair.

By return, the association asks Mum if she would be a keynote speaker at their international conference due to be held in Edinburgh. Strangely enough, the date is Milly's birthday. Mum – the renewed, vigorous, can-do Mum – dives deep into this project. Our neighbour Fiona comes over to listen intently to the drafts of her speech. Uncle Ian, king of spreadsheets and PowerPoints, helps Mum put the presentation together. As a former teacher, Mum knows exactly the points she wants to get across too. She also wants to include photos and two particular pieces of music.

One of the things that Michelle has noticed about me is the way I struggle to concentrate. It's a classic sign of PTSD. But in my case it has gone unattended for so many years that it's deeply embedded. Not being able to focus leaves me intellectually unfulfilled and frustrated. Yet this is something that can be fixed. Mum suggests that I go to see a new psychiatrist who specializes in trauma as I may need more targeted medication. The same doctor is already helping Mum.

I meet Dr Eileen Feeney for the first time on 13 July. Her office is at Woking Priory where I was once an inpatient. There's nothing institutional about Dr Feeney. She's a breath of fresh Irish air, attentive, engaged, spontaneous and warm. She agrees with Michelle, diagnosing attention deficit disorder, in addition to PTSD, and prescribing medication for it.

I finally move into my new house in the middle of July. On the first night I'm filled with an overwhelming sense of achievement. For now this house feels safe and secure. I've enjoyed furnishing it, getting everything exactly as I want it. It's a big day when Lovely Granny comes to see my new house for the first time. I've scrubbed, polished and tidied up ready for her arrival.

I open my front door to see my beautiful smiling Lovely Granny laden with a stunning bouquet of blue delphiniums. I welcome her in.

Her first words are 'Oh, Gemma, what a lovely big hall!'

'Lovely Granny,' I say, rather heatedly, 'this is the *lounge*.'

We laugh and it's added to the list of classic Lovely Granny moments.

Mum's EMDR is continuing. The process is never a straight line towards serenity. In early July, she finds herself crying a lot. She takes a walk to the place where we scattered Milly's ashes. It's peaceful and silent – no one there except Mum and Maisy.

Mum has taken with her a bunch of Milly's favourite sweet peas mixed with roses. She puts them in the river and watches them being swept away by a fast current. Maisy takes it into her head to chase after them along the riverbank for a while. Putting on her headphones, Mum listens to her processing playlist, replicating a session with Michelle, but in music. It starts reflectively and finishes happily with 'If I Had A Million Dollars'. She feels an enormous sense of relief, as if she has done a physical session.

It's temporary, of course. She remains very worried about me. My relationship with Dad is not doing well, and this causes her grief too, as she tries to mediate. My issues are to do with the way Dad withdrew into himself after the police started accusing him of Milly's murder. Now that I have seen him being strong, as he was at the trial, I'm angry for the years when he was not quite there for me. I know it's the police who did this to him. Yet there's no point in being angry with the police. That is like being angry with the wind.

All this time, despite everything that was revealed by the police and in the trial, Mum and Dad have stayed together. Of course I have been their priority ever since they lost Milly, and they would never endanger my mental state any more than they need to. I think that in some ways I have been a full-time project for them.

Working with Michelle has enabled Mum to visit the part of her trauma that was purely about herself and her marriage. Mum now understands that repressing her issues is like holding a knife to her heart. She has to deal with them. But she can't do it alone. Dad's famous reserve needs to be dismantled, and they need to do some hard work, separately and alone.

By the middle of August Dad has agreed to see a counsellor.

Things between me and Dad start to improve, and not long from now I shall see him back in action as the father Milly adored and would be proud of.

Now all we need to do is sort out Maisy's personality disorders.

The criminal trials of Rebekah Brooks and Andy Coulson are due to start on 9 September. We are asked if we would like to attend. You can guess our answer.

The trial means that Milly's back on the six o'clock news on 5 November. Rebekah Brooks is denying any knowledge of Milly's phone hacking even though she was editor of the *News of the World* when it happened. Brooks, her husband and colleagues are on trial for perverting the course of justice by hiding evidence. It emerges that, on 8 July 2011, seven boxes of notebooks were removed from a storage archive at News International, and the company had started a policy of deleting emails from previous years. On trial with the Brookses are former editor Andy Coulson, her deputy at the time of Milly's hacking, former managing editor Stuart Kuttner, and head of news Ian Edmondson.

The court case interests us, of course, but it irritates us more. Now that we've been in a courtroom ourselves, it's easier to translate what is important amid all the form and ceremony. It seems so petty. There seems to be so much game-playing.

In the end Rebekah Brooks is cleared of all charges against her. Andy Coulson is found guilty and sentenced to eighteen months in prison. The actual hacker, Glenn Mulcaire, gets another short sentence, suspended.

The judge, speaking of the *News of the World*'s 'unforgivable' actions regarding Milly, says, 'Their true motivation was not to act in the best interests of the child, but to get credit for finding her and thereby sell the maximum numbers of newspapers.'

★

My EMDR progresses through the rest of 2014. Sometimes it's hard. Sometimes it's beautiful. Through EMDR, I'm beginning to let the anger out and the sadness in. And that is when I begin to get closer to the part of my mind where Milly was. Through EMDR, I discover that my memories of Milly haven't been erased. They were there all along, masked and buried by the trauma.

And then in one session I hear her saxophone. The Pink Panther rides again. And I see and feel Milly again, as she was.

Now I think about Milly every day and will do so for the rest of my life. And I have access to my memories of our childhood together too.

So, I am getting better. Mum is getting better. We have learned to grieve. Mum and Dad are working through their issues. Things between Dad and me are getting back to where they should be.

Thanks to Michelle and EMDR, Christmas this year actually feels like Christmas. Lovely Granny and I stay at Mum and Dad's house. Various members of the family and close friends pop in. It's the first time we've done this. Mum's had a special candle customized with Milly's name in the wax. On Christmas Day, we light it for the first time. As we watch it burning, there's a sense that the warmth of its tiny flame is spreading through the room.

For the first time, the memory of Milly seems comforting rather than overwhelming.

I'm cooking all the time, almost obsessed with it. The amount of food, Mum observes, is 'somewhat extreme'. It feels good to provide for our family, to make delicious treats for them. I make roast goose on Christmas Day, then a pheasant casserole on Boxing Day. Dad gives Mum a magnificent cake stand. Together Mum and I make an orange spiced cake to put on top of it.

Good times, Mum writes in her diary.

72.

Bellfield is in the papers again. He's been awarded £4,500 compensation for the attack on him in 2009 by a fellow inmate of Wakefield Prison. The murderer has charged the prison service with failing to give him adequate protection, and he's won. The Ministry of Justice says that it is hugely disappointed by the decision of Durham County Court.

Instead of dwelling on that, for nothing good can come of it, Mum and I are making sure she's word perfect and ready for her EMDR conference speech. Just before the conference, she makes me sit down and listen to her lecture.

It's the first time I have heard the story of our lives from her perspective. It's extremely hard for me. I love Mum without any boundaries, and I want to be there for her, but this is different. I can't bear to hear how she suffered for all these years. It makes me feel how little I helped her. Her speech is so powerful, so moving, that it will take several EMDR sessions with Michelle for me to listen to it without crying or shouting.

On Milly's birthday, 25 June, I sit in the front row of the Edinburgh auditorium. It's amazing to me that my mother, who the previous year had virtually given up on life, is about to walk on to a stage and deliver a masterpiece of a lecture.

The audience sits silent, held by every word. I don't want the tears to be streaming down my face. I want to be strong and show Mum how inspirational she is. But I can't *not* cry and neither can the audience, which is turning into a sea of used tissues and red noses.

This would not be a Dowler event without a soundtrack. As light relief from all the emotion, Mum plays the song that helped us come to terms with receiving money from the *News of the World*: Milly's old favourite, 'If I Had A Million Dollars' by the Barenaked Ladies. Mum describes how she rediscovered the song after a moving EMDR session:

494

I suddenly realized that we now actually have a million dollars from Rupert Murdoch. Up until that point, we had left it more or less untouched, as it felt like blood money. But the song evoked all the happy memories of the past and the times we had laughed at the ridiculousness of the lyrics. Well, that well and truly started a new phase of our lives.

Here is a taste of the words:

> *If I had a million dollars*
> *If I had a million dollars*
> *I'd buy you a house*
> *I would buy you a house*
>
> *If I had a million dollars*
> *If I had a million dollars*
> *I'd buy you furniture for your house*
> *Maybe a nice chesterfield or an ottoman*
>
> *If I had a million dollars*
> *If I had a million dollars*
> *I'd buy you a K-Car*
> *A nice Reliant automobile*
> *If I had a million dollars I'd buy your lo-o-o-o-ve . . .*
>
> *If I had a million dollars*
> *If I had a million dollars*
> *I'd buy you an exotic pet*
> *Yep, like a llama or an emu . . .*
>
> *If I had a million dollars*
> *If I had a million dollars*
> *Well, I'd buy you a green dress*
> *But not a real green dress, that's cruel*
>
> *And if I had a million dollars*
> *If I had a million dollars*
> *I'd buy you some art*
> *A Picasso or a Garfunkel*
>
> *If I had a million dollars*
> *If I had a million dollars*

> *Well, I'd buy you a monkey*
> *Haven't you always wanted a monkey?*
> *If I had a million dollars I'd buy your love . . .*

As the song fades away, Mum reads out our family's shopping list:

1. *House . . . tick.*
2. *Chesterfield x 2 . . . tick.*
3. *Ottoman . . . tick.*
4. *Nice reliable automobile . . . tick.*
5. *Green dress . . . tick.*
6. *Some art . . . tick. (Mum has bought a picture called Poppies and Forget-me-nots. Poppies are my favourite and forget-me-nots are for Milly.)*
7. *Monkey . . . well, no.*
8. *Exotic pet . . . Maisy the spaniel? The only thing that's really exotic about Maisy is her, um, temperament.*

Mum shares with the audience one of her recent EMDR sessions:

In my back garden I have a pergola which I built with my dad many, many years ago. Over the pergola is a beautiful yellow rose.

The rose has a short flowering period of two to three weeks. However, each year when it flowered all I could see was the memory of two police officers pacing up and down underneath it, smoking and looking very concerned. We were waiting for Bob to return from London. Then they told us a body had been found nearby in the River Thames.

Michelle said, 'I think we need to process this.'

The rose seemed to evoke all the memories of being given bad news, the overwhelming anxiety it caused and the pressure of 'not knowing'.

After processing all the painful memories, over and over again, my mind went sort of blank, like a fresh sheet of paper, and then completely out of the blue I began to remember actually planting that rose with the girls, and Milly watering the rose with her little yellow watering-can. I kept getting glimpses of this image but it was hurting to sort of 'get it out'. It was like I had to break through a layer of grief to get to the happy memory.

Now when I look at that rose I can see us planting it again and I feel nice.

Mum finishes with another song on her processing playlist: 'Carry You' by Amy Grant. 'I think,' she smiles to the audience, 'it represents how I feel about my EMDR treatment with Michelle.'

Mum gets a full-on standing ovation, which lasts several minutes. I stand there too, brimming with pride. I want to nudge people and say, 'Hey! That's my mum up there! Isn't she bloody amazing?'

On my left is Dr Eileen Feeney, the psychiatrist who's been working with Michelle to piece Mum and me back together. We love Eileen too. Like Michelle, she has the natural ability to see what is going on, often without even asking. Now Eileen's crying her eyes out on one side of me. On the other is the incredible woman who originated and developed EMDR therapy, Dr Francine Shapiro. She's weeping too.

As for Mum, she looks around the room in wonder. I know what she's thinking.

What has she done? What has she been through to get here?

The conference spurs me into carrying on with my EMDR therapy. We systematically go through every incident that has caused me to feel worthless. There are hundreds. I have to address them all in order to clear every bit of damage done.

Working with Michelle opens closed doors between Mum and me. We find ourselves talking about things that have been forbidden for years. It turns out that each of us has been so afraid of upsetting the other that we have nursed many wounds that need light and warmth to heal. By the end of the month I'm finally telling Mum about how abandoned I felt at Milly's funeral. I explain what happened when Mum started making the noises of a wounded animal and Lovely Granny went to help her, leaving me alone with the fast-disappearing coffin. Mum cries for me and with me. And I cry for Mum.

I also ask some questions that have been buried in my mind since Milly's body was found. I ask if her hair was still attached to her skull. Mum also explains gently to me about what happens when a body decomposes, and that in the end only 90 per cent of Milly's remains were recovered. Grim as they are, I do get a sense of comfort from having the full facts at last. And there is such relief in being able to talk about it with Mum.

One November evening I get a text from Hannah Mac: *Are you at home now Gemma?*

I reply *Yes.*

She texts, *Don't go anywhere. I'll be with you in ten minutes.*

It sounds urgent, I think. *I'd better put the kettle on.*

Hannah arrives, looking very excited. In her hand is a little box. Smiling, she hands it to me. Like me, Hannah enjoys making things. She's very creative, and a bit of a perfectionist. Inside the box, under lots of shredded tissue paper, is a lolly stick with a handwritten message in black ink. It says, 'Beach Wedding 2015. Save the date.'

'Hannah!' I squeal. 'Congratulations!'

'There's something else, Gemma.'

I look back in the box. I find a pretty polished scallop shell.

'Turn it over.'

On the back of the shell is a piece of paper that I carefully unfold. It says, 'Will you be my bridesmaid?' There are two hearts drawn either side.

I give Hannah a Milly-style Guttural Hug. I'm as excited as a five-year-old at Christmas, but I want to mark the moment with dignity. I say, 'It will be an honour and a privilege to be your bridesmaid, Hannah.'

Since I lost Milly, I never thought I'd be asked to be a bridesmaid. And now I'm going to be a bridesmaid for Milly's dear friend.

Hannah has a beautiful ability to bring out the parts of my personality that are most like Milly's. We both love to sing, dance and perform. So we decide to re-enact the opening of the box for Mum on FaceTime.

Mum answers and we act out the scene.

'Mum, look what Hannah's given me.'

As usual, Mum's not wearing her glasses. She says, 'I can't make out what it is, Gemsie.'

I reply 'It's a lolly stick and it says, "Beach Wedding 2015. Save the date."'

Lots of squealing, congratulations and 'Lovelys' from Mum.

'We haven't finished yet, Mum.' I show her the shell. She still can't see so I read it to her: 'Will you be my bridesmaid?'

All Hannah and I can see are Mum's projectile tears. Mum always tries not to cry in front of friends so Hannah is alarmed.

After pulling herself together, which takes some time, Mum says, 'Hannah, I know you have done this for Milly. It means she is not forgotten.'

Now Hannah and I are weeping too.

73.

The start of 2015 looks so promising. In addition to being a brides-maid, one of the best things about Hannah's wedding is that I have a date. The relationship is still very new, yet for the first time I feel like myself. Having someone love me when I'm myself is all I've ever wanted. Now I feel loved, the way I know Grandad loved Lovely Granny. For once I start a new year with a sense of opti-mism and hope. Our flights and villa are booked ready for Hannah's wedding and we're busy choosing Mum an outfit.

In February 2015, Mum and I meet with a literary agent, Victoria Hobbs at A. M. Heath. Victoria's an attractive woman who immedi-ately puts you under the spotlight of her sharp mind. It's kind but it's intense. You could never fake or fudge anything in front of Victoria.

Her first question to me is, 'Why do you want to write a book, Gemma?'

Fortunately I know just why. You've read my reasons in the intro-duction. By the time the meeting is finished, Victoria has agreed to take me on. I walk out into the sunshine, shivering with excitement and also with fear. I'm suddenly extremely aware that I have a huge responsibility to get this right, for me, for Mum, for Dad and, most of all, for Milly.

Soon after, I have a rehearsal for being a published author. It's my turn to give a speech at an EMDR conference, this time in Brighton. I'm to do it on 21 March, the anniversary of Milly's disappearance.

I've always been fearless about public speaking. Mum says it's because I have a strong moral compass and so much to say. This presentation needs more than strong feelings. It needs research, reflection and rehearsal. I feel as if this presentation is about me as well as about Milly. I exist in my own right. For the first time, thanks to the EMDR, I am considering 'What does Gemma want?' rather than 'What does Gemma, sister of murdered Milly Dowler, want?' It's a huge difference.

With a PowerPoint, I tell my story, and Milly's: our happy life before she was abducted, the terror of losing her, the dark months of not knowing, the discovery of her body, the trial, the hacking. I enjoy working with words and images. However, seeing it all together like that, I wonder how we survived any one of those blows.

I don't dress like a victim for my presentation. I get out of my jeans and put on a romantic silk dress printed with large summer flowers. It's the dress of someone more innocent than I am, someone happier than I've been all these long, hard years. It's the dress of someone I want to be. When I tell our story, I want to be the girl who survived, the girl Bellfield couldn't ruin, the daughter Mum and Dad know I can be, the sister Milly would be proud of.

In Brighton, I deliver my speech without faltering. I hear my voice carrying across the room and I realize this is the same voice that I'm going to use for this book. This is my voice, whether on the page or in the microphone.

I also bring Milly's voice and personality into the room – not 'Tragic Milly Dowler' but Milly-Molly-Mandy Milly, Sausage Pot, Auntie Milly, Mildred, the sweet Old Soul that she was. I show her holding her rabbit Sooty, as the style guru in her fake leopard-skin hat, as the laid-back creative type with her customized everything, as the dancer and the singer and the Guttural Hugger.

I tell what happened to us after Milly was taken. Sometimes I use the press headlines to show what we were forced to read about my sister and ourselves. Sometimes I use private photographs that illustrate how our bodies as well as our minds were traumatized. I show how far we have come, now that Michelle has delivered me and Mum safely to the place of acceptance that we so desperately needed to reach. Michelle's there in the audience, and I'm so glad. I want her to hear how huge my gratitude is. I want her fellow practitioners to hear it too.

By the time I finish, everyone's in tears, and there's a standing ovation. I feel empowered to finish this book as fast and as well as possible. I present Michelle with the world's largest bouquet of English summer flowers.

After the conference, I send Mum an email. We see each other nearly every day, but I want to put something in writing.

As you know since September last year I have been working on our relationship. It has taken a lot of work on particular things that have been between us over the last thirteen years. I need you to remember that I love you no matter what happens. My love is unconditional. The difference now, Mum, is that I can love you without all the traumatic memories. I can truly be your daughter and you can be my Mum, without worrying about my future. However there is no chance I would have been able to get where I am today without your help and support. You were the one who found Michelle, and persuaded me to see her as well . . .

I love you Mum and always will. I'm going to Egypt and I will say hello to the fish for you. I do still need you, Mum, and always will do. Now we get the best parts of each of us.

Love you all the fishes in the Red Sea.

And she replies,

Gemma, you are an absolute inspiration . . . I could not be any prouder of you. I think Milly is with you in spirit and recently I have seen flashes in you that remind me deeply of her.

We feel as if we are finally moving on with living.

We have accepted that we'll probably never know exactly what happened to Milly but we are dealing with that. We count our blessings. The police are finally out of our lives. We are learning not to care about the discrepancies in their stories about the phone hacking. The press are out of our lives. We hope they won't need us again. Bellfield is out of our lives.

We are beginning to feel a little bit of positivity. It is literally incredible.

The book is going well.

On our calendar Hannah's wedding is encircled with stars and hearts.

Mum and Dad still haven't met my boyfriend and they are obviously dying to do so. We find a mutually convenient date. Mum starts excitedly planning the menu.

At that moment something happens, something that we have no reason to expect.

Suddenly things are worse than ever before.

8.

New Blows
May 2015 – March 2017

PLAYLIST

Alfie Boe	Tell Me It's Not True
David Essex from the original London cast recording of *Godspell*	The Finale
Céline Dion and Josh Groban	The Prayer
Paul Simon	Graceland
The Carpenters	Jambalaya
Robbie Williams and Olly Murs	I Wanna Be Like You
Emeli Sandé	Read All About It Pt III
Ben E. King	Stand By Me
Aloe Blacc	Mama Hold My Hand
Westlife	The Rose
Faith Hill	Somewhere Over The Rainbow
Westlife	You Raise Me Up
Roger Allam from the original cast recording of *Les Misérables*	Stars
Lady Antebellum	Hello World
LeAnn Rimes	Ten Thousand Angels Cried
Josh Groban with Ladysmith Black Mambazo	Lullaby
Lottie Mayor from the original stage recording of *Whistle Down the Wind*	Try Not To Be Afraid
James Taylor	The Water Is Wide

74.

Bellfield has been talking about what he did to Milly. No one ever thought this would happen.

This is the man who smirked 'No comment' in response to every question about Milly when interrogated by the police, and who got away with behaving in that way. This is the man who arrogantly turned his lumpy back to the camera in the police interview room, and who got away with it. This is the man who refused to speak even in his own defence at his trial for Milly's murder, who didn't even turn up for his sentencing and who got away with that too.

But the fact is that in late 2014 Bellfield starts to talk about Milly. From December 2014 to the end of February 2015, he keeps talking.

We don't hear about it until May of that year.

In the long view, a few months may not seem unreasonable. However, when you've lost a child, and have also lost the last hours in that child's life, even a minute is crucial. Not knowing is always more painful than knowing. Not knowing has been a huge part of our trauma.

Most paedophiles take what they want and then kill, usually within an hour or so. So we had always hoped that Milly did not spend a long time alive in the presence of Bellfield. We'd allowed ourselves to believe that Milly's dead body was already in the red Daewoo Nexia twenty minutes after Bellfield snatched her.

Now we learn that Milly's suffering at the hands of Bellfield was far worse and lasted much longer than we could have imagined. This new blow reactivates the shock of her disappearance, the horror of Minley Woods, the revulsion of finding out about her murderer.

It will murder our family all over again.

When Surrey Police finally start to tell us, it's a world-class fuck-up.

On 14 May, Mum and Dad are eating an early supper when a text arrives from Alice. She says there's some new information that's too sensitive to give over the phone or by message. Alice asks if Mum and Dad can come in for a meeting with Surrey Police at the end of the following week.

'Sensitive information', in our experience, can only be terrible information. Mum's physically sick as soon as she reads the message. She asks Alice to call. But Alice knows nothing more than that it concerns Bellfield. She cannot or is not allowed to say anything more.

After a sleepless night, Mum and Dad realize they can't possibly wait a week and that they shouldn't *have* to wait a week. The police don't get to decide that. Dad goes in to Woking police station the next day. He's told that Bellfield has confessed to Milly's murder. And that the murderer has provided certain other details.

The reason they're telling Mum and Dad, and now, is because Bellfield has shared his story with a paedophile prisoner. The police fear that the prisoner, who is about to be released, may go to the press.

After the trial and the hacking scandal, Surrey Police have learned to worry about what the press may say about them, especially about how they have dealt with the investigation and our family. They don't want to be caught out again not telling the Dowlers something acutely material to their daughter's case.

Dad's initial reaction, on hearing that Bellfield has confessed, is 'So bloody what? We already know he did it. So what's this *really* about?'

The police give Dad some background. It's mostly about how difficult this information has been to obtain. Bellfield would talk only to female officers. Unbelievably, the police have given in. Bellfield said they are not allowed to record the sessions or even take notes in his presence. The police have given in. Bellfield said he won't answer questions. He'd say only what he wants to say. The police have given in.

Bellfield's arrogance, while breath-taking, is not news to Dad either. He's seen the tapes of the earlier interviews. He's seen the man's demeanour in court.

As for the actual *content* of Bellfield's conversations with the female officers, Dad is told the material is so sensitive that we, Milly's family, cannot have it.

When Dad gets home, Mum cross-examines him. The strangely

selective information is a red rag to a bull for Mum, as is hearing about the way in which the police have apparently pandered to Bellfield's every whim. Mum's brain goes into overdrive. For her, the main questions are *why*, and *why now?*

Mum works it out: it must be *something about the information itself* that makes it radioactive.

Mum and Dad still haven't told me about this latest development. I'm spinning in my happy bubble after my success at the EMDR conference, working away on the book that is supposed to be the final word on this story. Mum and Dad cannot bear to distress me. Any mention of Surrey Police is bound to do that. A situation with Bellfield talking about Milly and Surrey Police withholding information? That is guaranteed to make me livid. Unwittingly, I force their hands by ringing to invite them over for a cup of tea and to meet my boyfriend. On the phone, Mum tells me what's just happened. I jump straight in my car and I'm with them in ten minutes.

As Mum puts it, I 'freak out completely'. I'm shouting and screaming. Tears shoot out of my eyes. The only words I can hear are 'sensitive information'.

Mum immediately phones Michelle Calvert, who alerts our psychiatrist Eileen Feeney. For the first time ever, we have a safety blanket of professionals caring for us.

Thank God. We're going to need them more than anyone could ever imagine.

On Monday, 18 May, Mum and I insist on a meeting of our own with the police. Dad doesn't believe we'll get anything more out of them, so he stays at home.

Mum is absolutely determined to get the answers to some very basic questions. She types out a list and puts it in her bag.

What are Bellfield's motives for confessing? Privileges?
How many murders has he confessed to?
How did he get Milly into his flat?
How quickly did he kill her?
What stops a fellow prisoner writing a book or selling this story to
a newspaper?

Unbeknown to me, Mum also tucks into her bag a large photo of Milly in a frame. It's her favourite – Milly driving the boat in Cyprus. It's one of our happiest memories of Milly: full of joy, confidence and a bit of mischief. Mum knows she's going to need Milly today. For extra courage, she takes Milly's favourite Beanie Baby, a little dog called Wrinkles. He looks a bit like Maisy.

At Woking police station we're greeted by a female officer we haven't met before. She comments that the weather is rather grim and that it's got dark all of a sudden.

I tell her, 'I'm pretty sure it's not as grim as what we're about to be told.'

There's no more small-talk after that.

In a meeting room, the same male and female officers whom Dad saw are waiting for us. We receive a minimal outline, nothing more than Dad was told. Every time we ask for more detail, they say they have nothing else to give us. It's too sensitive.

'That's not enough,' I say, over and over. 'There's more. There must be more.'

Eventually, our stubbornness extracts two new pieces of information. The first is that there are other cases involved in Bellfield's admissions. The second is that highly confidential covert searches will be taking place in densely wooded areas in the Metropolitan Police area. They will not say what the police are looking for or whether some items are Milly's. None of Milly's possessions – clothes, jewellery, telephone and rucksack – have ever been found. Yet we guess the police wouldn't be mentioning these searches unless something of Milly's is involved.

This isn't answering Mum's questions. It's just adding riddles. She pulls Milly's photograph out of her bag and places it on the table so that the officers are forced to look into my sister's blue eyes. Next to Milly, Mum sits Wrinkles the Beanie Baby. Mum's face shows utter determination.

'It is a mother's right to know the answers to these questions,' she says forcefully. 'How can you deny me that?'

Mum is taking the control that I wish I could. I'm not so brave. At the sight of Milly's face, in that place, I fall to pieces, whimpering with fear, frustration and the memories of nearly fourteen years of terrible conversations with Surrey Police.

The battle for information heats up. Mum powers through all the officers' objections. She insists on going through her list of questions. Few of the answers are forthcoming.

Mum changes tack: 'OK, if you're not going to answer *those* questions, then you have to answer this. *How* did he kill her?'

Mum points at the photograph. 'Do you *know* how he killed her?' Mum asks.

'Yes, Sally,' replies the female officer.

Mum shoots back, 'How?'

The officer replies, 'I can't tell you that, Sally. It's too sensitive. I'm a mother. I can't tell you that.'

Mum: 'If you're a mother, then surely you understand why I *must* know?'

I'm still silently sobbing and watching Mum in amazement.

'No, Sally.'

'I'm not leaving this police station until you tell me how my daughter was murdered.'

'No.'

'Right,' says Mum, briskly, 'let's do this by a process of elimination. Did he suffocate her?'

There's a stunned silence. Then a quiet 'No'.

I say, 'Did he stab her?'

Finally, the female officer breaks. Very quietly, she says, 'Strangulation.'

Strangulation. It is so personal. It's not quick like a gun-shot. It's not Bellfield's well-known technique of bludgeoning the back of a girl's head with a hammer.

We know more about strangulation than anyone should. The Hawker sisters told us that it takes three and a half minutes to kill someone that way.

I'm weeping uncontrollably.

Mum, grim-faced, keeps going: 'So how long did he keep Milly alive before he strangled her?'

After a great deal of prevarication, the female officer informs us that, although Bellfield initially took Milly into the flat at Collingwood Place, 'He killed her elsewhere.'

Elsewhere? What kind of elsewhere? A deserted warehouse, a lock-up garage?

All the possibilities are awful. The worst thing is that if he took her elsewhere, it means Bellfield didn't kill Milly quickly. It means she wasn't dead when he drove that red Daewoo Nexia away from Collingwood Place.

I feel as if we are falling into an abyss. Both Mum and I are screaming now.

Mum manages to repeat her question. 'So how long *was* she alive for?'

After another extended silence, we hear the words, 'Twenty-four to forty-eight hours.'

Two days in that monster's control? I can't look at Milly's sweet face on the table. I can't bear to open the lid of this new Pandora's box of secrets. I can't contemplate the possibility that my sister suffered for so long.

How did you bear it, Milly? I can't even bear hearing about it.

The walls of the anonymous grey room fall away. The horror of Milly's disappearance is suddenly fresh once more. I feel as if I'm in Minley Woods again, as if Milly has just been killed again, as if she'll never stop being killed.

Mum keeps firing questions through her tears. 'What did he strangle her with?'

What's left of the female officer mumbles, 'A scarf that belonged to the mother of Bellfield's girlfriend.'

The female officer explains that this scarf is among 'other trophies' buried in woodlands that the Metropolitan Police are now going to search for.

'Trophies?' I ask. 'Isn't that what you win at horse races?'

Mum quietly explains to me that some murderers like to keep the personal possessions of their victims. The police refer to those items as 'trophies'.

I'm silent with shock.

'So have you told us everything?' Mum asks the woman police officer. 'Was anyone else involved?'

'I'm a mother too,' the officer says again, looking Mum directly in the eye. The policewoman's own eyes are wet with emotion. 'Yes, you've been told everything there is to know.'

We're given the usual cautions with added emphasis, added blackmail: 'If you say anything it could mean that other crimes might not be solved and other victims might be left without justice.'

Just before the meeting finishes, a single ray of sunlight breaks through the dirty grey blinds. It brings with it a warmth I can feel on my skin.

'It's Milly,' I say aloud.

Mum says to the officer, 'I know how harrowing it must have been for you to tell us that. But thank you. It's the first time the police have told us the truth.'

Mum quietly takes Wrinkles and Milly's photo off the table and puts them into her bag. She helps me get up and puts her arm around me. We walk out to the car in silence. We drive a little way out of the police compound and pull into a layby.

We cannot say anything. We can't even cry.

Words and phrases tumble through my brain in no order.

The worst ones are 'scarf', 'strangulation' and 'forty-eight hours'.

75.

I don't remember how Mum and I end up in Walton. It must be on autopilot. There's a homing instinct in us to get back to Dad. By that time we're both in open hysterics. Poor Dad struggles to understand us. When we finally make it clear to him, he holds his head in his two giant hands and weeps. He needs his hands to support his head because otherwise the enormity of the information would surely flatten him. I feel as if we've hurt him so much. What father would want to know these things? But now that we know, he has to as well.

So here we are again. We have a few patchy, awful facts. In spite of what the policewoman said – and maybe *because* of what she said – we know instinctively that we've been denied other facts, possibly even worse ones. Mum has her tunnel eyes again. Dad's in shock. I can't stop crying. We're terrified of even speaking to one another. Ever since we first suspected our house was bugged by the police, and then after we discovered our phones had been hacked by the press, we have never known if it's safe to say aloud what we're thinking, even in our own kitchen.

The hours tick past, one, five, ten, twenty-four, thirty-six. Each slow passing hour marks the amount of time that we've been told Milly suffered at the hands of Bellfield. None of us can sleep. The forty-eight hours seem to last a lifetime. They continue until Wednesday, 20 May, when Mum, Dad and I have another meeting with the police. Mum doesn't ask. She sends a text saying the Dowlers will be arriving at Woking police station today at 3 p.m.

They must be shocked by our haggard appearances, but they say nothing. This time Alice comes too. It's the first time we've seen her since the trial. I wish it wasn't like this.

In advance of the meeting, I've sent a set of questions. That's so the police won't have the excuse that they need time to research or prepare replies.

They can't refuse to answer, I think.

I'm wrong. The police don't feel they owe us straight answers.

Their grounds for being evasive remain that 'other cases are involved'. There's also a new justification for not answering: it wouldn't be good for our mental health to know certain things.

It is, of course, far worse for our mental health to feel that we are being treated like children and not being told the full truth about Milly. The police are not our trusted therapists. They are the authors of a great deal of our pain. We don't trust our mental health in their hands.

Nor are we going to be fobbed off with 'This could affect other cases' today. Eventually the officers realize that we won't leave until we have more information. The female officer agrees to fetch some files. We're left staring at the other officer in silence until she comes back into the room carrying a small bundle of notes. Many lines and paragraphs are blacked out.

'By the way, I'm sorry,' the female officer says. 'I made a mistake on Monday about the amount of time he kept Milly alive. I've reread the notes. It wasn't forty-eight hours. I think it was all over and done with in about fourteen hours.'

All over and done with.

She looks at us as if we should be grateful. Yes, we are grateful that Milly's torture lasted fewer hours than she'd told us. Yet we are shocked that this officer could have got something so crucial so very wrong. It's now forty-eight hours since we saw *her* last. *When* did she realize that she'd misinformed us? Why did she not tell us *that second*? All that time, we've been living the minutes of Milly's suffering. Every second has been hell. I want to scream, yet I want information more. So I wait quietly to hear what she has to say now.

From the heavily redacted notes, she reads out Bellfield's account of what he did to Milly during those fourteen hours. It goes pretty much like this, except for a few details I still cannot bring myself to write down:

He calls her for help.
She crosses the road.
He forces her into Number 24 Collingwood Place.
Fingers her.
She says, Ouch.
Ties her up and covers her in a white sheet.

Hands behind back, sock in mouth.
Puts her in the passenger foot-well of red Daewoo Nexia.
Pulls the sheet back so he can see her face.
Her blazer and bag are left at Collingwood.
Driving.
She says, My gag has come out.
She says, My mum and dad don't have much money.
Drives to his mother's house.
Reverses down the long drive.
Removes the heavy tools from boot.
She says, Are you going to rape me?
He says, Shut up.
Forces her out of the foot-well to the car boot.
Rapes her in broad daylight face down over the boot latch.
The latch rips through her stomach.
She says, I'm bleeding.
Blood on the sheet under her.
Drives her to Little Benty, West Drayton.
Strips her.
Ties her up.
Locks her in a cupboard.
Returns to Collingwood to collect her bag and school blazer.
He wants to fuck her in it.
Returns and does that.
Afterwards, he locks her back in the cupboard.
Drives to where his girlfriend's staying in West Drayton.
Leaves girlfriend in early hours with dog.
Goes to Collingwood Place.
He and his dog are seen at Collingwood that night
walking by the entrance to bins.
Returns to Little Benty.
She is still alive.
At 5.30 a.m. strangles her with a brown silk scarf.
Later, dumps her naked body in Minley Woods.
Burns her clothes.

But for us, out of this whole catalogue of horror, one thing stands out. To hear what Milly said – *that*'s what strikes into our hearts.

After all these years since she was silenced, Milly speaks for the first time. And it's *her* voice we hear when the words are read. They are the words I know she'd use. They are the words I would say as well. They are Milly. They are true.

Mum's writing notes with shaking hands. Dad sits in stunned silence. For me, it takes every bit of energy not to scream as we hear what Bellfield did to Milly.

Mum asks if the confession has been evidenced. Has Bellfield's account been backed up? Have they checked with telephone mast records to confirm his movements? Have they checked out his statement against those of witnesses like his girlfriend, Emma Mills?

'You've known a while. You've had plenty of time to do this,' I point out bitterly.

They are 'assessing' evidence, the policewoman says. Mum asks, twice, just to make sure, 'Was anyone else involved?'

'No,' is the answer.

Dad wants to know about the covert searching for trophies in the woods. But the search is so covert that we're not allowed to know any more about it, other than that someone has been sent to covertly take a photograph of the general area, which is close to where we live.

Mum, Dad and I walk out of the police station on jelly legs.

The car does not seem safe, after what we've just heard. Home does not feel safe. Night does not feel safe, even with the three of us together. The whole world has become a dangerous place again. Everything has the potential to throw us overboard. Cupboards, scarves, car boots – all these things now seem sinister to us.

Suddenly I remember Hannah Mac's wedding. We're due to fly out to Majorca very soon. My dress is ready. Mum's is too. Dad always looks amazing in his formal clothes. The wedding is supposed to be one more sign that life goes on, and that we go on with it.

We won't be able to manage a flight, let alone a wedding now. Look at us. We can't eat. We can't sleep. We can't stop crying. Lovely Hannah Mac can't have ghosts at her wedding. I also know that I can't let her down without telling her the real reason why.

Mum asks Hannah's mother, Sara, to come over. The only way Mum can get through this is simply to read aloud her notes of the meeting. Sara has made a pledge that she will never cry in front of us. Now Sara breaks it.

Sara does not give the details to Hannah, who doesn't need those thoughts at her wedding. Hannah comes over to see us. The infection of our pain has spread. Hannah's about to be married to a wonderful man and now she cannot stop weeping and her beautiful face is tight with grief. She says she feels guilty about her tears. 'Gemma, I have no reason to cry. This is happening to *you.*'

I remind her that Milly and I always promised to be bridesmaids for each other. 'And you're like a sister to me. So I thought I'd be keeping my promise to Milly by being your bridesmaid.'

I give her a cuddle and hand her Milly's special pebble with the heart-shaped indentation. 'Please take this with you.'

We have one more request for the police, which is to do with my therapy and Mum's. EMDR necessitates reliving the worst moments of terror with the help of your therapist. We already know we have long hours of work ahead of us to process what we've just heard. So we ask if a written account of Bellfield's admissions can be made available.

That request will be considered, we are told.

At 3 p.m. the next day, Dad takes a call from the police. No, we cannot have the written account because of the investigations into other crimes. It might even affect the chances of finding another body. So Dad asks for a summary of just the part we *are* allowed to know. At 6 p.m. Alice delivers a single sheet of paper containing two short paragraphs.

It's entitled 'Verbal account given by LB'.

We feel as if we're about to learn the biggest secret that Surrey Police have ever kept from us.

But it's so brief. It's missing some of the facts we were given at the police station. It immediately begins to fester that many details have been left out – details that we cannot forget, having heard them. How did the police decide to edit them out? What *else* did they leave out? This piece of paper was supposed to resolve our doubts. Instead, it has made the 'truth' even more unstable. What is *not* written makes me more frantic with fear. No matter how many times I read it, I cannot make sense of it.

We worry the subject round and round, trying to enclose it in some kind of logic, some kind of clarity. But this is Surrey Police. Logic and clarity are not what they offer us.

There's to be a meeting of the 'Gold Group', we're told, to discuss the case.

We don't even know what a Gold Group is. We're too shell-shocked to ask.

It's a bank-holiday weekend, the first of the spring. Normally we'd be taking walks with Maisy, having Sunday lunch with Lovely Granny. There's plenty to do in the garden. Instead, our minds are working over the terrible grey areas that seem to be seething around the grim facts.

Mum goes to see Michelle, who, luckily, can explain what a Gold Group is: a meeting of top brass to deal with very important matters. The meeting, we know, is scheduled for the Tuesday after this bank holiday – 26 May. We spend the weekend drafting a letter to the Gold Group, so that our family's feelings can be present at the table, even if we're not allowed to be there in person.

Here's Mum's final draft. As ever, she starts with a thank-you, and has tried to be polite, hoping to be met halfway in courtesy, at least.

Firstly we would like to thank you for being brave enough to tell us the details. Galling as they are/were to hear we absolutely needed to know. For nearly fourteen years we have not known.

1. *For all we know, Bellfield may have already told quite a few prisoners, as obviously sharing the gory details with other paedophiles would be sexually exciting for him and them.*

2. *We are no longer prepared for Bellfield to have any control over us. During the trial he had control of the lines of questioning that his defence team took. He systematically tried to destroy our family one by one.*

3. *This information could be put in the press at any time, for example Gemma's wedding day (if she has one) or her Granny's funeral. We are NOT prepared to let this happen. We cannot live with that Sword of Damocles hanging over us.*

4. *As far as we see it, either Surrey Police press office releases the details in a controlled manner or we will do so ourselves.*

5. *We were due to fly to Majorca for Hannah's wedding. We have*

*cancelled going because nothing must be allowed to spoil her
beautiful day.*

6. *From experience we can say that mental torture is far more painful
than any physical pain and Bellfield and Surrey Police have given us
plenty of that already. It MUST stop.*

7. *There is one further question that I need answered: Is there any
indication that any other individuals were involved in Milly's
abduction, rape, torture, death or disposing of her body?*

8. *We understand that there may be other victims involved in these
disclosures but on this occasion we must put our needs first.*

9. *As we are sure you know, this matter is very urgent and we trust that
you are giving it the highest priority. Time is of the essence for us, as
each day that passes increases the pressure on our sanity and well-
being. We would wish you to prepare a controlled statement to the
press and media as soon as possible, or we will be forced to take action
ourselves.*

We email this to the police.

Mum's diary says: 'We spent this morning preparing a press
release detailing LB's confession and description of Milly's abduction, rape, torture, sexual abuse and strangulation. Just another
day in the life of the Dowlers.'

We know our press release will be hard for anyone to read. Yet
we also know the police will want to water down whatever we
write so our version contains absolutely everything.

Everything we know at this point, that is.

It may seem odd that we should want the world to know about the
torture and pain that Milly suffered. We have our reasons and I
want to explain them.

After these meetings with the police, Mum and I are rags of ourselves again. Our mental health has plummeted to the lows of the
first days of Milly's disappearance, or the trial. Bellfield is still controlling the situation, and us. The police have apparently facilitated
everything he wants. It seems to us that confessing to what he did
to Milly has only made Bellfield's life more comfortable and has
proven his power.

For once, we want to be in charge of managing what the public is told and when. In our minds, the police have made a mess of it. It's our turn, and it's our duty, to get it right. We want an account out there that is not neutralized by vague language. What happened to Milly was not neutral. It was evil beyond measure.

We also want to show how united we still are as a family, despite all the assaults on our peace of mind. We trust the public to be able to cope with this information. We think that they, like ourselves, are owed it. Why should Bellfield be protected from their disgust? Hundreds of cards to us, hundreds of thousands of pounds into Milly's Fund: these things have shown us that the decent people of Britain are on our side.

We know we are morally the owners of this information. But we are aware that there might be unpleasant consequences for us from the police if we release it on our own. We want them to agree with us, and to support us.

Why should our family yet again be left holding this unspeakable secret, unable to express our pain and outrage to anyone?

The Gold Group meeting takes place between 11 a.m. and 1 p.m. on 26 May. We drift around the house, waiting for the phone to ring. Another ray of sunshine comes through the window and warms my back. 'Milly's here again,' I tell Mum and Dad. 'I can feel her.'

At last the phone rings. It's what we've been waiting for, but we jump. Dad puts the female police officer on loudspeaker.

Rather than giving information, her priority is to know exactly what we want to go into the media so that she can assess what impact it will have on the investigation. She says this over and over again. Her job, she emphasizes, is being made very difficult by these demands of ours. She wants us to liaise with their media specialists.

Dad keeps his tone cooperative and courteous while insisting, 'It has to become public knowledge that this individual' – Dad rarely names Bellfield – 'has made a disclosure, an admission of killing Milly. People need to be under no illusion about him any more. And he needs to be aware that we know what's happened. And that really will, I think, start to put an end to this situation.'

Dad needs to remind the policewoman that there are people suffering here. People in this room. 'It's very critical, and I hope you were able to convey this at the meeting this morning. The real crux of all this is our continued mental health and well-being.'

'I do reassure you that was conveyed by me today,' the policewoman says, and speaks again of her tactics and responsibilities. 'You, Sally and Gemma are very much at the forefront of things for me.'

Dad says, 'That's very encouraging. Without being brutal, that's a minimum requirement from my perspective.'

The police officer reiterates how busy she is with committees and other work, but promises that she will see us tomorrow. She reiterates, 'Your demands are stopping me and my team of four officers from conducting the covert searches.'

Dad wants to make sure that tomorrow will be our last police meeting for a good long while. He understands that Bellfield is not going to give any more information unless it suits him. But we need to know *everything* it has suited him to say. 'Nothing I've heard or seen in the last thirteen – nearly fourteen – years tells me that it will ever be on your terms when the police are talking to him. The fact that female officers went in to see him – was not lost on us. Bloody obvious and very, very distressing.'

I speak now, in a trembling voice. I thank the policewoman for the information received so far. But I need more. What I need now is evidence from the police inquiry back in 2002: evidence of where his car was, where his phone was, in terms of when my uncle saw him. I need corroboration.

She undertakes to go back into the original inquiry to produce a timeline. She asks for more time to do it properly.

Mum agrees to supply the press release we've drafted so that the officer can show it to her legal team.

Dad sums it up. 'Our attitude now is due to thirteen years of, frankly, crap, if you'll pardon my language. We've been one of the most compliant families in an awful situation. I personally have not had a voice for nine of those years. But, by golly gosh, I've found it now. And, really, everybody needs to listen. Because, effectively, my personal feelings about this are very difficult to deal with.'

Dad being Dad, he now shows some empathy for the policewoman's position. He acknowledges, 'You're the unfortunate soul who's had to pick this up and run with it. The reality is that the track record of Surrey Police in the investigation is not good. Not good, is it? You've been handed what I consider to be one of the most poisoned chalices to deal with.'

Yet Dad stays on message. We need to get to the bottom of the situation. We need to know where our despair can end. 'There's not an elastic piece of time about this. My attitude is not going to get less assertive. Because I owe it to myself, I owe it to Gemma and Sally, and I owe it to Milly. I've got to do this for us, and for Milly's name and Milly's memory. We are utterly united about this as a family. Whatever's to come, and we're not blind to the difficulties ahead, whatever the reality is, this is our moment. And it's *your* moment.'

'Fair comment,' the policewoman says.

Arrangements are made for us to come, as usual, to the back door of the police station, the following evening.

Mum asks again for reassurance that the information Bellfield has provided is supported by the evidence of his phone records. We need to be sure. We need to be told specifically that this account of Milly's last hours is based on fact as well as the words of a murderer.

The policewoman promises that the timeline she gives us will be one that is corroborated by evidence. We finish the call.

'She's lying,' I say to Dad and Mum.

76.

Since hearing the news, Dad and I have been listening to one song on repeat: 'Tell Me It's Not True' from *Blood Brothers*. It's sung in a rich opera voice by Alfie Boe. Like us, the singer's just been told something unspeakable. He always thought he wanted the information, but now he has it, he cannot accept it or live with it.

Apart from her questions and the press release, Mum has been making other notes – notes not destined for Surrey Police eyes. Our emotions are not part of their project. It's not that Mum doesn't want to embarrass them: that seems impossible. She doesn't seek empathy from them: that's not on the agenda either. She just wants everyone to be honest, and that includes herself. She puts her unbearable thoughts on the page in the hope that this will tear them out of her heart and let her breathe again.

The honest truth is that the timing is too cruel. Milly has only just come back to life for Mum via EMDR. Those beautiful visualizations have made Milly real again. Now that Mum can picture her daughter so much more clearly, she can also see Milly's sufferings. There are no filters and no safety nets. She writes,

> Recently I went to see a musical from the seventies called Godspell. The finale song, with Jesus on the cross, starts, 'Oh God I'm bleeding, Oh God I'm bleeding . . .'
>
> All that I could hear replaying in my head over and over again was Milly singing to me, and me singing back to her.

> > 'Oh Mum, I'm bleeding
> > Oh Mum, I'm bleeding'
> > 'Oh Milly, you're bleeding'
> > (Music)
> > 'Oh Mum, I'm dying'
> > 'Oh Milly, you're dying'
> > 'Oh Mum, I'm dying'
> > (Music)

'Oh Mum, I'm dead'
'Oh Milly, you're dead
Oh Milly, you're dead
Oh Milly, you're dead.'

Mum finds it hard to leave the house. A simply query about her health makes her burst into tears, to the mystification of friends who know nothing of this huge new secret we're harbouring. Mum spends hours in the garden with her headphones on full volume.

I find a song called 'The Prayer', sung by Céline Dion, accompanied by Andrea Bocelli. It speaks to Mum and me as we would like to speak to Milly. The prayer is to someone who has gone, but whose light can still lead us to a safe place. We share the song with Dad. It soothes the rawness of our pain. Yet the trauma isn't settled enough to be processed by our brains yet. We don't have the words so music is the way we communicate with each other.

It feels as if we are carrying around a spinning ball of terror, like a nail bomb that will suddenly stop and release more of its deadly contents at any moment. But you never know when. So you can never feel safe.

Mum's garden is looking just about the best it ever has. Yet Mum is currently like one of the walking dead. The shadows under her eyes are so deep that you could fall into them. Dad has withdrawn into quiet desperation. I'm an explosion about to happen. You only have to look at our faces. All the signs are there: our emotional safety is in the hands of Surrey Police.

Milly's life wasn't safe in their hands. Neither is her death.

We're told that now, months after Bellfield's admissions, an officer has been out to the supposed site where the trophies are buried and covertly taken photos. Excavating the site will take twenty men two weeks if it's not covert and much longer if it is.

The police tell us these things with straight faces, as if they are not a mockery of logic, as if there's some doubt about the urgent need to substantiate the evidence of a man who has admitted to the rape and murder of a thirteen-year-old.

If the police are going to be a joke, then we are going to make our own bitter kind of fun. We decide to form our own Gold Group. We call in family and friends. Our Gold Group can't do worse than Surrey Police and we suspect it can do a hell of a lot better.

Here's the roll-call:

Mum – head of buying notebooks, lanyards and props
Lovely Granny – head of leaks and meetings in the street; also head of snacks
Dad – head of illegible notes, waffling and emergency ice-cream runs
Gemma – head of plainclothes covertness
Carole (court correspondent) – evidence demander
Fiona – head of poisonous biscuits
Sara – head of projectile vomiting
Uncle Ian – head of spreadsheets
Maisy – head of growling and barking
Sharpie factory – head of redactions (vast quantities needed as most documents heavily redacted)
Scully – legal guru and head of emergency retreats

We can't decide who should be head of intelligence so we blow up an inflatable seahorse and put a lanyard around its neck with this title. That sparks a whole new level of silliness, which in turn provides relief from the unbearable tension. We also decide that, due to the secrecy and covertness of everything, we should all have secret fish identifying names.

Milly loved fish. In primary school, she was asked to choose and draw her creature from the deep. 'My creature is a fish,' Milly announced, in her tottering six-year-old writing. And she drew a seascape full of beautiful fish, a mermaid and clear blue water.

If Milly were with us now, she would be her favourite Tasselled Wobbegong shark. She can't be here, so we shall form a shoal of people who love her. It will be as if we're swimming around Milly, protecting her from all the terrors of the deep. Those terrors include both Bellfield and Surrey Police.

When we 'fish folk' talk on the telephone, we shall refer to each other strictly by our secret names. This way, if anyone is listening in, he or she will be none the wiser and probably think we're mad. That's fine by us. We probably are a bit mad. We've been driven to it.

The Shoal roll-call includes:

Gemma – Great White Shark
Mum – Snapper
Dad – Barracuda
Lovely Granny – Lionfish
Uncle Pete – Piranha
Auntie Jenny – Jawfish
Eileen Feeney – Electric Eel
Michelle Calvert – Manta Ray

Over the next months, we shall find other people we trust, and they, too, will be added to the Shoal roll. In writing and publishing this book, we also acquire a Viperfish, a Masked Butterfly Fish, a Leopard Shark, a Deadly Dragonfish, a Flying Fish, a North Pacific Daggerfish and a Lemon Shark, all important, energetic members of the Shoal that encircles Milly, taking loving care of her memory.

Mum's in no state to attend the next police meeting, which is at 6 p.m. on Wednesday, 27 May.

I go with Dad. On the way, I say to him, 'I'm petrified that they're going to tell us something else.'

Dad reassures me: 'No, darling, it's all over. There can't be anything else.'

At Surrey Police, it's the same two officers, as well as a woman who deals with the media.

As far as we know, Dad and I are here to discuss the press release, which we've brought with us.

But that notion is soon stopped in its tracks. We know they have something else to tell us. We can see it from the looks on their faces.

Bellfield has told his blonde policewomen that, when he did what he did to Milly, he had an accomplice.

77.

Milly was tortured by *two* men? My heart constricts. I stumble out of the room and I'm sick in the bathroom.

When I come back in, my first words are, 'Mum's going to kill herself.'

I hear the police saying that they don't know if it's true about the 'alleged accomplice'. They have only Bellfield's word for it – the word of a liar. He might be making it up in order to hurt our family some more, or to get attention for himself. That, they say, is one of the reasons why they didn't tell us until now. There are legal ramifications . . .

I'm thinking, *How does this add up with the fact that they now say they're corroborating Bellfield's disclosures against the records? And if Bellfield spoke the truth about all those hours he tortured Milly, why would he be lying about this other man?*

The policewoman tells us that they still have to investigate the man Bellfield has named. Information about him may be in the original files. She needs to find out if anything adds up and assess whether it's worthwhile to take steps against him.

Worthwhile?

I'm re-traumatized, but I'm no longer the trembling sixteen-year-old cowed by the police in the so-called 'safe house' back in April 2002. I've been to the place where Milly's body was dumped. I've sat through Milly's funeral. I've watched Milly's murderer convicted at the Old Bailey. I've had my say with David Cameron and Rupert Murdoch, and I wasn't afraid of either of them. More importantly, I've at last had proper therapy that is starting to bring me back to myself. Because of Michelle Calvert's work, I've just – sort of – survived hearing about what really happened to Milly.

Now I'm fearless with the police. For all their conflicting justifications, I know that they've been utterly wrong in withholding this information from us. I know that I'm right to demand the truth. I don't care what they say, or how they threaten. Unlike at the trial, I risk nothing by saying what I think now.

I demand to know everything about the accomplice Bellfield has named, starting with, 'Is he in prison?'

No, he's not. He's out walking the streets.

'Where does he live?'

They can't share that.

Dad's been silent with shock. Now, under the table, his leg goes into an involuntary spasm, which causes him to leap out of his seat. His face is contorted with pain and he's stamping his spasming leg. He looks wild. Even I think, *Bloody hell, what's he going to do next?*

When he speaks his mind, I'm proud of him.

Dad has abandoned his normal gentlemanly, reasonable tone. His voice is rough with fury. 'This is shit from on high,' he says. 'I don't *care* about the legal ramifications. You cannot imagine the mental distress this is causing *me* to look after Sally and Gemma. You *see* Gemma's situation.'

The policewoman apologizes over and over. I say it's not her fault. I want to speak to her superior. The woman says that *she* made the decision not to tell us, mostly based on Bellfield being a known liar.

'This is not a bombshell,' says Dad. '*This* is a nuclear explosion . . . And right now, it's not about whether there was an accomplice involved, it's about the fact that you didn't bloody tell us. How are we supposed to *deal* with that?'

I say that the police must tell Mum about the accomplice themselves. 'And the next time you meet with her, it will be in a psychiatric hospital. She has taken forty milligrams of diazepam today. *Forty milligrams.*'

Dad says that, in the horrific context, Bellfield's having an accomplice seems perfectly credible. 'I don't have any doubts about it. Whether it can be proved or not is almost not here or there. In the grand scheme of things, what it boils down to is the fact that we are now faced with this – it's like walking to the edge of a cliff and jumping off. Then we pick ourselves up, climb back to where we were, and get pushed off again.'

I interrupt, shouting, '*He* did the damage. Bellfield. *He* took her.

527

Almost fourteen years ago. So who is dealing with that now? There's a finger pointing at you now. It is you, all of you. It's been you, constantly, eleven times knocking on his flat door, and him meanwhile getting on with moving his stuff, burning his mattress.'

I look at the policewoman. 'And when you came in and said you had told us the truth, we sat in that office and we cried and we said, "Thank you for being honest," because no one has ever done that. And I let my guard down stupidly, again, thinking that I could trust you to do the right thing.'

The policewoman apologizes once more.

'This doesn't mean another trial?' I ask. Fear infects my voice, which is quieter now.

The policewoman yet again explains the difficulties presented by evidence given by Bellfield, murderer and liar.

'OK, let's go through my questions then,' I say icily.

But she can't answer them now. She reminds us that Bellfield does not respond to questions. He gives only snippets of information when he feels like it.

It's too much. I ask the police officers to leave the room for a moment. Dad and I need to be alone. They go.

'For God's sake,' Dad breathes.

'Oh, my God,' I sob simultaneously.

We're both thinking of Mum, and what this is going to do to her.

I say, 'You know that joint suicide pact Mum was on about –'

'No,' says Dad. 'No, no, no, no, not that.'

'Dad, this other man, that is the exact thing Mum was on about last week.'

'I know. I know. I know.'

With shaking hands, I search my handbag for the diazepam.

Dad's voice is quiet and drained of hope. 'What *was* she thinking of? What *was* she thinking of, not telling us last week?'

We have to finish this, I think. 'Get them back in,' I say to Dad.

Warily, the officers re-enter, looking, as they well might, as if they would rather be swimming with sharks than talking with me and Dad.

Dad says, 'Right. Can we just go back to the question I've asked twice now? Is there *anything* else? I warn you now. If anything else is disclosed, you are in for real shit, I tell you. I know it's your decision but at the end of the day there's a chain of command in place. I've been cataloguing all of this. Thirteen days we've been at this – thirteen days, and you drop this . . . For Christ's sake, why the hell did you take that decision to withhold that?'

We are, Dad tells her, worse off than we were a week ago.

The policewoman apologizes unreservedly. The decision to withhold certain information was hers alone. She takes responsibility for the impact that it's had on us. 'I got it wrong. I understand trust and confidence is crucial for your family.'

'Tell you what,' says Dad. 'There's a big hole in the floor and they both just dropped through there.'

She offers to explain to us how these disclosures came about: Bellfield contacted Surrey Police because he wanted to make admissions to other offences.

I think, *So this was not about a paedophile informing the police after all. Nothing seems stable. Everything we've heard is up for renegotiation. There is no such thing as a fact.*

The woman explains that officers went to see Bellfield in February.

Not December? I thought we'd been told it was December.

Bellfield did not fully admit to the other offences. He gave some disjointed accounts. It was only at the end of an interview in February, when the tapes were turned off, that he made the disclosures about Milly. The officers wrote it down in their notebooks.

Bellfield did not implicate the other man in Milly's abduction or her murder. According to Bellfield, the man came to the last house where Bellfield held Milly, later on the night when she was taken. Bellfield said the man helped him move and dispose of Milly's body.

Both Dad and I are furiously scribbling down this information.

So now the accomplice is not a malicious lie by Bellfield but a person they are taking seriously?

My head hurts, trying to fasten all these shifting facts and interpretations on to one coherent truth. The diazepam is starting to work on me, making everything a little distant.

'Did he rape Milly when she was dead?' I ask. I don't even know if I'm talking about Bellfield or the alleged accomplice, or both. Poor Dad flinches.

No, he didn't say that, the policewoman explains. 'That's the problem. He's just spoon-feeding *his* information.'

I point out, 'That's precisely what you're doing to us, isn't it?'

'He is saying that he disposed of her property – her bag, her shoes. He's saying that there would be evidence on Milly's skirt – DNA. He's saying, "You wouldn't find the skirt, because I burned it."'

Bellfield also seems to have said that the alleged accomplice helped him burn Milly's things.

'So whose semen is on the skirt?' I ask baldly.

It is Bellfield's. But Bellfield says that the accomplice also raped Milly while she was still alive, on the evening of 21 March.

'Was she drugged?' I ask. By now, I'm hoping that she was.

Bellfield has not disclosed that. And it cannot be established.

Dad says, 'So. Is that *it*? Is there anything else? I'm asking this as a final question.'

The alleged accomplice is known to them, she tells us. He featured in the original inquiry with regard to the disposal of the Daewoo Nexia, which, they suspect, ended up in a scrapyard. This policewoman wasn't involved in Operation Ruby. She's now 'assessing' what Surrey Police did in the original inquiry with regard to the alleged accomplice.

'There's no evidence then,' I say sadly. The words 'original inquiry' to me just mean incompetence and vital missed opportunities.

Dad says to the policewoman, 'God, I feel bloody sorry for you. This is the legacy of the appalling initial bloody investigation that your colleagues did.'

Suddenly I'm weeping like a child, screaming over and over again, 'Why did you lie?'

Nothing dulls Dad's rage. 'It's beyond incompetence. There's one fact that will never ever leave me. Eleven times your officers knocked on the door of that individual's flat. If your former colleagues had done anything like a proper job, two more girls would not have been brutally murdered.'

It was nearly three. I remind them of the attempted murder of Kate Sheedy, who almost died.

Dad talks about his conversations with Phil McDonnell, father of Marsha, Bellfield's next victim after Milly. Phil's told Dad that if Surrey Police had done a proper job with the investigation about

Milly, then his daughter would be alive. 'I have to agree with him,' Dad says.

I ask, 'Does the paedophile, the one Bellfield shared his story with, know about the accomplice he has named?'

He does know.

'No wonder you're shitting bricks about the press release,' Dad observes.

I add, 'And if you think we're letting you anywhere *near* our press statement, you can jog on. Because I have had enough.'

'I've got no idea how to just assimilate this,' says Dad. 'My wife is on the bloody edge.'

'She is,' I confirm. 'She's got nothing left.'

'It's like a piece of elastic that stretches for ever,' Dad is saying quietly. 'It never breaks.'

'It's never-ending,' I agree.

I tell them how proud I am of Dad. He is standing strong and he's found his voice. 'And you haven't even given him the honesty that we as a family deserve. That *Milly* deserves. Milly! You remember what this whole damn thing is about?'

I replay the hideous scenario of Milly's last hours, the account we have pieced together over the last two weeks. I add in the role of the alleged accomplice, graphically.

My voice rises, thickened with tears. 'I'm so sick to my core that I shared my thoughts about Milly with you. About her being there when the sunlight broke into the room. She's so special. And I shared that with you too. You don't deserve to hear about her.'

Dad puts his arm around me.

I say, 'Literally, this is going to kill Lovely Granny.'

There's a brief silence in the room.

Dad demands to know what is happening, if anything, with this information that the police have had all these months. The woman officer reiterates that she needs to look back in the deep paperwork and the database, because she herself was not involved in the initial inquiry.

'Then find someone who is,' I say simply.

'They've run away, haven't they?' Dad says, and I agree.

I name a few of our old persecutors high up in the force, the ones who, in the early days, refused to consider anyone but Dad as the person behind Milly's disappearance; the ones who failed to send dogs to the station, the ones who let the rental history of 24 Collingwood Place go unresearched, the ones who told us that the irrelevant incident of Dad's magazine would never come out in court and be used against him. I add sarcastically, 'You don't need to go back in the files. Just ring a newspaper. Try the *Sun*. They know the run of events.'

The mood changes. Dad and I become coldly business-like. We give them twenty-four hours to come back to us with an evidenced timeline now including the alleged accomplice.

The policewoman wants at least a week to look back into the old files, thoroughly and properly. Bellfield has given no lead apart from a name.

Dad says, 'Every day is like a lifetime. Do you know what? There isn't enough of a lifetime left for a couple of us.'

The policewoman repeats, 'This is all the information I have.'

Dad says, 'The hardest thing is that if we had not been driving this situation, and pushing you like billy-oh, which we have been, had we not been doing this, we'd have been sitting in six months' time and we'd still be getting things in dribs and drabs. The thing is, there isn't the time. We're already out of time *yesterday*.'

'What do you need?' the policewoman asks.

Dad and I want to meet her superior officer tomorrow. 'As an absolute minimum.'

Dad doesn't know if I will be strong enough.

'I am coming with you,' I say.

'Someone will be coming,' I tell the policewoman, 'and you'd better hope it's not Lovely Granny.'

I ask, 'What happens if we bring a lawyer tomorrow?' My voice is hard.

There's a police media adviser in the room. I apologize for what she's had to hear. She explains she thought she was attending this meeting to discuss the press release.

Dad slams our draft on the table.

'It's got to be changed now, though,' I say pointedly. '*When we wrote that, we didn't have all the information.*'

'So you can have that,' Dad says, 'and have a good long hard think about it.'

I say, 'Then you can type up every single thing Bellfield said, as well as that timeline. I want your names on it . . . I know what you guys are like. You'll play games and say, "Oh, no, that was never said." '

They flinch at that. An investigation into Surrey Police's handling of the press hacking is still rumbling on and is not looking good for the force.

Dad says, 'As a family, we have been the most compliant, helpful, understanding, resilient people, bearing up under all the pressures. We've tried to do the right thing. But the problem is that this is like a Pandora's box. You open the box and *nobody*'s ever going to close it. You can be sure of that.'

Yet again the policewoman tries to take responsibility.

'If that sits just on your shoulders, then that says something about your superiors,' remarks Dad. 'Milly is the biggest case that Surrey Police have ever had. And if people in a senior capacity were not fully involved in all aspects of this, then I really want to know why.

'It's been horrible enough to lose Milly, but in some sort of bizarre world I'm now seeing, it's not just that that's horrible, it's everything around it that has compounded that. None of it actually fits together in any way, shape or form that a normal human being can comprehend. I'm not a policeman. I'm a bloke in the street. I think I'm an intelligent bloke in the street, but I'm struggling. I've got a wife and daughter who are struggling on such a level that I'm struggling to help them.'

I say suddenly, 'I don't want to be here any more.'

I start sobbing. Dad looks at me with concern. 'We need to go, sweetheart. Can you gather yourself a bit? I'm going to take you home, darling.'

I want the police to drive Dad home. I'm worried about him crashing the car in the state he's in.

'No, Gemma,' he says, 'why would I want any of these people anywhere near our house?'

We walk to the car.

I know that we are still sliding downwards.

I know that there are no brakes.

78.

Dad drives us out of the police station, and immediately pulls in to a layby. Our thoughts are churning with the same fear: what will happen when we tell Mum that Bellfield says he had an accomplice? I phone Eileen Feeney to check the maximum dosage of diazepam Mum can have.

At home, Mum's first reaction is, 'I *knew* it. I just knew it. I'm not going mad. *Why* do they drip-feed us with poison? *Why* do they make it so much worse by contradicting and withholding? Lies – that's all it is. Why don't they just tell us the whole truth about our daughter and spare us all these ridiculous tortuous meetings with different stories each time?'

Then Mum breaks down and weeps. We hold her. We stroke her hair. We give her more diazepam. What she needs is one of Milly's Guttural Hugs, something she's never going to have again.

Mum's too distraught to come with us the next day when Dad and I go to the meeting at the Mount Browne headquarters with one of Surrey Police's top brass.

In the past hours, I have moved from anger to fear. Bellfield's alleged accomplice is roaming the streets. Maybe even the streets where I walk. I think, *Oh, yes, the police say he is now part of the investigation. This investigation that's gone so well for the last nearly fourteen years. The investigation that left Bellfield out there to keep killing for years.*

I've made some notes. Not for the police but for me, to try to keep myself together. Working on the book, I'm learning about the power of words. Just having my thoughts written down makes me feel – even though it's not true – as if I have some authority, some agency here. The notes are crackling in my handbag while I listen to the police and their limp, limited phrases.

What really matters is that Milly is at peace now but God it hurts to think what she had to go through. I actually genuinely thought I had considered the worst scenario after processing my fears with Michelle Calvert. I felt

Milly could now rest in peace. I had processed it and was able therefore to stop being continually haunted by these nightmares.

But no. Now I can't stop picturing that her capture, torture, rape, sexual abuse and the disposal of her body was done not only by one psychopathic murderer but there was also another man who went to Little Benty where she was locked in a cupboard and raped her too.

Nothing new comes out of this meeting, but Dad and I have a chance to say what we think to a Surrey Police officer who is higher up the food chain than the unfortunate woman the day before.

The next day we receive a four-page letter from Surrey Police. It's not an apology for the painful shambles of the last fortnight. It's about our desire to issue a press release. In the third paragraph, there's a sentence: *It is information from Bellfield and we are not able to say whether any of it is true.*

This is not the first time that the police have sought to undermine what Bellfield has said. But, in this context, we feel that there's a simple and directed motive for it: to discourage us from releasing the information.

Surrey Police state that they will absolutely not support our request to release the information.

Then come the warnings. If we put the information out there, we, our friends and family are likely to be harassed by the media, hurt by images we see on television, subject to social media trolling, liable for legal ramifications if the information leads to Bellfield being harmed. If we put the information out there, our lives will be scrutinized and commented on; 'information from the trial' (so they're *still* using that over Dad) might be dug up and aired again.

That last is a particularly low blow. To us, it shows their desperation to keep us quiet.

Patronizingly, the letter suggests that our feelings over time may change and that we may regret releasing information that 'may prevent another family or victim achieving justice'. Our press release may even stop Bellfield talking so other crimes may not be solved.

The list of reasons goes over into a third page. We're told that our press release might give pleasure to other paedophiles; that it might give more 'control and kudos' to Bellfield in prison; that the trial of the *News of the World*'s former editor Andy Coulson could be prejudiced and, indeed, that people across the country might be dissuaded from helping the police with their inquiries.

All these things, the police imply, would be our fault if we insist on releasing the information.

If we insist, however, it's suggested that the police press office could help us write an abbreviated release with no material details. If we don't agree to that, then the police will not support our press release or take a joint approach with us.

Twice, the letter threatens legal ramifications for us if we can be seen to incite harm to Bellfield.

Mum reads the letter aloud to us from her phone. She has to keep stopping and checking as she thinks she must be misreading it.

Whatever the merits or motives of this threatening letter, we have to address it. On 1 June, Snapper, Barracuda and Great White Shark sit down for a family meeting to try to discuss a way forward. Why do we have to sit in our lovely kitchen and have a meeting like this? It is so very toxic to us now, the old familiar police pressure about not saying anything to anyone, first with the murder and then again with the phone hacking. Same old, same old. 'This is highly sensitive. You can't say anything or it could prejudice the case. You can't talk about it on the phone.'

Meanwhile, we're considering having our home swept for bugs.

That afternoon, Alice delivers the four-page timeline. This at last is the piece of paper that shows how the police investigation, such as it was, corroborates Bellfield's revelations. Handing it over to Dad, round the corner at the end of our road, she asks him if he's had time to reflect on the letter from the Gold Group.

Dad says, 'Yes. And we are not prepared to make any comment on it.'

We all read the timeline. The facts march across the page. They are only words, but they have such power. Our heads are spinning with unbearable images. We see and feel Milly's pain. We hear her words again. We remember again what we, in our desperation and ignorance, were doing during the hours of Milly's ordeal.

And, as things stand, a released paedophile can still sell this story to a newspaper at any time. At any time we could see the newsagent's racks filled with these facts, illustrated with photos of Bellfield and Milly, side by side again.

It's a very long, hard meeting at our kitchen table. Finally, I have an idea – what about asking Dominic Crossley, the lawyer who looked after the Core Participants, including us, during Leveson?

'Brilliant!' says Mum. We all like and trust Dominic. We know we can talk to him.

Dad and I telephone Dominic. Mum can't even be in the room for the call. She runs into the garden to wait it out. There's hope on her face when we come out to tell her Dominic has immediately agreed to help us and on a pro-bono basis.

The following day, Dad and I have a two-hour meeting with Dominic. Now fully briefed, he writes to Surrey Police. He tells them that his firm is instructed to represent our family and that all further communications from Surrey Police are to be addressed to him. He tells them that our trust and confidence in the force have all but disappeared. He makes them aware that recent correspondence and meetings with officers from Surrey Police have caused enormous and unnecessary distress and harm.

Dominic then tackles the threatening letter. He points out that the police have not apologized for exacerbating our deep and on-going pain by the way in which the disclosures have been provided to us. He concludes, 'It is our view that your letter is seriously misjudged.'

We love Dominic's use of understatement. Mum consults the fish ID book for a suitable name. Dominic becomes 'Deadly Dragonfish'.

Dominic tells the police that we are determined to ensure that the key Bellfield disclosures are placed in the public domain by the family and/or by a formal police statement before they inevitably enter it via Bellfield himself or the prisoners he has confided in. Dominic adds, 'The thought of an accomplice not being brought to justice as quickly as possible is extremely worrying for our clients.'

As a way forward, Dominic suggests a meeting with Surrey Police, an apology for the way the disclosures have been handled, an agreement that we shall receive full details of Bellfield's statements and also information concerning the current investigation into the new evidence he has provided, and any new disclosures, as well as details of the investigation into the accomplice he has named.

In the middle of these negotiations, we receive a letter from a TV company to say that a documentary about Bellfield will be screened on 24 June. It is called *Born to Kill*.

It's horrible. Yet it's the least of our worries now.

On Tuesday, 16 June, we receive Surrey Police's reply to Dominic's letter. It basically says nothing.

The trouble is, all this police drama is getting in the way of what really matters. In our re-traumatized state, Mum's processing with Michelle threatens to come undone, as she cannot tear her thoughts away from the violence Bellfield used on Milly. Her mind is filled with unbearable images. Mum cannot stop thinking about the pain, the perverted torture Milly suffered. At least this time she and I have Michelle to help us process what we've been told.

Yet no matter how much we process it, one detail will not go away. The fact that has wrecked us above all others is Bellfield saying that there were two of them. At least one of his girlfriends has revealed in interviews that Bellfield's special way of degrading them was to call in a friend or two to rape them.

Bellfield liked to keep his friends close, and he liked to operate in his own well-known manor. So that person who also abused Milly is still walking the streets, no doubt our streets.

It is like my old nightmare in which the man who hurt Milly is lurking nearby, and can help himself to me, too, at any time.

79

I can't be Hannah's bridesmaid in Menorca. Sorry, Milly.

xxxx Gemsie

We settle back into police time. We keep being reminded that Bell-field's revelations are part of a bigger investigation across several forces, coordinated by the Met. We're given deadlines by which we will have answers. We're told that the alleged accomplice will be arrested. On that understanding – that something will actually be done – we bide our time and hold on for answers.

The months drag on.

Instead of going to Hannah Mac's wedding, I have intense EMDR therapy with Michelle. Hannah sends a wedding video made just for us. At the end, the camera homes in on her closed hand. Hannah opens it, and there is Milly's special pebble with the heart on it.

There are so many things I have to process now. As they are for Mum, the images of Milly in Bellfield's power are very detailed in my mind. It takes hours and days of therapy to assimilate each one. I'm feverish all the time. Mum's just as bad.

We are getting nowhere with Surrey Police. No doubt they feel the same about us.

Dominic, Dad and I attend a series of frustrating and seemingly pointless meetings at which we try but fail to explain that our family cannot live with the prospect of the new information about Milly entering the public domain at an unknown date via Bellfield himself or via the prisoners to whom he has boasted.

Dominic is working on one other request: we want an assurance from Surrey Police that they will not speak to Bellfield again about Milly. We've told Dominic we don't want him enjoying any more of his porno-chats with the female officers he gets on demand. We want Milly as far away from him as possible.

We have told the truth of her last hours to the people who 'need' to know, the ones who cherish true memories of Milly, and who need to be saved from the misery of wondering what happened to her – even if the truth is worse than anything any of us could have imagined.

After long, painful talks with the people we trust, Mum, Dad and I finally agree that, for the moment, the press release is not the way forward. We will try to trust the police to deal properly with the accomplice Bellfield named. A wave of relief breaks over us. We can stop these bruising and demoralizing encounters with the police. We can focus on Milly and our healing.

The police at last release a document so that Mum and I can work through our re-traumatization. Unfortunately, it's not as simple as that. The new document's not consistent with what we've been told already. We discover new aspects to Bellfield's admissions. For example, he has mentioned Milly's ace of spades purse.

For years I had forgotten about that little purse. Bellfield's mention of it makes his admissions real and three-dimensional to us. And I suddenly feel like a terrible sister because I had forgotten about that purse and now it's Milly's murderer who has reminded me about it.

Other things have gone from the document, like Milly's words that Mum and Dad don't have much money. So we have little confidence that this account is complete. But it's all that we have, and Michelle starts helping us process it.

Meanwhile, Surrey Police are back in the news because of a trial at the Old Bailey, in which it's revealed that an officer of the force sold tips to the *Sun* over many years – including information about the investigation into Milly's disappearance.

The weeks go past. Then the months. Dominic, bless him, keeps up relentless pressure on the police, but there is still no sign of an arrest of the alleged accomplice. We have still not been told his name.

We were first informed about him in May. Now it's October. The police don't seem to take seriously, or perhaps don't care, that our cooperation was based on an understanding that they would do something about the intolerable situation with the accomplice Bellfield named. Every day that goes past might be the one in which a paedophile briefed by Bellfield sells Milly's story to a newspaper.

We're not sleeping. We're not eating. My sense of purpose is dissolving. I can't write. I can't even *remember* Milly and our once-happy family life, let alone put it on the page. I'm losing my chance to do something for Milly and for our family. Michelle and Eileen are keeping me and Mum alive by monumental efforts. We only really feel safe in their presence. Poor Michelle – we're draining her alive. She gives and gives, with her habitual grace and energy. We have no right to ask so much from her, and we are acutely aware of it.

We request a meeting with the Metropolitan Police. On 15 October we get a note from Dominic to say that the relevant officer is fully booked up until mid-November. But he would be prepared to see us one evening the following week. This would be simply for him to introduce himself to us – and not an opportunity for us to grill him.

We decide it's time to go over the heads of the police. We want to meet Theresa May, then the home secretary, whose responsibilities include the police. On 19 October, Mum sends her an email.

Dear Rt Hon Theresa May

A few months ago we received some extremely disturbing news from Surrey Police regarding the murder of Milly. The news is quite possibly the worst news anyone could ever be given about their daughter or sister. We are a family who have suffered for far too long under the scrutiny of the public eye as we are sure you are aware. We more than complied with the previous police investigation, and the subsequent legal trial. The recently disclosed information is of such a sensitive nature that we cannot write it down for fear of the press finding out. This has tested us to breaking point. We have now lost all faith and confidence in the ability of Surrey Police to investigate this new information.

We are appealing to you as a desperate heartbroken family. We are at our wits' end and do not know who else to turn to for assistance. Please can we request a personal meeting to discuss this matter as soon as possible.

Yours sincerely

Sally, Bob and Gemma Dowler

The response is very prompt. We're invited to see Theresa May on 22 October. The appointment is fixed for early evening to avoid any unwanted attention.

For the meeting, we have an agenda of ten items. But, first, we need to tell Theresa May about the last fourteen hours of Milly's life. We have composed our own script – as full a sequence of events as we've been able to glean from Surrey Police. In a room at the Home Office, Mum reads out the words. Apart from her steady voice, there's absolute silence in the room.

Theresa May has tears in her eyes by the time Mum finishes. We can feel her empathy and shock. We don't give her time to recover before moving on to a summary of the past six months. We explain the torture of being drip-fed the information. We explain the contradictions and outright lies. We tell her of our terror about the accomplice Bellfield named. We show her the threatening letter from Surrey Police.

We've also brought two photographs. One shows me and Mum a year before – healthy, glowing and getting on with our lives. The other shows us as we are now – sick-looking waifs with shadows under our eyes. Mum and I have lost fourteen kilos between us, weight we couldn't afford to lose.

Theresa May wants to know what she can do to help us.

We ask the home secretary to 'encourage' Surrey Police to release a statement about Bellfield and to arrest the alleged accomplice. She promises to do something. We leave satisfied that we have taken our case to the highest authority. I feel I've done all that can be done for Milly.

There is an immediate change of attitude at Surrey Police. Something, they assure us, is going to be done *very soon* about the accomplice Bellfield named.

Police time and Dowler time are very different, of course. So more weeks drag on.

The meeting with the home secretary has given us some heart, however. I decide it's time to get on with this book. Bellfield's revelations have made it all the more vital to tell our own story. So I prepare a PowerPoint presentation. I explain exactly what I want to say about Milly, about policing, about the justice system, about certain sectors of the press, about mental health.

I want the book to recreate the real Milly for a world that knows her only as a ghost-face, as the pretty young schoolgirl who was first missing, then murdered, then hacked. I want to replace 'Tragic Milly Dowler' with the amazing girl who was known and adored by so many people. So I go back to our family photograph albums, and to the memories Michelle has made safe again, to create a faithful portrait in words and images of the sister I loved.

When it's finished, I show my PowerPoint to Mum and Dad. They cry. But there are tears of relief too. Together, we make some adjustments. We show it to my literary agent, Victoria. She cries. So I know it's ready. We decide to show this confidential material to just one trusted publisher. The material is explosive, and we want it to stay under the radar until the book is finished. We don't want to be hacked again or second-guessed by the press. This is our story and we want to be allowed to tell it in the right way and in our own time.

So Victoria takes me to Michael Joseph, an imprint of Penguin, and I give my PowerPoint presentation. By the next day, I have a book deal.

I write a letter:

Dear Milly,

This is the first time I have written to you in years and years. I'm so sorry I haven't been in touch. I have been holding on to the tiniest glimmer of hope that you were still out there somewhere. He has told us what he did to you. My darling Milly, you must have been so scared. You were so brave, I know you would have been as you were always more brave than I was.

My sweetheart, I can't believe he did that to you. I want to ask you lots of questions about what happened to you, and where you disassociated. I hope your soul left your body when he turned left to take you to Hanworth. I think you carried on going straight and came home to us.

I'm so sorry that I'm holding you back from the freedom of this earth to the next place. I'm working really hard to try and get to you. I need to fully accept that you are gone. This is the hardest thing I have ever done. I was so young when I lost you, and as we both know although you were the younger you were more mature than I was.

I'm going to write a book, to describe the whole story of this tragedy. Milly I love you so much, I really miss you more than words can describe.

You had so much of your life to live. He took that from you and he has stopped me for nearly fourteen years as well.

I have had to try really, really hard to keep the pressure on the police to tell us what happened or what Bellfield says happened. I know that we will never have the whole story as you are the only one that knows the true details. Maybe one day, when I die, you will be able to tell me, and we shall dance in the fields of gold together.

Another year without Milly is about to begin. It is 2016. If she had been allowed to live, Milly would have reached the age of twenty-eight.

The man Bellfield named as his accomplice is still out on the streets.

80.

I don't want it to be my thirtieth birthday. But on 16 January, that's just what it will be. I can't bear to turn thirty still suffering from the fear that there's a man out there, in our own neighbourhood, who, Bellfield says, was involved in Milly's rape and torture, and in disposing of her naked body in a forest.

I have a little mantra in which I ask for Milly's forgiveness. I gaze at the photograph of the two of us as children in our sailor dresses, as if it's an icon, a picture with a special power. I ask Milly if it will be all right to celebrate my birthday in the middle of all these new events. I want her to tell me that it's OK to be alive when she is not, and that marking my thirtieth birthday – my fourteenth without her – will not make me any less of a loving sister or erase the pain of losing her.

I remember what Milly said to the Canadian boys in Cuba, just three months before she was taken: 'If you want to remember me, look at the sky. We will be seeing the same stars.'

So stars, and sparkling, will be the theme of my birthday party.

When Milly was still with us, the best part of birthdays or big nights out was always the getting ready, doing our make-up, trying on dresses, mutual surveillance of VPL or fake-tan streaks and a zero-tolerance policy on hair disasters. Milly was nothing if not frank about these things. As the party date approaches, I keep thinking about the fact that I won't have Milly to rule if my hair would look better down or up. She won't be making sure that the height of my heels is perfectly calibrated with the length of the skirt. If Milly were here with me, we would have had numerous dress rehearsals for our outfits. Milly would have been going for the Total Black, and shouting, 'More eyeliner!'

I cannot get away from the heart-breaking thought that Milly will not be there, working on dance routines, choosing the music, customizing the lighting scheme, decorating the cake. We should at this very minute be arguing about stupid little details. I should end up saying, as I always used to say, 'Hey! It's *my* party!'

My birthday approaches – in tandem with the long-delayed arrest of the accomplice that Bellfield has named in his confession. I want both things to come, and I also dread them.

The police are still warning us that our private lives will be offered up for scrutiny again once the arrest is made. We have been held for ransom too long over that. We're not falling for it again.

Finally the police tell us that, after thirteen months, the arrest has been scheduled. For my birthday. The arrest is what I want more than anything. Yet it's also what I desperately don't want to happen on the day of my party, which will be at Mum and Dad's house. I don't want my guests having to walk through the press to get to the front door. Mum's determined we shall have one day out of all the horror. We shall mark this milestone in my life with joy, not with fear and speculation about what's going on behind the scenes at Surrey Police headquarters. It feels by now that a part of my mind simply lives in those ugly corridors.

Following a quiet word from Dominic, the police agree to delay the arrest. Unfortunately it's not for one day, which is all we ask. Instead they say they will delay it for an unspecified period. Peace on my birthday is going to cost us.

Mum makes a cake. We decorate with lights. There's a bar area and a buffet. The garden is even more of a fairy tale than usual. We dress up in our finery. I've gone for Milly-style black, but with a sparkle – an awful lot of sparkle. Mum's sleek in black too, in a sophisticated flapper-style dress, which Milly would definitely have condemned as 'revampy'.

The guests arrive. The corners fill with beautifully wrapped gifts. The house fills with life and laughter. Milly's and my favourite music is playing on the sound system – Shania Twain, Spice Girls, S Club 7. Mum, Dad, Singing Uncle Pete and I have put together a little routine. We're playing, singing and dancing 'I Wanna Be Like You' from *The Jungle Book* film.

Mum has ordered herself a wireless microphone headset so she can move around and dance freely. Her performance consists of vigorous orangutan impressions, which have everyone helpless with laughter. Mum's the Queen of the Swingers, the Jungle VIP.

She shimmies, swings her arms, makes monkey hoots, plays the air harmonica and mimes playing the saxophone. *'I wanna be like you hoo-hoo!'*

I grab a microphone to sing Milly's old favourites, 'Spice Up Your Life' and 'Don't Stop Movin''.

Milly's here with us for one brief night, dancing too.

When I wake up the next morning, the arrest of the alleged accomplice is the only thing on my mind. Not just his arrest but how it's handled. I'm so afraid that the arrest will lead to nothing.

We are now informed that it will be taking place in the week commencing 21 January. They won't tell us which day. The police also tell Dominic that a journalist is in possession of some information regarding the recent disclosures.

I am wondering, *How? Could it have come from the police? Could it have come from one of the prisoners that Bellfield told? Is someone in the prison contacting the press on the outside?*

All these possibilities rage through our minds. Inevitably we begin to wonder if the press are hacking our phones again. The police inform us that the journalist has been told not to report anything because of the ongoing investigation and will receive a personal briefing in due course.

There does not seem to be any decent way that the information could have got to the newspaper. Yet, in a seeming reward, *the police are going to give it an exclusive?*

I stay at my parents' house. I've regressed to the state where I cannot be at home on my own. The stress is getting worse and worse. Eight months have now passed since we heard what Bellfield disclosed about Milly. The tension is horribly visible on all our faces. We have continued to lose weight. We've reverted to antidepressants. In spite of heavy medication, we are all sleep-deprived. I shout a lot. Mum cries a lot. Dad turns away a lot. We argue over the silliest of things.

Remember our family at the beginning of this book? Our family in the Christmas 2001 video, laughing, talking, joking and teasing round the table in Cuba? With everyone at ease, and everyone having their own special role? We are not that family any more. It is not just that we're missing Milly. Each of us has lost a part of ourselves. We've also lost the security and confidence that used to mark us out, which we once took for granted.

Dominic phones to say the police will not use Bellfield's name in any press release. This is because he is an informant. And informants have to be protected.

This is a step too far for Mum.

It's now that I clearly see the anger and pain she has been holding in. That morning, Mum has a panic attack that lasts two and a half hours. Anyone who's ever had a panic attack knows how harrowing it is. You fight for breath. You think it cannot possibly go on. Most attacks are mercifully brief, though they seem to last an eternity. Imagine feeling like that for two and a half hours.

I decide to video Mum's panic attack. I want to show Dominic what is happening to her. There's also a crazy thought in my mind that I shall show my mother's suffering to the police. It might be the only way to make them understand the agony they're causing by delaying the arrest of the named accomplice and keeping us muzzled.

The footage is harrowing. Mum's wrapped up in her home-knitted fish blanket, the one she made at the trial. She's pacing, screaming at invisible police. I think she's hallucinating that they are in the room with her. 'Do you see what you are doing to us? . . . *You* are the ones who are tearing us apart!'

Mum's behaving like an inconsolable child, so I offer her child comforts. I bring Taily Ted down from my room so she has something to cuddle. Mum weeps. 'My head, Gemsie, my head. It hurts so much. The pain never goes away.'

I bring her a cup of builders' tea and try to make her drink it. She eventually stops screaming, but it hurts to see the suffering on her wet, exhausted face.

When Dad gets home and sees Mum like this, his quiet, measured voice becomes powerful. He says, 'Enough is enough. I can't sit around and let this happen again to our family.'

We're not the only family involved, of course. So we ask the police to warn the families of Bellfield's other victims about what's coming. But we're afraid they won't. I can't find Kate Sheedy's number.

I have to leave it to the police. Later, when I find a way to contact her about this book, she tells me she wasn't warned. Sorry, Kate.

Dad arranges to meet with the McDonnell family to let them know personally.

I'm struggling to deal with the fact that, if the arrest goes ahead, I am sure the alleged accomplice will be let off the hook. The police don't exactly seem to be throwing their energies into investigating him. If they are, they're not telling us about it.

Lovely Granny is eighty-one this year. She's getting an hour's sleep at night because she's so worried about us. How can she survive more of this? I love Lovely Granny and I need her to be here. I want her to see me accomplish something in my life.

The waiting is destroying us. It feels as if we are waiting for them to find Milly's body again. It feels as if Milly has gone missing again and that we are still trying to find her. She's not at peace in the beautiful secret place where we scattered her ashes. Her death is in constant, cruel replay in our minds.

I keep remembering what the Hawkers said. It takes three and a half minutes to strangle someone to death.

At home, I desperately search on the internet for breaking news. There's nothing.

81.

Finally, on 27 January, the police arrest the man that Bellfield has named as his accomplice. In dawn raids, they also arrest five other members of Bellfield's gang from the old days of his long and unobstructed reign of terror in Surrey.

After ten hours, the police let the alleged accomplice go, claiming there's no evidence beyond what Bellfield has said.

I always knew this would happen. I think, *The police did not want to look deeply into the past. They wanted to put a lid on it. I just didn't think it would be quite so quick. At least, I realize, these six individuals now know that their former leader is a grass.*

But the whole thing seems token. It has taken place without actually addressing the confession and its full implications. If we had not been to see the home secretary, it probably wouldn't have happened at all.

Then the police issue *their* press release. Over the past months, since they first promised us an arrest, they've devoted a lot of time to various versions of what they were prepared to say. We have been almost speechless that they were crafting alternative drafts instead of arresting named accomplices or conducting any visible investigation. They use the version they prepared for the case of arrest with no further charges. They say simply that Bellfield has confessed to the abduction, rape and murder of Milly Dowler. There are no details of her long ordeal or the journeys she was forced to make. It seems to us that this press release was the only one that was ever destined for publication by the police.

At least they use Bellfield's name after all.

A small contribution from us is added at the end: *The effect of this information has been devastating for a family which has already had to endure so much.*

As is appropriate to their watered-down and long-delayed action, the police press release has just made everything more obscure. Some people are mystified as to why the police have said anything at all. Everybody already knows that Bellfield killed Milly. He was convicted of it at the Old Bailey.

So his confession is not a shock. The mention of rape is new. Yet, as Bellfield's methods with women have been well publicized, no one is surprised about that either. The mention of the alleged accomplice, which so tortures us, is so played down by the police as to amount to nothing that you could put your finger on. We wonder if journalists have also been warned of possible 'legal ramifications' if they write about the unnamed man.

There's bare mention of how long Milly's family or the police have known about Bellfield's disclosures. Of course, it wouldn't look particularly good for the police to be seen to have sat on such information for more than a year without acting.

There is hardly any coverage of the alleged accomplice in the news. The arrest has been successfully stage-managed so that no questions revolve back on the police.

Surrey Police have nothing else to say. The only person the press can interview is Colin Sutton, the former Metropolitan Police detective who caught Bellfield for the killings of Amélie and Marsha and who passed on the information to Surrey Police that the killer lived at Collingwood Place at the time Milly was taken. Without Colin Sutton, we think we'd probably never have known who murdered Milly.

Colin Sutton is shocked that Bellfield has spoken. Like Mum when she first heard, he thinks the first question that should be asked is *why* the murderer has supplied these details. He states that Bellfield is a very controlling man who never does anything unless he stands to gain by it. Sutton suggests that one reason for this timing may be that Bellfield is trying to present himself as showing remorse in case the law changes and allows him parole on the basis of having made a confession.

Colin Sutton thinks that Bellfield may have more to say.

We are not at peace. As Colin Sutton has suggested, the token arrest and the incompleteness of the police press release have left us vulnerable to further revelations. We know at least one journalist is looking deeper into the story.

There will be other reporters left less than satisfied with the way that Bellfield's crimes have been sketched out so briefly. There will be someone who notices that the named accomplice has been let off after what must seem a very cursory investigation. Then there's Bellfield's fellow paedophile with a big story to sell. Is he making contact with the press?

I think of all the things that the press have revealed to us about Bellfield's life in prison. I think about the way Milly's family is living now. I write in my diary:

This is England 2016

> *A prisoner who has three life sentences is allowed the following:*
> *PROTECTION and COMPENSATION if harmed*
> *TO HAVE SKY TV*
> *TO HAVE POCKET MONEY*
> *TO CHANGE HIS RELIGION TO ISLAM when his actions show that he is a man who believes in nothing except what he wants. Even his sister thinks this conversion was pragmatic and self-serving. She has told an interviewer he likes the Muslim prisoners' body oil.*
> *TO HAVE HIS NAME CHANGED BY DEED POLL AT TAXPAYERS' COST.*
> *TO BE ALLOWED TO MIX WITH OTHER CHILD-KILLERS AND MURDERERS and, as his confession shows, be allowed to brag graphically about the ways he raped my sister.*
> *TO BE ALLOWED ACCESS TO HUGELY EXPENSIVE LEGAL BOOKS, SO THAT HE CAN LEARN HOW TO PLAY THE SYSTEM. Of course, he doesn't have to work for a living any more, so he can spend as much time as he likes, at the taxpayers' expense, learning how to outwit the police.*
> *TO BE ALLOWED ACCESS TO LEGAL AID. By the time Milly's trial was over, we heard his defence had spent nearly a million pounds of the taxpayers' money. Our defence team told us that his side was procrastinating, because they were dumping costs on the state. I've been told that his team spent six times what was spent on the prosecution.*
> *TO BE ALLOWED TO SPEAK TO ONLY BLONDE POLICE OFFICERS.*
> *TO HAVE ACCESS TO A PEN AND PAPER AND A COMPUTER.*

TO HAVE HIS SAFETY CONSTANTLY MONITORED.
TO HAVE VISITS FROM HIS FAMILY.

Because of Bellfield, Mum won't be allowed visits from her younger daughter ever again.

We decide that what the police have done is not enough.

Two weeks after the arrests, we issue a press release of our own.

Why do we do it? Why do we ourselves not leave Milly in peace?

We do it because we want to touch the bottom.

Yes, it is a horrible choice to make. But why should we, who loved Milly the most, be burdened with keeping a festering secret? Why should we protect Bellfield with our compliance, our silence? Why should we, of all people, do what Bellfield wants?

I believe his disclosures are the truth. So do Dad and Mum.

As a family, we feel that the truth should be told.

We do it because we need to show just how evil and disgusting Bellfield is.

We do it because we have now suffered nearly fourteen years of fear and uncertainty. The police are supposed to protect the decent in society. Over the last year, we have been treated carelessly once too often.

We do it because we don't want to be taken by surprise when a paedophile sells his story to the press. If it comes from us, the information will come from the right place. We need to put Milly in a safe place where no one can attack her dignity again. If it comes from us, we believe that the press and the public will treat it with respect.

We trust the public. We know so much about the good side of the public. We have seen an entire community cry for us, help us, search for Milly, care for us, mourn for Milly. So many people have shown us – and Milly – love and respect.

We work hard on what we're going to tell them in our press release. We take professional advice. We decide what to include, and what to leave out, always thinking of Milly's dignity. Some of her words we keep to ourselves, as well as certain other details that might give pleasure to paedophiles or ghouls.

At last, our final draft is ready.

We don't tell Surrey Police what we're going to do. We don't need to hear all their stale threats again. They had their chance to do the right thing. Now it's ours.

Milly stands invisibly beside us when we sign that press release. You would not see her, but you need to know she was with us.

Emeli Sandé's song 'Read All About It' seems to tell our exact story. She sings,

> You've got the words to change a nation,
> But you're biting your tongue . . .
> You've got a heart as loud as lightning . . .
> So why let your voice be tamed?

82.

This is what we say:

Last month it was reported that Levi Bellfield had confessed to the police that he had abducted, raped and murdered Milly. It was the first time in thirteen years that Bellfield had actually made any admission to the police, previously having only ever said 'no comment'.

We feel we need to say something in addition to the information that has already been made public, as we do not think what has been revealed reflects the true heinousness of this man.

In May 2015 – nearly nine months ago – we were informed that Bellfield had requested to speak to Surrey Police about Milly. He made it clear to police that he would only speak to female police officers. Bellfield provided the officers with a harrowing account of Milly's final fourteen hours, giving details of her abduction, repeated rape, torture and then finally how he murdered her.

The reason we were told this information last May was because previously Bellfield had shared the information with other prison inmates and one of them was due to be released. This meant there was a risk that this information could be made public without us knowing about it.

Bellfield told the police that after abducting Milly and assaulting her at his flat a few yards from Walton Station, he then drove her to his mother's house. He reversed down a long driveway and then raped her in broad daylight over the boot of his car. Bellfield then moved her to another location, where the rape and torture continued for a number of hours, until the next day when he finally strangled her to death.

A few days after hearing this harrowing information from Surrey Police, they revealed to us that they were also investigating an alleged accomplice involved in the abduction and rape of Milly. Hearing Bellfield's account of how Milly spent her final hours before being murdered was shocking enough, but the news that there could have been another individual involved was devastating.

There are no words to describe the additional torment and pain we have been going through since we were told this information. We had to remain silent for eight months whilst the police conducted their investigation. Finally, when they made the arrest of the suspected accomplice, the person was questioned and released without charge in less than ten hours as there was no evidence found. Given it is now over thirteen years since Milly was murdered, the likelihood of obtaining evidence was very slim.

The pressure this has put us under as a family has been unimaginable and has taken its toll on all of us. We have had to fight every step of the way to get this far. In desperation last October we wrote to the Home Secretary to tell her of our concerns, and she met with us immediately.

Now we know the final hours of Milly's life, perhaps her soul, at long last, can finally rest in peace. The general public has always played a huge part in supporting us, for which we are eternally grateful and thankful. We believe that they should know what Bellfield did to our beautiful daughter and sister Milly.

Although we know that Bellfield will rot in jail for the rest of his life, we question how he can be allowed to 'call the shots' from his prison cell with legal representation paid for by the taxpayers' money.

In response to our press release, the police have only this to say to reporters:

The force has been in regular contact with the Dowler family during this investigation into the circumstances surrounding Milly's murder. We recognize this continues to be extremely distressing and our thoughts remain with them.

Meanwhile something lovely is happening.

Even in the wake of the police's first stunted announcement, the press did *not* indulge in a gruesome feeding frenzy about Milly. The vast majority of the press behaved like ladies and gentlemen of judgement and conscience.

And now that – thanks to our press release – they know a great deal more, they still keep on the right side of decent, even when reporting something that is horrific and obscene. It is possible, I guess, that they are simply shocked.

The media *do not* revel in salacious detail. They express

sympathy and respect for our family and compassion for Milly's final agony. They express their contempt for Bellfield.

The *Daily Mail* headlines, 'Coward who made Milly's family wait 14 years for a confession.' The *Sun* goes for 'FIEND FINALLY CONFESSES'.

The *Guardian* writes, 'Dowlers reveal Milly's horrific final hours.' The *Mirror* echoes our own wish: 'Perhaps at long last Milly's soul can now rest in peace.'

The other papers write similar headlines. Some print our press release in full. No one sensationalizes it. No one needs to.

Some papers pick up on what we left unsaid between our lines. The *Daily Mail* asks, 'Did police pander to a psychopath?' They quote Colin Sutton as saying that Bellfield should not have been allowed to dictate the terms of his confession and that Surrey Police should not have pandered to his ego and fantasies. 'It is typical of Bellfield to try to control everything. He probably thought "I can manipulate this situation better with female officers. I can make them squirm with what I say."'

The *Daily Telegraph* headlines, 'Milly family's agony over police delay.' They, too, interview Colin Sutton. 'My reading of their statement is that they feel they were only told about Bellfield's confession because of the cellmate's imminent release, and I find that surprising, because normally whatever information you've got, you pass on to the family.' He also warns, 'Everything Bellfield does is for his own interests. He will be enjoying inflicting more pain on the Dowler family and he will be enjoying the attention he is getting.'

All the papers speak of the urgent need to fully investigate the many other crimes that seem to lead to Bellfield's prison door. Attacks, both sexual and violent, on a long list of women, are brought up again, as they were after the two murder trials. Nine police forces are now looking into historical cases. Again, it's widely publicized that Bellfield was part of a gang that drugged and raped young girls.

We are pleasantly surprised by the kindness shown to us personally by the press. We have asked to be left alone, with Dominic contacting IPSO to insist on protection from harassment. It works. Nobody doorsteps us at home. Nobody tries to call us.

It seems as if the press have finally realized that Milly and our family have suffered enough. At last, it appears that the sexual torture of a thirteen-year-old girl is no longer considered a suitable subject for headlines.

The only thing the press get wrong is that some papers continue to put Milly's face next to Bellfield's. We don't want to see his face. Does *anyone* want to see that face? It's shut away in prison for ever now. I hope it stays off the pages of newspapers from this day forward.

Another interesting thing for us is how, in leaving *us* alone, the press now subject Bellfield's family to the kind of scrutiny previously reserved for us. The driveway of his mother's home is besieged by the press. It is photographed for the papers.

Something has been learned. Some of it can be attributed to sheer revulsion and outrage about what happened. Some has been learned, I think, via the closure of a whole newspaper, via trials for hacking, via press men and women seeing their colleagues go to prison.

At last, something has been learned, something like respect for my sister's memory.

Meanwhile our press release clearly rattles Bellfield's comfortable cage. He has enlisted the help of a solicitor. We're sad but not amazed to see that she's a beautiful young woman. We wonder who's paying her fees. Two days after our statement, she writes to Surrey Police about the 'alleged confession'. She says that Bellfield 'continues to deny any involvement in the murder'.

It seems to us that he's making an uncharacteristic mistake. He denies making a confession but at the same time claims that the police must have used hidden microphones when interviewing him. In other words, what those poor women police officers wrote down must be so close to perfect that Bellfield believes they recorded it. He wants to hear the tapes of these interviews. However – as he knows, as the police know, and as we know – he made sure that there were no such tapes. It's a typical Bellfield case of bitter smoke and ugly mirrors.

As usual, Bellfield finds ways to communicate, ways that he should not be allowed. A letter from him is printed in a newspaper.

Bellfield claims to be surprised and disappointed that Surrey Police broke the story about Milly. Citing the Police and Criminal Evidence Act 1984, he states that he has technically made no admissions to murder.

He also complains that Surrey Police 'can release such appalling information so publicly with no thought to the victims' families, and my family, who are innocent parties caught in the crossfire'.

So now Bellfield is blaming the police for making our family miserable? You can imagine the kind of comments the Shoal makes around the kitchen table.

Surrey Police issue a new press release to say that the force stands by its original statement of 27 January. The force acknowledges that it has received a letter from Bellfield's lawyer, adding, 'It will be considered in the same way as any other piece of correspondence.'

83.

Dear Milly, it's fourteen years since I last hugged you.

*xxx*x *Gemsie*

There has never been a good 21 March for our family since Milly was taken. But 2016 is one of the better ones. By now we've had almost a year to process what Bellfield said he did to my sister.

This 21 March, we decide to give Milly's memory a beautiful day. We want to bring back her life, not her death. For example, Milly's saxophone has come down from the loft. There was a time when I could not bear to see the brass keys Milly's fingers had touched. Now I can. We all can. So the sax is in the lounge, polished to a gleam, with one of her favourite pieces of music, 'Nobody Does It Better', beside it, as well as a photo of Milly playing.

Standing in front of the sax, Dad says, 'This is the first time I've felt Milly back in this house since she disappeared.'

Mum hugs him.

'It has brought the music back to her, and us,' he says wonderingly. 'It isn't painful any more.'

Soon after, Dad comes over to my house for a cuppa. Until now he's never been able to look at Mum's videos of our last Christmas in Cuba and Mexico. I've been watching them to help me write the first chapters of this book. I decide that it's time he saw them too. He doesn't put up a fight.

'Look how ridiculous we were!' he laughs. He notes how much younger he seemed then. How different Mum looked. Dad and I are crying – with laughter – at all the silliness, including Milly's sound effects and Lovely Granny the Drug Dealer.

It's the best hour I've shared with Dad since we lost Milly.

Mourning Milly has been and continues to be very complicated. First, there's the horror of what happened to her, and the traumatizing way the information was finally relayed to us. But then there are the beautiful complications of Milly herself. I cannot just mourn 'Milly'. That hardly covers it. She was so many things to me.

I mourn Milly telling me what to wear. I mourn Milly the sleepy-head in the pull-out bed in the mornings. I mourn Milly the picky eater and her cucumber sandwiches. I mourn Milly the exuberant dancer and singer. I have to address each of those Millys separately, bring her back to life, let her go and find the place she needs to stay in my heart. So does Mum. So does Dad.

Each time, it hurts.

Mourning Milly is a thousand-headed task.

If Milly hadn't been such a great little person, it would have been easier to let her pass. But she was exactly that great. So here we are, each with a never-closing hole in our heart – not one that we wish away – one we have learned to live with. Mum has a living metaphor for it. All year round, different flowers bloom in Milly's pot near the newt pond. But the pot is always there, and so is its inscription.

Mum thought of suicide during the worst times. Living meant being apart from Milly. Yet death would have meant being apart from me and Dad. So Mum, in the end, has chosen life.

I had choices too. There was a time when I could hardly bear to think about Milly because the pain was so great: I blocked her out, separated myself from her. Nor could I bear to confront what I had become in that state of loss: disturbed, angry, afraid to focus. Thanks to Michelle Calvert, it has stopped being toxic to remember my sister. Now I love thinking about her. There is so much to think about!

In our memories, Milly's no less beautiful, funny or loving than she was when she was alive. Her death has changed nothing of what we loved and love about her. This book has helped us all remember that Milly's no less precious just because she is no longer here.

We took so much pleasure in harvesting our memories of Milly for the early chapters.

As you will have noticed, we don't idealize her. That would be a waste of all her hilarious and creative naughtiness, of all the priceless acting out, of all the sweet eccentricity, of that 'Me do it!', of those Guttural Hugs. We don't want to waste a drop of lovely Milly.

For the fourteenth anniversary of her abduction, we decide to go, as a family, to the place where we finally scattered Milly's ashes. That place must stay a secret. Milly must be allowed some privacy, and so must we. But I'll share what we did, and how we felt.

Mum and Dad have often been to the place before. I always refused, even when Mum told me that kingfishers sometimes came there for Milly's anniversary. Mum felt they were messages from Milly herself.

I sleep very badly the night before the anniversary. I'm too fragile to drive, so Dad picks me up. It is to be a day of treats and sweetness, so we've been tasked to buy the ingredients for a pineapple upside-down cake on the way home. I make the cake in Mum's kitchen. We munch slices while it's still warm. Mum goes into the garden to pick primroses for Milly. I fasten the posy with my hair bobble. Mum chooses a pale green ribbon to tie a small bow.

Mum and Dad's card says, *To our beautiful little sausage Milly, forever in our hearts, my darling, with fondest love from Mummy and Daddy.*

It is signed with four kisses, one for each of us. The last kiss has a line under it to signify that the last member of our family is missing.

My card to Milly says, *Do not ever let anyone dull your sparkle.* I add two little sequins from my thirtieth-birthday party dress, and write, *Always be fabulous.* On the other side, I write, *Peace at last my darling Milly. You are safe now in my heart. I have preserved your memories well, and now the reward will be that I can truly feel them. I can truly feel you, the brightest star in a dark sky.*

I, too, draw four kisses, with the last one underlined.

We put Maisy in the car and drive to the secret spot where Milly's ashes were scattered. It is a place of trees, water and tranquillity.

As we walk towards the water, I'm suddenly fighting nausea and fear. I don't know what I'm afraid of, except that there will be pain. I haven't been here for years. I haven't confronted its sad memories yet. I have not processed them.

We reach the place. I read two short poems to Milly.

Mum tells me to climb down the boulder-strewn bank with Dad. He has to stand in the water to help me down. Fastidious Dad cannot bear to get muddy – through this long ordeal, that has not changed – so this is quite a sacrifice on his part.

I'm thinking about how mud-loving Milly would be laughing at us struggling to get down there. Milly would have loved Maisy, and laughed at her desperation to join us in the water.

There are no kingfishers. However, as I stand on the rock, two little ducks come over – a pair of mallards. They look at me expectantly. They are spoilt Home Counties ducks. They clearly think that the primroses in my hand are food for them.

Dad, standing in the water, reads out the words on his card. Then I read out mine.

The ducks listen attentively.

I bend down and cast the primroses and cards into the water. It carries them slowly away, followed by the greedy ducks.

'Sleep tight, Milly,' I murmur.

Dad and I scramble back up the bank. Dad disapproves of the health and safety lapses. But by now Mum and I are giggling, at Dad, at Maisy, at the ducks, at ourselves.

Then we go to see Lovely Granny, to tell her what we have done. We make her try on seven dresses for a party. Milly would have had strong views on this, of course.

Even without Milly to guide us, we think we make the right choice.

In April 2016 Surrey Police tell us that the inquiry into Bellfield's alleged accomplice is being closed down. There is no evidence apart from Bellfield's words, which he has now decided to retract.

Apparently it doesn't matter who helped Bellfield dispose of Milly's body, or of his red Daewoo Nexia. Or about the telephone-mast timings that apparently supported his admissions. Without investigation, there will be no further evidence. Without new evidence, there's nothing doing, and there are no apologies.

The apology we receive, sort of, in September 2016, is about something else. Surrey Police report on their internal inquiry into the hacking of Milly's phone fourteen years before. Operation Baronet concludes that the force knew about the hacking, that it should have been investigated, but that it was not.

Why was it not investigated? Well, there was fear of the consequences of taking on the *News of the World*, a paper that had something over so many people and was therefore not afraid of the police. However, Operation Baronet concludes that it was more likely that the hacking may not have been 'seen for what it was at the time'. It is, they say, 'a matter of deep regret'. Their failure to investigate was 'unacceptable'. The police have apologized to our family, the press release states, for the distress the matter has caused us.

I'm with Mum and Dad at their house when Dominic's email about Baronet arrives. He asks, 'Do you want to do a family press release?'

Do we want to do a press release?

Well, the thing is we're rather busy with getting on with our lives.

We're in the kitchen. The entire island is covered with photographs of Milly and the rest of our family. We're choosing the pictures for this book. The sun is so bright that Dad worries it might fade some of the photos, which will have to be scanned from original prints because Milly's early childhood was at a time before digital imaging. Other pictures are screen captures from Mum's little black-snouted video-cam, the one that recorded Milly's last Christmas in Cuba.

We're also taking out some of Milly's very important things that now live in a very special leather chest. It contains all the little notes and cards Milly sent us, her favourite *Milly-Molly-Mandy* books, a box of her saxophone reeds, a height chart we used to hang on the wall. (When Milly was taken, we were just starting to tease Mum that she was the shortest in the family.) The chest also contains the lock of Milly's hair found at Minley Woods and presented to us by Alice. Mum has placed in that box all the letters she and I have written to Milly over the years since she went. We've kept her schoolbooks, her reports, her music and a few of her clothes. There's also Milly's teddy in its Aran jumper knitted by Lovely Granny.

When you press that teddy's tummy, Mum's voice still says 'Night, night, Milly. I love you.'

For so long, I couldn't face any of those things. But lately, researching in Mum's personal archive of Milly-ness for this book has allowed me to get to know my sister all over again.

The memory of Milly is no longer terrifying. Sometimes it hurts us; sometimes it heals our pain; sometimes it does both. Mostly it's joyous. I can remember silly, naughty, endearing, eccentric Milly just as she was, not with her personality obscured by the clouds of mystery, tragedy and scandal. I am sad, endlessly sad, that she was taken from us. But now I can laugh when I watch her singing, dancing, mincing about on screen. Now I can appreciate how lucky we were to have Milly in our lives for thirteen whole years. I can also appreciate that what our family had was incredibly special.

Some people live to be eighty without living as fully as Milly did, or with as much love as our family has.

By this time I have written the chapters about the press hacking for this book. Writing has helped me put the *News of the World* in perspective. Hacking was briefly a big part of Milly's story. Yet the hacking would never have happened if a murderer had not snatched my sister and made her an object of interest to the press. And in the end the settlement from News International has helped us get on with our lives. If someone had to pay for what we've been through, there are plenty of people to look to. As it happens, the money came from the only institution that had actually profited financially from our pain. So, in a strange way, it almost seems right.

If you asked me whether we would go to trial again, even to see justice done to the alleged accomplice, no, we would not. We would not trust the promises of the police or the CPS. We would not be fit to go into a courtroom again. We know too much now about what might happen to us, and the advantages that would be given to the accused. We shall never again put ourselves into the hands of people we cannot trust.

Now, via compassionate and effective therapy, we have lived and relived Milly's last hours until we have achieved a kind of peace. Each of us still has our role to play in the tight, glowing circle of family life. The part that held Milly is not dark or empty – she's still here with us. Bellfield could not extinguish her light or the warmth we have for her. Meanwhile, this book is making its way into the world. It, too, will put so many things to rest.

So Dad tells Dominic, 'No, thank you, we don't want to issue a press release about Operation Baronet.'

There's a smile in his voice as he says it.

It's a smile that says, *The police are no longer relevant to our happiness.*

He comes back to the kitchen island, and looks at more pictures of Milly. 'This one's my favourite,' he says, lifting the photograph of me and Milly sitting on a bridge in Brecon in Wales. 'Or maybe this one . . .'

There are so many favourites.

Today it gives us such pleasure to see Milly's lovely face. We map out Milly's beauty from babyhood to 'Me do it!' toddler, to newt-loving tomboy, to Milly-Molly-Mandy Milly with the flicked-up hair, to dolphin girl, to cornrow queen, to Guttural Hugger, to willowy dancer to teen in jeans and fashion icon in black. There she is, our gorgeous girl.

We drink cup after cup of tea, careful not to spill a drop on the pictures we've laid out. It's so hard to cut them down to the number that the publishers have specified. We don't want to lose a second of Milly's thirteen years among us. We can hardly bear to edit out a single smile, a wink, a scowl or a laugh. There are literally a thousand different Millys fanned out on our table. They are all true to the core. You simply couldn't take a bad photo of Milly. And yet she was more beautiful than all of them.

Suddenly, this seems like the most enormous honour. *Who* gets to curate their sister for the world to see? It's a huge responsibility but most of all a privilege, this project of presenting Milly and our family to the people who will share the words I've written. We have to make her short life count towards a better future. Telling her story will, I hope, make people think more deeply about the law, the police and mental health.

Gradually we choose the images that best tell the story and define Milly most accurately. Reluctantly, we re-file some of the photographs. This won't be the last time we look at them. They'll come out often. One day I will show them to my own children. 'There's your auntie Milly,' I'll say. 'She was *amazing*. She loved newts. And Tasselled Wobbegong sharks. And singing and dancing. And Maltesers. And cheese and cucumber sandwiches. And me, and Mum and Dad. And Lovely Granny.'

Mum's enjoying herself. She has Milly with her, not the loss of Milly. The fact that she gave birth to Milly, nurtured her, loved her – these were wonderful things, *and still are.*

We lost all these wonderful things for so many years. Milly's death also changed my relationship with Mum into a desperate symbiosis, each clinging to the other for dear life. But while Milly lived among us, our relationship was simple and, like everything in our household, full of laughter.

We are getting back there.

Mum's dressed in yellow today. Mum's back in flower, in full petal, golden. I am so proud of her.

The sun smiles down on the garden, dappling the trees, including the one that held the tree-house where Milly and I used to make 'Beef Boginura' with old teabags and dirt, pretending to taste it and then praising it in French accents. The sun also shines through the branches of the Ginkgo biloba where a new family of blue-tits is nesting in the bird-box Milly built with Grandad's help.

Mum, Dad and I sit under those trees when we break for lunch, still chatting about Milly. The sunlight glistens on the newt pond, where a little brown creature perches on the rock-shelf Milly made.

We have gone from being a broken family who could barely speak to a group of loving adults laughing round the table.

Thirteen years ago, we cremated Milly and scattered her ashes in our secret place. We did not bury Milly's remains, because we were too afraid that the police would some day want to dig her up. Even when she was dead, that kind of disrespect kept on happening. People kept murdering Milly's memory all over again.

It had to stop, and it stops here, with this book about Milly and about how we survived what was done to her, something that she could not.

The process of writing this book has been a very turbulent one. Sometimes it has brought great joy, uncovering the buried treasure of memories. It has also brought a great deal of heartache. When I was reading the first draft, I was amazed at all the things we as a family have dealt with. I know I lived through them, yet seeing them written down was truly shocking, not just for me but for Mum, Dad and Lovely Granny too.

It has been a slow and sometimes painful process, like solving a very complicated three-dimensional puzzle. As it's gradually come together, it has also become a therapeutic process. Even during the darkest moments I have still been able to see there's a light at the end of the tunnel. Sometimes it was only a small glimmer, but it's always been there.

This is the light: the book will give me the final word on what really happened to my beautiful sister. It is for us to do this as we are the ones who lost the most precious thing in the whole world, a member of our family whom we loved dearly. Only we can tell the truth about how it really was.

I cannot guess how this book will be received. Yet I could not rest until I'd written it. Now it's done, so is my journey back to the person I set out to be before Milly was taken. I hope that this book gives Mum and Dad both their daughters back. Milly and Gemsie – we've both been missing for far too long.

This is the memorial I want for Milly, here in these pages.

I hope that you felt the love as you were reading them.

Appendix 1: Timeline

21 March 2002	Milly abducted
18 September 2002	Milly's body found in Minley Woods
8 October 2002	Service for Milly at Guildford Cathedral
4 February 2003	Marsha McDonnell murdered
21 March 2003	Milly's funeral
28 May 2004	Attempted murder of Kate Sheedy
19 August 2004	Amélie Delagrange murdered
22 November 2004	Bellfield arrested
29 November 2004	Death threat letter to Gemma from prisoner Paul Hughes
21 March 2006	Bellfield charged with murder of Amélie and attempted murder of Kate
26 May 2006	Bellfield charged with Marsha's murder
25 February 2008	Bellfield found guilty of murders of Marsha and Amélie, and the attempted murder of Kate Sheedy
30 March 2010	Bellfield charged with Milly's abduction and murder
4 May 2011	Bellfield trial for Milly's murder begins
23 June 2011	Bellfield found guilty of Milly's murder
4/5 July 2011	Phone hacking scandal breaks in the *Guardian*
10 July 2011	The *News of the World* closes
Spring 2013	Sally and Gemma start EMDR
May 2015	Surrey Police tell the Dowler family about Bellfield's admissions regarding Milly
27 January 2016	Arrest of accomplice named by Bellfield. Police issue a press release regarding Bellfield's disclosures
February 2016	The Dowler family issues their own press release
29 June 2017	This book is published in the UK

Appendix 2: EMDR and Psychotherapy with Gemma

Michelle Calvert
Clinical psychotherapist UKCP
EMDR clinical practitioner, EMDR Association UK and Ireland

Personal trauma fragments the individual's mind, heart and body. If someone is a child when the trauma happens, then the cracks go all the way down to the core.

The nervous system, emotional experience, thinking, reflecting and understanding are all gently forming in a child or young person. Newness is experienced with fresh eyes. There's no experience of life to protect, prepare or harden you. Everything is experienced with an intensity, as is your first kiss, your first goal, your first trip abroad, the first time you fall off your bike or are bullied.

Even an adult with life experience behind them will feel like a lost child as they stand among the fragments of their once-upon-a-time life and look at the pieces. For the Dowlers a grenade blew up their world. They could only stare at the pieces of what was once a beautiful life. Now everything looked different; nothing was familiar. Even lovely familiar joys like Christmas became like a strange theatre production.

When your sister, your daughter is abducted, tortured and murdered, it's like a stab from a poisoned blade. The knife stays in. The pain is ceaseless. It doesn't heal. For a seeming eternity there was, for the Dowlers, the not-knowing, the imagining, the small part of their hearts that still held a drop of hope, that believed in the magic of love, the small-child part of them that believed in fairies who would keep Milly safe. The prayers said to God to protect a child who was so beautiful and innocent to somehow bring her home.

A child like Gemma – good, obedient and thoughtful – believed in the adults' ability to make it all right, and that those in authority would take care of her and her family. For Gemma, the hope was dispelled not just once but again and again.

An adult can recognize, through their thoughts and emotions,

570

the charred remains of what life once was and know what is lost. Even then it's too much to bear. The blade stays in, and dissociation into numbness often follows.

Gemma could not make sense of any of it. Shock is painful for anyone. Shock that has no beginning or end, no sense, no story, no reprieve is unbearable. Where has the old life gone? Why is my mum not my mum any more? Why does she howl and collapse? Why is my dad silent and hollow? Why am I different? Surely someone will switch this channel over. Mum always made everything better. She put the plasters on Milly's and Gemma's knees. Dad always kept the family safe. School had its rules and Gemma knew what they were. Family and friends were kind. But for Gemma none of the old structures seemed to apply any more.

It was a struggle, wanting comfort, but knowing others were in pain; wanting normality, but there was none. Wanting friendships, love . . . wanting the life that had been wonderful and was taken by a shadow.

For Gemma, all the safety nets went at once. Life went from Disney to horror movie and she felt alone in it. She lived with a sense of fear that she could be snatched at any moment. No amount of screaming could tune her out of that terrible new world. For Gemma, the trauma was like moving between three existences. In my treatment work with her, I drew them on the page like circles, overlapping as in a Venn diagram.

In the 'red' place she was embodied in trauma. Her body felt like an electric wire, alive in pain and in rage. She saw the trees towering above, shadows and faces, bones and glass. Everything was jagged, raw, painful, foreboding, overbearing. She felt frightened and unsafe. Panic attacks came and escalated. Rage came and spiralled. All was fear and pain, out of control like a tornado, spiralling round and round. The image of a black vortex haunted Gemma. She was both the vortex and herself inside the vortex being funnelled down into a dark and terrifying place. All of her fears echoed her subconscious imaginings of what had happened to her little sister. Gemma is intuitive: she feels, she senses, she just knows . . .

When Gemma presented this part of herself in the therapy, she was lashing out at me, while at the same time wanting me to stop her and save her from herself. She had been hurt, disappointed, and the trust had almost gone. This anger masked a deep fear and sadness. It reminded me of when I once saw a beautiful grey horse caught on barbed wire, screaming. Fear made her pull away, kick out, which meant the wire tightened.

In the 'green' place, there was dissociation. It was like being suspended in a bubble. Nothing was felt: the body was numb; the mind acted without connection to the emotions. Hours might pass during which Gemma might have woken up, dressed, eaten and watched some television. But she didn't remember much of it, if any. She was connected to nothing but the numbness and the isolation in cold, lonely space. Everything and everyone felt very far away, even when they were bringing her a cup of tea or sitting with her. The shock just went on and on.

Alone in this disconnected place, Gemma's behaviour became more extreme in an effort to feel something. She might drink more . . . sometimes a lot more; she might take a lover. But nothing felt good or right . . . just strange, like watching theatre.

Gemma was shut down in that place, not a real person, an actress by no choice of her own, getting through whatever it was. I believe Gemma was in that state at every public event in order to be able to exist, to get through it minute by minute and stay upright.

In the green place her thoughts were largely of hate: self-hate; hate of the evil in the world; hate for everything seedy and filthy, dirty and rotten; hate for injustice; hate for everything taken.

The thoughts floated around her, echoing in the cavern of space:

I am nothing
I never saved my sister
I should have died instead
Where has my life gone?
Who am I?

In the 'blue' place, Gemma was her core: her true self kept safe from the trauma. When I first met her, the blue was like a flickering pilot light, weak but definitely there. That part was hiding, uncertain, like a nervous child, very timid, cowering.

In that place, she kept all the beautiful things: the whole memories, the sense of joy and happiness, existing like a shimmer of light or a scent on the wind. In that place, Gemma's heart could dare to take a few breaths of fresh air. Gemma was a wonderful nanny, and loved all the children she cared for, more so than they could imagine. Making tomato pasta for them or playing games at home, keeping them safe, protecting them: this was a happy, safe and loving place.

Gemma's a homemaker, and loves to keep everything clean and neat. She likes to make things pretty and stylish. Beauty, glitter and glamour are all good and joyful for Gemma. Her house smells of cakes and icing. Baking is something both Gemma and Sally love to do. Gemma is generous and she's kind. Gemma has the gift of intuition; she can sense a person.

As the therapy progressed the blue part grew stronger and stronger. Gemma began to get to know and like herself more. She began to see what others see: a loving, intuitive and generous girl. Gemma is immensely brave and she is determined to fight for her health and well-being. She's not going to shy away from anything. She wants to face it all. She's doing it for herself, but that's an odd notion to her. Is it OK for me to be healthy if Mum or Dad are not OK, because Milly is not OK?

In this place the thoughts whisper,

I want to have a life
I want a family
I am worth something
I was a good sister

A consultant psychiatrist at Woking Priory Hospital diagnosed Sally with post-traumatic stress disorder in 2012, and Gemma was diagnosed soon after. Their symptoms were almost textbook. The consultant referred Sally to me, saying, 'They need a magician.'

Gemma and Sally responded well to processing the trauma through EMDR. They responded well to me, possibly because my daughter was just thirteen at the time they were referred to me, the same age Milly was when she was taken.

I believe that somehow it was meant to be that I took this case.

It has been an honour to work with them. Sally is one of the most inspiring people I have ever met, and Gemma one of the most courageous.

Acknowledgements

This book owes so many epic thank-yous . . .

To Lovely Mum, for not giving up on our family. This book has made me realize that what we had was so special, and that was because of you.

To Lovely Dad, for being your amazing self, in spite of everything that the world threw at you. You were always there when Milly and I needed you.

To Lovely Granny, who put so much love into Milly and me, and who stood so stoutly between our family and everyone who tried to hurt us. Milly's Old Soul was your essence, Lovely Granny. Always remember that.

To Uncle Pete, Auntie Jenny, David and Daniel, for the sad songs and the happy ones.

To my 'surprise' Uncle Bree, Auntie Marilyn and Mark, for enriching our family life in so many ways.

To Auntie Linds, Uncle Ian and their daughters, Robyn and Laura, for a lifetime of love, support, holidays and karaoke, with extra thanks to 'Loley' for permission to print part of her last letter to Milly, and to Uncle Ian for the photos of the funeral flowers.

To Carole, our 'court correspondent', for being there when we needed you during the trial, for keeping Lovely Granny in one piece, and for allowing me to use part of the letter to Kenneth Clarke.

To Hesh, for embracing us with open arms, for taking my family's emotional burden on your shoulders, and for never judging me.

To the people who suffered with us, holding us up even when your own pain was acute: Hannah Mac, Sara and Mike, Julie, Fiona, Vicky, Lauren, 'Scully', Rebecca and many others. Hannah, our friendship was built from yours and Milly's, so it is going to last for ever.

To Eddie 'the Entrepreneur', Cara, Jess, Danielle, and all Milly's friends and teachers at Heathside.

To Kat and all those who put themselves through the ordeal of giving evidence at the trial.

To Michelle Calvert, without whom Mum and I would simply not have made it. As the doctor said, we needed a magician, not a therapist. That was you.

To our wonderful psychiatrist Eileen Feeney, who, no matter what happens, always seems to know what we need long before we recognize it in ourselves, and who chose her own secret fish ID.

To Michelle Lovric (Masked Butterfly Fish), my co-writer, who helped me find my voice. You showed me how to make our family come alive on the page, in all our true colours. Now our story's told, it will last for ever.

To Alice Barr and Jon Meaney, our family liaison officers, who were thrown into a uniquely awful situation, yet always managed to balance professionalism and humanity.

To Maria Woodall and the other officers at Surrey Police who genuinely tried to help. They know who they are.

To Colin Sutton and his team at the Met for the good old-fashioned detective work that finally took Milly's murderer off the streets.

A whole book could be written about the work of Milly's Fund and the many marvellous people who contributed heart, soul and sheer hard work, including – but not nearly only – Paul and Diana Lamplugh, our patron Chris Tarrant, our Trustees Sara and Hazel, Maria and Lovely Granny, who were our irreplaceable Mission Control. For Milly's Fund, Alice (cheered on by Jon) ran the 2003 Marathon. Other officers in Surrey Police raised money, too, in funny and creative ways, as did many members of the public.

To Mark Lewis (Mako Shark), who actually was there to speak for us, and to Dominic Crossley (Deadly Dragonfish), our human shield at the darkest times, and his ever-sensitive assistant Izzy.

To Linda at Dandini Flowers in Weybridge, for bringing us spring in winter.

To Dr David Ratcliffe, for being the most dependable and compassionate GP.

To our vet Andrew Manfield, for his discretion and sense of humour. He needs it, with Maisy.

To our personal trainer, Sam, who took so much heat from my boxing gloves during the trial.

To Jules, Louise and Lucy Hawker, for feeling able to talk openly to us about such awful experiences. We shared so much that evening. Thank you.

To David Trickey, for the real help he gave, and allowing me to use excerpts from his letters in this book.

To Craig Rickards, Milly's saxophone teacher, for the beautiful piece he composed for Milly's funeral and for permission to use his letter.

To Victoria Hobbs at A. M. Heath for just knowing the right place for this book and guiding me through the publishing process with humour, compassion and true Viperfish ferocity.

At Michael Joseph, thanks to my publisher Louise Moore for constant encouragement and empathy; to my editor Fenella Bates for listening so attentively and advising me so wisely. It is hard to believe we are the same age. Thanks also to Nicola Evans, Clare Parker and Amy McWalters, and also to our attentive copyeditor, Hazel Orme.

To Neil Reading (North Pacific Daggerfish), our press guru, for guiding us through the quicksands when we needed the truth out there.

To Lemon Shark, for her warmth, her insights and her publishing know-how.

This is also the place for kind wishes and compassionate thoughts for Kate Sheedy and the families of Amélie Delagrange and Marsha McDonnell. We think also of Rachel Cowles, Anna-Maria Rennie and Irma Dragoshi, who sadly came away from the painful Bellfield trials without receiving justice. We have shared something so terrible, but we have also survived, proving that love is stronger than evil. Kate's bravery and dignity have been an inspiration for me.

It would be impossible to thank all the members of the public who have offered real and emotional support through all our darkest days – the people who joined the searches, distributed posters, the people who left flowers, candles and teddy bears, the people who brought casseroles, who donated to Milly's Fund, and who wrote to us, especially after the trial. We have been conscious of their kindness and goodness. Most of all, they never let Milly be forgotten. They never buried her under scandal or sensation. They just knew our family had lost the most precious thing of all, and they honoured Milly, and our loss.

And that means that love has the last word.

Permissions

'If I Die Young' Words and Music by Kimberly Perry © 2010. Reproduced by permission of Sony/ATV Countryside, London W1F 9LD.

'Behind Blue Eyes' by The Who, written by Pete Townshend from the album *Who's Next* © 1971 Fabulous Music Ltd of Suite 2.07, Plaza 535, King's Road, London SW10 0SZ. International Copyright Secured. All Rights Reserved. Used by Permission.

'If I Had $1000000' by Steven Page and Ed Robertson. WB Music Corp. (ASCAP) and Treat Baker Music Inc. (SOCAN). All Rights Administered by Warner/Chappell North America Ltd.

Credits

'Endless Night' by Julie Taymor, Lebohang Morake, Jay Rifkin and Hans Florian Zimmer.

Inset images 1–36, 39, 45–8, 50–3, 56, 60, 61, 64, 65 © Sally Dowler; 37 ©Simon Walker/*The Times*; 38 © *Good Housekeeping*; 40 © Solent News & Photo Agency; 41 © The *Walton Informer*; 43 © The *Daily Telegraph*; 44 © Ian Dobson; 49 © Redseasnapper Duncan Spenceley; 54 © Dominic Lipinski/PA Archive/PA Images; 55 & p.358 © Priscilla Coleman/MB Media; 57 & 58 © Stefan Rousseau/PA Archive/PA Images; 59 © London News Pictures; 62 © The *Independent*; 63 © Greatrun.org; 66–68 © Craig Hibbert.